Craig B. Little

State University of New York, Cortland

Deviance and Control
Theory, Research, and Social Policy

Third Edition

F. E. Peacock Publishers, Inc.   Itasca, Illinois

Cover Illustration:
The Drummer, Paul Klee © Paul Klee Foundation Bern / A.K.G., Berlin / Superstock

ACKNOWLEDGMENTS

The author gratefully acknowledges permission to use material from the following sources:

Pages 30, 32, from HUSTLING by Gail Sheehy. Copyright © 1973 by Gail Sheehy. Used by permission of Delacorte Press, a division of Bantam Doubleday Dell Publishing Group, Inc.

Page 42, Table 2.1, from H. Reynolds, THE ECONOMICS OF PROSTITUTION, 1986. Courtesy of Charles C. Thomas, Publisher, Springfield, IL. Used by permission.

Page 76, Figure 3.1, from Alfred C. Kinsey et al., SEXUAL BEHAVIOR IN THE HUMAN MALE, 1948, p. 638. Reprinted by permission of the Kinsey Institute for Research in Sex, Gender, and Reproduction, Inc.

Page 119, Figure 4.3, adapted from R. E. L. Faris and H. W. Dunham, MENTAL DISORDERS IN URBAN AREAS, 1939. Used by permission of Vera S. Dunham.

Page 129, Figure 4.4. Reprinted with permission from: Scheff, Thomas J., BEING MENTALLY ILL: A SOCIOLOGICAL THEORY. Second Edition. (New York: Aldine de Gruyter) Copyright © 1984 Thomas J. Scheff.

Page 245, Table 7.1, from S. Araji and D. Finkelhor, "Abusers: A Review of the Research," in A SOURCEBOOK ON CHILD SEXUAL ABUSE, David Finkelhor with associates, eds., 1986, pp. 93–94. Reprinted by permission of Sage Publications, Inc.

Pages 247–48. Excerpt from THE BATTERED WOMAN by Lenore E. Walker. Copyright © 1979 by Lenore E. Walker. Reprinted by permission of HarperCollins Publishers, Inc.

Page 255, Figure 7.1, adapted from Richard J. Gelles, "Child Abuse as Psychopathology: A Sociological Critique and Reformulation," in the American Journal of Orthopsychiatry, 1973. Used by permission from the American Journal of Orthopsychiatry. Copyright 1973 by the American Orthopsychiatric Association, Inc.

Page 320, Table 9.1, from Dennis Gilbert and Joseph A. Kahl, THE AMERICAN CLASS STRUCTURE: A NEW SYNTHESIS, Fourth Edition, © 1993. Reprinted by permission of Wadsworth Publishing Co., Belmont, CA.

Pages 323 and 326, Figures 9.1 and 9.2, from Thomas R. Dye, WHO'S RUNNING AMERICA? THE BUSH ERA, Fifth Edition, © 1990, pp. 178, 251. Reprinted by permission of Prentice Hall, Englewood Cliffs, NJ.

To the memory of my mother Dorothy,
and to my father John

Contents

Preface

This new edition of *Deviance and Control* has been thoroughly updated and revised for the 1990s. In addition to incorporating the most recent data on each of the substantive deviance areas, it provides extensive coverage of the latest topics on the research agenda in the field. For example, in the "Street Crime and Delinquency" chapter there now is a section on gangs, and the new case studies in the "Elite Deviance" chapter include discussions of the most costly crime wave in American history, the savings and loan frauds; the world's most deadly industrial offense in Bhopal, India; and the Hamlet, North Carolina, chicken-processing plant fire that resulted in criminal conviction of the company's owner. In addition, the latest theoretical developments are incorporated throughout, ranging from new evidence concerning biogenetic explanations for homosexuality, controversy over the deterrence of family violence through criminal justice intervention, and exciting theoretical advances aimed at improving our understanding of crime.

Deviance and Control is intended to be the most comprehensive survey available of the field as a whole. Taken together, the individual chapters progress toward a strong sociological conclusion: The kinds and amounts of deviance in a society depend substantially on how the society is organized. The chapters on specific behaviors accumulate evidence that most deviance is embedded deeply in the social and economic structures of our society. Realizing this fact helps identify points of social policy leverage, even as it exposes limits on the effectiveness of those social policies intended to control deviance that are most easily implemented. A recurrent theme is that measures intended to control deviance often come with high costs in terms of dollars, freedom, and rights to privacy. Therefore, citizens and policy makers must balance the intended benefits of social control strategies against the losses their implementation might inflict on individuals and the society's fundamental values.

Readers are encouraged to be attentive to the interconnections of various deviant behaviors—both with each other and the society's "legitimate" social institutions. For example, alcoholic beverages are associated with suicide, violence in the family, and street crime, but the production, promotion, and sale of alcohol is also a major national and international industry. Likewise, the roots of violent gangs and the savings and loan crime wave can both be related to the deindustrial transformation of the American economy in which factory work, the socioeconomic base of working-class communities, declines in importance while the financial service industry expands. With this viewpoint in mind, we conclude that greater attention to a social justice perspective on deviance is apt to be more fruitful than the criminal justice and medicalized modes now in vogue.

Chapter 1 surveys theories of deviance and approaches to social control with the intention of demonstrating the connections between them. The organizing principle is their levels of analysis—biological, psychological, social psychological, and sociological. In the subsequent chapters these levels of analysis are employed to order the discussion of each deviant behavior. The final chapter, Chapter 10, presents a model to explain how social policies intended to control deviant behavior emerge. Reflecting on the material from the proceeding chapters, the social justice alternative to the currently predominant criminal justice and medical approaches is sketched in greater detail. Some readers may find it appropriate to peruse Chapter 10 immediately after Chapter 1 before going on to the separate discussions of deviance in Chapters 2 through 9.

Over the years, numerous teachers, colleagues, and students have contributed guidance, motivation, and critical reactions to this project. To them I am most grateful. Earlier editions of *Deviance and Control* benefited from the help of Harold Firestone, Fred Halley, Arnold Linsky, Elaine Little, Earl Rubington, Kathryn Russell, Robert Simmonds, Richard Stephens, Stuart Traub, and Lynn Zimmer. Those to whom I owe a special debt of thanks for advice on this edition are Richard Gelles, Walter Hopkins, Darrell Irwin, Richard Jones, Tim Prenzler, and Lynn Zimmer.

Research assistants Staci Call and Kathi Zucker spent many hours tracking down facts and sorting out details. Thanks are once again due to the SUNY Cortland Memorial Library staff, and especially to Eileen Williams, for their cheerful, able assistance. Gilda Haines provided a variety of essential secretarial services. Of particular note is the exceptional work of Gloria Reardon whose skillful copy editing has improved the book immeasurably. Ted Peacock, Jura Avizienis, and the other diligent people at F. E. Peacock Publishers provided advice and support from start to finish. Thanks, finally, to my wife Elaine and my daughter Heather for your inspiration, love, and encouragement.

The comments and suggestions from readers of previous editions have enhanced this edition of *Deviance and Control*. I welcome hearing from faculty and students. You can reach me at my e-mail address:
LITTLEC@SNYCORBA.CORTLAND.EDU

Craig B. Little
Cortland, New York

1 | Explanations of Deviance and Control

Why people behave as they do has been a question long asked by parents and teachers, police and politicians, psychologists and sociologists. More to the point, they often want to know why some people are better behaved than others. This suggests that people who have a reputation for misbehavior are different from the rest of us in important ways. The underlying assumption is that deviants are different. From this point of view, the task of those seeking to explain deviance is (1) to discover what characteristics distinguish deviants from nondeviants, and (2) to develop a logical explanation (a theory) consistent with the differences observed. A great many social scientists have devoted time and effort to understanding deviant behavior using this strategy, and some of what their research tells us about deviance is described in this book.

Of course, deciding what constitutes proper behavior as compared to misbehavior is not easy. For example, as almost anyone who attended elementary school knows, while some teachers are very permissive, others are very strict. Students are quick to pick up these distinctions, and most learn easily that the same behavior, such as talking softly in class, may be grounds for punishment by the strict teacher but lead to no sanction by the permissive teacher. In other words, there is nothing inherently deviant about talking in class. Rather, the deviant quality of the behavior is conferred upon it by the teacher who backs up her definition of classroom-talking with the power to punish. Even an extreme form of misbehavior, like killing, can be looked at in this way as well. While some killings are clearly defined as deviant, others are justified (killing in self-defense) and some others are approved (executions).

Looking at deviant behavior from this perspective suggests that it is important to ask what factors lead to the definition of certain activities as deviant in a particular time and place. For example, the history of laws regarding drinking in the United States illustrates that the same behavior—selling alcoholic beverages—may be legal, as it was prior to 1919 and after 1933, or illegal, as it was during the period of the Prohibition amendment. In response to this observation, students of deviance might seek to explain why the sale of alcoholic beverages was outlawed in 1919 and why that decision was later reversed. Social scientists have directed their attention to questions of this kind, as well as to questions about the causes underlying particular patterns of behavior.

DEVIANCE AND DEVIANTS

Two broad perspectives on the study of deviance are suggested by what we have said so far. One of the more obvious but important points is that understanding deviance involves studying both those who break rules *and* those who make rules. Studying the *rule breaker* begins with such questions as: Why does a person become a homosexual? Research in response to this question has yielded some fascinating theories and evidence that suggest genetic transmission, family dynamics, the process of sexual identity formation, and social learning among many possible causes. Studying the *rule makers* stimulates questions like: Why is homosexuality considered to be deviant, rule-breaking behavior at all? Has it always been so considered in human societies? How did rules against homosexuality come about, and how are they changing? Are rules against homosexuality applied equally to everyone in the society? Here the issue is, essentially, how the rules that establish an activity as deviant come to be made and how they are enforced.

These two types of questions point to an important distinction when trying to evaluate explanations of deviance. The first question—"Why does a person become a homosexual?"—is aimed at understanding a deviant person. We might call it a *type-of-person* question that leads us to explore the etiology (causes) of the deviant's activity. The second question—"Why is homosexuality deviant at all?"—is directed at understanding how the behavior is classified. It is a *type-of-behavior* question that leads us to analyze the development of rules and laws. Both concerns are legitimate aspects of the field of deviant behavior. However, being aware that some theories are attempts to explain deviants' behaviors while others deal with the labeling of behaviors as deviance should demonstrate that the reason very different theoretical perspectives are sometimes applied to the same kind of deviant behavior is that fundamentally different questions can be asked about it. Some theories focus on the causes of deviants' behaviors, and others emphasize why and how certain behaviors come to be labeled deviance.

DEFINITIONS OF DEVIANCE AND THE FIELD OF INQUIRY

Precisely defining deviant behavior is impossible, but struggling toward a definition provides insight into the ambiguity at the heart of the concept. Howard S. Becker (1963) has identified two broad American traditions in the sociological study of deviance which differ in their approaches to defining deviant behavior. The first simply concerns whether a particular activity objectively breaks the rules or not. If a person's behavior violates the rules—written laws or widely shared understandings of what constitutes rule-breaking behavior—then that behavior is defined as deviant. In this straightforward, legalistic view, if an activity breaks the rules, it is deviant. Otherwise, it is not.

The second approach emphasizes how others perceive and react to an activity, regardless of whether there is an explicit rule against it or not. For example, there is not a rule or law against stuttering when one speaks. However, as stutterers know to their discomfort, other people often react to them by breaking off conversations, avoidance, or other negative responses such as treating them in a condescending way that implies they lack intelligence. In other words, people often treat stutterers as though they are deviant. Thus, from this point of view, deviance is not defined in relation to rules or laws. Rather, an activity is considered deviant if it simply arouses negative reactions in others.

Objective Rule-Breaking and Perceptions by Others

Now consider the implication of defining deviance either in terms of objective rule-breaking or the perception of others. The *objective rule-breaking* orientation assumes that the rule in question is very clear and agreed upon by most people in the society. This approach to defining deviance seems to work best when dealing with serious problems such as murder, assault, or theft. There is consensus in American society that these things are not to be tolerated, and there are clear laws against them which are more or less strictly enforced.

The objective rule-breaking approach does not seem to work as well if we realize that many times when the law is broken (objective rule-breaking occurs), the rule-breaking is treated as though it were not deviant at all. For example, not long ago in many jurisdictions there were "blue laws" prohibiting stores from opening on Sunday. However, these laws were seldom obeyed or enforced. Indeed, in some localities, the store operator who kept a retail business closed on Sunday would have been the deviant in the eyes of other operators and customers, regardless of the law. In this case, it can be argued that keeping a store open is deviant from an objective rule-breaking point of view but not deviant according to the perceptions of most others.[1]

We might also consider cases when people do not actually break the law but are treated by others as though they had. For example, even without a law stating that occasionally we must mow our lawns, failure to do so may after a while earn us the hard glances, scandalized whispers, or ostracism of our neighbors. Similarly, members of some religious sects, commune dwellers, stutterers, the handicapped, and numerous others have found themselves treated as if they were rule breakers even though they had not broken any specific rules.

An understanding of deviance clearly requires attention to objective rule-breaking. But as the examples above suggest, defining deviance only in terms of the objective rules may lead us to overlook some kinds of behavior that produce very significant negative reactions from others. Moreover, in our consideration of deviance we should be sensitive to cases when, despite the law being broken, there is not much negative reaction to the infraction. It is important, then, to consider both how a given behavior relates to social rules and how others react to it.

TYPES OF DEVIANCE

Conforming behavior neither objectively breaks any rules nor is perceived by most others as deviant. It is important to remember that even most individuals who be-

come labeled deviants—whether they are hippies, whores, murderers, or thieves—
actually engage in conforming behavior *most* of the time. Conforming behavior is
the norm in most social groups, and even individuals labeled as deviant usually
abide by both the formal and informal rules most of their lives. Students of deviance are, of course, less interested in conforming behavior than in various types of
deviance, except to the degree that conformity is the standard against which deviance is measured. Using the two concepts of objective rule-breaking and reactions
of others, it is possible to distinguish three types of deviance: pure deviance, secret
deviance, and falsely accused deviance.

Most of what we commonly call crime is *pure deviance*—both objectively rule-
breaking and perceived by others as deviant. In American society ordinary crime is
well represented by the FBI's eight "Index" crimes that provide the data for the annual crime rates widely cited from the *Uniform Crime Reports* (UCR). They are:
murder, aggravated assault, rape, robbery, burglary, larceny, auto theft, and arson.
Numerous other behaviors such as counterfeiting or kidnapping would fit into the
criminal category. When most Americans think of criminal behavior, they probably
have in mind activities such as the eight Index crimes.

Sometimes an activity is definitely against the rules, but it is either so well hidden that nobody sees it or, if it is seen, nobody seems to do anything about it. Becker (1963) called such behaviors *secret deviance*. For example, fairly common sexual activities such as swinging, fetishism, and sodomy are illegal in many jurisdictions
but usually take place in private without the knowledge of nonparticipants. In these
cases the behavior in question would be perceived as deviant by others, but others
do not see the behavior taking place.

Closely related to the concept of secret deviance in some respects is what is
called *victimless crime*. Edwin Schur (1965) coined this term to refer "essentially to
the willing exchange, among adults, of strongly demanded but legally proscribed
goods or services" (169). He described abortion, homosexuality, and drug addition
as examples. To these might be added prostitution, illegal gambling, and numerous
other forms of vice. Their primary characteristic is a transaction between two parties, both of whom desire to enter into the relationship.[2] Because neither party in
the interaction desires to make a complaint, laws against these exchanges are relatively difficult to enforce. Thus, in the absence of active pursuit by vice squads,
most activities of this sort simply go on with little intrusion by the law enforcement
authorities.

Keeping deviant behavior secret may also be related to the ability of the person
engaging in the activity to cover up the transgression. The deviance committed or
controlled by the powerful, therefore, is often secret deviance.[3] Power implies the
ability to affect the social control machinery—to "fix the ticket"—in order to avoid
prosecution and public humiliation. And power, embodied in very high social status,
also permits some people to transcend the potentially debilitating stigma of a deviant label. For example, leaders of organized crime, whose interests are usually embedded in both the world of vice *and* legitimate business, are often revered and
treated with great respect within their own ethnic communities and beyond them.

In another case, Schwartz and Skolnick (1964) found that physicians with malpractice convictions suffered relatively little professional, economic, or social damage compared to less powerful lawbreakers. Likewise, judges have been reluctant to apply severe sentences to business executives convicted of corporate crimes, responding to their lawyers' pleas that their clients, although lawbreakers, are not "real" criminals.

Finally, there are instances when there has been no objective rule-breaking, but the behavior is perceived as deviant by others. Probably the most common examples of this situation are what is sometimes called *alternative lifestyles*. Religious cultists, commune dwellers, political zealots, hobos, and tramps all sometimes find themselves persecuted by others as if they had broken laws even though they have not. Becker calls law abiders who nonetheless become pinned with a deviant label the *falsely accused*. A broad category of behavior that Thomas Scheff (1966) calls *residual rule-breaking* also fits into this type. In Scheff's discussion of mental disorders, residual rule-breaking is behavior "for which our society provides no explicit label, and which, therefore, sometimes lead(s) to labeling of the violator as mentally ill..."(34). In other words, residual rule-breaking is not strictly prohibited in a way that allows us to categorize the violator as a murderer, thief, or arsonist; but others do find the behavior so annoying or disconcerting that they seek removal from their midst of the person who engaged in it. Standing too close in normal conversations, refusing to reply when spoken to, or uncontrolled laughter at inappropriate moments are incidents of residual rule-breaking. Excessive residual rule-breaking—the persistent violation of everyday informal rules of interaction—can, under certain circumstances, according to Scheff, become officially labeled as mental illness.

False accusation, or deviant labeling without legal conduct, is more likely to be the lot of the relatively defenseless. These types of deviance therefore are often the deviance of the powerless. The behavior receives the reprehension of others, not because it is strictly illegal—for it is not—but because it is different and those who engage in it lack the power to resist a stigmatizing deviant label. In contrast, the rich or famous may be able to avoid being labeled mentally ill even when they engage in behaviors that would earn others this designation. Terms like *eccentric* or *free spirit* excuse odd behavior and often protect the powerful from negative responses to their deviance.

THEORY, RESEARCH, AND SOCIAL POLICY

The words *theory* and *research* sometimes have a forbidding connotation that implies highly complex statements and equally esoteric procedures of scientific investigation. At root, however, there need not be anything mysterious about either. In fact, even though we hardly know it, at a fairly basic level we all theorize about human behavior and conduct research on it every day. We theorize when we try to explain something. A theory, in its broadest sense, is simply an explanation for some event or phenomenon. Thus, in response to the observation that little Billy is an active child who is always getting into everything, a grandmother may reply, "He comes by it naturally; he's just like his father was at that age." The grandmother has stated a theory of Billy's behavior—specifically, a genetic theory implying that hereditary characteristics shared with a parent explain the behavior. To be sure, the theory is not precisely formulated, as it would be by a social scientist, and it stands untested by research. Still, by recognizing that a theory has just been proposed and then trying to understand the mechanism that it implies (heredity, in Billy's case), we can learn to think clearly about different kinds of explanations.

Research can take many forms, ranging from simple observation to elegant, controlled experiments. However, regardless of the strategy or technique, observation is the basic component of all research. In this sense, as we experience the world around us—often unconsciously making comparisons, searching for regularities, identifying differences—we engage in research. The major differences between our everyday observations and those of the social scientist are that the social scientist's are apt to be more systematic and made more precise by the use of techniques to assure representativeness of the sample of the population studied and careful training to minimize biased data gathering.

The findings from research observations may be used in at least two ways. First, the results of observations can become the basis for generating a theory. For example, by carefully recording many people's accounts of how they initially came to smoke marijuana, Becker (1963) constructed the theory that marijuana smoking is an activity usually learned from others. The second way to use research findings is to test a theory. We might start with a theory that poor economic conditions lead to higher rates of mental disorders (a "stress" theory of mental disorder). To test this theory, we could examine the relationship between economic indicators (e.g., levels of employment) and mental hospital admission rates over a long period of time. One researcher who did this (Brenner, 1973) found evidence to support the theory. In either case—*generating* theory or *testing* theory—research is a way of linking our explanations for social phenomena with actual occurrences in the world around us.

While research is important in constructing and testing theories, it might be reasonable to ask: Why are theories so important? Why is it important to be able to understand and evaluate them? The answer that is most central to the goals of this book has to do with the role of theory in the formulation of social policy. Put simply, the accepted theory about what causes a particular pattern of behavior can guide our attempts to control or change it. For example, if we accept a theory that the strange behavior of some people is due to demonic possession, we might devise a social policy that emphasizes religious exorcism, ritual, or punishment to drive away the evil spirits. (This happened in 17th-century colonial America during the witchcraft hysteria.) Throughout most of this century, theories of bizarre behavior have conceptualized it as illness or disease; therefore, hospitalization and medical treatment have dominated social policy toward mental disorders. On the other hand, if we theorize that publicly labeling and stigmatizing a person who exhibits odd behavior as mentally ill actually *increases* the person's tendencies to act strangely (Scheff, 1966), we might initiate a social policy designed to minimize the humiliation and isolation of mental hospitalization by releasing mental patients to local community care facilities. Such a "deinstitutionalization" policy, largely consistent with labeling theory, has been followed in the United States for nearly 40 years.

We usually think of theory as being the guide to social action, but this is not always the case. Sometimes, social policy makers (our society's elite class, politicians, or government officials) may decide on a particular course of action and then promote a theory to rationalize it. For example, there is evidence that the *real* reason for releasing mental patients back to their communities has been to lower the burdens on the states for the cost and responsibility of psychiatric care (Scull, 1977). However, a labeling theory like Scheff's which suggests deinstitutionalization as a way of avoiding the damaging stigma of hospitalization might be embraced by policy makers to rationalize and mask the real reasons for increased reliance on community-based outpatient facilities.

Theories, then, are important because they serve both to guide and to rationalize social action or interaction. In a democracy, where citizens are presumably able to influence social policy decisions by pressuring legislators and voting, the capacity to understand and evaluate theories is essential. Deciding the best course for social policy requires informed, reasoned judgment about the theories implied by various social policy courses. To avoid being hoodwinked, we must understand theories sufficiently to decide when they are being used to guide social policy and when they are being used as smoke screens by social policy makers to hide the true intentions of the laws they pass. From this viewpoint, full, meaningful participation in a democratic society demands learning how to think carefully about theories of behavior in order to exercise true freedom of choice as a citizen.

Chapters 2 through 9 of this book each have a section devoted to explanations (theories) of various types of deviance and the evidence (research findings) that relates to those explanations. The following overview of several different levels of explanation provides a framework for organizing such theories into sensible categories.

LEVELS OF EXPLANATION

Explanations of deviant behavior range from those attributing the cause to the basic constitution of the individual (the person's nature), through how the individual is socialized (the person's nurture), to larger environmental explanations such as the opportunities available to advance social status (the opportunity structure) and the transmission of cultural values (the subculture). Broadly speaking, it can be useful to think of the different kinds of causal variables used in explanations of deviant behavior in terms of their levels of analysis, such as those outlined in Table 1.1: (1) biogenetic, (2) psychological, (3) social psychological, and (4) sociological. In the next few pages we will briefly discuss each of the four levels of analysis and indicate the kinds of causal variables exemplifying them in various theories in the deviance literature.

Table 1.1   Levels of Explanation of Deviant Behavior

Level	Kinds of Causal Variables	Examples
Biogenetic	Head shape or other physical anomaly Atavism Somatotype	Phrenologists Lombroso (1911) Sheldon (1949) Glueck & Glueck (1956)
	Chromosome composition (XYY theory)	Jacobs et al. (1965)
	Genetic transmission	Mednick et al. (1984)
Psychological	Instinctual drives (and/or their suppression)	Ardrey (1961) Freud (1930)
	Mental pathology	Glueck & Glueck (1959)
	Maternal deprivation Intelligence and impulsivity	McCord & McCord (1956) Wilson & Herrnstein (1985)
Social Psychological	Socialization Superego development Low self-control	 Henry & Short (1954) Gottfredson & Hirschi (1990)
	Social learning Imitation	Akers et al. (1979) Bandura et al. (1961)
	Influences of significant others Differential association	 Sutherland & Cressey (1970)
	Labeling	Scheff (1966)

Biogenetic

Biogenetic explanations focus on physiological characteristics of the individual. In the late 1700s and early 1800s phrenologists theorized that irregularities in the shape of a person's brain, as manifested in bumps that could be felt on the head, were a significant cause of criminal behavior. Likewise, Lombroso's (1911) famed theory of *atavism* claimed that some criminals were, physically and mentally, degenerate throwbacks to prehuman, apelike forms. More recently, others have tried to establish a causal relationship between body type and deviance, especially delinquent behavior (Sheldon, 1949; Glueck and Glueck, 1956). Although there probably is a tendency for delinquents to be mesomorphs (muscular body types) rather than ectomorphs (lean, delicate body types) or endomorphs (round, fat body types), it is doubtful that mesomorphy "causes" delinquency (Sutherland and Cressey, 1970; Mannheim, 1965). Rather, delinquents are more apt to be mesomorphs for the same reason that baseball players are; boys with athletic builds are more likely

Table 1.1	(continued)	
Level	Kinds of Causal Variables	Examples
Sociological	Social structure	
	"Needs" of the society	
	Functionalism	Durkheim (1938)
		Erikson (1966)
	Social change	
	Social disorganization	Faris & Dunham (1939)
	Anomie	Durkheim (1951)
	Opportunity structure	Cloward & Ohlin (1960)
	Anomie	Merton (1968)
	Social ecology	Cohen and Felson (1979)
	Culture	
	Transmission of values and attitudes	Shaw & McKay (1942)
	Delinquent subculture	Cohen (1955)
	Subculture of violence	Wolfgang & Ferracuti (1967)
	Control	
	Social bond	Hirschi (1969)
	Deterrence	Braithwaite & Geis (1982)
	Reintegrative shaming	Braithwaite (1989)
	Political economy	
	Class structure	Quinney (1970)
		Chambliss (1975)
	Class conflict	Taylor et al. (1973)

to be successful at both activities. Each of these biogenetic theories of deviance has been largely discredited by research.

A more recent controversial biogenetic theory postulates a relationship between chromosome composition and antisocial behavior, especially sexual violence (Jacobs et al., 1965). This theory states that a propensity to violence in some males is due to the presence of an extra Y (male) chromosome in the cells of their bodies. The extra Y chromosome is thought to add an aggressive tendency to these men's psychophysiological constitutions. At this point, although the chromosomes and violence hypothesis has not been entirely discredited, the weight of the evidence suggests that no such simple syndrome is apt to account for violent behavior (Fox, 1971; Hook, 1973; Witkin et al., 1976; Reiss and Roth, 1993).

A number of other theories of deviance either explicitly state or imply that the behavior is at least partly due to a genetically inherited physiological predisposition.

There is some evidence to support them, at least for certain types of deviance (Ellis, 1983; Mednick et al., 1984). For example, the results of one study on rates of alcoholism in families showing that 52% of alcoholics had at least one alcoholic parent suggest the possibility that genetic inheritance may be a factor (Catanzaro, 1967: 34). Of course, to establish unequivocally the role of genetic transmission, the contribution of nongenetic factors such as family structure or parental attitudes toward drinking would have to be isolated. Most researchers conclude that even when genetic predispositions are relevant, the person's socialization and environment still must be taken into account for an adequate explanation of the deviance (Peele, 1986; Fishbein, 1990).

Psychological

Psychological-level theories also emphasize the individual's personal traits, especially those such as instincts or intelligence that might be important to behavioral predispositions. For example, in *Civilization and Its Discontents*, Freud (1930) postulates that numerous types of deviance including intoxication, religious fanaticism, withdrawal, and madness can be attributed to sublimation of humans' basic sexual, aggressive instincts. Ardrey (1961, 1966) argues that much of the violence in human societies is rooted in man's inherited aggressive instincts deriving from his prehistoric need to gain and defend territory.[4] In addition to instinctual drives, psychological-level explanations of deviance have involved variables such as mental pathology (Glueck and Glueck, 1959), maternal deprivation (McCord and McCord, 1956), hormonal imbalance, epilepsy (Shah and Roth, 1974), intelligence and impulsivity (Wilson and Herrnstein, 1985).

Social Psychological

Psychological explanations depend upon factors that become part of a person's personality at birth, or very shortly thereafter. Social psychological theories emphasize variables that emerge as a result of the person's interactions with others. For example, some theorists suggest that deviance is a product of a person's failure to develop sufficient internal controls during the socialization process. Punitive child-rearing practices involving the excessive use of punishment and external controls seem to retard superego development. In Freudian terms, individuals with weak superegos do not possess the internal restraints or sense of guilt to prevent them from engaging in antisocial, illegal, or excessively violent behavior (Coser, 1967). On the other hand, it has been hypothesized that love-oriented child-rearing techniques run the risk of creating a too-strong superego. In such a person a heightened potential for guilt inhibits outwardly directed hostility in the face of frustration, and it can lead to inwardly directed responses such as depression or even suicide (Henry and Short, 1954). Gottfredson and Hirschi (1990) theorize that low self-control is common to a broad range of deviant behaviors, and the origin of low self-control, established before a child is eight years old, is to be found in ineffective child rearing. To the extent that child-rearing practices differ by class, we might expect to find that different types of deviance vary by class as well.

Another social psychological approach emphasizes imitation and role modeling. For example, Albert Bandura and his colleagues (Bandura, 1962; Bandura, Ross, and Ross, 1961, 1963; Bandura and Walters, 1959) have developed a social learning theory which maintains that exposure to adult deviant role models, even exposure through the media (e.g., television violence), leads young children to learn and imitate such behavior. Similarly, Edwin H. Sutherland's famous theory of differential association states that a person will learn to violate rules through associating with rule breakers more than with people who follow the rules (Sutherland and Cressey, 1970). What is learned includes both skillful techniques (how to pick a lock, juggle the account books, or pick up a "john") and psychological defenses to reduce or eliminate guilt (rationalizations, projections, etc.). These defenses are often referred to as *neutralizations* (Sykes and Matza, 1957), or rationalizations for having broken a particular rule. They are employed by deviants ranging from teenage vandals to corporate executive criminals whose illegal, unsafe factories kill and main thousands, for example (Hills, 1987).

Still another example of the social psychological level of analysis is labeling theory. In this approach, the single most important event leading a person to be locked into a deviant role is said to be official labeling. When a person is officially identified as a drunk, a thief, a prostitute, crazy, or having any other disvalued status, the label helps convince that person that he or she is indeed different, possibly bad, even dirty. Sometimes the label also closes off legitimate opportunities for the person to go straight. Thus, for example, prostitutes become caught in a sequence of revolving-door justice where they are picked up on the street for hustling "tricks," go to court and are fined or placed on bail for prostitution, and then find themselves stigmatized and back on the street with no better opportunities to make a living than before. To earn money for bails, fines, and simply to live, they have few alternatives other than continued prostitution.

Sociological

Theories at the sociological level of analysis tend to emphasize how different social structures or social environments exert pressures on people to engage in deviant activity. One of the earliest sociological theories of deviance is Emile Durkheim's (1938) *functional* analysis of crime.[5] He argues that since deviance is present in all societies, it must serve some positive function or else it would not persist. Put another way, because deviance is present in all known societies, it must fulfill some of their needs for survival. Durkheim suggests that deviants do serve a positive role in a society: They help to define and publicize the rules for others, create increased social cohesion by acting as outsiders that people collectively can react against, and sometimes they act as forebearers of social change. He concludes that because deviance is useful to society, every society has its "normal" rate of deviant behavior.

Another group of American sociologists working in the first half of the 20th century thought that conditions such as suicide, mental disorders, and delinquency seemed to be concentrated in certain areas of cities (Cavan, 1923; Faris and Dunham, 1939; Shaw and McKay, 1942). They hypothesized that the reason for higher rates of deviance in these locations was the *social disorganization* to be found in them. These theories argued that rapid social changes in American cities, epitomized by massive immigration, industrialization, and urbanization, had led to a weakening of social norms, and weakened norms, reflected in social disorganization, were the underlying cause of deviance. The social disorganization theorists sought evidence in support of their theory by relating certain indices of social disorganization in a particular area of a city, such as the proportion of foreign-born residents, property values, and types of dwellings, to rates of deviance found there. They did find that areas with the greatest social disorganization had higher rates of deviance, but other theorists have since questioned the way in which they measured disorganization, suggesting the presence of class bias (Mills, 1942).

Durkheim, the French sociologist who made the first detailed argument for a functionalist theory of deviance, also introduced the concept of *anomie* (normlessness) to explain differing rates of suicide among nationalities and other social groupings. Durkheim's (1951) anomie theory is based on the idea that people's desires for ever-increasing social status must be limited and restrained by societal norms. If their desires are not restrained, they will never be satisfied and are doomed to perpetual unhappiness. In a sense, Durkheim was saying that norms tell people what they can reasonably expect in their social positions; in effect, norms teach them to "know their place" in the society. When the norms in a society are seriously disturbed because of economic upheaval (e.g., boom or bust cycles), desires are not restrained, resulting in increase anomie and, according to Durkheim, higher rates of suicide. Chapter 5 on suicide will explain Durkheim's theory of anomic suicide more fully, putting it into the context of his contributions to understanding this behavior and why some societies have more suicide than others.

An American sociologist, Robert K. Merton, further developed Durkheim's anomie theory and applied it to several other kinds of deviant behavior. The key variable in Merton's theory is what others have called *opportunity structure* (Cloward and Ohlin, 1960). Merton (1968) states that in some societies there is an imbalance between cultural goals (things that people generally think are valuable and worth striving for) and institutionalized means (the legitimate, legal ways to attain the valued goals). In American society there tends to be great emphasis on attaining material wealth like cars, good clothes, a home, appliances, and so on. These are culturally valued symbols of success in the United States. Everyone is expected to strive for these goals and each of us is constantly urged, through advertising, to pursue them. However, the means to reach these goals are not universally available. Not everyone has the same educational or occupational opportunities. This overemphasis on the goals without adequate availability to all of the means for achieving them puts intense pressure on some individuals to use illegitimate, illegal means instead. Merton suggests that higher rates of deviance (especially crime) are apt to be found at points in the society where the disjunction between cultural goals and legitimate opportunities is greatest. Put another way, an imbalance of emphasis in the social structure creates the condition for a breakdown of norms, or anomie.

Some theorists at the sociological level of analysis postulate the *cultural transmission* of values and attitudes that actually support rule-breaking. Much of the theory and research in the area of juvenile delinquency has centered on the question of the values to which delinquents adhere. While there are certainly those who argue against cultural transmission (Sykes and Matza, 1975), other theorists describe a delinquent subculture that, in distinct contrast to the culture of the society at large, actually values negativistic, nonultilitarian, malicious behavior (A. Cohen, 1955). Similarly, Wolfgang and Ferracuti (1967) ascribe higher rates of homicide in areas such as the American South or "among a relatively homogeneous subculture group in any large urban community (52)" to a value system that constitutes a subculture of violence. In other words, the deviance is theorized to result from a unique set of norms and values shared by members of a particular group through their culture.

Control theory assumes that people will commit deviant acts unless they are restrained in some way. While most of the theories previously described respond to the question, Why does the deviant do it? control theory responds to the question, What prevents the nondeviant from committing deviant acts? From this perspective, deviance is not problematic, and all of us, given free reign, would commit whatever deviant acts gave us some pleasure, satisfaction, or benefit. People limit their deviant behavior to the extent that they are subject to mechanisms of social control, including not wanting to disappoint others, guilt, fear of getting caught, and the desire to maintain their reputations. Thus, rather than focusing upon conditions such as genetic predisposition, psychological trauma, family upbringing, or social pressures that might impel a person into deviance, control theory concentrates on the social mechanisms that deter people from deviant activity.

Hirschi's (1969) formulation of control theory states that a person's bond to the society is what restrains him from committing deviant acts. When people have a sense of attachment, commitment, and involvement with law-abiding others in the society and have learned to believe in the morality of the law, it is unlikely they will be deviant. They will conform because they have a "stake in conformity" (Toby, 1957).

Another variation of control theory concentrates on conventional techniques of punishment and deterrence. For example, Braithwaite and Geis (1982) argue that although sanctions such as fines or imprisonment have not been particularly effective deterrents against ordinary street criminals, such measures have a high probability of success in reducing high-status corporate crime. They reason that since corporate crimes such as price fixing or health and safety violations are often based on the rational, calculated determination of possible gain, making the risks clearly outweigh the benefits would make law-abiding behavior the normal, rational decision. Moreover, high-status individuals who have the most to lose from traditional criminal penalties like fines and the public humiliation of imprisonment would be most deterred by those measures. This reasoning suggests that a society's capacity to successfully shame those who contemplate deviance might also affect the overall rate of deviance in the society. Braithwaite (1989) has proposed that societies relying upon shame and, following successful shaming, reintegration of the deviant will have the lowest rates of crime. Compared to the United States, Japan appears to fit the model of a society that relies upon reintegrative shaming to keep its crime rates low.

Some contemporary sociological theories emphasize class structure as central to the development and application of criminal law in capitalist societies (Quinney, 1970; Spitzer, 1975). Beginning with the premise that society is dominated by a ruling elite, these sociologists show how rules (laws) are formulated in the interest of the elite and then are applied to protect the powerful, to threaten the powerless, and to maintain the inequitable status quo. From this perspective, deviance is best understood in relation to *class conflict*. The powerful are presumed to manipulate the legislation and execution of laws in their interests through control of the criminal justice system, and the powerless are seen as more vulnerable to the application of criminal sanctions (Chambliss, 1975). Thus the appearance of more deviance in the lower classes is attributed mainly to class discrimination in the making and enforcement of the laws.

Theories of deviance operate at different levels of explanation, ranging from biogenetic to sociological. Each of the levels of explanation we have described is represented several times in subsequent chapters. However, not every type of explanation has been applied to every type of deviance we will examine. Any particular form of deviance may seem to be more amenable to certain explanations than others. For example, prostitution has not been explained by biogenetic theories, but social psychological (learning theories) and sociological (functionalist) explanations of it have been widely accepted. In the theory and research on homosexuality, however, biogenetic explanations (heredity and hormones) have been given significant consideration. The sections on explanations of the various forms of deviance represent the types of theories and the levels of explanation most predominantly applied in each case. You might find it helpful to occasionally refer to Table 1.1 for a reminder of the organizing framework as you read subsequent chapters.

APPROACHES TO SOCIAL CONTROL

The study of deviance is not limited to the search for explanations. Indeed, from the viewpoint of social policy, the central question has been: What should be done about deviance? How should we punish, isolate, reform, treat, rehabilitate, humiliate, or make an example of the deviant? These are issues of social control—"the organized ways in which society responds to behavior and people it regards as deviant, problematic, worrying, threatening, troublesome or undesirable in some way or another" (Cohen, 1985: xi).

Deviance and control are opposite sides of the same coin. Functionalists argue that the deviant often contributes to social life by helping to publicize the rules, by leading the way to social change, by creating social solidarity among those he or she offends, and by establishing the normative boundaries of a group, community, or society (Durkheim, 1951; Erikson, 1966). In our appreciation for the functions of deviance, however, we must not forget that the deviant cannot provide these services alone. The deviant helps to establish the rules by example. So it is with the unruly schoolboy whose mission in life seems to be to show others in the class where the normative boundaries are by repeatedly crossing over them into deviant mischief. But for the deviant boy to perform his "functions" he needs someone to call attention to his misdeeds and apply negative sanctions as a punishment and a warning. Without agents of social control (parents, teachers, psychiatrists, social workers, police, judges, and a host of others) who identify, capture, treat, reform, or punish the deviant, the deviant is of little or no social consequence. Indeed, without its counterpart in social control, deviance does not exist.

Changing Modalities of Control

The history of criminal punishment most clearly conveys the outlines of the major Western transformations in social control. Until the end of the Middle Ages in the 15th century, most deviance was handled informally in families and villages. In cases not involving the Church, the chief deterrent was the fear of private vengeance by victims or their relatives. Jails were not used as punishment; when sanctions were applied by city or village officials, they tended to be corporal or capital punishment for the poor and fines for the wealthy (Rusche and Kirchheimer, 1939). As city-states developed into nation-states, governments took on more of the responsibility for punishing crime. Punishments, however, tended to remain brutal. Even through the 18th century, those convicted of crimes were apt to face hanging, decapitation, physical dismemberment (cutting off a finger, hand, ear, etc.), branding, or public disgrace in the pillory of the town square. Punishment focused on the body of the condemned (Foucault, 1977). Social control was characterized by public displays of retribution, with minimal involvement by the state and none by the penological experts.

During the 19th century this changed. The change is best represented by the emergence of large-scale institutions of control, including the prison and the asylum (Rothman, 1971). With their predominance, the place of control moved from the public square of the community to within the walls of institutions run by penal or therapeutic experts and professionals (wardens, penologists, phrenologists, psychiatrists, and therapists). By the mid-1800s the major changes were clear; Cohen (1985) notes the following:

- The increasing involvement of the state in the building and administration of bureaucratic institutions for the punishment, custody, or cure of deviants.
- The dominance of professional experts who concentrate on differentiating and classifying deviant and dependent groups according to "scientific" criteria.
- The placement of deviants into segregated "asylums."
- A decline in punishment involving public displays of physical harm.

There is little dispute that these changes occurred; there is less agreement about the reasons why. Durkheim (1933) hypothesized that more simple, homogeneous societies held together by "mechanical solidarity" are dominated by "repressive" law that focuses on punishment. In contrast, complex, heterogeneous societies that cohere by "organic solidarity" are characterized by "restitutive" law that seeks to correct or restore rather than punish. Others have linked the changes more to the specific historical developments of political economy. Spitzer and Scull (1977) document how changes in English crime control are embedded in the larger capitalist transformation from a society dominated by rural landed aristocracy to one dominated by industrial factory owners. With the increasing importance of factory labor came a greater need to control workers' behavior and invest in "human capital." Therefore, underlying the changes in approaches to social control was an increasing rationalization of the system aimed at achieving the goals of discipline and productivity over punishment (Spitzer, 1979).

Large, bureaucratic, segregating institutions of social control—often called *total institutions* (Goffman, 1961)—remained the unchallenged mode until the 1960s. Then there began a "deinstitutionalization" movement intended to return social control to the community. The ideology of this destructuring movement called for decentralization, decriminalization, deinstitutionalization, deprofessionalization, self-help, and the removal of stigma and labels (Cohen, 1985). The apparent reality of the trend is best exemplified by the sharp reductions in mental institutions over the past three decades. The reasons for "decarceration" range from the alleged failures of the treatment model, to the noninterventionist social policy implications of labeling theory, to the need of governments to relieve themselves of excessive financial burdens (Cohen, 1979; Scull, 1977). The result has been an increase in community-oriented social control strategies that often include the private sector and an emphasis on self-help.

None of this, however, has meant an overall reduction in the social control of deviance. Rather, it has meant more. As Cohen (1979) puts it,

> [T]he major results of the new movements towards "community" and "diversion" have been to increase rather than decrease the *amount* of intervention directed at many groups of deviants in the system and, probably, to increase rather than decrease the total *number* who get into the system in the first place. In other words: "alternatives" become not alternatives at all but new programs which supplement the existing system or else expand it by attracting new populations." (347)

In this expanding system of social control, next to the older, exclusive, coercive, authoritarian total institutions now stand newer inclusive, treatment-oriented, professionally administered, community-based facilities and normatively oriented, self-help organizations such as Alcoholics Anonymous (Davis and Anderson, 1983).

Levels of Social Control

Theories of deviance can be organized according to their levels of explanation as we have done. Because strategies in response to deviance are closely related to the explanations of the behavior toward which they are directed, it is likewise possible to employ these four levels—biogenetic, psychological, social psychological, and sociological—when thinking about social control. In Table 1.2 we do this by including

Table 1.2   Levels of Social Control

Level	Control Target	Examples
Biogenetic	Genetic or neuro-endocrinological abnormalities	Medical intervention (e.g., pharmacological or surgical treatment)
Psychological	Disturbed personality	Psychotherapy; psychotropic drugs
Social Psychological	Learned patterns of behavior	Therapeutic: behavior modification; therapeutic communities emphasizing resocialization
		Punitive: use of the criminal justice system to punish and deter (e.g., fines, probation, parole, incarceration, capital punishment)
Sociological	Social structure Social ecology conducive to deviance	Building social spaces to reduce crime through lighting, architecture, surveillance, etc.; neighborhood watches
	Unequal opportunity structure	Educational and employment reforms (e.g., greater resources for education, job training, day care of children, flexible work hours)
	Economic and social inequalities, particularly as they affect families neighborhoods, and communities	Fundamental redistribution of of wealth and power (e.g., progressive income, corporate and inheritance tax reform; political activism and organization; voter registration reform)
	Ideology Prejudice, racism, sexism, patriarchy	Transmission and validation of alternative values (e.g., acceptance of diversity, racial and sexual equity) through education, legal reform (e.g., equal rights legislation), the public media, and personal example

the levels of the social control strategy that correspond to the levels of explanation of deviant behavior. In addition, for each level of control we identify the target of control, ranging from individual physiology to social organization, and we give specific examples of how the control strategy can be implemented.

At the biogenetic level, the target of control might be genetic or chemical abnormalities in the individual that allegedly cause the deviance. For example, if evidence supports the theory that some men are harmfully aggressive because they have excessive levels of the male hormone testosterone, the control strategy would dictate the search for medical interventions—probably in the form of drug treatment—to correct the problem. Note that the appropriateness of a control strategy depends upon the corresponding theory of what causes the deviance and the strength of the evidence supporting the theory. In addition, the use of a strategy depends upon what is politically and morally acceptable according to the prevailing standards of the society. For example, *if* it could be shown that some men rape because of abnormally high levels of testosterone, castration of these men might be one effective form of control consistent with both the theory and the evidence. However, castration might very well *not* be a viable option from a moral or political viewpoint. The irreversibility of the procedure may make it morally unacceptable, or physical mutilation might be repugnant as a control alternative to a vast majority of people, and this would make it politically impossible to implement as social policy.

At the psychological level a disturbed personality is the control target, and psychotherapy and/or psychotropic drugs are the typical interventions. Social psychological control strategies focus on learned patterns of behavior. The therapeutic model uses behavior modification techniques, often in a therapeutic group setting such as residential drug treatment centers. The punitive model—especially when guided by assumptions of deterrence—employs various levels of punishment imposed by the criminal justice system. The main supposition is that deviant behavior can be deterred by increasing its risks and costs relative to its rewards.

The sociological level of social control receives the greatest attention in this book. The approaches at this level tend to emphasize the *prevention* of deviance. In contrast, controls at the other levels tend to emphasize *reaction* to deviance, usually in the form of treatment or punishment, only after it has occurred. Sociological strategies focusing on social structure range from thoughtful arrangement of buildings and public spaces to make them less inviting sites for crime to large-scale changes aimed at redressing economic and social inequalities that affect families, neighborhoods and communities. An assumption supported repeatedly by evidence in the subsequent chapters of this book is that the most effective, efficient social controls are the informal ones exerted on people when they are closely linked to others in networks of kin, neighborhoods, and communities. Such relationships provide stability growing out of mutual obligations, a sense of commitment, and the rewards of caring, human concern. The global economic forces in contemporary America tending to break down families and neighborhoods—from the automobile to corporate policies affecting factory closings, the frequent transfer of employees, and lack of child care for working parents—contribute to deviance by weakening the bonds of informal control. As a result, we have come to rely more and more on formal, after-the-fact control mechanisms administered by medical and criminal justice professionals.

The Social Policy of Control: Problems and Prospects

Throughout the 19th and 20th centuries governments have become more involved in social control. They have done so as they have taken greater responsibility for public safety and public welfare. By the early 1970s, however, the costs of this expanding burden were becoming apparent—especially with the increased emphasis placed on building up the military while simultaneously cutting taxes. In the face of budget deficits at state and national levels, officials have tried to reduce the public costs of social services and social control. One result has been to reduce or eliminate certain social control functions such as the care and custody of mental patients, which produced the deinstitutionalization and community mental health movements. This approach has relied heavily on the use of medical advances, in particular drugs to control the behavior of those who would previously have been in mental hospitals. Other strategies have included turning activities like policing or the administration of minimum-security prisons over to companies in the private sector; relying more heavily on volunteer modes of social control such as citizen policing or neighborhood watch organizations; and attempts to prevent deviance by the increased use of surveillance techniques.

While governments have relinquished some of their social control functions, others have intensified. In particular there is greater reliance upon imprisonment and capital punishment. Present trends in social control present a two-handed image: the iron fist of incarceration or execution for the criminally deviant remains firm and growing in favor; for those who are less threatening and are not simply abandoned, the velvet glove of professional, therapeutic treatment extends its grasp. Among the highlights of current developments in social control we can see the following:

- Withdrawal of government resources devoted to the custody and care of "social junk" (the mentally ill, poor, aged, and otherwise dependent) and a greater tendency to allow them to be abandoned and end up in urban streets and alleys (Spitzer, 1975).
- Increased use of medical technology such as psychotropic drugs to control in the community those who were formerly institutionalized.
- Increased intrusion by the technology of surveillance (TV monitors, bugging devices, spies, drug testing) into everyday life and the expansion of businesses that provide the techniques (Lowman, Menzies, and Palys, 1987; Marx, 1988).
- A vast expansion of the private security of industry to provide specialized services such as the protection of corporate property (Shearing and Stenning, 1983).
- An increase in dependence upon nongovernmental, private, and self-help control strategies, such as neighborhood watch groups, citizen patrols, auxiliary

police, privately supported substance abuse treatment facilities, and privately contracted community mental health services.

- Increased resources, both public and private, devoted to the imprisonment of "social dynamite" (the criminal and the "dangerous").
- A return to the ultimate exclusion, capital punishment, but in a more "humane," medicalized guise by lethal injection.

This is one set of social control policy choices now in place. The remainder of this book is intended to help you understand them better, to evaluate the relationship of various theories and research findings to them, and to assess the alternatives. The grim list above does not, in fact, exhaust the possibilities. Indeed, from the theory and research complied in this book there emerges an option to our present course.

Society, Deviance, and Social Justice

Each of the next eight chapters takes up in detail a specific form of deviance and the approaches to its control. As you are reading about each topic, however, you should try to keep in mind the interconnections among them. Many deviant behaviors have common correlates. For example, alcohol is associated generally with violent behavior and is mentioned prominently in conjunction with suicide, family violence, and street crime. Likewise, understanding the role of illegal street drug markets in the economies of urban, ghetto neighborhoods is essential to understanding patterns of street crime in America. Thus, Chapter 6, "Alcohol and Other Drugs," is closely connected with Chapter 8, "Street Crime and Delinquency."

At a more global level, very different deviant behaviors can be linked. A basic premise of this book is that societies in large measure get the kinds and amounts of deviance they are organized to produce. This is not to say that people in America *want* to experience, for example, a rise in street gang violence or to be looted by the world's most massive crime wave such as the multi-billion dollar savings and loan frauds. It is to say, though, that the deterioration of America's inner cities, giving rise to more urban gang violence, and the increase in financial industry crime have common roots in recent socioeconomic trends. You will note in the section on gangs in Chapter 8 that many street gang researchers attribute current gang patterns to the deindustrialization of America's inner cities. As companies move their manufacturing overseas and American factories close, the legitimate avenue to economic security for working-class young people with minimal education disappears. Likewise, the economic basis for stable families and communities deteriorates and the conditions for gangs become ideal. In Chapter 9 you will read that the savings and loan crime wave may only be the leading edge of a corporate crime trend. As deindustrialization continues and the financial services industry becomes more prominent in the American economy, researchers in this field predict increases in this type of crime. Thus, the reorganization of American society—its transition from an industrial to a postindustrial economy—is affecting patterns of deviant behavior at opposite ends of the economic spectrum.

Finally, as noted above, two approaches in reaction to deviant behavior presently dominate social control policies in America. One is the punitive mode, which calls for more law enforcement, harsher sentencing, and more prisons in which to warehouse street criminals. The second is the therapeutic mode, which tends to classify and treat deviance as medical pathology. The final chapter of this book, drawing insights of research and theory, offers an alternative to the practice of social control. The social justice model calls on us to pay far greater attention to the *prevention* of harmful deviance by attending to its underlying causes, rooted in inequality and injustice. Prostitution and high rates of violence in families are linked to inequalities between women and men; street crime, drug abuse, gang activity, and homelessness are related to the disintegration of poor families, neighborhoods, and communities. A social justice approach would devote far more societal resources to eliminating social and economic inequalities.[6] At the other end of the social spectrum, where corporate criminals pollute, steal, and kill, the reach of the criminal law has indeed fallen short. Social justice demands that the harmful deviance of the powerful receive much greater attention from the criminal justice system than it has in the past.

SUMMARY

This chapter has introduced the study of deviance and social control as a field of inquiry. We began by distinguishing between explanations aimed at understanding the behavior of deviant individuals (*deviants*) and explanations dealing with how a particular sort of behavior becomes labeled deviant (*deviance*). Another way to put this distinction is to note the difference between type-of-person theories directed to the question, Why does the person act that way? and type-of-behavior theories responding to the question, Why are certain activities treated as deviant while others are not? There is widespread agreement that some deviant activities, many of them called crimes, are wrong and ought to bring some negative reactions. Many other deviant activities fail to generate a strong public consensus about how they should be treated. This suggests that interest-group conflict, politics, and power are frequently central to understanding deviance.

Next we turned to the importance of theories (explanations) and research (systematic observations) for the formation of social policies directed at changing or controlling deviance. Because theories frequently serve as guidelines or rationalizations for social action or inaction, citizens in a democratic society must be able to understand and evaluate the theories surrounding various social policy choices. Research is both a source for generating theories and a means for testing them. A brief review of approaches to explaining deviance was organized according to levels of analysis: biogenetic, psychological, social psychological, and sociological. These levels move generally from locating the cause within the individual (nature) to locating the cause in the social environment (nurture).

Finally, we reviewed approaches to social control. Present social policies reflect both the continued use of exclusionary, total institutions that arose during the 19th century and more recent developments in therapeutic, community-oriented treatment and self-help. The net result has been an expansion of social control techniques and the number of people who become enmeshed in the system of social control. Social control strategies can be categorized into the same four levels of analysis that were applied to theories of deviance. This book places particular emphasis on the sociological level and on social policies aimed at better coping with the most harmful kinds of deviance. The underlying premise is that the types and amounts of deviance in a society depend to a large extent on how the society is organized. Some of the most harmful forms of deviance in American society stem from common socioeconomic roots. A global perspective opens our eyes to the connections between activities as varied as urban street gangs and the recent savings and loan crime wave. The chapter concluded with a preview of the social justice alternative to the control of deviance that is presented in the final chapter of this book.

This analysis should be useful in understanding the theories, research, and control strategies discussed in the chapters that follow on specific types of deviance. When trying to grasp a particular explanation of deviance, it is usually helpful to ask yourself the following questions:

- Does the explanation deal with how a *person* becomes deviant or how the *behavior* becomes deviance?
- What is the *level of analysis* of the explanation? Does it emphasize the individual's *nature* or socioenvironmental *nurture*?
- What variable in the theory is proposed as the main *cause* of the deviance? Lack of social integration? Anomie? Blocked legitimate opportunity? Social learning? Social class?
- What are the *social policy* implications of the theory? What theory of deviance underlies a given *control strategy*? Is a particular group or class apt to benefit from the *approaches to social control* supported by a given theory?
- Based on knowledge gained from theory and research, what *social control policies* are apt to be most effective? What are the apparent *benefits* and *costs* of the policy alternatives?

ENDNOTES

1. An interesting question can be raised when old, discarded laws like the blue laws become the objects of renewed attention and attempts at enforcement. For example, see Chambliss (1973). This issue is discussed later at various points in this book.

2. While Schur (1965) identifies the transactional nature of victimless crimes as their underlying commonality, there is heated debate revolving around his label for them. For an excellent exchange on the issue of whether "victimless" crimes really have no victims, see Schur and Bedeau (1974).

3. Of course, the most famous recent examples of failure on the part of the powerful to maintain the secrecy of their deviance include the collapse of the Nixon administration brought about by the Watergate episode and the exposure of the Iran-Contra affair in the Reagan administration.

4. Ethology is the study of how animal behavior relates to that of humans. Ardrey (1961) finds ethological evidence for his theory in the study of territoriality among fish, birds, and subhuman primates. A similar argument is advanced by Lorenz (1966).

5. While Durkheim applies his functional analysis specifically to crime, the logic of the argument holds equally well for the broader category, deviance. For example, see Erikson (1966).
6. Economic inequalities, in particular, have grown astonishingly in recent years. For an account of the growing gap between rich and poor, see Chapter 9.

REFERENCES

Akers, R. L., Krohn, M. D., Lanza-Kaduce, L. and Radosevich, M.
1979   "Social Learning and Deviant Behavior." *American Sociological Review* 44: 636–655.

Ardrey, R.
1961   *African Genesis.* New York: Atheneum.
1966   *The Territorial Imperative.* New York: Atheneum.

Bandura, A.
1962   "Social Learning through Imitation." In *Nebraska Symposium on Motivation.* Lincoln: University of Nebraska.

Bandura, A., Ross, D., and Ross, S. A.
1961   "Transmission of Aggression through Imitation of Aggression Models." *Journal of Abnormal and Social Psychology* 63: 575–582.
1963   "Imitation of Film—Mediated Aggressive Models." *Journal of Abnormal and Social Psychology* 66: 3–11.

Bandura, A., and Walters, R. H.
1959   *Adolescent Aggression.* New York: Ronald.

Becker, H. S.
1963   *Outsiders.* New York: Free Press.

Braithwaite, J.
1989   *Crime, Shame, and Reintegration.* New York: Cambridge University Press.

Braithwaite, J., and Geis, G.
1982   "On Theory and Action for Corporate Crime Control." *Crime and Delinquency* 28: 292–314.

Brenner, M. H.
1973   *Mental Illness and the Economy.* Cambridge, MA: Harvard University Press.

Catanzaro, R. J.
1967   "Psychiatric Aspects of Alcoholism." Pp. 31–45 in David J. Pittman (ed.), *Alcoholism.* New York: Harper & Row.

Cavan, R.
1923   *Suicide.* Chicago: University of Chicago Press.

Chambliss, W. J.
1975   "Toward a Political Economy of Crime." *Theory and Society* 2: 149–170.

Cloward, R., and Ohlin, L. E.
1960   *Delinquency and Opportunity: A Theory of Delinquent Gangs.* New York: Free Press.

Cohen, A. K.
1955   *Delinquent Boys.* Glencoe, IL: Free Press.

Cohen, L. E., and Felson, M.
1979   "Social Change and Crime Rate Trends: A Routine Activities Approach." *American Sociological Review* 44: 588–608.

Cohen, S.
1979   "The Punitive City: Notes on the Dispersal of Social Control." *Contemporary Crisis* 3: 339–363.
1985   *Visions of Social Control: Crime, Punishment and Classification.* Cambridge, England: Polity Press.

Cohen, S., and Scull, A. (eds.)
1983   *Social Control and the State.* New York: St. Martin's.

Coser, L. A.
1967   "Violence and the Social Structure." Pp. 53–71 in *Continuities in the Study of Social Conflict.* New York: Free Press.

Davis, N. J., and Anderson, B.
1983   *Social Control: The Production of Deviance in the Modern State.* New York: Irvington.

Durkheim, E.
1938   *The Rules of Sociological Method.* Translated by S. A. Solovay and J. H. Mueller; edited by G. E. G. Catlin. New York: Free Press.
1951   *Suicide: A Study in Sociology.* Originally published 1897. Translated by J. A. Spaulding and G. Simpson. Glencoe, IL: Free Press.

Ellis, L.
1982   "Genetics and Criminal Behavior." *Criminology* 20: 43–66.

Erikson, K. T.
1966   *Wayward Puritans.* New York: John Wiley.

Faris, R. E. H., and Dunham, H. W.
1939   *Mental Disorders in Urban Areas.* Chicago: University of Chicago Press.

Fishbein, D. H.
1990   "Biological Perspectives in Criminology." *Criminology* 28: 27–72.

Foucault, M.
1977   *Discipline and Punish: The Birth of the Prison.* New York: Pantheon.

Fox, R. G.
1971   "The XYY Offender: A Modern Myth?" *Journal of Criminal Law, Criminology, and Police Science* 62: 59–73.

Freud, S.
1930   *Civilization and Its Discontents*. Translated by J. Riviere. London: Hogarth Press.

Glueck, S., and Glueck, E.
1956   *Physique and Delinquency*. New York: Harper & Row.

Glueck, S., and Glueck, E.
1959   "Mental Pathology and Delinquency." Pp. 122–126 in *The Problem of Delinquency*. Boston: Houghton Mifflin.

Goffman, E.
1961   *Asylums*. Garden City, NY: Anchor.

Gottfredson, M. R., and Hirschi, T.
1990   *A General Theory of Crime*. Stanford, CA: Stanford University Press.

Henry, A. F., and Short, J. F. Jr.
1954   *Suicide and Homicide*. New York: Free Press.

Hills, S. L.
1987   *Corporate Violence: Injury and Death for Profit*. Totowa, NJ: Rowman and Littlefield.

Hirschi, T.
1969   *The Causes of Delinquency*. Berkeley, CA: University of California Press.

Hook, E. B.
1973   "Behavioral Implications of the Human XYY Genotype." *Science* 179: 139–150.

Jacobs, P. A., Bunton, M., Melville, M. M., Brittain, R. P., and McClemont, W. F.
1965   "Aggressive Behavior, Mental Subnormality, and the XYX Male." *Nature* 208: 1351.

Lombroso, C.
1911   *Crime, Its Causes and Remedies*. Translated by H. P. Horton. Boston: Little, Brown.

Lorenz, K.
1966   *On Aggression*. Translated by M.K. Wilson. New York: Harcourt, Brace and World.

Lowman, J., Menzies, R.J., and Palys, T. S.
1987   *Transcarceration: Essays in the Sociology of Social Control*. Brookfield, VT: Gower.

Mannheim, H.
1965   *Comparative Criminology*. Boston: Houghton Mifflin.

Marx, G.T.
1988   *Undercover: Police Surveillance in America*. Berkeley, CA: University of California Press.

McCord, W., and McCord, J.
1956   *Psychopathology and Delinquency*. New York: Grune and Stratton.

Mednick, S. A., Gabrielli, W. F. Jr., and Hutchings, B.
1984   "Genetic Influences in Criminal Convictions: Evidence from an Adoption Cohort." *Science* 224: 891–893.

Merton, R. K.
1968   "Social Structure and Anomie." Pp. 185–214 in *Social Theory and Social Structure*. New York: Macmillan.

Mills, C. W.
1942   "The Professional Ideology of Social Pathologists." *American Journal of Sociology* 49: 165–180.

Peele, S.
1986   "The Implications and Limitations of Genetic Models of Alcoholism and Other Addictions." *Journal of Studies on Alcohol* 47: 63–73.

Quinney, R.
1970   *The Social Reality of Crime*. Boston: Little, Brown.

Reiss, A. J. Jr., and Roth, J. A.
1993   *Understanding and Preventing Violence*. Washington, DC: National Academy Press.

Rothman, D. J.
1971   *The Discovery of the Asylum*. Boston: Little, Brown.

Rusche, G., and Kirchheimer, O.
1939   *Punishment and Social Structure*. New York: Russell.

Scheff, T. J.
1966   *Being Mentally Ill*. New York: Aldine.

Schur, E.
1965   *Crimes without Victims*. Englewood Cliffs, NJ: Prentice-Hall.

Schur, E. M., and Bedeau, H. A.
1974   *Victimless Crimes: Two Sides of a Controversy*. Englewood Cliffs, NJ: Prentice-Hall.

Schwartz, R. D., and Skolnick, J. H.
1964   "Two Studies of Legal Stigma." Pp. 103–117 in H. S. Becker (ed.), *The Other Side*. New York: Free Press.

Scull, A. T.
1977   *Decarceration: Community Treatment and the Deviant, A Radical View*. Englewood Cliffs, NJ: Prentice-Hall.

Shah, S., and Roth, L. H.
1974   "Biological and Psychophysiological Factors in Criminality." Pp. 101–173 in D. Glaser (ed.), *Handbook of Criminology*. Chicago: Rand McNally.

Shaw, C. R., and McKay, H. D.
1942   *Juvenile Delinquency and Urban Areas*. Chicago: University of Chicago Press.

Shearing, C. D., and Stenning, P. C.
1983   "Private Security: Implications for Social Control." *Social Problems* 30: 493–506.

Sheldon, W. H.
1949   *Varieties of Delinquent Youth: An Introduction to Constitutional Psychiatry*. New York: Harper & Row.

Spitzer, S.
1975   "Toward a Marxian Theory of Deviance." *Social Problems* 22: 635–651.

1979   "The Rationalization of Crime Control in Capitalist Society." *Contemporary Crises* 3: 187–206.

Spitzer, S., and Scull, A. T.
1977   "Social Control in Historical Perspective: From Private to Public Responses to Crime." Pp. 265–286 in D. F. Greenberg (ed.), *Corrections and Punishment*. Beverly Hills, CA: Sage.

Sutherland, E. H., and Cressey, D. R.
1970   *Criminology*, 9th edition. Philadelphia: Lippincott.

Sykes, G. M., and Matza, D.
1957   "Techniques of Neutralization: A Theory of Delinquency." *American Journal of Sociology* 22: 664–670.

Taylor, I., Walton, P., and Young, J.
1973   *The New Criminology*. New York: Harper & Row.

Toby, J.
1957   "Social Disorganization and Stake in Conformity." *Journal of Criminal Law, Criminology, and Police Science* 48: 12–17.

Wilson, J. Q., and Herrnstein, R. J.
1985   *Crime and Human Nature*. New York: Simon and Schuster.

Witkin, H. A., Mednick, S. A., Schulsinger, F., Bakkestrom, E., Christiansen, K. O., Goodenough, D. R., Hirschhorn, K., Lundsteen, C., Owen, D. R., Phillip, J., Rubin, D. B., and Stocking, M.
1976   "Criminality in XYY and XXY Men." *Science* 193: 547–555.

Wolfgang, M. E., and Ferracuti, F.
1967   *The Subculture of Violence*. New York: Tavistock.

2 | Heterosexual Deviance

To survive as a species, humans must engage in sexual relations, and most people feel the effects of a biologically based sexual drive for a significant portion of their lives. While a fundamental human sex drive undeniably exists, it is equally clear that human sexual behavior takes highly diverse forms. The sexual appetite is channeled, molded, restricted, repressed, or stimulated by a huge number of beliefs, customs, and sanctions in various cultures around the world. The extent of human cultural diversity is displayed most dramatically in the customs and taboos surrounding basic human functions such as eating, an activity necessary for short-term survival of individuals, and sex, an activity necessary for long-term survival of the species. One way in which people identify their own group in contrast to another is the set of taboos or customs that dictate what foods are allowable, proper, or desirable to consume. Taboos against mixing meat and dairy products or eating beef, or preferences for steak and kidney pie or spaghetti and meatballs, immediately identify certain groups. Likewise, norms vary widely regarding sexual behavior: attractiveness (fat or thin, old or young, big breasts or small), availability of sexual partners (permissive or severely limited access), marital-sexual arrangements (varying from strict monogamy to polygamy), and acceptance of nonprocreative sexual practices (sexual foreplay, homosexuality, or masturbation), to name a few.

Because differential standards of conduct have evolved in different cultures in regard to even the most basic human functions, simple, general definitions of deviant sexual behaviors are impossible. Moreover, standards of sexual behavior are apt to change over time in any society. Beginning in the 1960s, there was within a generation in the United States a dramatic increase in the availability of sexually explicit materials and more permissive attitudes toward premarital intercourse, mouth-to-genital sex, and masturbation, with corresponding increases in these behaviors. There also was a more open treatment of human sexuality, especially female sexuality, and a considerable shift away from the double standard which is more lenient for males (Hunt, 1974). Smith (1990) observes, however, that "at least since the early 1970s there appears to have been no liberal shift, and even some conservative movement, in attitudes on homosexuality, extra-marital sex, and pornography."

The appearance in the early 1980s of two sexually transmitted diseases, herpes and AIDS, has apparently reversed some of the trends initiated in the sexual revolution of the 1960s and early 1970s. For example, a 1986 survey of 2,600 college students found that 19% approved of an occasional one-night stand, 48% in 1966 (Van

Gelder and Brandt, 1986). National surveys have found that the proportion of never-married women who reported having had sexual intercourse increased from 28% in 1971 to 46% in 1979 and then stabilized at about 43% in 1982 (Darrow, 1987). Changes in sexual behavior have been most pronounced among homosexual men who have reported sharp reductions in their high-risk sexual activity as knowledge of the AIDS epidemic has spread and the death toll attributed to it has risen (Feldman, 1985; Martin, 1987). For heterosexuals, evidence seems to indicate far less change. Although 98% of Americans polled in 1986 had heard of AIDS, only 11% reported having changed their sexual behavior. Based on surveys of college women between 1975 and 1989, one study concludes that "there has been little change in sexual practices in response to new and serious epidemics of sexually transmitted diseases, with the exception of an increase in the use of condoms (which still does not reach 50 percent)" (DeBuono et al., 1990). Nonetheless, there are reports of a "chill" in the sex industry (primarily prostitution), and predictions of a "new Victorianism" (Chaze, 1987; Cornish, 1986; Leishman, 1987).

This chapter focuses on heterosexual involvement in several types of activities that are generally regarded as deviant. Two caveats are in order. First, as we will show in Chapter 3 on homosexuality, human sexuality is best conceived of as a continuum of preferences and behaviors, with most people's sexuality falling somewhere between purely heterosexual and purely homosexual. Moreover, the activities discussed in this chapter are not limited exclusively to people who think of themselves as heterosexuals. We have chosen to concentrate on heterosexually oriented forms because they predominate in our society and generally present the most pressing issues for social policy. Second, studies of the precise effects of AIDS on heterosexual behaviors have yet to be published. For instance, there is some anecdotal evidence that prostitution of all types has diminished somewhat, but accurate estimates do not exist (Leishman, 1987). In any case, recent arrest data and casual observation in any American large city confirm that many "johns" continue to pay women for sex.

PROSTITUTION

If asked to visualize a prostitute in our mind's eye, most of us would probably imagine a lone "painted" woman, seductively clothed, walking the streets of a city. Such an image does in fact conform in part to reality—although we shall see that not all prostitutes are ostentatious-appearing streetwalkers, or even female. Rather than relying on appearance, prostitution is better defined by the unique properties of what a prostitute does. One expert defines prostitution as any sexual exchange in which the reward for the prostitute is neither sexual nor affectional (James, 1977: 369). Thus anyone, including a young boy, a wife, or a girlfriend, who exchanges sexual access solely for material gain (money, clothes, promotion, or entertainment) is a prostitute.

While this definition makes logical sense, as a practical and legal matter we can define prostitution more precisely. First, although gigolos (males who provide sexual services to women for pay) and male homosexual prostitutes unquestionably exist (Luckenbill, 1986), they receive relatively little attention from the law. Historically, prostitution by any definition has overwhelmingly involved women as the sexual providers in the relationship. For this reason, in this chapter we will deal only with female prostitution. Second, sexually active women who receive gifts from lovers can be distinguished from prostitutes by taking their image into account. Heyl (1979: 2) favors Polsky's (1967: 191) definition: "Prostitution is the granting of nonmarital sex *as a vocation*.... Although women accepting gifts regularly from lovers may be engaged in a commercialized relationship, they usually do not view it that way. Prostitutes, on the other hand, see the sex-money exchange as the business transaction that constitutes their job." Therefore we will confine our discussion of prostitution to women who exchange sex for money as a business.

Historical and Cultural Perspectives

Although there are no firm grounds for the claim that prostitution is the world's oldest profession, it does appear that relationships approaching prostitution have existed for a very long time. We say "approaching" because arrangements that might appear to be prostitution by Western cultural standards are sometimes not viewed that way in other societies. For example, in Urga, Mongolia, merchants and lamas (monks) took women as companions on short journeys. After one group of women was paid and discharged, the men sought others as replacements. However, from the buyers' point of view these were not prostitutes but temporary wives. Similar arrangements existed among some American Indian tribes, where it was customary for a woman to accompany a man on an extended hunting trip to satisfy his material and sexual needs in exchange for a share of the meat. The arrangement would be terminated at the end of the hunt.

Some writers have classified as prostitution the Eskimos' hospitality tradition of a male host offering his wife's services to a visitor, in exchange for which she received a small gift. By Western cultural standards this may appear to be a case of prostitution, but according to Eskimo culture it is not (Bullough and Bullough, 1978). Accounts of other non-Western practices such as prescribed promiscuity, religious rituals, serial marriage, or polygamy might be interpreted as prostitution, depending on the viewpoint of the observer. The point is that since prostitution is so much a matter of definition according to the standards of a particular society, cross-cultural generalizations about its development in preindustrial societies are difficult.

In Western history references to prostitution date back to ancient Greece, where there was widespread prostitution of various types, ranging from cultivated, upper-class courtesans (hetaera) to lower-class streetwalkers who sound similar in classical accounts to those encountered in urban areas today. During the earliest Greek period prostitution was condoned, along with homosexual behavior and very sexually explicit art. Later, in Plato's time, there was a growing hostility toward sex. The historical ambivalence of the Greeks toward prostitution, with early tolerance—even encouragement—and later hostility, seems to have been paralleled in

Roman attitudes. In early Rome there were temple prostitutes, brothels, and street-walkers, but upper-class courtesans were not romanticized as in early Greece. The popular attitude was to treat the prostitute as a low-status person and her occupation as a necessary evil.

During the early Christian period, stigmatizing attitudes toward prostitution, and indeed all sexual activity, hardened. At the same time, prostitution continued to flourish, with the reluctant toleration by the Church. Bullough and Bullough (1978) observe that

> The fact that Christianity, with its open and avowed hostility toward sexual intercourse, tolerated prostitution as a necessary evil indicates how deeply the subordination of women and the double standard are set in Western culture. Though Christians attempted to ameliorate some of the conditions of the prostitute, they never challenged traditional attitudes enough to grant sexual equality or to regard women, except for the virginal unmarried woman, as other than part of the family unit. (66)

During the later Middle Ages, prostitution became widely accepted, and most attempts to eliminate it were abandoned. Sexual inequality, the acceptance of women as sex objects, and the impossibility for an unmarried woman to support herself by other means all contributed to widespread prostitution and, apparently, resigned attitudes toward it.

From the 15th century to the present day, European public policy and attitudes toward prostitution have varied considerably. Toward the end of the 15th century, an epidemic of syphilis, coupled with the reform ideology of the Protestant movement, fostered attempts at repression. By the 17th century the syphilis epidemic had declined and courtesans among the elite—such as Madame de Pompadour, mistress of Louis XV—were frequently accepted in the royal courts. Prostitution among the lower classes increased, in brothels and in the streets. Through the late 18th and early 19th centuries, despite renewed epidemics of venereal disease, prostitution was tolerated in practice. The emphasis was on regulation rather than reform or elimination. Toward the mid-19th-century Victorian era, a less flamboyant approach toward sexuality in general brought a return of reformist attitudes toward prostitution.

Present-day images of the prostitute and the historical attitudes that serve as a foundation for the continued existence of prostitution are rooted in recurrent themes and conditions present from the outset of Western civilization. Historically, women were viewed as subordinate to men and as asexual in nature—two conditions that served as the foundation for the sexual double standard. Under this standard, widespread sexual activity is tolerated or encouraged on the part of men, while the withholding of sexual favors is demanded on the part of most "good" women. Inevitably, a small population of enterprising women has been pushed into the business of meeting the high demand. Today, with persistent occupational double standards under which women receive lower pay than men for comparable work, and with households headed by women much more likely to be living in poverty, prostitution may seem to be an employment option for some women who otherwise would be trapped in the welfare system or the lowest-paying jobs (Hobson, 1987).

Prostitution in the United States Today

Types. Prostitutes are available to fit almost any sexual demand with a wide range of prices for services. The business styles include but are not limited to streetwalkers, bar girls, studio models and escorts, masseuses, hotel and convention prostitutes, house prostitutes, and call girls. Between the extremes the relative status of the types is not clear, but streetwalkers are at the lower end of the hierarchy and call girls at the top. A comparison of these two extremes indicates the differential risks, degree of independence, styles of client relationships, economic opportunities, and future prospects of women in the trade.

Streetwalkers are the most visible of prostitutes, although they account for only about 20% of all forms in the United States (Campbell, 1991). In most large urban areas they usually are found in "red light" districts or "adult entertainment" areas on streetcorners or in doorways, awaiting potential customers who walk or drive by. The "stroll" is "the street territory on which streetwalkers ply their trade" (Carmen and Moody, 1985: 208). Usually, streetwalkers are approached by men, the price and type of sexual service are negotiated, and agreement is reached on where to meet for the exchange—usually a cheap hotel that provides rooms for prostitution or even the client's car. The fee usually ranges from $20 to $100 a "trick" with an average of about half a dozen "johns" each afternoon or night.

Street prostitutes usually come from poor families and often are members of a racial or ethnic minority or runaways from white families. They have a high incidence of drug use, but contrary to myth, most are not heroin addicts (Carmen and Moody, 1985: 39). They are sometimes both the dispensers and the victims of violence. Because for short periods of time they are apt to carry substantial amounts of cash, these women are targets of muggers. Increasingly, street prostitutes are robbing their clients, sometimes acting in teams—one member steals from the john while he is engaged in sex with the other one. The street hooker lives in a world of pimps, roach-infested hotels, vice officers, "pros wagons," night courts, bail bondsmen, prostitution lawyers, and day-to-day existence with a criminal record. The risk of arrest is great; the likelihood of long-term financial success is small; and the physical toll is enormous.

Gail Sheehy (1973) puts it well:

> It sounds unbelievably glamorous. Come to the big city and make a minimum of $200 a night doing what comes naturally. Work six nights a week while you're young and pretty. It's the fastest way to make money in the shortest time. How else can a girl earn $70,000 a year? There are several critical facts the recruiter fails to mention. The average *net* income for a streetwalker is less than $100 a week. "To the pimp she's nothing but a piece of meat," says one police veteran of prostitution vans. And she ages very quickly. Prostitution is a physically punishing business. Right from the start a working girl begins to worry about her age. This is one profession in which seniority is not rewarded. (12–13)

Until very recently, most urban street prostitutes were part of a "stable" of from two to a dozen women overseen by a pimp. The characteristic pattern was for the woman to turn over the money she earned to the pimp in exchange for his expertise in administering her professional and personal life. He would pay bail bondsmen or otherwise attend to the consequences of brushes with the law and allow her to share the status he derived from his lifestyle, which usually included fancy clothes, a customized car, and the aura of a celebrity. He also would provide her with a secure sense of belonging, which seems to explain, in part, why street prostitutes so readily became attached to pimps, despite the overbearing, inequitable, sometimes violent aspects of the relationship. Women in American society have traditionally been socialized to feel that they need a man to care for them, and there is no reason to suspect prostitutes felt otherwise. S. Hall (1972) quotes this description of the pimp-prostitute relationship by a pimp named Silky, which provides insights into how he operated with his women and why they stayed with him:

> It's almost inevitable that a prostitute ends up with a player. It's hand and glove. Birds of a feather. The two just go together. Their heads are in the same place. We have the same thought patterns about life. We live the same life. Most girls look at everyone besides pimps as tricks. Some people think that pimps are whores because they take money, and that whores are tricks because they pay the pimps. It's true that without money a girl can't be mine, no way. A date can't have her unless he pays her. That is a similarity. But the relationship between a pimp and a whore is also a man-woman relationship. Our personal relationship is number one. Money is part of that relationship because money is a rule and a law of life.
>
> A girl who is a prostitute becomes good at manipulating men. Because I am aware, I don't allow her to manipulate me. With me, she has the one relationship that isn't a "use" relationship. She needs a pimp for her personal life. He's the only one who can understand, appreciate and handle her. (5–6)

The pimp-prostitute relationship was both utilitarian and emotional. In it could be found the complexities of economic and interpersonal influences that characterize gender relations throughout the society. Indeed, there are many respects in which life on the streets replicates *and* magnifies the gender inequities higher up on the socioeconomic scale. Romenesko and Miller (1989) conclude in their study of female street hustlers that "Traded as chattel, often stripped entirely of property in the process of exchanging 'men,' and finally disowned when competition from other more naive, more attractive, and more obedient women becomes too strong, street women find themselves doubly jeopardized by capitalistic-patriarchal structures that are pervasive in 'straight' society and profound upon the street" (109).

In the past few years, the widespread use of crack cocaine in American cities has brought "a shift in women's relationships with men on the streets, with crack perceived as having replaced traditional pimp/prostitute relationships" (J. Miller, 1994: 1). The amount of drug use and drug addiction among street prostitutes has always been high. With the availability of crack, however, has come a sex-for-crack pattern of prostitution that sharply curtails the customary pimp role (Ratner, 1993). This might at first suggest greater independence for prostitutes, but because men largely control drugs and other resources on the streets, street prostitutes have become increasingly subject to sexual degradation and vulnerable to violence as drug dealing has become comparatively more lucrative than pimping (Miller, 1993). The crack-induced demise of the pimp-prostitute relationship has made street prostitution even more dangerous than it already was.

In contrast to the streetwalker, the call girl is at the pinnacle of the profession. She is usually white, attractive, socially sophisticated, discreet, and independent. Her business is arranged mostly by telephone as she receives calls for "visits" or "dates" with customers. A call girl may begin building up a "book" of clients by taking the extra customers of another girl who receives a share of the fee, or current customers may refer friends or business associates to her. While there usually is some contact with other call girls, this mode of prostitution is not enmeshed in a web of threatening or parasitic relationships like those that surround the streetwalker.

Sheehy (1973) quotes from an interview with a "liberated" call girl:

> Take a woman of my age. Twenty-five. Divorced. After a woman has lived with a man and reaches a certain age, she needs sex. That's why being a working girl is so great. I take only champagne tricks, $100 an hour. My men are all very well dressed and successful with styled hair and young wives in Southampton, that group. They're men I would date if I weren't in the business. It's a protection for me because I'm always afraid of getting involved. I don't want another unhappy marriage. So being a call girl is like taking out sexual insurance. I get paid for it. Plus when I want to enjoy it, I enjoy it…. (205)

Sheehy describes another call girl this way:

> Today she is determined to build up a good book in New York. Her goal is to chin up the social ladder toward a rich husband. By now she has assembled a $6,000 wardrobe, paid off most of her furniture, and has almost "done her teeth." The apartment belongs to another working girl who is living with a client in Italy. The address, the chandeliered lobby, the patina of hand-polished bronze elevators—all these things are critical if one is to maintain a champagne clientele. But she pays off no one. (Once a girl begins paying off, there is no end to the overhead.) In the interest of discretion, she allows no more than five of her most distinguished clients per week past the nosy doorman…. Now that she has had a taste of independent high living on $600 to $1,000 a week, her sights have been raised. She wants to hit the top as a call girl. She keeps telling herself it is the true liberation. There is only one thing missing in her two years in New York; she has not seen or held a man for anything but business. (211–212)

Extent of Prostitution. Obviously, there is no way to count accurately the number of prostitutes in the United States, even if a satisfactorily precise definition existed. One widely cited source estimates that as many as 500,000 women earn nearly $20 billion per year in the occupation (Simon and Witte, 1982). Prostitution also exacts a major commitment from the criminal justice system. According to FBI statistics (U.S. Department of Justice, 1993), in 1992 56,808 women were arrested for "prostitution and commercialized vice." Moreover, James (1977) estimates that a substantial portion of the female arrests for "curfew and loitering law violations" or "vagrancy" probably involve at least suspicion of prostitution, and approximately 30% of female jail inmates are there on a prostitution charge.

Clients. The sexual behavior of 101 male clients with female street prostitutes studied in Camden, New Jersey (Freund et al., 1991), provides some insight into these patrons and their activities. Most of the clientele were mature men of about 40, on average residents of the area for about 20 years, and currently or previously married. Racially, they were similar to the composition of the general population of the area and had been clients of local prostitutes for an average of about five years. Most were regular or repeat clients—93% monthly or more frequently, and 63% at least weekly. About half the clients reported sex with the same prostitute or groups of prostitutes. They primarily met on the street, and 43% of the sexual encounters took place in clients' cars. Vaginal sex (43%) and oral sex (39%) were the most common sexual activities; condoms were used in 72% of the vaginal sexual activity and 33% of the oral activity.

Venereal Disease and AIDS. Despite widespread public concerns that prostitutes spread venereal disease, the rates among prostitutes are low—less than 5%, compared to a 25% rate among high school students aged 15–19 (Carmen and Moody, 1985: 12). Studies of the presence of HIV (the AIDS virus) antibodies in female prostitutes in the United States and Europe have found that unless a prostitute abuses drugs by injection, HIV infection is not likely (Acheson, 1987: 663). A study of prostitutes' clients in New York which focused on AIDS yielded consistent results; of 101 men tested, 3 tested positive for AIDS (Leishman, 1987). One of these three "reported more than 2,200 sexual contacts, and after four interviews finally said that he had once been the receptive partner in anal sex" (46). The other two men were also suspected of having been exposed to high-risk factors rather than having contracted the disease from a prostitute.

In another study of 284 intravenous drug users, those who did *not* claim prostitution were significantly *more* likely to be infected by the AIDS virus (Banks, Brown, and Ajuluchukwu, 1991). This should not be surprising, for sex is these women's business and they know it well enough to take precautions. Many women on the street are particularly insistent about the use of condoms in any kind of sex (Freund et al., 1991). At the same time, because drug use is so prevalent among American street prostitutes, in some locations the prevalence of HIV infection among them is high. In a Centers for Disease Control study (1987), 78 percent of the prostitutes claimed they used condoms with customers, but only 16 percent of them said they did so with nonpaying partners. This suggests that the lovers of prostitutes may be a greater risk to prostitutes than their clients. In developed countries, drug use is the most common reason for exposure to HIV among street prostitutes, followed by unsafe sex with a nonpaying, injecting partner (Plant, 1990). As a result of findings such as these, the exact role of prostitution in the heterosexual spread of AIDS remains unclear (Campbell, 1991).

Although prostitution may have fallen off in the United States in areas hit hardest by the AIDS epidemic, especially New York and San Francisco, activity has not been much affected in most cities. Indeed, in some legalized brothels in Nevada, business has increased. Customers are apparently encouraged by strict prohibitions against drug use, regular weekly medical exams, and rules making condoms mandatory for all sex acts.

Because of their high volume of sexual activity, prostitutes appear to be a good target for AIDS education campaigns. This is especially true in settings such as the jurisdictions in Nevada where prostitution is legal. There, according to Campbell (1991):

> Prostitutes have an opportunity for interaction with customers when they conduct the routine inspection and are able to reject a customer on the basis of his health alone. In addition to making a judgment about his health, prostitutes give instructions to customers to wash with Betadine and to put on a condom. Here, then, the scope of prevention becomes broadened to include not just the prostitute's health but her customer's as well. (1375)

Explanations of Prostitution

Functions. The earliest attempt to explain the prevalence of prostitution was made by Kingsley Davis (1937), who posed the question this way: "Why is it that a practice so thoroughly disapproved, so widely outlawed in Western civilization, can yet flourish so universally?" (744). He begins by noting that human sexual behavior has social significance beyond mere reproduction. Because human females are sexually receptive year-round, sex is a permanent part of human social life, and it can be used for purposes other than erotic gratification. Indeed, the employment of sex for nonsexual ends characterizes not only prostitution but all our institutions involving sex, such as courtship and marriage. Looked at this way, prostitution is not unique simply because of its use of sex for nonsexual reasons.

Prostitution does differ from legitimate sex-linked institutions such as marriage because it does not encourage or demand relative permanence or emotional feeling—qualities that are conducive to stable families in which children may be reared. Since prostitution does not exist for the legitimate ends of reproduction or child rearing, it is broadly condemned. According to Davis, "Commercial prostitution stands at the lowest extreme; it shares with other sexual institutions a basic feature, namely the employment of sex for an ulterior end in a system of differential advantages, but it differs from them in being mercenary, promiscuous and emotionally indifferent. From both these facts, however, it derives its remarkable vitality" (749).

Davis argues that when rules restricting sexual activity to marriage are strong, opportunities for sex are greatly diminished. Prostitution is one way to meet male sexual demands in a society with rules that inhibit the supply of available females. Moreover, it allows relatively few females to satisfy many men and does so without requiring any commitment beyond the men's ability to pay. The prostitute-client relationship is commercial, impersonal, and transitory. Prostitution is, then, an institution complementary to the traditional marriage and family because it provides an outlet for immediate sexual gratification without directly threatening the family. It follows that as sexual norms are liberalized and women are less closely tied to the traditional family, prostitution should decline. However, while Davis foresees a simultaneous reduction in both family stability *and* prostitution, he does not predict the total elimination of either.

> ...even if present trends continue, there is no likelihood that sex freedom will ever displace prostitution. Not only will there always be a set of reproduction institutions which place a check upon sexual liberty, a system of social dominance which gives a motive for setting sexual favors, and a scale of attractiveness which creates the need for buying these favors, but prostitution is, in the last analysis, economical. Enabling a small number of women to take care of the needs of a large number of men, it is the most convenient sexual outlet for many, and for the legions of strangers, perverts, and physically repulsive in our midst. It performs a function, apparently, which no other institution fully performs. (755)

Social Psychological Development. A functionalist theory like Davis's is aimed at explaining why a practice like prostitution exists. We can, of course, seek an answer to a very different sort of question: Why do certain women become prostitutes? One approach in response to this question has been to assume that something must be fundamentally wrong—even sick—with a woman who sells sex. Various psychoanalytic or psychological studies of prostitutes have reported motivations such as being oversexed or frigid, latently homosexual, or having other difficulties in psychosexual development (see for example, Greenwald, 1970; or Winick and Kinsie, 1971). However, the evidence to support these assertions is weak and contradictory. For example, in a study specifically aimed at uncovering evidence concerning theories of psychological abnormalities, Gebhard (1969) found that among 127 prostitutes there was no unusually high incidence of frigidity, homosexuality, or hatred of men.

One researcher (Heyl, 1979) has ruefully observed that analyses of prostitutes based on the Freudian concepts of Oedipal/Electra complexes, penis envy, or infantile regression would make more sense if applied to their male clients. After all, the prostitute's motivation is obviously utilitarian—she does it to earn a living. The client's motivation, being less utilitarian, might be more appropriately explained by *his* psychosexual development. Nevertheless, the extant research at the psychological level focuses overwhelmingly on the prostitute rather than the client.

Aside from psychoanalytic motivations, the reasons for becoming a prostitute can be classified under three headings: (1) predisposing factors, (2) attracting factors, and (3) precipitating factors. *Predisposing factors* typically include parental abuse and neglect, especially early sexual abuse (N. Davis, 1971; D. Gray, 1973; Simons and Whitbeck, 1991). Coincident with disruptive family backgrounds, women who become prostitutes typically leave home permanently and have their first sexual experiences at an earlier age than other women. These factors are especially characteristic of street prostitutes and to some extent, although to a lesser degree, for call girls. At a more general level, Rosenblum (1975) has argued that for call girls, socialization into the female sex role is a predisposing factor, and the attitudes that both they and nondeviant women learn toward sex and men are not qualitatively different:

> Desirability for both the call girl and the nondeviant woman is most basically measured by physical appearance and the ability to make a man feel "masculine." Neither the call girl nor the nondeviant woman have high expectations about receiving sexual gratification (though to differing degrees), and both expect some type of "pay off" for their desirability (though the prostitute's payment is more tangible). The difference between the utilization of and the expectations regarding sexuality is only one of degree. The decision to become a call girl simply requires an exaggeration of one aspect of the situation experienced as a nondeviant woman. (180)

Attracting factors in prostitution for women include comparative career advantages such as independence, adventure, money, and sexual gratification. In a review of 26 studies of prostitution, James (1977: 390-391) found that "economics" was mentioned as an important conscious motivation in 14 of the studies and "adventure" was mentioned in 10. Because of social and occupational discrimination, few occupations widely available to women promise the high economic payoff that prostitution does, especially for call girls, who have the least risk of arrest or physical harm. Geis (1972) notes that

> ...prostitution may be regarded as an entrepreneurial endeavor, at least on certain levels of its pursuit, replete with all of the advantages that self-employment offers (including the opportunity to easily avoid payment of income taxes). One has no bosses, and retains the right to choose whether one cares to work at given times. Perhaps, in an ironic way, prostitution can be seen as much as anything else as fulfilling the vocational wish, expressed today by so many altruistically inclined young persons, that they "like to work with people." (177)

The *precipitating factors* that motivate a woman to take up prostitution vary greatly. Economic pressures, an unhappy love affair or marriage, having a marginal occupation like cocktail waitress in bars catering to men who are "cruising," or positive contact with a pimp or other prostitutes may all contribute to drifting into "the life." The general pattern reported repeatedly in studies of street prostitutes is estrangement from home while quite young (N. Davis, 1971) and a supportive relationship with a pimp or other prostitutes who provide for the insecure novice what appears to be a secure place in a well-defined (even if authoritarian) social world (Gray, 1973).

Street prostitution is often one among several activities—including drugs, fraud, forgery and theft—that constitute the illegal work of street hustling. E. Miller (1986) found three recruitment paths to street hustling in her Milwaukee study: (1) introduction through familial networks, the most likely route for black women; (2) drug use, most typical for Hispanics; and (3) running away from home, not associated with race or class. In another study (Carmen and Moody, 1985), the interviewer asked: "Were you forced into the life by a pimp?" The responses puncture the myth that women are typically coerced into prostitution by individual men. Usually, economic need comes first. Two of the answers were:

> I was all by myself, had nowhere to go. I was hungry, couldn't go home, and I had no money to eat or live. So I came on the streets and started working to make some money, and now I'm not hungry and have a place to live. No one had to put me on the streets. The money is cool, but at least I don't have to be hungry or sleep in the streets, or worry about where my next meal is coming from, or where I'm going to sleep.— Vickie.

> No. The reason why I became a prostitute is because of the money. I could not find a job and I needed money. And my man, he doesn't force me to come out on the streets—it's because I want to. I find it's an easier way to make a living and to have more things out of life. I was never forced into prostitution. If I don't want to come out, he doesn't make me. I'd rather work the streets and get all the things I want.—Blanche. (103–104)

Career Movement and Labeling. How does a woman begin to see herself as a prostitute? This question goes beyond establishing the *factors* associated with becoming a prostitute to the description of the *process* through which a deviant identity is established. Nanette J. Davis (1971) suggests three stages in the process of career movement and role commitment:

1. The process of drift from promiscuity to the first act of prostitution.
2. The transition between conventional sexual behavior and deviance.
3. The professionalization of deviance.

In stage 1, promiscuity may be used as a status tool to gain attention—especially if the young woman comes from an unstable home. She becomes identified by others (and comes to see herself) as different or a troublemaker. The drift from promiscuity to the first act of prostitution generally occurs in late adolescence, when she gradually becomes aware that the already-established pattern of promiscuous behavior can be profitable: "It was either jump in bed, and go with every Tom, Dick, and Harry, and just give it away, so I decided to turn tricks instead…. The money was so easy to get" (Davis, 1971: 305). Being institutionalized in a correctional facility appears to speed up the process leading to self-conception as a prostitute, since incarceration with established prostitutes facilitates the learning of techniques and attitudes required to take up the role.

In stage 2, transitional deviance, many young women show a pattern of behavior alternating between conventionality and deviance. They may make verbal commitments to stop prostituting and return to home, school, or job. There is motivational ambivalence between the fears of acquiring the inevitable stigma as a prostitute and the desire to establish economic independence. A few at this stage may move permanently in the direction of conventional behavior, due to negative experiences with a pimp, a client, or the police. Economic motives seem to provide the strongest reason for others to increase their frequency of prostitution. Those who continue may use their links with pimps and other prostitutes to provide "in-service training" that includes:

> (1) Willingness to satisfy a broad range of client requests, requiring certain social and sexual skills; (2) elimination of fears regarding clients who are defined as "odd" (sado-masochists); (3) adaptation to police surveillance and entrapment procedures; (4) avoid-ance of drunken clients, or those unable or unwilling to pay; and (5) substitution of a "business" ethic for the earlier one of "gaming" or excitement concerns. (Davis, 1971: 315)

In state 3 of deviant involvement, professionalization, there is what Davis calls the "unequivocal perception of a deviant self." Prostitution has become the daily routine in which sex is the vocation. The woman is now firmly implanted in a social network of johns, pimps, other prostitutes, and police with whom she must deal regularly and skillfully. For example, the actual social relations between prostitutes and police are far less hostile than their legal relationship would imply. The veter-an prostitute will provide services for vice officers such as counseling or instructing troublesome hookers, acting as an informant, and providing sex for the officers themselves or others such as judges or politicians. Thus prostitutes are able to attain one of their primary goals by helping vice officers attain theirs. The successful pros-titute avoids arrest by providing services for officers: information, friendship, emo-tional support, and sex (Atkinson and Boles, 1977: 227).

The Political Economy of Prostitution

Prostitution and the Law.   Legal sanctions, in the United States as well as most so-cieties, are directed almost exclusively at the prostitute; little or no attention is di-rected toward the client. This is not to say that men who purchase the services of prostitutes are acting legally. In most jurisdictions, being a client of a prostitute is strictly illegal, but male clients are almost never arrested or prosecuted. For ex-ample, during a two-month period in New York City when a 1967 law took effect that called for arrest of *both* prostitutes and patrons, only 6% of the arrests were for patronizing. Of the 508 convicted cases, only 8% were for patronizing, and there was a distinct lack of media publicity regarding the men who were arrested, "obviously extending a courtesy to patrons which [the media] do not extend to prostitutes" (Roby, 1969: 99).

Strong forces exist to support differential enforcement of the law in a way that protects patrons. The reason is to be found in the relative statuses of the prostitute and the client. Generally speaking, the prostitute is from a lower- or working-class background, while the customer is middle class. Moreover, the client is more thor-oughly attached to valued institutions in the society. As Flexner (1920) accurately observed long ago:

> The professional prostitute being a social outcast may be periodically punished without disturbing the usual course of society.... The man, however, is something more than a partner in an immoral act; he discharges important social and business relations, is a fa-

ther or brother responsible for the maintenance of others, has commercial or industrial duties to meet. He cannot be imprisoned without damaging society. (108)

In other words, regardless of the obvious injustice, those with influence due to their more valued status receive preferred treatment before the law.

Aside from the preferential treatment of clients compared to prostitutes, there is further legal discrimination. As we have already noted, the lower-status street prostitute is much more likely to be arrested than the higher-status call girl who serves an elite clientele. Clearly, having the resources to operate discreetly provides considerable protection from the law. And even the cast of characters who reap the greatest profits from their association with the street prostitute—including pimps, doormen, hotel operators, and commercialized-vice landlords—go relatively untouched by the law. The heaviest burden of the law and the resulting stigma fall on the women who have the fewest political and economic resources for resistance.

Commercialized Vice and the American Way. A careful examination of the prostitute and her occupation reveals a paradox. The prostitute herself is an outcast, an outsider—a true deviant with a spoiled identity who must manage as best she can to find compensation for her loss of social standing in her income and the relationships that make up her subculture. At the same time, prostitution as an occupation is consistently integrated with numerous fundamental American beliefs and institutions.

Prostitution is supported by widely shared discriminatory attitudes toward women. First is the sexual double standard, which portrays men as having "natural" sexual needs to "sow their wild oats" or engage in extramarital sex, while women are idealized as asexual, unpromiscuous, and faithful. To the degree that such a double standard exists, a relatively few women (the "bad girls," the sluts, and the whores) will be required to service relatively many men, thus creating obvious pressures for some women to take economic advantage of the supply-demand imbalance.

Second, learning the traditional female sex role that emphasizes sexual attractiveness and pleasing men for a "payoff" is consistent with sex as a vocation. Moreover, when women are subtly taught that they need to be attached to a man for economic security and emotional fulfillment, the stage is set for the domination exercised over many prostitutes by pimps.

Third, the inferior status of women to men and resultant job discrimination make prostitution an economically viable—even attractive—opportunity for many. Financial advantage is not the sole motivator, but the information presented in this chapter clearly establishes it as a potent force.

Finally, an array of people profit from prostitution indirectly, and it is in their interest to have the activity go on relatively undisturbed by serious attempts to eliminate it. Lemert's (1951) assessment is as good as any, since:

If [the prostitute] works on her own, the cab driver and the bellhop have to be paid. The disreputable medical examiner and the abortionist take a portion of the prostitute's income, as do the attorneys who obtain her release when she is arrested. Apart from the attorney's fees, money has to go to the "fixer" who sees to it that she escapes prosecution or conviction. The bail bondsman levies his toll, and often the policeman on the beat is not loath to practice crude extortion on the prostitute either in trade or money…. Real-estate owners and managers are able to earn far more on their investments and properties by renting to prostitutes or vice-resort operators than to other tenants. Better class hotels, along with the cheaper ones, owe part of their revenue to the prostitute, as well as taxicab companies, laundries, amusement parks, vacation resorts, and contraceptive manufacturers and distributors. The sale of liquor has always been intimately connected with prostitution, brought out by the large number of contacts between prostitutes and customers made in taverns and bars…. In other words, prostitution has been, and remains integrated into many functions or organizations which are sanctioned enterprises in the community and important in our economy. (91)

Despite the deviant status of the women who practice it, prostitution cannot be separated from the ideology or the legal and economic institutions of American society. Prostitution persists—even thrives in some places—because it provides relatively risk-free economic benefits to the powerful by women who are economically and emotionally drawn to the life, regardless of the high risks, punishing lifestyle, and rampant exploitation of many who provide the service.

Feminism and the Prostitution Rights Movement

Before the early 1970s, there were no prostitution rights organizations in the United States. Margo St. James, an ex-prostitute, founded COYOTE ("Call Off Your Old Tired Ethics") in 1973 as an attempt "to sever prostitution from its historical association with sin, crime, and illicit sex, and place the social problem of prostitution firmly in the discourse of work, choice and civil rights" (Jenness, 1990: 403). COYOTE's goals are the repeal of all laws against prostitution, the treatment of prostitution as a legitimate service occupation, and the protection of the civil rights of such "sex workers." Advocates argue that these goals are consistent with a feminist agenda because they advocate women's rights of occupational choice, women's control over their own bodies, and elimination of the sexual double standard (Jenness, 1993).

Not all feminists agree (Shrage, 1989). Since the emergence of COYOTE, counterorganizations have sprung up. One of them is WHISPER (Women Hurt in Systems of Prostitution Engaged in Revolt), which, according to Weitzer (1991) "denies that women freely choose prostitution, that prostitution is a valid career, and that it can ever be organized humanely. Prostitution is based on male domination, women's commodification, and 'enforced sexual access and sexual abuse.' Hardly a victimless crime, it is 'a crime against women by men' since it violates women's human dignity. Buying sexual favors is by definition 'violence against women'" (35).

On balance, it appears that the ranks of the COYOTE advocates have remained small and the movement has hardly had the impact of others such as the one for gay rights. Nevertheless, the issues raised by the COYOTE/WHISPER debate concerning prostitution are paralleled in related domains, including pornography and rape.

SOCIAL POLICY ON PROSTITUTION

Except in Nevada, prostitution is illegal in the United States. Nevertheless it continues to exist, regardless of its status under the law. This is not to say that social policy is powerless to affect the attractiveness of prostitution to some women. Much of the information presented above suggests that their economic situations motivate women to take it up, and therefore, social policies should be directed toward creating more alternatives for making a living. These include economic development of poor communities to stabilize families and improve the situations in which young people are reared; better social services to help families in need; more educational and employment opportunities, especially for young people; and an end to pay inequities for women. Hobson (1987) makes the point well:

> Remedies for prostitution need to be linked to social policy reforms around poverty, unemployment, and child welfare; more specifically, the growing feminization of poverty—as a result of divorces and nonmarital pregnancies—needs to be addressed. Changing the course of prostitution history will require beginning with a recognition that prostitution is not a private contract between consenting adults but an issue that is intrinsically bound up with long-term agendas for social and sexual equality. (236)

Present strategies to control prostitution in the United States fall into four broad categories identified by Helen Reynolds (1986). In the *laissez-faire model* characteristic of San Francisco, although prostitution is illegal, neither enforcement nor prosecution is pursued vigorously. In contrast, the *control model* adopted in the North Dallas neighborhood calls for a heavy investment of police time and energy in enforcement and prosecution. The *regulation model* followed in Nevada makes prostitution legal, but only in licensed brothels. A *zoning model*, such as that of Boston's "Combat Zone," is similar to the laissez-faire approach, but the activity is only tolerated by the police within a small, concentrated area of the city. Table 2.1 summarizes how these approaches influence the prostitution markets and attempt to control them.

Cracking down through stiffer law enforcement does not eliminate prostitution. Such efforts merely push the activity to another area. Especially in large cities, law enforcement tends to be counterproductive and discriminatory: even though two people (prostitute *and* john) have broken the law, neither is likely to make a complaint. However, when arrests occur it is usually the street prostitute who feels the force of the law, at considerable public expense. Carmen and Moody (1985) found that "(T)he cost of arrest, detention, and prosecution is about $2,500 per arrest. The average number of prostitutes arrested is approximately twenty thousand in New York City alone" (193). This adds up to $50 million dollars a year in New York City and approximately $150 million nationally being devoted to law enforcement that is hardly an effective deterrent.

An alternative would be *decriminalization,* or the repeal of all laws regulating sex between consenting adults, regardless of its form or whether money changes hands. Unlike the current criminalization policy in most jurisdictions, the goal

Table 2.1   Comparison of Evidence from Examples of Prostitution Models (Reynolds, 1986)

Model and Example	How Well Example Fits the Model	Types of Prostitution Found	Pimps	Visibility of Prostitution	Related Crime	Police Corruption
1. Laissez-faire model: San Francisco	Fits well in some parts of the city, particularly the adult tourist areas and minority neighborhoods; not all parts of San Francisco have obvious prostitution.	Massage parlors, escort services, bar prostitutes, hotel prostitutes, call girls	For most streetwalkers and some other types; not for highly paid and independent prostitutes (hotel and call girls)	Very visible in adult tourist areas, along with adult bookstores and movie theaters	Often found with streetwalkers	Some, as police have discretion to arrest or not; one officer convicted of recruiting juveniles for a pimp
2. Control model: North Dallas neighborhood	Fits well in the neighborhood with strict social control, especially compared to another neighborhood with little social control	Bar and hotel prostitution, some call girls	None in evidence in controlled neighborhood	None, except some subtle solicitation in hotel bars	Little	Little, since police priorities are not directed toward this type of prostitution
3. Regulation model: Rural Nevada	Fits very well for the only type of market allowed by regulation: brothels	Brothels; other types of prostitution in rural Nevada effectively suppressed	Not allowed to live in same county as prostitutes	Only signage visible, but signage can range from subtle to blatant	Very little	Little, since rules have been established; however, sheriff can change rules or influence licensing, making some corruption likely
4. Zoning model: Combat zone in Boston	Fits well, although model called for regulated prostitution within the zone and Boston has no legal prostitution	Streetwalkers and bar prostitutes, mainly in the Combat Zone	For most (if not all) prostitutes in the Combat Zone	Visible loitering and solicitation in vicinity of adult bookstores and movie theaters	Often occurs if no police patrol; can be controlled by police presence	Likely due to police power of discretion and history of police corruption in the Combat Zone

Source: Reynolds, 1986: 186.

would not be to stop prostitution. Short of authoritarian measures that are untenable in a pluralistic democracy, eradication is unrealistic. Rather, the intentions of decriminalization would be:

- To repeal laws that have discriminated against women.
- To free enforcement resources for attention to truly harmful crimes against persons or property.
- To relieve the courts of a massive burden.
- To release the women entrapped by it from the stigmatizing, humiliating effects of revolving-door "justice."

Combined with zoning regulation to control solicitation in unwanted times and places, this approach to public policy would be realistic, efficient, and just (Lowman and Mathews, 1992).

The first priority for social policy should be to assure that no woman is faced with prostitution as the only realistic, economically viable alternative to starvation or homelessness for herself and her children. Practically this means greater resources devoted to the provision of social services, the elimination of sexist attitudes such as the double standard, and an end to economic discrimination against women in the workplace. Beyond that, those who choose, for whatever reasons, to make recreational sex a business should be left to do so with a minimum of official attention from the criminal justice system.

PORNOGRAPHY

The word *pornography* is derived from the Greek *pornographas*, meaning literally "the writing of harlots." Today most people would probably agree that pornography is sexually oriented material intended to arouse vulgar, shameful, lewd, or disgusting thoughts. In the abstract, then, pornography is fairly easy to define. The difficulty arises when trying to determine whether any particular book, painting, film, videotape, or record is pornographic, because any attempt to define pornography in terms of its effects (sexual arousal) requires an accounting of the audience and the setting, in addition to the pornographic work itself. For example, to many adolescent, middle-class boys a generation ago, women's lingerie ads or photographs of bare-breasted women in *National Geographic* magazine were sexually arousing enough to stimulate masturbation and, for some, to generate vulgar, disgusting thoughts. Would it then be correct to define these materials as pornographic? The point is that pornography is very much in the eye of its beholder, and this is at the heart of the problem that social scientists and lawyers alike have encountered when trying to apply a definition. The subjectivity and value judgment involved in designating material as obscene or pornographic is well illustrated by Supreme Court Justice Potter Stewart's statement in a 1946 decision that, although he probably could never succeed in defining intelligently the types of material he would call pornographic, "I know it when I see it." Subsequent Supreme Court decisions have applied the analogous principle of "they'll know it when they see it" by ruling that local community standards of decency should be the definitional guideline.

In 1967, a commission on obscenity and pornography was appointed by President Lyndon Johnson to assess the extent and effects of such materials and to make legislative recommendations. Since to study the effects of pornography requires a precise definition, the commission was no less perplexed than lawyers and judges had been. In the end, it decided to use the term *erotic materials* in place of *pornography* or *obscenity*:

> In the absence of well-defined and generally acceptable definitions of both obscenity and pornography, the Commission conceptualized the relevant stimuli as erotic materials, sexual materials, or sexually explicit stimuli over a range of media (photographs, snapshots, cartoons, films, and written materials in books, magazines and typewritten stories) which are capable of being described in terms of the sexual themes portrayed: e.g., "a man and a woman having sexual intercourse," or "mouth-sex organ contact between man and woman." (U.S. Commission on Obscenity and Pornography, 1970: 181)

While pornography and obscenity revolve around erotic or sexual themes, it does not follow that all erotica are pornographic or obscene. Beyond the explicit, objective content of the material, pornography requires a subjective value judgment on the part of the viewer that it is vulgar, shameful, or offensive. The designation of material as pornographic is complex, because as a population Americans disagree even over which sexual acts are themselves vulgar or shameful.

Cultural and Historical Context

Erotica has existed from earliest recorded history. Sculptures of female fertility goddesses, phalluses, and copulating couples date back thousands of years. Elaborate visual erotica existed at least as long ago as the whorehouse murals found in Pompeii and the ancient Hindu temple erotic sculptures found in India. Written descriptions of sexual activities date at least from the Roman poet Ovid's *The Art of Love* at about the time of Christ and the Oriental *Kama-Sutra* of Vatsayama from Western India in the fourth century A.D. The existence of such materials was certainly not regarded in those times as a major social problem worthy of large-scale efforts to control them. Indeed, erotic art and writing were frequently integrated into the religious customs and beliefs of the society (Hyde, 1964).

Western prohibitions against sexually oriented materials are relatively recent. In part this is because, until the invention of the printing press and relatively cheap methods of papermaking, and the higher literacy rates that followed, erotica was not readily available to the general population. Even after the invention of printing, the Roman Catholic Church, the most powerful censor in history, bothered little about erotic books per se. It was only when "the bawdy was combined with heresy or a satire or attack upon the church, as in the *Decameron*, that the work was ecclesiastically proscribed or at least not permitted to be read by the faithful until it had been 'expurgated'" (Hyde, 1964: 164). The earliest English legal cases aimed at erotic writing were based on charges of sedition against the crown or blasphemy against the church, rather than any "threat to public morals" posed by sexually oriented themes.

In mid-19th-century Victorian England, the first obscenity legislation passed was aimed specifically at the importation and dissemination of "lewd" works. Beyond printing technology and increased literacy, Muedeking (1977) suggests several other factors that encouraged erotica and thus stimulated its legal control in England. These included:

> ...The rise of the state (Crown) and the decline of the Church as the supreme institution and the corresponding necessity for the state to replace custom with uniform laws for the control of behavior; the fear of satirical erotica undermining the authority of the state; and the development of a lucrative underground market in erotica (which, interestingly enough, arose out of the very existence of antipornography laws). (485–486)

In the United States, the relative lack of concern for erotica paralleled that in Britain until the mid-1800s, when Anthony Comstock, a reformist zealot, took it upon himself to ensure enforcement of an 1868 New York obscenity statute. By rallying the support of various groups, including the Young Men's Christian Association, Comstock mounted sufficient political pressure to get himself appointed by the president to the Post Office Department as a censor. He was authorized, under the 1865 Federal Mail Act, to open any letter or package and judge whether its contents were obscene. In most states obscenity statutes were passed to supplement the federal legislation concerning the mails.

Obscenity became a constitutional issue in 1957, when the Supreme Court ruled in a 5 to 4 decision in *Roth* v. *United States*:

> Obscene material is material which deals with sex in a manner appealing to prurient interests. I.e., material having a tendency to excite lustful thoughts....[to] the average person, applying contemporary community standards, the dominant theme of the material taken as a whole appeals to prurient interest.... All ideas having even the slightest redeeming social importance—unorthodox ideas, even ideas hateful to the prevailing climate of opinion—have the full protection of the guarantees [of the First Amendment].... But implicit in the history of the First Amendment is the rejection of obscenity as utterly without redeeming social importance.

For a time this ruling undermined existing obscenity statutes, allowing greater openness and availability of sexually oriented materials. However, other Supreme Court decisions, especially *Miller* v. *California* (1973), appeared to be aimed at restraining the "permissive" trend. Briefly, the key sections of these rulings state that:

- There can be no "national" definition of what is "offensive"—communities and states may set their own standards.
- "Obscene" material is not protected by the First Amendment right of free speech.
- It is not necessary to prove that obscenity is harmful in order to prohibit it.
- To show that material has "redeeming social value" is not sufficient as a defense against an obscenity charge.

In sum, concern for the legal control of sexually oriented materials is a relatively recent phenomenon in Western culture. However, as availability has increased so have public concern, legal statutes, and judicial rulings. Today, the definition and control of pornography have become persistent public and political issues.

Extent and Types of Pornography

The production of sexually oriented materials is a testament to human ingenuity. Indeed, in the typical American urban "sex shop," erotica that appeal to every one of the human senses can be found. Only a partial shopping list includes books, pictures, magazines, movies, live shows, records, audio and video tapes, lotions, creams, prophylactics in a wide variety of colors and shapes, flavored douches, dildos, leather goods intended for bondage, and even inflatable life-size dolls complete with fake genitalia.

Although no accurate accounting exists against which availability can be judged, casual impressions yield the conclusion that the numbers of retail and mail order outlets for erotica have increased substantially in the past 25 years. The report of the U.S. Commission on Obscenity and Pornography (1970) indicated that the sexually oriented materials business in the United States may have grossed as much as $2.5 billion. Given the huge growth in cable television and home video businesses that did not even exist in 1970, the figure is much greater today. Recent estimates put the total at between $6 billion and $9 billion annually. Sexually explicit videocassettes comprise about 50% of the market and are estimated alone to gross over $100 million a year (Potter, 1989). The latest pornography outlets include computer CD-ROM disks, interactive computer games, and distribution over electronic-mail networks. Federal prosecutions for pornographic distribution in cyberspace have begun (Abernathy, 1993).

The key question in the debate over what to do (or not to do) about pornography is whether pornography causes harm. The 1970 commission report concluded that exposure to sexual materials, while arousing to both males and female, is harmless. Its conclusions, however, were based on studies that used nonviolent though sexually explicit stimuli. Such materials might be within what many people would think of as erotica. In contrast, much sexually explicit material in magazines, movies, television, and videotapes today is also degrading, dehumanizing, and violent in its attitudes toward women. Sexually explicit materials do not all have the same effects (Donnerstein, Linz, and Penrod, 1987; Malamuth and Donnerstein, 1984), and leading researchers in the field are careful to specify the exact nature of the materials they use in their efforts to assess harm, as shown in Figure 2.1.

Effects of Sexual Materials

The U.S. Commission on Obscenity and Pornography undertook, in 1967, the first comprehensive research program to provide information on the effects of exposure to explicit materials. The research procedures included surveys, experiments, and studies of rates and incidence of sex offenses at the national level. The commission's conclusions about the effects of exposure to sexual images, reported in

---

Figure 2.1   Types of Stimulus Materials used in Research on the Effects of Pornography

---

I. *Nonviolent, low-degradation sexually explicit stimuli.*

Material most consistent with the definition of erotica. Depictions of mutually consenting sexual activity, pictures, verbal descriptions, and films.

II. *Nonviolent, high-degradation sexually explicit stimuli.*

Material degrading and demeaning to women, depicting them as willing recipients of any male sexual urge (excluding rape) or as oversexed and highly promiscuous. Examples: X-rated film *Debbie Does Dallas* and many "stag" or "peep show" films.

III. *Violent pornography.*

Sexually explicit material that depicts sexual coercion in which a man uses force against a woman to obtain sexual gratification. There are scenes of rape and other forms of violent sexual assault. Victims are often portrayed as "enjoying" the assault.

IV. *Nonexplicit sexual aggression against women.*

Similar to violent pornography except less sexually explicit. These materials typically contain rape scenes that are not sexually explicit, but the idea that women benefit from sexual abuse is a recurring theme.

V. *Sexualized explicit violence against women.*

Materials usually R-rated because they lack specific portrayals of sex, but usually more graphically violent than X-rated aggressive pornography. Depictions may include images of torture, murder, and mutilation common in the "slasher" film genre.

VI. *Negative-outcome rape depictions.*

Materials that show graphic and brutal rapes, but unlike most forms of violent pornography there is no indication that the victim enjoys being raped. There may be either explicit or nonexplicit depictions of sexual activity.

Source: Adapted from Donnerstein, Linz, and Penrod, 1987: 3–5.

1970, have generally been confirmed in subsequent studies (Kutchinsky, 1983; Byrne and Kelley, 1984). However, these findings apply *only to nonviolent sexual materials* (Type I in Figure 2.1) *with exposure over a short time.* The commission's summary report is reprinted below.

> **Psychosexual Stimulation.** Experimental and survey studies show that exposure to erotic stimuli produces sexual arousal in substantial portions of both males and females. Arousal is dependent on both characteristics of the stimulus and characteristics of the viewer or user.
>
> Recent research casts doubt on the common belief that women are vastly less aroused by erotic stimuli than are men. The supposed lack of female response may well be due to social and cultural inhibitions against reporting such arousal and to the fact that erotic material is generally oriented to a male audience. When viewing erotic stim-

uli, more women report the physiological sensations that are associated with sexual arousal than directly report being sexually aroused.

Research also shows that young persons are more likely to be aroused by erotica than are older persons. Persons who are college educated, religiously inactive, and sexually experienced are more likely to report arousal than persons who are less educated, religiously active, and sexually inexperienced.

Several studies show that depictions of conventional sexual behavior are generally regarded as more stimulating than depictions of less conventional activity. Heterosexual themes elicit more frequent and stronger arousal responses than depictions of homosexual activity; petting and coitus themes elicit greater arousal than oral sexuality, which in turn elicits more than sadomasochistic themes.

Satiation. The only experimental study on the subject to date found that continued or repeated exposure to erotic stimuli over 15 days resulted in satiation (marked diminution) of sexual arousal and interest in such material. In this experiment, the introduction of novel sex stimuli partially rejuvenated satiated interest, but only briefly.

Effects upon Sexual Behavior. When people are exposed to erotic materials, some persons increase masturbatory or coital behavior, a smaller proportion decrease it, but the majority of persons report no change in these behaviors. Increases in either of these behaviors are short-lived and generally disappear within 48 hours. When masturbation follows exposure, it tends to occur among individuals with established but unavailable sexual partners. When coital frequencies increase following exposure to sex stimuli, such activation generally occurs among sexually experienced persons with established and available sexual partners. In one study, middle-age married couples reported increases in both the frequency and variety of coital performance during 24 hours after the couples viewed erotic films.

In general, established patterns of sexual behavior were found to be very stable and not altered substantially by exposure to erotica. When sexual activity occurred following the viewing or reading of these materials, it constituted a temporary activation of individuals' preexisting patterns of sexual behavior.

Other common consequences of exposure to erotic stimuli are increased frequencies of erotic dreams, sexual fantasy, and conversation about sexual matters. These responses occur among both males and females. Sexual dreaming and fantasy occur as a result of exposure more often among unmarried than married persons, but conversation about sex occurs among both married and unmarried persons. Two studies found that a substantial number of married couples reported more agreeable and enhanced marital communication and an increased willingness to discuss sexual matters with each other after exposure to erotic stimuli.

Attitudinal Responses. Exposure to erotic stimuli appears to have little or no effect on already established attitudinal commitments regarding either sexuality or sexual morality. A series of four studies employing a large array of indicators found practically no significant differences in such attitudes before and after single or repeated exposures to erotica. One study did find that after exposure persons became more tolerant in reference to other persons' sexual activities although their own sexual standards did not change. One study reported that some persons' attitudes toward premarital intercourse became more liberal after exposure, while other persons' attitudes became more conservative, but another study found no changes in this regard. The overall picture is almost completely a tableau of no significant change.

Several surveys suggest that there is a correlation between experience with erotic materials and general attitudes about sex: Those who have more tolerant or liberal sexual attitudes tend also to have greater experience with sexual materials. Taken together, experimental and survey studies suggest that persons who are more sexually tolerant are also less rejecting of sexual material. Several studies show that after experience with erotic material, persons become less fearful of possible detrimental effects of exposure.

Emotional and Judgmental Responses. Several studies show that persons who are unfamiliar with erotic materials may experience strong and conflicting emotional reactions when first exposed to sexual stimuli. Multiple responses, such as attraction and repulsion to an unfamiliar object, are commonly observed in the research literature on psychosensory stimulation from a variety of nonsexual as well as sexual stimuli. These emotional responses are short-lived and, as with psychosexual stimulation, do not persist long after removal of the stimulus.

Extremely varied responses to erotic stimuli occur in the judgmental realm, as, for example, in the labeling of material as obscene or pornographic. Characteristics of both the viewer and the stimulus influence the response: for any given stimulus, some persons are more likely to judge it "obscene" than are others; and for persons of a given psychological or social type, some erotic themes are more likely to be judged "obscene" than are others. In general, persons who are older, less educated, religiously active, less experienced with erotic materials, or feel sexually guilty are most likely to judge a given erotic stimulus "obscene." There is some indication that stimuli may have to evoke both positive responses (interesting or stimulating) and negative responses (offensive or unpleasant) before they are judged obscene or pornographic.

Criminal and Delinquent Behavior. Delinquent and nondelinquent youth report generally similar experiences with explicit sexual materials. Exposure to sexual materials is widespread among both groups. The age of first exposure, the kinds of materials to which they are exposed, the amount of their exposure, the circumstances of exposure, and their reactions to erotic stimuli are essentially the same, particularly when family and neighborhood backgrounds are held constant. There is some evidence that peer group pressure accounts for both sexual experience and exposure to erotic materials among youth. A study of a heterogeneous group of young people found that exposure to erotica had no impact upon moral character over and above that of a generally deviant background.

Statistical studies of the relationship between availability of erotic materials and the rates of sex crimes in Denmark indicated that the increased availability of explicit sexual materials has been accompanied by a decrease in the incidence of sexual crime. Analysis of police records of the same types of sex crimes in Copenhagen during the past 12 years revealed that a dramatic decrease in reported sex crimes occurred during this period and that the decrease coincided with changes in Danish law which permitted wider availability of explicit sexual materials. Other research showed that the decrease in reported sexual offenses cannot be attributed to concurrent changes in the social and legal definitions of sex crimes or in public attitudes toward reporting such crimes to police, or in police reporting procedures.

Statistical studies of the relationship between the availability of erotic material and the rates of sex crimes in the United States present a more complex picture. During the period in which there has been a marked increase in the availability of erotic materials, some specific rates of arrest for sex crimes have increased (e.g., forcible rape) and others have declined (e.g., overall juvenile rates). For juveniles, the overall rate of arrest for sex crimes decreased even though arrests for nonsexual crimes increased by more than 100%. For adults, arrest for sex offenses increased slightly more than did arrests for nonsex offenses. The conclusion is that, for America, the relationship between the availability of erotica and changes in sex crime rates neither proves nor disproves the possibility that availability of erotica leads to crime, but the massive overall increases in sex crimes that have been alleged do not seem to have occurred.

Available research indicates that sex offenders have had less adolescent experience with erotica than other adults. They do not differ significantly from other adults in relation to adult experience with erotica, in relation to reported arousal or in relation to the likelihood of engaging in sexual behavior during or following exposure. Available evidence suggests that sex offenders' early inexperience with erotic materials is a reflection of their more generally deprived sexual environment. The relative absence of experience appears to constitute another indicator of atypical and inadequate sexual socialization.

In sum, empirical research designed to clarify the question has found no evidence to date that exposure to explicit sexual materials plays a significant role in the causation of delinquent or criminal behavior among youth or adults. The Commission cannot conclude that exposure to erotic materials is a factor in the causation of sex crime or sex delinquency. (U.S. Commission on Obscenity and Pornography, 1970: 24–27)

Aggressive Pornography

The overall findings of the 1970 commission stood largely unshaken for about ten years. Then mounting criticism of its conclusions in a more conservative political climate initiated a new wave of research and policy-making activity. The report of the Attorney General's Commission on Pornography (U.S. Department of Justice, 1986), appointed during the Reagan administration with the aim of contradicting the 1970 commission's findings, cited research indicating that pornography might be harmful and called for social policies to suppress it. While declaring that the scientific evidence was inconclusive, the report nevertheless expressed the belief that pornography causes crime. However, many of the scientists whose work was cited protested that it had been misused to reach this conclusion (Pally, 1991).

Is exposure to sexually explicit materials harmful? On balance the evidence is mixed. Nonaggressive sexually explicit materials (erotica) do not appear to increase male aggression toward women; however, pornographic material that tends to portray women as sexual objects and includes coercive sex does increase calloused attitudes toward women, especially if the exposure to such material is over a long period of time (Zillmann and Bryant, 1984). The evidence for harmful effects becomes more compelling with increases in the aggressive content. Citing Malamuth and Donnerstein (1982), Byrne and Kelley (1984) found that exposure to pornography characterized by negative affect, coercive imagery, and rape myths "can result in an increase in aggressive-sexual fantasies, aggressive behavior, acceptance of anti-female attitudes, and, specifically, in male aggression against females" (9).

Hard-core pornography with aggressive themes does appear to be harmful. It particularly raises levels of aggression in already-angered men (S. Gray, 1982). It also can reinforce insensitive, negative attitudes toward women such as the myth that women enjoy violent encounters (Donnerstein, Linz, and Penrod, 1987: 103), and it appears to contribute to a cultural climate that encourages rape (Baron and Straus, 1984). Two points should be stressed, however. First, we should not conclude that it is the erotic or sexual component of aggressive pornography that is the source of these negative effects. Indeed, the heavy weight of the evidence suggests that "violence against women need not occur in a pornographic or sexually explicit context to have a negative effect on viewer attitudes and behavior" (Donnerstein, Linz, and Penrod, 1987: 112). For example, Linz (1989) found that viewing violent slasher films for both long- and short-term studies lessens sensitivity toward rape victims. Thus, in regard to their impact on women, sexually oriented materials per se are far less the culprit than those that are violently oriented. Content analyses have shown that women in R-rated films are depicted receiving violence twice as often and sexual violence two and a half times more often than women in X-rated videos are (Yang and Linz, 1990). Second, systematic content analyses of pornographic magazines and movies have found that even in recently available materials, aggressive themes are prevalent in only a small minority. Overall, the link between pornography and rape is weak at best (Altimore, 1991; Gentry, 1991; Kutchinsky, 1991).

Explanations of Pornography

Functionalism. Ned Polsky (1967) has argued that the same functionalist theory applied by Kingsley Davis (1937) to prostitution can be used to explain the persistence of pornography. Davis sees prostitution as a necessary outlet for the expression of disapproved sexual activities that are impersonal, transitory, and nonfamilial, while Polsky sees pornography, under certain conditions, as a *functional alternative* to prostitution:

> Prostitution and pornography occur in every society large enough to have a reasonably complex division of labor; and although pornography develops in only a rudimentary way in preliterate societies (by means of erotic folktales and simple pictorial or sculptural devices), whenever a society has a fair degree of literacy and mass-communication technology then pornography becomes a major functional alternative to prostitution.
>
> In saying that prostitution and pornography are, at least in modern societies, functional alternatives, I mean that they are different roads to the same desired social end. Both provide for the discharge of what society labels antisocial sex, i.e., impersonal, nonmarital sex: prostitution provides this via real intercourse with a real sex object, and pornography provides it via masturbatory, imagined intercourse with a fantasy object. (185)

In addition, pornography can function as a sexual outlet in situations where people are isolated from the opposite sex, such as prisons or the military. Some of the most famous works in erotic literature were written by the Marquis de Sade and Jean Genet in prison, apparently for their own entertainment.

True to the functionalist theoretical tradition that began with Durkheim, Polsky suggests that judging, labeling, and stigmatizing pornography and pornographers is part of the process of defining the moral boundaries that distinguish a community. The interactions between pornographers and those who seek to control them help to serve notice as to the limits that community standards of behavior will tolerate. A social function of pornographers and their products, in other words, is to explore, discover, map, and publicize the outer limits of acceptable sexual conduct.

Adolescent Sexual Socialization and Guilt. Most pornography is directed toward a male audience. Even casual observation reveals that most patrons of X-rated movies and adult book stores are white, working- to middle-class, young to middle-aged men. We might fruitfully ask: What draws these particular men to the forbidden sights, sounds, and fantasies depicted in contemporary pornography?

The answer appears to lie in (1) the dominant themes of the materials, (2) the setting in which they are viewed, and (3) the psychosexual histories of the viewers. First, the sexual activities portrayed in most pornography today are generally deviant. That is, they sharply diverge from the normative ideal that sex should be confined to marriage, and in that setting only a limited repertoire of activities (ideally, coitus) should be performed. Typically, X-rated movies or adult books revolve around nonmarital sex, multiple partners, oral-genital activity, homosexual contacts, sadism, bondage, and so on. Contemporary pornography focuses, literally, on sex organs in a manner that treats both women and men simply as objects to be manipulated for sexual release. Above all, the appeal is to male sexual gratification devoid of interpersonal commitment. Women are displayed as playthings—lustful, insatiable, ever ready and eager to satisfy the orgasmic urge of the man. The world of pornography is oriented toward male sexual fantasies inhabited by an endless population of forbidden women.

Of course, for most white, middle-class males, the fantastic domain of pornography and their actual sexual lives bear little resemblance. Genuinely desirable women are taught to withhold or at least to be discreet in dispensing sexual favors. Indeed, for many middle-class adolescents, especially 20 to 30 years ago, the earliest and most prevalent sexual activity was masturbation—often with the aid of erotica as a stimulant. As Polsky (1967) has put it, "people given to using pornography do so for the most part as a means of facilitating masturbation. This is the primary use of pornography. It is summed up in the classic description of pornographic books as 'the books that one reads with one hand'" (187).

Yet, masturbation, particularly when it is facilitated by the mental fantasies provoked by the lust-filled world of pornography, is an anxiety-provoking, guilt-laden activity. A pattern of gratification through masturbation facilitated by pornography forges a link between the guilt of forbidden sexual fantasies and sexual stimulation. As Gagnon and Simon (1967) claim, guilt and anxiety may become closely associated with sexual behavior. Contemporary pornography could be especially arousing to middle-class males for whom sneaking into an X-rated movie or smuggling home a dirty novel or videotape produces anxiety. In this way guilt and anxiety, often associated with the consumption of pornography, themselves become aphrodisiacs with strong appeal.

Sexism and Violence. Shortly after the Commission on Obscenity and Pornography published its report, a curious contradiction was pointed out by James Q. Wilson (1971). He noted that the U.S. National Commission on the Causes and Prevention of Violence had concluded in 1969 that media violence, especially in movies and television, was apt to have the adverse effect of stimulating violent behavior, while the Commission on Obscenity and Pornography had concluded in its 1970 report that pornography does not contribute to individual "harms." How can we account for the apparent discrepancy between the two findings? Wilson is careful to allow that part of the problem is due to the immense difficulties in doing valid, accurate research on problems such as the effects of media violence or pornography. However, in the end he argues that social science may never be able to provide sufficient evidence to make it the sole basis for social policy:

> In the cases of violence and obscenity, it is unlikely that social science can either show harmful effects or prove that there are no harmful effects. It is unlikely, in short, that considerations of utility or disutility can be governing. These are moral issues and ultimately all judgment about the acceptability of restrictions on the various media will have to rest on political and philosophical considerations. (243)

In short, Wilson believes that social scientific evidence can never be adequate to resolve what are essentially political issues. Thelma McCormack (1978) has taken Wilson's observation of the contradictory findings of the two commissions a step further to suggest that the very research on which the conclusions are based is a reflection of female subordination in a male-dominated society.

In studies of the effects of media violence, the primary violent themes involve men against men. Often they include homosexual undertones, as in boxing films showing "two male boxers slugging it out in the ring, periodically locked in embrace, bare body touching bare body, moving steadily toward a climax in which the loser is subdued and prone on the floor" (McCormack, 1978: 551). Such themes can produce anxiety in male viewers about their sexual identity. In pornography, however, the predominant theme is to portray powerless women satisfying the narcissistic virility of superpotent men. Thus, violence themes in the media are anxiety-producing and threatening to males, while pornographic themes reinforce male self-images of superiority and machismo. McCormack points out that

> The humiliation of women and insecurity about sexual identity match the two conclusions merging from the areas of research examined, one condoning pornography as an innocent pleasure without serious social consequences; the other condemning media violence as leading to senseless and brutal acts in everyday life. The contradiction which seemed so puzzling and which we attempted unsuccessfully to resolve in favor of one or the other now turns out to be the central fact. On a deeper level, the contradiction disappears. The unifying variable is machismo. (552)

It follows, according to McCormack's reasoning, that in a male-dominated society the themes of media violence would be disapproved, while the themes of erotica would be judged harmless. In a sexually stratified society, that which causes harm to men is to be condemned, while that which portrays women as powerless sex objects is judged harmless.

Customers and Crime. Although the consumers of pornography are overwhelmingly male, they are not an otherwise homogeneous group. A recent study of pornography patrons at a midwestern adult bookstore yielded two typologies that reveal a broad range of activities and identities (Tewksbury, 1990). In respect to their "role enactments," customers were divided into porno watchers, masturbators, sex seekers, sex doers, and the naive. Their identities included heterosexual-imaged, homosexual-imaged, and a mix of these two. The observations serve to remind us that the consumption of sexually explicit materials covers the full range of sexual orientation and activities.

Pornography has been alleged to be linked to other commercialized forms of vice. A study of 26 retail pornography outlets in Philadelphia (Potter, 1989) supports this contention, concluding that in this city there is an overlap between retail pornography and other forms of vice, and, regarding illicit sexual services, retail pornography outlets are part of organized criminal networks. Gambling or gambling referral was provided in over a third of the stores sampled, and drugs or drug information were dispensed in nearly 70% of them. In particular, the data revealed that pornography and prostitution were intimately related as businesses, but Potter points out that "This does not mean that it is pornography, as a product, which creates this pattern of interaction. Certainly, pornographic materials are available in other settings, such as video rental stores or newsstands. Rather, it is a combination of factors, including location, clientele, and marketing strategies which result in this overlap in the provision of illicit goods and services" (248).

Status Politics. The public display and availability of pornography has on occasion become a major political issue in a community. The rallying cry of conservatives who seek severe restrictions usually amounts to, "Pornography is leading us to our downfall." Some feminists have also taken a prohibitionist stand, arguing that violent pornography is harmful and therefore ought to be legally banned. Others insist upon the right of adults to see, hear, or read whatever they please, under the protection of the First Amendment freedoms. However, like most inflammatory political issues in American history, from the temperance movement which culminated in the Prohibition amendment to the present right-to-life movement, antipornography crusades are largely symbolic of more far-reaching differences of opinion and lifestyle.

Following the logic of Gusfield's (1963) analysis of the American temperance movement, Zurcher and Kirkpatrick (1976) argue that antipornography campaigns are most likely to arise in communities where what has long been regarded as middle-class respectability is threatened by social change. People who are "established, stable, and solid" are being challenged by "the new, upstart, and the sophisticated." In a word, those who believe in the old way of the life and its values feel their status slipping as the new way of life and its values gain prestige. Naturally, those who feel their status ebbing wish to fight back. The most efficient, effective way to do so is to focus attention on a single, narrow issue that becomes symbolic of the broader divergence of beliefs. Thus an antipornography crusade is a symbolic defense of a traditional way of life that encompasses religiosity, antiliberalism, belief in the weakness of human nature, and the need to reverse a trend of moral decline.

Zurcher and Kirkpatrick found antipornography crusaders to be "status discontents" who were struggling to maintain the prestige of their lifestyle in a battle of status politics:

> The traditional life-style with which they were comfortable and to which they were committed was increasingly being challenged by social change. Conporns (antipornography crusaders) felt strongly that the prestige and power of their style of life was being undermined and was not being represented, particularly by the mass media, as viable. The issue of pornography had become, for the Conporns, a suitable summary symbol of the challenges and a focus for resistance to them. (275)

Of course, struggles for recognition and status are not limited to traditionalist versus modernist or conservative versus liberal. Almost never are the lines of interest clearly drawn. Exemplifying this fact is the position on pornography of some women in the feminist movement, which closely parallels McCormack's hypothesis concerning why, until recently, pornography was declared harmless by predominantly male social researchers. Pornographic themes designed to appeal to males are alleged to support, in fantasy, male self-images of superiority and machismo. Susan Brownmiller (1979), a leading feminist, puts it this way:

> We are not opposed to sex and desire and we certainly believe that explicit sexual material has its place in literature, art, science and education. No, the feminist objection to pornography is based on our belief that pornography represents hatred to women, that pornography's intent is to humiliate, degrade and dehumanize the female body for the purpose of erotic stimulation and pleasure. We are opposed to the presentation of the female body being stripped, bound, raped, tortured, mutilated and murdered in the name of commercial entertainment and free speech. (9A)

The underlying reason for this emphatic opposition is in the feminist understanding of how pornography represents the hierarchical relationship between women and men. Catherine MacKinnon (1992) says:

> In pornography, there is, in one place, all of the abuses that women had to struggle so long even to begin to articulate, all the *unspeakable* abuse: the rape, the battery, the sexual harassment, the prostitution and the sexual abuse of children. Only in the pornography is it called something else: sex, sex, sex, sex and sex, respectively. Pornography sexualizes rape, battery, sexual harassment, prostitution and child sexual abuse; it thereby celebrates, promotes, authorizes and legitimizes them. More generally, it eroticizes the dominance and submission that is the dynamic common to them all. It makes hierarchy sexy and calls that "the truth about sex" or just a mirror of reality. Through this process,

pornography constructs what a woman is as what men want from sex. This is what pornography means. (461)

Both prostitution and pornography have been characterized as victimless crimes by some social scientists and social policy makers. Such a characterization should not be taken lightly or uncritically. It is true that these activities do involve willing customers who are unlikely to make a formal complaint to law enforcement authorities. The client or customer, therefore, could hardly be called a victim. However, the sexist and too-often violent themes that frequently characterize relationships involving prostitution or images portrayed in pornography suggest a more general victimization of women in our sexually stratified society. Moreover, prostitutes or porn actors are often no more than poorly paid bit players in much larger money-making schemes, despite the fact that they have the most to lose in terms of personal danger or damaged reputation. These are cases in which the "deviant" might best be considered the victim.

SOCIAL POLICY: THE DILEMMAS OF CENSORSHIP

In the early 1980s the control of pornography once again became a significant public issue—one that persists into the 1990s. Restrictions have been proposed on both the local and national levels. A prototype of the former was the 1983 antipornography ordinance drafted by feminists Andrea Dworkin and Catherine MacKinnon that was introduced in Minneapolis, passed by the city council, but vetoed by the mayor, who objected to it on the grounds that it conflicted with the First Amendment right to free speech (Warring, 1986). Subsequent attempts to enact similar ordinances have been made in other cities. An antipornography statute adopted in 1984 by the Indianapolis City-County Council was ruled unconstitutional on the grounds that it violated the guarantees of both free speech and press. On the national level, the move toward legal controls is embodied in the U.S. Attorney General's Commission (1986) recommendations: (1) beefing up existing obscenity laws by adding heavy fines and mandatory jail terms, (2) increasing government surveillance of individuals suspected of trafficking in pornography, (3) regulating media such as cable television more stringently, and (4) drafting model statutes restricting the sale of sexually oriented materials.

The moves toward legal controls and censorship have met with criticism. First, the proponents of antipornography statutes focus on *sexual* content, despite the evidence that "violent images, rather than sexual ones, are most responsible for people's attitudes about women and rape" (Donnerstein and Linz, 1986: 59). Second, censorship is a two-edged sword; while suppressing pornography, it can be used simultaneously to suppress other materials (Dworkin, 1993). As Betty Friedan puts it:

There is a dangerous attempt to use a feminist smoke screen and even to claim that this antipornography suppression legislation is a weapon against sex discrimination and a weapon to liberate women from the degradation of pornography. Now, I speak as someone who has no particular liking for pornography....I do find terribly dangerous the move to suppress sexually explicit material in books or television. My own book, *The Feminine Mystique*, which had something to do with putting a name to the problems oppressing women…was suppressed as pornographic in libraries in the Midwest….If the antipornographic legislation, the suppression of pornography, was passed, the first targets of it would be feminist books….like *Our Bodies, Ourselves*…giving women control of their own bodies. (National Coalition against Censorship, 1986: 24–25)

Moreover, questions of sexuality ought to be a part of the investigation and discussion of gender relations. Warring (1986) says, "A climate of censorship promotes a chain of sexual silences. When inquiry into the male fantasies that dominate the representational system is discouraged, so is inquiry into classes of fantasy that are less likely to achieve representation—fantasies of sexual minorities and women" (106–107).

The evidence also does not support censorship directed broadly at sexually explicit material. Donnerstein, Linz, and Penrod (1987) observe that "The most well-documented finding in the social science literature is that all sexually violent material in our society, whether sexually *explicit* or not, tends to promote aggression against women" (179). Content analysis has found that R-rated films contain far more violence against women than X-rated ones. There is indeed a serious problem of violence directed at women in the American media. However, the censorship necessary to suppress it would be extraordinarily broad and potentially damaging to democratic free speech (Dworkin, 1993).

One alternative to censorship would be to educate people about the effects of media images by incorporating information on them in television documentaries or school curriculums. There is evidence that when people are informed of the negative effects of media violence, either before or after exposure, the effects are not so severe (Donnerstein, Linz, and Penrod, 1987). Certainly parents ought to be encouraged to delay their children's exposure to graphic depictions of violence found in many mass-released films and on cable television. Given the importance of protecting free speech in a democracy, however, social policy ought to concentrate on better informing the public before seeking stricter laws.

Ultimately, the appeal of pornography—particularly materials that depict degrading and violent behavior toward women—ought to be recognized as a reflection of gender inequality. The less women are regarded as sex objects subordinate to male whims (no matter how violent), the less hospitable the environment for pornography. Changing these attitudes is a long-term endeavor that includes relentless attacks on gender inequality in all its forms—in the law, the workplace, the community, and the home. The control of pornography should be seen as part of the political process in American society whereby women assert their human rights to social and cultural equality.

RAPE

Without question, rape is a sexual crime (Bell, 1991). Rape occurs whenever one person forces sex upon another without consent. Although it is clearly a sexual act, numerous studies of rape and rapists (many cited below) confirm that rape does *not* occur primarily to serve the sexual needs of the offender. Instead, rape is an act of *power, domination, and violence.* As Groth (1983) puts it, "Rape is not primarily the aggressive expression of sexuality but rather the sexual expression of aggression" (1352).

Types of Rape

In the United States, the legal concept of rape does not include all incidents of forced sex, and most state statutes explicitly exclude husbands who rape their wives. Also excluded are cases of more subtle coercion such as many "date rapes." One way to understand types of rape is to imagine them along a continuum between "illegal rape" at one extreme and "legal rape" at the other, as shown in Figure 2.2. Official statistics imperfectly reflect the magnitude of the rape problem in our society because these data include only rapes officially defined as illegal. Almost certainly there are more legal rapes annually than the illegal variety. Official statistics on rape are also faulty because they include only incidents reported to the authorities, and many victims are reluctant to report them.

Illegal Forcible Rape.   For official statistical purposes, the definition of rape in the United States is: "The carnal knowledge of a female forcibly and against her will. Included are rapes by force and attempts or assaults to rape. Statutory offenses (no force used—victim under age of consent) are excluded" (U.S. Department of Justice, 1993: 381). In 1992 109,060 such rapes were reported to police, according to the FBI's 1993 *Uniform Crime Reports.* This was up 38% since 1983, in part because women have become more willing to report rapes. Arrests for forcible rape in 1992 totaled 33,332 offenders, 52% white and 47% black.

More revealing of the actual amount of forcible rape is the National Crime Survey of victimization conducted annually by the Bureau of Justice Statistics using a sample of nearly 49,000 households. The 1991 study (U.S. Department of Justice, 1992) estimated 173,000 incidents of rape nationally, over 58% higher than the FBI figures. Overall, the highest rates of victimization were for young women between 16 and 19 years old. Black women were three times more likely to be victimized than whites. The highest risk category was black women aged 25–34, who were over six times more likely to be raped than white women the same age. Illegal rape is overwhelmingly an *intra*racial crime. Over three-quarters of black single-offender victims identified their assailant as black; over 80% of white victims were accosted by white offenders. There is no evidence that black rapists prefer white victims (South and Felson, 1990). The victims are typically poor and come from the same marginalized communities as the men who are most apt to rape them. In 52% of the cases, rape victims said the offender was a stranger; 48% of forcible rapes involved nonstrangers. Overall, only about 60% of those victimized reported the crime to the police. The most common reasons for not doing so were that the victim viewed it as a personal matter or feared reprisals.

Figure 2.2   Types of Rape Arranged along an Illegal/Legal Continuum

Illegal Rape			Legal Rape

• -- •

△	△	△	△
"Official" illegal forcible rape	Date rape	Workplace rape	Marital rape

---

Official data concerning illegal rape underestimate the true magnitude and nature of the problem. They exclude many rapes, such as those in marriage, that are beyond the reach of the law. Often women themselves do not regard sexual violence directed against them by husbands as rape. They also tend to ignore instances where women have sex against their will but the technique is extortion rather than physical force—for example, when a women is told directly or indirectly by her supervisor that a positive job evaluation is contingent upon sexual favors. Moreover, the official data give the impression that rape is almost entirely a problem of poor, minority women being victimized by poor, minority men. While it is true that officially recorded rape is an especially serious problem in economically depressed communities, a significant number of unrecorded or "legal" rapes involve middle- to upper-class victims and perpetrators.

Date Rape. Researchers have long known that male sexual aggression can be a part of dating. Kirkpatrick and Kanin (1957) found in a survey of women on a university campus that during one academic year "20.9 percent were offended by forceful attempts at intercourse and 6.2 percent by 'aggressively forceful attempts at sex intercourse in the course of which menacing threats or coercive infliction of physical pain were employed' " (53). A follow-up study about 20 years later found similar results (Kanin and Parcell, 1977). In a recent survey 341 women and 294 men were asked to describe their dating experiences. The findings revealed that 77.6% of the women and 57.3% of the men had been involved in some form of sexual aggression; and 14.7% of the women and 7.1% of the men reported having been involved in sexual intercourse against the woman's will (Muehlenhard and Linton, 1987: 186). A survey of a national sample consisting of 6,159 women and men attending 32 representative institutions of higher education (Koss, Gidyez, and Wisniewski, 1987) indicated that 27.5% of the women reported experiencing and 7.7% of the men reported perpetrating an act that met the legal definitions of rape (including attempts) since the age of 14. Few of these victims or perpetrators had been involved in the criminal justice system, so their experiences were not reflected in official crime statistics.

The data indicating that date rape is common on American college campuses have recently been called into question, and the resulting debate has been intense. Gilbert (1992) cautions that some surveys of sexual exploitation "are highly sophisticated examples of advocacy research. Elaborate methods are employed under the guise of social science, to persuade the public and policy maker that the problem is vastly larger than commonly recognized" (8). Equally insistent are the arguments that rape incidence estimates from official sources seriously underestimate the problem; acquaintance rape, in particular, is far more common than has been documented in crime surveys (Koss, 1992). On a more theoretical level, one recent critic worries that by allegedly exaggerating the extent of date rape on college campuses, "Today's rape-crisis feminists threaten to create their own version of the desexualized woman [Germaine] Greer complained of 20 years ago....It is the passive sexual role that threatens us [women] still, and it is the denial of female sexual agency that threatens to propel us backwards" (Roiphe, 1993: 68).

While one-on-one sexual assault in dating situations is reason for concern, evidence of gang rape creates even greater revulsion. Peggy Reeves Sanday (1981) provides the following example:

> The 17-year-old freshman woman went to the fraternity "little sister" rush party with two of her roommates. The roommates left early without her. She was trying to get a ride home when a fraternity brother told her he would take her home after the party ended. While she waited, two other fraternity members took her into a bedroom to "discuss little sister matters." The door was closed and one of the brothers stood blocking the exit. They told her that in order to become a little sister (honorary member) she would have to have sex with a fraternity member. She was frightened, fearing they would physically harm her if she refused. She could see no escape. Each of the brothers had sex with her, as did a third who had been hiding in the room. During the next two hours a succession of men went into the room. There were never less than three men with her, sometimes more. After they let her go, a fraternity brother drove her home. He told her not to feel bad about the incident because another woman had also been "upstairs" earlier that evening (Large southern university). (2–3)

Sanday, an anthropologist, interprets such incidents, often perpetrated by fraternities or male athletic teams, as providing a context for ritualized male bonding and sexualized power at the obvious expense of the women victimized. At the most base sexual level, she argues, "by sharing the same sexual object, the brothers are having sex with each other as well" (110). Sanday further shows that such incidents are too often treated with institutional and legal leniency, thus perpetuating female degradation, fear, and second-class citizenship.

Certain factors combine to increase the risk of sexual aggression in a dating situation. These include the male's initiating the date, paying all the expenses, and driving; miscommunication about sex; heavy alcohol or drug use; and "parking." The male's acceptance of traditional sex roles, interpersonal violence and adversarial attitudes about relationships, and rape myths (such as "women really enjoy being raped") also contributes. The length of time the dating partners have known one another seems unrelated to the risk of sexual aggression (Meuhlenhard and Linton, 1987). To these should be added the warning for women to be wary of male institutions that "appear to commodify women, viewing them as bait, as servers, and as sexual prey" (Martin and Hummer, 1989: 457).

Workplace Rape. People in subordinate positions are vulnerable to exploitation in numerous ways. This is often the case for women in their jobs. In the workplace "exploitation rape" includes "any type of sexual access gained by the male being able to take advantage of the female's vulnerability because she is dependent upon him for economic or social support" (Box, 1983: 128). The typical inequalities between men and women in the workplace often permit male supervisors to use economic threats (not hiring, retaining, or promoting) to coerce women to have unwanted sexual intercourse (Messerschmidt, 1986: 146). Rather than the use of physical force to gain sexual access, workplace rape often involves a more subtle form of extortion. This type of unwanted, forced sexual intercourse is especially pernicious because its use of economic rather than physical coercion may make it more "acceptable" in the eyes of perpetrators, victims, and the law. If it is covered in the law at all, it is defined as sexual harassment rather than rape.

Marital Rape. "In the United States, the marriage license is, in effect, a raping license" (Yllo and Finkelhor, 1985). When that statement was written, well over two-thirds of the states had laws making it impossible to charge a man with raping his wife. By 1990, seven states still recognized a spousal exemption to rape in marriage: Louisiana, Missouri, Pennsylvania, South Carolina, South Dakota, and Utah (Augustine, 1990). Twenty-six states, more than half, maintain a partial marital exemption.(Ruch, 1992). Nevertheless, sexual violence inflicted by husbands on wives is frequently a behavioral reality (Gelles, 1977). In one random sample survey of over 900 women from the general population, 14% of those who had been or were married reported forced sexual activity by their husbands (Russell, 1982). Another recent study of 323 women found that 10% had been subject to force or threat in sexual relations with their husbands (Finkelhor and Yllo, 1983). These authors concluded that "It appears that marital rape is, in fact, the most common form of rape. Yet it remains the least recognized and its victims the most silenced" (Yllo and Finkelhor, 1985: 149).

Evidence accumulating on marital rape confirms the predominant role of aggression in sexual assaults. Most marital rapes are associated with other forms of domestic violence (Frieze, 1983). In a sample of 146 women who had experienced marital violence, 23% said they had also experienced marital rape. This study also found that "there is no distinct syndrome that differentiates raping marriages from nonsexual battering marriages" (Bowker, 1983: 351–352). There is strong evidence that men sometimes use rape and violence during rape to punish the victim for a grievance. Indeed, injury in such violent sexual encounters is more likely if the offender and victim are an estranged couple (Felson and Krohn, 1990).

The trauma of marital rape is deep and lasting. Surveys of women raped by their husbands find such effects as a loss in the ability to trust any man, negative attitudes toward men, lack of desire for sexual relations, low self-esteem, and marital breakdowns (Russell, 1982; Holmstrom and Burgess, 1983). One victim's words captured the pain:

> The physical abuse was horrible, but that was something I could get over. It was like a sore that heals. When he forced me to have sex, that was more than just physical. It went all the way down to my soul....He just raped me...my whole being was abused.... I feel if I'd been raped by a stranger, I could have dealt with it a lot better.... When a stranger does it he doesn't know me, I don't know him. He's not doing it to me as a person, personally. With your husband, it becomes personal. You say, this man knows me. He knows my feelings. He knows me intimately and then to do this to me. It's such a personal abuse. (Yllo and Finkelhor, 1985: 156)

Effects of Rape

Women who have been raped experience both short-term and long-term psychological difficulties (King and Webb, 1981). As would be expected in respect to any traumatic experience, some women are more resilient than others. In one study that followed the recovery of victims during a year after the rape and compared them to nonvictims, 75–80% of the victims were more anxious, fearful, suspicious and confused than nonvictims (Kilpatrick, Resnick, and Veronen, 1981). Postrape trauma appears to be greatest for both the oldest and the youngest victims, with young women "particularly vulnerable to long-term sexual dysfunction" (Bourque, 1989).

The effects of rape go beyond the trauma of its immediate victims. The fear of rape is a constraining influence on the activities of most women; the potential of victimization keeps women in their homes at night, dependent on men for protection, passive and modest in order to remain inconspicuous—in short, the fear of rape restricts women's freedom (Griffin, 1979). Younger women fear rape more than any other crime, possibly because of its association with other serious crimes such as homicide. Warr (1985) calls fear of rape "a potent constraining force" and maintains that "it is difficult to imagine many other social problems that affect so many people in such a direct way" (249).

Explanations of Rape

Offender Motives. Rape is not a crime of sexual desire; the underlying motive is power and domination. Groth (1983) has identified three types of rape:

1. Anger rape, in which sexuality is a means for expressing pent-up rage, and harm is the intent.
2. Power rape, in which the rapist is trying to affirm his sexual identity through domination.
3. Sadistic rape, in which there is a fusion of aggression and sexuality.

To these could be added ritualized male bonding and camaraderie in the case of gang rape (Holmstrom and Burgess, 1983; Sanday, 1990).

Sexual dysfunction is a factor in about one-third of all rape cases. Typical but by no means universal personality characteristics of perpetrators include low self-esteem, insecure masculinity, poor social skills, chronic unhappiness, and a need to aggress. Many rapists themselves have been victims of sexual assault in their formative years (Kruttschnitt, 1989).

Learning and Cultural Context. The most consistent finding concerning rapists and those with a proclivity to rape in American society has been their acceptance of rape myths (Malamuth, 1981; Scully, 1990). Men learn myths such as "Women mean 'yes' when they say 'no'" or "Most women eventually relax and enjoy it" in their cultures. In a study of the reasons given by convicted rapists for committing the crime (Scully and Marolla, 1984), it was found that "Justifications particularly, but also excuses, are buttressed by the cultural view of women as sexual commodities, dehumanized and devoid of autonomy and dignity....(T)he sexual objectification of women must be understood as an important factor contributing to an environment that trivializes, neutralizes, and perhaps, facilitates rape" (542). Thus, it would be wrong to presume that rape is merely the idiosyncratic outcome of a twisted mind or a result of men's natural sexuality. As Box (1983) says, "The engine of rape is not to be found between a man's loins, but in his mind, and this in turn reflects cultural definitions of gender" (161).

If a propensity to rape were universal among men, we would find rape present in all cultures. The cross-cultural evidence is to the contrary. In a study of 156 tribal societies, Sanday (1981) found that 47% could be classified as "rape free," 18% were "rape prone," and the remaining 35% were in an intermediate category. The "rape prone" societies contain "a cultural configuration that includes interpersonal violence, male dominance, and sexual separation" that evolves when societies are "faced with depleting food resources, migration, or other factors contributing to a dependence on male destructive capacities as opposed to female fertility" (25). Sanday concludes:

> Sexual violence is one of the ways in which men remind themselves that they are superior. As such rape is part of a broader struggle for control in the face of difficult circumstances. Where men are in harmony with their environment, rape is usually absent....(V)iolence is socially and not biologically programmed. Rape is not an integral part of male nature, but the means by which men programmed for violence express their sexual selves. (25–26)

Because rape is associated with the acceptance of attitudes favorable to violence toward women, Sutherland's principle of differential association offers an excellent explanation for the occurrence of rape. By this principle, a man will become a rapist when he has learned an excess of definitions favorable to rape over definitions unfavorable to rape (Sutherland and Cressey, 1970). Definitions of rape—both favorable and unfavorable to it—are learned directly from others and indirectly through the media as part of socialization. Cultures in which boys and men are frequently exposed to rape-favorable attitudes during most of their lives can be expected to have a higher incidence of rape.

Gender and Economic Inequality. Economic inequality in a society contributes to the prevalence of rape and the patterns it takes (Schwendinger and Schwendinger, 1981). When women's economic position is subordinate to men's, they are more susceptible to sexual extortion. This is especially true in the American workplace, where women are more apt to be in lower organization positions (secretaries, clerks, etc.) and to earn on average only about 70% of men's pay for equivalent jobs. Economic inequality leaves open the door for workplace rape, a form that is far more frequent among men in positions of power and least likely to result in intervention by the law. In contrast, poor young men in communities with high unemployment rates and few economic opportunities are apt to make the women in their midst the target of the enormous frustrations and deep anger they feel. Economic inequality among men is one reason why, in the official population of rapists (those legally tried and imprisoned), men from racial and ethnic minorities and the lower social classes are overrepresented. As Box (1993) notes, "These are just the men who are much more likely to commit those types of rapes—mainly 'anger' and less so 'domination'—which the law recognizes as rape and is prepared sometimes, depending on the social characteristics of the victim and the suspect, to prosecute" (152–153).

In the same way the rate of rape varies across societies, it also varies among the states. Using official rape data, Baron and Straus (1987) were able to identify several factors that influence the incidence of officially recorded rape. They find that gender inequality (economic, political, and legal), social disorganization (mobility, single-parent households, etc.), the proportion of the population residing in urban areas, the circulation of pornography, overall economic inequality, and the unemployment rate have direct effects on the incidence of rapes known to the police. After further specification of their findings they conclude that "the fundamental causes of rape are to be found in violence, sexism, and social disorganization" (Baron and Straus, 1987: 483).

Social Control

Crime itself can be a means to social control (Black, 1983). In no case is this more evident than rape. We have already considered how the fear of rape controls women by increasing their dependency and restricting their freedom. Brownmiller (1975) has taken this position to its logical extreme: "From prehistoric times to the present, I believe, rape has played a critical function. It is nothing more or less than a conscious process of intimidation by which *all men* keep *all women* in a state of fear" (5). To the extent that this suggests that *all* men are equally prone to rape or that the proclivity to rape is a biologically endowed male trait, it is contradicted by the evidence presented above. However, to the extent that the intimidating fear of the reality of rape persists in American society, it contributes to a system of male domination and patriarchy that ultimately *does* benefit all men—regardless of whether or not they actively support such a system (LaFree, 1989).

The legal status of rape in American society reflects underlying themes of male domination and control. The historical basis for legal prohibitions that still make it impossible in a number of jurisdictions for a husband to be charged with raping his wife was in 17th-century English law, which declared that "the husband cannot be guilty of a rape by himself upon his lawful wife, for by their mutual matrimonial consent and contract the wife hath given up herself in this kind unto her husband, which she cannot retract" (*Harvard Law Review*, 1986: 1255). Legal precedents over the years further established that wives were considered *property*—"their husband's chattel, deprived of all civil identity." Although today most judges do not refer to women as property in their decisions, these assumptions underlie contemporary rape-exemption statutes. Most important, the effect of these statutes is deeply discriminatory against women, beneficial to males who subject their wives to sexual aggression in marriage, and symbolic of how the law operates more generally to control women in the interests of men (Smart and Smart, 1978).

SOCIAL POLICY ON RAPE

Strategies to prevent rape can stress either the individual or the institutional level. The first type concentrates primarily on educating women to avoid rape rather than stopping men from committing rape. Women are taught to recognize and avoid dangerous situations, encouraged to learn skills of self-defense, and advised on what to do when faced with imminent rape. Contrary to popular myth, studies have found that women faced with a potential rapist are more apt to avoid rape if they resist—especially with multiple strategies such as running away, physical force, and yelling (Bart, 1981; Levine-MacCombie and Koss, 1986). Kleck and Sayles (1990) note that since only about 3% of rape incidents involve serious additional injury, "it is the rape itself that is nearly always the most serious injury that the victim suffers" (149).

Most prevention strategies have focused on potential or actual rape victims. Swift (1985) calls for an approach aimed at equalizing the power balance between the sexes and reducing the tolerance for and practice of violence in American society. Rape law reforms, such as "victim shield" laws which prevent evidence about the victim's past from coming before the jury, have met with mixed success (Goldberg-Ambrose, 1992). The research we have cited demonstrates that gender inequality, sexism, acceptance of rape myths, and insensitive attitudes toward violence all contribute to a social climate that is conducive to sexual aggression. Long-range social policy ought to include the following:

- Legislation intended to guarantee general sexual equality in the economy, in politics, and before the law.
- Law reform aimed at condemning sexual assault no matter where it occurs—on the streets, in the workplace, or between spouses at home.

- Law reform aimed at ensuring that the victim and accused are treated equally and fairly. At present, the trial of an accused rapist often results in defense attempts to embarrass, taint, and otherwise blame the victim. In many cases rape victims are dissuaded from prosecution by their unwillingness to tolerate such tactics in the courtroom.
- Educational interventions aimed at improving individual men's attitudes about women and reducing sex-role stereotyping. A primary goal should be to diminish the association of masculinity with violent behavior.
- Medial strategies that include pressuring advertisers and media executives to use television and movies in reducing sex-role stereotypes and sensitizing people to the harmful pervasiveness of violence in American society.
- Economic and social policies that provide genuine opportunities for people, especially young men, in marginalized communities, thereby reducing their frustration and rage that too often finds release in sexual aggression and violence.

SUMMARY

Prostitution, pornography, and rape are not exclusively heterosexual in nature. In this chapter we have concentrated on their heterosexual forms because these are the most common and the most pressing in respect to social policy. Prostitution has a long history with alternating periods of relative toleration and attempts at suppression. Today in the United States women exchange sex for money in a wide range of settings, from wealthy to poor, from legally regulated to illegal. The most common form remains illegal street prostitution, populated disproportionately by women in marginal economic situations and members of racial and ethnic minorities.

Some have argued that prostitution persists because it serves socially useful functions. More likely, it persists because it is tied to a political economy that restricts opportunities for women in a cultural environment that retains a sexual double standard and exaggerates male sexuality. Under these conditions, with the male demand for commercial sex high and the supply of women motivated to provide the service great, prostitution is apt to remain a widespread economic activity.

Pornography and, particularly, attempts to suppress it have much shorter histories than prostitution. From the invention of the printing press, the wide availability of mass media has made pornography not only more prevalent but more controversial. The key question for public policy has been: Is pornography harmful? The answer depends first on how pornography is defined. Sexually explicit materials (erotica), while arousing to most people, do not appear to encourage violence or have other harmful effects. However, a mounting body of research evidence consistently shows that depictions combining sex with aggression—whether "sexually explicit" or not—are harmful. Such materials can encourage the acceptance of rape myths and even stimulate potential rapists. The focus of concern ought to be violent images, especially when combined with sexual ones, but not sexually explicit images per se.

Unlike prostitution or pornography, rape is a crime of overt aggression. While the rates of officially recorded illegal forcible rapes are high, still more rapes remain unreported, including those that occur on dates, in the workplace, and in marriage. Marital rape, the most frequent type, still is not subject to prosecution in some states. Rape is not an idiosyncratic act of uncontrolled male sexuality; it is supported by a sociocultural context of gender inequality, the fusion of sexuality and violence in the media, the acceptance of rape myths, and discrimination in the legal system.

The unifying theme of this chapter has been that patterns of deviant activity cannot be explained merely by ascribing them to individual pathology. Rather, activities such as prostitution, pornography, and rape are tied to the class interests, economy, sexual stratification, cultural beliefs, and legal system of the society in which they are found. To be successful, social policies intended to control prostitution, pornography, and rape must acknowledge the need to make fundamental changes in the structure and ideology of American society.

REFERENCES

Abernathy, J.
1993   "Sex and the Single Hacker." *Village Voice* 38 (March 16): 49.
Acheson, E. D.
1987   "AIDS: A Challenge for the Public Health." *Lancet*, March 22: 662–666.
Altimore, M.
1991   "The Social Construction of a Scientific Myth: Pornography and Violence." *Journal of Communication Inquiry* 15: 117–133.
Atkinson, M., and Boles, J.
1977   "Prostitution as an Ecology of Confidence Games: The Scripted Behavior of Prostitutes and Vice Officers." Pp. 219–232 in C. D. Bryant (ed.), *Sexual Deviancy in Social Context*. New York: New Viewpoints.
Augustine, R.I.
1990   "Marriage: The Safe Haven for Rapists," *Journal of Family Law* 29: 559–590.
Banks, S. E., Brown, L. S. Jr., and Ajuluchukwu, D.
1991   "Sexual Behaviors and HIV Infection in Intravenous Drug Users in New York City." *Journal of Addictive Diseases* 10: 15–23.
Baron, L., and Straus, M. A.
1984   "Sexual Stratification, Pornography, and Rape in the United States." Pp. 185–209 in N. M. Malamuth and E. Donnerstein (eds.), *Pornography and Sexual Aggression*. New York: Academic Press.
1987   "Four Theories of Rape: A Macrosociological Analysis." *Social Problems* 34: 467–489.

Bart, P. B.
1981   "A Study of Women Who Both Were Raped and Avoided Rape." *Journal of Social Issues* 37: 123.
Bell, V.
1991   "Beyond the Thorny Question: Feminism, Foucault and the Desexualization of Rape." *International Journal of the Sociology of Law* 19: 83–100.
Black, D.
1983   "Crime as Control." *American Sociological Review* 48: 34–45.
Bourque, L. B.
1989   *Defining Rape*. Durham, NC: Duke University Press.
Bowker, L.
1983   "Marital Rape: A Distinct Syndrome?" *Social Casework* 64: 347–352.
Box, S.
1983   *Power, Crime and Mystification*. New York: Tavistock.
Brownmiller, S.
1975   *Against Our Will: Men, Women, and Rape*. New York: Simon and Schuster.
1979   Article in *Philadelphia Inquirer*, August 1, p. 9-A.
Bullough, V., and Bullough, B.
1978   *Prostitution: An Illustrated Social History*. New York: Crown.
Byrne, D., and Kelley, K.
1984   "Pornography and Sex Research." Pp. 1–15 in N. M. Malamuth and E. Donnerstein (eds.), *Pornography and Sexual Aggression*. New York: Academic Press.

Campbell, C. A.
1991   "Prostitution, AIDS, and Preventive Health Behavior," *Social* Science *and Medicine* 32: 1367–1378.

Carmen, A., and Moody, H.
1985   *Working Women: The Subterranean World of Street Prostitution.* New York: Bessie/Harper & Row.

Centers for Disease Control
1987   "Antibody to Human Immunodeficiency Virus in Female Prostitutes." *Morbidity and Mortality Weekly Report* 36: 157–161.

Chaze, W. L.
1987   "Fear of AIDS Chills Sex Industry." *U.S. News and World Report* 102 (February): 25.

Cornish, E.
1986   "Farewell, Sexual Revolution. Hello New Victorianism." *Futurist* 20: 2,49.

Darrow, W.
1987   "Behavioral Changes in Response to AIDS," Symposium International de Reflexion sur le Side, Center for International Conferences, Paris, October.

Davis, K.
1937   "The Sociology of Prostitution." *American Sociological Review* 2: 744–755.

Davis, N. J.
1971   "The Prostitute: Developing a Deviant Identity." Pp. 297–322 in J. M. Henslin (ed.), *Studies in the Sociology of Sex.* New York: Appleton-Century-Crofts.

DeBuono, B.A., Zinner, S. H., Daamen, M. and McCormack, W. M.
1990   "Sexual Behavior of College Women in 1975, 1986 and 1989." *New England Journal of Medicine* 322: 821–825.

Donnerstein, E. J., and Linz, D. G.
1986   "The Question of Pornography." *Psychology Today* 20: 56–59.

Donnerstein, E., Linz, D., and Penrod, S.
1987   *The Question of Pornography: Research Findings and Policy Implications.* New York: Free Press.

Dworkin, R.
1993   "Women and Pornography." *New York Review of Books*, October 21: 36ff.

Feldman, D. A.
1985   "AIDS and Social Changes." *Human Organization* 44: 343–348.

Felson, R. B. and Krohn, M.
1990   "Motives for Rape." *Journal of Research in Crime and Delinquency* 27: 222–242.

Finkelhor, D., and Yllo, K.
1983   "Rape in Marriage: A Sociological View." Pp. 119–130 in D. Finkelhor, R. Gelles, G. Hotaling, and M. Strauss (eds.), *The Dark Side of Families: Current Family Violence Research.* Beverly Hills, CA: Sage.

Flexner, A.
1920   *Prostitution in Europe.* New York: Century.

Freund, M., Lee, N., and Leonard, T.
1991   "Sexual Behavior of Clients with Street Prostitutes in Camden, NJ." *Journal of Sex Research* 28: 579–591.

Frieze, I. H.
1983   "Investigating the Causes and Consequences of Marital Rape." *Signs* 8: 532–553.

Gagnon, J. H., and Simon, W.
1967   *Sexual Deviance.* New York: Harper & Row.

Gebhard, D. H.
1969   "Misconceptions about Female Prostitutes." *Medical Aspects of Human Sexuality* 3: 28–30.

Geis, G.
1972   *Not the Law's Business? An Examination of Homosexuality, Abortion, Prostitution, Narcotics and Gambling in the United States.* Washington DC: National Institute of Mental Health.

Gelles, R. J.
1977   "Power, Sex, and Violence: The Case of Marital Rape." *Family Coordinator* 26: 339–347.

Gentry, C. S.
1991   "Pornography and Rape: And Empirical Analysis." *Deviant Behavior* 12: 277–288.

Gilbert, N.
1992   "Realities and Mythologies of Rape." *Society* 29: 4-10.

Goldberg-Ambrose, C.
1992   "Unfinished Business in Rape Law Reform." *Journal of Social Issues* 48: 173–185.

Gray, D.
1973   "Turning-Out; A Study Of Teenage Prostitution." *Urban Life and Culture* 1: 401–425.

Gray, S. H.
1982   "Exposure to Pornography and Aggression toward Women: The Case of the Angry Male." *Social Problems* 29: 387–398.

Greenwald, H.
1970   *The Elegant Prostitute.* New York: Ballantine.

Griffin, S.
1979   *Rape: The Power of Consciousness.* San Francisco: Harper & Row.

Groth, A. N.
1983   "Rape: Behavioral Aspects." Pp. 1351–1356 in *Encyclopedia of Crime and Justice.* New York: Free Press.

Gusfield, J. R.
1963   *Symbolic Crusade: Status Politics and the American Temperance Movement.* Urbana: University of Illinois Press.

Hall, S.
1972   *Gentleman of Leisure: A Year in the Life of a Pimp.* New York: New American Library.

Harvard Law Review
1986   "To Have and to Hold: The Marital Rape Exemption in the 14th Amendment." 99: 1255–1273.

Heyl, B. S.
1979   *The Madam as Entrepreneur: Career Management in House Prostitution.* New Brunswick, NJ: Transaction.

Hobson, B. M.
1987   *Uneasy Virtue: The Politics of Prostitution and the American Reform Tradition.* New York: Basic Books.

Holmstrom, L. L., and Burgess, A. W.
1983   "Rape and Everyday Life." *Society* 20: 33–40.

Hunt, M.
1974   *Sexual Behavior in the 1970's.* Chicago: Playboy Press.

Hyde, H. M.
1964   *A History of Pornography.* New York: Dell.

James, J.
1977   "Prostitutes and Prostitution." Pp. 368–428 in E. Sagarin and F. Montanino (eds.), *Deviants: Voluntary Actors in a Hostile World.* Morristown, NJ: General Learning Press.

Jenness, V.
1990   "From Sex as Sin to Sex as Work: COYOTE and the Reorganization of Prostitution as a Social Problem." *Social Problems* 37: 403–420.

1993   *Making It Work: The Prostitutes' Rights Movement in Perspective.* New York: Aldine de Gruyter.

Kanin, E. J., and Parrell, S. R.
1977   "Sexual Aggression: A Second Look at the Offended Female." *Archives of Sexual Behavior* 6: 67–76.

Kilpatrick, D. G., Resick, P. A., and Veronen, L. J.
1981   "Effects of a Rape Experience: A Longitudinal Study." *Journal of Social Issues* 37: 105–122.

King, H. E., and Webb, C.
1981   "Rape Crisis Centers: Progress and Problems," *Journal of Social Issues* 37: 93–104.

Kirkpatrick, C., and Kanin, E.
1957   "Male Sex Aggression on a University Campus." *American Sociological Review* 22: 52–58.

Kleck, G., and Sayles, S.
1990   "Rape and Resistance." *Social Problems* 37: 149–162.

Koss, M. P.
1992   "The Underdetection of Rape: Methodological Choices Influence Incidence Estimates." *Journal of Social Issues* 48: 61–75.

Koss, M. P., Gidyez, A., and Wisniewski, N.
1987   "The Scope of Rape: Incidence and Prevalence of Sexual Aggression and Victimization in a National Sample of Higher Education Students." *Journal of Consulting and Clinical Psychology* 55: 162–170.

Kruttschnitt, C.
1989   "A Sociological Offender-Based Study of Rape," *Sociological Quarterly* 30: 305–329.

Kutchinsky, B.
1983   "Obscenity and Pornography: Behavioral Aspects." Pp. 1077–1083 in *Encyclopedia of Crime and Justice.* New York: Free Press.

1991   "Pornography and Rape: Theory and Practice? Evidence from Crime Data in Four Countries Where Pornography Is Easily Available." *International Journal of Law and Psychiatry* 14: 47–64.

LaFree, G. D.
1989   *Rape and Criminal Justice: The Social Construction of Sexual Assault.* Belmont, CA: Wadsworth.

Leishman, K.
1987   "Heterosexuals and AIDS: The Second Stage of the Epidemic." *Atlantic Monthly*, February: 39–58.

Lemert, E. M.
1951   *Social Pathology.* New York: McGraw-Hill.

Levine-MacCombie, M. J., and Koss, M. P.
1986   "Acquaintance Rape: Effective Avoidance Strategies." *Psychology of Women Quarterly* 10: 311–320.

Linz, D.
1989   "Exposure to Sexually Explicit Materials and Attitudes Toward Rape: A Comparison of Study Results." *Journal of Sex Research* 26: 50–84.

Lowman, J., and Mathews, H.
1992   "Street Prostitution Control: Some Canadian Reflections on the Finsbury Park Experience." *British Journal of Criminology* 32: 1–17.

Luckenbill, D. F.
1986   "Deviant Career Mobility: The Case of Male Prostitutes." *Social Problems* 33: 283–296.

MacKinnon, C. A.
1992   "Pornography, Civil Rights and Speech." Pp. 456–511 in C. Itzin (ed.), *Pornogra-*

phy: Women, Violence and Civil Rights. New York: Oxford University Press.

Malamuth, N. M.
1981   "Rape Proclivity among Males." *Journal of Social Issues* 37: 138–157.

Malamuth, N. M., and Donnerstein, E.
1982   "The Effects of Aggressive-Pornographic Mass Media Stimuli." Pp. 103–136 in L. Berkowitz (ed.), *Advances in Experimental Social Psychology*, Vol. 15. New York: Academic Press.

Malamuth, N. M., and Donnerstein E. (eds.)
1984   *Pornography and Sexual Aggression.* New York: Academic Press.

Martin, J. L.
1987   "The Impact of AIDS on Gay Male Sexual Behavior Patterns in New York City." *American Journal of Public Health* 77: 578–581.

Martin, P., and Hummer, R. A.
1989   "Fraternities and Rape on Campus." *Gender and Society* 3: 457–473.

McCormack, T.
1978   "Machismo in Media Research: A Critical Review of Research on Violence and Pornography." *Social Problems* 25: 544–555.

Messerschmidt, J. W.
1986   *Capitalism, Patriarchy, and Crime: Toward a Socialist Feminist Criminology.* Totowa, NJ: Rowman and Littlefield.

Miller, E. M.
1986   *Street Woman.* Philadelphia: Temple University Press.

Miller, J.
1994   *Gender and Power on the Streets: The Ecology of Street Prostitution in an Era of Crack Cocaine.* (in press).

Muedeking, G. D.
1977   "Pornography and Society." Pp. 463–502 in E. Sagarin and F. Montanino (eds.), *Deviants: Voluntary Actors in a Hostile World.* Morristown, NJ: General Learning Press.

Muehlenhard, C. L., and Linton, M. A.
1987   "Date Rape and Sexual Aggression in Dating Situations: Incidence and Risk Factors." *Journal of Counselling Psychology* 34: 186–196.

National Coalition against Censorship
1987   *The Meese Commission Exposed: Proceedings of a National Coalition against Censorship.* New York: Author.

Pally, M.
1991   *Sense and Censorship: The Vanity of the Bonfires.* New York: Americans for Constitutional Freedom.

Plant, M.
1990   *Aids, Drugs and Prostitution.* London: Tavistock/Routledge.

Polsky, N.
1967   *Hustlers, Beats and Others.* Chicago: Aldine.

Potter, G. W.
1989   "The Retail Pornography Industry and the Organization of Vice." *Deviant Behavior* 10: 233–251.

Ratner, M. S. (ed.)
1993   *Crack as Pimp: An Ethnographic Investigation of Sex-for-Crack Exchanges.* New York: Lexington.

Reynolds, H.
1986   *The Economics of Prostitution.* Springfield, IL: Charles C. Thomas.

Rigor, S., and Gordon, M. T.
1981   "The Fear of Rape: A Study in Social Control." *Journal of Social Issues* 37: 71–92.

Roby, P. A.
1969   "Politics and Criminal Law: Revision of the New York State Penal Law on Prostitution." *Social Problems* 17: 83–109.

Roiphe, K.
1993   "Date Rape's Other Victim." *New York Times Magazine,* June 13: 26ff.

Romenesko, K., and Miller, E. M.
1989   "The Second Step in Double Jeopardy: Appropriating the Labor of Female Street Hustlers." *Crime and Delinquency* 35: 109–135.

Rosenblum, K. E.
1975   "Female Deviance and the Female Sex Role: A Preliminary Investigation." *British Journal of Sociology* 26: 169–185.

Ruch, L. O.
1992   "Sexual Violence against Women." *Journal of the History of Sexuality* 2: 634–641.

Russell, D. E. H.
1982   *Rape in Marriage.* New York: Macmillan.

Sanday, P. R.
1981   "The Socio-Cultural Context of Rape: A Cross-Cultural Study." *Journal of Social Issues* 37: 5–27.
1990   *Fraternity Gang Rapes: Sex, Brotherhood and Privilege on Campus.* New York: New York University Press.

Schwendinger, J. R., and Schwendinger, H.
1981   "Rape, Sexual Inequality and Levels of Violence." *Crime and Social Justice* 16: 3–31.

Scully, D.
1990   *Understanding Sexual Violence: A Study of Convicted Rapists.* Boston: Unwin Hyman.

Scully, D., and Marolla, J.
1984   "Convicted Rapists' Vocabulary of Motive: Excuses and Justifications." *Social Problems* 31: 530–544.

Sheehy, G.
1973   *Hustling: Prostitution in Our Wide-Open Society*. New York: Delacorte Press.

Shrage, L.
1989   "Should Feminists Oppose Prostitution?" *Ethics* 99: 347–361.

Simon, C., and Witte, A. D.
1982   *Beating the System*. Boston: Auburn House.

Simons, R. L., and Whitbeck, L. B.
1991   "Sexual Abuse as a Precursor to Prostitution and Victimization among Adolescent and Adult Homeless Women." *Journal of Family Issues* 12: 361–379.

Smart, C., and Smart, B.
1978   *Women, Sexuality and Social Control*. London: Routledge and Kegan Paul.

Smith, T. W.
1990   "The Sexual Revolution?" *Public Opinion Quarterly* 54: 415–435.

South, S. J., and Felson, R. B.
1990   "The Racial Patterning of Rape." *Social Forces* 69: 71–93.

Sutherland, E. H., and Cressey, D. R.
1970   *Criminology*, 9th edition. Philadelphia: J. B. Lippincott.

Swift, C. F.
1984   "The Prevention of Rape" Pp. 413–426 in A. W. Burgess (ed.), *Rape and Sexual Assault: A Research Handbook*. New York: Garland.

Tewksbury, Richard
1990   "Patrons of Porn: Research Notes on the Clientele of Adult Bookstores." *Deviant Behavior* 11: 259–271.

U.S. Commission on Obscenity and Pornography
1970   *Report of the Commission*. Washington, DC: U.S. Government Printing Office.

U.S. Department of Justice
1986   *Report, U.S. Attorney General's Commission on Pornography*. Washington, DC: Author.
1987   *Sourcebook of Criminal Justice Statistics—1986*. Washington, DC: Bureau of Justice Statistics.
1992   *Criminal Victimization in the United States, 1991*. Washington, DC: Bureau of Justice Statistics.

1993   *Uniform Crime Reports: Crime in the United States*. Washington, DC: Federal Bureau of Investigation.

U.S. National Commission on the Causes and Prevention of Violence
1969   *Progress Report of the National Commission on the Causes and Prevention of Violence to President Lyndon B. Johnson*. Washington, DC: Author.

Van Gelder, L., and Brandt, P.
1986   "AIDS on Campus." *Rolling Stone* 483: 80 ff.

Warr, M.
1985   "Fear of Rape Among Urban Women." *Social Problems* 32: 238–250.

Warring, N.W.
1986   "Coming to Terms with Pornography: Toward a Feminist Prospective on Sex, Censorship, and Hysteria." Pp 85–112 in *Research on Law, Deviance and Social Control*, Vol. 8, Greenwich, CT: JAI Press.

Weitzer, R.
1991   "Prostitutes' Rights in the United States: The Failure of a Movement." *Sociological Quarterly* 32: 23–41.

Wilson, J. Q.
1971   "Violence, Pornography and Social Science." *The Public Interest* 22: 45–61.

Winick, C., and Kinsie, P. M.
1971   *The Lively Commerce: Prostitution in the United States*. New York: Quadrangle.

Yang, N., and Linz, D.
1990   "Movie Ratings and the Content of Adult Videos: The Sex-Violence Ratio." *Journal of Communication* 40: 28–42.

Yllo, K., and Finkelhor, D.
1985   "Marital Rape." Pp. 146–158 in A. W. Burgess (ed.), *Rape and Sexual Assault: A Research Handbook*. New York: Garland.

Zillman, D., and Bryant, J.
1984   "Effects and Massive Exposure to Pornography." Pp 115–138 in N. M. Malamuth and E. Donnerstein (eds.), *Pornography and Sexual Aggression*. New York: Academic Press.

Zurcher, L. A., Jr., and Kirkpatrick, R. G.
1976   *Citizens for Decency: Antipornography Crusaders as Status Defense*. Austin: University of Texas Press.

3 | Homosexuality

H omosexual behavior has existed in most cultures throughout history, but heterosexual intercourse has been the statistical and cultural norm in all known societies (Carrier, 1980). This is not to say that homosexual attractions, behaviors, and identities are unnatural for everyone. Indeed, as we will show, for some people a sexual orientation toward others of the same sex is an unplanned, unavoidable, unchangeable aspect of their identity. Despite people's inability to determine or alter their sexual orientation, societal reactions to those whose orientations are homosexual have usually been negative; throughout history, people who display and act on such an orientation have faced disapproval, discrimination, and even death (Crompton, 1978). Thus, although for certain people homosexuality may be natural and unavoidable, it is deviant behavior in three senses—statistically, normatively, and in the negative reactions it regularly evokes. The theories of deviance and control discussed in this chapter can provide a better understanding of homosexuality, reactions to it, and social policies that affect it.

ATTRACTION, BEHAVIOR, AND IDENTITY

Homosexual acts are easily defined. They are sexually oriented physical contacts between same-sex individuals that may include kissing, body rubbing, mutual masturbation, oral-genital stimulation, or anal intercourse. However, not everyone who engages in a homosexual act may consider herself or himself a homosexual (Berger, 1983). In other words, it is possible to engage in homosexual behavior without having a homosexual identity. In this chapter we will use different terms to take this reality into account. *Homosexual behavior* refers simply to the activity, regardless of identity. *Homosexuality* applies to those who are sexually attracted to others of the same sex, who are inclined to act on that attraction by engaging in sexual behavior with same-sex partners, and who recognize and accept their sexual orientation as part of their identity.

Homosexuality can be present in both men and women. Consistent with most current usage, we will use *homosexual* in specific references to both males and females, and in general references to males whose sexual attraction and behavior are oriented toward other males and whose identities include this orientation. *Lesbians* are the female counterpart of homosexuals. The term *gay* is often used in reference to homosexuals, and we will apply it both to these men and to lesbians. Gays are people who have generally decided to be open about their homosexuality. In a social sense they would be said to have "come out of the closet," but their open approach to their homosexuality often includes a political dimension aimed at reducing prejudice and discrimination. The gay rights movement includes both homosexuals and lesbians who seek to change laws, economic policies, and attitudes that negatively affect them.

HISTORICAL AND CULTURAL ATTITUDES

Western observers have often found homosexual behavior in small-scale, preindustrial societies. Evidence from a survey of 76 such societies in the early 1950s indicated that in 64% of them, "homosexual activities of one sort or another are considered normal or at least socially acceptable for certain members of the community" (Ford and Beach, 1951: 130). In many cultures, high status is attached to those who fulfill roles associated with homosexual behavior.

In general, the most common acceptable form of homosexuality in preindustrial societies is the *berdache*, a male who dresses like a woman, performs women's tasks, and adopts the feminine role in sexual behavior with male partners. For example, among the Siberian Chuckch, a *berdache* is not only acceptable, but is seen by others as a prestigious shaman or healer who is believed to be endowed with supernatural powers. In other societies, such as the Tanala of Madagascar or the Mojave Indians of California and Arizona, the man-woman *berdache* is regarded by others in the community without either ridicule or praise.

The other pattern of homosexual activity frequently found in preindustrial cultures is a sexual liaison between men or boys who are otherwise heterosexual. For example, Ford and Beach found that among the Sivans of Africa, all men and boys engage in anal intercourse, and "They adopt the feminine role only in strictly sexual situations and males are singled out as peculiar if they do not indulge in these homosexual activities.... Both married and unmarried males are expected to have both homosexual and heterosexual affairs" (131–132). Sometimes, as among the Aranda of Australia or the Koraki of New Guinea, older men engage in anal intercourse with young boys. Such a practice may be a temporary arrangement in lieu of a heterosexual marriage or part of initiation rites from puberty into manhood. Among women in preindustrial cultures, approved forms of homosexual relations appear to be far less common than among men. This may be because males' homosexual behavior is more regulated than females' is. Usually, even when male homosexual behavior is approved, its practice is limited by rules governing the special social role, age, or ritual time period for which it is a appropriate (Carrier, 1980: 120). Lesbianism seems to have been mostly ignored in custom and law. Therefore its actual incidence may be greater than it appears from the anthropological record.

While acceptable forms of homosexual behavior clearly are found in preindustrial societies, such acceptance is not universal. In 28 of the 76 societies Ford and Beach surveyed, "homosexual activities on the part of adults are reported to be totally absent, rare, or carried on only in secrecy" (129). In numerous cultures (for example, the Cuna, Trukese, Chiricahua, and Sampoil), children who show any inclination toward homosexuality are harshly punished. In some others, such as the Rivala Bedouins, homosexuality is sufficient cause for the death penalty.

In Western cultures, the situation is equally complex; approval and disapproval of homosexual behavior may exist at the same time or at different times. The Hebrew moral code strongly condemns homosexuality. In classical Greece it appears that homosexuality and homosexual prostitution were fairly widespread and accepted, among intellectuals especially (Licht, 1955), but the attitude of the general public was far less favorable (Karlen, 1980). A similar situation of elite acceptance and public disfavor seems to have existed in the Roman Empire.

The extent of homosexual behavior during the Middle Ages is unknown, although there is some evidence that it may have been commonly practiced among some clergy (McIntosh, 1968: 187) and medieval rulers (Rowse, 1977) while it was still being generally condemned by the masses, in accordance with church doctrine. From ancient times an impressive number of men who were avowedly homosexual or strongly suspected of homosexual conduct made their mark on history, including Socrates, Plato, Julius Caesar, Alexander the Great, Michelangelo, Christopher Marlowe, and William Shakespeare. However, it must be remembered that these personages from the past exemplify those who engaged in some (not necessarily exclusively) homosexual behavior. They generally did not correspond to the stereotyped homosexual role associated with homoerotic behavior today because such a role did not emerge until the end of the 17th century in England (McIntosh, 1968: 189).

The term *lesbian* comes from the Greek isle of Lesbos, the birthplace of the ancient lesbian poet Sappho. Historical knowledge of lesbianism is extremely limited because, as Bullough (1979) says, "almost all of our historical information—religious, legal, literary, or political—is male-centered, written by men for other men. We do not know how most women in the past saw themselves, since almost all we know about them comes from the writing of men" (117). There is no clear reference to lesbian activity in the Bible, only occasional accounts in English and American literature prior to the 19th century, and virtually no attention directed at it by the law. A 1649 case in Plymouth Colony is the only prosecution in American history for a lesbian act. Bullough declares that historically "lesbians have suffered more discrimination because they are women than because they are homosexuals" (117).

Since the 18th century, public attitudes toward homosexual behavior in Western societies have tended to be hostile. There is some grudging tolerance, however, especially in occupational categories such as artist. Indeed, it appears that Western governments, sometimes going against the tide of popular opinion, have led the way in relaxing laws against homosexual behavior by consenting adults in private. England, West Germany, and Canada have instituted such reforms. The United States remains the most severe Western society in its legal and public condemnation of homosexual behavior.

Summing up this brief cultural and historical review, a majority of small-scale, preindustrial societies recognize and tolerate—and some even encourage—limited homosexual behavior. At the same time, in no case is it ever the predominant mode of sexual activity among adults. Far greater attention has been paid to the rules and rituals surrounding the homosexual behavior of males than has been given to that of females. In complex Western societies there seems to have been a certain amount of homosexual behavior (even literary praise), while most of the populace has not been very tolerant of it at all.

SEXUALITY AS A CONTINUUM: DEFINING HOMOSEXUALITY

While defining a homosexual act is rather easy, defining a person as homosexual is not. For instance, is it reasonable to classify individuals as homosexual or lesbian if only once or twice in their lives they engage in homosexual acts and their sexual activity is otherwise heterosexual? If not, how many homosexual acts are required to label someone a lesbian or homosexual? Clearly, these questions suggest that homosexuality and heterosexuality are not discrete, either-or categories. In fact, the most sophisticated researchers in the field have concluded that human sexuality is best conceived of as lying along a continuum ranging from exclusively heterosexual to exclusively homosexual, and a great many people's sexuality falls somewhere in between.

The difficulty inherent in classifying human sexuality into either-or, heterosexual or homosexual categories was demonstrated by Alfred Kinsey and his colleagues, in a frequently cited research finding that 37% of white American males and 13% of females interviewed said they had had at least one homosexual experience to the point of orgasm between adolescence and old age (Kinsey, Pomeroy, and Martin, 1948; Kinsey et al., 1953). Should we then conclude that over a third of the American males interviewed were homosexual? And if not, what frequency of homosexual experience or other criteria should be the defining characteristics of a homosexual? These and related issues led Kinsey to devise a seven-step continuum of human sexual preferences ranging from 0, denoting a person who has never had any overt homosexual experience, to 6, denoting an individual who has had no history of overt heterosexual experience (see Figure 3.1).

According to Kinsey's (1948: 650–656) estimates, about three-quarters of all American men in any given year are exclusively heterosexual (0), and about half of them will be in this category throughout their lives. At the other extreme, about 5% rate exclusively homosexual (6) in any given year, and about 4% will be in this category throughout their lives. Thus, for nearly half the males the rating actually falls somewhere between exclusively heterosexual and exclusively homosexual. Findings from five sample surveys conducted between 1970 and 1990 suggest that, at a minimum, 5% to 7% of U.S. men report some same-gender sexual conduct during adulthood, and the majority of men who do so report some male-female sexual contacts also (Rogers and Turner, 1991). About 2% to 4% of married men are potentially homosexually active, and among all homosexuals, between 10% and 20% will at some time in their lives get married (Ross, 1989).

Figure 3.1   The Kinsey Heterosexual-Homosexual Rating Scale

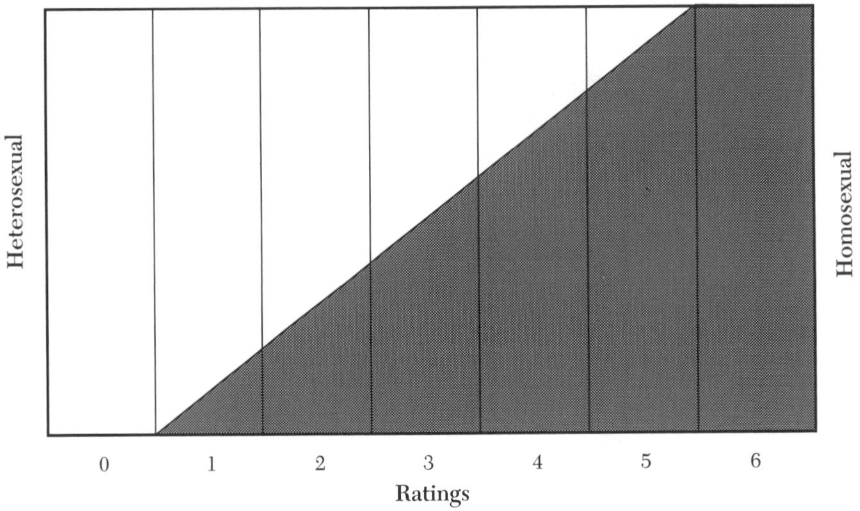

Based on both psychologic reactions and overt experience, individuals rate as follows:

0   Exclusively heterosexual with no homosexual.

1   Predominantly heterosexual, only incidentally homosexual.

2   Predominantly heterosexual, but more than incidentally homosexual.

3   Equally heterosexual and homosexual.

4   Predominantly homosexual, but more than incidentally heterosexual.

5   Predominantly homosexual, but incidentally heterosexual.

6   Exclusively homosexual.

Source: Kinsey, Pomeroy, and Martin, 1948: 638.

The viability of the Kinsey continuum has been reaffirmed through its en-
lightening use in more-recent major studies of the physiology of homosexual behavior by Masters and Johnson (1979) and of homosexual lifestyles by Bell and
Weinberg (1978).

Homosexual Physiology

After 14 years of clinical study of hundreds of males and females engaging in homosexual behavior in their institute laboratory, William Masters and Virginia Johnson produced an excellent base for comparison with their previous, well-known
findings on heterosexual activity. Generally speaking, they found no differences

between homosexuals and heterosexuals in physiological capacity to respond to similar sexual stimuli:

> ...there is no statistically significant difference between sexually experienced male homosexual and male heterosexual study subjects in facility to respond to orgasmic levels to similar techniques of masturbation, partner manipulation, and fellation. Similarly...there is no statistically significant difference in facility or orgasmic attainment between sexually experienced female homosexual and heterosexual study subjects in response to masturbation, partner manipulation, and cunnilingus. (Masters and Johnson, 1979: 205–206)

One dominant pattern of sexual behavior consistently observed by Masters and Johnson in the interaction of committed male or female homosexual couples was infrequently present in the sexual activity of committed heterosexual couples. Usually, committed homosexual couples *took their time* in sexual interaction in the laboratory. They appeared to be more relaxed and gave the impression of more complete subjective involvement in the sexual activity than their heterosexual counterparts (64). Masters and Johnson speculate that one reason for this apparent enhanced sexual communication between attached homosexual couples may be public hostility. In a hostile environment, partners may place great value on their established relationships which may increase communication in both matters nonsexual and sexual. This conclusion is certainly compatible with the suggestion by labeling theorists that harsh societal reactions tend to solidify the relationships between members of a group who are the objects of public opprobrium or disgrace.

These researchers also found remarkable similarities in dealing with sexual problems by heterosexuals and homosexuals. Masters and Johnson conclude, therefore, that:

> Over the past 15 years, it has become apparent that the individual's sexual orientation does not significantly alter his or her problem of sexual dysfunction. Impotence and anorgasmic states have just as devastating an effect on homosexual as on heterosexual men and women. Fears of performance and spectator roles can make a sexual cripple of any sexually dysfunctional individual, homosexual or heterosexual. Sexual fakery is freely practiced by representatives of both sex preferences. (406)

Overwhelmingly, then, this research underscores the conclusion that "from a functional point of view homosexuality and heterosexuality have far more similarities than differences" (403).

Homosexual Diversity

A number of common, widespread beliefs about homosexuality are challenged in a study of almost 1,000 men and women with homosexual orientations (Kinsey scale 5 or 6) compared with almost 500 heterosexuals (Kinsey scale 0 or 1), Allen P. Bell and Martin S. Weinberg (1978) found, for example, that:

- A majority of men and women with homosexual preferences are not "out of the closet" but keep their sexual orientations covert.

- Homosexual men and women cannot be sexually stereotyped as either hyper-active or inactive.
- Search for sexual contacts is infrequent among lesbians and among homosexual men who "cruise" in public places; most conduct their sexual activity in the privacy of their homes.
- Over one-third of the homosexual women and about one-fifth of the men have been married at least once.
- Above all, homosexual men and women exhibit great diversity in their lifestyles and personal adjustment, not at all unlike the diversity found among those whose sexual orientation is predominantly heterosexual.

To underscore the range of sexual experience among the men and women in their sample, Bell and Weinberg (1978) devised a typology with five categories (see Table 3.1). Their descriptions of the categories follow.

1. *Close-Coupleds.* These individuals had close relationships in two senses: They were closely bound to a partner, and the pair tended to look to each other rather than to outsiders for interpersonal and sexual gratification. The fact that many more homosexual women (39%) than men (14%) are in this category is consistent with the widely established observation that lesbians tend to form more stable, enduring attachments than their male counterparts. Close-coupleds had the fewest reported sexual problems, the fewest difficulties at work, and generally had attained a very high level of personal adjustment and well-being.

2. *Open-Coupleds.* These individuals lived with special sexual partners but also sought satisfactions with people outside the partnership. Both men and women did more than the average amount of cruising. Open-coupleds were less happy, less self-accepting, and more worried, tense, or depressed than close-coupleds.

3. *Functionals.* "If close- and open-coupled respondents are in some respect like married heterosexuals, the functionals come closest to the notion of 'swinging singles'" (223). Sex played a large part in the lives of these men and women, as reflected in their high level of sexual activity with many partners. They were least likely to regret being homosexual, cruised frequently, and were involved in the gay subculture. While their adjustment is characterized as cheerful, self-reliant, optimistic, and comfortable with their sexuality, the close-coupleds surpassed them in overall well-being.

4. *Dysfunctionals.* This group "most closely accords with the stereotype of the tormented homosexual" (225). They reported more sexual problems, difficulties with the law, and emotional instability than any other group. Although males spent a fair amount of time cruising and had a relatively high number of sex partners, sexual anxiety and performance failures were quite frequent. "If we had numbered only dysfunctionals among our respondents, we very likely would have had to conclude that homosexuals in general are conflict-ridden social misfits" (226).

5. *Asexuals.* Both men and women in this group showed a lack of involvement with others. Of all the groups they had the lowest levels of sexual activity,

Table 3.1   A Typology of Sexual Experience among Homosexual Men and
Women (Bell and Weinberg, 1978)

	PERCENT IN CATEGORY	
Type	Men	Women
Close-coupleds	14%	39%
Open-coupleds	25	24
Functionals	21	14
Dysfunctionals	18	8
Asexuals	23	16
	101%°	101%°
Total number	485	211

Source: Adapted from Bell and Weinberg, 1978.
°Total percentages exceed 100 due to rounding.

number of partners, and ratings of their sex appeal. They had narrow sexual reper-
toires and a fair number of sexual problems. Their lifestyle was solitary, and, despite
complaints of loneliness, they seemed to be not very interested in establishing stable relationships. Overall, they were moderate in their psychological adjustment
and the extent to which their homosexuality caused them difficulty.

Conclusions.   The findings of the Bell and Weinberg study show that homosexual
and lesbian adults are a very diverse group. Indeed, the conclusion that the types of
relationships and personal adjustments found among homosexuals and lesbians
parallel quite closely those among heterosexuals is probably justified. There is no
question that the chief difference between heterosexuals and homosexuals is the nature of their sexual orientation. The Masters and Johnson (1979) research reinforces this point in regard to physiology by emphasizing that *other than sexual orientation*, heterosexual and homosexual function or dysfunction are remarkably
similar. Likewise, any simplistic picture of homosexual lifestyle and personal adjustment is no more accurate or acceptable than such an image of heterosexuals
would be. Of course, living in a hostile environment places significant social and psychological burdens on homosexuals, and we can only imagine how most heterosexuals would adapt under the same handicaps. All of the evidence suggests that in the
absence of widespread negative stereotypes, fear, prejudice, and discrimination,
homosexuals and lesbians are the equals of heterosexuals in the potential for satisfying social relationships and psychological adjustment. In the words of Bell and
Weinberg (1978), "homosexual adults who have come to terms with their homosexuality, who do not regret their sexual orientation, and who can function effectively sexually and socially, are no more distressed psychologically than are heterosexual men and women" (216).

Lesbians and Homosexuals Compared

Regardless of their sexual orientations, lesbians and homosexuals are subject to many of the same influences, attitudes, and constraints that distinguish between women and men more generally in the society. For instance, like other women, most lesbians become aware of their sexual needs and express them somewhat later than men do. With respect to gender identity, many lesbians appear to have rejected the traditional feminine role or to have chosen male roles because they had no visible lesbian role models as children (Cooper, 1990). Like most women, lesbians are usually less promiscuous than their male counterparts. Indeed, "Being a female homosexual is like being a female in general, both sexually and socially. There is a tendency to greater conformity, stability of relationships, and an absence of indiscriminate sexual involvements" (Saghir and Robins, 1980: 292).

A major difference between lesbians and homosexuals is in their previous heterosexual experience. About 70% to 80% of Kinsey scale 5–6 females have experienced heterosexual intercourse, while only 20% to 25% of Kinsey scale 5–6 males have (Marmor, 1980). This is probably due to the combination of differences in male and female sexual physiology and the pressures felt by women to conform to male heterosexual demands, especially in adolescence. In neither case is there evidence that homosexual activity is typically initiated through seduction by an older female or male (Gagnon and Simon, 1973; Bell, Weinberg, and Hammersmith, 1981). Lesbian identity formation is complex, and theories suggest its development goes into adulthood (Weille, 1993).

While lesbians are unquestionably subject to discrimination, they are more readily tolerated than homosexual men. In a male-dominated society, heterosexual men may feel threatened by homosexuals, who represent a weak or ambiguous link in the chain of sexual stratification. The hatred manifest in verbal and physical aggression directed at homosexual men ("gay bashing") has roots in the same gender inequality that influences attitudes contributing to violence against women. Moreover, lesbians may be regarded by most men as simply in a sexual limbo—"waiting for the right man to come along." Heterosexual male-oriented pornography often contains explicit lesbian sexual activity (usually followed by the male or males portrayed as bringing the women to climax) but almost never depicts the behavior of male homosexuals. As Gagnon and Simon (1973) put it:

> [S]ince [heterosexual] males are the producers of most sexual fantasies, it is perfectly possible for them to conceive of the lesbian as simply being unawakened heterosexually, merely waiting for the right man to appear. Since thinking about the aroused female is a significant source of sexual arousal for the [heterosexual] male, the source of her arousal is a matter of indifference. (177)

In contemporary society, therefore, many outcomes of sexuality are similar for males and females, regardless of their sexual orientation. Heterosexual men and homosexual men share a propensity for promiscuity and overt displays of sexuality. Women, heterosexual or lesbian, resemble one another in the development of their sexuality, in the patterns of their relationships, and in their likelihood of being treated as sex objects in the fantasies of most heterosexual males.

SUBCULTURAL PATTERNS: HOMOSEXUAL LIFESTYLES

Just as there is no single set of personality traits characterizing all homosexuals and lesbians, there is no typical lifestyle. A large number of homosexual men and women lead quiet, unassuming lives, pursuing their work or careers with no outward sign of their sexual preferences or relationships. Numerous others assume a double persona, playing conventional work and family roles when on the job or in the presence of relatives and reserving for their leisure hours any overt identification with the mannerisms, dress, language, and gathering places of the gay subculture (Warren, 1974). Unattached males who have "come out of the closet" are most frequently participants in the gay world.

Coming Out

As we have indicated, having engaged in homosexual activity does not necessarily mean that individuals will identify themselves as homosexual. Actually, the male homosexual role is neither universal nor ancient. McIntosh (1968) points out that "the role does not exist in many societies, that it only emerged in England towards the end of the 17th century, and...although the existence of the role in modern America appears to have some effect on the distribution of homosexual behavior, such behavior is far from being monopolized by persons who play the role of homosexual" (192). Many people (probably most) who experience homosexual desires, fantasies, and even activities do not thereby decide that they are homosexual. Adoption of a homosexual identity is a process that, beyond attraction to same-sex people, requires a person to neutralize the common negative stereotypes of the homosexual or lesbian role and to recognize that, despite hostile public images, homosexuality can be seen as neither sick nor evil but as positive or desirable.

Coming out, the assumption of a homosexual identity, is not likely to take place immediately once a person is physically attracted to someone of the same sex. Dank (1971) found in a survey of 180 self-identified homosexuals that on the average there was a six-year interval between recognizing homosexual feelings of attraction and deciding that they were homosexual. Often the necessary component in identifying oneself as homosexual was positive interaction with people who had already assumed the homosexual role. Contact with such people could occur in a number of social contexts. Dank's 180 respondents were asked to identify the social contexts in which they came out and the distribution he found is shown in Table 3.2 This ordering of contexts suggests that for men, an intense, personal relationship with a homosexual and contact with the gay subculture often precipitate coming out. Dank gives the reply of one respondent:

> I knew that there were homosexuals, queers, and what not; I had read some books, and I was resigned to the fact that I was a foul, dirty person, but I wasn't actually calling myself a homosexual yet....I went to this guy's house and there was nothing going on, and

Table 3.2   Social Contexts in Which Respondents "Came out" (Dank, 1971)

Social Context	Percent	Number[a]
Having a love affair with a homosexual man	30%	54
Frequenting gay parties and other gatherings	26	46
Frequenting parks	24	43
Frequenting gay bars	19	35
In the military	19	34
Read for the first time about homosexuals and/or homosexuality	15	27
Having a love affair with a heterosexual man	12	21
Living in all-male quarters at a boarding school or college	7	12
Seeing a psychiatrist or professional counselor	6	11
Just arrested on a charge involving homosexuality	4	7
Patient in a mental hospital	2	3
Living in a YMCA	1	2
Just fired from a job because of homosexuality	1	2
Was not having any homosexual relations	20	36

Source: Dank, 1971: 184.
[a]Total number of social contexts is greater than 180 (number of respondents) because of overlap in contexts.

> I asked him, "Where is some action?" and he said, "There is a bar down the way." And the time I really caught myself coming out is the time I walked into this bar and saw a whole crowd of groovy, groovy guys. And I said to myself, there was the realization, that not all gay men are dirty old men or idiots, silky queens, but there are some just normal-looking and acting people, as far as I could see. I saw gay society and I said, "Wow, I'm home." (187)

The process appears to be similar for lesbians who come to realize a lesbian identity. For instance, Ponse (1984) quotes one woman:

> I was working in an office…and we started buddying around together and drinking and all, and she was the one who broke me in…I was running around with her and this is what started me. All of a sudden I realized that I liked what I was doing. At this point I was running around with gay people and at this time I knew that was the way it was going to be. And then I met _____ and that was my life. When I got out of the service, there wasn't any doubt in my mind….I just think you're a lesbian or a homosexual and that's it….I think it's all the way around, sexually and emotionally, yeah, all the way around. (27)

Coming out, then, depends both upon a person's internal sexual feelings *and* the definitions and explanations of those feelings available in his or her social environment. For example, if homosexuality is commonly seen by friends of acquaintances as a mental illness (a negative definition or explanation), development of a homosexual identity will be inhibited. However, if others important to a person define homosexuality more as an alternative way of life, that person's problems with accepting a homosexual identity will be diminished. Goode (1978) nicely summarizes the combination of things that frequently precipitate adoption of a gay self-concept.

> One is *a persistent lack of erotic and/or emotional interest in the opposite sex.* Second: the continuing failure of one's ability to explain away one's homosexuality. Third: having a deep, significant, meaningful homosexual experience with someone whom one respects and loves. Fourth: having an intimate, particularly one who is gay, explain to one that one *is*, in fact, gay. And lastly: dramatically realizing that there are many attractive, desirable, "normal" men and women—who don't fit one's preconception of the homosexual—who are gay. (380–381)

Meeting Places: Bars, Baths, and Tearooms

Among those with homosexual identities, men are more apt than women to socialize in relatively overt homosexual gathering spots. Multiple temporary liaisons are the more frequent pattern of a sexual activity among young male gays, and the settings in which this interaction occurs constitute an important slice of the gay subculture. Bars are a primary locus for the male homosexual community in many cities, providing an opportunity to get together during leisure hours and seek out partners for sexual encounters. The gay bar has been described, rather tamely, by one observer as "the homosexual equivalent of the USO or the youth club, where the rating and dating process may unfold in a controlled and acceptable manner" (Achilles, 1967: 231–232).

The gay bar scene is divided into several subtypes which emphasize the patrons' particular sexual tastes. In metropolitan areas such as Boston, Chicago, Washington, D.C., and San Francisco, large populations of homosexuals support specialized establishments, including western, leather, S-M, dance, and "piss-elegant" bars.[1] The patron makes a conscious decision as to the population group with whom he chooses to identify and expects to find it at a particular bar. As E. W. Delph (1978) notes,

> The piss-elegant patron does not expect leather people at his bar. Both consider the presence of the other ludicrous. Communications and interaction are seriously impeded by the appearance of incongruous identities. After all, the patron wishes to socialize with individuals with whom he can interact and relate to in a comfortable, taken-for-granted way....
>
>   The stand-up, cruising bar is spartanly equipped....Physical aspects of the bar focus attention on cruising. Spacious empty areas not only accommodate large numbers of patrons, but permit enough "runway" space to allow the continual flow of individuals to incessantly ply back and forth among the crowd, exhibiting and posturing physical virtues while searching for the desired, erotic object of the evening. In a popular bar such as Kellers, for example, the pool table is covered on weekends to conserve desperately needed space. It also adds another surface to which to lean (and posture). A narrow bar at best, Kellers becomes so crowded that even getting inside the bar is difficult. Bodies

mash tightly against each other, encouraging touch even if by accident. Squeezing through the throng, touching as one goes, is a crucial input in Kellers' popularity. The compactness of the bar and the fact that the patron is physically pressed against several other men generate sensuousness and a feeling of belonging, in spite of a lack of verbal intercourse. (113–116)

Until the mid-1980s, gay baths were popular settings for male impersonal sex in many American cities. The basic establishment usually included a locker room, towels for hire, steam room, and private bedroom cubicles (also for hire). More elaborate facilities included a snack bar, restaurant, television room, discotheque, and a shop purveying cosmetics and sexual devices. This environment provided nearly ideal conditions for impersonal sex: "protection; ample accessible opportunities; a known shared, organized reality; bonding of experience; congeniality; and a comfortable physical setting" (Weinberg and Williams, 1975: 124). Of course, there are medical risks in the numerous sexual contacts between men in settings like gay bars and baths, sometime involving hundreds of different partners. In general, the greater the number of partners, the greater the incidence of sexually transmitted diseases of all sorts—including, of course, AIDS. It is in this context that gay bathhouses became a focal point of controversy.

When it became apparent in the early 1980s that AIDS is a sexually transmitted virus, there was a growing demand for the closing of gay baths as a matter of public health. Some gay organizations resisted, arguing that this was an interference with the rights for gays to associate as they pleased. The bath owners also resisted, to protect their lucrative businesses. In 1984 bathhouses were ordered closed in San Francisco, followed shortly by several other American cities. Randy Shilts (1987) decries the delay of action:

> What made the San Francisco closure so anticlimactic…was that it came so late. Most of the people still frequenting San Francisco bathhouses in late 1984 were already infected with the AIDS virus. The saved lives were most likely those of a few thousand uninformed gay tourists. In fact, by the time the baths were closed and a truly comprehensive education program started in San Francisco, about two-thirds of the local gay men destined to be infected with LAV/HTLV-III already carried the virus. Any victories wrung from AIDS education or bathhouse closure would be Pyrrhic indeed. (491)

Though less prevalent now than prior to 1985, gay baths still exist in many cities throughout the United States. Not all states or localities have laws that ban them, and in some jurisdictions that do, the bathhouses continue to operate illegally.

Tearooms are public toilet facilities, such as those in parks or subways, where impersonal, transitory homosexual encounters frequently take place. According to Laud Humphreys (1975), who studied "the tearoom trade," "Public restrooms are chosen by those who want homoerotic activity without commitment for a number of reasons. *They are accessible, easily recognized by the initiate, and provide little public visibility*" (2–3). In the tearoom, sex can be had with a variety of partners quickly and anonymously, without any social obligation beyond the immediate physical exchange. Moreover, as with having many heterosexual partners, the dangers of being caught and exposed when having sex in a public place acts as a powerful aphrodisiac that magnifies the psychological payoff.

The types of participants in tearoom activity tell something about their probable motives and the diversity among those who seek homoerotic activity—many of whom, it should be emphasized, do not participate in the more overt homosexual subculture. For the Humphreys study, tearoom visitors were classified into four types. The most common participants (38%), known in the gay subcultural argot as *trade,* were or had been married and worked at jobs which would be threatened if their homosexual activity should be unmasked. Often these men found sexual relations with their wives curtailed and unsatisfactory. Thus, to protect both their marriages and their jobs, they apparently found the quick, impersonal sex of the tearoom an acceptable form of release. Humphreys found "no indication that these men seek homosexual contact as such; rather they want a form of orgasm—producing action that is less lonely than masturbation and less involving than a love relationship (115).

Ambisexuals (24%), the second type, were also likely to be married. However, unlike the trade, they recognized that their homosexual activity was indicative of their psychosexual orientations and thought of themselves as bisexual or ambisexual. These men effectively led two lives—one straight and the other gay—which they kept separate "much as a surreptitious gambling habit might be hidden from...family and neighbors" (122).

The *gay* men in Humphreys's classification (14%) were strongly attached to uniquely homosexual institutions. They were unmarried and made no pretense of living straight lives, as the ambisexuals and trade did. Humphreys (1975) notes that:

> Although these men correspond most closely to society's homosexual stereotype, they are least representative of the tearoom population.... That any of them patronize the tearooms at all is the result of incidental factors: they fear that open cruising in the more common homosexual market places of the baths and bars might disrupt a current love affair; or they drop in at a tearoom while waiting for a friend at one of the "watering places" where homosexuals congregate in parks. They find the anonymity of the tearooms suitable for their purposes, but not inviting enough to provide the primary setting for sexual activity. (125)

The *closet queens* (24% of Humphreys's sample) earned their appellation in the gay argot because they accepted their same-sex orientation strongly but felt an equal pressure to avoid exposure (often related to their jobs) and not come out into the homosexual subculture. They were socially isolated and often unhappy. Their situation amply demonstrates how the stigma of being identified openly as homosexual can drive some people into misery and further underground in the deviant activity. Sometimes the closet queen would cruise the streets to pick up young boys for furtive, one-night stands:

> Although painfully aware of their homosexual orientations, these men find little solace in association with others who share their deviant interests. Fearing exposure, arrest, the

stigmatization that might result from participation in the homosexual subculture, they are driven to a desperate, lone-wolf sort of activity that may prove most dangerous to themselves and the rest of society. (129)

Conclusions. Discussion of these meeting places for homosexual encounters suggests at least three themes in the subculture. First is the wide diversity of both the participants in homosexual behavior and the variety of settings in which it takes place. Many homosexuals lead very quiet lives, consisting mainly of ordinary socializing with friends at home. Of those who do frequent the "sexual marketplaces," not all identify themselves as homosexual. Over 60% of Humphreys' tearoom participants did *not* identify with the gay subculture. Put simply, not all homosexual activity takes place within the gay subculture, and all who engage in homosexual activity do not identify themselves as gay.

Second, the stigma attached to gay identity by a substantial proportion of people in the society all too often pressures those with homosexual feelings into temporary, impersonal contacts to secure sexual satisfaction. Fear of being labeled a homosexual is, for some, a powerful deterrent against coming out. Driven underground by this fear, they become traders in the most transitory, anonymous, and silent of public sexual marketplaces. The settings and circumstances of deviant behavior can only be adequately understood as they relate to the wider culture's norms and values.

Third, these meeting places are marvels of highly ordered, complex systems of nonverbal interaction. To be sure, the cues of body language, dress gesturing, positioning and the like play a significant role in most heterosexual encounters. However, when guarantees of anonymity and speed become prime motivators for bringing sexual activity to its conclusion, silent interaction emerges as a surprisingly efficient means of communication.

AIDS and Changing Sexual Behavior

Men who engage in promiscuous, unprotected homosexual activity are at extraordinarily high risk of contracting acquired immunodeficiency syndrome (AIDS). In 1992 alone, 45,472 cases of AIDS were reported in the United States (U.S. Bureau of the Census, 1993), and, according to the U.S. Department of Health and Human Services (1993), through July 1993, 315,390 cases of AIDS had been reported since the first diagnosis of AIDS in the United States in 1981, and 61 percent of all adult cases reported had involved "men who have sex with men" (homosexuals and bisexuals). In a study comparing homosexual men who showed evidence of having been infected with the HIV virus that causes AIDS to those who had not, several sexual practices were found to increase risk substantially. These included "receptive anal intercourse with ejaculation by nonsteady sexual partners, many sexual partners per month, and other indicators of high levels of sexual activity" (Darrow et al., 1987: 479).

In the light of this evidence, which has been widely publicized, especially in the gay community, we would expect sexual behavior among many homosexual men to have changed. Several studies show that it has. A 1983 survey of 655 gay men in San Francisco (McKusick, Horstman, and Coates, 1985), about two years after the viral cause of AIDS had been established, found that although men visiting bathhouses showed little change in their behavior, "other groups showed substantial reductions in frequency of sexual contacts from bars, baths, T-rooms, or parks. Men in monogamous relationships showed little change in sexual behavior within their relationship. Men in nonmonogamous relationships and men not in relationships reported substantial reductions in high-risk sexual activity" (493). In another study 745 gay men aged 20 to 65 were interviewed in New York City about changes in their behavior since a year after they heard of AIDS, and their sexual activity was reported to have declined 78%. According to Martin (1987), "The frequency of sexual episodes involving the exchange of body fluids and mucous membrane contact declined by 70 percent, and condom use during anal intercourse increased from 1.5 to 20 percent" (578). Other studies have found similar changes (Darrow, 1987; Klein et al., 1987). The factor that most sharply distinguishes homosexual men who practice risky sex from those who do not is drug use within sexual contexts (Siegel et al., 1989).

Despite the high rate of AIDS infection among homosexual men in the United States, the spread of the disease in this group has been dropping—largely because homosexual men are lowering their risk by changing their behavior.[2] The changing behavior has been facilitated by the social and communications networks established in conjunction with the gay rights movement; gay organizations and the gay press have been important avenues for communicating the risks of contracting the HIV virus and how to lower them (Doll and Bye, 1987). This is in sharp contrast to the problems of stemming the tide of AIDS infection among intravenous drug users who, as a group, are much more difficult to warn and educate because they generally lack ties to organizations (Velimirovic, 1987). One prominent researcher concluded in 1989 that if present patterns continued, AIDS would be a disease of the poor and minorities, and the lives of gay men would be redirected toward less erotic and more couple-oriented relationships (Gagnon, 1989). This conclusion was borne out in the 1993 report of the U.S. surgeon general on HIV infection and AIDS. Through 1992 47% of all reported AIDS cases were among blacks and Hispanics, though they represented only 21% of the U.S. population. The incidence of AIDS cases was found to be increasing among women and adolescents, and the highest rate of increase was among men and women who acquire HIV through heterosexual contact (Centers for Disease Control, 1993: 24–25).

While most homosexual men do appear to be rationally altering their behavior in accordance with the evidence on AIDS, the same cannot be said of the reactions to the disease of many who identify themselves as heterosexual. Even though it has been established that AIDS is not transmitted by casual contact, public reaction has bordered on hysteria. At one time children with AIDS were excluded from school; health care workers refused to treat AIDS patients; and undertakers refused to embalm those who died. Conrad (1986) describes AIDS as "an illness with a triple stigma: it is connected to stigmatized groups (homosexuals and drug users); it is sexually transmitted; and, like cancer, it is a terminal, wasting disease" (53).

The close association of homosexuality with AIDS has had profound effects on the gay community. Homosexuality has been restigmatized; fears and threats have forced many gay men back into the closet; and, in general, homophobia and discrimination have increased. The difficulties touch even the most basic relationships. The clearest finding in a survey of over 400 parents of gay men was that "the AIDS outbreak reopened old wounds for parents who had already come to terms with their child's homosexuality" (Robinson, Skeen, and Walters, 1987: 49). After a period of increasing acceptance in the 1960s and 1970s, homosexuals again have found themselves having to cope with an extremely hostile social environment (Shilts, 1987).

One-Sex Environments: Prisons and the Military

Total institutions are residential facilities such as prisons, mental hospitals, or monasteries in which the inhabitants are separated from the outside world and much of the daily round of life is strictly controlled. The term was coined by Erving Goffman, who notes that "Their encompassing or total character is symbolized by the barrier to social intercourse with the outside and to departure that is often built right into the physical plant, such as locked doors, high walls, barbed wire, cliffs, water, forests, or moors" (4). Frequently, as in prisons or military training camps, the institutional setting is total, and inmates or recruits are strictly segregated by sex for prolonged periods. Under such conditions the potential of and pressures for homosexual behavior are heightened.

Homosexuality in Prisons. The alternative sexual patterns for prison inmates are reduced to three: abstinence, masturbation, and homosexual activity. Although there are no precise estimates of how many male prisoners rely on each of these, a reasonable guess would suggest that 30% to 45% of inmates engage in homosexual activity (Buffum, 1972: 13). The patterns of homosexual behavior in the male prison constitute a subculture within a subculture, in which rather clearly defined rules and roles create a definite hierarchical structure.

At the top, in the prison argot, are "wolves" or "jockers"—aggressive, frequently older men who always take the inserter role. They do not see themselves as homosexual but view their activity as a transitory substitute for heterosexual relations. Indeed, their aggressive activity is taken as a confirmation of their masculine identity and an enhancement of their status in the prison stratification system. The "punks" are pressured into the homosexual receptor role by force and fear, or they turn to it as a form of homosexual prostitution for monetary gain. In either case, the punk role is usually taken by young, slightly built inmates and carries with it the low status accorded its association with feminine weakness. "Queens" or "fags" are those who partake of preferential homosexuality. They usually have homosexual experience prior to incarceration and are subject to the same stigma their sexual preference would arouse in the culture outside the prison.

Two of the prison roles revolving around homosexual activity, wolves and punks, are clearly products of the unique prison environment. In neither case do the men who assume them have a homosexual identity prior to imprisonment. It is reasonable to ask, then, what the long-term effects of their prison-situated homosexual activity are after release. In a small (nine-subject), detailed study directed at this question, Sagarin (1976) found that of aggressive participants "who actively sought a homosexual experience and not only had willingly entered into it but also had inflicted it on others, all returned to heterosexuality. On the contrary, all of those who had been forced and subdued into homosexuality, who insisted that it had hurt and disgusted them and they had entered it most unwillingly, continued the pattern and pursued it in their post-prison years" (254).

This finding again emphasizes the importance of distinguishing homosexual behavior from homosexual identity. It is also consistent with the evidence from Chapter 2 that rape is not primarily a means for sexual gratification; rather, it is the sexual expression of domination and aggression. As Sagarin puts it:

> For the aggressors, the subduing of another was not primarily a search for sexual outlet, affection, or even release from tension. It was a means for the reaffirmation of masculinity in a subculture in which few other methods were available for such expression....For aggressors, the prison homosexuality was a temporary expedient, and because they always thought of it in that fashion, they could emerge with their heterosexuality untouched, their masculinity undiminished, their normalcy unquestioned, their self-image untarnished. (254)

Clearly, then, the social and psychological importance of the homosexual act is not intrinsic to it; rather, the important thing is how the act is defined by others and by oneself.

As for the subdued, Sagarin finds no evidence of latent homosexuality in their pasts that might explain their postprison persistence. Instead, it appears that homosexuality can be a learned way of life, and the learning takes place even in unpleasant situations. Sagarin says,

> It takes place through adaptation and accommodation, through an effort to suppress fear and disgust in order to make the act less repugnant, and it is reinforced by the definition of others and by the concepts of latency that are today widely known even in relatively less educated groups. Furthermore, the experience of going from heterosexual to homosexual identification and life pattern can take place after the onset of maturity: it need not be during adolescence, as has frequently been suggested. (256)

Female penal institutions generally differ physically from those for males. Women's prisons often have no walls, use dormitories as opposed to cells, and are smaller. These structural differences account, in part, for the pattern of sexual relationships common in women's prisons. Prison lesbianism rarely takes the form of forcible subjugation; rather, there is a tendency to develop relatively stable inmate "family" systems in which "married" couples are represented by homosexual pairings. In some cases these pseudofamilies extend beyond the husband and wife roles to daughter or grandmother roles as well. Apparently this pattern of attachments is consistent with the widely diffused feminine ideal of linking sexuality with affection and the maintenance of nurturing, emotionally supportive relationships. However, one recent study (Propper, 1982) found that not all make-believe family participation by imprisoned women involves overt homosexual behavior, nor does all lesbian activity take place within pseudofamily roles.

Both male and female patterns of homosexual behavior in prisons tend to be adaptations for the creation of structure in the absence of other symbols of status or identity. The pattern in women's prisons emphasizes affectionate stability akin to the typical family while men in prison create, sometimes coercively, a hierarchical stability revolving around strict sexual role assignment and patterns of domination. Prisoners retain their sexuality regardless of the loss of personal identifiers such as clothing or family and work relationships in the identity-stripping process and isolation of imprisonment. It should be no wonder that when people are deprived of alternative bases for the creation and maintenance of social structure, homosexual activity becomes a focal point around which some kind of social organization can be developed.

Homosexuality in the Military. Another single-sex environment in which particular concern about homosexuality has been expressed is the armed forces. Indeed, in the 1990s, the question of gays in the military has been a high-profile issue in flux. Changes in the strict exclusionary policy of the past appear inevitable, but the mechanism—whether through executive order, legislative action, or the courts—remains to be seen (Stiehm, 1992). Until very recently the U.S. military, in line with federal employment policies, legally regarded homosexuals as unfit to serve. However, a substantial number of male homosexuals have been inducted during periods of conscription, and both male and female homosexuals have joined the armed forces voluntarily. Like homosexuals in any other form of employment, most of them do their jobs well, and their sexual orientations have not invited disciplinary attention. One study of male homosexuals (Saghir and Robins, 1973) found that 16% who were called up in a draft were not selected because they identified their sexual preference; 4% were rejected due to prior arrests; and the great majority who entered the service experienced no problems. Eventually only 6% of those inducted received less than honorable discharges. That so many gays have had distinguished careers in the military is all the more remarkable, given the zeal with which the services have historically pursued them (Shilts, 1993).

Particularly when the draft is in effect, homosexuals are placed in a difficult double bind. If they admit their homosexuality prior to induction, the result will be a deferment and a stigmatizing blotch on their records that will likely mar future employment opportunities. If, fearing such an outcome, they go into the military, there remains the risk of discovery and a less than honorable discharge. Such a separation from the military makes them ineligible for veterans' benefits and also threatens careers. Williams and Weinberg (1971) conclude:

The majority of homosexuals who serve do so with honor, and it seems foolish to pursue this group with the ardor that authorities exhibit. If an individual's sex life does not interfere with his service activities, it should be of no concern to military authorities. If it is of such a type that causes problems, then homosexuals should be separated but not necessarily in a way that is punitive. Punitiveness should be based on the nature of the offense without regard to the serviceman's sexual orientation. The automatic use of less than honorable discharges in the military's disposition of homosexuals is in our eyes immoral. (187)

EXPLANATIONS OF HOMOSEXUALITY

Theories concerning homosexuality cover the full range of possibilities, from the biogenetic and psychoanalytic to societal reaction and the politics of the gay rights movement. In this section we will present various perspectives on the development of sexual preference and then turn to the debate over what "causes" homosexuality. The section concludes with considerations of labeling, homophobia, and the political struggle for acceptance by the gay and lesbian community.

Heredity and Hormones

If the identification of a homosexual gene could be determined, it would provide the most elegant explanation possible of homosexuality. The probabilities of a person being homosexual would be statistically calculable, just as hair or eye color are based on genetic endowment. The crucial difference, however, is that hair and eye color are relatively fixed physical characteristics, while homosexuality is a complex, emergent mix of attitudes and patterns of behavior. Studies of identical twins have shown that if one is homosexual or lesbian, the other is quite likely to be so too (Kallman, 1952a, 1952b; Heston and Shields, 1968; Bailey and Pillard, 1991; Bailey et al., 1993). While numerous problems of the research on homosexual twins—including selective samples and small sample size—do not permit definite conclusions, evidence is accumulating that a hereditary factor may play a part in some types of homosexual behavior.

Recent research has examined the physiological mechanisms through which sexual orientation may be influenced in some people. Differences in hypothalamic structure between heterosexual and homosexual men have been discovered (LeVay, 1991), and a preliminary but methodologically sophisticated study of DNA markers on the X chromosome indicated that, with a statistical confidence level of more than 99%, "at least one subtype of male sexual orientation is genetically influenced" (Hamer et al., 1993). However, such research evidence demands extreme caution in interpretation (King, 1993). While it appears increasingly certain that biogenetic predispositions underlie the homosexual orientations of at least some gay men and women, sexual orientation is extremely complex, and the expression of biogenetic propensities is always influenced by interaction with social and environmental factors. We remain a long way from a complete biogenetic understanding of what causes human sexual orientation.

Psychoanalytic Perspectives

In psychoanalytic explanations it is generally assumed that homosexuality is symptomatic of pathology or sickness. The detailed dynamics of scenarios that produce the alleged abnormality vary, but from this perspective homosexuality is viewed as an illness to be treated and, it is hoped, cured. In males, fear of castration (castration anxiety) is thought to be heightened in some cases by the sight of a woman as a sexual partner without a penis. Thus certain men are repulsed by women and attracted to men. Another alternative explanation is that an overbearing mother and a weak, unassertive father can combine to alienate a son from masculine identification (Bieber, 1962).

Among females, a variation of the male's castration anxiety forms the foundation for psychoanalytic theories of lesbianism. Lacking a penis, the female may suffer from "penis envy" and the trauma of realizing that she may have already been castrated or at least not have been born fully equipped. One possible consequence might be that a girl would identify so closely with her father that she fails to incorporate a feminine orientation. Generally speaking, in the case of boys or girls, the psychoanalytic perspective hypothesizes that if there is a too-intense attachment to the parent of the opposite sex, guilt and fear associated with the incest taboo create revulsion against all heterosexual contact. The result may be homosexuality.

Criticism of psychoanalytic theories has been intense. Of the many problems we will briefly mention only three. First, the explanations are *post hoc*; that is, they are derived by examining case studies of homosexuals and then piecing together possible reasons for sexual orientation. Rarely are there attempts to compare homosexuals to heterosexuals or studies to test the theories by predicting sexual orientation, given certain conditions. Second, just how the personalities of homosexuals are "disordered" or "sick" is very unclear. In one famous study (Hooker, 1957), for example, a panel of psychiatrists and clinical psychologists was unable to distinguish homosexuals from heterosexuals on the basis of personality tests. Third, psychiatric case studies of homosexuals are usually based upon people who have gone to a psychiatrist precisely because they are troubled. It would not be surprising to find evidence of personality or social maladjustment among people who place themselves in a psychiatrist's care, whether they are homosexual or heterosexual. Certainly the majority of homosexuals and heterosexuals never come to the attention of psychiatrists. In a word, psychiatric conclusions regarding sexuality in general, and homosexuality in particular, are probably based upon very biased samples of cases.

Learning Theory

Implicit in psychoanalytic explanations is the assumption that some sort of disorder, in either the person's upbringing or psyche, motivates homosexuality. The fundamental imagery of the homosexual portrayed in these theories is that of a person driven into deviance by an abnormal condition. In sharp contrast, explanations that rely on learning theory assume that homosexual behavior can be learned and reinforced like any other behavior. The initial homosexual experience, according to this viewpoint, is usually not the result of some drive or need but instead a matter of chance. For example, the preadolescent sex play common between boys or between girls may provide an experience or attachment that is pleasurable and rewarding. Learned fears or inhibitions regarding heterosexual relations also may make a person more receptive to homosexual activity.

The effect of rather isolated but pleasurable homosexual experiences can be reinforced and enlarged through fantasies imagined during self-masturbation. Akers (1973) describes the process:

> Through both direct reinforcement and reinforcement through masturbatory imagery, then, the homosexual experience may be repeated. Each time that it results in positive outcomes, the probability of repeating it increases. Rewarded repetition and practice enhance the ability to attain pleasure from the homosexual acts of mutual masturbation, fellatio, and anal intercourse. Inhibitions toward homosexuality continue to decrease. Depending on how frequent and how pleasurable simultaneous heterosexual experiences are, each succeeding successful homosexual episode increases the probability of further homosexual involvement. (160)

Beyond learning the techniques and learning to enjoy homosexual behavior, individuals may (but do not necessarily) learn to play homosexual or gay roles. In the process of coming out, they learn to organize their lives around their alleged deviant images. In interaction with others who share their homosexual identification, participants in the subculture learn how to manage their shunned status, to rationalize their behavior to themselves and others, and to get along with others in a hostile world.

The Development of Sexual Preference

To counter many of the criticisms of psychoanalytic and learning research, Allen Bell and his colleagues (1981) designed a comprehensive study comparing 979 homosexual (Kinsey scale 5–6) with 477 heterosexual (Kinsey scale 0–1) men and women. A number of stereotypes or myths are *not* supported by their findings:

- Parents' relationships with their son or daughter are *not* central to the development of sexual preference.
- Homosexual preference is *not* caused by poor peer relationships.
- Labeling by others does *not* significantly influence sexual preference.
- Atypical experiences with persons of the opposite sex do *not* lead to homosexual preference.
- Seduction by an older homosexual or lesbian does *not* play a role in the development of homosexual sexual preference.

This study found that sexual preference typically originates very early in a person's development—by adolescence and prior to sexual activity. Homosexual "feelings" (attractions) usually occurred three years or so prior to initial homosexual activity with another. Homosexual men and lesbians do not lack in heterosexual experiences during childhood and adolescence, they simply do not find them gratifying. Gender nonconformity (boys not engaging in "male-oriented" activities; girls not engaging in "female-oriented" ones) during childhood was found to be strongly related to later homosexuality in adulthood. Bell, Weinberg, and Hammersmith (1981) conclude that

> …homosexuality is as deeply ingrained as heterosexuality, so that the differences in behaviors or social experiences of prehomosexual boys and girls and their preheterosexual counterparts reflect or express, rather than cause, the eventual homosexual preference. In short, theories that tie homosexuality to an isolated social experience cannot be expected to account well for such a basic part of one's being as sexual preference appears to be. (190–191)

These findings are not inconsistent with a possible biological basis for sexual preference. The authors note that "If there is a biological basis for homosexuality, it probably operates more powerfully for exclusive homosexuals than for bisexuals…[and] it probably accounts for gender nonconformity as well as for sexual orientation" (216–217). Regardless of a biological predisposition, it is evident that sexuality is a deep-rooted, fundamental human characteristic that is neither easily within a person's control nor easily subject to alteration. To discriminate against people or otherwise treat them badly in reaction to a characteristic for which they are not willfully responsible is the height of injustice—especially if they inflict no harm on others or do not involve others against their wills. Such injustice has historically been the lot of homosexuals and lesbians.

The Essentialist/Constructionist Debate on Causes

The question of what "causes" homosexuality—its etiology—is a fundamental issue that is presently receiving a great deal of research attention. At the core of the debate is what is commonly called essentialist versus constructionist arguments. According to Risman and Schwartz (1988),

> The essentialist model holds that each individual has a *true*, or essential, sexual self which does not change. In contrast, constructionists suggest that homosexual behavior is something which some individuals DO: it is not who they ARE. Constructionist argue that social opportunities and meaning systems—rather than core personality traits—influence choice of sexual partners. (127)

Although advocates of both positions sometimes seem to insist that only one model or the other must be correct, and therefore the other is wrong, it is likely that there is a good deal of truth to both. On the essentialist side are the findings that homosexual orientation is found in about 5 percent of all societies, it is largely unchangeable, and, increasingly, it is found to have a biogenetic component (Whitam and Mathy, 1986). Constructionists emphasize the relatively modern emergence of the gay social role and accounts by gays of their own identities as evidence in support of their position (Risman and Schwartz, 1988; Troiden, 1988). In fact, it is likely that eventually it will be proven that sexual *orientation* does have a strong physiological basis, but sexual *identity* is far more mutable and open to choice (Reiter, 1989). The way people *behave* sexually, in turn, results from a complex interaction of their sexual orientations and their emergent sexual identities.

Societal Reaction

The societal reaction approach, sometimes called *labeling theory*, emphasizes the consequences of negative sanctions directed against deviants. Weinberg and Williams (1974) found that

> ...for the majority of homosexuals in the societies we studied (the United States, Denmark, and the Netherlands) the impact of the legal situation is not *direct*. Instead, we believe the most universal (though not necessarily the most serious), effect of legal repression is to symbolize society's rejection of the homosexual. This rejection seems to be a major source of the homosexual's problems. (268)

Widespread adaptations to this rejection include the development of the homosexual subculture to provide social support and the emergence of militant homophile (gay) movements which attempt to confront directly and politically the laws that symbolize rejection.

Homophobia, or intense fear and hatred of homosexuals, is part of the general cultural climate in the United States. Even in periods when homophobia is not overt, it lies dormant, ready to reemerge with the stimulus of a crisis such as the AIDS epidemic. Homophobia's origins are to be found in Judeo-Christian tradition dating back thousands of years. The persecutions of homosexuals that have surfaced periodically in Western history include brutalization and murder by the ancient Hebrews, burning in the Middle Ages, and the genocide of Hitler's Germany. In the latter case, over 50,000 alleged homosexuals were arrested and sent to concentration camps. In Germany and the occupied countries during World War II, between 100,000 and 400,000 died in this manner (Crompton, 1978).

Homophobia usually has its origins in one or more of the following factors: (1) insecurity about one's own sexuality and gender identity, (2) a strong religious indoctrination that condemns homosexuality, and (3) ignorance about sexuality in general, especially homosexuality. A recent study of people's attitudes toward homosexuality found that the fear of homosexual males appears to reflect concern for maintaining the "proper" male and female roles. In addition, those who favored maintenance of sex-segregated institutions tended to be the most homophobic. Thus, homophobia may serve to maintain a sharp psychological boundary between social and sexual interaction for those who strongly support single-sex institutions (Britton, 1990).

Marmor (1980) argues that ignorance about the causes of homosexuality may be the most important source of homophobic reactions:

> Many people still tend to think of homosexuality either as a pattern that is freely chosen by a conscious act of will or as something that is "caught" from others, either as a result of seduction or by an "infectious" imitation or "modeling" of oneself after homosexuals

to whom one has been exposed. These latter myths have played a powerful role in the recent "backlash" taking place in a number of states with regard to the legal rights of homosexual teachers. (19)

Fighting ignorance about homosexuality must be a major strategy in the effort to reduce homophobia. However, getting the facts out about causation will probably not be enough. Ultimately, the reduction of homophobia will require honest portrayals associating gays with positive values and favorably reflecting their contributions to the society (Kirk and Madsen, 1989).

The Politics of Definition and Control

In December 1973 the American Psychiatric Association (APA) officially declared that homosexuality "by itself does not necessarily constitute a psychiatric disorder." From 1951 to 1973 homosexuality had been categorized in the APA's *Diagnostic and Statistical Manual* in the context of sexual deviation. The action by the APA Board of Trustees was accompanied by a "Position Statement of Homosexuality and Civil Rights" which clearly recognizes the power of society's most potent official labelers, especially psychiatrists, to influence the lives of their "clients." In this statement, Spector (1977) reports,

> ...the board deplored all public and private discrimination against homosexuals and urged the enactment of civil rights legislation to protect homosexuals and the repeal of all discriminatory legislation against homosexual behavior. It further deplored the use of "pejorative connotations derived from diagnostic or descriptive terminology used in psychiatry" as the basis for such discrimination. (53)

Almost immediately, opposition to the change in nomenclature, led by psychoanalysts Irving Bieber and Charles Socorides, mobilized. This group circulated a petition which gathered the 200 members' signatures required to throw the board's decision open to a referendum of the entire APA membership. A vote was scheduled for April 1974, and both sides campaigned strenuously. The issue of whether to officially classify homosexuality as a mental disorder was being decided politically by the members of a prestigious professional society in a hotly contested vote on the issue. Over 10,000 of the APA's 18,000 members voted in the referendum, and the Board of Trustees' decision was upheld by 58% of them.

We might rightfully ask: What's so important about a definition? Some thought on the question leads to the realization that the theoretical images concocted to explain deviance are very much matters of definition, rarely decided by unanimous agreement, and result from passionate political struggles. This episode also directs attention to the pivotal position of the professions concerned with human behavior, especially psychiatry, psychology, sociology, and medicine, as battlegrounds for issues of social control in a modern society.

The Gay and Lesbian Rights Movements

Although homosexuality has existed throughout recorded human history, the origins of the gay and lesbian rights movements are a great deal more recent. The earliest social movement to advance the civil rights of gay people was organized in Germany in 1897. There is tragic irony in this, of course, because homosexuals were transported to Nazi death camps along with millions of Jews, gypsies, and other "social undesirables" during World War II. In the United States in the 1950s, gays experienced the extreme hostility of the government and the media in the context of the reactionary politics of the Senate Subcommittee on Investigations led by Senator Joseph McCarthy. Adam (1987) describes the effect:

> Like the German militarists of the Weimar period or the British at the time of Napoleon, the McCarthyites drew together personal feelings of self-esteem expressed in terms of "manhood" with national self-esteem and belligerence. Working within a gender discourse that associated maleness with toughness and effectiveness, in opposition to supposedly female weakness and failure, male homosexuality symbolized the betrayal of manhood—the feminine enemy within men. (58)

Being labeled a homosexual during this period could have the same dire consequences for a person's career as being labeled a communist.

The 1960s ushered in the civil rights movement, with the goal of eliminating racial discrimination. The birth of the American gay rights movement is usually said to have followed a police raid of the Stonewall Inn, a New York City gay bar, on June 27, 1969. Rather than remaining docile, the patrons fought back. Within weeks, the Gay Liberation Front had been organized in New York; marches and demonstrations followed, and the movement spread to numerous other cities and most college campuses across the county (Humphreys, 1972). While the male homosexual movement and its female lesbian counterpart frequently joined forces in the fight for acceptance, they had distinct identities. The lesbian movement found itself in a complex dialogue with feminism from the 1970s on into the 1990s. By the mid-1980s the gay rights movement had demonstrated its political potency, both locally and nationally, at the polls. It became a vital organizational foundation for AIDS-prevention education and campaigns to end discrimination in housing, employment, and the military.

SOCIAL POLICY: THE ACCEPTANCE OF DIVERSITY

Homosexuality has long been considered within the orbit of legal control in the United States. Until 1962, sexual behavior between two persons of the same sex was a criminal offense in all 50 states. It has now been decriminalized in about half of them, and in the others penalties of up to 20 years in prison still are possible (Rivera, 1982; Reinig, 1990). Three main consequences flow from criminal laws against homosexuality in the U.S. First, even though enforcement is usually sporadic and selective, criminal laws make constant the threat and fear of criminal prosecution. Second, the criminal laws support secondary legal sanctions such as immigration and military policies that affect homosexuals and lesbians. And third, they help to maintain and legitimize an antigay climate that at times can turn ugly and violent (Russo and Humphreys, 1983; Schneider, 1987).

In addition to criminal sanctions in some jurisdictions, lesbians and homosexuals have no explicit federal legal protection regarding employment. In numerous cases teachers who are homosexual or lesbian have been given "due process" and then fired, and the courts have upheld the dismissals. Homosexuals and lesbians have been subject to dishonorable discharge from the military if discovered. Generally, homosexual parents lose child custody cases, and present immigration law calls for the exclusion of homosexuals as "sexual psychopaths." Citizenship can be denied anyone applying who is found to be homosexual.

Even when not directly subject to the legal threats, lesbians and homosexuals are subject to threats of informal employment discrimination. One study of discrimination against lesbians estimated that almost one-third of 1,151 respondents anticipated employment discrimination; 13% actually experienced some; and 8% lost or nearly lost their jobs as a result of being discovered (Levine and Leonard, 1984). The most common response among both women and men homosexuals has been to remain closeted in their work lives. Often they make employment decisions, such as self-employment or finding work in certain more tolerant industries, in the light of anticipated discrimination.

Research evidence overwhelmingly suggests that sexual orientation is not a matter of willful choice. For some people in this society, and probably in every society, same-sex attraction is natural and unavoidable. The challenge then becomes to expand the capacity of the society to tolerate the diversity presented by all its minorities—including lesbians and homosexuals. Acceptance minimally ought to include elimination of criminal statutes that underlie and legitimize other forms of discrimination and prejudice. More positively, federal discrimination laws ought to include sexual orientation as a category protected against discrimination in employment, housing, and other matters. Finally, because ignorance about sexuality is often at the heart of homophobia, social policy ought to include support of education to improve people's knowledge about it.

SUMMARY

Homosexual behavior is culturally and historically widespread. Although in most societies there seem to be some individuals who engage in homosexual activities, they are not the statistical or cultural norm. Moreover, in many times and places homosexual behavior has been the object of strong negative attitudes and sanctions. Male homosexuality has received greater attention from historians than lesbianism because males have tended to write history about other men. In Western culture lesbianism seems to have been somewhat more tolerated than male homosexuality.

Human sexuality is best understood as arrayed along a continuum between purely heterosexual and purely homosexual attractions, behaviors, and identity throughout a person's life. Only about half of American men are exclusively heterosexual or homosexual in their behavior over their lifetimes. Predominantly homosexual men and women are remarkably similar physiologically to their predominantly heterosexual counterparts, and homosexuals and lesbians are as diverse in their lifestyles as heterosexuals are. Some are in close, stable, long-term relationships; others have promiscuous sex lives; and still others lead a solitary, isolated existence. The range is not unlike that among heterosexuals. Indeed, in many ways lesbian women resemble women in general and homosexual men resemble men in general. For instance, lesbians tend to have more stable relationships and fewer sex partners than male homosexuals.

Coming out is the acceptance of a homosexual or lesbian identity. Many, though by no means all, who have come out of the closet participate in the gay subculture. For males in urban areas this subculture consists mainly of encounters in gay bars, baths, and tearooms. Since the AIDS epidemic, there have been marked changes in male homosexual activity. While the spread of AIDS among homosexual men is subsiding, the number already infected with the HIV virus will cause a huge death toll for at least a decade. Gay organizations have facilitated the distribution of AIDS warnings and educational materials that have helped bring about changes in the sexual practices of homosexuals to reduce risk. The social effects of AIDS include increased homophobia in the society and a return to the closet for some homosexuals.

There is growing evidence for a biological origin of homosexuality, especially for those on the extremes of the Kinsey scale of sexual preferences. Psychoanalytic theories emphasizing family dynamics have been largely discredited as an explanation. Sexual orientation, whether heterosexual or homosexual, appears to develop very early in life, typically prior to adolescence. Homosexual orientation does not result from seduction by an older homosexual or lesbian. Sexuality is a fundamental characteristic of a person's being that is neither within a person's control nor easily changed.

Societal reactions to homosexuality are often negative. The most extreme is homophobia. This intense fear and hatred of homosexuals grows out of the homophobic's own sexual insecurity, indoctrination, or ignorance. It is morally unacceptable to persecute someone for an aspect of their identity for which they bear no responsibility—particularly if they do no harm to others in realizing that identity. Thus homosexual behavior between consenting adults ought not to be subject to legal sanctions of invidious medical labeling. The struggle in the American Psychiatric Association over the medical definition of homosexuality is a vivid example of how the control of deviance emerges from a political process. The effectiveness of the gay rights movement is a testament to how those who have been labeled deviant can resist and even reverse this designation. Social policies should focus on decriminalization of homosexual activity between consenting adults and encourage greater acceptance of diversity in the society.

ENDNOTES

1. "Piss-elegant" refers to a style of presentation that is seen as "pseudo" authentic and thus false. The style emphasizes conservative attire and formal manners and is closely associated with the "closeted" homosexual and middle-class virtues. The style is also associated with pecuniary (monied) success, which many participants have not attained. "Elegance"—meaning monied manners—is pretended and hence

labeled "piss." Patrons of these bars do not refer to themselves as "piss-elegant," although they employ the term when referring to others they wish to derogate.

2. The death toll from AIDS among homosexual men will continue to rise, probably for as long as a decade, because of the lengthy latency period before symptoms appear. However, "A wide range of data amassed over the past year reveal that the virus has stopped spreading in surveyed groups of gay men. In several cities it continues to infect black and Hispanic drug addicts and their babies at a disturbing rate" (Boffey, 1988: 1).

REFERENCES

Achilles, N.
1967   "The Development of the Homosexual Bar as an Institution." Pp. 228–244 in J. H. Gagnon and W. Simon (eds.), *Sexual Deviance*. New York: Harper & Row.

Adam, B. D.
1987   *The Rise of a Gay and Lesbian Movement*. Boston: Twayne.

Akers, R. L.
1973   *Deviant Behavior: A Social Learning Approach*. Belmont, CA: Wadsworth.

Bailey, J. M., and Pillard, R. C.
1991   "A Genetic Study of Male Sexual Orientation." *Archives of General Psychiatry* 48: 1089–1096.

Bailey, J. M., Pillard, R. C., Neale, M. C., and Aggie, Y.
1993   "Heritable Factors Influence Sexual Orientation in Women." *Archives of General Psychiatry* 50: 217–223.

Bell, A. P., and Weinberg, M. S.
1978   Homosexualities: *A Study of Diversity Among Men and Women*. New York: Simon and Schuster.

Bell, A. P., Weinberg, M. S., and Hammersmith, S. K.
1981   *Sexual Preference: Its Development in Men and Women*. Bloomington: University of Indiana Press.

Berger, R. M.
1983   "What Is a Homosexual? A Definitional Model." *Social Work*. 28: 132–135.

Bieber, I.
1962   *Homosexuality: A Psychoanalytic Study of Male Homosexuals*. New York: Basic Books.

Boffey, P. M.
1988   "Spread of AIDS Abating, but Deaths Will Still Soar." *The New York Times* 2/14/88: 1.

Britton, D. M.
1990   "Homophobia and Homosociality: An Analysis of Boundary Maintenance." *Sociological Quarterly* 31: 423–429.

Buffum, P. C.
1972   *Homosexuality in Prisons*. Washington, DC: U.S. Government Printing Office.

Bullough, V. L.
1979   *Homosexuality: A History*. New York: New American Library.

Carrier, J. M.
1980   "Homosexual Behavior in Cross-Cultural Perspective." Pp. 100–122 in J. Marmor (ed.), *Homosexual Behavior: A Modern Reappraisal*. New York: Basic Books.

Centers for Disease Control and Prevention
1993   *The Surgeon General's Report to the American Public on HIV Infection and AIDS*. Washington, DC: Health Resources and Services Administration.

Conrad, P.
1988   "The Social Meaning of AIDS." *Social Policy* 17: 51–56.

Cooper, M.
1990   "Rejecting 'Femininity': Some Research Notes on Gender Identity Development in Lesbians." *Deviant Behavior* 11: 371–380.

Crompton, L.
1978   "Gay Genocide from Leviticus to Hitler." Pp. 67–91 in L. Crew (ed.), *The Gay Academic*. Palm Springs, CA: ETC Publications.

Dank, B. M.
1971   "Coming Out in the Gay World." *Psychiatry* 34: 180–197.

Darrow, W.
1987   "Behavioral Changes in Response to AIDS," Symposium International de Reflexion sur le Side, Center for International Conferences, Paris, October.

Darrow, W. W., Echenberg, D. F., Jaffe, H. W., O'Malley, P. M., Byers R. H., Getchell, J. P., and Curran, J. W.
1987   "Risk Factors for Human Immunodeficiency Virus (HIV) Infections in Homosexual Men." *American Journal of Public Health* 77: 479–483.

Delph, E. W.
1978   *The Silent Community: Public Homosexual Encounters*. Beverly Hills, CA.: Sage.

Doll, L. S., and Bye, L. L.
1987   "AIDS: Where Reason Prevails…" *World Health Forum* 8: 484–488.

Ford, C. S., and Beach, F. A.
1951   *Patterns of Sexual Behavior.* New York: Harper & Row.

Gagnon, J. H.
1989   "Disease and Desire." *Daedalus* 118: 47–77.

Gagnon, J. H., and Simon, W.
1973   *Sexual Conduct: The Sources of Human Sexuality.* Chicago: Aldine.

Goffman, E.
1961   *Asylums: Essays on the Social Situation of Mental Patients and Other Inmates.* Garden City, NY: Anchor.

Goode, E.
1978   *Deviant Behavior: An Interactionist Approach.* Englewood Cliffs, NJ: Prentice-Hall.

Hamer, D. H., Hu, S., Magnuson, V. L., and Pattatucci, A. M. L.
1993   "A Linkage between DNA Markers on the X Chromosome and Male Sexual Orientation." *Science* 261: 321–328.

Heston, L. L., and Shields, J.
1968   "Homosexuality in Twins: A Family Study and Registry Study." *Archives of General Psychiatry* 18: 149–160.

Hooker, E.
1957   "The Adjustment of the Male Overt Homosexual." *Journal of Projective Techniques* 21: 18–31.

Humphreys, L.
1972   *Out of the Closets: The Sociology of Homosexual Liberation.* Englewood Cliffs, NJ: Prentice-Hall.
1975   *Tearoom Trade: Impersonal Sex in Public Places.* Chicago: Aldine.

Kallman, F. J.
1952a   "Comparative Twin Study of the Genetic Aspects of Male Homosexuality." *Journal of Nervous and Mental Disease* 115: 283–298.
1952b   "Twin Siblings and the Study of Male Homosexuality." *American Journal of Human Genetics* 4: 136–146.

Karlen, A.
1980   "Homosexuality in History." Pp. 75–99 in J. Marmor (ed.), *Homosexual Behavior: A Modern Reappraisal.* New York: Basic Books.

King, M.
1993   "Sexual Orientation and the X." *Nature* 364: 288–289.

Kinsey, A. C., Pomeroy, W. B., and Martin, C. E.
1948   *Sexual Behavior in the Human Male.* Philadelphia: W. B. Saunders.

Kinsey, A. C., Pomeroy, W. B., Martin, C. E., and Gebhard, P. H.
1953   *Sexual Behavior in the Human Female.* Philadelphia: W. B. Saunders.

Kirk, M., and Madsen, H.
1989   *After the Ball: How America Will Conquer Its Fear and Hatred of Gays in the 90s.* New York: Plume.

Klein, D. E., Sullivan, G., Wolcott, D. L., Landsverk, J., Namir, S., and Fawzy, I. F.
1987   "Changes in AIDS Risk Behaviors among Homosexual Male Physicians and University Students." *American Journal of Psychiatry* 144: 742–747.

LeVay, S.
1991   "A Difference in Hypothalamic Structure between Heterosexual and Homosexual Men." *Science* 253: 1034–1037.

Levine, M. P., and Leonard, R.
1984   "Discrimination against Lesbians in the Work Force." *Signs* 9: 700–710.

Licht, H.
1955   "Male Homosexuality in Ancient Greece." Pp. 267–349 in D. W. Corey (ed.), *Homosexuality: A Cross-Cultural Approach.* New York: Julian Press.

Marmor, J.
1980   "Overview: The Multiple Roots of Homosexual Behavior." Pp. 3–22 in J. Marmor (ed.), *Homosexual Behavior: A Modern Reappraisal.* New York: Basic Books.

Martin, J. L.
1987   "The Impact of AIDS on Gay Male Sexual Behavior Patterns in New York City." *American Journal of Public Health* 77: 578–581.

Masters, W. H., and Johnson, V.
1979   *Homosexuality in Perspective.* Boston: Little Brown.

McIntosh, M.
1968   "The Homosexual Role." *Social Problems* 16: 182–192.

McKusick, L., Horstman, W., and Coates, T. J.
1985   "AIDS and Sexual Behavior Reported by Gay Men in San Francisco." *American Journal of Public Health* 75: 493–496.

Money, J.
1980   "Genetic and Chromosomal Aspects of Homosexual Etiology," Pp. 59–72 in Judd Marmor (ed.), *Homosexual Behavior: A Modern Reappraisal.* New York: Basic Books.

Ponse, B.
1984   "The Problematic Meanings of Lesbian." Pp. 25–33 in J. D. Douglas (ed.), *The Sociology of Deviance.* Boston: Allyn and Bacon.

Propper, A. M.
1982   "Make-Believe Families and Homosexual Activity among Imprisoned Girls." *Criminology* 20: 127–138.

Reinig, T. W.
1990   "Sin, Stigma and Society: A Critique of Morality and Values in Democratic Law and Policy." *Buffalo Law Review* 38: 859–901.
Reiter, L.
1989   "Sexual Orientation, Sexual Identity, and the Question of Choice." *Clinical Social Work Journal* 17: 138–150.
Risman, B., and Schwartz, P.
1988   "Sociological Research on Male and Female Homosexuality," *Annual Review of Sociology* 14: 125–147.
Rivera, R.
1982   "Homosexuality and the Law." Pp. 323–336 in P. William, J. D. Weinrich, J. C. Gonsiorek, and M. E. Hotvedt (eds.), *Homosexuality: Social, Psychological and Biological Issues.* Beverly Hills, CA: Sage.
Robinson, B., Skeen, P., and Walters, L.
1987   "The AIDS Epidemic Hits Home." *Psychology Today* 21: 48–52.
Rogers, S., and Turner, C. F.
1991   "Male-Male Sexual Contact in the USA: Findings from Five Sample Surveys, 1970–1990." *Journal of Sex Research* 28: 491–519.
Ross, M. W.
1989   "Married Homosexual Men: Prevalence and Background." *Marriage and Family Review* 14: 35–57.
Rowse. A. L.
1977   *Homosexuals in History: A Study of Ambivalence in Society, Literature and the Arts.* New York: Macmillan.
Russo, A., and Humphreys, L.
1983   "Homosexuality and Crime." Pp. 866–872 in *Encyclopedia of Crime and Justice.* New York: Free Press.
Sagarin, E.
1976   "Prison Homosexuality and Its Effects on Post-Prison Sexual Behavior." *Psychiatry* 39: 245–257.
Saghir, M. T., and Robins, E.
1973   *Male and Female Homosexuality.* Baltimore: Williams and Wilkins.
1980   "Clinical Aspects of Female Homosexuality." Pp. 280–295 in J. Marmor (ed.), *Homosexual Behavior: A Modern Reappraisal.* New York: Basic Books.
Schneider, W.
1987   "Homosexuals: Is AIDS Changing Attitudes?" *Public Opinion* 10: 6–7/59.

Shilts, R.
1987   *And the Band Played On.* New York: St. Martins.
1993 *Conduct Unbecoming: Lesbians and Gays in the U.S. Military.* New York: St. Martins.
Siegel, K., Mesagno, F. P., Chen, J., and Christ, G.
1989   "Factors Distinguishing Homosexual Males Practicing Risky and Safer Sex." *Social Science and Medicine* 28: 561–569.
Spector, M.
1977   "Legitimizing Homosexuality." *Society* 14(5): 52–56.
Stiehm, J. H.
1992   "Managing the Military's Homosexual Exclusion Policy: Text and Subtext." *University of Miami Law Review* 46: 685–710.
Troiden, R.
1988   *Gay and Lesbian Identity: A Sociological Analysis.* Dix Hills, NY: General Hall.
U.S. Bureau of the Census
1993   *Statistical Abstract of the United States: 1993,* 113th edition. Table 203. Washington, DC: U.S. Department of Commerce.
U.S. Department of Health and Human Services
1993   *HIV/AIDS: Surveillance Report,* 2nd qtr. ed., 5 (July). Washington, DC: Author.
Velimirovic, B.
1987   "AIDS as a Social Phenomenon." *Social Sciences and Medicine* 25: 541–552.
Warren, C. A. B.
1974   *Identity and Community in the Gay World.* New York: Wiley.
Weille, K. H.
1993   "Reworking Developmental Theory: The Case of Lesbian Identity Formation." *Clinical Social Work Journal* 21: 151–160.
Weinberg, M. S., and Williams, C. J.
1974   *Male Homosexuals: Their Problems and Adaptations.* New York: Oxford.
1975   "Gay Baths and the Social Organization of Impersonal Sex." *Social Problems* 23: 124–136.
Whitam, F. L., and Mathy, R. M.
1986   *Male Homosexuality in Four Societies: Brazil, Guatemala, the Philippines, and the United States.* New York: Praeger.
Williams, C. J., and Weinberg, M. S.
1971   *Homosexual and the Military: A Study of Less than Honorable Discharge.* New York: Harper & Row.

4 | Mental Disorders

Historically, images of madness have not followed a smooth path from the supernatural to the enlightened. However, despite occasional halts and temporary reversals, the supposed causes of madness have generally moved (1) from an emphasis on the sacred (possession by gods, demons, witches) to the secular, (2) from the moralistic search for flaws in the individual to naturalistic explanations emphasizing scientific research findings, and (3) from locating the causes exclusively within the person (spiritual possession or physiological illness) to a greater recognition of the impact of a person's external social environment.

IMAGES OF MADNESS

Mental Disorder in Western History

Throughout most of Western civilization, magic or demonic possession dominated popular images of the reasons for bizarre and incomprehensible behavior. The ancient Greeks believed that madness was due to possession by malignant demons or gods. Even the gods themselves were subjected to possession, as when Hercules went insane from possession by Lyssa, the goddess of madness, or Orestes's madness was ascribed to the Furies.

Contemporaneously with these views, Hippocrates, the Greek physician, proposed an organic theory of madness in a treatise entitled "On the Sacred Disease." Dealing primarily with epilepsy, Hippocrates attacked explanations relying on diabolical possession and, in a more modern manner, claimed that an organic disturbance in the brain causes madness. In contrast, Plato emphasized the psychological biography of a person, and examined how family relationships and education in the formative years explain adult behavior. Hippocrates's emphasis on organic dysfunction and Plato's on social psychological explanations still represent viable alternative hypotheses which contemporary researchers use in trying to understand the causes of mental disorders.

In the Middle Ages (roughly from the collapse of the Roman Empire in the 5th century A.D. through the beginning of the Renaissance in the 14th century), the Church was the primary institution presiding over a difficult era marked by wars, famine, plague, and pestilence. Madness often expressed itself in mass hysteria, flagellants, and dance manias which were popularly attributed to demonic possession. The Renaissance (roughly the 14th through the 16th centuries) saw continued emphasis on demonology, especially witchcraft, as an explanation of madness. In the face of great opposition, a few thinkers, such as Johann Weyer, who is today considered the father of modern psychiatry, tried to counter the accusation and vicious treatment of alleged witches by offering psychological reasons for their behavior. However, his views would have to wait several centuries before receiving popular support.

In the 17th and 18th centuries the insane were increasingly placed in the same institutions with the poor, the crippled, and the delinquent. In an age called the Enlightenment, madness, along with other social problems, was believed to be conquerable by reason, even if the insane had to be captured, caged, and forced into submission. In the United States asylums specifically for the insane emerged during a period of idealistic reform in the 1800s (Rothman, 1971). The reliance on segregating the insane in asylums in both England and the United States represented a revolution in the theory and practice of social control which was closely tied to the advent of a mature capitalist market economy and expanding government (Scull, 1989; Sutton, 1991). In 19th-century England, theories of madness moved from what Skultans (1975) describes as "psychiatric romanticism," in which the moral force and will of the individual were called upon to combat insanity, to "psychiatric Darwinism," which cited inherited character and constitutional flaws as root causes of madness.

Analysis of the internal dimensions of the mind (ego, superego, and id) and the individual's relationship to an external social context are both embodied in 20th-century Freudian psychology. Researchers have discovered organic causes and treatments for numerous mental disorders such as Hippocrates's "sacred disease," epilepsy. Psychiatrists, other physicians, psychologists, and sociologists continue to seek explanations and effective treatments for functional mental disorders that have no apparent organic causes.

Cross-Cultural Perspectives

The most obvious outward sign or symptom of mental disorder is odd behavior. However, not everyone who behaves oddly at one time or another is diagnosed as mentally ill. Moreover, a person can get away with acting very strangely in some situations without any particularly incriminating outcome. In fact, under certain circumstances behaving oddly is considered normal. For example, people dress and cavort during Mardi Gras week in New Orleans in a way that would bring a very negative response at other times of the year. Behavior is rarely if ever evaluated out of its situational context.

In New Orleans, the standards for judging behavior change rather dramatically from time to time during the year. Likewise, people's activities are differently evaluated from place to place—that is, in different cultures. The idea that behavior can only be understood in the context of a particular situation or culture is called *cultural relativity*. According to the principle of cultural relativity, any behavior may be viewed as normal in one culture but as aberrant, even as a sign of mental disorder, in another. From a cultural relativist position, the reason for labeling a person's behavior as crazy or mad may lie in the culturally filtered eye of the beholder, rather than in a malfunction of the physiology or psyche of the person whose behavior is being judged. It appears from this viewpoint that there are no absolute standards or symptoms for determining the presence or absence of mental illness. Indeed, taking cultural relativity to its logical extreme, we might legitimately ask: Is there such a thing as mental illness? We will return to this question shortly.

People in various cultures *do* evaluate similar behaviors differently, a fact that supports the cultural relativist position. As we mentioned in Chapter 3, numerous Native American tribes adopted a social role called the *berdache*, "men-women" who at puberty adopted the dress and work of women (Benedict 1934: 263). This special role provided a socially acceptable outlet for men who fail to conform to prevailing definitions of masculinity and who, in another culture, might be persecuted or prosecuted. Likewise, the shamans (medicine men) of some Native American, Siberian, African, and other cultures may exhibit trance-like states, hallucinations, seizures, and violent behavior that is dangerous to themselves and others, but in these cultures they are held in esteem for their special powers. The same behavior would not be tolerated in many other cultures.

Anthropologists have also found that a certain type of deviant behavior may appear to be unique to a specific culture. For example, a person running *amok* in Malaysia indiscriminately kills anyone in his path. Some members of the Chippewa and Cree tribes of Canada are said to have been afflicted with the *windigo* psychosis, which, under conditions of extreme deprivation and isolation, leads the victim to cannibalize his own family and rampage wildly until hunted down. Haiti has its magical death, or voodoo. Numerous cultures, including those of the Navajos, the Mexican Zapotecs, medieval Western Europe, and colonial New England, have had versions of witchcraft.

It is tempting to conclude from this sort of ethnographic evidence that mental disorder is a phenomenon that is so relative to a particular culture that we cannot possibly discover sufficiently common symptoms to classify it as a definite type of "illness" found in all human populations. However, experts on culture and personality, such as Anthony Wallace (1970, 1972), do not interpret cultural differences in reactions to similar behavior or the tremendous variety of symptoms among different cultures as evidence that there is no common mental-disorder process to which human beings are generally vulnerable. We can sum up the prevailing weight of anthropological opinion in the following three points.

First, different cultures do encourage different styles of mental disorders. Symptoms vary according to the individual's cultural experience and symbolic mode of presenting them. Paranoid delusions expressed as fear of devils, demons, and other supernatural spirits in a preindustrial culture are replaced by radio, radar, and voices from outer space in modern Western society. Nevertheless, the behaviors that fit within the major categories of mental illness developed by Western psychiatry (organic psychoses, functional psychoses, personality disorders, etc.) seem to be universal.

Second, there are no societies in which mental disorders are unknown, but societies do vary in overall frequency and relative frequency of various types of mental disorder. Explaining these differences is one of the more interesting questions for anthropologists and sociologists.

Third, the causes of mental disorders, whether rooted in genes, psychic experience, or social interaction seem to be ubiquitous in human groups. Despite what appear to be common underlying causes, explanations of mentally disordered behavior and reactions to it vary widely. Depending on the culture, reactions to bizarre behavior may include continued integration in the group by assignment to a special role; enforced exclusion through institutionalization; intensive magical, psychological, or medical therapy; and even total indifference.

DEFINITIONS AND TYPES OF MENTAL DISORDERS

Until recently in American culture, the stigmatizing labels *mad, crazy, lunatic, idiot, insane, mentally defective,* and so on were reserved for rather severe exhibitions of abnormal behavior. In many other cultures today, the mentally disordered are distinguished from others only after the most obvious demonstration of their incapacity to function normally in day-to-day living with others. However, 20th-century Western civilization is characterized by a broadening definition of mental disorders. Behaviors only mildly disruptive to the flow of everyday life, such as personality disorders or minor examples of conduct disturbance, have become a significant concern among those who diagnose and treat psychopathology.

While the definition of mental disorder has varied over time and among different cultures, the modern tendency has been for more types of disorders to be included in diagnostic manuals and for a broadening of the definition of previously included types. Given shifting standards among different times and cultures, a brief, precise definition of mental disorder is difficult. However, in most times and places a person has been classified as mentally disordered when he or she exhibits what seems to be uncontrolled, irrationally motivated behavior considered by most others to be sufficiently abnormal and irresponsible in its sociocultural context to require special treatment, isolation, or social control.

In this definition, mental disorder is recognized through the way a person behaves—the outward manifestation of mental disorder is how a person acts. Beyond that, the definition takes into account the apparent motivation for the behavior, the context in which it occurs, and a judgment or reaction to it on the part of others. Mentally disordered behavior is usually distinguished from criminal behavior on the basis of motive and responsibility. In the case of the criminal the motive is usually rather clear, and the individual is held accountable. A criminal is thought to be responsible for violation of the law, and punishment is therefore the appropriate response. The mentally deranged behave with unclear motives and, upon being judged irresponsible, require treatment or exclusion from everyday social situations in which their behavior is upsetting or potentially dangerous to others.

Types of Mental Disorders

The accepted standard for classifying mental disorders is the *Diagnostic and Statistical Manual of Mental Disorders,* third edition revised, published by the Amer-

Figure 4.1   Major Categories of Mental Disorders according to DSM–III–R
Classification

1. Disorders usually first evident in infancy, childhood, or adolescence (e.g., hyperactivity, anorexia nervosa, stuttering).
2. Organic mental disorders (e.g., senility, substance-induced damage).
3. Psychoactive substance use disorders (e.g., abuse of alcohol, barbiturates, opioids, etc.).
4. Schizophrenia.
5. Delusional (paranoid) disorders.
6. Other psychotic disorders not elsewhere classified.
7. Mood disorders (depression, mania).
8. Anxiety disorders (e.g., phobias, anxieties, compulsive behavior).
9. Somatoform disorders (psychogenic pain, hypochondriasis).
10. Dissociative disorders (hysterical neuroses, dissociative type).
11. Sexual disorders (e.g., fetishism, exhibitionism, sexual dysfunction, etc.).
12. Factious disorders.
13. Impulse control disorders not elsewhere classified (e.g., pathological gambling, kleptomania, pyromania, etc.).
14. Adjustment disorders.
15. Psychological factors affecting physical condition.
16. Other conditions not attributable to a mental disorder that are a focus of attention or treatment (e.g., academic problem, marital problem, phase of life or other circumstantial problem, etc.).
17. Personality disorders (e.g., narcissistic, antisocial, etc.).

Source: American Psychiatric Association, *Diagnostic and Statistical Manual of Mental Disorders*, 3rd edition, revised, 1987: 3–10.

ican Psychiatric Association in 1987 (DSM–III–R). This reclassification divides mental disorders into the 17 major categories listed in Figure 4.1. The main change in the third edition, which was published in 1980, was that neuroses and their various subtypes, a major category in the preceding editions, were no longer listed separately. The former neurotic subtypes are now included with categories 7–10, mood, anxiety, somatoform, and dissociative disorders. The revision, DSM–III–R, makes a few additional changes in the major categories of mental disorders. For example, the former category, affective disorder, has been changed to the more descriptive mood disorders. In addition, three new experimental categories which have aroused substantial controversy are identified in the latest version of DSM–III–R: late luteal phase dysphoric disorder, the behaviors associated with premenstrual syndrome; sadistic personality disorder; and self-defeating (masochistic) personality disorder. These may be included as categories in the next edition planned for sometime in the 1990s. Because DSM–III and its revision are still relatively new, much research on mental disorders is based upon the older classification scheme. Thus, some of our discussion in this chapter will necessarily rely upon the earlier, and for our purposes still valid, system in DSM–II (1968).

Traditionally, mental disorders have been divided into two major categories: organic brain syndromes and functional disorders not attributable to physiological changes in the brain. The symptoms in both of these categories may be similar, including hallucinations, impairment of memory and judgment, lowered intellectual function, and social failure. The major distinction between the two is whether or not the disorder is clearly related to physical brain damage. The origin of functional disorders is generally assumed to be psychosocial. Indeed, the use of the word *functional* implies that these mental disorders arise from a person's attempts to adjust to psychological or social stresses and strain. Abnormal behavior thus "functions" as a form of adaptation to a difficult situation.

Organic brain syndromes are further divided into subtypes according to the agent that produced the brain damage. Included among organic disorders are (1) senile or old-age psychoses, (2) paresis or dementia paralytica caused by syphilis infection, (3) alcoholic psychoses, (4) drug addictions, and (5) syndromes caused by various infections (encephalitis, meningitis, typhoid fever) or congenital cranial anomalies (Down's syndrome, birth trauma). As Table 4.1 shows, organic brain syndromes, exclusive of alcoholic and drug disorders, comprise about 9% of resident state and county psychiatric patient disorders in the United States. If patients with alcoholic and drug disorders, and a portion of those classified as mentally retarded are included, it can be said that close to one-fifth of all resident psychiatric patients in the United States have organic disorders.

Because functional disorders are presumed to have psychosocial causes, this major psychiatric category has received the most attention from social scientists. According to traditional diagnostic classification, functional disorders have been further divided into subcategories: neuroses, psychoses, personality disorders, psychophysiologic disorders, transient situational personality disorders, and behavior disorders of childhood and early adolescence. Neuroses have been distinguished from psychoses as being less socially debilitating and rarely requiring long-term institutionalization. Compulsive behavior, phobias, hysteria, amnesia, hypochondria, and disturbances of speech, hearing, and sight have usually been classified as neuroses. Psychoses are comparatively more severe and intense and have been more likely to lead to institutionalization.

Psychoses are subdivided into two major types: schizophrenia and mood disorders (manic-depression). Schizophrenia is characterized by withdrawal, disorientation in time and place, inability to perform expected roles, hallucinations, occasionally incomprehensible speech, and other inappropriate social behaviors such as unwarranted laughing or odd gestures. Schizophrenia is the most frequent diagnosis of mental disorder for institutionalized patients, and it applies to about half of those in public psychiatric facilities in the United States.

The other major category of psychosis, manic-depression, is usually more transitory and has a better prognosis than schizophrenia. Manic-depressives may be extremely agitated and excited in the manic stage, or withdrawn, guilt-ridden, and self-destructive in the depressive stage. The person with this disorder may vacillate

Table 4.1   Number and Percent Distribution of Resident Patients by Diagnosis, State and County Mental Hospitals, United States, 1991

Major Diagnostic Categories	Number	Percent
Organic		
Organic disorders°	8,329	9.4%
Alcoholic disorders	2,406	2.7
Substance-related disorders	1,623	1.8
Mental retardation	3,242	3.7
Functional		
Schizophrenia and related disorders	43,780	49.5
Depressive (mood) disorders	9,929	11.2
Personality disorders	1,242	1.4
Pre-adult disorders	1,656	1.9
Other psychoses	3,688	4.2
Other		
Undiagnosed	8,603	9.7
All other	3,893	4.5
Total	88,391	100.0%

Source: U.S. Department of Health and Human Services, 1993: 46.
°Excludes alcohol and other substance-related disorders.

between mania and depression or remain in only one state. As Table 4.1 shows, the diagnosis of depressive disorders, which is made for about 11 percent of institutionalized patients, applies to far fewer patients than schizophrenia does. However, depression is more frequently diagnosed among the well-to-do, and the data in Table 4.1 comes from public facilities, whose patients are disproportionately in the lower classes. Therefore, the percentage of depressive disorders may be underrepresented, while that of schizophrenia may be overrepresented. We will return to this point shortly when we discuss explanations of mental disorder.

The remaining subcategories of functional disorders cover a very broad range of behaviors which are diagnosed as affecting only a small percentage of institutionalized mental patients. Personality disorders may be diagnosed for behaviors ranging from "perfectionism," stuttering, and nail biting to aggressive, antisocial acts like arson or murder. Psychophysiologic disorders include conditions that affect single organ systems such as weight loss, cramps, asthma, and other physical problems which are caused by emotional upset. Transient situational personality disorders are reactions to extreme situations such as a major disaster. Preadult (childhood and early adolescent) disorders include behavioral problems specific to this age category.

Is Mental Illness a Disease?

Some types of socially unacceptable behavior unquestionably arise from disease. Organic disorders, such as mental retardation caused by physical abnormalities of the brain, and the psychosis caused by syphilis fit the medical definition of illness. Indeed, the fundamental criterion of disease is a proven or demonstrated lesion—an identifiable abnormality of cells, tissues, organs, or bodies. Most people alleged to suffer from mental disorders do *not* have a demonstrable lesion that defines the "illness." Rather, in the case of functional mental disorders—by far the most prevalent kind diagnosed—there is no pathological lesion. The defining characteristic of most mental illness is how the patient *acts*, rather than any physical abnormality. Thomas Szasz, a well-known psychiatrist, reasons that it is inappropriate therefore to define or treat what is typically called mental illness as a disease. He argues that most "mental illness" is not a disease at all; indeed, the whole concept of mental illness as a disease is a myth: "Mental illness is not something a person has but something he does or is" (Szasz, 1974: 267).

If most mental illness is not a disease, then what is it? According to Szasz, the "symptoms" of mental disorder really represent basic conflicts between the individual exhibiting them and the people who uphold the accepted social norms of the community. Szasz does not deny that such norm-breaking behavior exists—even in fairly severe form. Rather, he objects to calling it *illness*, preferring instead to refer to *problems of living*. This he hopes would lead psychiatrists to realize that they are not "doctors" in a traditional sense and ought not to treat their "patients" as though they suffered from real diseases (Szasz, 1987).

Such an iconoclastic position is a threat to psychiatry, a profession which owes much of its prestige to close association with scientific medicine. The professional stakes of how mental disorders ought to be defined are high. As we will show later in this chapter, the most fundamental theoretical conflicts regarding the explanation of mental disorder depend on the perspective taken in its definition—whether it is defined as disease according to the medical model or as normative conflict (rule-breaking behavior) as suggested by the work of Szasz and labeling theorists.

THE DISTRIBUTION OF MENTAL DISORDERS

Counting Cases

Our discussion of the types of mental disorders and their institutionalized rates should not leave the impression that we have accurately estimated the extent of mental disorder in the United States. To begin, while the diagnostic categories may appear exhaustive and mutually exclusive in the abstract, in practice psychiatric diagnosis has been shown to be lacking in reliability and validity (Scheff, 1984). In one review of six studies that compared the agreement rates of psychiatric diagnosis, agreement on the diagnosis was found to vary from 56% to 88% (Conover, 1972). In another well-known study by Rosenhan (1973), eight sane people gained admission to psychiatric hospitals by faking minor, nondescript symptoms. In each case the pseudopatient was diagnosed as schizophrenic and, after admission, gave no further evidence of symptoms. They remained hospitalized an average of 19 days, and each was discharged with a diagnosis of schizophrenia "in remission." In no case was the pseudopatient discovered by the hospital staff. In a subsequent experiment, it was demonstrated that when members of the hospital staff were told that a pseudopatient would attempt to gain admission, they frequently identified genuine patients as pseudopatients. In addition to the difficulties of reliably identifying psychiatric illness, various conflicts inherent in the multiple goals of mental health facilities (for example, cost containment, patient care, research, and the like) can contribute to diagnostic instability (Brown, 1987).

To discover the extent of mental disorder in a population, therefore, it is first necessary to evaluate the problem of unreliable, invalid diagnosis. No entirely satisfactory solution exists to counter this difficulty. When assessing research results for guidance in social policy decisions, it is vital to examine carefully the criteria used to determine cases. A study's working definitions heavily influence its results.

Researchers have long recognized that institutionalized patients in psychiatric hospitals do not constitute the total number of people afflicted with mental disorders in a population. Restricting the definition of cases to patients admitted to institutionalized psychiatric treatment excludes those who may have symptoms but have not received care. An extensive psychiatric survey of midtown Manhattan in the early 1960s showed that only about one-fourth of those judged to resemble psychiatric cases had ever been in treatment (Srole et al., 1962: 147). The use of treatment facilities also varies with their availability and public attitudes toward their use (Dohrenwend and Dohrenwend, 1969: 5–7). Thus, while the enumeration of treated cases is important in planning psychiatric services, institutionalized patient data do not estimate accurately the occurrence or distribution of mental disorders throughout a population. For information on the "true" prevalence of mental disorder, we must turn to surveys of general populations or communities designed to uncover untreated cases.

A review of 24 North American true-prevalence studies in both rural and urban areas (Dohrenwend, 1975) leads to unsettling conclusions about our ability to grasp the overall extent of functional psychiatric disorder. In some communities, rates of less than 2% were reported, while in others the rates exceeded 50%. Analysis reveals that these vast differences are due primarily to variable data collection procedures, especially definitions of what constitutes a case of psychiatric disorder. The best current data on the true prevalence of mental disorders in the United States come from estimates calculated by the National Institute of Mental Health (NIMH) of the results of epidemiological catchment area surveys in various urban and rural areas. These surveys use the NIMH Diagnostic Interview Schedule (DIS), which is based on DSM–III–R and covers the organic disorders of alcohol and drug abuse and the functional disorders of schizophrenia, affective disorders, anxiety and somatoform disorders, and antisocial personality, as well as cognitive impairment. Table 4.2 presents the data on the number of Americans who, at a given time, could be expected to have suffered these disorders during the previous six months, based on the results of these surveys (Bourdon et al., 1992). The table indicates that in any six-month period, approximately 35.8 million adults, or 19.5% of the population, suffer from one or more mental disorders, according to DSM–III criteria.

It should be emphasized that these figures are estimates. In the end, the true prevalence of mental disorders remains an elusive statistic clouded by methodological inconsistency in definitions and data collection. However, as results of these surveys indicate, only a portion of psychiatric cases treatable according to DSM–III criteria ever receive treatment, and therefore statistics based on institutionalized rates underestimate the true prevalence of mental disorders.

SOCIOCULTURAL FACTORS IN MENTAL DISORDERS

Age

In most studies that report the relationship between age and rates of mental disorder, the young have shown the lowest rates of psychopathology. This fairly clear pattern of findings with regard to minimum rates of disorder is not matched by an equally definitive age at which maximum rates of mental disorder are likely. In an exhaustive review of 24 studies, Dohrenwend and Dohrenwend (1969) reported that in 5 of them the maximum rates of mental disorder were found in adolescence, in 12 of them the maximum rate was in the middle years, and in 7 it was in the oldest group.

Further analysis of results by age for psychosis, neurosis, and personality disorders does not add any more useful information. No age group consistently shows a higher rate for any of these types of mental disorder. While some very specific types, such as senile psychosis in the elderly, are obviously related to age, we can conclude that no consistent relationship between age and mental disorder emerges from current findings.

Sex

Comparisons of numerous studies reveal no consistent sex differences in overall rates of functional psychoses (Dohrenwend and Dohrenwend, 1976). Overall, men and women are equally prone to mental disorders in general, and they appear to be similarly susceptible to being diagnosed schizophrenic. There are, however, differences between men and women on other major subtypes. Manic-depressive psychosis is generally higher among women, as are rates of neuroses, while rates of personality disorder are consistently higher for men.

In their discussion of those findings, Dohrenwend and Dohrenwend (1976) raise an important issue for future research:

> These results cannot easily be explained by role theories arguing that at some time and place one or the other sex is under great stress and, hence, more prone to psychiatric disorder in general. Instead, the findings suggest that we should discard undifferentiated, unidimensional concepts of psychiatric disorder and with them false questions about whether women or men are more prone to "mental illness." In their place we would sub-

Table 4.2   Six-Month Prevalence of Selected Mental Disorders, Estimated Number and Percent of the U.S. Civilian Population, 1990

Type of Disorder	Number in Millions	Percent
Organic		
Alcohol abuse/Dependence	8.6	4.8%
Drug abuse/Dependence	3.7	2.0
Functional		
Schizophrenia	1.7	.9
Affective disorders	10.7	5.8
Anxiety/Somatoform	16.4	8.9
Antisocial personality	1.5	.8
Cognitive impairment (severe)	3.1	1.7
Any diagnostic interview schedule disorder	35.8	19.5

Source: Bourdon et al., 1992: 665.

stitute an issue posed by the relatively high female rates of neurosis and manic-depressive psychosis, with their possible common denominator of depressive symptomatology, and the relatively high male rates of personality disorders with their possible common denominator of irresponsible and antisocial behavior. The important question then becomes, What is there in the endorsement and experiences of men and women that pushes them in these different deviant directions? (453)

Recent studies estimating the true prevalence of overall mental disorders show some tendency for women to have higher rates of emotional problems than men in Western societies. However, women also seek psychiatric help more often than men with similar emotional problems (Kessler, Reuter, and Greenley, 1979). Thus men and women differ in their propensity to define emotional problems as warranting psychiatric attention. It has been estimated that "between 10% and 28% of the excess female psychiatric morbidity measured in treatment statistics could be due to this sex difference in problem recognition" (Kessler, Brown, and Broman, 1981: 49).

Race

Relatively few studies allow for comparison between rates of mental disorders for whites and blacks. The evidence from eight studies which do permit analysis of the data by race show no consistent pattern at all; four reported higher rates for whites and an equal number reported higher rates for blacks (Dohrenwend and Dohrenwend, 1969). Neither race is clearly more prone to mental disorder. Nonwhites do show higher levels of psychological distress, and the differences between whites and blacks are especially evident among people with low incomes (Kessler and Neighbors, 1986). For both African Americans and whites, the overall amount and severity of psychiatric disorder is inversely related to their socioeconomic status— that is, low socioeconomic status is associated with high prevalence rates of overall psychiatric disorder, regardless of race (Williams, Takeuchi, and Adair, 1992). Rates of involuntary hospitalization also have been higher for nonwhites than for whites (Linsky, 1970). For males in particular, this is not because nonwhites have higher rates of disorders but because whites and nonwhites characteristically differ in their means of entry into treatment. Nonwhite males are more likely to initiate treatment through police involvement, and with this first step the probability of involuntary hospitalization is high (Rosenfield, 1984).

Rural-Urban Setting

It is commonly thought that, due to the stresses and pressures of urban life, mental disorders are more prevalent in cities than in rural areas. This belief is enhanced by the fact that the rates of *hospitalized* mental disorders are greater in urban areas. However, as we have noted, rates of institutionalized disorders probably reflect the availability of treatment facilities and community attitudes toward abnormal behavior more than the true prevalence of disorders in the general population. For example, researchers have found that rural people are more resistant to the use of treatment facilities and more apt to allow those whose behavior is questionable to remain in the community (Eaton and Weil, 1955; Eaton, 1974).

According to the evidence from community surveys that have attempted to estimate the true prevalence of mental disorders in rural and urban settings, urban rates tend to be higher, but only slightly so. More interesting are the findings for subtypes of disorders. Manic-depressive psychoses clearly appear to be more prevalent in rural areas; the rates for schizophrenia, personality disorders, and neuroses are higher in urban settings. We will examine explanations for these differences when we discuss sociological theories of mental disorder in the following section. The evidence must be considered cautiously, however, because no studies have adequately accounted for the possibility that higher urban rates might be due in part to migrants from rural to urban areas who bring with them certain types of psychopathology.

Social Class

No finding in psychiatric epidemiology is more consistent and clear-cut than that the highest rates of overall mental disorder are found in the lowest social classes. The most widely cited study confirming this relationship is the 1950s survey by August B. Hollingshead and Frederick C. Redlich in New Haven, Connecticut, reported in *Social Class and Mental Illness* (1958). Using an index of five social classes, as determined by area of residence, occupation, and education, they analyzed all patients in public and private psychiatric hospitals as well as all who were undergoing treatment but were not institutionalized. In the general population the lowest social class (class V) made up about 18% of the total, but about 38% of the patients were

Figure 4.2   Class Position and Types of Mental Illness (Hollingshead and Redlich, 1958)

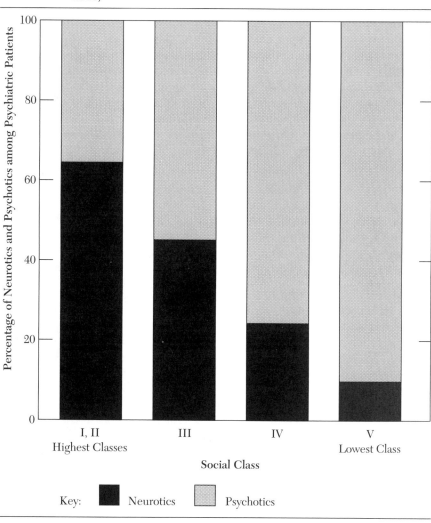

Source: Adapted from Hollingshead and Redlich, 1958: 223.
Note: Percentage of neurotics and psychotics among total psychiatric patients, by social class (age and sex adjusted).

in this class. The seriousness of the mental disorder was also related to social class in this study. As Figure 4.2 shows, neurosis is far more likely to be the diagnosis for patients in the two higher classes (I and II), and psychosis is the more frequent type of diagnosis in the lower classes.

Certain aspects of Hollingshead and Redlich's findings have been replicated using more recent national data on the incidence of admissions to public and private psychiatric hospitals.[1] From the data in Table 4.3 it seems reasonable to assume that public hospitals are more likely to receive patients from the lower social classes, while private hospitals handle more affluent patients. These 1986 data show that overall organic disorders, especially those associated with alcohol, are more frequently diagnosed in public institutions, while depressive disorders and neuroses are higher among private psychiatric patients. Among functional disorders, schizophrenia is the more likely diagnosis in public institutions, and affective disorders are diagnosed far more often in private hospitals.

True prevalence studies of noninstitutionalized populations also agree with the evidence presented above. A review of these studies by Dohrenwend (1975) indicated that:

- The highest rates of overall psychiatric disorder have been consistently found in the lowest social class.
- The highest rates of schizophrenia and personality disorders are generally found in the lowest social class.
- The rates of neurosis and manic-depressive psychosis are not as consistent, but there is a tendency for these disorders to be more prevalent in the higher social classes.

Social class is also related to commitment status and the outcome of psychiatric treatment. In a comparison of studies that distinguished between involuntary and voluntary commitment, Nicholson (1986) found that those involuntarily committed tended to be older, male, nonwhite, and with fewer educational and economic resources compared to those who entered hospitals voluntarily. Patients of higher social status also have been found to show comparatively greater improvement following psychiatric treatment (Gift et al., 1986). In addition, numerous studies have shown that people in the lower social classes may be exposed to higher levels of social stress and be more sensitive to stress in ways that contribute to their higher rates of mental disorders (Kessler and Cleary, 1980; Link, Dohrenwend, and Skodol, 1986).

Conclusions. Research evidence on the relationship between sociocultural factors and mental disorders can be summarized as follows:

- There is no consistent relationship between age and overall rates of mental disorder.
- Men and women are equally prone to mental disorder overall. However, women have higher rates of affective disorders and neuroses, while men consistently have higher rates of personality disorders. Women have higher rates of treated disorders because they are more likely than men to seek help for emotional problems.
- There is no consistent relationship between race and rates of mental disorder. Nonwhites, however, are more likely to be involuntarily hospitalized than whites are.

Table 4.3   Percent of Total Admissions for Inpatient Services to State and County Mental Hospitals and to Private Mental Hospitals, by Primary Diagnosis, United States, 1986

| | PERCENT OF ADMISSIONS, BY DIAGNOSIS | |
Diagnostic Category	State and County Mental Hospitals	Private Mental Hospitals
Organic		
Organic brain syndromes	3.2%	3.2%
Alcoholic disorders	16.5	7.6
Drug disorders	6.4	7.0
Functional disorders		
Schizophrenia	36.5	11.4
Affective disorders	16.7	48.3
Personality disorders	2.0	1.1
Adjustment disorders	6.3	3.4
All others	12.4	14.9
Total	100.0%	100.0%
Number	285,159	174,520

Source: Mannersheid and Sonnenschein, 1990: 159.

- Rates of mental disorders tend to be slightly higher in urban areas. Schizophrenia, personality disorder, and neuroses rates are higher in urban areas, while depressive psychosis rates are higher in rural areas.
- Overall, the highest rates of mental disorders are in the lower class. Lower-class patients are more likely to be diagnosed as schizophrenic or as having personality disorders, while upper-class patients are more likely to be diagnosed as depressive or neurotic. Social class is associated with hospital commitment status, treatment outcome, exposure to stress and sensitivity to stress linked to mental disorders.

EXPLANATIONS OF MENTAL DISORDER

Nature versus Nurture: The Genetics or Environment Issue

There is undeniable, impressive evidence which points to the role of heredity in the *etiology* (the causation) of mental disorders. In early studies of schizophrenia by a geneticist, it was found that over 68% of children whose parents were both schizophrenic later developed schizophrenia (Kallman, 1938). If only one parent was schizophrenic the odds dropped to about 1 in 6, and they continued to decline as the relationship to schizophrenic relatives became more distant (Kallman, 1946). Subsequent genealogical studies (Book, 1953) and investigations of twins (Heston, 1966; Gottesman and Shields, 1972) have added to the evidence of hereditary factors, even when social conditions in the home of schizophrenic parents were controlled in the research design. An overview of current studies designed to establish the role of genetic predisposition to schizophrenia concludes that "genetic factors are at least as important in the etiology of schizophrenia as they are in the etiology of diabetes, hypertension, coronary artery disease, and ulcers" (Kendler, 1983: 1422). Although the evidence for the inheritability of schizophrenia is strong, a single genetic link has not been discovered. The evidence for the inheritance of affective disorders is mixed, possibly due to problems of definition and diagnosis (Lochlin et al., 1988). The field of psychiatric genetics remains both active and controversial (Pardes et al., 1989; Kidd, 1991).

Whereas at one time the genetics-environment issue centered on the either-or question of which one was *the* cause of mental disorder, most investigators now agree that people's genetic endowment and their social experiences in the environment interact in precipitating mental disorder. Certain genotypes clearly appear to be more prone to disorders, but the actual occurrence of psychopathology in the individual's life also depends upon environmental factors. Still to be settled are questions about the relative weight of heredity or the environment, especially differences in various types of mental disorders, and questions about precisely how the genetic transmission operates and is stimulated to produce disorders.

Social Disorganization: The Ecological Approach

A pioneering sociological study called *Mental Disorders in Urban Areas* by Robert Faris and H. Warren Dunham was published in 1939. They collected data on admissions to all public and private mental hospitals in Chicago and then plotted on maps the rates of mental disorder for various areas of the city. Using this "ecological" technique, they discovered (as shown in Figure 4.3) that overall rates of mental disorder (then called "insanity rates") generally were highest in the poor, transient areas near the center of the city and declined as the zones approached the more affluent, more stable suburbs. This is, of course, consistent with the findings of subsequent researchers presented in our discussion of social class. Perhaps more important than the basic empirical findings are the issues Faris and Dunham raised as they posed possible explanations for their results. The alternatives they offer remain fundamental concerns in the sociology of mental disorder and, indeed, the entire field of deviant behavior.

With any study it is possible that the findings observed happened by chance. Accordingly, Faris and Dunham first confront the alternative that the distribution of rates they found in Chicago was a peculiar occurrence. However, based on evidence from another city and the degree and consistency of differences, they reject the *chance hypothesis*. As we have noted, the weight of virtually all studies since supports their rejection of this alternative.

The second possibility, called the *selection hypothesis*, states "that the patterns of rate distribution represent only a concentration of cases of mental disorder which

Figure 4.3   "Insanity" Average Rates, 1922–1934, Chicago, by Zones and Divisions Based on 1930 U.S. Census Tracts (Faris and Dunham, 1939)

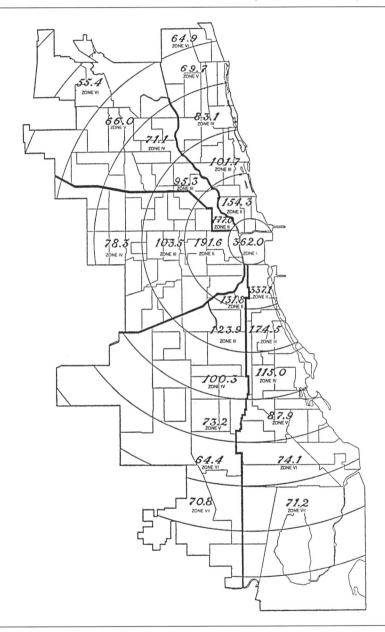

Source: Adapted from Faris and Dunham, 1939: 36.
Notes: Rates based on 100,000 1930 population, age 15 and over. Subcommunities based on U.S. Census tracts of Chicago; zone I drawn at one-mile radius from center of the city; zones II–VII inclusive drawn with two-mile radius.

have been institutionalized because of poverty" (Faris and Dunham, 1939: 161). It could be that mental disorders are in fact evenly distributed throughout all areas of the city, but only the poor, because they are relatively powerless, are institutionalized. The suggestion has also been made that the visibility of and tolerance for bizarre behavior varies among different communities, thus making institutionalization more likely in some than in others. Faris and Dunham reject the selection hypothesis on the grounds that they managed to cover most cases, both affluent and poor, by surveying admissions to both public and private hospitals. However, the selection hypothesis remains a viable alternative favored by many sociologists today. In fact, Dunham (1964) displays considerable scientific integrity in critiquing his own classic work; reversing his earlier position, he declares the likely validity of the selection hypothesis. The selection hypothesis continues to provide a focus for contemporary theoretical debate (Dohrenwend et al., 1992).

Faris and Dunham next considered the *drift hypothesis*: "An interpretation frequently made of the concentration in the center of the city of insanity rates, and the schizophrenic rates particularly, is that persons who are mentally abnormal fail in their economic life and consequently drift down into the slum areas because they are not able to compete satisfactorily with others" (163). A more recent variation suggests that in a society where upward mobility is highly valued, the healthy and competent are able to work their way out of the slums, leaving behind a residue of less-able people, a relatively high proportion of whom have psychiatric disorders. Faris and Dunham rejected the drift hypothesis in their 1933 study because it appeared that most people with mental disorders were not downwardly mobile but instead had been long-term residents of lower-class areas. However, the drift hypothesis—especially its residue variation—remains an alternative favored today by some theorists.

The possibility finally accepted by Faris and Dunham is the *social and life-conditions* or *stress hypothesis*. Stated in its more general form, the greater stress and strains of life in the lower class are assumed to increase the chances for mental breakdown and thus cause the higher rates of mental disorder in the central city. More specifically, these authors hypothesize that in socially disorganized parts of the city interpersonal contacts are most likely to be disrupted, and this in turn leads to greater social isolation and higher rates of schizophrenia. Because rates of manic-depressive psychoses do not consistently decrease with distance from the city's center, it is suggested that the etiology of this disorder, in contrast to schizophrenia, might be found in extremely intimate and intense social contacts more characteristic of rural settings. A later study (Eaton and Weil, 1955) of the Hutterites—a very close-knit, communal, family-oriented, rural sect living in the northwestern United States and southwestern Canada—revealed unexpectedly high rates of depression, thus supporting this hypothesis.

Because Faris and Dunham did their study in Chicago, where they were strongly influenced by social disorganization theorists (see Chapter 5), it is not surprising that their conclusion favored the social and life-conditions hypothesis. It best reflects the social disorganization tradition of which they were a part. However, each of the alternatives they raised has remained a viable explanation and the stimulus for much research and theoretical debate today. The most sophisticated study to date (Dohrenwend et al., 1992) concluded that "social selection may be more important for schizophrenia and that social causation (the stress hypothesis) may be more important for depression in women and for antisocial personality and substance abuse in men" (946). Whenever evaluating the results and interpretations from any study of rates of mental disorder, or any deviant behavior, we must carefully consider the applicability of the selection, drift, or stress hypothesis.

Social Structural Strain

Conditions in the Economy. We have noted that the highest rates of mental disorder generally are found in the lower socioeconomic strata of American society. If we accept the stress hypothesis, it seems reasonable to propose that some of the unique conditions of lower-class life eventually lead to greater mental disorder. Following this line of reasoning, sociologist M. Harvey Brenner has conducted several studies exploring the hypothesis that as the state of the economy worsens, rates of mental hospitalization will increase. An analysis of the relationship between the employment index and fluctuations in mental hospital admissions rates in New York over a 127-year period supported this hypothesis (Brenner, 1973). Periods of low employment were consistently followed by higher rates of mental hospital admissions. A subsequent study using national data from 1940 to 1973 showed that increases in the unemployment rate were followed by increases in mental hospital admissions (Brenner, 1976). Using a sophisticated technique for making estimates, Brenner concluded that a 1% increase in the unemployment rate sustained over a period of six years could be associated with an increase of over 4,000 state mental hospital admissions.

While the three decades Brenner studied largely preceded implementation of the deinstitutionalization movement for mental health patients, the basic proposition that mental hospitalization will increase during economic downturns and decrease during upturns seems irrefutable. How that relation should be interpreted is open to question, however. Brenner's theory is similar to the stress or social and life-conditions explanation of Faris and Dunham. Brenner (1973) states:

> This hypothesis assumes that social disorganization, reflected in turn in symptoms and intolerance of deviance, will result from the inability of individuals to perform socially designated roles. Inability to fulfill one's social role frequently results from downward shifts in economic activity, during which more people are losing than are gaining income, prestige, and power. The economy provides the fundamental means whereby the individual fulfills the majority of his aspirations, as well as the more immediate social obligations he faces. His inability to maintain his usual or intended life-style and social position indicates that he is unable to meet the requirements of other people who form the network of his social relations, responsibilities, and requirements. (11)

Nevertheless, Brenner's use of the phrase "intolerance of deviance" suggests that the selection hypothesis is also a plausible explanation. This hypothesis implies that higher hospital admission rates follow economic downturns because admission standards change or unusually high frustration is directed at those who behave oddly. Brenner also notes, correctly, that the state of the economy has considerable impact on people's abilities to fulfill their aspirations—particularly those associated with improving their social status. This idea relates closely to anomie theory, which focuses on the possible effects of a discrepancy between people's aspirations and the avenues open for achieving them.

Anomie. In his famous essay "Social Structure and Anomie," Robert K. Merton (1938) shows how social conditions exert pressure on certain people to engage in deviant behavior. Briefly, he argues that a condition of *anomie* (normlessness) arises when a culture encourages its members to value goals which they are actually unable to attain under its accepted laws or norms. Thus, anomie is present when members of the lower class are constantly informed through the popular culture that material rewards such as home ownership and fancy cars are positively valued, while at the same time experience tells them that the legitimate means for achieving these goals, such as good educations and well-paying jobs, are not readily accessible to them. A likely result of this anomic condition—the discrepancy between means and ends—is for individuals to maintain their desires to achieve the culturally valued goals but to reject the legitimate means for achieving them in favor of illegitimate ones. Merton labels the adaptation to this situation *innovation*, which in fact usually amounts to what we more commonly call *crime*.

In contrast to innovation, Merton refers to mental disorders as a *retreatist* form of adaptation. Retreatist behavior is also likely when a person desires culturally valued goals but is denied the means to attain them—a situation which calls for "innovative" rule-breaking to reach the goals. But what if a person has so thoroughly internalized prohibitions against breaking the law that he or she simply cannot illegally innovate? In this case the individual is trapped in a double bind, desiring the goals but finding available neither legitimate nor illegitimate means to secure them. The result, says Merton, is a rejection of *both* the culturally valued goals and the legitimate means. The person escapes the conflict of discrepant goals and means by retreating into the alien, privatized world of psychosis. Thus Merton conceives of mental disorder as an escapist adaptation akin to chronic drunkenness, drug addiction, isolation, or the ultimate retreat, suicide.

Subsequent studies (see Kleiner and Parker, 1963), guided by Merton's insights, show that psychopathological groups usually have larger discrepancies between achievements and aspirations than normal control groups. Indeed, Parker and Kleiner (1966) found that the discrepancy between aspirations and achievements, which they call *goal-striving stress*, was significantly higher in the institutionalized mentally ill population than in the community population; higher among psychotic patients than neurotics; and higher among people in the community with a greater incidence of psychoneurotic symptoms.

It appears, then, that when avenues to achievement are blocked, the resulting frustration may become manifest in a greater incidence of mental disorder, and there is some evidence that depression is the type of disorder most likely to arise from blocked opportunities. Linsky (1969) designed a study to explore the relationship between depression and opportunities available for occupational success relative to aspirations. He found that depression was highest in communities where relative opportunities were the least. He concludes by saying, "It appears that chronic stress attendant on life in communities with opportunity structures incapable of satisfying the aspirations of the residents increases the frequency of depression" (131).

Family Structure and Dynamics

As we noted in our brief discussion of heredity as a cause of mental disorders, there is some evidence that people who develop mental disorders are more likely to have a psychopathological parent. Proponents of genetic transmission theory accept these findings as support for their position. Alternatively, some theorists suggest that the higher incidence of mental disorders among children from a home in which a parent is mentally ill may be due to maladaptive patterns of adjustment learned in this situation. For example, in his analyses of how people in families interact, British psychiatrist R. D. Laing (1969) shows how patterns of interaction and methods of dealing with everyday problems seem to be learned and passed on from parents to children. Therefore, in addition to genetic transmission in families he raises the equally plausible possibility of social psychological transmission through socialization.

Other researchers have found certain modes of socialization which seem to be prevalent among those who are later diagnosed as schizophrenics. Parents, particularly the mother, tend to be unstable, domineering, and demanding (Weinberg, 1967). Myers and Roberts (1959) found that patients had close attachments to parents of the opposite sex but hostile relationships to parents of the same sex. There is no clear evidence that mental disorder is related to birth order of children in the family. However, the preschizophrenic child tends to be isolated from other siblings because of age, physique, or some other factors. Family structure in the family of origin may have some influence on the likelihood of later mental disorder. For example, parental absence during childhood, regardless of the reason, is associated with higher scores on a measure of depression (Amato, 1991). While tendencies such as these appear, there is no single family type or pattern of socialization that inevitably produces or inhibits the later development of psychopathology.

The picture of family dynamics provided by researchers who have studied families in which one member develops schizophrenia is of an overwhelming series of difficulties which exceed the person's ability to cope. In their study of poor families in San Juan, Puerto Rico, Rogler and Hollingshead (1965) describe the interrelated crises experienced by schizophrenic persons during the 12 months preceding the perceived onset of the disorder.

> Systematic comparisons of the six types of perceived personal problems reported by the sick persons (and families) with those of the well persons (and families) demon-

strate that each of the diagnostic family types in the sick group encountered many more problems than the well families during the problematic year. There are more economic difficulties and more severe physical deprivation in the sick than in the well families. There are far more interspouse conflicts among the sick families than the control families; difficulties with members of the extended family are more frequent and more severe. The sick families report more quarrels and fights with their neighbors. There are more physical illnesses in the schizophrenic families. Finally, more sick persons than well persons, male as well as female, note a disparity between their own perception of the difficulties they encountered and the ways they think their spouses viewed these same problems. Stated otherwise, the schizophrenic men and women think their spouses do not understand the personal difficulties they face, as well as the men and women in the control group do. In general, the person who is diagnosed as suffering from schizophrenia perceives himself as bombarded by a multiplicity of personal and family problems he is not able to handle. The behavioral evidence shows, however, that he struggles to solve them by every means available to him. (409–410)

It is difficult to say with assurance which of these difficulties are causes and which are consequences of the mental disorder. However, the authors of this study do feel that in contrast to childhood and adolescent experiences, "a rash of insoluble, mutually reinforcing problems" which trap the person in the period prior to onset of the disorder clearly distinguish those who become schizophrenic.

Despite serious problems arising in the family because of failure on the part of a disturbed person to perform his or her social roles successfully, family members have been found to be remarkably resistant to seeking professional help (Yarrow et al., 1955). Thus, while in certain cases family dynamics may contribute to the precipitation of mental disorder, at the same time families frequently have a very high tolerance for deviance that permits them to avoid contact with professionals until the disturbed person's behavior becomes very disruptive to family life (Sampson, Messinger, and Towne, 1962).

More recent research has attended to family roles in relation to the mental disorders of spouses (Warren, 1987). We have noted that women tend to have higher rates of depression than men and that people's abilities to fulfill their aspirations also influence levels of depression. Ross and Huber (1985) found that economic hardship increases both spouses' levels of depression; the husband is most affected by level of personal earnings and the wife by her education and the children. This suggests that failure in relation to role expectations is apt to affect the depression levels of husbands and wives. Generally, the greater a person's power, the less the likelihood of depression. In a study of marital power, Mirowsky (1985) concludes that "each spouse is least depressed if marital power is shared to some extent.... The division of marital power in the average marriage is closer to the level that minimizes the husband's depression than it is to the level that minimizes the wife's depression" (557).

Studies of Psychological Distress

Psychological distress takes two major forms: depression and anxiety. The first is characterized by feeling sad, demoralized, hopeless, listless, and the like; the second involves being tense, worried, irritable, and fearful (Mirowsky and Ross, 1989). While psychological distress is not a mental disorder at the level of psychosis, it clearly relates to people's mental state of well-being, and it affects every individual occasionally throughout life. Indeed, over the past several decades, numerous community surveys have documented evidence that symptoms of psychological distress are widespread (Gurin, Veroff, and Ford, 1960; Srole et al., 1962; Leighton et al., 1963; Dohrenwend and Dohrenwend, 1969; Mirowsky and Ross, 1989). Probably the most important finding from such surveys is that psychological distress is *not* uniformly distributed throughout American society.

Mirowsky and Ross (1989) argue that there are four established social patterns in the distribution of psychological distress:

1. Women are more distressed than men;

2. Married people are less distressed than the unmarried;

3. Undesirable life events are associated with distress;

4. Higher income, education, and occupational prestige are associated with less distress.

With respect to undesirable life events such as illness, death of a family member, or loss of a job, we might assume that the number of such events experienced in a given period will determine the level of distress. In fact, however, the level of distress depends more on the context of the negative events and whether the person's response is active and instrumental rather than passive and fatalistic (Kessler, Turner, and House, 1989; Wheaton, 1990; Aneshensel, Rutter, and Lachenbruch, 1991). Mirowsky and Ross (1989) point to the importance of maintaining a sense of control:

> Of all the things that might explain the social patterns of distress, one stands out as central: the sense of control over one's own life.... The patterns of distress reflect the patterns of autonomy, opportunity, and achievement in America. The realities of class and status have a profound influence on the sense of control. Education, family income, unemployment, and economic hardship all affect the sense of control and, through it, depression, anxiety, malaise, and even paranoia and schizophrenia. (167)

Where individuals are located in the social scheme and how their positions affect their capacity to sense control over their lives is powerfully related to their psychological distress or, conversely, their mental well-being. This suggests several fruitful targets social policy makers might address to facilitate the reduction of psychological distress:

• Improved education to increase people's capacities to cope effectively with problems and earn a decent livelihood.

- Good jobs to provide adequate incomes, a measure of autonomy, and accommodation to family demands such as child care.
- Supportive relationships based on equity and fairness rather than dominance and exploitation.

Labeling Theory

A contemporary sociological theory of mental disorder introduced by Thomas Scheff in his book *Being Mentally Ill* (1984; originally published 1966) has generated much controversy and debate. Scheff states that there is very little verified theory about the causes of functional mental disorders, and a major deficiency in most current explanations is a failure to incorporate sufficiently the role of social processes. Scheff's goal is to explain stable, recurring, functional mental disorders—as opposed to isolated, idiosyncratic episodes or organic pathology—by emphasizing the effects of how others react to a person's odd behavior.

The theory defines mental illness in terms of rule-breaking behavior. Many kinds of rule-breaking in our culture are given specific labels—crime, perversion, drunkenness, and the like. However, there are numerous other forms of rule-breaking that have no explicit labels. Frequently this type of rule-breaking involves violation of everyday norms which define how to interact courteously and get along with others. Repeatedly interrupting the conversation of others or refusing to speak when spoken to may not be against the law, but such actions do constitute a form of rule-breaking behavior. Odd, annoying behavior of this sort Scheff calls *residual rule-breaking*. He argues further that much of what commonly becomes labeled mental illness fits in the category of residual rule-breaking. Put another way, residual rule-breaking, under certain circumstances, may be defined by others as symptomatic of mental illness.

The nine propositions of Scheff's theory are presented in the following paragraphs, with brief examples of evidence that seems to support them.

Proposition 1. *Residual rule-breaking arises from fundamentally diverse sources* (Scheff, 1984: 41). People may violate everyday interaction norms for many reasons. Scheff discusses four: organic (e.g., drug ingestion or lack of food or sleep), psychological (e.g., childhood trauma or peculiar upbringing), external stress (e.g., battle fatigue, disaster, or exam period) and volitional acts of innovation or defiance (e.g., avant-garde works of art or civil disobedience). It is important to bear in mind that the precise reasons why residual rule-breaking first occurs are less important to Scheff's theory than how others do or do not react to it.

Proposition 2. *Relative to the rate of treated mental illness, the rate of unrecorded residual rule-breaking is extremely high* (45). Many people who engage in residual rule-breaking are never labeled mentally ill, by either themselves or others. Odd behaviors such as withdrawal, aggressiveness, or hallucinations often are unrecognized, ignored, or rationalized. Furthermore, there is evidence (some of which we have already discussed), that communities frequently contain many "psychiatrically impaired" persons who have never been hospitalized or treated.

Proposition 3. *Most residual rule-breaking is "denied" and is of transitory significance* (47). This proposition is closely linked to the preceding one. Strange behavior by a student in the dorm might be rationalized as due to the stress of exams. The behavior passes and not much is made of it; it does not become a basis for labeling the person as mentally ill. The critical question for the theory is: Under what conditions *does* residual rule-breaking become officially labeled mental illness?

Proposition 4. *Stereotyped imagery of mental disorder is learned in early childhood* (54). Underlying this proposition is the assumption that being mentally ill is a social role which can be learned and imitated like any other role such as that of mother, father, or teacher. Evidence for this assumption often may be seen among children in schoolyards who are as apt to "play crazy" as they are to play house.

Proposition 5. *The stereotypes of insanity are continually reaffirmed, inadvertently, in ordinary social interaction* (55). As depicted in the media, mental disorder generally is portrayed in such images as violence, bizarre facial expressions or physical movements, or incoherent speech. Negative references such as "Ex-Mental Patient Kills Six" frequently appear as headlines or are heard in news broadcasts. Even our everyday speech is laced with clichés ("You're nuts," "Are you out of your mind?") which reinforce stereotyped images of insanity.

Proposition 6. *Labeled deviants may be rewarded for playing the stereotyped deviant role* (65). A person who becomes a psychiatric patient often gets positive reactions by displaying insight into the causes of the illness during psychiatric interviews. This is not unlike the notion that "The first step to a 'cure' is to recognize that you are sick." Patients who thoroughly subordinate themselves to the hospital officials and staff—those who make the least trouble and keep their place—are apt to receive the most favorable (albeit condescending) responses. Assuming that a person *does* need help, accepting the label is rewarded with help and care.

Proposition 7. *Labeled deviants are punished when they attempt to return to conventional roles* (66). The stigma of being an "ex-mental patient," regardless of past diagnosis and treatment or present condition, is a difficult burden. Prior mental hospitalization virtually guarantees rejection for certain jobs. A highly publicized case involved Senator Thomas Eagleton, who was dropped as the candidate for vice-president of the United States on the 1972 Democratic ticket after his brief period of mental hospitalization several years earlier became public knowledge.

Proposition 8. *In the crisis occurring when a residual rule-breaker is publicly labeled, the deviant is highly suggestible, and may accept the proffered role of insane as the only alternative* (67). Most people become confused, anxious, and easily manipulated when they are under a great deal of stress. Imagine your own feelings when you are unexpectedly called upon in class. Magnify these feelings to suit the gravity of a serious accusation that you are out of your mind. At this point you may very well begin to agree with the accusation as you experience more anxiety, confusion, and loss of self-control.

Proposition 9. *Among residual rule-breakers, labeling is the single most important cause of residual deviance* (69). Put otherwise, this proposition states that the labeling reaction of others to residual rule-breaking is the most critical factor in a person being viewed by others and himself or herself as mentally ill.

In Scheff's theory, the likelihood of being labeled a mental patient depends upon how severe the societal reaction is to the residual rule-breaking. The severity of the societal reaction depends on: (1) the degree, amount, and visibility of the rule-breaking; (2) the rule-breaker's power and social distance from agents of social control (police, doctors, psychiatrists); and (3) the tolerance level of the community and the availability in the culture of alternative nondeviant roles which help to rationalize residual rule-breaking.

Figure 4.4 shows the relationships among the propositions of the theory. It begins in the upper left-hand corner with residual rule-breaking arising from diverse causes (proposition 1). While most residual rule-breaking is denied and transitory (proposition 3), you can follow the sequence of events proposed to occur when public labeling (proposition 9) does take place. Note that some of the relationships take the form of a vicious circle. For example, in the lower right-hand portion of the chart, the person begins to believe herself or himself deviant (8F), becomes anxious, loses self-control, (8G), and engages in episodes of compulsive behavior (8H). This in turn reinforces the person's own developing conception of self as indeed deviant. Similar deviation-amplifying feedback loops can be seen at various points in the diagram.

Labeling theory minimizes the assumption that one who is labeled mentally ill is suffering from a disease. The theory, therefore is controversial, because it represents an attack on the psychiatric perspective that is grounded in a medical model of illness. Labeling theory claims that being mentally ill is more a social role than a medical disease. As we might expect, an assault on the psychiatric establishment is sure to stir an intense response. Walter Gove (1975), a leading proponent of the psychiatric view, evaluated the labeling perspective and concluded that:

- There is very little evidence of psychiatric victimization or tendency to diagnose a person mentally ill without thorough screening.
- People normally try to deny the existence of mental illness when bizarre behavior occurs, turning to that label only as a last resort.
- Contrary to the labeling theory prediction, it is not people with the least resources who are most apt to enter the mentally ill role.
- Mental hospitalization does not have the deleterious consequences suggested by labeling theorists.

Scheff (1984) has responded with his own assessment of the evidence. After a review of 18 studies directly related to labeling theory, he concludes that 13 support its propositions and 5 fail to do so. In a similar review of 26 studies, Khron and Akers (1977) find that 23 are consistent with the labeling perspective, while 3 are not. Townsend (1980) claims that "the best empirical evidence suggests that psychiatric and social factors interact to determine case outcome and that the latter frequently outweigh the former in their effects" (268). Gove (1982), in an updated review, concludes "The labelling theory of mental illness points to some real

Figure 4.4   Flow Chart for the Stabilization of Deviance in a Social System (Scheff, 1966)

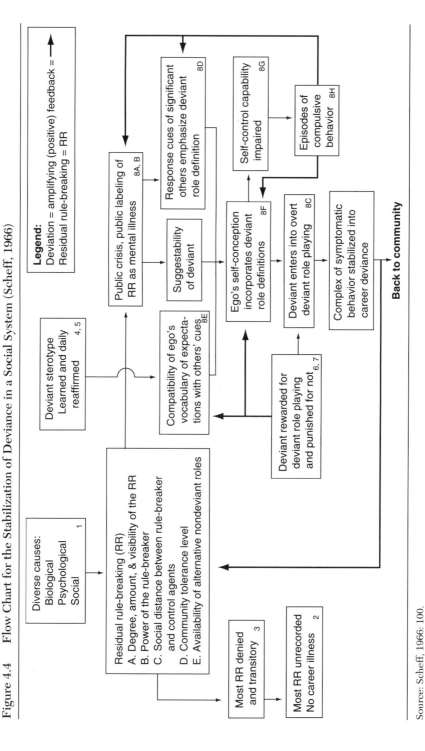

Source: Scheff, 1966: 100.
Note: Numbers refer to Scheff's propositions: width of rules and arrows for deviation-amplifying feedback indicates relative importance.

processes, but these processes were more important in the past than they are in the present. In fact, a careful review of the evidence demonstrates that the labelling theory of mental illness is substantially invalid, especially as a general theory of mental illness" (295). Some recent studies report findings consistent with labeling theory (Link, 1982) while others do not (Weinstein, 1983; Whitt and Meile, 1985).

One group of researchers has proposed a modified labeling perspective which claims that even if labeling does not directly produce mental disorders, it can lead to negative outcomes for mental patients. This approach, taken by Link et al. (1989), further asserts that

> ...socialization leads individuals to develop a set of beliefs about how most people treat mental patients. When individuals enter treatment, these beliefs take on new meaning. The more patients believe that they will be devalued and discriminated against, the more they feel threatened by interacting with others. They may keep their treatment a secret, try to educate others about their situation, or withdraw from social contacts that they perceive as potentially rejecting. Such strategies can lead to negative consequences for social support networks, jobs, and self-esteem. (400)

The research evidence is consistent with this modified labeling theory. Thus labeling theory, though controversial, continues to generate useful insights for our understanding of mental disorders.

Central to critiques of labeling theory such as Gove's is the idea that both public attitudes toward mental illness and approaches to institutionalization and treatment have changed considerably since the 1950s and early 1960s, the period in which Scheff's theory was developed. While the data and evidence appeared to support his propositions then, significant changes have since occurred that bear on the theory. This should be kept in mind in the brief discussion of public reactions to mental disorders that follows.

PUBLIC ATTITUDES TOWARD MENTAL DISORDERS

Studies of attitudes toward mental disorders have attempted to measure public knowledge of various aspects of mental illness, responses to statements about the mentally ill, and the desire to maintain social distance from the mentally ill. The earliest of these studies indicated that fear, stigmatization, and rejection characterized public feeling about the mentally ill; knowledge about types of mental disorder was scant; and optimism about treatment, and opinions of psychiatrists were quite low (Star, 1955, 1961; Bingham, 1951). Two other well-known studies done during the 1950s, one in Canada (Cumming and Cumming, 1957) and one in the United States (Nunnally, 1961), concluded that public attitudes were dominated by denial, isolation, and insulation of mental illness, and the public was largely uninformed about mental illness. The Nunnally study included a large-scale content analysis of television, radio, newspapers, and magazines which demonstrated that mental patients were heavily stereotyped as dangerous and unpredictable. This study was very influential in support of Scheff's postulate about the stereotyped imagery of mental disorders.

Subsequent research has reported greater public knowledge and more positive public attitudes toward mental illness. Summarizing this research, Gove (1975) says,

> ...recent research shows that persons are now more knowledgeable about mental illness and are better able to identify the mentally ill (see Spiro et al., 1973; Crocetti et al., 1974, for a review of the evidence). Furthermore, as Aviram and Segal (1973: 127) and Crocetti et al. (1974) have shown, there has been a consistent decline over time in the extent to which the mentally ill are rejected. Most striking is the finding by Simmons (1969: 33) that, among 13 types of deviance, ex-mental patients were less likely to be rejected than eleven of the other types, including atheists, gamblers, beatniks, alcoholics, and adulterers. In fact, the only category of deviance that was even likely to be rejected was intellectualism. Thus, although the data from the 50s support the societal reaction view that those perceived as mentally ill are excluded from social interaction, the recent evidence suggest that this view now rests on a questionable empirical base. (38–39)

While public attitudes toward the mentally ill may not be as harsh as in the past, recent studies show that rejection still prevails despite research showing that the mentally ill have only a moderate tendency to be more criminal or dangerous than others in the general population (Rabkin, 1974; Steadman and Felson, 1984; Nieradzik and Cochrane, 1985; Teplin, 1985; Link, Andrews, and Cullen, 1992). We are well advised to be cautious about assuming that there have been tremendous increases in positive public attitudes toward the mentally ill (Brockman, D'Arcy, and Edmonds, 1979).

Mental health workers themselves believe that most people are more fearful and have more negative attitudes toward the mentally ill than they actually do. Studies confirm that psychiatric patients' expectations that they will be devalued and discriminated against produce the negative effects predicted by labeling theory (Link, 1987a; 1987b; Link, Andrews, and Cullen, 1992). Likewise, when patients perceive their psychiatric disorders as illness they are significantly more inclined to adopt a "sick role" than if they view their disorder in nonmedical, psychosocial terms (Augoustinos, 1986). Fortunately, there is evidence that increased contact with mental patients is associated with reduced fear of them (Link and Cullen, 1986). This could be a potentially positive finding in light of the trend toward deinstitutionalization and community-based mental health care, which increases the social visibility of those in treatment.

MENTAL OR PSYCHIATRIC HOSPITALS

In American society hospitalization for mental disorders has very different effects upon those who experience it compared to those who are hospitalized for physical illness. One reason is that patients in mental or psychiatric hospitals are frequently placed there involuntarily. For example, in 1986 about 69% of the 343,000 patients admitted to state and county mental hospitals were involuntary commitments (Center for Mental Health Services data). Sociological interest in mental institutions stems primarily from their stigmatizing effect on both inmates and staff, combined with their difficult multiple goals of custody, treatment, and rehabilitation.

As we noted in Chapter 1, Erving Goffman (1961) describes the mental hospital as a *total institution,* similar in many important respects to prisons, bootcamps, boarding schools, or monasteries. The key attribute of total institutions is "the handling of many human needs by the bureaucratic organization of whole blocks of people" (6). Institutions are "total" when they become virtually the entire physical and social environment for their inmates. Thus the total institution is "a social hybrid, part residential community, part formal organization" (12). As a total institution in the business of processing people, the mental hospital is characterized by the bureaucratic structure of its staff, the great social distance separating the staff and patients, and, all too frequently, depersonalization and powerlessness as routine experiences for patients.

In the study by Rosenhan (1973) already cited, the eight researchers who had themselves committed to 12 different mental hospitals around the United States feigned a relatively minor hallucinatory symptom, and all but one were admitted with a diagnosis of schizophrenia. They remained undetected as pseudopatients in the hospitals an average of 19 days, whereupon they were released with diagnoses of schizophrenia in remission. During their stay, the pseudopatients carefully observed the interactions among patients and the staff. Their experiences as psychiatric patients generally support other sociological observations. Rosenhan (1973) gives the following example:

> Consider the structure of the typical psychiatric hospital. Staff and patients are strictly segregated. Staff have their own living space, including their dining facilities, bathrooms, and assembly places. The glassed quarters that contain the professional staff, which the pseudopatients came to call "the cage," sit out on every dayroom. The staff emerge primarily for caretaking purposes—to give medication, to conduct a therapy or group meeting, to instruct or reprimand a patient. Otherwise, staff keep to themselves, almost as if the disorder that afflicts their charges is somehow catching. (254)

Those with the most power (e.g., psychiatrists) spent the least time with and had least to do with patients, while those with the least power (orderlies, nurses) were most involved with them. When patients attempted to interact with the staff, they were often totally ignored as though they did not even exist. The powerlessness of the patients was evident in their loss of legal rights, lack of personal privacy, and restricted freedom of movement.

Rosenhan attributed the depersonalization of the patients primarily to negative attitudes toward the mentally ill and those who treat them, as well as the hierarchal structure of the mental hospital. In addition, he suggests that heavy reliance on psychotropic medication may also contribute to depersonalization by convincing hospital staff that pills or injections are sufficient treatment and further patient contact may not be necessary. The extensive use of physical treatment techniques such as psychosurgery, insulin, electroshock, hydrotherapy, and drugs has been reported by others as well.

Table 4.4   State and County Mental Hospitals Compared to Private Psychiatric Hospitals, United States, 1980, 1981

Characteristic	State and County Mental Hospitals	Private Psychiatric Hospitals
Number of inpatient additions, 1981	370,693	162,034
Average daily census, 1981	122,073	15,281
Race, 1980		
White	72%	87%
Nonwhite	28%	13%
Admission status, 1980		
Voluntary	42%	87%
Involuntary (noncriminal)	51%	13%
Involuntary (criminal)	7%	0%
Payment source, 1980		
No payment	47%	1%
Insurance	10%	68%
Type of therapy, 1980		
Drug therapy	65%	64%
Individual	7%	24%
Family/couple	50%	94%
Group	50%	56%
Activity	48%	74%

Source: Taube and Barrett, 1985.

While the conditions in psychiatric hospitals reported by researchers may strike us as inhumane and counter to a rehabilitative goal, they should not be ascribed entirely to the staffs who care for patients in these institutions. Indeed, as Perrucci (1974) suggests, staff members are frequently victims of stigmatizing public attitudes simply because they work in state hospitals; he met people in the community who wondered aloud if the doctors and other staff "weren't as crazy as the patients." This sort of stigma, coupled with problems wrought by dwindling resources, adds to the difficulty of working in a mental institution. The public attitudes within which the hospital must operate and the bureaucratic structure of its organization substantially account for the depersonalization and apparent callousness attendant on institutionalization.

It cannot be assumed that all such hospitals are the same. The greatest variations are between public state and county mental hospitals that generally serve the less affluent and the private psychiatric hospitals that serve those who are better off. The information in Table 4.4 draws some of the major distinctions. Note that compared to private hospitals, public hospitals have a higher proportion of nonwhite patients (28% to 13%); a much higher proportion who have no means to pay (47% to 1%); and a much higher proportion of noncriminal involuntary commitments (53% to 13%). These data suggest that the kind of psychiatric hospital a person enters is strongly associated with his or her socioeconomic status. Recall from Table 4.3 that diagnosis varies by hospital type, with public hospitals having higher diagnosis rates than private hospitals for alcoholic disorders (17% to 8%) and schizophrenia (37% to 11%), while their rates for affective disorders are lower (17% to 48%). Once a person has been admitted and diagnosed, the type of treatment received also is apt to differ considerably. While the use of drug therapy is about the same, patients in private facilities are far more apt to receive individual therapy, family or couple therapy, or activity therapy.

SOCIAL POLICY ON TREATMENT AND LEGAL RIGHTS

Deinstitutionalization and Community Mental Health

Since the early 1960s there has been a pronounced change in the treatment of people with mental disorders, with far less reliance on mental hospitals and much greater utilization of community-based facilities. For example, in 1955 about half of the psychiatric patient care episodes in the United States were in state mental hospitals, compared to about one-fifth in 1971. Outpatient services accounted for only 23% of psychiatric care episodes in 1955 but for 42% in 1971. Use of federally funded community mental health centers has risen dramatically since their construction and staffing were authorized by legislation passed in 1963 (Bachrach, 1976). Between 1970 and 1980 the total number of state and county mental hospitals dropped from 310 to 280, and the number of federally funded community mental health centers rose from 196 to 691. More startling are the data for the period 1969–1979, when hospital facilities experienced a 31% drop in annual patient episodes, while the community centers had a 291% increase (Mechanic and Rochefort, 1990).

As Table 4.5 shows, since 1970 there has been a slight decline in the rate of admissions to psychiatric hospitals, combined with a dramatic reduction in the length of hospitalization; almost as many people continue to be hospitalized annually, but for much shorter stays. Thus, while state and county hospitals remain important in the mental health care system, treatment in nontraditional institutions such as general hospitals, nursing homes, board-and-care homes, halfway houses, and the like has become much more prevalent (Mechanic and Rochefort, 1990).

An adequate definition of deinstitutionalization, according to Bachrach (1989), would include three primary processes:

1. *Depopulation*, the shrinking of the state hospital resident population.
2. *Diversion*, the deflection of patients to community-based facilities.
3. *Decentralization*, the broadening of responsibility for patient care to multiple-service providers.

Table 4.5   Psychiatric Hospital Use Rates, United States, 1970–1991

Year	Admissions per 1,000 Population	Days in Hospital per 1,000 population
1970	3.3	862
1975	3.2	490
1976	3.1	429
1977	3.0	390
1978	2.7	345
1979	2.9	334
1980	2.8	326
1981	2.7	304
1982	2.7	292
1983	2.6	274
1984	2.4	234
1985	2.5	224
1986	2.5	217
1987	2.6	214
1988	2.8	209
1989	2.9	201
1990	2.9	190
1991	2.9	179

Source: U.S. Bureau of the Census, *Statistical Abstract of the United States: 1988:* 99; *1992:* 114; *1993:* 124.

The overall trend during the past 25 years has been toward shortened hospitals stays and greatly increased use of outpatient care in community-based facilities such as community hospitals and mental health centers.

Much of the support for this changing philosophy in mental health care has come from labeling theorists like Scheff and observers like Goffman who brought their sociological perspective to the problems of institutionalization in psychiatric hospitals. These researchers consistently concluded that hospitalization is stigmatizing and patients may become so integrated into the hospital routine that they cannot function outside the institution. Hospitalization also breaks patients' family and community ties, making return to the community difficult. Thus hospitalization, the culmination of the process of labeling those with mental disorders, may in fact lead them to assume the mentally ill role. Many mental health professionals have argued that keeping patients in the community, away from the custodial environment of the hospital, has greater therapeutic value. They allege that growing public acceptance of the mentally ill and the widespread use of psychoactive drugs have made implementation of this philosophy possible.

From a more critical perspective, some observers, such as Scull (1977), have argued persuasively that the real impetus behind the "decarceration" or deinstitutionalization movement was the government's desperate need to cut the costs of so-cial control, custodial care, and rehabilitation. Certainly federal policy has provid-ed economic incentives for decreased reliance on hospitalization through Supple-mental Security Income and Medicaid, which match federal funds with state financing of community care. Thus deinstitutionalization has been powerfully mo-tivated by the eagerness of state legislatures to pass the cost of mental health care on to the federal government (Warner, 1989; Wegner, 1990). Other developments have also contributed. The availability of neuroleptic drugs permits people whose unmedicated behavior would be unacceptable by community standards to appear more controlled. Courts have also heightened concern for the civil rights of insti-tutionalized patients (Gudeman and Schore, 1984.) However, one response to ju-dicially mandated higher standards for institutionalized care (such as requirements to avoid overcrowding) has been for states to turn patients out into the streets.

Issues to Be Resolved. Despite the alluring arguments in favor of community men-tal health care and the statistical evidence that deinstitutionalization is in fact taking place, many problems remain to be faced. A few of the most significant issues can be presented in the form of questions:

1. What patients should be selected for community care? Community mental health care has brought a tendency to give more attention to those with less severe dis-orders, who are easier to care for in community facilities. In addition, the success of community-based treatment depends upon the quality of patient support and ser-vices. People from lower-class, minority communities are apt to return to environ-ments and facilities that are less conducive to successful care than upper-class, non-minority patients. Overall, deinstitutionalization has had positive effects for women and the elderly more than for men and younger people, and for whites more than for nonwhites (Wagenaar and Lewis, 1989). Community care has worked best for "acute-ly ill patients, who responded quickly to antipsychotic medicines, and for those who could return to homes, jobs, and families" (Shadish, Lurigio, and Lewis, 1989: 2).

2. How should treatment in the community be organized? This question has to do with the sites, hours of availability, and personnel required for treatment. Crit-ics have pointed to the overreliance on psychoactive drugs as a treatment modality in community mental health.

3. How can patients be supported in the community? Are employment, hous-ing, social activities, and other social resources available?

4. How can community resistance to the presence of the mentally ill be re-duced? Patients discharged from mental hospitals often are not welcomed back into the community with open arms, and it is possible that return to a hostile com-munity is no less detrimental than isolation in a hospital's back wards. There are also problems of the pressures exerted on families who become responsible for the care and rehabilitation of relatives released from hospitals.

None of these issues, among numerous others, has been entirely resolved. Bachrach (1976) places the problems of the deinstitutionalization movement in a helpful theoretical context by employing a functionalist perspective. She argues that *"the deinstitutionalization movement in the United States represents a search for functional alternatives to the mental hospital"* (19; italics in original). In other words, the policy of moving patients out of mental institutions and back to their communities is guided by the assumption that the job of care and rehabilitation of the mentally ill can be done as well or better in a community setting. However, while the apparent, manifest functions of mental hospitals are care and rehabilitation, these institutions also serve some less obvious, latent functions. For example, in certain cases mental hospitals (1) provide necessary long-term custodial care for the chronically disturbed; (2) remove the patient from a hostile environment, thus serving as a haven or asylum in the most positive sense; (3) protect society from certain dangerous individuals; and (4) provide a centralized place for research and for the training of mental health professionals. As a result, the large-scale dissolution of mental hospitals has met with resistance from the families of mental patients, the communities to which the patients must now turn for care, and the mental health professionals whose interests are tied to mental hospitals. Thus, says Bachrach,

> *...many of the problems confronting the deinstitutionalization movement result from the failure to provide functional alternatives for some basic functions serviced by the mental hospital.* The logical conclusion that follows from a functionalist point of view is that *mental hospitals must not and cannot be eliminated until alternatives for the functions of asylum and custodial care have been provided."* (19; italics in original)

The problems to be overcome for the success of deinstitutionalization still are formidable. As Scull (1990) observes:

> Work with the chronically crazy is not only poorly paid, frustrating, and all-too-often lacking in intrinsic rewards, it is also professionally *declasse* and stigmatized. Chronic schizophrenics are mostly an unattractive lot, statistically unlikely to become more than marginally contributing members of society even under the best of circumstances. In a large fraction of the population, their condition attracts fear, loathing, and hostility, and such sympathy as their plight evokes scarcely weighs heavily enough in the balance sheet to offset the liability their persistent and permanent dependency represents in the competition for scarce resources.... The sidewalk psychotic may be esthetically offensive to the sensibilities of the more fortunate, destructive of some of the remaining civilities of urban existence, and occasionally a real threat to the economics or physical well-being of the community as a whole. The mentally disturbed hidden from view in more domestic surroundings may impose all-but-intolerable burdens on family members. But neither set of problems seems acute or threatening enough to prompt collective responses proportional to the gravity of the need. (309–310)

We can conclude that deinstitutionalization and the community mental health movement have laudable goals that are consistent with much sociological theory and observation about the detrimental effects of hospitalization for mental disorders. At the same time, while implementation of this movement has occurred rapidly, it has met with resistance and has had limited effectiveness. A functional analysis indicates that it would be an error to anticipate total elimination of mental hospitals until their functions are assumed adequately by alternative structures. Nowhere have the perceived failures of the deinstitutionalization movement been raised more pointedly than in the revelations and debate over homelessness in the past decade.

Homelessness among the Mentally Ill

The indictments of the homeless state of a significant portion of the mentally ill have been shrill: "To put the situation as simply as possible, we are confronted system-wide with antiquated and depopulated state hospitals, inadequate and over-burdened outpatient clinics, and city streets full of the devastated victims of dein-stitutionalization, an unenlightened policy that has been made into a tragic mockery by the forces of inertia and economic and political self-interest" (Pepper and Ry-glewicz, 1982: 391). Some charge that the "madness in the streets" originated with the ideals of the 1960s counterculture and attacks on civil commitment procedures (Isaac and Armat, 1990), while others point to policy shifts in federal and state financing of mental health care (Johnson, 1990). Estimates of the extent to which de-institutionalization has contributed to the homelessness problem vary widely. In one study of 78 shelter "guests" in an urban area, about 90% received primary psychiatric diagnoses: 40% psychoses; 29% chronic alcoholic; and 21% personality disorders. One-third had previously been hospitalized for psychiatric care (Bassuk, Rubin, and Lauriat, 1984). In contrast, an Ohio study found the prevalence of homeless people with mental health problems to be closer to 20% (Roth, Bean, and Hyde, 1986). The wide variation probably has to do with the locations of study populations, the screening techniques used, and the unreliability of psychiatric diagnosis. From various studies, consensus is emerging that about 30% of the homeless might be classified as mentally ill (Wright, 1988; Shlay and Rossi, 1992), although some think this estimate is too high (Snow, Baker, and Anderson, 1988; Piliavin, Westerfelt, and Elliott, 1989).

To be sure, while some homeless people have serious mental disorders, not all do. In the end, the problem of homelessness itself—regardless of the extent to which it is specifically related to mental disorder—must be addressed. Homeless people are best seen as individuals burdened with interrelated problems that include a high level of need for mental health services, along with many other unmet needs. This suggests the advisability of an integrated response to their needs, as proposed by Roth, Bean, and Hyde (1986):

> Homeless people, whether mentally ill or not, need shelter, food, health care, job training and ultimately employment or at least an income…. [S]ystems which develop or provide housing, income, job training, employment, health care and psychiatric services must come together to provide an array of services necessary for each individual. Providing psychiatric services to a mentally ill homeless person leaves the person still homeless, just as providing food to a hungry homeless person leaves the person still homeless. (213)

All of this, of course, requires a commitment of resources, the distribution of which is a central issue in most social policy debates. The process that began in

1963 under the community mental health law presumed a broad spectrum of community services would accompany deinstitutionalization. Indeed, there is rather clear evidence that where such services are provided, they work. In a study of schizophrenic patients released from two cities—one American and one Canadian—with widely different community-based resources, those in the Canadian city, which provided extensive services, had fewer readmissions, higher levels of employment, and higher levels of well-being (Beiser, 1985). The finding for the American city in this study mirrors that for the country as a whole, as Bassuk (1984) points out:

> The community mental health movement failed primarily because the Federal and state governments never allocated the money needed to fulfill its promise. American society is currently trying to solve the problem cheaply, giving the mentally ill homeless at best emergency refuge and at worst no refuge at all. The question raised by the increasing number of homeless people is a very basic one. Are Americans willing to consign a broad class of disabled people to a life of degradation, or will they make the commitment to give such people the care they need? In a civilized society the answer should be clear. (Bassuk, 1984: 45)

Mental Disorder and the Law

On a day-to-day basis, officials in communities must make decisions about what to do with people whose behavior is disruptive to others, sometimes clearly illegal, and occasionally dangerous. At the same time these officials are providing for the peace and safety of the community, they must assure the individual rights of anyone accused of being disruptive or dangerous. Advocates for mental patients have focused on their rights to have treatment, to refuse treatment, to choose the least restrictive alternative, and to enjoy normal daily living (Freddolino, 1990).

Simultaneous protection of the rights of the community and individuals' rights underlies the social policy issues with which psychiatrists and lawyers and legal authorities must deal. We will discuss three kind of decisions involving the convergence of psychiatry and the law—involuntary commitment, incompetency to stand trial and the insanity defense.

Involuntary Commitment. Every state provides for the legal, involuntary commitment of certain persons to a psychiatric hospital. The underlying principle of such laws is the assumption that some people may pose a danger to themselves and others, and this requires their removal from the community. While this principle makes sense in theory, it is frequently very difficult to interpret in practice. How do we determine that a person is a danger to himself or others? In extreme cases, such as clear physical threats to others or attempted suicide, the determination may be straightforward. However, involuntary commitment has occurred frequently with far less convincing evidence of threat. Complaints that lead to involuntary commitment often come from those who find the accused person's behavior disturbing, odd, or in disagreement with their own standards. The problem, then, is to be sure that simply being different is not grounds for removing a person's freedom and rights through involuntary hospitalization.

Until recently, in many states the process of involuntary commitment was severely criticized for ignoring individual rights, especially during court hearings. The legal hearing is supposed to provide the means for protecting the rights of the individual, but, as Mechanic (1980) notes, judges were apt to accept routinely the advice of psychiatrists in commitment cases: "The court has other business to attend to, and judges frequently assume that a legal hearing would not be conducive to the patient's mental health.... Thus the commitment process often has had the form of due process of law but was actually vacuous because the decision was frequently predetermined" (190).

In one study of court procedures Scheff (1964) found that medical examiners spent an average of ten minutes on each case and almost always recommended detention. Furthermore, court hearings were usually brief and perfunctory:

> In one urban court (the court with the largest number of cases) the only contact with the judge and the patient was in a preliminary hearing. This hearing was held with such lightning rapidity (1.6 minutes average) and followed such a standard and unvarying format that it was obvious that the judge made no attempt to use the hearing results in arriving at a decision. He asked three questions uniformly: "How are you feeling?", "How are you being treated?", and "If the doctors recommend that you stay here a while, would you cooperate?" No matter how the patient responded, the judge immediately signified that the hearing was over, cutting off some of the patients in the middle of a sentence. (22)

In response to such practices, American commitment laws and procedures have been revised over the past two decades. The changes, now adopted in every state, apply to three aspects of civil commitment. First, the criteria for commitment have been narrowed from "in need of treatment for mental illness" to "being dangerous to oneself or others by virtue of mental illness." Second, the commitment period has been changed from indeterminate to a relatively brief, determinate period—for example, 72 hours or several days. Third, commitment procedures have been changed to emphasize due process, including right to counsel, burden of proof, and the like, to safeguard the rights of those civilly committed (Mills, 1986).

These reforms have enhanced the rights of those thought to be mentally ill and avoided many abuses of the past. Nevertheless, new problems are associated with the deinstitutionalization movement. Now, it is alleged, many people with serious mental disorders remain unassessed and untreated, and some who cannot be hospitalized against their will end up in jails, prisons, or inadequate community treatment facilities (Mills, 1986; Gove, 1985). Social policy—economic and legal—has reduced reliance on the asylums of the past, and in many ways this is good. However, we ought not to allow efforts to guarantee the legal protection of individuals' rights to encourage or excuse the abandonment of community responsibilities to provide help for those who need it.

Some have argued for the elimination of involuntary commitment on the grounds that the "benefits of abolition or severe limitation of involuntary commitment will be an increase in liberty that is not outweighed by the increased harms, a reduction in the role confusion and onerous tasks of mental health professionals, the enhancement of treatment, and the freeing of wasted resources" (Morse, 1982: 86). Others claim that this would be a strong case if present alternatives were not often worse. As public institutions are replaced by profit-making enterprises, "care" has become marginal at best, and at worst it is totally nonexistent. For many with mental disorders, the outcome of noncommitment is homelessness. In the absence of adequate resources outside psychiatric hospitals to assist those in need, involuntary commitment remains a necessary alternative. After a lengthy study of how mental disorder is handled by the law, Warren (1982) reluctantly concludes:

> Justice is not done in involuntary civil commitment, and yet I argue for its retention….[I]n the existing social system, I believe, human needs are better served by involuntary commitment than by the most probable alternatives: abandonment to the streets, or subhuman existence in uncontrolled for-profit institutions. Personal liberty, in my view, is a chimera where there is in truth no effective liberty. (211)

These arguments against and for involuntary commitment do not exhaust the alternatives. We need not necessarily forsake justice in the interest of servicing human needs, as suggested by Warren. One promising tactic is outpatient commitment, an approach that can exert some measure of social control over the mentally ill by using the least restrictive means (Sheid-Cook, 1991). More broadly, policy makers should seek to *change* the existing social system that forces the difficult choice of justice or abandonment. Put simply, this means allocating adequate resources to human services outside hospitals to assist those in need. Involuntary commitment is unjust, and leaving those in need to fend for themselves is inhumane, especially in an affluent society. Neither is acceptable.

Incompetency to Stand Trial. During the summer of 1977, New York City police undertook one of the biggest, most widely publicized manhunts in the United States to date. They were searching for a serial murderer known as Son of Sam who in one year shot six young women in the head, killing them, and wounded several others. The shootings were apparently motiveless and random. Following his capture the killer, David Berkowitz, was described in the press as "completely wacko," "nutty as a fruitcake," "paranoid," and "bizarre."

Public reaction to this case was particularly intense, and the fear was frequently expressed that Berkowitz might enter an insanity plea at this trial and end up in a psychiatric hospital rather than a prison. In fact, using the insanity defense at a trial is far less common than a pretrial decision that the person charged is incompetent to stand trial. The incompetency question is raised in less than 10% of criminal cases and is found to be warranted in about 25% to 30% of these (Morse, 1983). Berkowitz was judged competent to stand trial and was later found guilty, but similar psychiatric screening procedures have been used to bar trials for other famous cases such as the Boston Strangler or New York's "mad bomber," who set off 37 explosives over 16 years in a campaign against the city's electric and gas company. The incompetency ruling has been found in less celebrated cases as well.

The rationale for the incompetency ruling is that a defendant must be able to cooperate in preparing for the case for his own defense. If a person lacks the capacity to understand the charges and proceedings because of mental disease or deficiency, it would be unfair to go on with a trial because the right to an adequate defense would be denied. When a person is committed to a mental hospital due to incompetency, the goal is not to "cure" the defendant but simply to restore competence so the trial can go on.

While the incompetency ruling is clearly intended to guarantee an individual's right to a fair trial, it can also be used to deny a defendant's rights as well. Mechanic (1980) summarizes this argument:

> A judgment of incompetency to stand trial thus allows for the indefinite detention of persons believed to be dangerous, of those who cannot take care of themselves, and of those who are public nuisances.... Many such defendants are clearly mentally ill, and lawyers and judges often feel that a determination of incompetence is in their best interest. Critics of the process feel that this legal provision effectively allows the community to deny persons their legal right to a trial, to determinate sentence, and to due process of law. (207)

Indeed, there is evidence that after deinstitutionalization, incompetency to stand trial has been used in some cases as an alternative to civil commitment (Arvanites, 1986). Judging from the public reaction to particularly brutal crimes, it appears that many people criticize the incompetency procedure because they feel it denies the community an opportunity for retribution.

The Insanity Defense.   When a case comes to trial, the law presumes that the person accused was aware of the wrongful behavior being charged. Historically, the most widely used criterion for establishing responsibility was the M'Naghten rule formulated by the English House of Lords in 1843. The rule has been modernized in the Modern Penal Code of the American Law Institute to read:

> (1) A person is not responsible for criminal conduct if at the time of such conduct as a result of mental disease or defect he lacks substantial capacity either to appreciate the criminality of his conduct or to conform his conduct to the requirements of the law.
> (2) As used in this Article, the terms "mental disease or defect" do not include an abnormality manifested only by repeated criminal or otherwise antisocial conduct. (#4.01) (Goldstein, 1983: 739)

The legal issues surrounding interpretation of the insanity defense are too complex to outline here. There are, however, two aspects which point to the difficulty of judging whether an insanity verdict is appropriate. First, as studies such as Rosenhan's pseudopatients experiment have shown, diagnosis of insanity is a very inexact procedure. Indeed, at many trials where the insanity defense is used, eminently qualified psychiatrists called as expert witnesses for the prosecution and defense differ in their diagnoses of the defendant's sanity. In these cases it becomes obvious that diagnosing insanity is not the same straightforward procedure as diagnosing many physical ills.

Second, even when it can be agreed that a defendant suffers from a psychiatric disorder, that does not constitute evidence that the psychiatric disorder caused the unlawful behavior. Mechanic (1980) summarizes this problem well:

> The judgment of whether it is reasonable to regard the defendant as responsible for his behavior cannot be made on technical or scientific grounds. If, for example, a schizophrenic patient is apprehended committing a crime and when arrested is seen to be in a hallucinogenic state, one would be tempted to attribute his unlawful behavior to schizophrenia. However, most hallucinating schizophrenics do not commit crimes, and many nonschizophrenics do. Thus, the fact that schizophrenia is a concomitant of the unlawful act in no sense establishes a causal relationship between them. In some cases, of course, the link is obvious, as when a mental patient hears voices which tell him to commit an irrational and meaningless offense. But in such circumstances one hardly needs a psychiatrist to make the necessary observations. (211–212)

Lawyers claim that the insanity defense is not an easy one to uphold successfully. Indeed, it is used in less than 2% of cases, probably because even if it is successful, it does not bring freedom. The trial lawyer F. Lee Bailey has been quoted as saying, "Juries don't like the phraseology. The phrase 'not guilty' sticks in their craw when a jury is faced with colorful evidence. And jurors often say, 'I know this guy is nuts, but we're not going to put him in some institution where some psychiatrist can let him out'" (Alpern and Agrest, 1977). A recent public opinion survey found that people generally dislike the insanity defense because they want lawbreakers punished, regardless of insanity, and they believe that the defense fails to protect the public. People also vastly overestimate the use and success of the insanity plea (Hans, 1986). Nevertheless, occasional celebrated cases where the defendant is successful in avoiding prison elicit a public outcry calling for legal changes to eliminate the "not guilty by reason of insanity" verdict or make it more difficult to attain.[2]

SUMMARY

Mental illness presents especially difficult problems of definition and diagnosis that have become issues in the development of theory, research, and social policy. We began this chapter with a review of historical and cross-cultural evidence, concluding that in virtually all times and places, apparently uncontrolled, irrationally motivated behavior has existed. People have sometimes thought that such behavior is due to supernatural causes or illness; their reactions to it have ranged from punishment, to indifference, to treatment. According to contemporary American professional psychiatric usage, mental disorders are of two major types—organic (brain disease or damage, alcoholic psychoses, drug-induced psychoses) and functional (not attributable to any clear physiological impairment). Within the functional category are the psychoses (schizophrenia, manic-depression, and personality disorders) and the neuroses (phobias, anxieties, hysterias). A strong case has been made by critics of the psychiatric approach that functional mental disorders are not diseases at all and should not be treated as such because they have no established physiological cause.

From our examination of findings on the distribution of mental disorders among various social categories, the major variable identified is social class. The highest rates of mental disorder are in the lower classes; these patients are more likely to be diagnosed as schizophrenic or with personality disorders while upper-class patients are more likely to be diagnosed as depressive or neurotic. Social class is related not only to type of diagnosis but to the type of hospitalization and treatment and the treatment outcome for the patient.

Biogenetic explanations of certain mental disorders, particularly schizophrenia, have received strong research support. Heredity as a predisposing factor and a person's social experiences probably interact in the precipitation of some mental disorders. At the sociological level, in respect to social environment, the stress of living under conditions of social disorganization was one of the earliest causes proposed and tested by theorists Faris and Dunham. They found that rates of mental disorder are highest in the urban center and decrease toward the periphery. Their work is also important because it clearly identifies four alternative hypotheses that have guided the design and interpretation of many research studies since. The hypotheses are:

1. *Chance.* The distribution of highest rates of mental disorder in the city's center might merely be an odd occurrence.

2. *Selection.* Those who have the least power to resist being labeled (inner-city, poor residents) are more likely to be identified as mentally ill and institutionalized. This is an early version of societal reaction or labeling theory.

3. *Drift.* Those who are the least mentally competent move into the city center, which tends to be a collecting point for social failures, while those who are most able to do so move away. The result is a higher density of the socially and mentally impaired who contribute to the high rates of mental disorders.

4. *Stress.* Social and life conditions aggravated by poverty and social disorganization in the central city are very stressful, causing higher rates of mental illness.

Largely consistent with the stress theory of mental disorders are findings that rates of mental hospitalization increase with downturns in the economy. Likewise, Merton's anomie theory suggests that blocked opportunities to reach their goals may lead some people to retreat into the imaginary world of mental disorder, especially depression. Studies consistently find that when people are in situations that promote feelings of having little control over their lives, they are far more likely to suffer symptoms of psychological distress.

At the social psychological level of explanation we considered family socialization and coping with problems of day-to-day life. Scheff's labeling theory is a social psychological explanation arguing that influential others such as psychiatrists, in the process of officially designating a person mentally ill, can actually increase the person's aberrant symptoms, self-conceptualization as mentally disordered, and likelihood of taking on more permanently the mentally ill role. Labeling theory has been controversial because it challenges directly the psychiatric perspective based on a medical model of mental disorder.

We considered mental hospitals for their effects on both patients and the people who work in them. The climate of negative public opinion and the bureaucratic structure of the modern psychiatric institution contribute to the difficult problems of depersonalization and largely custodial treatment. When the national policy of deinstitutionalization for mental patients is analyzed from a functionalist perspective, deinstitutionalization represents a search for functional alternatives to the psychiatric hospital that has yet to be successful. While the movement has sharply reduced the length of stay of hospitalized patients, it has not followed up with adequate resources for community-based care.

Finally, we considered the points at which psychiatry and the law meet in respect to involuntary commitment to a mental institution, incompetency to stand trial, and the insanity defense. Reforms in civil commitment procedures have combined with the deinstitutionalization movement to emphasize the social policy dilemmas posed by the goals of protecting individual rights to freedom and community responsibilities to provide for those in need.

ENDNOTES

1. *Prevalence* refers to the number of cases in a population at any point in time. In contrast, *incidence* means the number or rate of new cases or admissions over a span of time, for example, during a given year or month.
2. Where the authority of medicine and that of the law converge in the power to incarcerate the individual, we find some of the most complex questions for social policy (Freeman and Roesch, 1989). The brief discussion here hardly does them justice. A thoughtful consideration could begin with Morris (1980), whose analysis leads to the controversial recommendations that the ruling on incompetency to stand trial and the insanity defense ought to be abolished.

REFERENCES

Alpern, D. M., and Agrest, S.
1977   "Will He Stand Trial?" *Newsweek* (August 20): 27–28.
Amato, P. R.
1991   "Parental Absence during Childhood and Depression in Later Life." *Sociological Quarterly* 32: 543–556.
American Psychiatric Association
1968   *Diagnostic and Statistical Manual: Mental Disorders*, 2nd edition. Washington, DC: Author.
1980   *Diagnostic and Statistical Manual of Mental Disorders*, 3rd edition. Washington, DC: Author.
1987   *Diagnostic and Statistical Manual of Mental Disorders*, 3rd edition, revised. Washington, DC: Author.

Aneshensel, C. S., Rutter, C. M., and Lachenbruch, P. A.
1991   "Social Structure, Stress, and Mental Health: Competing Conceptual and Analytical Models." *American Sociological Review* 56: 166–178.
Arvanites, T. M.
1986   "Commitments for Incompetency to Stand Trial: An Emerging Functional Equivalent to Civil Commitment." *Dissertation Abstracts International* 47: 2314-A.
Augoustinos, M.
1986   "Psychiatric Inpatients' Attitudes toward Mental Disorder and the Tendency to Adopt a Sick-Role." *Psychological Reports* 58: 495–498.

Aviram, U., and Segal, S.
1973   "Exclusion of the Mentally Ill: Reflection on an Old Problem in a New Context." *Archives of General Psychiatry* 29: 126–131.

Bachrach, L. L.
1976   *Deinstitutionalization: An Analytical Review and Sociological Perspective.* Washington, DC: National Institute of Mental Health.
1989   "Deinstitutionalization: A Semantic Analysis." *Journal of Social Issues* 45: 161–171.

Bassuk, E. L.
1984   "The Homeless Problem." *Scientific American* 241: 40–45.

Bassuk, E. L., Rubin L., and Lauriat, A.
1984   "Is Homelessness a Mental Health Problem?" *American Journal of Psychiatry* 141: 1546–1549.

Beiser, Morton
1985   "Does Community Care for the Mentally Ill Make a Difference? A Tale of Two Cities." *American Journal of Psychiatry* 142: 1047–1052.

Benedict, R.
1934   *Patterns of Culture.* Boston: Houghton Mifflin.

Bingham, J.
1951   "What the Public Thinks of Psychiatry." *American Journal of Psychiatry* 107: 599–601.

Book, J. A.
1953   "A Genetic and Neuropsychiatric Investigation of a North Swedish Population." *Acta Genetic et Statistica Medica* 4: 1–100, 133–139, 345–414.

Bourdon, K. H., Rae, D. S., Locke, B. Z., Narrow, W.E., and Regier, D. A.
1992   "Estimating the Prevalence of Mental Disorders in U.S. Adults from the Epidemiological Catchment Area Survey." *Public Health Reports* 107: 663–668.

Brenner, M. H.
1973   *Mental Illness and the Economy.* Cambridge, MA: Harvard University Press.
1976   Estimating the Social Costs of National Economic Policy: Implications for Mental and Physical Health, and Criminal Aggression. Washington, DC: U.S. Government Printing Office.

Brockman, J., D'Arcy, C., and Edmonds, L.
1979   "Facts and Artifacts? Changing Public Attitudes toward the Mentally Ill." *Social Science and Medicine* 13A: 673–682.

Brown, P.
1987   "Diagnostic Conflict and Contradiction in Psychiatry." *Journal of Health and Social Behavior* 28: 37–50.

Conover, D.
1972   "Psychiatric Distinctions: New and Old Approaches." *Journal of Health and Social Behavior* 13: 167–180.

Crocetti, G. M., Spiro, H. R., and Siassi, I.
1974   *Contemporary Attitudes toward Mental Illness.* Pittsburgh: University of Pittsburgh Press.

Cumming, E., and Cumming, J.
1957   *Closed Ranks: An Experiment in Mental Health Education.* Cambridge, MA: Harvard University Press.

Dohrenwend, B. P.
1975   "Sociocultural and Social-Psychological Factors in the Genesis of Mental Disorders." *Journal of Health and Social Behavior* 16: 365–392.

Dohrenwend, B. P., and Dohrenwend, B. S.
1969   *Social Status and Psychological Disorder: A Causal Inquiry.* New York: Wiley.
1976   "Sex Differences and Psychiatric Disorders." *American Journal of Sociology* 8: 1447–1454.

Dohrenwend, B. P., Levav, I., Shrout, P. E., Schwartz, S., Naveh, G., Link, B. G., Skodol, A. E., and Stueve, A.
1992   "Socioeconomic Status and Psychiatric Disorders: The Causation-Selection Issue." *Science* 255: 946–952.

Dunham, H. W.
1964   "Anomie and Mental Disorder." In M. B. Clinard (ed.), *Anomie and Deviant Behavior: A Discussion and Critique.* New York: Free Press.

Eaton, J. W., and Weil, R. J.
1955   *Culture and Mental Disorders.* Glencoe, IL: Free Press.

Eaton, W. W.
1974   "Residence, Social Class and Schizophrenia." *Journal of Health and Social Behavior* 15: 289–299.

Faris, R. E. L., and Dunham, H. W.
1939   *Mental Disorders in Urban Areas.* Chicago: University of Chicago Press.

Freddolino, P. P.
1990   "Mental Health Rights Protection and Advocacy." *Research in Community and Mental Health* 6: 379–407.

Freeman, R. J., and Roesch, R.
1989   "Mental Disorder and the Criminal Justice System: A Review." *International Journal of Law and Psychiatry* 12: 105–115.

Gift, T., Strauss, J. S., Ritzler, B. A., Kokes, R. F., and Harder, D.
1986   "Social Class and Psychiatric Outcome." *American Journal of Psychiatry* 143: 222–225.

Goffman, E.
1961   *Asylums*. New York: Doubleday-Anchor.
Goldstein, A. S.
1983   "Excuse: Insanity." Pp. 735–742 in *Encyclopedia of Crime and Justice*. New York: Free Press.
Gottesman, I. I., and Schields, J.
1972   *Schizophrenia and Genetics: A Twin Study Vantage Point*. New York: Academic Press.
Gove, W. R.
1975   *The Labelling of Deviance: Evaluating a Perspective*. New York: Halstead.
1982   "The Current Status of the Labelling Theory of Mental Illness." Pp. 273–300 in W. R. Gove (ed.), *Deviance and Mental Illness*. Beverly Hills, CA: Sage.
Gove, W. R., Tovo, M., and Hughes, M.
1985   "Involuntary Psychiatric Hospitalization: A Review of Statutes Regulating the Social Control of the Mentally Ill." *Deviant Behavior* 6: 287–318.
Gudeman, J. E., and Shore, M. F.
1984   "Beyond Deinstitutionalization: A New Class of Facilities for the Mentally Ill." *New England Journal of Medicine*. 331: 832–836.
Gurin, G. G., Veroff, J., and Ford, S.
1960   *Americans View Their Mental Health*. New York: Basic Books.
Hans, V.
1986   "An Analysis of Public Attitudes toward the Insanity Defense." *Criminology* 24: 393–413.
Heston, L. L.
1966   "Psychiatric Disorders in Foster Home Retarded Children of Schizophrenic Mothers." *British Journal of Psychiatry* 112: 819–825.
Hollingshead, A. B., and Redlich F. C.
1958   *Social Class and Mental Illness*. New York: Wiley
Isaac, R. J., and Armat, V. C.
1990   *Madness in the Streets: How Psychiatry and the Law Abandoned the Mentally Ill*. New York: Free Press.
Johnson, A. B.
1990   *Out of Bedlam: The Truth about Deinstitutionalization*. New York: Basic Books.
Kallman, F. J.
1938   *The Genetics of Schizophrenia*. Locust Valley, NY: J.J. Augustine.
1946   "The Genetic Theory of Schizophrenia." *American Journal of Psychiatry* 103: 309–322.
Kendler, K. S.
1983   "Overview: A Current Perspective on Twin Studies of Schizophrenia." *American Journal of Psychiatry* 140: 1413–1425.
Kessler, R. C., Brown, R. L., and Broman, C. L.
1981   "Sex Differences in Psychiatric Help-Seeking: Evidence from Four Large Scale Surveys." *Journal of Health and Social Behavior* 22: 49–64.
Kessler, R. C., and Cleary, P. D.
1980   "Social Class and Psychological Distress." *American Sociological Review* 45: 463–478.
Kessler, R. C., and Neighbors, H. W.
1986   "A New Perspective on the Relationships among Race, Social Class, and Psychological Distress." *Journal of Health and Social Behavior* 27: 107–115.
Kessler, R. C., Reuter, J. A., and Greenley, J. R.
1979   "Sex Differences in the Use of Psychiatric Outpatient Facilities." *Social Forces* 58: 557–571.
Kessler, R. C., Turner, J. B., and House, J. S.
1989   "Unemployment, Reemployment, and Emotional Functioning in a Community Sample." *American Sociological Review* 54: 648–657.
Kidd, K. K.
1991   "Trials and Tribulations in the Search for Genes Causing Neuropsychiatric Disorders." *Social Biology* 38: 173–178.
Kleiner, R. J., and Parker S.
1963   "Goal Striving, Social States and Mental Disorder: A Research Review." *American Sociological Review* 28: 189–203.
Krohn, M. C., and Akers, R. L.
1977   "An Alternative View of Labeling versus Psychiatric Perspectives on Societal Reaction to Mental Illness." *Social Forces* 56: 341–361.
Laing, R. D.
1969   *The Politics of the Family and Other Essays*. New York: Vintage.
Leighton, D. C., Harding, J. S., Macklin, D. B., MacMillan, A. M., and Leighton, A. H.
1963   *The Character of Danger: Stirling County Study*, Vol. 3. New York: Basic Books.
Link, B. G.
1982   "Mental Patient Status, Work, and Income: An Examination of the Effects of a Psychiatric Label." *American Sociological Review* 47: 202–215.
1987a   "The Social Rejection of Former Mental Patients: Understanding Why Labels Matter." *American Journal of Sociology* 92: 1461–1500.
1987b   "Understanding Labeling Effects in the Area of Mental Disorders: An Assessment of the Effects of Expectations of Rejection." *American Sociological Review* 52: 96–112.

Link, B. G., Andrews, H., and Cullen, F. T.
1992   "The Violent and Illegal Behavior of Mental Patients Reconsidered." *American Sociological Review* 57: 275–292.

Link, B. G., and Cullen F. T.
1986   "Contact with the Mentally Ill and Perceptions of How Dangerous They Are." *Journal of Health and Social Behavior* 27: 289–303.

Link, B. G., Cullen, F. T., Struening, E., Shrout, P. E., and Dohrenwend, B. P.
1989   "A Modified Labeling Theory Approach to Mental Disorders: An Empirical Assessment." *American Sociological Review* 54: 400–423.

Link, B. G., Dohrenwend, B. P., and Skodol, A. E.
1986   "Socio-Economic Status and Schizophrenia: Noisome Occupational Characteristics as a Risk Factor." *American Sociological Review* 51: 242–258.

Linsky, A. S.
1969   "Community Structure and Depressive Disorders." *Social Problems* 17: 120–131.
1970   "Who Shall Be Excluded: The Influence of Personal Attributes in Community Reaction to the Mentally Ill." *Social Psychiatry* 5: 166–171.

Lochlin, John C., Williamson, L., and Horn, J. M.
1988   "Human Behavior Genetics." *Annual Review of Psychology* 39: 101–133.

Mannerscheid, R. W., and Sonnenschein, M. A., (eds.)
1990   *Mental Health, United States, 1990*. Washington, DC: National Institute of Mental Health.

Mechanic, D.
1980   *Mental Health and Social Policy*, 2nd edition. Englewood Cliffs, NJ: Prentice-Hall.

Mechanic, D., and Rochefort, D. A.
1990   "Deinstitutionalization: An Appraisal of Reform." *Annual Review of Sociology* 16: 301–327.

Merton, R. K.
1938   "Social Structure and Anomie." *American Sociological Review* 3: 672–682.

Mills, M. J.
1986   "Civil Commitment of the Mentally Ill: An Overview." *Annals* 484: 28–41.

Mirowsky, J.
1985   "Depression and Marital Power: An Equity Model." *American Journal of Sociology* 91: 557–592.

Mirowsky, J., and Ross, C.
1989   *Social Causes of Psychological Distress*. New York: Aldine de Gruyter.

Morris, N.
1980   *Madness and the Criminal Law*. Chicago: University of Chicago Press.

Morse, S. J.
1982   "A Preference for Liberty: The Case against Involuntary Commitment of the Mentally Disordered." Pp. 60–109 in C. A. B. Warren, *The Court of Last Resort: Mental Illness and the Law*. Chicago: University of Chicago Press.
1983   "Mentally Disordered Offenders." Pp. 1046–1050 in *Encyclopedia of Crime and Justice*. New York: Free Press.

Myers, J. K., and Roberts, B. H.
1959   *Family and Class Dynamics in Mental Illness*. New York: Wiley.

Nicholson, R. A.
1986   "Correlates of Commitment Status in Psychiatric Patients." *Psychological Bulletin* 100: 241–250.

Nieradzik, K., and Cochrane, R.
1985   "Public Attitudes towards Mental Illness—The Effects of Behavior, Roles, and Psychiatric Labels." *International Journal of Social Psychiatry* 31: 23–33.

Nunnally, J. C.
1961   *Popular Conceptions of Mental Health, Their Development and Change*. New York: Holt, Rinehart and Winston.

Pardes, H., Kaufman, C. A., Pincus, H. A., and West, A.
1989   "Genetics and Psychiatry: Past Discoveries, Current Dilemmas, and Future Directions." *American Journal of Psychiatry* 146: 435–443.

Parker, S., and Kleiner, R. J.
1966   *Mental Illness in the Urban Negro Community*. New York: Free Press.

Pepper, B., and Ryglewicz, H.
1982   "Testimony for the Neglected: The Mentally Ill in the Post-Deinstitutionalization Age." *American Journal of Orthopsychiatry* 53: 388–392.

Perrucci, R.
1974   *Circle of Madness: On Being Insane and Institutionalized in America*. Englewood Cliffs, NJ: Prentice-Hall.

Piliavin, I., Westerfelt, I., and Elliott, E.
1989   "Estimating Mental Illness among the Homeless: The Effects of Choice-Based Sampling." *Social Problems* 36: 525–531.

Rabkin, J.
1974   "Public Attitudes toward Mental Illness: A Review of the Literature." *Schizophrenia Bulletin* 10: 9–33.

Rogler, L. H., and Hollingshead, A. B.
1965   *Trapped: Families and Schizophrenia*. New York: Wiley

Rosenfield, S.
1984   "Race Differences in Voluntary Hospitalization: Psychiatric vs. Labeling Perspectives." *Journal of Health and Social Behavior* 25: 14–23.

Rosenhan, D. L.
1973   "On Being Sane in Insane Places." Science 179: 250–258.
Ross, C. E., and Huber, J.
1985   "Hardship and Depression." Journal of Health and Social Behavior 26: 312–327.
Roth, D., Bean, G. J., and Hyde, P. S.
1986   "Homelessness and Mental Health Policy: Developing an Appropriate Role for the 1980s." Community Mental Health Journal 22: 203–214.
Rothman, D. J.
1971   The Discovery of the Asylum: Social Order and Disorder in the New Republic. Boston: Little, Brown.
Sampson, H., Messinger, S. L., and Towne, R. D.
1962   "Family Processes and Becoming a Mental Patient." American Journal of Sociology 68: 88–96.
Scheff, T. J.
1964   "Social Conditions for Rationality: How Urban Courts Deal with the Mentally Ill." American Behavioral Scientist 8: 21–24.
1966   Being Mentally Ill: A Sociological Theory. Chicago: Aldine.
1984   Being Mentally Ill: A Sociological Theory, 2nd edition. New York: Aldine.
Scull, A. T.
1977   Decarceration: Community Treatment and the Deviant: A Radical View. Englewood Cliffs, NJ: Prentice-Hall.
1989   Social Order/Mental Disorder: Anglo-American Psychiatry in Historical Perspective. Berkeley: University of California Press.
1990   "Deinstitutionalization: Cycles of Despair." Journal of Mind and Behavior 11: 301–311.
Shadish, W. R., Jr., Lurigio, A. J., and Lewis, D. A.
1989   "After Deinstitutionalization: The Present and Future of Mental Health Long-Term Care Policy." Journal of Social Issues 45: 1–15.
Shlay, A. B., and Rossi, P. H.
1991   "Social Science Research and Contemporary Studies of Homelessness." Annual Review of Sociology 18: 129–160.
Sheid-Cook, T. L.
1991   "Outpatient Commitment as Both Social Control and Least Restrictive Alternative." Sociological Quarterly 32: 43–60.
Simmons, J. L.
1969   Deviants. Berkeley, CA: Gendessary.
Skultans, V.
1975   Madness and Morals: Ideas on Insanity in the Nineteenth Century. Boston: Routledge and Kegan Paul.

Snow, D. A., Baker, S. G., and Anderson, L.
1988   "On the Precariousness of Measuring Insanity in Insane Contexts." Social Problems 35: 192–196.
Spiro, H. R., Siassi, I., and Crocetti, G.
1973   "Ability of the Public to Recognize Mental Illness: An Issue of Substance and Issue of Meaning." Social Psychiatry 8: 32–36.
Srole, L., Langer, T. S., Michael, S. T., Opler, M. K., and Rennie, T. A. C.
1962   Mental Health in the Metropolis. New York: McGraw-Hill.
Star, S. A.
1955   "The Public's Idea about Mental Illness." Paper presented at the National Association for Mental Health Meetings, Chicago, Ill.
1961   The Dilemmas of Mental Illness Cited in the Joint Commission on Mental Illness and Health Action for Mental Health. New York: Science Editions.
Steadman, H. J., and Felson, R. B.
1984   "Self-Reports of Violence: Ex-Mental Patients, Ex-Offenders, and the General Population." Criminology 22: 321–342.
Sutton, J. F.
1991   "The Political Economy of Madness: The Expansion of the Asylum in Progressive America." American Sociological Review 56: 665–678.
Szasz, T. S.
1974   The Myth of Mental Illness: Foundations of a Theory of Personal Conduct, revised edition. New York: Harper & Row.
1987   Insanity: The Idea and Its Consequences. New York: Wiley.
Taube, C. A., and Barrett, S. A. (eds.)
1985   Mental Health, United States, 1985. Washington, DC: National Institute of Mental Health.
Teplin, L. A.
1985   "The Criminality of the Mentally Ill: A Dangerous Misconception." American Journal of Psychiatry 142: 593–599.
Townsend, J. M.
1980   "Psychiatry versus Societal Reaction: A Critical Analysis." Journal of Health and Social Behavior 21: 268–278.
U.S. Bureau of the Census
1987   Statistical Abstract of the United States: 1988;
1992   1992; 1993. 1988, Table 156; 1992, Table 769;
1993   1993, Table 181. Washington, DC: U.S. Department of Commerce.
U.S. Department of Health and Human Services
1993   Additions and Resident Patients at End of Year, State and County Mental Hospi-

tals, by Age and Diagnosis, by States, United States, 1991. Rockville, MD: National Institute of Mental Health.

Wagenaar, H., and Lewis, D. A.
1989   "Ironies of Inclusion: Social Class and Deinstitutionalization." *Journal of Health Politics, Policy, and Law* 14: 503–522.

Wallace, A. F. C.
1970   *Culture and Personality*, 2nd edition. New York: Random House.
1972   "Mental Illness, Biology and Culture." Pp. 363–402 in Francis Hsu (ed.), *Psychological Anthropology*. Cambridge, MA: Schenkman.

Warner, R.
1989   "Deinstitutionalization: How Did We Get Where We Are?" *Journal of Social Issues* 45: 17–30.

Warren, C. A. B.
1982   *The Court of Last Resort: Mental Illness and the Law*. Chicago: University of Chicago Press.
1987   *Madwives: Schizophrenic Women in the 1950s*. New Brunswick, NJ: Rutgers University Press.

Wegner, E. L.
1990   "Deinstitutionalization and Community Based Care for the Chronic Mentally Ill." *Research in Community and Mental Health* 6: 295–324.

Weinberg, S. K.
1967   *The Sociology of Mental Disorders*. Chicago: Aldine.

Weinstein, R. M.
1983   "Labeling Theory and the Attitudes of Mental Patients: A Review." *Journal of Health and Social Behavior* 24: 70–84.

Wheaton, B.
1990   "Life Transitions, Role Histories, and Mental Health." *American Sociological Review* 55; 209–223.

Whitt, H. P., and Meile, R. L.
1985   "Alignment, Magnification, and Snowballing: Processes in the Definition of 'Symptoms of Mental Illness'." *Social Forces* 63: 682–697.

Williams, D. R., Takeuchi, D. T., and Adair, R. K.
1992   "Socioeconomic Status and Psychiatric Disorder among Blacks and Whites." *Social Forces* 71: 179–194.

Wright, J. D.
1988   "The Mentally Ill Homeless: What Is Myth and What Is Fact?" *Social Problems* 35: 182–191.

Yarrow, M. R., Schwartz, C. G., Murphy, H. S., and Deasy, L. C.
1955   "The Psychological Meaning of Mental Illness in the Family." *Journal of Social Issues* 11: 11–24.

5 | Suicide

Humans have been described as the most tragic of all creatures because they alone recognize their own mortality. Philosophers and social scientists have long been fascinated with the question of why some people, possessing this awareness, willfully end their own lives, and their efforts to understand suicide have helped us grasp the essentials of our humanity. The distinctly human aspect of suicide is reflected in the declaration of the 20th-century existentialist philosopher Albert Camus (1955) that "There is but one truly serious philosophical problem, and that is suicide. Judging whether life is or is not worth living amounts to answering the fundamental question of philosophy."

At the end of the 19th century sociologists were motivated to study suicide by Emile Durkheim's efforts to establish social reality as a distinct object of study. Durkheim began his study by contriving a foil: Why would sociologists, who are interested in collective social phenomena, choose to study suicide, probably the most intensely individualistic and personal of human acts? His response was that even a highly personal decision such as taking one's own life is, in part, the product of social and cultural conditions. As you will see in this chapter, suicide rates often follow quite regular patterns among various societies, subcultures, and social categories. Furthermore, it appears that the number and quality of a person's social relationships with others frequently is central to the decision to choose death over life.

HISTORICAL AND CULTURAL ATTITUDES

Anthropological evidence has established that in most small-scale, preindustrial societies, suicide rates are relatively low (LaFontaine, 1975: 85). In many such societies suicide has been considered a taboo to be approached with fear, superstition, or magic rituals. For example, the Baganda women of Uganda, afraid the ghosts of suicides might impregnate them, ward off the evil by throwing grass and sticks on the place where a suicide was buried. The Gisu of Africa attribute suicide to the anger of their ancestors; they say that an immediate sacrifice to the ancestors is a necessary precaution following a suicide to rid the community of evil. The body of the suicide is not accorded the normal burial ritual but is thrown in the thick brush to be forgotten (LaFontaine, 1960). Farberow (1975: 3) suggests two other reasons for revulsion from suicide. The act may indicate contempt for the community because the suicide rejects further participation in it, and it represents an economic loss to the society by depriving it of a useful mother, warrior, or worker.

Suicide is not, however, universally abhorred among preindustrial people. Indeed, in certain societies the act has been positively valued and encouraged under some circumstances. A Netsilik Eskimo is quoted as saying: "For our custom up here is that all old people who can do no more, and whom death will not take, help death to take them. And they do this not merely to be rid of life that is no longer a pleasure, but also to relieve their nearest relations of the trouble they give them" (Leighton and Hughes, 1955: 327). A similar recognition of the possible positive social functions of suicide is a significant aspect of the debate over euthanasia in contemporary Western societies.

Suicides or suicide attempts in some societies also provide a means of symbolizing anger, unhappiness, unjust treatment, or protest. For example, Giddens (1971: 156) notes that among the Trobriand Islanders, the Kuma and the Dobu of New Guinea, suicide attempts may be used as a way of registering displeasure with a spouse. In this context, suicide or attempted suicide is a rational social act intended to pressure others to respond in a desired way. In general, then, viewing suicide from a cross-cultural perspective makes it evident that suicide is not always an unreasoned act committed by a pathological individual.

Suicide in Western Societies

Throughout the history of Western civilization, attitudes toward suicide have varied a great deal. Among Jews of the Old Testament, suicide was considered wrong except under very extreme conditions such as the disgrace of capture or torture. Jewish law generally condemned suicide, and when it occurred victims and their families were not accorded the usual rites of burial and mourning. During the Greek and Roman periods, spanning the 5th century B.C. to the 4th century A.D., the lower classes found suicide repugnant, while the upper classes developed an attitude of indifference and even approval under certain circumstances. These included preserving one's honor, avoidance of pain or shame, expressing bereavement at the loss of a loved one, or dying for a patriotic cause (Farberow, 1975: 4–5).

During the early Christian era, the Romans enacted laws against suicide to curb financial losses when their soldiers or slaves killed themselves. Punishments included forfeiture of the estate when a person under arrest committed suicide, which also prevented loss to state revenues. In the same historical period Christians condemned suicide but, paradoxically, they frequently became willing martyrs. About the 4th century A.D., suicide became virtually unknown because of strong denunciation and punishment by the Church. Sanctions against suicide included confiscation of the victim's property, degradation of the corpse, and refusal of burial in consecrated ground. A common practice in England was to bury the suicide at a crossroads by night, with a stake driven through the heart. In other parts of Europe the corpse was dragged through the streets and hanged on a gallows (Rosen, 1975: 14).

In the mid-18th century, intellectuals began to question some of the dogmatic attitudes toward suicide that had characterized the Middle Ages. Three trends evident in this shift of opinion continue to the present day. First, there was opposition to the traditional Christian attitude that suicide is sinful and morally obnoxious. Second, scholars became interested in how national character relates to suicide, thus presaging the contemporary interest in environmental factors such as climate, urbanization, and economic conditions. Third, there was a tendency to consider self-destruction as a medical problem frequently associated with madness, hereditary psychopathology, or brain disease (Rosen, 1975: 21). The tendency to associate suicide with mental illness probably accounts for the fact that up to the present day, suicide can be stigmatizing for the victim's family.

VARIATIONS IN SUICIDE RATES

International Rates

Because of variations in reporting procedures and the unreliability of the data among countries, it would be unwise to draw conclusions from only slight differences in national suicide rates. There is, however, a broad range in the suicide rates for various countries of the world, from less than 1 per 100,000 population to almost 50 per 100,000 annually (see Table 5.1). In general, there is a tendency, with a few exceptions, for more highly industrialized societies to have higher suicide rates and poorer, developing countries to have lower rates.

At first we might be inclined to predict higher suicide rates for those who are poor and have the worst living conditions. The logic of this prediction would be that a dismal, downtrodden existence makes life seem less worth living; therefore, more suicides would occur. However, the international data obviously do not support such an argument. Indeed, Durkheim noticed long ago that poverty seems to offer some "protection" against suicide. In addition to comparisons between nations, higher white than nonwhite suicide rates in the United States, South Africa, and other countries tend to support Durkheim's claim that poor groups will have lower suicide rates than the more affluent. Several theories to be discussed later in this chapter offer explanations for these findings.

Suicide Rates in the United States

Some researchers have treated suicide and homicide as extreme types of aggressive, violent behavior (Henry and Short, 1954). It is proposed that in the case of suicide, violence is directed inwardly against the self, while homicide is an extreme form of outwardly directed aggression. Because suicide and homicide can be conceptualized as alternative modes of aggressive behavior, their rates are frequently compared over time, as shown in Figure 5.1. Between 1965 and 1991, American suicide rates remained remarkably stable, with only occasional tendencies to rise or fall. In contrast, homicide rates rose over most of the period, declined from a peak reached in 1980, and rose again after 1985, reaching a new peak in 1991.

In general, homicide is an act committed by relatively young people between the ages of 15 and 35. It is likely that some portion of the rising homicide rate through the 1960s and 1970s was due to the growing proportion of people in the

Table 5.1   Suicide Rates of Selected Countries per 100,000 Population, Various
Years, 1984–1990

Developed Countries	Rate	Date	Developing Countries	Rate	Date
Hungary	39.9	1990	Puerto Rico	10.3	1990
Finland	28.8	1990	Argentina	7.4	1987
Austria	26.3	1990	Chile	5.5	1987
Denmark	24.1	1990	Costa Rica	5.0	1988
Belgium	22.3	1990	Ecuador	4.6	1988
France	20.9	1989	Venezuela	4.2	1987
Sweden	18.6	1989	Panama	3.8	1987
Czechoslovakia	18.6	1989	Brazil	3.1	1986
Luxembourg	17.8	1990	Mexico	2.2	1986
Yugoslavia	16.5	1989	Paraguay	1.5	1986
Japan	16.3	1990	Guatemala	0.5	1984
Germany (Federal Republic)	15.8	1990	Egypt	0.2	1987
Iceland	15.7	1990			
Norway	15.6	1989			
Bulgaria	14.7	1990			
New Zealand	14.7	1988			
Australia	13.3	1988			
Canada	13.3	1989			
Poland	13.0	1990			
United States	12.4	1988			
Hong Kong	10.5	1989			
Scotland	10.4	1989			
Netherlands	10.2	1989			
Northern Ireland	9.9	1990			
Portugal	8.8	1990			
Ireland	7.9	1989			
Israel	7.8	1989			
United Kingdom	7.8	1990			
Italy	7.6	1988			
Spain	7.2	1987			
Greece	3.8	1989			

Source: *United Nations Demographic Yearbook, 1991*, 1992: 438–459, Table 21.

U.S. population who were born in the 1950s baby boom and had reached the age at
which they were most likely to commit homicide. In contrast, suicide rates generally increase with age. Until the mid-1970s the American population was on average
proportionately younger; therefore, while homicide rates increased, suicide rates remained quite stable. In the 1990s, however, it is becoming clear that as a result of
declining birth rates and longer life expectancy, there will be proportionately fewer
young people and more older people in the U.S. population. Thus we might expect

Figure 5.1   Suicide and Homicide Rates per 100,000 Population, United States, 1965–1991

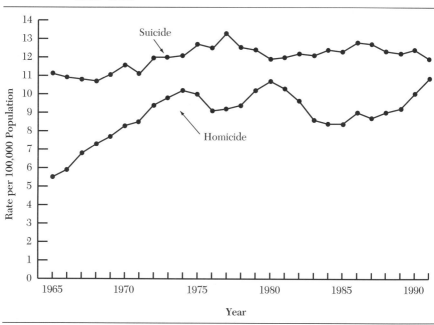

Source: U.S. Bureau of the Census, *Statistical Abstract of the United States* (various years *1967–1993*).

that, over the next decade or so, homicide rates will stabilize and possibly even drop, while suicide rates will begin to rise.

The tendency for suicide rates to be higher among older people is not unique to the United States; it is a worldwide phenomenon. Most industrialized countries tend to have a much older age distribution in their populations than less-industrialized nations, which generally have high birth rates and younger populations. Thus, in accounting for the differences in suicide rates among the countries listed in Table 5.1, age distribution may be an important consideration. Countries with "young" populations tend to have low suicide rates, and those with "older" populations have higher rates.

Evaluating Official Statistics

In 1990 in the United States, 30,906 deaths were officially recorded as suicides, a rate of 12.4 per 100,000, making suicide the eighth-ranking cause of death among Americans, according to the *Statistical Abstract of the United States: 1993* (U.S. Bureau of the Census, 1993). Looked at another way, suicide is the fifth leading cause of years of potential life lost before the age of 65 (*MMWR*, 1986). We should take care not to infer, however, that these statistics accurately reflect the true amount of suicidal behavior; the most obvious omission is the large number of attempted suicides, estimated to be around 200,000 per year. But even if we consider only completed suicides, we can justifiably be concerned with the validity and reliability of suicide statistics.

Official statistics on suicide, or any other social phenomenon, are the product of decisions by professionals (police, doctors, coroners) as to how to define, classify, and record each individual case they observe. Statistics such as annual suicide rates are the collective result of a very large number of individuals' intuitions and interpretations, with a correspondingly large possibility for unreliability and error. The first difficulty in deciding whether to classify a death as a suicide stems from the definition of the term. There is general agreement that "intention to die" is fundamental to suicide. But what are the grounds for inferring intent? Examining a corpse, how can a medical examiner determine whether or not the person intended to take his or her own life? Should only the physical evidence, such as the victim's wound or stomach contents, be considered? Or should the medical examiner also try to account for the victim's psychological state prior to death?

A wide variety of behaviors may be reasonably defined as suicidal. For example, cigarette smoking has been described as a form of slow-motion suicide. It is clear that smoking increases significantly the risk of life-threatening illnesses, and a case might be made for classifying all lung cancer victims who were long-term, heavy smokers as suicides. At the other extreme, it might be argued that intent is clear only when a suicide note is left by the deceased. Studies have shown, however, that only a minority (one-sixth to one-third) of suicides leave notes, so using the existence of a note as the only criterion for classifying a death as a suicide would underestimate seriously the actual number of suicides. In practice, coroners and medical examiners apply their own idiosyncratic working definitions to the cases they observe. In the absence of a suicide note, one medical examiner's suicide may be another's accident. This source of variation increases the unreliability of official statistics to an unknown extent.

Reporting systems also affect statistics—the more standardized and efficient the reporting system, the more accurate the resulting rates will be. Urban areas and more technologically advanced societies are likely to have much better reporting systems for all sorts of social phenomena than rural areas and developing countries do. This alone might account for some of the difference between urban areas, which tend to have higher official rates of suicide, and rural areas, which tend to have lower rates. A thorough, efficient reporting system that includes every case recorded as a suicide will produce higher official rates than an inefficient, slipshod system that fails to record many cases.

For many people, the suicide of a family member is a social disgrace. Therefore it may be to the advantage of survivors to cover up any evidence that suicide was the cause of death, or they may convince the medical examiner to officially classify a possible suicide as death by some other cause. It has been suggested that religious sanctions lead certain groups to underreport suicides, though the Catholic Church, which formerly would not permit those who died by suicide to be buried with church sanction, no longer discriminates against them.

Those who contemplate suicide are usually aware of how choosing this method of death might represent a loss of face, both to themselves and to friends or relatives close to them. Suicide also may lead to an economic loss for the survivors, because taking one's own life frequently negates insurance coverage for beneficiaries. For these reasons, researchers speculate that many people who resort to suicide disguise their self-destructive intent by planning their deaths to look like accidents. It is likely that a certain number of fatal falls, drownings, and automobile accidents are really suicides. Pokorny, Smith, and Finch (1972) found in a detailed examination of 28 auto crash fatalities that 4 of them were suicides. In another study the research suggested that about 20% of those involved in auto accidents might have certain depressive or self-destructive potentialities (Tabachnick and Gussen, 1973: 175). It appears that a significant number of the approximately 47,000 annual fatalities in U.S. motor vehicle accidents could be added to the 31,000 classified as suicides if it were possible to understand the victim's intent in every case.

Our conclusion in this consideration of official statistics is that disagreements about definitions, inconsistent working procedures, varied reporting systems, and efforts by the suicide's relatives or the victim to mask intent to die all contribute to the unreliability of official suicide data. Since it appears likely that there are pressures to classify an ambiguous death as something other than a suicide, official statistics are likely to underestimate the true incidence of suicide.

SOCIAL CORRELATES OF SUICIDE

Sex, Age, and Race

Suicide rates in the United States vary widely by sex (many more males than females), by age (from virtually none among black females under 15 to a rate of more than 50 per 100,000 for white males over 65), and by race (fewer blacks than whites in both sex and age categories). Figure 5.2 illustrates these relationships.

Sex. Men and women differ in several respects with regard to suicidal behavior in the United States. Men kill themselves at a much higher rate than women, according to official statistics (as shown in Figure 5.2). In 1990 the official male suicide rate per 100,000 was 20.4, while for females it was only 4.8. This difference in suicide rates generally is found in other countries as well.

Although men *complete* suicide at a higher rate than women, women have a higher rate of *attempted* suicides. One likely explanation is to be found in the different suicidal methods they use. As Table 5.2 shows, about two-thirds of U.S. male suicides in 1990 were committed with firearms, while female suicides were more likely to be committed either with firearms (42%) or by poisoning (36%). Since using a gun is swifter and more lethal than, for instance, taking an overdose of sleeping pills, the preferred method for males is more likely to result in death.

There are a number of plausible explanations for the different choices of suicide method by men and women. In American society males have been socialized to

Figure 5.2   Suicide Rates by Sex, Age, and Race, United States, 1990

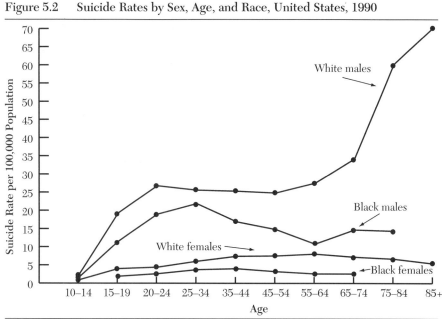

Source: U.S. Bureau of the Census, *Statistical Abstract of the United States, 1993*, 1993: 99.

identify firearms with strength and masculinity. Women may choose poisoning, in part as a matter of vanity, since having one's head split apart by a bullet is not a very attractive image, even in death. Indeed, women who do shoot themselves tend to aim at their bodies rather than their heads (Lester, 1972: 40). It also seems likely that women, more frequently than men, use suicidal threats or attempts as a means of manipulating others or as a cry for help to draw attention to their problems (Farberow and Shneidman, 1965).

Age. Overall, suicide rates rise with age. Among children under five years old, suicide is virtually unknown. In 1990, official suicide rates in the United States ranged from under 1 per 100,000 among 10- to 14-year-old black females to a peak of 70.3 among white males 85 years of age and older. Generally speaking, those who *attempt* suicide are younger than those who *complete* suicide (Shneidman and Farberow, 1957), and older people tend to use more lethal methods than those who are younger (Lester, 1972). Apparently the young are more apt than the old to use suicide attempts as a "cry for help."

Two trends in respect to age are noteworthy. First, for those aged 15–24, suicides have become the third leading cause of death, ranking behind only accidents and homicide (U.S. Bureau of the Census, 1993: 93). Possible reasons for this increase are considered below in our discussion of adolescent and young-adult suicide.

Table 5.2   Suicides by Sex and Method Used, United States, 1990

	PERCENT OF TOTAL SUICIDES BY SEX	
Method	Males	Females
Firearms	66%	42%
Poisoning	13	36
Hanging and strangulation	15	12
Other	6	10
Total	100%	100%
Number	24,724	6,182

Source: U.S. Bureau of the Census, *Statistical Abstract of the United States, 1993* 1993: 98.

The second trend is a somewhat smaller decrease in the suicide rate for males over 45 since the 1960s (Monk, 1987). The main reason probably has to do with increases in social security benefits and health-care improvements that have made life for the elderly easier and more fulfilling (Stack, 1982).

Race. Whites generally have higher suicide rates than nonwhites in the same society. This is true both in the United States and in other biracial countries such as South Africa, consistent with the earlier observation that the suicide rates of poorer countries are lower than in affluent countries. Indeed, it appears that racial differences in suicide rates have far less to do with race per se than with the relatively poor or powerless status of most nonwhites as compared with whites.

Before turning to the question of status we should note a significant trend in the suicide rate among young black males. You can see in Figure 5.2 that black suicide rates for the age categories up to 34 years old rather closely parallel the high rates for white males. On the basis of 25 interviews with young black suicide attempters, Hendin (1969) concludes that they had violent, murderous impulses—implying that the higher suicide rates may be a further manifestation of aggressive rage that some young blacks direct inwardly. Breed (1970) suggests that the suicides of young, lower-class, single black men are frequently "fatalistic"—suicides that originate in feelings of inferiority, powerlessness, and subjugation to arbitrary authority.

Since the 1980s, another variation on the fatalism theme adopted by minority youths has prevailed. The callous attitudes toward the worth of their own and others' lives expressed by many young people living in urban ghettos seem to have blurred the distinction between homicide and suicide. In a world marked by low expectations of longevity and a code of murderous revenge, to be a killer often assures one's own imminent violent death. Thus a fatalism that leads to self-destruction is common to both those who kill others and await their own turns as victims and those who simply kill themselves. At the same time, restraints such as overt racism and discrimination, which previously tended to produce solidarity among young blacks, have become weakened (Davis, 1982). Uplifted but unmet aspirations, coupled with the loosening of communal and family ties, have combined to increase the likelihood of suicide by young, black and other minority males. In any case, racial differences in suicide rates appear due more to social than to racial factors. Indeed, as South (1984) observes, "as nonwhites gain economic status relative to whites, their suicide rates more and more resemble those of whites" (178).

Occupation, Marital Status, and Religion

Occupation and Social Status. The relationship between suicide rates and occupation or social status in the United States has not been clearly established. Examining data at the end of the 19th century, Durkheim (1951; originally published 1897) concluded that suicide rates were highest among high-status people and lowest for those of low status. Some studies since Durkheim's time have agreed with this finding (Kalish, 1968; Stengel, 1964), but at least one (Powell, 1958) found higher suicide rates in upper-level *and* lower-level occupational groups, with the smallest suicide rate for those at the middle. Subsequent researchers found in Chicago and Detroit that higher class position, as defined by occupation, is associated with lower suicide rates (Maris, 1969; Stack, 1980). Evidence is also accumulating that low economic or social status is related to high suicide rates, at least in the United States. Stack (1982) found that in American society, "poverty can contribute to high suicide rates through such means as the frustrations associated with low incomes, relative deprivation, poor mental and physical health, higher unemployment, greater alienation from work, and higher rates of marital dissolution than in higher classes" (48).

Aside from status, there are certain occupational characteristics that seem to increase the probability of suicide. Occupations found to have exceptionally high suicide rates include pharmacist, physician, dentist, cab driver, police officer, farmer, and fisherman (Powell, 1958; Maris, 1969). We can speculate that jobs requiring either intense, involved interaction with others or, at the other extreme, working at relatively solitary pursuits will increase the likelihood of suicide. One study of dentists suggests that their high suicide rates may be due to social tension and stress growing out of disappointing comparisons of their own prestige with the status of physicians (Hilliard-Lysen and Riemer, 1988). It is also apparent that people who are downwardly mobile and losing occupational status have higher suicide rates (Breed, 1963). A large number of studies have established a firm association between unemployment and suicidal behavior, but the nature of the association is problematic (Platt, 1984). It has yet to be shown whether unemployment is directly related to suicide in some people or whether *both* unemployment and suicide are caused by a prior third condition such as a psychiatric illness, especially depression.

Marital Status. Married people are far less apt to kill themselves than those who are single, divorced, or widowed. Moreover, married people with children are less apt to commit suicide than those who have none. Taken together, these facts suggest that family relationships and responsibilities may act as a buffer protecting against suicidal impulses. More generally, it appears that people who have trouble establishing and maintaining warm, mutually interdependent social relationships are more likely to make serious, lethal suicide attempts (Worden, 1976).

Religion. Durkheim predicted that religious groups with strong social cohesion, such as Jews and Catholics, would have lower suicide rates than those with weaker group ties, such as Protestants. More recent findings generally support his conclusion regarding religious integration: Catholics have lower suicide rates than non-Catholics (Breault, 1986; but also see Bankston, Allen, and Cunningham, 1983). Catholics and evangelical Protestants have lower rates than institutional Protestants (Pescosolido and Georgianna, 1989), and Islam has an independent effect in lowering suicide (Simpson and Conklin, 1989), although such relationships may be dependent on the regional social context (Pescosolido, 1990). In a study of the effects of religious commitment on suicide that used rates from 25 nations, high religious commitment was associated with low suicide, but only for females, the group traditionally most committed to religion (Stack, 1983).

Economy and Culture of the Society

The effects of the economy on suicide rates have drawn attention since Durkheim first noted the relationship. One recent study found that in the United States a higher unemployment rate has been associated with higher suicide rates for males (Yang, 1992), while other research has demonstrated that historically the national business cycle has been significantly related to levels of suicide (Wasserman, 1989).

Japan, which scored extraordinary economic success in recent years, has also had one of the world's highest suicide rates. It has been argued that a number of the same cultural traits that account for Japanese economic success also contribute to its high suicide rate. These traits include an emphasis on faith and loyalty over reason, along with attention to the goals of the collective over those of the individual. While the government encourages a strong desire to succeed, many Japanese do not have access to the avenues for success, such as an elite higher education. The disappointments inherent in these economic realities are further exacerbated by Japanese cultural attitudes toward aggression, suicide, and death. In Japan there is a strong prohibition on other-directed aggression; death is glorified and suicide is romanticized (Iga, 1986). This suggests that the ways in which people respond to frustrations in their lives are powerfully shaped by their culture (Huff-Corzine, Corzine, and Moore, 1991).

Suicide among Adolescents and Young Adults

Suicides among young people increased sharply in the United States between 1960 and 1980, when they leveled off at a high plateau. In 1990, 4,869 officially recorded suicides were in the 15–24 age group, for a rate of 13.2 per 100,000. Increases in the suicide rate for this age group have been steepest for white males, comparatively less for black males, and only slight for females (Shaffer, 1987). Like older women and men, young females attempt suicide more frequently than they complete it, usually employing less lethal methods such as drugs or poisoning, while young males complete suicide more frequently and tend to use more lethal methods, particularly firearms. One study has shown that the involvement of both firearms and alcohol has increased greatly in young male suicide victims. Brent, Perper, and Allman (1987) found that "Suicide victims who used firearms were 4.9 times more likely to have been drinking than were those who used other methods of suicide. The availability of firearms and the increased use of alcohol among youth may have made a significant contribution to the increase in the suicide rate among the young" (3369). Other reasons proposed for the increase in youthful suicides include (1) the loosening of family ties, particularly due to increasing divorce (Stack, 1990); (2) greater tolerance of suicide as an acceptable option, possibly associated with weakening religious faith; and (3) increased media publicity which appears to precipitate the clustering of self-inflicted deaths (Hawton, 1986).

Predisposing factors in adolescent suicide include depression (but less than in adults), previous suicide attempts, alcohol and drug abuse, and the experience of acute stress (Holden, 1986; Wodarski and Harris, 1987). There is strong evidence that among adolescents, both suicide attempters and suicide completers have experienced a long, intensifying accumulation of problems in their lives (Jacobs, 1971; Curran, 1987; Little, 1994). Social psychological profiles of those who have committed suicide suggest that the victims had poor problem-solving skills for dealing with stressful conditions (Sadowski and Kelly, 1993). A breakdown of relationships, lack of achievement, and inability to cope with situations over which the young person has no control have also been cited as motivations (Peck, 1987). Because young people who are suicidal often have poor communication skills for dealing with personal or interpersonal conflicts, they may resort to dramatic acting-out.

Unlike all other age groups, young married people have comparatively higher suicide rates than those who are single (Seiden, 1969; Petzel and Cline, 1978). Many youthful marriages may have been a means of escape from unhappy parental homes, which are frequently associated with the backgrounds of suicidal individuals. High divorce rates among people who are married very young also suggest that early marriage is apt to be particularly stressful and unstable.

Evidence concerning the suicide rates of college students as compared to their nonacademic peers is inconsistent, partly because it is difficult to obtain accurate data (Arnstein, 1986). However, attempted and completed suicides in this group have long been of concern. The question of why is troublesome, given the advantaged position and generally supportive environment of the typical college student. One possible explanation is that while suicidal students often are academically successful and have objective evidence of their success (such as grades), many of them are reported to lack confidence in their ability, to feel as though their success is an accident, or to fear they eventually will be "found out." This nagging anxiety about one's genuine ability and worth has been called the "fraud complex" (Munter, 1966).

It is significant that the rise in suicides among young people persisted through the relative quiet and stability of the 1950s, the outwardly directed period of protest and social upheaval in the 1960s, the more inwardly directed drug culture and narcissism of the 1970s, and the acquisitive, "me-oriented" perspective of the 1980s. Moreover, youth suicide rates have remained high in the 1990s. Media reports have related tension-producing situations such as campus unrest or increased drug use to this trend, but researchers familiar with youthful suicides have disagreed with this explanation. Farnsworth (1972) suggests that the problem runs much deeper:

> Contrary to what might have been expected, the rise of student despair, alienation, experimentation with drugs for recreation, loss of confidence, and disillusionment with societal modes of regulation has not caused a wave of suicides. Private hopelessness or despair, rather than distress concerning public developments that is shared with one's peer group, is the paramount motive for suicide. (ix, x)

This is not to say that the rise in youthful suicide is unrelated to changes in American society. Hendin (1976) persuasively points to what he sees as an emotional atrophy in the family.

> Society is fomenting depression in the trend toward the devaluation of children and the family. The increasing emphasis on solitary gratification and immediate, tangible gain from all relationships encourages an unwillingness in parents to give of themselves or tolerate the demands of small children. It is not surprising that the family emerges through the eyes of many students as a jail in which everyone is in solitary confinement, trapped within their own particular suffering. The frequent absence of intimacy, affection, warmth, or shared concern, the prevalence of families in which no one had gotten what he needed or wanted has had a profound impact on this generation.
>
> Out of this disaffection has come a rising number of young people who are drawn to numbness because it has been their only security for a lifetime. Whenever the newness of coming to college, of graduating, of finding a person or a pursuit that interferes with that security and threatens to break the bond of deadness that held them to their parents, these students may be overwhelmed by suicidal desires. Certainly in their suicidal attempts these young people are moving toward becoming finally and forever what they felt they were meant to be. (332–333)

Other High-Risk Groups

A review of evidence from three large studies by Saunders and Valente (1987) established that homosexual men and lesbians make from two to seven times more suicide attempts than comparable heterosexuals. A history of previous attempts is a strong predictor of subsequent suicide. Homosexual men and women also are high on other predisposing factors such as alcohol or drug abuse and interrupted social ties, such as loss of personal support networks of families and friends, social isolation, or the end of a love relationship. In general, gay men and lesbians closely fit Durkheim's observation that alienated, poorly integrated groups are at high risk for suicide.

In general, suicide rates are higher for people with chronic or life-threatening illnesses; the likelihood of suicide is great for persons with AIDS, generally considered a young adult disease. A study of New York City residents in 1985 demonstrated that the risk of suicide in men with AIDS aged 20–59 was 36.60 times that of men that age without this diagnosis and 66.15 times that of the general population (Marzuk et al., 1988: 1333). The most serious implication of this finding may be the need for caution in proposals calling for mass population screening for antibodies to the AIDS virus. Unless appropriate counseling is available and the follow-up needed to identify faulty diagnoses can be assured, some people may be placed needlessly at high risk for suicide.

Despite the justifiable attention to suicide rates among the young, the elderly maintain by far the highest suicide rates in the United States. The data on suicide suggest that the highest-risk individual for suicide would be an "old-old" (over 75), divorced or widowed, white male who uses a firearm to kill himself (McIntosh, 1992). Compared to the young, whose ratio of attempted to completed suicides may be as high as 300 to 1, the elderly have a ratio of about 4 attempts to each suicidal death. Thus an attempt by an elderly person is much more likely to result in a fatality. Because the elderly are an increasing age cohort in the U.S. population, suicides in people over age 65 will continue to be of concern (Klagsbrun, 1991). Thorny ethical issues such as the role of physicians in assisted suicide and "the right to die" are often associated with this age group.

BIOPHYSICAL EXPLANATIONS OF SUICIDE

Suicide is a sign—probably the ultimate sign—of hopelessness and helplessness. The presence of a psychiatric disorder, especially depression, is consistent with the commonsense notion that a person who commits suicide must be terribly unhappy; untroubled people are unlikely to kill themselves. Therefore it should not be surprising that in a large number of studies, psychiatric illness (especially depression) has been found to be associated with suicide (Monk, 1987). Sainsbury (1986) presents evidence of three types:

1. Consistently over several studies, it has been shown that about 1 in 6 (15%) of patients diagnosed with depressive illness will ultimately die by suicide.

2. Evidence from interviews with relatives and examination of medical records indicate a high percentage of suicides (30% to 60%) have suffered from treatable mental illness—especially depression.

3. A number of studies show that a large percentage of attempted suicides are depressives.

One of the largest studies of suicide yet undertaken involved interviews with informants (mostly close relatives) of 266 suicides, compared to groups of nonfatal suicide attempters and people who had died of natural causes. Maris (1981) reports that "About 75 percent of the natural deaths had no major mental disorders, whereas only 27 percent of the completers and 14 percent of the nonfatal attempters were symptom-free....About 40 percent of...suicide completers had been hospitalized for mental problems at least one or more times in their lives, compared with 50 percent of...nonfatal attempters" (233).

In addition to such epidemiological evidence, several studies suggest that it is possible to identify some suicidal persons according to levels of biochemical neurotransmitters in spinal fluid which are related to both depression and aggression (Asberg, Nordstrom, and Traskman-Bendz, 1986). In some cases, genetic factors may predispose individuals to suicide (Kety, 1986). Psychiatric illness, biochemical markers, and genetic predisposition undoubtedly play roles in many suicides, although apparently not in all. Knowledge of these correlates is important to understanding who in a given population is at most risk as a potential suicide; it may also be useful in planning policies for suicide prevention. However, like predispositions and immediate precipitating events, conditions in the social environment can either suppress or excite a person's urge to self-destruction—whether that urge is chronic or transient.

SOCIAL PSYCHOLOGICAL EXPLANATIONS

Durkheim's Theory of Social Integration and Regulation

One of the earliest and certainly most influential theories to explain suicide was proposed by the French sociologist Emile Durkheim in the late 1800s. In *Suicide* (1951; originally published in French in 1897), he observed many of the same sorts of tendencies in official suicide rates that we see now. Rates of poor countries are lower than those of affluent countries; the married have lower rates than other marital statuses; and so on. Durkheim therefore reasoned that if suicide rates show consistent patterns among social categories, there must be social characteristics to explain the consistencies.

Durkheim proposes four types of suicide—egoistic, altruistic, anomic, and fatalistic. *Egoistic suicide* occurs when a person has lost (or possibly never had) close social ties with others. The person is not well integrated into the society, and life has become meaningless. Those most apt to commit egoistic suicide include the aged, who are less integrated into the society as they retire and their family and friends become more remote or die.

Altruistic suicide occurs when a person literally gives up life for the benefit of the society or group. Examples are Japanese kamikaze pilots during World War II who made suicidal crash attacks on enemy targets, or a soldier who jumps on a live grenade to save his unit. In the case of altruistic suicide, the person's integration into the group is extremely high—so high, in fact, that one's life is worth sacrificing for the group.

Durkheim describes anomie as an endemic condition of modern social life which is most severe in periods of rapid social change, especially economic upheaval in a society. He suggests that in cycles of economic boom or bust, there is rapid upward or downward mobility. People are moving from one social category to another at a much higher than normal rate, and as they move they lose their social bearings. In their new positions they are less sure of the rules to guide their behavior and relationships with others, and social norms lose their power to regulate their expecta-

Figure 5.3   Predictions of Types of Suicide Based on Level of Social Integration and Regulation (Durkheim, 1951)

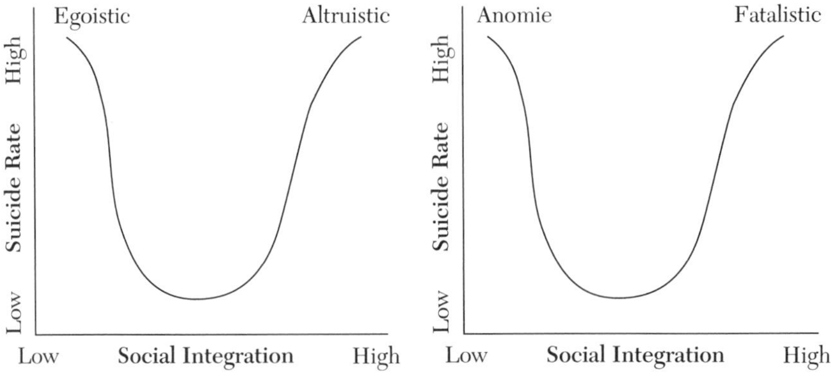

tions for themselves and for others. Durkheim proposes that in this relatively insecure, normless, anomic social environment, higher rates of *anomic suicide* will occur.

Durkheim briefly mentions *fatalistic suicide*, in which a person is overwhelmed by feelings of powerlessness in the face of "oppressive discipline." He gives the example of the suicide of slaves, who obviously suffer from excessive regulation of their lives. Similarly, fatalism is proposed as a possible explanation of increases in the suicide rate among young blacks (Breed, 1970).

At a more general level, Durkheim theorized that two sociological variables—the degree of a person's integration into social life and the amount of regulation over the person's behavior—are keys to understanding suicide rates. Low integration leads to high rates of egoistic suicide, and extremely high integration leads to altruistic suicide.[1] Moderate levels of integration are related to low suicide rates, as are moderate levels of regulation. High suicide rates are associated both with the lack of social regulation which produces anomie and with the feelings of powerlessness felt by people who are tightly regulated and made subject to arbitrary authority (see Figure 5.3).

Two recent studies have used cross-national comparisons to test Durkheim's theory. The first measured levels of religious, family, and political integration in 42 nations and found that together these variables explain 76% of the variation in the suicide rates (Breault and Barkey, 1982). The second employed data from 52 nations to establish that, consistent with Durkheim's predictions, suicide is correlated in the predicted directions—higher (+) or lower (-) rates—with the following indicators of family solidarity: divorce (+); presence of children (-); employment of women outside the home (+); and agricultural employment (-). In addition, suicide is lower in poorer countries and higher in those that are more affluent (Conklin and Simpson, 1987).

Status Integration

Most sociological theories of suicide since Durkheim's have been attempts to extend his insights concerning social integration. Jack P. Gibbs and Walter T. Martin (1964) examined the relationship between social or status integration and suicide. To measure status accurately for a true test of Durkheim's theory, they define status integration as the degree of stability in a person's social relationships. Further, they propose that stable social relationships depend on the degree to which people are free of the conflicting demands of incompatible status expectations. For example, a male nurse or a female engineer is apt to experience role conflict due to the incompatible expectations for his or her sex and occupational status. Gibbs and Martin reason that when statuses conflict, as they do for a male nurse, people will try to avoid or get out of such socially uncomfortable situations. Thus in 1964, when male nurses were very rare, they could anticipate difficult social relationships, poor social integration with others, and relatively high suicide rates. Today there are more male nurses, but in 1992, 94.3% of all registered nurses still were female (U.S. Bureau of the Census, 1993: 405).

The authors thus predict that the less frequently a status or configuration of statuses (e.g., male nurses) is occupied, the higher the suicide rate will be. As you can imagine, collecting data adequate to test the theory is difficult because suicide rates are not readily available for all possible status combinations of sex, age, race, occupation, education, and so on. However, Gibbs and Martin do present some findings that are largely consistent with their predictions, and others have subsequently reported positive results (Stack, 1987; Stafford and Gibbs, 1988). While status integration theory has been subject to criticism since it was first offered (Douglas, 1967; Chambliss and Steele, 1966), and some major problems have arisen in attempted tests, it remains an important stimulus for further research (Gibbs, 1982; Stafford and Gibbs, 1985).

Social Disorganization

Explanations of social behavior, like all human creations, are affected by the environment in which they are produced. So it is with early 20th-century American theorists who worked in a country experiencing rapid immigration, industrialization, and urbanization. Many whose intellectual home was at the University of Chicago linked the rapid social changes in American society with a variety of social problems, including mental illness, delinquency, and suicide.

Numerous studies from this perspective concentrated on analyzing different areas of a city, frequently Chicago, to establish correlations between the amount of social disorganization in an area and the rates of deviance in it. The sequence of events was proposed to go something like this. Areas with high residential mobility and transient populations lack the traditions to create stable communities. Such areas, which are especially apt to appear in periods of rapid social change, suffer from social disorganization—they lack strong social values and traditions to control the behavior of the residents. As a result, people in them are especially prone

Figure 5.4   Predicted Relationship between Social Disorganization and Suicide

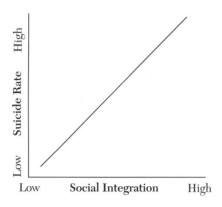

to high rates of personal disorganization. Personal disorganization, in turn, leads to higher rates of deviance, including suicide (see Figure 5.4).

Ruth Shonle Cavan's (1928) study of suicide relies heavily on this reasoning. Like Faris and Dunham's (1939) ecological study reported in *Mental Disorders in Urban Areas* (discussed in Chapter 4), Cavan's findings could be interpreted with the drift hypothesis as an alternative to social disorganization. Indeed, Cavan actually seems to accept the drift hypothesis as a distinct possibility:

> It is not to be thought that these institutions [dope peddlers, bars, houses of prostitution, rooming-houses and pawnshops] and types of conduct typical of the highly suicidal areas cause suicide. Rather they are symptoms of a general condition of personal and social disorganization which in the end may lead to suicide. There is in these areas a concentration of unsatisfied and disorganized persons, and therefore the probability of more suicide than in communities well organized as to community life and the characters of individuals. (104–105)

The concentration of unsatisfied and disorganized persons in these areas may, of course, occur because such people are unsuccessful in the mainstream society and "drift" into the skid row areas of cities, thus contributing to the high suicide rates there.

Cavan is careful to avoid suggesting that social disorganization is the *only* cause of suicide, however. Rather, she argues that social disorganization increases the likelihood that it will occur.

> In even the most stable social organization there is probably some personal disorganization, some people who cannot fit themselves wholly to the demands of customs and institutions. In times of social disorganization the difficulty is increased, and many people who would travel happily along under normal conditions find themselves unable to adjust to conflicting standards. It is these people, unable, under adverse social conditions,

to work out a satisfying personal life organization, who contribute to the increased suicide rates in communities where social disorganization prevails. (107–108)

Whether many of the suicide-prone will act on their predispositions depends largely on their social environment. Under ideal social conditions, only the most seriously vulnerable may succumb; when conditions become more severe and stressful, some who otherwise would adjust short of suicide may find conditions intolerable.

Frustration and Aggression

Some theorists have studied homicide and suicide as related phenomena, and their rates are often compared, as in Figure 5.1 above. The source of the supposed relationship derives from the assumption that both homicide and suicide are forms of aggression resulting from frustration; the fundamental difference is that homicide is a form of aggression directed outwardly, against another, while suicide is an aggressive act directed inwardly, against one's self. Beginning with this assumption, Andrew F. Henry and James F. Short, Jr. (1954) seek to answer the question: Why is there a tendency for people in some social categories (e.g., blacks) to have high homicide rates and low suicide rates while others (e.g., whites) have low homicide rates and high suicide rates?

Henry and Short first turn to the matter of blame for frustrations. On the one hand, if you have been ascribed a relatively low status in the society or feel powerless to control what happens to you, then when you feel frustrated in reaching your goals you are not likely to turn inward and look to yourself as the source of your frustration or the target of your aggression. Thus for a black person in a racially stratified society, for example, the blame for frustration obviously must lie elsewhere, and aggression is more likely to be directed outwardly. On the other hand, if you have a relatively high ascribed status and have the advantages on your side as you try to reach your goals, who is there to blame other than yourself if you fail and are frustrated? Thus whites in American society are more likely to direct aggression inwardly than outwardly.

The general principle proposed by Henry and Short incorporates the concept of external restraint. Low-status people are subject to a high degree of external restraint or control by others; high-status people are less subject to external restraint. Henry and Short reason that high external restraint of a population is associated with low suicide rates (and high homicide rates). Likewise, low external restraint is associated with high suicide rates (and low homicide rates).

Henry and Short next examine the role of child-rearing practices to explain inwardly and outwardly directed aggression. Researchers studying the different methods people use to raise children have found that working-class parents tend to use physical punishment, while middle- and upper-class parents resort more to reasoning, threatened isolation, and "love-oriented" discipline. Further, it has been found that discipline by physical punishment is apt to hinder the formation of strong internal controls and a potential for feeling guilt, while child-rearing techniques emphasizing loss of love rather than physical punishment lead to the formation of a

strong internal control and superego (sense of guilt). A person with the strong internal restraint of a well-developed superego is less likely to direct aggression against
others. Weak internal restraint, in the form of a weak superego, means that there are
lowered barriers against directing aggression outwardly against others. Henry and
Short predict, then, that strong internal restraints will be associated with higher
suicide rates (and lower homicide rates) and that weak internal restraints will be associated with lower suicide rates (and higher homicide rates).

In sum, Henry and Short's theory is based on the concepts of external and internal restraint. Lower-status people who are subject to high external restraint and
are socialized to have low internal restraint will be more likely to direct aggression
against others (homicide), and therefore, less likely to direct aggression against the
self (suicide). Higher-status people who experience lower external restraint but are
socialized with higher internal restraint will tend to blame themselves more for
frustrations and be more inhibited in directing aggression against others. Therefore,
they will have higher suicide rates and lower homicide rates.

Henry and Short's explanation of differential rates of suicide and homicide is,
like most such explanations, consistent with much of the data on suicides—but not
all of it. Whites generally do have higher suicide rates than blacks, but the high
rate of suicide among young black males is not explained by the theory. Suicide
rates by social class are even less consistent. One complicating factor is the apparently high suicide rates among both very high-status and very low-status people.

Imitation as an Explanation of Suicide

There is a popular notion that some individuals may be moved to kill themselves in
imitation of the act of suicide by others. A celebrated example is the self-inflicted
death of Marilyn Monroe in 1962, which was followed by a perceptible rise in the
suicide rate. However, research evidence that imitation is a significant factor in suicide was found to be contradictory and inconclusive (Lester, 1972) until an analysis
of British and American data between 1947 and 1968 (Phillips, 1974) indicated
quite clearly that the suicide rate increases immediately after a suicide has been
publicized. The greater the publicity, the larger the subsequent rise in suicides in
the area. Later studies have explored the effects of television as a stimulus to higher suicide rates, with both positive (Bollen and Phillips, 1982; Phillips, 1982; Phillips
and Bollen, 1985; Phillips and Carstensen, 1986) and negative (Baron and Reiss,
1984; Horton and Stack, 1984; Kessler and Stripp, 1984) findings. While imitation
certainly is not a major cause of suicide, it does appear that a highly publicized suicide—of a prominent person, in particular—may encourage others to imitate the act
(Wasserman, 1984).

The media have been implicated in suicide in another way somewhat related to
the notion of imitation. Country music songs are often filled with images of family
strife, breakup and loss, alcohol abuse, and alienation from work. We might speculate that in areas where country music is popular, people's suicidal moods would be
nurtured by their listening habits. A study of 49 U.S. metropolitan areas led to the
conclusion that the greater the airtime devoted to country music, the greater the

suicide rate for whites, the most likely racial group for country music listeners (Stack and Gundlach, 1992).

Societal Reaction and Social Meaning

Societal Reaction. Since suicide attempts have been described as a cry for help (Farberow and Shneidman, 1965), it makes sense that how others respond to a threat or attempt affects the decision to commit suicide. Attempted suicides far outnumber completed ones, and it appears that suicide attempts frequently are arranged in a way that allows a fairly high probability of rescue. When others respond sympathetically to the cry for help, the suicidal person's life often changes sufficiently to inhibit further attempts.

Kobler and Stotland (1964) argue against a view of suicide in which the person is driven to self-destruction by a death instinct. Instead, they emphasize the reactions of others to a person who has demonstrated suicidal intent:

> Our conception views suicidal attempts and verbal or other communications of suicidal intent as efforts, however misdirected, to solve problems of living, as frantic pleas for help and hope from other people: help in solving the problems, and hope that they can be solved. Whether the individual actually commits suicide—and this is our central concern—seems to depend in large part on the nature of the response by other people to his plea. If the response is hopelessness and helplessness, suicide is more likely to occur. It is our conviction that an implicit or explicit fear or expectation of suicide is most often communicated by a hopeless, helpless response, and that this communication is important in facilitating suicide. (1)

As evidence for their position, Kobler and Stotland describe "an epidemic of suicide" in a psychiatric hospital whose staff was experiencing low morale and deteriorating self-confidence. In this situation, the staff was unable to respond favorably to patients who entered the hospital with the expectation of being helped. Indeed, it appears that the hospital staff subtly communicated their expectation that the patients would kill themselves. The patients, having their own feelings of hopelessness and helplessness thus reinforced and focused, apparently responded to the expectation by committing suicide.

Social Meaning. Most of the theories and ideas discussed up to this point (with the exception of the societal reaction perspective) examine and attempt to explain official suicide statistics. Recalling our discussion concerning the problematic definition of any particular death as a suicide and the barriers to consistent or complete reporting of suicidal deaths, we might be justified in questioning the validity of theories which take as their primary task the explanation of official suicide rates. Jack D. Douglas, who takes this position, reasons further that careful observations and descriptions of actual suicide cases can help explain why people commit suicide.

Applying this approach, Douglas (1967) infers some common patterns of meaning that people attach to their suicidal actions:

- Suicide as a means of transforming the soul from this world to the other world. The person sees suicide as a vehicle of escape and a way of fundamentally changing relationships to others in the world after death.
- Suicide as a transformation of the substantial self in this world or the other world. By attempting or committing suicide, suicidal persons attempt to change others' image of them and convince others of how serious, sincere, or committed they are.
- Suicide as a means of achieving fellow feeling. Suicide or a suicidal attempt is intended to elicit sympathy from others.
- Suicide as a means of getting revenge. The suicidal act may be used to make others feel responsible or guilty.

Thus Douglas claims that suicide cannot be explained without studying the concrete situations in which it takes place. We must understand the meanings suicidal persons attach to their actions if we are to explain why they occur. This can only be done, he argues, through the comparative study of suicidal cases as opposed to the statistical study of suicide rates.

Edwin Shneidman, a leading contemporary expert on suicide, has explored its meaning in depth—primarily in interviews with people who have survived highly lethal attempts. He identifies the common characteristics of committed suicide, beginning with the observation that suicide is not a random or pointless act but a way out of a problem, dilemma, or difficulty. Thus he offers this definition: "Currently, in the Western world, suicide is the conscious act of self-induced annihilation, best understood as a multidimensional malaise in a needful individual who defines an issue for which the act is perceived as the best solution" (Shneidman, 1986: 4). In the face of intolerable psychological pain, the suicidal individual's goal is to cease consciousness—to escape the distress that is felt so acutely.

According to Shneidman, "Suicide is best understood not so much as an unreasonable act—every suicide seems logical to the person who commits it given that person's major premises, style of syllogizing, and constricted focus—as it is a reaction to frustrated psychological needs" (5). In the face of an apparent insolvable dilemma, coupled with frustrated psychological needs, the common emotion is a feeling of hopelessness/helplessness. This feeling, and the difficulties the suicidal individual faces, are made more intractable because the common cognitive state is *constriction*, or an incapacity to see alternatives other than suicide as solutions. Suicide appears to be the only way out. However, despite the bleakness there remains an ambivalence; the person wants *both* to die and to survive. Shneidman says,

> Perhaps the most interesting finding from large numbers of retrospective psychological autopsies of unequivocal suicidal deaths is that in the vast majority there were clear clues to the impending lethal event. These clues to suicide are present in approximately 80% of suicidal deaths.... It is a sad and paradoxical thing to note that the common interpersonal act of suicide is not hostility, not rage or destruction, not even withdrawal, but communication of intention. (11)

Shneidman presents evidence to support his claim that suicide is commonly consistent with the lifelong coping patterns of the individual, which often include previous episodes of disturbance, low capacity to endure psychological pain, a tendency toward a constricted view of problems, and earlier escapist approaches to solutions. Suicide is not best understood as a psychosis, neurosis, or character disorder; nor does a universal psychodynamic formulation for suicide exist. The immediate goal for intervention is to relieve the suicidal person's disturbance—to reduce the anguish, tension, and pain. Shneidman suggests one way to do this, "by addressing in a practical way those in-the-world things that can be changed if ever so slightly." The therapist should contact others close to the patient, as well as employers, government agencies, and so on, and should act as an ombudsman protecting the patient's interests and welfare. In the long term, the goal should be to help the suicidal person become aware of alternatives, "to increase the options for action and to increase the ways available within and to the person to have more options—in a phrase, to widen the blinders" (14).

Suicide Notes as Explanations

On the face of it, the study of suicide notes would seem to be a highly effective way to explore the meaning of suicides. At a person's self-chosen moment of death we might expect some profound statement of purpose and explanation. In fact, however, this is usually not the case. Reviewing the results of suicide note studies over 25 years, Shneidman (1976) observes:

> Suicidal notes are not like letters or diaries, which are written at leisure, often away from the scene of action. Suicide notes would seem to be comparable to battle communiques, filled with the emotion of the current scene and describing some special aspects of the contemporary dramatic event. And yet, as one reads hundreds of suicide notes, it becomes clear that many of them tell pretty much the same story. What is most disappointing is that most suicide notes, written at perhaps the most dramatic moment of a person's life, are surprisingly commonplace, banal, even sometimes poignantly pedestrian and dull. It is obviously difficult to write an original suicide note; it is almost impossible to write a note that is really informative or explanatory. (258)

Approximately one-sixth to one-third of persons who are officially labeled suicides leave suicide notes. However, studies comparing the characteristics of those who do leave notes with those who do not show no significant differences in age, sex, marital status, socioeconomic status, mental condition, and numerous other factors (Shneidman and Farberow, 1957; Tuckman, Kleiner, and Lavell, 1959). At the same time, it is impossible to say whether suicides who write notes have fundamentally different attitudes from those who do not.

In studies comparing genuine and simulated suicide notes, it has been shown that genuine notes are characterized by narrow reasoning, greater hostility and self-blame, more use of specific names and instructions to survivors, less introspection and more use of the various meanings of the word love (Shneidman, 1976: 260). Indeed, the content of genuine suicide notes is generally typical enough that, after some practice, it is possible to distinguish real from simulated suicide notes with a fairly high rate of accuracy.

The repetitive themes in genuine suicide notes are also apparent from researchers' attempts to classify them. For example, Jacobs (1967) found that nearly all of 112 suicide notes he examined fell into one of six categories:

1. *First-form notes*. Notes begging forgiveness or indulgence on the part of survivors.
2. *Sorry illness notes*. "...Before I get a stroke on top of my other troubles of my legs I decided that this would be easier for me... Please forgive me. I cannot endure any more pains."
3. *Not-sorry illness notes*. "Dear Jane: You are ruining your health and your life just for me, and I cannot let you do it...."
4. *Direct accusation notes*. "You Bob and Jane caused this—this all."
5. *Will and testament notes*. "I hereby bequeath all my worldly goods and holdings to Bill Smith...."
6. *Notes of instruction*. "I have gone down to the ocean. Pick out the cheapest coffin Jones Bros. has. I don't remember the cost. I'll put my purse in the trunk of the car."

Despite expectations that suicide notes might help explain self-destruction, the promise has been largely unfulfilled. At the time a person is about to commit suicide—at the end of hope—expression of the most deeply meaningful aspects of the act is probably impossible. Shneidman (1976) says, "In other words, that special state of mind necessary to perform a suicidal act is one which is essentially incompatible with an insightful recitation of what was going on in one's mind that led to the act itself" (264).

COMPREHENSIVE ATTEMPTS TO EXPLAIN SUICIDE

Suicidal Careers

On the basis of psychological autopsies compiled in interviews with victims' survivors, Ronald Maris formulated the concept of suicidal careers. His findings of factors associated with suicide, consistent with many of those found in other studies, are arranged in their chronological relationships throughout the life cycle. Table 5.3 summarizes these results. Maris (1981) emphasizes the finding that *The primary factors in the etiology of suicide are* age, negative interaction, drug and alcohol use, hopelessness-depression-dissatisfaction, the number of suicide attempts, and use of lethal methods. *The secondary factors are* sex, religion, early trauma, suicide in the family of origin, sexual deviance, work problems, physical illness, and conceiving of death as an escape" (325).

The Suicide Syndrome

There is no single theoretical formulation that will explain every suicide. As we have seen in this chapter, numerous types of suicide have been proposed (for ex-

Table 5.3   A Life-Cycle Model of Factors Associated with Completed Suicide (Maris, 1981)

Background	Early Life	Midlife Until 5 Years Before Death	Late Life— A Few Months to Just Before Death
Age (older)	Suicide in family	Repeated depression	Hopelessness and depression in managing the human condition
Sex (male)	Early trauma and a multiproblem family of origin	Drug and alcohol problems	Number of suicide attempts
Religion (Protestant)		Prolonged negative interaction	Use of lethal means
		Work problems	Poor mental or physical health
		Sexual deviance	
		Repeated life failure	
		Social isolation	

Source: Adapted from Maris, 1981.

ample, Durkheim's egoistic, altruistic, anomic, and fatalistic), with differing social conditions and personal motivations surrounding each. Even in a communal situation such as the mass suicide by cult members in Jonestown, Guyana, the suicides were not homogeneous—some were apparently altruistic, while others were fatalistic (Black, 1990). Still, Warren Breed (1972) made a worthwhile attempt to assemble a set of characteristics which appear to be present in at least half of American suicides, forming a sort of basic suicide syndrome. These characteristics also suggest possible modes of intervention to prevent an impending suicide.

First, many suicidal persons have a great deal of *commitment* to "making it" by accumulating things and being upwardly mobile; they have very high aspirations for themselves and have thoroughly internalized cultural norms of success. However, they have much lower commitments to people.

The second characteristic is *rigidity*—an inability to bend or change either one's roles or one's goals. In the face of difficulties or failure, the person does not have the flexibility to try new paths, to adjust goals to fit a new situation.

The third is *failure*. For men, this frequently includes being fired from a job, passed over for promotion, demoted, or some other frustration in their work lives. Among women, analogous difficulties have traditionally occurred in family-related activities, including troubles in relationships with spouses and problems with children. Often there are multiple failures, such as those of the unemployed man whose wife leaves him.

The fourth characteristic is *shame* as a response to failure. These persons feel their shortcomings deeply, anticipate negative reactions from others, and experience a disastrous blow to their self-esteem. They feel that the self-image they present to others has been shattered, and the depression often found in suicide follows. Such a person wishes to "run away and hide." The solution, of course, is to change one's commitments and adjust one's goals, but this is impossible for the rigid person.

The fifth characteristic is *social isolation*. As self-esteem declines, interactions with others become more difficult. The person withdraws. "Once a committed person feels shame over failure and cannot create a new life because of his rigidity, he feels worthless and, moreover, feels that other people also see him as worthless" (Breed, 1972: 8).

What can a suicide preventer or rescuer do? The five components of the syndrome do suggest tactics for altering a potential suicidal career, consistent with most of the information presented in this chapter. While intervention on behalf of the most rigid persons may be difficult, many who manifest the suicide syndrome can be helped to cope with the crisis. Breed concludes, "In some cases the 'failure' is illusory, and the wise helper can point this out, thus reducing the shame and isolation. The helper can also counsel experimentation with *switching goals, roles*, and *social contacts*, and a reduction in commitment (placing the eggs in different baskets)" (17).

SUICIDE PREVENTION AND SOCIAL POLICY

Crisis Intervention Programs

The main vehicles for implementing suicide prevention strategies in the United States have been programs that attempt to provide crisis intervention, usually by telephone. Generally, calls to a crisis hot line are answered by sympathetic volunteers who have received some training by professionals and can provide help, usually in the form of referrals to services. Some of the religiously affiliated services, such as the Save-a-Life League in New York City, have been operating since the early 1900s. A sharp increase in the prevention movement during the 1960s resulted in the establishment of over 200 nonreligiously affiliated suicide prevention programs.

How effective are such programs in the prevention of suicide? Research results are not encouraging. The most carefully designed study (Lester, 1974) found no significant relationship between suicide rates and the presence of suicide prevention centers in cities. An overall assessment of existing research concludes that while centers do attract a high-risk population, on balance the evidence does not indicate any effects on community suicide rates (Hendin, 1982; Dew et al., 1987). One notable exception is a study (Miller et al., 1984), which compared suicide rates in counties that added centers between 1968 and 1973 with those that did not, an association between centers and the reduction of suicides was found among young white females, by far the most frequent callers to crisis lines or suicide prevention centers. The authors conclude that over 600 lives per year are probably being saved, given the present availability of centers.

Thus even if such programs appear to have limited effectiveness in suicide reduction, they unquestionably fulfill useful functions by directing people in need to a variety of helpful services. Many prevention centers have served as excellent educational and training facilities or have stimulated research. However, it is almost certain that they do not attract as callers the majority of suicide attempters or eventual completers. This shortcoming led Hendin (1982) to the following analysis:

> Suicide is a problem of considerable magnitude. It is estimated that there are several hundred thousand suicide attempts in this country each year....Follow-up studies have shown that about 10% of an attempted-suicide population go on to kill themselves within a ten-year period. Other retrospective studies in the United States have shown that between 20% and 65% of those who kill themselves have a history of prior attempts. These findings indicate that the attempted suicide population contains much of the eventual suicide population, plus an even larger number of people who will not go on to kill themselves. (185–186)

By using our current knowledge about those most likely to eventually commit suicide, it is possible to identify high-risk cases among attempted suicides. This strategy focuses efforts on the people most likely to require intensive suicide intervention. Hendin concludes with this recommendation:

> The identification and treatment of the high-risk population might involve as many as ten thousand new cases a year throughout the country, but such a program would still be far more manageable—and probably more fruitful—than one attempting to identify and somehow treat the literally millions who call in to suicide prevention centers. Such treatment would have to include individual psychotherapy, the use of psychotropic medications when indicated, and in many cases the use of volunteers to work as befrienders in combination with a therapist. The efficacy of such an approach could first be tried and tested in a limited way in order to avoid the sequence of enthusiasm and disillusion that characterizes the history of the suicide prevention centers. (186)

Other Preventive Measures

A longer-term prevention strategy is education about the clues to potential suicides through schools, the workplace, and the media (Shneidman, 1986). Particularly in respect to youth suicide, school-based case-finding and educational programs have the potential to be effective. An evaluation of a youth suicide prevention school program in California found, after the first two years, significant gains in the understanding of suicide prevention techniques among students who took the course (Nelson, 1987).

Prevention also could be enhanced by attention to the methods used in suicide. Clearly, the most lethal is by firearms (see Table 5.2 above); suicide by this means has been increasing dramatically in the United States. In 1950, about 50% of male and

21% of female suicides used firearms; in 1990, 66% of males and 42% of females used this means. This represents about a 30% increase for males and a 100% increase for females. One researcher estimated that all of the increase in suicide rates between 1953 and 1978 could be accounted for by suicides by firearms (Boyd, 1983).

The firearms suicide rate is particularly high for young males (Boyd and Mo-scicki, 1986). In 1990, the official rate of firearm mortality by suicide for males 15 to 19 years old was 13.5 per 100,000 for whites and 8.8 for blacks; for males age 20 to 24 it was 17.5 for whites and 13.2 for blacks. The rate for females in the same age categories was much lower, about 2.3 for whites and 1.3 for blacks. Brent et al. (1991) found that the odds that potentially suicidal adolescents will kill themselves increase by a factor of 75 when a gun is kept in the home.

A related factor is the increased availability of firearms in the United States. Monk (1987) reports that the combined domestic production and imports of firearms for civilian use was 2.16 million in 1960 and 6.4 million in 1980, an increase of 200%.

Comparative evidence by states indicates that reduced access to guns by civilians is associated with lower rates of suicide by firearms (Lester, 1987), and international comparisons suggest that suicide rates are affected by the relative access of different lethal means. Particularly in regard to youth suicides, controlling access to firearms may be the most effective method for reducing rates of suicide by this means (Shaffer, 1987; Rich et al., 1990).

SUMMARY

Suicide, a distinctly human phenomenon, has pricked the curiosity of social theorists because of the remarkably stable patterns of suicide rates among different social groups. Attitudes toward suicide have ranged from disdain to encouragement throughout history, and the dominant reaction has been some combination of fear and disapproval. Indeed, the stigma still attached to the act contributes to the difficulties in amassing accurate official statistics about it. Still, it is possible to identify several persistent variations in suicide rates that are sufficiently great to ensure their validity, despite shortcomings in the data. For example,

- Suicide rates are generally higher in developed, industrialized countries than in developing ones.
- In the United States and other multiracial countries, whites have higher suicide rates than nonwhites.
- Suicide rates are generally highest among the old, although rates among young people have been increasing dramatically over the past 30 years.
- Women *attempt* suicide more frequently, but men have the highest *completed* suicide rates.

Psychological depression, drug and alcohol abuse, homosexuality, early family problems, and a suicidal close family member are all predisposing factors in suicide.

At the sociological level of explanation, Durkheim proposed the importance of social integration and regulation. Extremes of either integration or regulation in his theory account for one of four types of suicide (egoistic, altruistic, anomic, or fatalistic). Thus old people, who by virtue of retirement and loss of friends and relatives through death become less well integrated into the society, are more apt to commit egoistic suicide (caused by low social integration). At the other extreme, the soldier who jumps on a live grenade to save his comrades demonstrates his intense integration into his group by sacrificing his life for it (altruistic suicide). Gibbs and Martin's status integration theory and Cavan's social disorganization approach are additional sociological explanations.

Other social psychological theories include Henry and Short's analysis of the relationship between suicide and homicide. They conceptualize both as manifestations of aggression in the face of economic frustration. The poor and the powerless, when frustrated, are more apt to direct their aggression outwardly (homicide) while the well-to-do and powerful are more apt to blame themselves for whatever shortcomings they experience and thus direct aggression toward themselves (suicide). Henry and Short combine this idea with evidence about how different child-rearing practices encourage or inhibit people's tendencies to lash out against others. Also at the social psychological level we considered the role of imitation as a suicide motivator, such as the "suicide epidemic" that resulted in a small mental hospital when subtle cues from a demoralized hospital staff conveyed to patients the expectation that they would commit suicide.

Although there are undeniable social regularities in suicide rates, a full understanding of the act requires trying to infer the meaning that people attach to their suicidal actions. Douglas's approach to the social meaning of suicide, Shneidman's account of the common characteristics in suicides, and the study of suicide notes were considered in this light. Findings from Maris's large study based on psychological autopsies of suicides provide a model of the typical suicidal career, and consistent with the information in this chapter is Breed's suicide syndrome. Breed's set of characteristics often associated with suicidal individuals includes commitment to upward mobility, rigidity, failure, shame, and social isolation.

Social policy on suicide prevention largely takes the form of suicide crisis intervention programs. Research findings suggest that both educational programs and greater restrictions on the availability of lethal means, particularly firearms, could be effective social policies for suicide prevention.

ENDNOTES

1. In a comparatively more recent formulation, Straus and Straus (1953: 469) suggest that suicide rates will be relatively high in closely integrated social structures, with the addition that higher homicide rates will be associated with more loosely integrated social structures.

REFERENCES

Arnstein, R. L.
1986   "The Place of College Health Services in the Prevention of Suicide and Affective Disorders." Pp. 335–361 in G. L. Klerman (ed.), *Suicide and Depression Among Adolescents and Young Adults*. Washington, DC: American Psychiatric Press.

Asberg, M., Nordstrom, P., and Traskman-Bendz, L.
1986   "Biological Factors in Suicide." Pp. 47–71 in A. Roy (ed.), *Suicide*. Baltimore: Williams and Wilkins.

Bankston, W. B., Allen, H. D., Cunningham, D. S.
1983   "Religion and Suicide: A Research Note on Sociology's 'One Law'." *Social Forces* 62: 521–528.

Baron, J. H., and Reiss, P. C.
1985   "Same Time, Next Year: Aggregate Analysis of the Mass Media and Violent Behavior." *American Sociological Review* 50: 347–363.

Black, A., Jr.
1990   "Jonestown—Two faces of Suicide: A Durkheimian Analysis." *Suicide and Life-Threatening Behavior* 20: 285–306.

Bollen, K. A., and Phillips, D. P.
1982   "Imitative Suicides: A National Study of the Effects of Television News Stories." *American Sociological Review* 47: 802–809.

Boyd, J. H.
1983   "The Increasing Rate of Suicide by Firearms." *New England Journal of Medicine* 308: 872–874.

Boyd, J. J., and Moscicki, E. K.
1986   "Firearms and Youth Suicide." *American Journal of Public Health* 76: 1240–1242.

Breault, K. D.
1986   "Suicide in America: A Test of Durkheim's Theory of Religious and Family Integration." *American Journal of Sociology* 92: 628–656.

Breault, K. D., and Barkey, K.
1982   "A Comparative Analysis of Durkheim's Theory of Egoistic Suicide." *Sociological Quarterly* 23: 321–331.

Breed, W.
1963   "Occupational Mobility and Suicide among White Males." *American Sociological Review* 28: 179–188.

1970   "The Negro and Fatalistic Suicide." *Pacific Sociological Review* 13: 156–162.

1972   "Five Components of a Basic Suicide Syndrome." *Life-Threatening Behavior* 2: 3–18.

Brent, D. A., Perper, J. A., and Allman, C. J.
1987   "Alcohol, Firearms, and Suicide among Youth." *Journal of the American Medical Association* 257: 3369–3372.

Brent, D. A., Perper, J. A., Allman, C. J., Moritz, G. M., Wartella, M. E., and Zelenak, J. P.
1991   "The Presence and Accessibility of Firearms in the Homes of Adolescent Suicides: A Case-Control Study." *Journal of the American Medical Association* 266: 2989–2995.

Camus, A.
1955   *The Myth of Sisyphus and Other Essays*. New York: Vintage Books.

Cavan, R. S.
1928   *Suicide*. Chicago: University of Chicago Press.

Chambliss, W. J., and Steele, M. F.
1966   "Status Integration and Suicide." *American Sociological Review* 31: 524–532.

Conklin, G. H., and Simpson, M. E.
1987   "The Family, Socio-Economic Development and Suicide: A 52 Nation Comparative Study." *Journal of Comparative Family Studies* 18: 99–112.

Curran, David K.
1987   *Adolescent Suicidal Behavior*. New York: Hemisphere.

Davis, R.
1982   "Black Suicide and Social Support Systems: An Overview and Some Implications for Mental Health Practitioners." *Phylon* 43: 307–314.

Dew, M. A., Bromet, E. J., Brent, D., and Greenhouse, J. B.
1987   "A Quantitative Literature Review of the Effectiveness of Suicide Prevention Centers." *Journal of Consulting and Clinical Psychology* 55: 239–244.

Douglas, J. D.
1967   *The Social Meanings of Suicide*. Princeton, NJ: Princeton University Press.

Durkheim, E.
1951   *Suicide*, originally published 1897. Translated by J. A. Spaulding and G. Simpson. New York: Free Press.

Farberow, N. L.
1975   *Suicide in Different Cultures*. Baltimore: University Park Press.

Farberow, N. L., and Shneidman, E.
1965   *The Cry for Help*. New York: McGraw-Hill.

Faris, R. E. L., and Dunham, H. W.
1939   *Mental Disorders in Urban Areas*. Chicago: University of Chicago Press.

Farnsworth, D. L.
1972   "Foreword." In E. S. Shneidman (ed.), *Death and the College Student*. New York: Behavioral Publications.
Gibbs, J. P.
1982   "Testing the Theory of Status Integration and Suicide Rates." *American Sociological Review* 47: 227–237.
Gibbs, J. P., and Martin, W. T.
1964   *Status Integration and Suicide*. Eugene: University of Oregon Press.
Giddens, A.
1971   *The Sociology of Suicide*. London: Frank Cass.
Hawton, K.
1986   *Suicide and Attempted Suicide among Children and Adolescents*. Beverly Hills, CA: Sage.
Hendin, H.
1969   *Black Suicide*. New York: Basic Books.
1976   "Growing Up Dead: Student Suicide." Pp. 322–333 in E. S. Shneidman (ed.), *Suicidology: Contemporary Developments*. New York: Grune and Stratton.
1982   *Suicide in American*. New York: W. W. Norton.
Henry, A. F., and Short, J. F.
1954   *Suicide and Homicide*. Glencoe, IL: Free Press.
Hilliard-Lynsen, J., and Riemer, J. W.
1988   "Occupational Stress and Suicide among Dentists." *Deviant Behavior* 9: 333–346.
Holden, C.
1986   "Youth Suicide: New Research Focuses on a Growing Social Problem." *Science* 233: 839–841.
Horton, H., and Stack, S.
1984   "The Effect of Television on National Suicide Rates." *Journal of Social Psychology* 123: 141–142.
Huff-Corzine, L., Corzine, J., and Moore, D. C.
1991   "Deadly Connections: Culture, Poverty, and the Direction of Lethal Violence." *Social Forces* 69: 715–732.
Iga, M.
1986   *The Thorn in the Chrysanthemum: Suicide and Economic Success in Modern Japan*. Los Angeles: University of California Press.
Jacobs, J.
1967   "Phenomenological Study of Suicide Notes." *Social Problems* 15: 60–72.
1971   *Adolescent Suicide*. New York: Irvington.
Kalish, R. A.
1968   "Suicide." *Bulletin of Suicidology*. December, 37–43.
Kessler, R. C., and Stipp, H.
1984   "The Impact of Fictional Television Suicide Stories on U.S. Fatalities: A Repli-

cation." *American Journal of Sociology* 90: 151–167.
Kety, S.
1986   "Genetic Factors in Suicide." Pp. 41–45 in A. Roy (ed.), *Suicide*. Baltimore: Williams and Wilkins.
Klagsbrun, S. C.
1991   "Physician-Assisted Suicide: A Double Dilemma." *Journal of Pain and Symptom Management* 6: 325–328.
Kobler, A. L., and Stotland, E.
1964   *The End of Hope: A Socio-Clinical Study of Suicide*. New York: Free Press.
La Fontaine, J.
1960   "Homicide and Suicide among the Gisu." Pp. 94–129 in P. Bohannan (ed.), *African Homicide and Suicide*. Princeton, NJ: Princeton University Press.
1975   "Anthropology." Pp. 77–91 in S. Perlin (ed.), *A Handbook for the Study of Suicide*. New York: Oxford University Press.
Leighton, A., and Hughes, C. C.
1955   "Notes on Eskimo Patterns of Suicide." *Southwestern Journal of Anthropology* 11: 327–338.
Lester, D.
1972   *Why People Kill Themselves: A Summary of Research Findings on Suicidal Behavior*. Springfield, IL: Thomas.
1974   "Effect of Suicide Prevention Centers on Suicide Rates in the United States." *Health Services Reports* 89: 37–39.
1987   "Availability of Guns and the Likelihood of Suicide." *Sociology and Social Research* 71: 287–288.
Little, C. B.
1994   "Adolescent Problems and Suicidal Behavior." Unpublished paper.
Maris, R. W.
1969   *Social Forces in Urban Suicide*. Homewood, IL: Dorsey.
1981   *Pathways to Suicide: A Survey of Self-Destructive Behaviors*. Baltimore: Johns Hopkins University Press.
Marzuk, P. M., Tierney, H., Tardiff, K., Gross, E. M., Morgan, E. B., Hou, M., and Mann, J.
1988   "Increased Risk of Suicide in Persons with Aids." *Journal of the American Medical Association* 259: 1333–1337.
McIntosh, J. L.
1992   "Epidemiology of Suicide in the Elderly." *Suicide and Life Threatening Behavior* 22: 15–35.
Miller, H. L., Coombs, D. W., Leeper, J. D., and Barton, S. N.
1984   "An Analysis of the Effects of Suicide Prevention Facilities on Suicide Rates in

the United States." *American Journal of Public Health* 74: 340–343.

Monk, M.
1987   "Epidemiology of Suicide." *Epidemiological Reviews* 9: 51–69.

Morbidity and Mortality Weekly Reports (MMWR)
1986   "Premature Mortality Due to Suicide and Homicide—United States, 1983." *Morbidity and Mortality Weekly Reports* 35: 357–365.

Munter, P. K.
1966   "Depressions and Suicide in College Students." Pp. 20–25 in L. McNeer (ed.), *Proceedings of Conference on Depression and Suicide in Adolescents and Young Adults.* Fairlee, VT: Vermont Department of Mental Health.

Nelson, F. L.
1987   "Evaluation of a Youth Suicide Prevention School Program." *Adolescence* 22: 813–825.

Peck, D. L.
1987   "Social-Psychological Correlates of Adolescent and Youthful Suicide." *Adolescence* 22: 863–879.

Pescosolido, B. A.
1990   "The Social Context of Religious Integration and Suicide: Pursuing a Network Explanation." *Sociological Quarterly* 31: 337–357.

Pescosolido, B. A., and Georgianna, S.
1989   "Durkheim, Suicide, and Religion: Toward a Network Theory of Suicide." *American Sociological Review* 54: 33–48.

Petzel, S. V., and Cline, D. W.
1978   "Adolescent Suicide: Epidemiological and Biological Aspects." *Adolescent Psychiatry* 6: 239–266.

Phillips, D. P.
1974   "The Influence of Suggestion on Suicide: Substantive and Theoretical Implications of the Werther Effect." *American Sociological Review* 39: 340–354.

1982   "The Impact of Fictional Television Stories on U.S. Adult Fatalities." *American Journal of Sociology* 87: 1340–1359.

Phillips, D. P., and Bollen, K. A.
1985   "Same Time, Last Year: Selective Data Dredging for Negative Findings." *American Sociological Review* 50: 364–371.

Phillips, D. P., and Carstensen, L. L.
1986   "Clustering of Teenage Suicides After Television News Stories about Suicide." *New England Journal of Medicine* 315: 685–689.

Platt, S.
1984   "Unemployment and Suicidal Behavior: A Review of the Literature." *Social Science and Medicine* 19: 93–115.

Pokorny, A. D., Smith, J. P., and Finch, J. R.
1972   "Vehicular Suicides." *Life-Threatening Behavior* 2: 105–119.

Powell, E. H.
1958   "Occupations, Status, and Suicide: Toward a Redefinition of Anomie." *American Sociological Review* 23: 131–139.

Rich, C. L., Young, J. G., Fowler, R. C., Wagner, J., and Black, N. A.
1990   "Guns and Suicide: Possible Effects of Some Specific Legislation." *American Journal of Psychiatry* 147: 342–346.

Rosen, G.
1975   "History." Pp. 3–29 in S. Perlin (ed.), *A Handbook for the Study of Suicide.* New York: Oxford University Press.

Sadowdki, C., and Kelly, M. L.
1993   "Social Problem Solving in Suicidal Adolescents." *Journal of Consulting and Clinical Psychology* 61: 121–127.

Sainsbury, P.
1986   "Depression, Suicide, and Suicide Prevention." Pp. 73–88 in A. Roy (ed.), *Suicide.* Baltimore: Williams and Wilkins.

Saunders, J. M., and Valente, S. M.
1987   "Suicide Risk among Gay Men and Lesbians: A Review." *Death Studies* 11: 1–23.

Seiden, R. H.
1969   *Suicide among Youth.* Washington, DC: U.S. Government Printing Office.

Shaffer, D.
1987   "Strategies for Prevention of Youth Suicide." *Public Health Reports* 102: 611–613.

Shneidman, E. S.
1976   "Suicide Notes Reconsidered." Pp. 253–278 in E. S. Shneidman (ed.), *Suicidology: Contemporary Developments.* New York: Grune and Stratton.

1986   "Some Essentials of Suicide and Some Implications for Response." Pp. 1–16 in A. Roy (ed.), *Suicide.* Baltimore: Williams and Wilkins.

Shneidman, E. S., and Farberow, M. L.
1957   *Clues to Suicide.* New York: McGraw-Hill.

Simpson, M. E., and Conklin, G. H.
1989   "Socioeconomic Development, Suicide and Religion: A Test of Durkheim's Theory of Religion and Suicide." *Social Forces* 67: 945–964.

South, S.
1984   "Racial Differences in Suicide: The Effect of Economic Convergence." *Social Science Quarterly* 65: 172–180.

Stack, S.
1980   "Occupational Status and Suicide: A Relationship Reexamined." *Aggressive Behavior* 6: 243–244.
1982   "Suicide: A Decade Review of the Sociological Literature." *Deviant Behavior* 4: 41–66.
1983   "The Effect of Religious Commitment on Suicide: A Cross-National Analysis." *Journal of Health and Social Behavior* 24: 362–374.
1987   "The Effect of Female Participation in the Labor Force on Suicide: A Time Series Analysis, 1948–1980." *Sociological Forum* 2: 257–277.
1990   "The Effect of Divorce on Suicide in Denmark, 1951–1980." *Sociological Quarterly* 31: 359–370.
Stack, S., and Gundlach, J.
1992   "The Effect of Country Music on Suicide." *Social Forces* 71: 211–218.
Stafford, M. C., and Gibbs, J. P.
1985   "A Major Problem with the Theory of Status Integration and Suicide." *Social Forces* 63: 643–660.
1988   "Change in the Relation between Marital Integration and Suicide Rates." *Social Forces* 66: 1060–1079.
Stengel, E.
1964   *Suicide and Attempted Suicide.* London: Penguin.
Straus, J. H., and Straus, M. A.
1953   "Suicide, Homicide and Social Structure in Ceylon." *American Journal of Sociology* 58: 461–469.

Tabachnick, N., and Gussen, J.
1973   *Accident or Suicide? Destruction by Automobile.* Springfield, IL: Thomas.
Tuckman, J., Kleiner, R. J., and Lavell, M.
1959   "Emotional Content of Suicide Notes." *American Journal of Psychiatry* 116: 59–63.
United Nations
1992   *United Nations Demographic Yearbook, 1991,* Table 21. New York: Author.
U.S. Bureau of the Census
1992, 1993 *Statistical Abstract of the United States: 1992, 1993. 1992:* Table 125; *1993,* Tables 126, 128, 136, 137, 138. Washington, DC: U.S. Department of Commerce.
Wasserman, I. M.
1984   "Imitation and Suicide: A Re-examination of the Werther Effect." *American Sociological Review* 49: 427–436.
1989   "The Effects of War and Alcohol Consumption Patterns on Suicide: United States, 1910–1933." *Social Forces* 68: 513–530.
Wodarski, J. S., and Harris, P.
1987   "Adolescent Suicide: A Review of Influences and the Means for Prevention." *Social Work* 32: 477–483.
Worden, J. W.
1976   "Lethality Factors and the Suicide Attempt." Pp. 131–162 in E. S. Shneidman (ed.), *Suicidology: Contemporary Developments.* New York: Grune and Stratton.
Yang, B.
1992   "The Economy and Suicide: A Time-Series Study of the USA." *American Journal of Economics and Sociology* 51: 87–99.

6 | Alcohol and Other Drugs

People have used mind-altering substances for ages, predating recorded history. The discovery that alcohol is produced from overripe fruits almost certainly dates back to the Stone Age, and it appears from archeological evidence that one of the earliest uses for cultivated grain may have been in beer making. Ancient peoples long before Christ ingested opium, mescal buttons (mescaline), hallucinogenic mushrooms, and numerous other substances with the intention of altering moods or perceptions. During more recent recorded human history, there have been very few societies in which the use of drugs has been totally absent. Indeed, the use of alcohol among the world's societies comes close to being universal. Drug use is neither exclusively modern nor a phenomenon restricted to complex urban societies (Edwards, Arif, and Jaffe, 1983).

Of course, there are drugs that do not alter moods or perceptions. Antibiotics, aspirin, penicillin, and numerous others are prescribed and taken with only the most minor mind-altering effects, if any. It also is possible to alter one's state of mind without ingesting or injecting a substance; practitioners of transcendental meditation or hypnosis and avid long-distance runners who experience a "runner's high" are examples. However, for our purposes, the definition of drugs will be limited to physical substances ingested or injected into the body with the intention of altering moods or perceptions. The intention may be linked to a medical or therapeutic rationale (as with using morphine to reduce pain or Prozac to relieve depression or anxiety), to recreation (as with drinking alcohol or smoking marijuana at a party), or to physical dependence (as with the perceived need of the alcohol or heroin addict).

AN OVERVIEW OF DRUG USE

Drugs will never have exactly the same effects upon all people in all places or in the same person at all times. It is commonly recognized that some people are able to hold their liquor better than others, for example. Some become mellow when drunk, while others become aggressive. These and other differences depend on factors such as the person's physique, cultural beliefs about drinking and drunkenness, and the setting in which the drinking takes place. Some people become habituated or addicted to a particular drug rather quickly, while others are able to use the same substance in a controlled manner indefinitely (Zinberg, 1984). Put simply, drugs do not themselves alter states of consciousness in specific ways. Rather, drug effects result from an interaction of numerous conditions which can vary enormously from one drug-taking situation to the next. To understand drug effects we must take account of the social setting in which the drug-taking occurs, including whether or not the use is legal.

The major variables influencing drug effects include the following identified by Erich Goode (1978: 190–194).

1. *Identity*. What users believe they are ingesting can make a difference. Frequently people think they have ingested one thing (e.g., marijuana, mescaline, LSD), when a bogus alternative has been substituted by a dealer. As numerous experiments have shown, the placebo effect of expecting a certain feeling or mood change can often stimulate that change in the absence of any active substance.

2. *Dose*. Generally, the more of a drug ingested, the more extreme the effect. However, in some cases, low doses may have the opposite effects. In many people, for example, very low doses of alcohol increase the capacity to do certain intellectual tasks, possibly by lowering anxiety levels. Larger doses may dull the senses to the point of making the same task impossible.

3. *Potency and purity*. With drugs such as LSD, only a tiny amount has to be taken to produce extreme psychoactive effects. Far-less-potent drugs such as alcohol require far greater amounts to have marked effects. Moreover, it is well known that many drugs available illegally on the street have been cut with inert substances by as much as 95%. In combination, potency and purity account in part for the variation in the amount of a substance needed to produce a certain level of effect.

4. *Mixing*. When certain drugs are taken at the same time as another drug, they have stronger effects than either one taken separately. Probably the best known combination is alcohol and barbiturates, which increases the likelihood of deadly depressant effects.

5. *Route of administration*. Some drugs may be ingested in a variety of ways; marijuana may be smoked, eaten (mixed with food or sprinkled on it), drunk (as a tea), or swallowed as a tablet. Different methods of administering the same substance may produce different effects. Other alternatives are sniffing (glue), snorting (cocaine), or injection (heroin). Often the mode chosen is more dependent on cultural custom than differences in potency or effect.

6. *Habituation*. Continuous use of many, but not all, drugs produces increased tolerance of the drug, so more of it is needed to produce the desired effect. Increased experience with a drug also brings greater assurance of how to handle and even enjoy strange sensations.

7. *Set and setting*. "Set" includes the various subjective factors—expectations, mood, anxiety level, tiredness, and so on—that characterize the person taking a drug. To these variables must be added the setting: alone in one's room, a party, a bar, an airplane, a formal dinner, a football game. The same person

drinking the same quantity of the same alcoholic beverage in different settings may experience vastly different alterations of mood and behavior.

To sum up, drugs alone do not have specific effects. Drug effects result from a combination of the substance's chemical properties, the physical and mental condition of the drug user, and the setting in which the drug is taken.

Characteristics of Alcohol as a Drug

In a number of the examples used so far in this chapter, alcohol is treated as a drug. Doctors and researchers who specialize in alcohol abuse consider alcohol to be as much a drug as marijuana or even heroin, despite its popular image as a substance quite apart from these more "dangerous" drugs. Official agencies, such as the National Institute on Alcohol Abuse and Alcoholism, and private groups like Alcoholics Anonymous also take the position that alcohol is a mind-altering chemical substance which fulfills every reasonable criterion to be labeled a drug.

Alcohol is a depressant of the central nervous system. It can produce several conditions that are usually regarded as measures of a drug's potential harmfulness. Alcohol can lead to what clinicians term *psychological dependence*. This to say that a person may develop a powerful desire to drink—especially in particular social situations—even though he or she is not physically addicted. Like other mind-altering drugs, alcohol is used mostly for recreational purposes, to enhance other enjoyable activities, and most people use the drug reasonably. Also, like other mind-altering drugs, alcohol can be used in a way that creates problems for the user and others; in some people it can lead to *physical dependence*, or addiction. People who drink large amounts of alcohol every few days may acquire a *tolerance* for it, so that in order to achieve the same effects, increasing amounts must be ingested. When people addicted to alcohol stop drinking it, they suffer severe *withdrawal symptoms* (tremors, delirium, and convulsions). For an alcohol addict, the experience of stopping cold, or immediate cessation, is a harrowing one which dramatizes its toxic physical effects. The short-term toxicity of alcohol is apparent in the ease of overdosing to the point of acute sickness, loss of consciousness, or even death.

Alcohol, then, has the potential to produce effects as serious and diverse as any other drug. Psychological dependence and physical dependence characterized by the tolerance-withdrawal syndrome are possible outcomes for excessive users. An estimated 18 million Americans over 18 years old experience problems with alcohol abuse; alcoholism will afflict between 3% and 10% of all Americans at some point in their lives (Vaillant, 1983; U.S. Department of Health and Human Services, 1987). More people are excessive users of alcohol than of any other mind-altering substance. Alcohol abuse and dependence is the most common of all mental disorders, and alcohol abuse is more highly associated with violence and crime than any other drug (Bucholz and Robins, 1989). The most typical addict in America is not a heroin junkie but an alcoholic.

Drug Use as Deviance: Laws and Perceptions

Obviously, not all drug-taking is considered deviant. Medications that alter states of consciousness may be taken legally under the direction of a physician, with no deviant stigma attached to the taker. Indeed, some mind-altering substances, such as caffeine, nicotine, and alcohol, may (with certain age restrictions) be taken freely in the United States without legal sanction or severe negative reactions from others. Employers permit (and often encourage) coffee breaks because caffeine is a performance-enhancing drug. In American society, some people are *encouraged* to take controlled mind-altering drugs—for example, those that seem to improve behavior or make otherwise difficult people easier to deal with, such as Ritalin for schoolchildren, antidepressant drugs like Prozac, and other antipsychotic drugs. Even an illegal drug such as marijuana may be used among some groups of people with no negative stigma or sense of impropriety.

These observations suggest that two dimensions of drugs are particularly important when considering them from a sociological viewpoint. First is the drug's legal status: legal or illegal. Second is how the drug's use is perceived by others: Is it considered proper, normal use, or improper, deviant abuse? These two dimensions should be examined together (as in Table 6.1) when considering drug use as deviance. By combining a drug's legal status and perceptions of use, we can see that:

- Many drugs may be taken legally without the user ever being stigmatized as deviant.
- Taking legal drugs may result in negative reactions from others if the dosage is extreme, or it interferes with the user's ability to perform normal social roles.
- A drug may be illegal, but its use may be so widespread that it is regarded as normal and acceptable. Marijuana is an example, particularly in regard to its use and the perception of its use by many young people and those who become regular users in the 1960s and 1970s.
- Some drugs are both illegal and widely considered improper and dangerous to use.

We should be aware that the legal status of any drug can change over time. For example, the manufacture, sale, or transportation of alcohol was illegal in the United States between 1919 and 1933, but it has been legal under certain restrictions since. Likewise, cocaine was a frequent ingredient in patent medicines in 19th-century American society; it was even part of the original formula for Coca-Cola. A drug's image among large segments of the population can also change. Marijuana gained sharply in rate of use and popular acceptance from the early 1960s to the early 1980s, after which it began to level off, declining into the early 1990s.

America's Drug Problem

Most Americans use mind-altering substances regularly. Some frequently used drugs, such as caffeine, nicotine, and alcohol, are legal. Others, such as marijuana,

Table 6.1   Legal Status and Perceptions of Drug Use in the United States

Perception of Use: Attachment of Stigma	LEGAL STATUS	
	Legal	Illegal
Proper use: Low or no stigma	Drugs prescribed by physician in the prescribed dose	Marijuana (particularly among some young people)
	Coffee, nicotine	Use of illegally obtained prescription drugs, often on the job
	Alcohol (in moderation)	
	Methadone (prescription)	
Improper use: High stigma	Overdose or extended unprescribed use of a prescription drug (e.g., Valium)	Cocaine
		Heroin
		LSD
	Alcohol (regular drunkenness or alcoholism	STP

cocaine, and heroin, are illegal. Millions of prescriptions are written annually for a host of other drugs that have mind-altering potential. *All* of them, whether illegal or not, can be harmful if abused. Excessive, prolonged use of caffeine can cause heart problems; the nicotine addiction of tobacco smokers is responsible for over 300,000 deaths each year; and alcohol abuse or addiction kills thousands and costs billions annually in the United States. Cocaine, heroin, and to a lesser extent marijuana can be harmful to excessive users. However, the greatest costs of the "illegals" must be measured in terms of (1) their connection to crime, (2) the drain on criminal justice resources attempting to control them, and (3) the poisoning of foreign relations by international drug trafficking (Nadelmann, 1989; Chambliss, 1992).

There *is* a drug problem in this country, but there is also a great deal of mystification and misinformation about it, due to political and media exploitation (Orcutt and Turner, 1993). Regardless of its political appeal, the goal of a "drug-free America" is doomed by inconsistency and simplicity. It is inconsistent because only the "illegals" are taken seriously, despite the enormous problems associated with all drug abuse. While government programs and groups like Mothers Against Drunk Driving (MADD) urge less drinking, the alcohol industry inundates the media with advertising to increase it. There was inconsistency also in the public insistence of the Reagan and Bush administrations on a "war on drugs" while they allowed the making of secret deals with international drug merchants in order to finance illegal interference in wars in Central America. Law enforcement crackdowns intended to restrict the supply of illegal drugs regularly consumed by about 10% of Americans have had little effect (Kraar, 1988; Kupfer, 1988). Indeed, current drug policies may induce problems worse than the ones they are intended to solve. For example, AIDS is spread among intravenous (IV) drug users, increasing the threat of the disease to the general population. Most people who inject drugs choose this as the most efficient way to administer a substance to which they are addicted and which is expensive because it is prohibited, and users share needles because they are not available without prescription. Thus it is not so much heroin *use* as it is heroin (and needle) *prohibition* that causes the high rate of HIV infection among heroin users. In the face of these realities, a simple "Just say no" campaign directed at children cannot be an effective solution to the drug problem. The theory and research presented in this chapter point to social policy alternatives that are more likely to succeed.

MAJOR DRUGS AND THEIR EFFECTS

The number of chemical substances known to have the potential to alter states of consciousness runs into the thousands. However, only a relative few are regularly used nontherapeutically in the general population. Recognizing that the examples we provide are far from exhaustive, we will concentrate on the most readily available and most commonly used drugs, particularly those that are illegal or frequently abused.

Drugs may be classified in any number of ways; Table 6.2 presents some characteristics of the typology we will use in our discussion. The principal headings in this typology, which is based on the psychoactive properties and typical mind-altering effects of drugs, are:

1. Central nervous system stimulants.
2. Central nervous system depressants.
   a. Analgesics.
   b. Sedative-hypnotics.
3. Hallucinogens.
4. Others (marijuana, hashish).

Central Nervous System Stimulants

Stimulants of the central nervous system produce wakefulness and alertness. Caffeine (in coffee, tea, and some soft drinks) and nicotine (in tobacco products) are two widely used, largely unrestricted, legal stimulants. Amphetamine is prescribed by physicians to treat depression, fatigue, appetite control, and hyperactivity in children. The prescription amphetamine most often used illegally in the United States is found in Desoxyn, Methedrine, Dexedrine, and Benzedrine. Because amphetamine increases alertness, much nonmedical use, rather than being recreational, is concentrated in certain occupational categories such as truck driver or assembly-line worker. College students are also more likely than the general public

Table 6.2   A Typology of Drugs and Their Effects

Drug Type	Subtype	Examples	Perceptual Effects	Psychological Dependence	Physical Dependence	Tolerance
Central nervous system stimulants		Amphetamine, cocaine, caffeine, nicotine	Produce arousal, alertness, inhibit fatigue and lethargy	Yes	Possible	Yes (sensitization with cocaine)
Central nervous system depressants	Analgesics	Narcotics: opium, morphine, heroin, codeine. Also, Percodan, Methadone, Demerol	Reduce perception of pain	Yes	Yes	Yes
	Sedative-hypnotics	Alcohol, barbiturates, Valium, Librium, Miltown, Quaalude, Sopor, Parest	Produce drowsiness, relaxation, sleep	Yes	Yes	Yes
Hallucinogens (psychodelics)		LSD, mescaline, psilocybin, STP, DMT, peyote	Variable central nervous system effects	Yes	No	Yes
Others		Marijuana, Hashish	Variable effects	Possible	No	No

Sources: Goode, 1978: 197–198; Clinard and Meier, 1985: 174–175.

to use amphetamine. In one survey, during the six months prior to questioning, 3% of household members surveyed said they had used stimulants nonmedically, compared to 21% of college students (New York State Division of Substance Abuse, 1981).

Extended amphetamine use can lead to malnutrition and dehydration due to appetite suppression. The drugs are usually ingested orally as pills but can be injected intravenously. Large-dose intravenous users, called "speed freaks," have a tendency to be highly irritable and even violently dangerous when "crashing" from several hours or days of "speeding." While amphetamine does not cause physical dependence, repeated use does lead to tolerance and the potential for abuse.

Cocaine, also a central nervous system stimulant, is an illegal drug that has undergone rapidly increasing use in the United States. Medically, cocaine is prescribed as a local anesthetic; its original recreational use produced effects when "snorted" through the nose. In moderate doses, cocaine usually makes the user more active, talkative, self-confident, and happy. Its effects are short-lived—a half hour or so. While it produces no physical dependence, to maintain a stable effect over time, users must follow each dose of the drug with a large subsequent dose (Zimmer and Morgan, 1995).

Because of the relatively high price of cocaine, it acquired an upper-status, chic image among illicit drug users in the 1970s; between the mid-1970s and mid-1980s the number of people who said they had ever used cocaine went from 5.4 million to 22.2 million. Its use spread to all segments of the population, especially after the introduction of crack, a crystallized form. In 1985, about 5.8 million Americans said they had used cocaine within the past 30 days, and emergencies and deaths associated with its use grew threefold between 1981 and 1985. Both the increased use and medical incidents are related to changing routes of administration and availability. For example, freebasing (inhaling the vapors of purified cocaine) increased from less than 1% of users in 1977 to 18% in 1985. Crack, the crystallized form of cocaine which is usually smoked, represents a new marketing technique that dramatically lowered the price of a cocaine "high," thus removing the price barrier that previously inhibited experimentation by the young (Kozel and Adams, 1986).

Cocaine use has followed the downward trends in lifetime, annual, and current prevalence rates for virtually all drugs in recent years. Among the total population in 1991, 0.9% reported ever having used cocaine and 1.9% reported ever having used crack (U.S. Bureau of the Census, 1993: 137). These rates, however, are based on self-reports to the National Household Survey on Drug Abuse conducted by the U.S. Substance Abuse and Mental Health Services Administration, and they vary widely by age, sex, and race. There are reports that a decline in *daily* use of cocaine had not occurred by 1990 (Kandel, 1991). In other words, heavy use of various forms of cocaine, particularly crack, appears to have increased. Among seriously delinquent youth, their involvement simultaneously in IV drug use, prostitution, and sex-for-crack exchanges places them at extraordinarily high risk of HIV infection (Inciardi et al., 1991; Ratner, 1993).

Cocaine has become a highly lucrative business for dealers and exporting countries. During 1980, U.S. cocaine imports were estimated to be around 100,000 pounds. An illicit retail dealer could then sell the drug, cut with various other substances, for between $100 to $140 per gram. The National Narcotics Intelligence Consumer's Committee estimated that in 1980 cocaine imports had a retail value between $27 and $32 billion. Van Dyke and Byck (1982) note that

> If the cocaine trade were included by *Fortune* in its list of the 500 largest industrial corporations, cocaine would rank seventh in volume of domestic sales, between the Ford Motor Company and the Gulf Oil Corporation. Based on U.S. estimates, the monetary value of Bolivia's cocaine exports may now surpass the value of the country's largest legal industry, tin. Colombia's more highly refined cocaine exports total about $1 billion annually, half the value of the coffee crop. (128)

In the late 1980s, about 80% off the cocaine coming into the United States flowed through Colombia, whose drug trade was then valued at about $4 billion (*Economist*, 1988: 63). In 1990, the retail value of cocaine sold in the United States was over $17 billion (Office of National Drug Control Policy, 1991).

Central Nervous System Depressants

Analgesics. Opiates, derived from the opium poppy, have long been used to reduce physical pain and mental suffering. Narcotic use and addiction are not recent phenomena in this country but date back to the Civil War. Morphine, a very effective painkiller used liberally during the Civil War, created an addiction so extensive it was called "the soldier's disease." Later, with no legal restraint, opium and morphine were often used as active ingredients in the patent medicines peddled at traveling medicine shows with the claim that they would cure everything from warts to insomnia. Prior to passage of the Harrison Narcotic Act in 1914, which required prescription by a registered physician for purchase, narcotics were readily available. Having no particular trouble obtaining drugs to support their habits, addicts did not form a distinct social group or subculture.

Narcotics include opium, morphine, heroin, codeine, and numerous synthetics such as Percodan, Methadone, or Demerol. They may be smoked, eaten, or injected. If used frequently, users may rather quickly become tolerant of them and physically dependent. Withdrawal from narcotics is accompanied by restlessness, nausea, cramps, vomiting, and anxiety. Contrary to popular myth, withdrawal is not nearly as uncomfortable or dangerous as is withdrawal from alcohol or barbiturates. Although in the public image a racial-ethnic minority, urban, streetwise heroin junkie is the focal point of the drug problem in American society, narcotics addiction does not fit neatly into categories of race, ethnicity, or social class. For example, rates of narcotics addiction for doctors and nurses are sufficiently high that it can be regarded as an occupational hazard.

The incidence of first-time heroin use rose sharply from the mid-1960s to the early 1970s and has since dropped off. Many of today's heroin users were initiated into its use during this period (Kozel and Adams, 1986: 972). Recent increases in heroin-related morbidity (incidence of disease) and mortality rates are apparently related to the growing availability of low-price "black tar" heroin. The sharing of contaminated needles in intravenous drug use has also increased the possibility of death from AIDS for heroin users. In several urban areas such as New York City, IV drug users have replaced homosexual men as the highest risk group for AIDS (Boffey, 1988).

Ethnographic profiles of heroin users in the past decade have provided some valuable insights into the facts of daily life surrounding this drug. It is estimated that while between 300,000 and 400,000 heroin users have not received treatment, they have not fallen into depravity as a result (Hanson et al., 1985). A considerable proportion of regular users of psychoactive substances, including heroin and cocaine, continue to function effectively at work and in other areas of social life (Winick, 1991). Street addicts go through different phases in their addiction careers. Involvement in criminal activity more frequently precedes drug use (Faupel, 1991), but it is not the drug per se that leads addicts into crime. The crimes of drug abusers—such as the heavily discounted sale of stolen property—actually make them valued members of ghetto communities as suppliers of otherwise expensive goods (Johnson, 1985). Such accounts paint a picture of heroin addiction, street addicts, and their communities that is far more complex than the typical drug-crazed image of popular culture (Stephens, 1991).

Sedative-Hypnotics. This class of drugs is the most commonly used in the United States. When they are taken recreationally, as in the case of alcohol, the intent is usually relaxation. Medically, barbiturates and the newer benzodiazapines are prescribed to relieve anxiety and produce sleep.

A number of characteristics of the sedative-hypnotics make them potentially dangerous drugs. First, they tend to disorient the user's perception of time. As a result, a person unaware of how frequently the drug is being taken may easily take a lethal overdose. Second, sedative-hypnotics dull physical reactions. The tragic effects of this characteristic are apparent from the statistics on alcohol-related automobile accidents and fatalities. Berry and Boland (1977: 118) estimate that alcohol abuse is present in *at least* 50% of all fatal auto accidents, and the economic cost of motor vehicle accidents attributable to alcohol abuse approaches $5 billion annually. Third, both alcohol and barbiturates are addictive and habitual users increase their tolerance rapidly. The withdrawal symptoms are severe, painful, and longer lasting and more life threatening than for any other class of drugs. Fourth, particularly in the case of barbiturates, there is only a small difference between a dosage necessary for a high and one that is potentially lethal. Added to the greater likelihood of miscalculation brought on by a disoriented time perspective, this increases the chances of death due to overdose. Fifth, the effects of two or more sedative-hypnotics taken together can be more intense than simply the sum of separate doses. This multiplier or interaction effect of drug mixing is best known in regard to barbiturates taken with alcohol.

Sedative-hypnotics, particularly tranquilizers prescribed to treat anxiety, were major contributors to what one observer in the early 1970s called "an epidemic of *legal* drug use" in the United States (Rogers, 1971). Through advertising in medical journals, pharmaceutical companies urge doctors to prescribe an array of drugs such as Quaalude, Parest, Sopor, Ribrium, Valium, Miltown, Equanil, and Placidge to quiet people's nerves.

Since the mid-1970s, however, there has been a sharp downturn in the use of these and may other pharmaceuticals. For example, Valium, the largest selling prescription drug in America, which was prescribed by doctors over 61 million times in 1975, had dropped to 33.6 million prescriptions by 1980 (Goode, 1984: 47). Greater caution and reluctance on the part of physicians to prescribe these drugs resulted from the federal Comprehensive Drug Abuse Prevention and Control Act, which rates drugs according to "abuse potential" and medical utility.

While the trend is clearly down for some types of psychotherapeutic drugs, medical use is still widespread, especially among adults over 25 and women. Nationally in 1982, 16% of women and 16% of all persons aged 50 or older reported prescription use of a psychotherapeutic drug within the last month. Apparently replacing Valium as the most popular prescription drug of the 1990s have been antidepressants such as Prozac. By 1993, Prozac had accounted for $1.2 billion in sales and had been prescribed for more than 6 million people in the United States since its introduction in 1988 (Freudenheim, 1994). The judgment of experts like Peter Schrag (1978) remains relevant; he argues that Americans are taught to believe in a "pill for every problem" approach to dealing with their personal troubles. Rather than searching for the causes and solutions for their anxieties in the social, political, and economic environments, they learn to blot out their symptoms with a small tablet, effortlessly swallowed.

Hallucinogens

The use since ancient times of natural hallucinogens or psychedelics such as psilocybin from mushrooms has usually been in conjunction with religious rituals, the way Native Americans have used peyote from cactus. Today, LSD (lysergic acid diethylamide) is the most widely used drug in this class, because it is relatively easy to produce synthetically and low in cost. LSD is the most potent of known psychoactive substances; only 50 to 200 micrograms—a quantity barely visible to the naked eye—is required for an average "trip." It has extreme effects on mood and perception; users describe them as ranging from beautiful and revealing to frightening. In addition to seeing spectacular images of brilliant colors and shimmering sounds, a user may lose the sense of time, feel indistinguishable from the setting, and experience sharp disorientation to the physical and social worlds.

Despite the unquestioned potent psychoactive properties of hallucinogens, little is known about the dangers of their use. We know that no physical dependence or addiction is possible with them; people do not get physically hooked as with the depressants. Tolerance does occur, and regular users require increasingly larger doses to maintain the same level of effect. But because tolerance to most hallucinogens builds quickly and thoroughly, there is little chance of developing "dependence." After several consecutive days of use, there is almost no psychoactive effect. There have been reports of psychotic or panic reactions to hallucinogens—bad trips—that may have contributed to accidental deaths or suicides, but, contrary to popular opinion, such incidents are quite rare. Fort (1969) estimates that damaging behavior connected with psychedelics may occur between 1 and 10,000 and 1 in 100,000 experiences with the drugs. The long-term physical effects of LSD have not been determined. There is evidence that the substance can cause genetic damage in laboratory animals given large doses, but there is no evidence of similar effects in humans who generally ingest fairly small amounts.

Sensational attention was accorded the usage of psychedelic drugs in the media during the 1960s and early 1970s, but they have never been widely used in the general population. There is some evidence that the incidence rose slightly through the mid-1970s and then began to decline. Even at its peak, probably fewer than 10% of Americans ever used a hallucinogen, and most committed users tend to use these drugs for only a few years and then stop. In 1990, 9% of American high school seniors said they had ever used hallucinogens, compared to 16% in 1975 and 12% in 1986 (Johnston et al., 1987; Kandel, 1991).

Other Drugs: Marijuana

Marijuana, or cannabis, is the *illegal* drug used most widely for recreational purposes in the United States. National surveys have established that about 80 million Americans have used marijuana at least once, and slightly less than 15 million say they have used it within the past month (Kandel, 1991). It is most often smoked but occasionally used in foods or tea, and it comes from a plant that grows wild in many parts of the world. The flowering part and upper leaves of the female plant are dried and crushed into a tobaccolike consistency or a powder. The psychoactive ingredient in marijuana is THC (tetrahydrocannabinol), which can vary from a trace in the case of cannabis grown in the United States to 5% in varieties grown in Jamaica or Southeast Asia. Hashish is a still more potent form usually imported into the United States from the Middle East.

The subjective effects of marijuana vary; Americans have reported one or more of the following: euphoria, disoriented time perspective, heightened appetite, relaxation, inability to concentrate, a tendency to think that many things are funny, giggling, increased appreciation of art or music, and rambling and unfocused thoughts. Many of these feelings or perceptions are apparently conditioned by cultural expectations, because in other societies marijuana may produce quite different sensations. For example, in Jamaica rural laborers smoke the drug while they work (as opposed to during relaxation) and they report almost none of the same effects North American users do (Rubin and Comitas, 1975). When very large doses of synthetic THC are taken, the effects can be more intense, including hallucinations and transient psychotic episodes.

Marijuana is a nonaddictive substance and produces neither tolerance nor physical dependence. There have been claims that marijuana use, especially frequent long-term use, causes a number of pathological conditions, including brain damage, genetic abnormalities, lowered level of testosterone, cancer, paranoia, short-term memory loss, and lack of motivation. The evidence in respect to any of these alleged harms is generally weak. Probably the only definite evidence of physical damage from smoking marijuana is the finding that chronic use appears to irritate and reduce the efficiency of the lungs in the way cigarette smoking does (Morgan, Riley, and Chesher, 1993). Marijuana use does not inevitably lead to the use of other illegal drugs such as heroin. It is the first illegal drug that most people take and, for the most part, the only illegal drug they will ever use.

TRENDS AND PREVALENCE OF DRUG USE

The late 1960s and early 1970s was a watershed period for American drug use. Prior to 1962 an average of only 2% of the population reported ever having had experience with an illicit drug. Between 1962 and 1967, greater numbers of youth and young adults began using marijuana, although throughout this period the use of stronger illicit drugs, such as heroin, cocaine, or hallucinogens, remained at very low levels. The lifetime experience with illicit drugs among youths and young adult men and women doubled in all regions of the United States during this period. Marijuana use grew faster among whites than other racial groups, eradicating the racial differences from earlier years. Well into the 1970s drug-use rates among the young continued to climb. By 1977 more than half the young adults ages 18–25 and more than one-fourth of the youths ages 12–17 who were surveyed reported having used marijuana at least once (Cisin, Miller, and Harrell, 1977: 15–16).

The recent tendency, even among young people, has been downward. For example, 11 percent of high school seniors reported using marijuana daily in the previous month in 1978, and by 1991 the proportion had dropped to 2% (Reuter, 1992). Findings from the National Household Survey on Drug Abuse, presented in Table 6.3, show that in 1992 alcohol was the drug most people reported having used in the previous year, followed by cigarettes and marijuana. Among young adults (18–25 years old), 78% said they had used alcohol and 23% reported using marijuana in the previous year. This age group had the highest use rates for every other category of drugs listed; for alcohol, they were virtually tied with adults ages 26–34. The percentages in Table 6.3 also make it apparent that age is a key to understanding American patterns of drug use. It remains true that "age so overshadows...[other] demographic factors that it is tempting to conclude that some degree of illicit substance use (e.g., marijuana experimentation) may be a typical maturational experience for many of today's youth and young adults—a part of 'growing up'"(Cisin, Miller, and Harrell, 1977: 9–10). Overall, Kandel (1991) concludes, "Illicit drug use is a youth phenomenon. The proportion in the general population ever having used any illicit drug is more than twice as high among those aged 18 to 34 as among those 35 and older" (376–377).

Despite the association of drug use with youth, there has been a trend in the past few years for higher percentages of adults age 26 and older to report they have ever used various drugs. This is because each year a new group of persons enters the

Table 6.3   Percent Reporting Having Used Drugs in Previous Year, Age 12 and
Over, United States, 1992

| | PERCENT OF AGE GROUP | | | |
Substance	Youths (12–17)	Young Adults (18–25)	Adults (26–34)	Older Adults (35+)
Stimulants				
Cocaine	1%	6%	5%	3%
Nonmedical prescription	1	2	2	0.3
Depressants				
Alcohol	33	78	79	63
Nonmedical prescription	1	2	1	0.6
Tranquilizers	1	3	2	1
Heroin	0.1	0.5	0.2	0.1
Hallucinogens				
All types	2	5	1	0.1
Others				
Marijuana/hashish	8	23	14	3
Cigarettes	18	41	39	29

Source: U.S. Department of Health and Human Services, 1993.

older adult category, and they bring with them their experience of first having tried marijuana as youths during the 1970s. As a result, "having tried marijuana is no longer limited to the very young, and current use is no longer extremely rare in the 'middle age' years" (Miller, 1983: 29).

Denise B. Kandel, a leading expert, notes the following trends in drug use:

> The lifetime and period-specific prevalence rates observed in 1990 represent important downward changes in the usage of drugs, which began in 1980 for most illicit drugs and in 1985 for cocaine. These peak periods in usage followed striking increases in the use of illicit drugs in the 1960s and 1970s....In my opinion, the downward trend is real and affects most segments in society, although the decline may occur at different rates in different groups. The trends have been sharpest among whites, and not as strong among blacks, especially those 26 to 34 years old. Among Hispanics, past-year prevalence appears to increase slightly after the age of 25. However, with increasing age, fewer individuals in every ethnic group remain current users of drugs following initiation. (1991: 384, 389)

Kandel points out that drug use among disadvantaged groups, such as school dropouts and the unemployed, has not followed the downward trends observed in the general population (408).

DRUGS, CRIME, AND AIDS

Drugs and crime are intimately linked in the popular imagination, usually incorrectly. In general, there is little evidence that most drugs "cause" violence or crime directly by unleashing aggressive or other asocial tendencies (Chaiken and Chaiken, 1990). To repeat a point made earlier, drug effects depend on numerous interacting variables in the individual, the dosage, and the setting. As we will show below, this is even true of alcohol, the drug more strongly associated with violent behavior than any other, illegal or legal (Nadelmann, 1989; Reiss and Roth, 1993).

The connection between drugs and crime (especially violence), however, is much more closely linked to the effects of drug prohibition and the massive criminal justice enforcement directed at their control. According to Reiss and Roth (1993):

> The illegality of some psychoactive drugs raises their street price above levels that would exist in an open market. The raised price is associated with two different kinds of encounters, each of which carries a risk of violence. First, some drug users commit robberies or burglaries to obtain drugs or money for purchasing drugs. Second, the artificially raised prices create excess profits for drug dealers, which raises the stakes in disputes about marketing practices. Since these illegal markets are not subject to legal dispute resolution mechanisms, violence may be a first resort. (200)

Drug dealing, with its associated violence and crime, becomes concentrated in poor communities where the lack of legitimate employment opportunities makes the criminal drug trade attractive (Johnson et al., 1990). The illegal drug markets in these communities become magnets for risk-seekers carrying weapons; for the increased involvement of youth gangs in the drug market; and for the disorganization and breakdown of crime and violence-inhibiting controls in these neighborhoods. The growing ranks of the impoverished in American society increases the population of those whose bleak life prospects heightens their involvement with illicit drugs—both as takers and in the criminal drug markets.

AIDS poses another threat identified with illicit drugs. Stall, Watters, and Case (1989) describe this threat as follows:

The AIDS epidemic has transformed and elevated to a new order of magnitude the risks associated with intravenous drug use. For the first time, the act of sharing needles now carries with it a risk far greater than those of a one-time drug injection or the legal ramifications of that act. Moreover, the dangers of sharing needles have now spread to even those who may have never once used drugs (i.e., to the sexual partners and unborn children of intravenous drug users). The effects of HIV among IV drug users may even come to touch all residents of some localities. This will happen if state and local governments are forced to increase taxes or costs for medical and social services and/or to curtail valued government services in order to meet the medical costs created by IV drug users with AIDS (1).

In New York City an estimated 200,000 people inject heroin at least once a week. Present seropositivity rates for HIV among IV drug users range from about

50% in New York City to 24% in Baltimore to 15% in San Francisco, with minorities generally having higher rates (Booth, 1988; Peterson and Bakeman, 1989; Watters, 1989; Vlahov et al., 1991). There is frequent sexual activity unprotected by condoms between intravenous (IV) drug users and multiple partners, some of whom are not IV users themselves (Feucht, Stephens, and Roman, 1990; Kane, 1991). As a group, IV drug users are difficult to impact with AIDS prevention messages, and policies to build bridges to this population, as opposed to the use of alienating criminal justice sanctions, are essential (Conviser and Rutledge, 1989; Inciardi, 1990; Oppenheimer, 1991). Methadone treatment, for example, has been found to be effective in reducing IV drug use and needle sharing among heroin addicts (Ball, Myers, and Friedman, 1988). Other interventions include the free distribution of bleach and new needles and treatment on demand (Booth, 1988).

THE COSTS AND CONSEQUENCES OF ALCOHOL ABUSE

No one knows how many alcoholics there are in the United States. Nine million is the figure often cited, but between the problems of defining precisely who is or is not an alcoholic and then accurately counting the cases, this is only a very gross estimate. Studies of various business and government agencies indicated that at least 6% to 10% of an employee population suffered from alcoholism in its early, middle, or late stages (U.S. Senate Hearings, 1977). The lifetime prevalence rate of 14% for alcohol dependence disorders in the general population is more than double that for all illicit drugs combined (Kandel, 1991: 380).

Alcohol is involved in about one quarter of all admissions to general hospitals in the United States; nearly half of convicted criminal justice offenders used alcohol just before committing their offenses; and alcohol plays a major role in the four most common causes of death in males aged 20–40—accidents, suicides, homicide, and cirrhosis of the liver (Vaillant, 1983; U.S. Department of Health and Human Services, 1987). The economic costs of alcohol misuse and alcoholism in 1990 were conservatively estimated at approximately $98.6 billion (Institute for Health Policy, 1993: 16). Reduced productivity was the most costly type of loss, followed by mortality and treatment expenses. Alcohol was the direct, main cause of death for nearly 20,000 people in 1990; the total number of deaths attributable to alcohol as a direct or contributing cause (e.g., in auto accidents or homicides) was almost 100,000. This compares to no more than 30,000 premature deaths due to the direct and indirect effects of illegal drugs and about 400,000 premature deaths from tobacco (Reuter, 1992). Alcohol misuse is present in about 40% of nonpedestrian and pedestrian traffic facilities (*Alcohol Health and Research World*, 1974: 20). A Los Angeles study of nearly 5,000 homicide victims found that alcohol was detected in the blood of 46% of them; in 30% it was at the level of intoxication in most states (Goodman et al., 1986). In a New York City study, Haberman and Baden (1978) found that 58% of cases of unnatural deaths "had an identified problem with alcohol, narcotics, or both; 41% were classified as alcoholics and 28% as narcotics abusers" (2–3). They also reported the following findings:

> Well over half of all homicides of adults in New York City may involve substance abusers as victims, perpetrators, or both. About one-half of all violent deaths are associated with alcohol use, and about the same amount of alcohol use may occur among the offenders in cases involving narcotics users; at present more than two-thirds of the violent deaths in New York City are associated with the use or abuse of these substances. (8)

The amount of resources devoted to the social control of alcohol-related problems is also reflected in arrest data. In 1992, over 2 million abuse violations accounted for 22% of *all* arrests in the United States. A downward trend in arrests for public drunkenness has followed the reclassification of alcohol abuse as a disease rather than a crime in some states, but driving under the influence, drunkenness, and liquor law violations still contribute heavily to national arrest rates.

Less obvious than the toll in death, disease, and treatment or control costs is the burden those with drinking problems place on their families. The spouses of alcoholics, the largest share of whom are women, often go through lengthy periods of denial, self-blame, and stigma management in trying to maintain their marriages and families (Weinberg and Volger, 1990; Wiseman, 1991). The disease model has expanded to encompass not only the alcoholic but also family members, many of whom are said to be afflicted with the "disease" of codependency. For some women, in particular, the tendency to define relationships with alcoholics in terms of codependency becomes a trap; they find themselves forever defined as suffering from an illness and in need of a lifelong process of recovery parallel to that of the alcoholics they love (Asher, 1992).

Trends in Alcohol Use

Despite these enormous costs, the overall trends in alcohol consumption and related hazards in the United States have been in a downward direction. Since the mid-1960s, Americans have generally been drinking more wine and beer and fewer distilled spirits (Hilton and Clark, 1987). The 1987 government report *Alcohol and Health* estimated the annual consumption of pure alcohol per person age 14 and over at 2.65 gallons, the lowest since 1977. (To ingest this amount of alcohol would require drinking 50 gallons of beer, 20 gallons of wine, or more than 4 gallons of distilled spirits.) The percentage who would be classified as moderate to heavy drinkers had declined from 33% in 1979 to 29% in 1985. Cirrhosis of the liver mortality, the most direct health risk from chronic alcohol use, was the lowest since 1959 (U.S. Department of Health and Human Services, 1987). The prevalence of alcohol use among high school students, college students, and other young adults declined only very slightly from the mid-1970s to the mid-1980s (Johnston et al., 1987). Between 1985 and 1990, however, reported use of alcohol during the preceding year by youths (ages 12–17) dropped from 52% to 41%, and by young adults (ages 18–25) it dropped from 87% to 80% (Kandel, 1991).

EXPLANATIONS OF ALCOHOL ABUSE

Alcoholism: The Medical Model

The concepts of alcoholism is both imprecise and contested, and it has been impossible to establish exactly what causes the condition, when it begins in a given individual, and whether a person, once afflicted, can ever be rid of it. This, of course, makes alcoholism different from many other medical conditions such as the common cold or appendicitis. Nevertheless, the medical model of alcoholism has been firmly established by the recognition it has received from prestigious professional and public organizations such as the American Medical Association, the American Psychiatric Association, and the World Health Organization. In 1970 alcoholism was officially designated a disease in the Hughes Act, which established the National Institute of Alcohol Abuse and Alcoholism.

The medical model of alcoholism generally assumes the sequential presence of several factors:

1. An individual predisposition to alcoholism that makes the alcoholic essentially different from the nonalcoholic.
2. Excessive consumption that becomes compulsive.
3. A progressive pattern with a distinct series of phases.
4. Physical dependence (addiction).
5. An assumption that, once afflicted, the only "cure" is to abstain forever.

The Role of Heredity.   For years, studies have indicated a tendency for alcoholism to "run in families." However, if a behavioral characteristic such as excessive drinking appears to be passed down in families, it is not necessarily true that it is transmitted genetically. For example, alcoholism might run in families because alcoholic parents, by their behavior, inadvertently teach their children to drink excessively.

One way to sort out whether alcoholism is familial or genetic in origin is to see whether children of alcoholic parents who are reared away from them have a higher risk of becoming alcoholics than children of nonalcoholic parents. Such a study by Goodwin (1976) indicated that this was the case, even if the children and their parents were separated in early life. Evidence continues to accumulate that heredity is a causal factor in at least some cases of alcoholism (Loehlin, Willerman, and Horn, 1988). Strong evidence for biological vulnerability is provided in findings that certain trait markers are common to those who are at risk of developing alcoholism. These include decreased intensity of reaction to modest ethanol doses for the sons of alcoholics; decreased amplitude of certain brain waves; and different patterns of electroencephalograms (Schuckit, 1987).

On the basis of Swedish research (Cloninger, Bohman, and Siguardsson, 1981), two types of predisposition to alcoholism have been proposed: *milieu-limited*, a susceptibility that occurs in both sexes, is less severe, and requires environmental provocation for onset, and *male-limited*, which occurs only in biological sons of severely alcoholic fathers and gives rise to the early onset of severe alcoholism. Because the milieu-limited type is more frequently involved in alcoholism, environmental factors are considered essential to most cases. We should be cautious to avoid drawing inappropriate conclusions from this evidence, however. It does not mean that all children of alcoholic parents will become alcoholic; nor does it say that not having alcoholic parents is a guarantee against becoming alcoholic. Most "new" alcoholics do *not* have an alcoholic parent. Goodwin (1976) concludes that "severe forms of alcohol abuse may have a genetic predisposition but heavy drinking itself, even when responsible for occasional problems, reflects predominantly nongenetic factors" (74). While some people may run a greater risk of becoming alcoholics due to their genetic backgrounds, genetic predisposition provides only a small portion of the total explanation for alcoholism or alcohol-related problems (Peele, 1986). An adequate explanation of alcoholism must take into account heredity, psychological, and environmental risk factors (Donovan, 1986; Tarter and Edwards, 1987).

The Jellinek Classification and Alcoholics Anonymous. The traditional model of alcoholism has been heavily influenced by the proposal of E. M. Jellinek (1952 and 1960) for a classification of alcoholics and a series of stages from prealcoholism to alcoholism. His four main types of alcoholism, designated by Greek letters, are divided into two disease and two nondisease categories. *Gamma alcoholism* is characterized by increased tissue tolerance to alcohol, adaptive cell metabolism, withdrawal symptoms, and loss of control. *Delta alcoholism* is very closely related to gamma, but "inability to abstain" is substituted for "loss of control." Both of these are considered diseases. In contrast, *Alpha alcoholism* consists of habitual drinking due to psychological dependence, with no serious physical complications. *Beta alcoholism* is characterized by physical complications from alcohol use but with neither physical nor psychological dependence. Alpha and Beta alcoholism are not diseases in the Jellinek formulation. Gamma alcoholism is considered most typical in the United States, and it has become the type targeted by Alcoholics Anonymous.

Jellinek's proposal is that alcoholics progress through a series of stages, from the prealcoholic phase, which might last a few months to several years, to three alcoholic phases, and termination in severe medical complications. The sequence is as follows:

- *Phase I, prealcoholic.* Alcohol is used as a drug to "treat one's nerves." Larger amounts are continually needed to produce the desired effect.
- *Phase II, early alcoholic.* Blackouts during heavy drinking begin. Other symptoms include preoccupation with alcohol: sneaking drinks, accompanied by feelings of guilt; and defense mechanisms such as denial or rationalizations for drinking.
- *Phase III, the crucial phase.* The drinker experiences *loss of control* and a physical demand for alcohol.

- *Phase IV, the chronic or final phase.* This is characterized by uncontrolled "benders," uncontrollable craving, delirium tremens (d.t.'s) and other severe medical problems such as cirrhosis of the liver, malnutrition, and brain damage.

Jellinek took great care to present his model and its proposed stages as tentative working hypotheses, and they remain central to the popular image of alcoholism. They quickly became a part of the ideology of Alcoholics Anonymous (AA), one of the first and most successful social support groups, which had been founded at New York City in 1935 by two former drinkers. The medical model has been remarkably persistent, even in the face of findings that contradict its basic premises (Faulkner, Sandage, and Maguire, 1988). This traditional model is presently under attack from various perspectives. Several critics argue that the medical model is not well supported by substantive scientific findings and has been maintained because it serves variously interested parties such as AA, the temperance movement, and medical associations and research institutes (Robinson, 1976; Schneider, 1978). Public acceptance of the disease image is enhanced by its connection in AA to a repentant role for the alcoholic (Trice and Roman, 1970). Because fundamental middle-class values are invoked in the demand for strict self-control and total abstinence, the medical model fosters a moralistic stance. Other critics (Orcutt, 1976; and Hills, 1980) emphasize the negative consequences of AA's permanent assignment of the alcoholic role: "there is no such thing as a *former* alcoholic— only a *sober* alcoholic." Orcott (1976) observes that the increasing influence of the medical ideology on alcoholism may have the undesirable consequence of locking the alcoholic into a nonresponsible, but stigmatized role" (419).

The traditional view of alcohol dependence is being challenged by evidence from a broad range of studies that have provided the foundation for a different type of model (Pattison, Sobell, and Sobell, 1977). The traditional and alternative models are summarized for comparison in Table 6.4. While the alternative model recognizes alcohol dependence as a serious health problem, it takes a much more flexible view of the development of dependence and does not insist that total abstinence is essential for a person once labeled *alcoholic*. It remains to be seen whether the traditional view, inspired by Jellinek's work as incorporated into the AA ideology, will be dislodged from the central place it has had in popular images of alcoholic dependence.

Sociocultural Models of Alcoholism

Social Stress and Normative Constraints. Robert Bales explains differences in rates of alcoholism among various social or cultural groups in terms of social stress. He proposes that certain social structural conditions may create stress for members of a particular group. For example, the high rate of alcoholism among men in 19th- and early-20th-century Ireland arose first from tension and frustration in a society that denied young men opportunities for sexual or status fulfillment. However, the reaction to the stress is even more likely to take the form of excessive alcohol consumption if the cultural norms of the society encourage drinking—even intoxica-

Table 6.4   Comparison of Traditional and Alternative Models of Alcohol
Dependence

Traditional Model	Alternative Model
1. There is a unitary phenomenon which can be identified as alcoholism.	1. Alcohol dependence summarizes a variety of syndromes defined by drinking patterns and the adverse physical, psychological, and/or social consequences of such drinking. These syndromes, jointly denoted as "alcohol dependence," are best considered as a serious health problem.
2. Alcoholics and prealcoholics are essentially different from nonalcoholics.	2. An individual's pattern of alcohol use can be considered as lying on a continuum, ranging from pathological to severely pathological. Any person who uses alcohol can develop a syndrome of alcohol dependence. Continued drinking of large doses of alcohol over an extended period of time is likely to initiate a process of physical dependence which will eventually be manifested as an alcohol withdrawal syndrome.
3. Alcoholics may sometimes experience a seemingly irresistible physical craving for alcohol, or a strong psychological compulsion to drink.	3. Recovery from alcohol dependence bears no necessary relation to abstinence, although such a concurrence is frequently the case. The consumption of a small amount of alcohol by a person once labeled as "alcoholic" does not initiate either physical dependence or a physiological need for more alcohol by that individual.
4. Alcoholics gradually develop a process called "loss of control" over drinking and possibly even an inability to stop drinking.	4. The development of alcohol problems follows variable patterns over time and does not necessarily proceed inexorably to severe or fatal stages.
5. Alcoholism is a permanent and irreversible condition.	5. Alcohol problems are typically interrelated with other life problems, especially when alcohol dependence is long established.
6. Alcoholism is a progressive disease which follows an inexorable development through a distinct series of phases.	

tion—as a means for relieving stress, especially if the culture fails to provide alternative tension-reducing outlets.

While Bales's theory (1946) appears to be logical and consistent, only recently has it been subjected to a systematic test. In a series of three studies, Arnold S. Linsky and his colleagues used a large archive of state-level indicators of stress, drinking norms, and alcohol-related problems to test Bales's theory. Three separate indicators of stress—"stressful life events," status integration, and relative economic opportunities—were correlated with alcohol-related phenomena, and stress was found to account for 27% of the variation of cirrhosis death rates, 14% of the variation in alcoholism and alcoholic psychosis death rates, and 47% of the variation in alcohol consumption rates (Linsky, Straus, and Colby, 1985: 72). They also found the least heavy drinking in states where local norms discourage alcohol use (Linsky, Colby, and Straus, 1986), and, consistent with Bales, that the relationships between stress and alcohol problems are *strongest* in the context of strong cultural support for alcohol use (Linsky, Colby, and Straus, 1987). Harris and Fennell (1988) found further that the relationship between job stress and alcohol consumption is affected by the person's beliefs regarding the efficacy of alcohol to relieve stress. This research points to the importance of social and cultural factors in the explanation of drinking behavior and suggests that social policies designed to reduce consumption ought to include the reduction of social stressors such as factory closings, unemployment, and geographic mobility, along with policies that discourage alcohol as a mode of tension reduction.

Cultural Variation, Ambivalence, and Integration. Ogden Nash captured a common popular belief about the effects of alcohol with the couplet, "Candy is dandy/But liquor is quicker," referring to the strategy a man might use to assure the amorous response he was seeking from a woman. The implication is that alcohol leads people to let down their guard and let loose—in short, alcohol is presumed to cause people to lose their inhibitions. That the psychological consequences of drinking alcohol in large quantities include the dulled senses and lowered reaction time that are characteristic of depression cannot be denied. However, it does not follow that alcohol necessarily leads to any particular social behavior. In regard to alcohol and violent behavior, for example, Reiss and Roth (1993) state that "the evidence from three decades of studies of animals and humans clearly demonstrates that there is no simple dose-response relationship" (189). Indeed, among the world's various cultures, examples can be found in which alcohol appears to be associated with virtually opposite responses. For instance, MacAndrew and Edgerton (1969), in their comparison of drunken behavior in a large number of societies, found that drinking might characteristically lead (1) to violence in one culture (the Abipone Indians of Paraguay) but passiveness in others (the Yuruna Indians of South America); (2) to increased sexual activity in one (the Tarahumara of Mexico) but no change in sexual activity in others (the Camba of Bolivia); and (3) to gregarious sociable interaction in one (the Mixtecs of Mexico) but solitary withdrawal in another (the Aritama of northern Colombia).

Such differences in social behavior "under the influence" indicate that alcohol does not directly cause certain attitudes or actions and "being drunk" may be better conceived as a learned social role. As MacAndrew and Edgerton put it:

> Rather than viewing drunken comportment as a function of toxically disinhibited brains operating on impulse-driven bodies, we have recommended that what is fundamentally at issue are the *learned* relations that exist among men living together in a society. More specifically, we have contended that the way people comport themselves when they are drunk is determined *not* by alcohol's toxic assault upon the seat of moral judgment, conscience, or the like, but by what their society makes of and imports to them concerning the state of drunkenness. (165; italics added)

Just as there are cultural differences in people's responses to drunkenness, there are variations in rates of alcoholism among ethnic groups. It is *not* true that groups in which drinking occurs frequently will inevitably have high rates of alcoholism. For example, both Orthodox American Jews and Italian Americans drink alcohol with relative frequency, but their rates of alcoholism are low. Actually, more important than the average frequency of drinking as a correlate with rates of alcoholism are the norms that guide drinking when it occurs. Generally, rates of alcoholism are relatively low in groups which by custom integrate drinking with social and religious practices, thus providing clear guidelines for when, how much, and in what situations one should drink (Mizruchi and Perrucci, 1970). As Chafetz (1971) observes:

> Apparently, in cultures which use alcohol but have a low incidence of alcoholism, people drink in a definite pattern. The beverage is sipped slowly, consumed with food, taken in the company of others—all in relaxing, comfortable circumstances. Drinking is taken for granted. No emotional rewards are reaped by the man who shows prowess of consumption. Intoxication is abhorred. Other cultures with a high incidence of alcohol-related problems usually assign a special significance to drinking. Alcohol use is surrounded with attitudes of ambivalence and guilt. Maladaptive drinking, drinking without food, and intoxication are common. (3–4)

Orthodox Jews have been taken as a striking example of the effectiveness of the cultural integration of drinking as a mechanism for preventing alcohol problems. In a classic study, Snyder (1958) observed that Jews probably have very low rates of alcohol abuse because their culture calls for frequent ritualistic drinking which is integrated with family religious practices. Even as Jewish Orthodoxy has declined, the rate of alcohol problems remains low among Jews—a fact that Glassner and Berg (1980) attribute to four "protective processes":

1. Association of alcohol abuse with non-Jews.

2. Integration of moderate drinking norms, practices, and symbolism during childhood by means of religious and secular rituals.

3. Restriction of most adult primary relationships to moderate drinkers.

4. A repertoire of techniques (such as joking about their moderation) to avoid excessive drinking under social pressure.

In contrast, cultural groups with high rates of alcoholism, such as the Irish, are said to emphasize drinking as an activity in itself, often at special locations (bars or pubs) that are separate from other aspects of daily life and rituals (Bales, 1946). Moreover, heavy drinking is apt to be taken as a symbol of manliness, and this reinforces heavy alcohol use as an activity that differentiates men and women. In this sense, drinking—especially heavy drinking—becomes a disintegrating ritual that sets the stage for mixed cultural messages and guilt about alcohol consumption. Attempts to wash away the guilt by overindulgence may contribute to alcohol-related problems in these cultures.

If it is correct that ambivalent, inconsistent, mixed cultural messages about drinking behavior can be said to account for some measure of alcoholism, then some of the alcohol problems in American society can be attributed to a general cultural ambivalence toward alcohol use. Side by side in American society—and frequently in sharp conflict throughout our history—have been temperance groups calling for total abstinence and the banning of alcohol consumption and other forces, including the movies, television, and the liquor industry, enticing people to drink by portraying alcohol as the beverage of the sophisticated and the successful, or the working person who knows how to have a good time. Certainly American culture as a whole does not provide its members with a clear, verified set of guidelines in regard to drinking. This is readily understandable, given the widely varying cultural origins of the American people. The divergence of subcultural norms has not only contributed to ambivalent attitudes and behaviors involving drinking by individuals, but has at times been at the core of national political conflict.

The Social Functions of Drinking.   People in American society are usually quite frank about the intent or even the need to serve alcoholic beverages at social gatherings. Many of us have had occasion to observe that the party will get going after people have a few drinks and loosen up. This fits with the popular belief of alcohol as a disinhibitor; it suggests that a manifest function of drinking is to provide social lubrication—to encourage people to unwind and interact more easily, freely, and naturally. However, as we have noted, drunken behavior varies widely across different cultures, and disinhibition is only one of the numerous possible reactions to drinking, depending on the expectations conveyed by one's culture. In American culture, alcohol is widely believed to be a social lubricant, and people normally react as if it were.

Drinking serves a related social function, latent or less openly acknowledged, that in our society (among others) amounts to temporary suspension of our responsibility for our own behavior. Our beliefs about the disinhibiting effects of alcohol allow us to excuse what would otherwise be considered impolite, outrageous, or even dangerous behavior with the simple phrase, "I guess I was drunk." As MacAndrew and Edgerton (1969) put it, in such societies:

> …the state of drunkenness is a state of societally sanctioned freedom from the otherwise enforceable demands that persons comply with the conventional proprieties. For a while—but just for a while—the rules (or, more accurately, *some* of the rules) are set

aside, the drunkard finds himself, if not beyond good and evil, at least partially removed from the accountability nexus in which he normally operates. In a word, drunkenness in these societies takes on the flavor of *"time out"* from many of the otherwise imperative demands of everyday life. (89–90)

In this sense, drinking is the functional equivalent of ritualized occasions found in societies the world over in which people are briefly permitted to ignore some of the norms that apply to their age, sex, or social status. Mardi Gras, a period of mer-rymaking revelry prior to Lent, appears to fit this cultural pattern. Possibly, when the routine rhythm of social life is punctuated with ritually continued periods of rule vi-olation, the norms of everyday life are made more tolerable for those who are op-pressed and more evident to all. However, in its power to excuse, drinking in our culture may go beyond suspending judgment and responsibility for relatively harm-less transgressions like loud, discourteous, or disruptive behavior. It may, in the minds of some, provide very subtle license for such harmful acts as reckless driving, sexual harassment, rape, wife beating, or child molesting (McCaghy, 1968). Thus, calling "time out" by resorting to the widely accepted excuses "I'm going to get drunk," "I am drunk," or "I was only drunk" serves an important social function in our society: It provides a ready means to cut loose and disavow transgressions. At the same time, this opportunity to deny responsibility may subtly provide some with the license to avoid a measure of the psychic costs (guilt and shame) usually attached to particularly harmful or odious behavior. Taken to this extreme, drinking may be said to be *dysfunctional* in our society. This is certainly the case for direct victims of alcohol abuse such as those killed or injured in drunk driving accidents or those who suffer the daily tribulations of living with an alcoholic family member.

The Politics of Definition. To drink or not to drink has been a political issue in the United States since its founding. In fact, there may be no better example of how deviance is a product of political struggle among various interest groups than Joseph Gusfield's interpretation of the American temperance movement, *Symbol-ic Crusade* (1963). Positions favoring drinking or abstinence have provided a sig-nificant way of distinguishing among subcultures in American society. As we have noted, various religious or ethnic groups have different norms in regard to alco-holic beverages, establishing whether or not, what, when, where, how much, and with whom to drink. Drinking thus is similar to numerous other consumption habits that distinguish various groups and provide people the means to establish their group identity. Thus consumption taboos (e.g., no smoking or alcohol use among de-vout Moslems) or patterns of consumption (e.g., smoking marijuana among some segments of American society) provide a means for group members to say to one an-other as well as to outsiders, "This is our custom—our way of showing who we are." To the things people characteristically consume as food or drink we could add other cultural identifiers, such as their customary clothing (blue jeans or jacket and tie), music preferences (soul, country and western, or classical), or style of speaking (southern dialect or Boston accent).

In mid-19th-century American society, abstinence from drinking was one symbol of middle-class status. At the same time, for the waves of immigrants entering this country from Ireland, eastern Europe, and Italy, drinking alcohol was one of the cultural customs they shared. Thus, in the late 1800s, temperance emerged as a means of distinguishing "native" Americans from immigrants; Protestants from Catholics; middle class from lower class. The political struggle to make temperance the law of the land through an amendment to the Constitution occurred because it had become a *symbol* of social status. Establishing the dominance of that symbol in law became important because "public support of one conception of morality at the expense of another enhances the prestige and self esteem of the victors and degrades the cultures of the losers" (Gusfield, 1963: 5). Passage of the 18th (Prohibition) Amendment in 1919 signaled the dominance of nativist, American Protestantism, just as its repeal in 1993 symbolized the fall of this group from its privileged position. In Gusfield's words,

> The Eighteenth Amendment was the high point of the struggle to assert the public dominance of old middle-class values. It established the victory of Protestant over Catholic, rural over urban, tradition over modernity, the middle class over both the lower and upper strata.
>
> The significance of Prohibition is in the fact that it happened. The establishment of Prohibition laws was a battle in the struggle for status between two divergent styles of life. It marked the public affirmation of abstemious, ascetic qualities of American Protestantism. In this sense it was an act of ceremonial deference toward old middle-class culture. If the law was often disobeyed and not enforced, the respectability of its adherents was honored in the breach. After all, it was *their* law that the drinkers had to avoid.
>
> If Prohibition was the high point of old middle-class defense, Repeal was the nadir.... In the Great Depression both the old order of nineteenth-century economics and the culture of the temperance ethic were cruelly discredited.
>
> The repeal of the Eighteenth Amendment gave the final push to the decline of old middle-class values in American culture. (7)

Thus we can see that behind the drive to establish a particular behavior as officially deviant may lie overarching conflicts of interest and the struggle of status-group politics.

Public Attitudes and Social Policy. Using commonly held ideas to explain deviant behavior exerts a powerful influence on the public policies designed to control it. For example, if people generally believe that alcoholism is the result of some moral failing deep within the alcoholic, they are apt to advocate public responses to drunkenness that emphasize either criminal punishment or repentance. If, instead, the common wisdom attributes alcoholism to psychological or biological illness, public policy is apt to emphasize medical intervention and the decriminalization of drunkenness.

Several researchers have identified changes of this sort. Gusfield (1967) argues that since the early 1800s drinking has undergone two "moral passages," or changes, in the public image of the heavy drinker. The first was from the "repentant drinker" to the "enemy drinker," which transformed the alcoholic from an object of pity to an evil to be stamped out. Central to the effort to stamp out alcoholism was the temperance movement, which was also motivated by status politics. The second major transition of public attitudes was from the "enemy drinker" to the "sick drinker." Linsky (1971) found a similar movement in the explanations of alcoholism and alcohol problems found in popular magazines. Since 1900 there has been a distinct decline in the use of moralistic "free will" and "social criticism" explanations, which place the blame for alcoholism on the corruption of individuals, groups, or institutions. Naturalistic (nonmoralistic) psychological, biological, and sociological explanations have become increasingly prevalent and now dominate the popular imagery.

The American history of changing public attitudes and laws in regard to alcohol stands as testament to Durkheim's (1966) observation that no act or individual is intrinsically deviant; rather, deviance is a product of the collective definition dominant among members of a group at any given moment. Above all, the collective definition that confers the label *deviant* upon any particular behavior or individual can be, and often is, altered over time.

Often with such alterations in deviance definitions come changes in public policy. In 1971, Congress passed the Uniform Alcoholism and Intoxication Treatment Act, urging treatment of public inebriates within the health care system rather than the criminal justice system. As a result, public drunkenness is increasingly (although not completely) being handled through medical intervention (detoxification or drying-out centers and related rehabilitation programs).

The ultimate consequences of this trend are at the moment unclear. On the one hand, it seems futile and unjust to cycle skid row alcoholics in and out of drunk tanks to serve life imprisonment sentences "on the installment plan." James P. Spradley (1970) goes so far as to argue that "incarceration in jail, intended as a *punishment* for public drunkenness, is a *cause* of public drunkenness" (5) because the indignities of being processed and serving time provide an alibi for hitting the bottle upon release. After 30 days in jail, in the words of Spradley's title, *You Owe Yourself A Drunk*. At the same time, the effects of decriminalization and subsequent medicalization of the problem have yet to be demonstrated. It can even be argued that reconceptualizing the problem of public drunkenness has merely substituted a system of medical control (consistent with the public image of the alcoholic as sick) for a system of legal control (outmoded as the public image of alcoholic as enemy fades into the past). It does appear that when assigned the task, medical units formally process drunks they encounter much faster than comparable police units do (Pastor, 1978).

It is clear that the shift away from criminal prosecution of public inebriates is far from complete (Finn, 1985). In 1992, public drunkenness still accounted for over 590,000 arrests annually in the United States, making this crime fourth only to driving under the influence of alcohol, larceny-theft, and drug abuse violations in the number of arrests (U.S. Department of Justice, 1993: 229). Note that these drunkenness arrest figures do not include arrests for driving under the influence, disorderly conduct, or vagrancy, all of which are likely to involve alcohol abuse.

While the problem of alcoholism remains serious in American society, there have been positive signs that Americans are drinking more responsibly. Per capita consumption has decreased slightly; industry sources reveal that sales of alcoholic beverages have declined; and organizations such as MADD (Mothers Against Drunk Driving) and SADD (Students Against Driving Drunk) have apparently had a significant impact on attitudes and behaviors. There is an emphasis on high school educational programs to encourage responsible drinking and public information campaigns designed to encourage informal intervention by friends to prevent drunk driving. Such direct, assertive intervention efforts have been shown to be effective (Collins and Frey, 1992). There is little evidence that legal changes that focus on formal control and prohibition, such as the 21-year-old age requirement, are effective in lowering consumption; instead, there is "considerable evidence that restrictive legislation drives younger drinkers underground, resulting in overall higher consumption rates" (Mooney, Gramling, and Forsythe, 1992). When young people are forced to drink illegally, they do most of it at alcohol-dominated gatherings with maximum intake among same-age peers, out of the view of more experienced drinkers. Rather than a new temperance movement intended to eradicate alcohol from the society, the tendency in public consensus and official policies is to accept alcohol as a normal part of life, while focusing on associated problems such as drunk driving. Thus, as Lender and Martin (1987) predict, in the future the alcohol question "will be a matter not of eliminating alcoholism but of keeping drinking and any problems it creates within limits society can tolerate. This attitude, no matter how unpalatable to some, may represent the new consensus on drinking in America. In some ways, it may represent a more flexible return to the orderly communal ideals of the past" (204).

MARIJUANA USE

Despite the illegality of marijuana, it is, with the exception of alcohol and tobacco, the drug Americans most frequently report ever having used. Not surprisingly, it has been the object of considerable sociological theorizing about why people become regular marijuana users, why they discontinue its use, and how the law should treat the drug and its users.

The Social Learning Explanation

In a manner no different from that used with other types of deviant behavior, much of the research on marijuana use has focused on the question, "Why do they do it?" The answer has frequently been assumed to reside in the individual's psychological motives or need to escape, and avoid facing the realities and responsibilities of daily living. The approach of Howard S. Becker challenges the assumption that some pathological motive must lie behind a behavior such as regular marijuana smoking. He maintains that people frequently have their first experience with marijuana quite by chance when they find themselves in the presence of others who have the drug and can show them how to use it. They probably are not motivated to try it by some deep need to escape. Instead, most marijuana users are *first* motivated to try it out of some vague mixture of curiosity, opportunity, and momentary peer pressure to join in the experience with the group. In the words of Becker (1963):

> Attempts to account for the use of marijuana lean heavily on the premise that the presence of any particular kind of behavior in an individual can best be explained as the result of some trait which predisposes or motivates him to engage in that behavior. In the case of marijuana use, this trait is usually identified as psychological, as a need for fantasy and escape from psychological problems the individual cannot face.
>
> I do not think such theories can adequately account for marijuana use. In fact, marijuana use is an interesting case for theories of deviance, because it illustrates the way deviant motives actually develop in the course of experience with deviant activity. To put a complex argument in a few words: instead of the deviant motives leading to the deviant behavior, it is the other way around; the deviant behavior in time produces the deviant motivation. Vague impulses and desires—in this case, probably most frequently a curiosity about the kind of experience the drug will produce—are transformed into definite patterns of action through the social interpretation of a physical experience which is itself ambiguous. (41–42)

Of course, simply trying marijuana does not guarantee that a person will become a regular user. Becker extends his argument to show how a novice may go through three steps which "leave him willing and able to use the drug for pleasure when the opportunity presents itself" (46). The first step is to *learn the technique* of smoking marijuana (the way it is most often ingested in American society). This includes such particulars as learning how to roll a joint, how to inhale the smoke, how to hold it in the lungs, and how often to do so. Only by learning the proper technique will the drug produce its effects. Those who fail to learn how will not become regular marijuana users.

The second step is to *learn to perceive the effects*, which can be quite subtle. To perceive them, the first-time user is often coached by tutors: "How do you feel? A little bit dizzy? Kind of silly? Are you hungry?" These cues tell the novice what to look for, what to attribute to the substance being smoked.

The third step is to *learn to enjoy the effects*. To feel dizzy, thirsty, or hungry or to misjudge time or spatial relationships are not intrinsically pleasurable experiences. Indeed, some people find the effects of marijuana smoking unpleasant or even frightening; they will not become regular users. Learning to define the effects of marijuana favorably is facilitated by the encouragement of the others with whom one smokes. Only by learning from others what to expect and how to perceive those sensations as pleasant and desired will an experimenter become a regular user.

Becker thus constructs a social learning theory based on the premises that drug use, like any other behavior, is learned, and peer-group influences are highly important to the learning. In regard to substance use, social learning theory proposes that differential association—more frequent interaction and identification with peer groups, family members, and others who accept it than with those who do not—sets the stage for the experience, reinforcement, definitions, and imitation of such use, including alcohol and marijuana (Akers et al., 1979). Recent studies have shown that the greater the number of adolescent friends who use marijuana, the lower the likelihood that a person will expect negative outcomes from use and the greater the person's expectations of positive experiences (Orcutt, 1975). Researchers have repeatedly found that use of marijuana by peers is the most important predictor that a person will become a marijuana user (Kandel et al., 1976; Marcos, 1986), as well as a drug user more generally (Newcomb, Maddahian, and Bentler, 1986; Akers et al., 1989; McGee, 1992). If their friends use marijuana most adolescents will also do so, irrespective of social, psychological, or familial characteristics. One comprehensive test of social learning theory used survey data on adolescent drinking and marijuana use (Akers et al., 1979). The major social learning variables—differential association, differential reinforcement, definitions, and imitation—combined to account for 68% of the explanation of marijuana use and 55% of alcohol use. The most powerful explanatory variable was differential association.

The importance of peer influences in marijuana use is further demonstrated by the similarity of social characteristics that separate smokers from nonsmokers. In a sample of students from 20 New York City colleges, Johnson (1973) found a remarkable sociopolitical homogeneity among users which strongly suggested that marijuana smoking had evolved into an integral part of one segment of the youth subculture. Among nonreligious, politically liberal men who were daily cigarette smokers, 97% had tried marijuana and 62% smoked it at least weekly. This is in contrast to religious, politically conservative, noncigarette-smoking women, only 4% of whom had tried marijuana and none of whom smoked it weekly. In a more recent study, researchers found that lifestyle factors such as educational values, religious commitment, and time spent in peer-oriented activities are more important than race or ethnicity in explaining adolescent drug use (Wallace and Bachman, 1991).

Experimenting with marijuana has become virtually the norm in American society; about half of young adults have done so by the time they reach age 25. Most of them, however, have not been—nor are they likely to be—heavy users. We might ask, therefore, what differentiates those who eventually advance to heavy use. Kaplan et al. (1986) addressed this question in a large study involving over 1,000 young adults who reported using marijuana at least once. Heavy use was defined as daily or near daily use of marijuana for at least a month. The highest correlate with heavy use was the age of first trying it; the younger novices are, the more likely are they to become heavy users. As Kaplan et al. put it, younger age at first use "reflects earlier weakening of social control and involvement with delinquent peers, increasing both the opportunity and motivation to try marijuana and then to escalate use" (57). Feelings of distress around the time one first tries marijuana are negatively related to later use; if trying the drug has adverse consequences, the likelihood of escalated use declines.

Current evidence points consistently to the role of social learning in differential association with drug-using peers as a key to explaining marijuana use among young people. Indeed, some social learning theorists argue that the principles of this approach apply to other substances, both legal and illegal, ranging from alcohol to hallucinogens (Akers, 1973).

Reasons for Discontinuing Use

While some marijuana users have continued to use the drug regularly beyond adolescence into their 30s and 40s, a typically large proportion of youthful users cease smoking as they get older. This is not surprising, since the adolescent worlds of users and nonusers are, despite the distinction in drug-taking, remarkably similar, and users themselves tend to see their use as transient (Glassner and Loughlin, 1987). Marijuana use in the United States typically begins to decline after the 18–25 age category (see Table 6.3 above). Studies of former marijuana users in college indicate strongly that it is not aging per se or a rejection of values common to the marijuana-smoking youth culture that accounts for cessation, but instead significant status changes such as marriage, entry into parenthood, and change of associates after graduation (Henley and Adams, 1973; Yamaguchi and Kandel, 1985). Tom, a 24-year-old, married business major working as a bank executive, is a typical case cited by Brown et al. (1984).

> Tom first tried marijuana when a freshman in college because he says "Everyone was trying it." He reports that he did not get much from the drug at first, but later would become very high, more extroverted and happier than usual, similar to getting drunk. He smoked about one a week for five years, except during his sophomore year, when he "smoked pot every day for six to nine months." He never smoked alone, only with friends.
>
> In his junior year, Tom began limiting his marijuana smoking to weekends because he started going with the girl he later married. She did not smoke, and though he found it no fun to smoke alone, after graduation he stopped completely when he procured a bank position saying, "I was afraid a bust would ruin my career." He says it was not difficult to give up marijuana, although he missed it somewhat at first and might use it again "sometime" in the future. (533–535)

Tom's case, consistent with the survey findings from large numbers of people, underscores the importance of social position and associations, both for the use of marijuana and the cessation of its use. Smoking pot is an activity that almost always begins and continues in the context of strong social group supports. A marijuana user who moves away from these supports into a new social context is apt to stop using it. Thus to Becker's three learning tasks for regular marijuana use—learning the smoking technique, learning to perceive the effects, and learning to enjoy them—we should add an additional condition. The person must continue to associate with groups that have norms and values favorable to recreational pot smoking. The upshot is that from initiation through regular use to cessation, marijuana smoking is a social activity that can be better explained by factors in social situations than by searching for pathological traits in individuals.

Medicine and Morals: Marijuana as a Public Issue

Concern for legal control over marijuana use is largely a 20th-century phenomenon. State legislation to outlaw its possession, sale, or use dates back to the 1920s, and by 1930 16 states prohibited use of the drug. The Marijuana Tax Act of 1937 was the key piece of federal legislation aimed at controlling marijuana on a national level. Until the 1970s, state penalties for use, possession, or sale tended to be very severe, including lengthy jail sentences for possession and even capital punishment for second offenses of selling the drug to minors. By the early 1980s most states had reduced penalties for simple possession, and in 11 jurisdictions there was some form of decriminalization (Inciardi, 1981: 146). In some states possession of marijuana is a low-level misdemeanor with penalties akin to those for parking violations. Perhaps more important, the laws against individual possession or use of marijuana are barely enforced in most jurisdictions—even as the incidence of use among young people has been declining (Musto, 1987). Still, the nascent decriminalization movement of the 1960s and 1970s did not meet with widespread success in the 1980s. The legalization debate is likely to continue without a clear-cut resolution.

Should marijuana use be legalized? One rational way to approach this social policy question is to conduct a cost/benefit analysis of continued criminalization versus decriminalization. James Inciardi (1981) proposes a sensible framework for such an accounting:

> On the one hand, there are the physiological and psychosocial costs of marijuana use—undesirable personality changes, antisocial behavior patterns, alterations in properly coordinated motor activity, psychological dependence liabilities, and the undetermined spectrum of health consequences from the drug's long term chronic use. Viewing these as physical, psychic, and social costs of marijuana use, their prevention could be considered as the *benefits* of criminalization policies *if* existing marijuana statutes were indeed effective in deterring those who might otherwise use the drug.
>
> By contrast, there is a perplexing series of personal, social and economic costs which can be attributed to the very bearing of current antimarijuana laws. The *personal costs* include the temporary, long-term, or even permanent disruptions in users' lives which result from arrest, conviction, sentencing, and incarceration. The *social costs* involve society's loss of productive (or potentially productive) citizens when official adjudication interrupts, prevents, or otherwise limits the pursuit of occupational careers, places users into nonproductive treatment or correctional settings, or when the prisonization and criminalization processes associated with incarceration introduce users to more serious and predatory criminal violations. The *economic costs* can be defined by the total budgetary allocations to the three segments of the criminal justice system—police, courts, and corrections—for the enforcement of the marijuana laws and the processing and management of offenders. (146–147)

Even if such evidence is carefully researched and assembled, it is unlikely that it would convince a substantial number of people to change their minds—either for or against decriminalization—because legalization is more than a simple matter of personal harm or social costs. Marijuana is a symbol. As a consumption habit, it bears significance not unlike the use of alcohol as an identifier of the immigrant, urban, Catholic in the late 19th and early 20th centuries. Marijuana is symbolically linked in the popular mind to a segment of the youth culture originating in the 1960s that was identified as liberal (even radical), sexually promiscuous, and socially irreverent (Goode, 1969). This fact, not objective evidence of costs or benefits, is the bottom line of the decriminalization debate. Perhaps the strongest indication is that although experts representing a broad spectrum of opinion about overall U.S. drug policy agree that the prohibition against use of marijuana for medical purposes is absurd, the prohibition remains (Krauss and Lazear, 1991). To the extent that marijuana remains symbolically attached to the youth culture, and this collectivity remains politically impotent, marijuana legalization remains unlikely. In a manner closely akin to our consideration of Prohibition and its repeal, the debate over marijuana draws us to recognize the inherently political aspects of deviance and the politics of strategies to control it.

THE POLITICAL ECONOMY OF DRUGS

The Promotion of Drugs: The Case of Alcohol

The promotion, production, and sale of alcoholic beverages is big business. The global alcohol market has been estimated at roughly $170 billion, about $40 billion of it in the United States (Cavanagh and Clairmonte, 1985: 1). As can readily be seen in television, newspapers, magazines, and billboards, this industry aggressively advertises its products, not only in the United States but worldwide. Any conclusions about a national or international drug problem must take the global economy into account.

Alcohol has been a part of most cultures for hundreds or thousands of years. Prior to colonial contact, most preindustrial societies considered drinking as a regular part of life. There it was controlled by customs and rituals, and only infrequently did it result in pathological consequences (Singer, 1986: 114). Alcohol use was common; alcohol abuse was rare. Problems of alcohol abuse in these societies have arisen when local customs controlling alcohol use have been destroyed and locally produced alcohol has been replaced by products commercially promoted and distributed. When the consumption of alcohol is driven by the profit motive of outside producers rather than the customary patterns established over many generations, excessive drinking becomes far more common.

In industrializing societies, problems of alcoholism have tended to become especially acute for lower-status or working-class men who drink to relieve social stress or use drinking as a means of expressing class solidarity (Park, 1983). Indeed, employers in the 19th century encouraged working-class alcohol abuse as a means of labor control, not unlike the encouragement of opiate use to control Chinese railroad laborers on the western frontier (Singer, 1986: 123). Likewise, in the contemporary, labor-intensive agricultural economy, migrant workers may be paid with rations of alcohol. Drunken or drugged workers are less likely to object vigorously to poor working conditions.

Paralleling the destruction of traditional customs that controlled drinking and the encouragement of drinking as an integral part of industrial development has been the enormous growth and power of the alcohol industry. Huge corporations, as opposed to local breweries or stills, are the producers of most of the world's alcohol today. In pursuit of profits, these companies have focused on consolidation of the global market and have aggressively sought to expand alcohol consumption. The transformation from small local firms to the giant corporations that dominate today's national and international markets can be seen in respect to the U.S. brewing industry. In the short span of 20 years, from 1961 to 1981, the top six U.S. breweries jumped from control of 38% of the American market to 83%. The largest company, Anheuser-Busch, moved from 9.5% to 30.4% of the market in this period (Cavanagh and Clairmonte, 1985: 54). Similar market restructuring has occurred in the wine and spirits industries. The results include concentration on output and retailing; increased opportunities for collusive business practice; and conglomeration with other industries such as soft drinks and tobacco, which allows profits to be funneled from one corporation to another for development and marketing. As these transnational corporate conglomerates grow, they have more resources and become more adept at using international networks to promote their products. They are especially successful at mass-marketing techniques that associate social drinking with images of youth, sports, leisure, fun, and "style" (Singer, 1986).

Faced with declining consumption among established drinkers in the United States, probably as a result of increased health and safety concerns, the industry has responded by targeting new markets, especially among minorities, the young, and women, particularly women in professional occupations. It has also targeted people in less-developed countries (Ridlon, 1988). The strategy of exporting and aggressively promoting unhealthful products when health consciousness or legal restrictions limit marketing opportunities in this country follows the precedent established in respect to cigarettes, infant formula, and pesticides, among other products (Michalowski and Kramer, 1987; Schmeisser, 1988). In response to a similar strategy by the alcohol industry, less-developed countries increased their alcohol imports between 1972 and 1980 by a factor of four, from $325 million to $1.3 billion per year (Slevaggio, 1983).

In sum, alcohol is the world's most widely used mind-altering substance. The drug's use has been long established; but, worldwide its abuse has been growing. To understand this we must appreciate the transformation of alcohol production from local breweries, vintners, and stills to giant transnational corporations that search the world for opportunities to *increase profits* by advertising their products with mass-marketing techniques. The encouragement of drug use is a significant part of the contemporary global economy. As the case of opiates and heroin illustrates, such encouragement has existed since the beginning of international commerce almost 400 years ago.

The Prohibition of Drugs: Opiates and Heroin

When considering the control of drugs, we usually think of (1) restricting access to certain legal drugs by placing their distribution under the supervision of a physician, or (2) attempting to deter their use by making them illegal to use, possess, or sell. Of course, attempts to limit drug use in either manner are relatively recent phenomena. Up until the end of the 19th century, virtually any substance, including opiates, was available to anyone who could pay the going market price, and the primary controls on use were social and informal. Particularly during the 1800s, the United States was populated with thousands of addicts, in all social classes, who fed their habits quietly and unobtrusively from the endless, unrestricted supply of legal drugs.

Perhaps even more astonishing in historical perspective is the fact that Western European nations, including the United States, were until relatively recent times actively and openly engaged in the promotion of opiate drug traffic. William J. Chambliss (1978) has pieced together the story of how, between the 15th and 19th centuries, opiates became an important commodity in the worldwide domination of capitalist economic systems through the expansion of colonial empires. His account provides an excellent example of how historical experience in the promotion of the opiate trade laid the foundations of habits, institutions, and economic relationships that now make reversal of our policy toward drugs a difficult task at best.

Opium has been used since antiquity. It comes from the juice of a poppy that grows chiefly in a warm, mountainous region stretching from Turkey to Southeast Asia. The Turks, who grew most of the ancient world's supply, carried small quantities of the substance to the East over trade routes. Chambliss points out, however, that widespread use throughout the world—especially in the Far East—came with expansions of the capitalist world economy outward from Europe. Beginning in the 1500s, the Portuguese, the Dutch, and the English colonized much of Asia as they searched for products, raw materials, new markets, and labor. The Portuguese were the first to recognize the potential of the opium trade in Asia to provide a substitute for a portion of the gold and silver they sought. After driving out the Asian traders, they began purchasing the drug from Turkish and Indian traders and then trading it for such local products as spices and tea, which they could sell at a good profit in Europe.

As the European powers fought over Asian colonies during the next three centuries, the Dutch gained the upper hand in Indonesia and much of Southeast Asia. The colonial powers expanded into the interior of Asia, using the opium trade as a way to pay for the spices, tea, and silk they acquired. Turkey was gradually replaced as the main opium-growing area by India, where it was mainly produced by the British East India Company, a private firm granted political and economic power over the colony by the British government. According to Chambliss (1978: 118), the company's representatives in Asia and the colonial governments were responsible for spreading opium addiction throughout Asia, especially among the Chinese.

The Chinese government, recognizing the economic and human price of a country infested by opium, attempted to resist by restricting imports. When British pressure to expand the opium trade persisted, war ensued. The Opium War between England and China (1839–1842) and a subsequent conflict in 1856 eventually forced Chinese legalization of opium smoking and trading. As a consequence, the potential market was vastly increased, and British traders proceeded to spread the opium habit to the interior of China. Chambliss (1978: 120) points out that "the market was truly overwhelming and couched in the nicest of terms when the head of one of the major opium-trading companies noted that opium was a 'comfort to the hard-working Chinese'" (Owen, 1934: 243).

Eventually Chinese growers began to compete with British traders, thus diminishing British profits in the opium trade. However, British capitalism in China flourished in the second half of the 19th century, in large part due to the profits and labor advantages provided by the opium trade. By the end of the century, Chambliss notes, "it was often said that China had become a nation of opium smokers" (120).

Meanwhile, European colonial powers were tightening their hold on Asia. A combination of famine, war, and a poor economic situation in the latter part of the 19th century caused a large number of opium-smoking Chinese of South China to emigrate to cities of Southeast Asia such as Saigon and Bangkok. Chambliss traces the development:

> In every major city of Southeast Asia from Rangoon to Saigon, colonial and local governments developed opium dens. The opium trade as carefully, albeit corruptly, organized by an unholy alliance between colonial officials, local governments, and a new class of entrepreneurs who were given government franchises to import and sell opium. Opium sales provided 40–50% of the income of colonial governments. (McCoy, 1972: 63 and Wen, 1961: 52–75) Opium profits helped finance the railways, canals, roads, and government buildings as well as the comfortable living conditions of colonial bureaucrats.... Opium became the mainstay of the government revenues. It was simultaneously the main thread on which the working class hung and was ensnared into providing labor for the European trade with these nations. It was opium, not religion, that was the opiate of the masses in Southeast Asia. By the 1940s there were in Indochina (Cambodia, Laos, and Vietnam) over 2,500 opium dens providing 45% of all tax revenues and an immeasurable percentage of the unclaimed salaries to both local and colonial government officials. (McCoy, 1972: 76) (121–122)

Although the American opium trade was not quite as extensive as that of the British, it was large and profitable and contributed to industrial development by providing significant capital. Profits from opium trading were invested in the textile mills which proliferated in New England following the introduction of the power loom in 1814. Chambliss points out "the neat paradox that opium helped create a labor force for capitalist expansion in Asia and America and the profits from the opium trade provided the capital for the development of the factory system in New England" (122). Moreover, the introduction of opium and heroin in the United States came with the importation of Chinese coolies to work the gold and silver mines of the West and build railroads across the continent. At this time, opium smoking was an ideal medium for dulling the pain of workers who were laboring without the comfort of their families under the most horrible conditions. The employers considered the laborers' opium smoking an advantage. By controlling the importation and distribution of opium, they made a profit selling it to workers, and the threat of withdrawing the supply was enough to forestall many potential labor complaints.

By the late 1800s, Western mining and railroad construction declined, massive European immigration was supplying a large body of cheap labor and reducing the need for a drugged, suppliant army of laborers. The British now controlled the bulk of the opium market, thereby further reducing American participation. In 1886, the United States passed the first antiopium legislation ever, making it illegal to trade in the substance. This is not to say, however, that the opium and heroin business disappeared. After the interruptions of the two World Wars, the heroin industry continued to grow until recently. In 1980, it was estimated that the annual gross sales of heroin in the United States were between $7 and $9 billion (McNicoll, 1983: 19). In 1991, it was put at $12.2 billion (Office of National Drug Control Policy, 1991).

Analogous to the tendency toward corporate takeovers and the trend toward concentration of economic power in "legitimate" American business, the illicit heroin industry was undergoing a transitional period during the late 1970s and 1980s. During that time there was warfare among competing groups of middlemen supplying drugs in Latin America and Europe. Despite this instability and the huge resources poured into the American war on drugs, most drugs, including heroin, are as readily available on the streets today as they were 30 years ago. What Chambliss said of the heroin industry in 1978 remains true:

> …[I]t will continue to thrive, to expand, to reap large profits and to support large numbers of law enforcement people, politicians and specialists in illegal business.
> The heroin industry is a mainstay of the political economy of much of the capitalist world and it shall not be eliminated any more readily than the automobile, banking or construction industries. (138–139)

Two things must be emphasized from this account of the rise of the opiate industry. First, the history of political and economic policy toward any particular behavior, no matter how severely condemned and sanctioned today, may reveal that it was at one time legal, exploited, and even encouraged. To understand today's social problems requires a historical perspective. Second (and related to the first), we should bear in mind that each generation establishes modes of exploitation that may come back to haunt their progeny. The early colonial capitalist empires promoted and profited from the opiate trade, with no concern for the addicted. Today governmental attempts to stem that trade face a massive international network whose roots took hold with legitimation by those same governments 200 years ago. "For whatsoever a man soweth, that shall he also reap" (Galatians 6: 7).

DRUGS AND SOCIAL POLICY

Throughout this chapter we have suggested that there are no easy answers to the problems associated with drugs. The reasons have to do with both demand and supply. Around the world, in nearly every culture, during almost every historical era, people have used mind-altering substances. To eliminate their use is inconceivable, as the failed American experiment with the prohibition of alcohol suggests (Levine and Reinarman, 1991). Moreover, certain drugs, even addictive drugs such as alcohol and tobacco, are at the heart of major "legitimate," transnational industries with enormous profits and power to protect their interests. The demand for drugs is great, and for some of them it is heightened by effective mass marketing. Likewise, in regard to supply, drugs are big international business—the alcohol and tobacco industries, the pharmaceutical companies that make huge profits from mood-altering drugs like Prozac, the international cartels that deal in marijuana, cocaine, or heroin. The retail value of illegal drugs sold in the United States in 1990 has been estimated at over $40 billion (Office of National Drug Control Policy, 1991). In either case—with legitimate or illegal drugs—as long as there is demand, the suppliers will find ways to meet it and profit from it.

The major thrust in U.S. policy in respect to illicit drugs—particularly marijuana, cocaine, and heroin—has been aimed at supply. One approach has been to eliminate the drugs through crop control at the source countries. This has proved extremely difficult because, for example, stopping coca leaf production in one country merely pushes production to another. Moreover, drug production and trafficking have become *the* major industry in Latin America countries such as Colombia, where thousands of people, from peasant growers to wealthy drug merchants and the politicians they bribe, have no interest in curtailing the drug trade. For Peru alone, it is estimated that the drug economy is worth at least $2 billion (Morales, 1989). Indeed, agencies within the U.S. government have appeared to work at cross-purposes. The Justice Department may seek to undermine and limit drug trafficking, while the State Department and the CIA encourage it by dealing with the drug traffickers (Mills, 1986; Cockburn, 1987; Kwitny, 1987; Wisotsky, 1987; Chambliss, 1992).

Interdiction efforts to stop drugs from entering the country have a poor record of success because of the huge U.S. borders to protect, the large number of people who cross them regularly, and the relatively small bulk of the illicit substances that agents are seeking to intercept. Supply reduction strategies sponsored abroad are doomed to failure (Falco, 1992). Even if interdiction could succeed, it is likely that Americans would then turn to drugs grown or produced synthetically within this country; about half of the marijuana consumed here is domestically grown (Weisheit, 1990). Moreover, control attempts ranging from attacking international drug-dealing organizations to street-level enforcement directed against local pushers have had only limited effectiveness. In sum, the realities of demand and supply in a global market involving both licit and illicit drugs makes the elimination of drug use feasible only in a worldwide police state. U.S. attempts to enforce prohibition have proved inefficient, costly, and counterproductive (Nadelmann, 1992).

Are there any viable social policy options? Some directions are suggested by answers to the following questions.

1. Are drugs harmful? Yes. Drugs have the *potential* to be harmful, especially when used in excess. This is true whether the drug in question is alcohol, marijuana, cocaine, heroin, or many of the legal drugs currently available either by prescription or over the counter. Depending on a host of variables—dose, individual physiology, mode of ingestion, social setting, and the like—mind-altering substances can have various effects. They may either impair or improve the performance of certain tasks; have damaging or beneficial physiological effects; or become habit-forming or addictive in time, for some people. Some drugs, such as heroin used intravenously, impose secondary harms on addicts because prohibitions against it encourage dangerous forms of use, such as needle-sharing.

2. Does drug use inevitably lead to excess? No. For example, millions of people throughout the world use alcohol responsibly in a controlled manner, even though it has the potential to be addictive. Likewise, millions of people have used illicit drugs such as marijuana, cocaine, or opiates occasionally or even regularly without becoming addicted (Zinberg, 1984; Wisotsky, 1986; Winick, 1991).

3. Are those who are addicted to drugs likely to be crazed or criminal? No. Prior to the late 19th century there were no restrictions on drug sale or use in the United States. Narcotics, especially morphine, were used extensively in patent medicines, and thousands of Americans, from Civil War soldiers to middle-class housewives, were addicts (Goode, 1989). Crime was not associated with addiction, as it is today in the United States. This results when addicts must obtain illegal drugs on an expensive black market (Anglin, 1983) and turn to crime to pay the high cost of supporting their habit.

4. Can drug use be eliminated from American society? No. The facts of both demand and supply militate against elimination. Prohibition is a fanciful goal. Goode (1984) has put it well. *"The only realistic approach to the drug problem is to develop methods not to eliminate drug use or even reduce it drastically, but to live with it and make sure that drug users do not seriously harm themselves and others"* (276; italics in original).

5. Is there presently a reasonable balance in American drug control policy? No. Our drug policy has been overwhelmingly focused on supply-side reduction through massive criminal justice effort (Bayer, 1991). During the 1980s, the federal budget for drug control increased from $1.5 billion at the start of the decade to $6.7 billion in 1990. Enforcement, as opposed to treatment and prevention, accounted for between 70% and 80% of these resources. Arrests for drug offenses and prison populations both have swelled, at enormous cost (Reuter, 1992). American drug policy could benefit greatly by borrowing from successful foreign models such as the Dutch "harm reduction" strategy, which minimizes the role of criminal justice enforcement. In its place there is an emphasis on treating drug addiction within a public health model that provides for education, prevention, and outreach with service to addicts (Oppenheimer, 1991). This is particularly essential in respect to IV drug use; building bridges to addicts in order to encourage behavioral changes is a

key to stemming a major avenue for the AIDS epidemic to spread further to the general population.

Some Rational Approaches

The theory and research cited in this chapter point to some sensible approaches to drug policies, briefly described in the following paragraphs:

Be *honest* about the effects of drugs. Hysterical, inaccurate claims about the effects do more harm than good (Reinarman and Levine, 1989). To claim or even imply that smoking marijuana inevitably leads to hard-drug use is patently false, and the experience of literally millions of Americans tells them so. Scare tactics based on exaggeration or false information ultimately hamper the credibility of attempts to convince people of the genuine harmful effects of drugs.

Second, *discourage all drug abuse*. This includes alcohol and tobacco, as well as illicit drugs. The techniques to discourage abuse should include accurate public education through the schools and media; package warning labels; limits—possibly even bans—on advertising; high taxation to discourage use; and legal controls on when, where, and how the drug can be publicly consumed. For example, the opening times of bars could be curtailed, as they are in England, and alcohol could be made available only when ordered with food. Liquor stores could have limited hours. Prohibitions on where tobacco can be used in public are expanding, with public support. Enforced for the most part informally, these laws demonstrate the possibility for controlled use as an alternative to outright prohibition.

Third, step back from a counterproductive emphasis on criminal control of all drugs and *move toward decriminalization* of drug use. Police measures, from local to international in scale, have proven to be massive failures at enormous costs in terms of dollar and civil liberties (Goode, 1984; Brecher, 1986; Hamowy, 1987; Nadelmann, 1988; 1989). This is *not* to say that drugs like heroin ought to be legally uncontrolled and freely available to anyone, any more than alcohol should be. Rather, we ought to:

- Eliminate the pressure on addicts to support their now-illegal habits through other illegal activities—especially property crimes (Johnson et al., 1985).
- Try to undermine the massively overpriced international market in illicit drugs.
- Avoid criminalizing the nonaddicted user.
- Make it possible for addicted users to live relatively normal lives until they are willing or able to attempt detoxification.
- Resist further intrusions into citizens' private lives through the expansion of random drug testing (Zimmer and Jacobs, 1992).
- Experiment with noncriminal alternatives to controlled use (Kaplan, 1983; Trebach, 1982, 1987).

In addition, we ought to emphasize—through public education of the sort that has been remarkably effective in respect to cigarettes, despite massive countermeasures by the tobacco industry—that drug use of any sort carries with it risks, and for a person who chooses to be a user the price can be high. Decriminalization of drugs does not necessarily imply advocacy of their use.

Fourth, for drug users, especially addicts, *provide substantial support for a wide variety of treatment programs*. Addiction treatment of all sorts—whether for alcohol, tobacco, cocaine, crack, or heroin—is difficult and uncertain (Vaillant, 1983; Peele, 1985). We ought to be open-minded and willing to experiment with approaches such as narcotic addict maintenance programs, therapeutic communities, and support groups like Alcoholics Anonymous.

Fifth, we all need to recognize our responsibility as citizens to help create social environments—in our families, friendships, communities, and the nation—that *provide opportunities for human fulfillment*. Some people undoubtedly take drugs to block out the pain of despair. America's urban ghettos are filled with people for whom street commerce in illicit substances and services is the most attractive and economically rewarding employment available. The markets for illegal drugs have historically been found in low-income, minority communities, and it is their residents who suffer most the daily burdens of high addiction and drug-related crime (Kornblum, 1991). Social policies must be aimed at alleviating physical and psychological misery at the bottom of the class structure (Skolnick, 1992). The reasons both buyers and sellers pattern their lives around drugs must be minimized. Throughout the society we need to encourage moral values of health, moderation, self-control, social consciousness, and personal responsibility for our actions (Peele, 1988).

SUMMARY

The meaning of the term *drug* varies widely; in this chapter, drugs are considered to be physical substances ingested or injected into the body with the intention of altering moods or perceptions. Drugs alone do not have specific effects. Drug effects grow out of an interaction of factors, including the chemical properties of the substance, the physical and mental condition of the user, and the setting in which the drug is taken.

Alcohol is a drug, a central nervous system depressant that is potentially addictive. Frequent users acquire a tolerance for it, and alcohol addicts suffer severe withdrawal symptoms. The other major drugs and their effects were also reviewed. Historically in the United States, the period from 1962–1967 marks the initiation of widespread marijuana use. Use rates of almost all recreational drugs then climbed, but that trend has peaked in recent years, and rates for some recreational drug use have begun to decline. Age overshadows all other demographic characteristics (race, rural-urban, social status) in differentiating drug users. Young adults have the highest rates in every recreational drug-use category except cigarettes.

Drugs are linked to crime primarily through the creation of artificially high prices and violence-prone illegal markets, encouraged by hard-edged prohibition policies that rely on the criminal justice system. Even alcohol, the drug most associated with violence in American society, has various effects on people depending on numerous individual and social factors. The illegal drug markets that are usually found in poor, minority communities place a terrible burden on those who have the least resources to help them cope. The highest rates of AIDS infection are now found among intravenous drug users, who are becoming a conduit for introduction of the disease into the general population. Public health measures, including clean needle distribution, methadone maintenance programs, adequate treatment facilities, and education need to replace the law enforcement approach that presently marginalizes IV drug users.

We began our explanations of drug abuse with alcoholism. At a biogenetic level of explanation, some evidence supports the likely role of hereditary predispositions to alcoholism among some people. The best-known conceptualization of alcoholism is the Jellinek disease model, which has been part of the Alcoholics Anonymous ideology for many years. There have been recent criticisms of and challenges to this traditional model. At the sociological level of explanation we considered the role of social stress and normative constraints on drinking. Differences in the drinking patterns of ethnic groups point to the importance of norms and cultural integration in respect to alcohol abuse. How people act when they are drunk varies greatly from culture to culture. Being drunk is not simply a matter of losing one's inhibitions. Moreover, there are cultural differences in rates of alcoholism. Usually, alcoholism rates are low in groups whose customs integrate drinking with social and religious practices that provide clear guidelines for when, how much, and in what situations one should drink. In American culture, drinking seems to perform the latent function of allowing a time out from normal expectations of proper behavior.

The history of changing laws regarding alcohol is an excellent example of the political side of the deviance defining process. Prohibition and its repeal were the outgrowth of intense political struggles among various interest groups. Not only laws governing alcohol use, but public images of alcoholism have changed over time and have influenced public policy.

One of the principal explanations of marijuana use has been social learning theory. The evidence strongly points to the role of social learning in differential association with peers as a key to understanding marijuana use among young people. Likewise, cessation of marijuana use is heavily influenced by one's social situation. The issue of decriminalizing marijuana is intensely political. Marijuana's role as a youth culture symbol and the moral overtones of the argument are apt to drown out rational cost/benefit analyses in the public debate.

The role of huge transnational corporations in the promotion of alcohol introduced a discussion of the political economy of drugs. Worldwide, the local production of alcohol is being replaced by aggressively advertised and marketed products produced by the corporations making up the international alcohol industry. In pursuit of profits, these companies are targeting the young, women, and people in less developed countries as potential users.

Our review of the history of opiates revealed that attempted legal restrictions on trafficking and use are rather recent. Indeed, throughout much of the period from the 16th to the 20th centuries, Western countries, especially Britain and the United States, actively promoted the lucrative opium trade. Today's international heroin industry is rooted in a prior political economy of exploitation.

We also considered some guidelines for sensible social policies regarding drug use: honest, accurate public information; discouragement of all drug abuse; movement toward decriminalization; a shift of emphasis away from criminal enforcement toward harm reduction; support for a wide variety of treatment programs; and greater attention to alternative means for human fulfillment throughout the society.

REFERENCES

Akers, R.
1973   *Deviant Behavior: A Social Learning Approach.* Belmont, CA: Wadsworth.
Akers, R. L., Greca, A. L., Cochran, J., and Sellers, C.
1989   "Social Learning Theory and Alcohol Behavior Among the Elderly." *Sociological Quarterly* 30: 625–638.
Akers, R. L., Krohn, M. D., Lanza-Kaduce, L., and Radosevich, M.
1979   "Social Learning and Deviant Behavior: A Specific Test of a General Theory." *American Sociological Review* 44: 636–655.
Alcohol Health and Research World
1974   "The Economic Costs of Alcohol Misuse." *Alcohol Health and Research World*, Winter: 19–26.
Anglin, M. D.
1983   "Drugs and Crime: Behavioral Aspects," Pp. 636–643 in *Encyclopedia of Crime and Justice.* New York: Free Press.
Asher, R. M.
1992   *Women with Alcoholic Husbands: Ambivalence and the Trap of Codependency.* Chapel Hill: University of North Carolina Press.
Bales, R. F.
1946   "Cultural Differences in Rates of Alcoholism." *Quarterly Journal of Studies on Alcohol* 6: 482–498.
Ball, J. C., Myers, C. P., and Friedman, S. R.
1988   "Reducing the Risks of AIDS through Methadone Maintenance and Treatment." *Journal of Health and Social Behavior* 29: 214–226.
Bayer, R.
1991   "Introduction: The Great Drug Policy Debate—What Means This Thing Called Decriminalization?" *Milbank Quarterly* 69: 341–363.
Becker, H. S.
1963   *Outsiders: Studies in the Sociology of Deviance.* New York: Free Press.

Berry, R. E., and Boland, J. P.
1977   *The Economic Cost of Alcohol Abuse.* New York: Free Press.
Boffey, P. M.
1988   "More Drug Treatment Centers Are Urged." *The New York Times*, June 5, p. 28.
Booth, W.
1988   "AIDS and Drug Abuse: No Quick Fix." *Science* 239: 717–719.
Brecher, E. M.
1986   "Drug Laws and Drug Law Enforcement: A Review and Evaluation Based on 111 Years of Experience." Pp. 1–27 in B. Segal (ed.), *Perspectives on Drug Use in the United States.* New York: Haworth.
Brown, J. W., Glaser, D., Waxer, E., and Geis, G.
1974   "Turning Off: Cessation of Marijuana Use after College." *Social Problems* 21: 527–538.
Bucholz, K. K., and Robins, L. N.
1989   "Sociological Research on Alcohol Use, Problems, and Policy." *Annual Review of Sociology* 15: 163–186.
Cavanagh, J., and Clairmonte, F. F.
1985   *Alcoholic Beverages: Dimensions of Corporate Power.* New York: St. Martin's Press.
Chaiken, J. M., and Chaiken, M. R.
1990   "Drugs and Predatory Crime." Pp. 203–239 in M. Tonrey and J. Q. Wilson (eds.), *Drugs and Crime.* Chicago: University of Chicago Press.
Chafetz, M.
1971   "Introduction." Pp. 1–4 in *First Special Report to the U.S. Congress on Alcohol and Health.* Washington, DC: National Institute on Alcohol Abuse and Alcoholism.
Chambliss, W. J.
1978   "The Political Economy of Smack: Opiates, Capitalism and the Law." Pp. 115–141 in R. J. Simon (ed.), *Research in Law and Sociology*, Vol. I. Greenwich, CT: JAI Press.

1992   "The Consequences of Prohibition: Crime, Corruption, and International Narcotics Control." Pp. 15–32 in H. H. Traver, and M. S. Gaylord (eds.), *Drugs, Law and the State*. New Brunswick, NJ: Transaction.

Cisin, I., Miller, J., and Harrell, A. V.
1977   *Highlights from the National Survey on Drug Abuse: 1977*. Washington, DC: National Institute of Drug Abuse.

Clinard, M. B., and Meier, R. F.
1985   *Sociology of Deviant Behavior*. New York: Holt, Reinhart and Winston.

Cloninger, C. R., Bohman, M., and Siguardsson, S.
1981   "Inheritance of Alcohol Abuse." *Archives of General Psychology* 38: 861–868.

Cockburn, L.
1987   *Out of Control*. New York: Atlantic Monthly Press.

Collins, M. D., and Frey, J. H.
1992   "Drunken Driving and Informal Social Control: The Case of Peer Intervention." *Deviant Behavior* 13: 73–87.

Conviser, R., and Rutledge, J. H.
1989   "Can Public Policies Limit the Spread of HIV among IV Drug Users?" *Journal of Drug Issues* 19: 113–128.

Donovan, J. M.
1986   "An Etiologic Model of Alcoholism." *American Journal of Psychiatry* 143: 1–11.

Durkheim, E.
1966   *The Rules of Sociological Methods* originally published in 1938. Translated by S. A. Solovay and J. H. Mueller; edited by G. E. G. Catlin. New York: Free Press.

Economist
1988   "Getting Gangsters Out of Drugs." April 2; pp. 11–12.

Edwards, G., Arif, A., and Jaffe, J.
1983   *Drug Use and Misuse: Cultural Perspectives*. New York: St. Martins.

Falco, M.
1992   "Foreign Drugs, Foreign Wars." Daedalus 121: 1–14.

Faulkner, W., Sandage, D., and Maguire, B.
1988   "The Disease Concept of Alcoholism: The Persistence of an Outmoded Scientific Paradigm." *Deviant Behavior* 9: 317–322.

Faupel, C. E.
1991   *Shooting Dope: Career Patterns of Hard-Core Heroin Users*. University of Florida Press.

Feucht, T. E., Stephens, R. C., and Roman, S. W.
1990   "The Sexual Behavior of Intravenous Drug Users: Assessing the Risk of Sexual Transmission of HIV." *Journal of Drug Issues* 20: 195–213.

Finn, P.
1985   "Decriminalization of Public Drunkenness: Response of the Health Care System." *Journal of Studies on Alcohol* 46: 7–23.

Fort, J.
1969   *The Pleasure Seekers: The Drug Crisis, Youth and Society*. Indianapolis: Bobbs-Merrill.

Freudenheim, M.
1994   "The Drug Makers Are Listening to Prozac." *The New York Times*, January 9: p. F7.

Glassner, B., and Berg, B.
1980   "How Jews Avoid Alcohol Problems" *American Sociological Review* 45: 647–664.

Glassner, B., and Louglin, J.
1987   *Drugs in Adolescent Worlds: Burnouts to Straights*. New York: St. Martin's.

Goode, E.
1969   "Marijuana and the Politics of Reality." *Journal of Health and Social Behavior* 10 (June): 83–94.

1978   *Deviant Behavior: An Interactionist Approach*. Englewood Cliffs, NJ: Prentice-Hall.

1989   *Drugs in American Society*, 3rd ed. New York: McGraw-Hill.

Goodman, R. A., Mercy, J. A., Loya, F., Rosenberg, M. L., Smith, J. C., Allen, N. H., Vargas, L., and Klots, R.
1986   "Alcohol Use and Interpersonal Violence: Alcohol Detected in Homicide Victims." *Journal of Public Health* 76: 144–149.

Goodwin, D.
1976   *Is Alcoholism Hereditary?* New York: Oxford.

Gusfield, J. R.
1963   *Symbolic Crusade*. Urbana: University of Illinois Press.

1967   "Moral Passage: The Symbolic Process in Public Designations of Deviance." *Social Problems* 15: 175–188.

Haberman, P. W., and Baden, M. M.
1978   *Alcohol, Other Drugs and Violent Death*. New York: Oxford University Press.

Hamowy, R.
1987   *Dealing with Drugs: Consequences of Governmental Control*. Lexington, MA: Lexington Books.

Hanson, B., Beschner, G., Walters, J. M., and Bovelle, E.
1985   *Life with Heroin: Voices from the Inner City*. Lexington, MA: Lexington Books.

Harris, M. M., and Fennell, M. L.
1988   "A Multivariate Model of Job Stress and Alcohol Consumption." *Sociology Quarterly* 29: 391–406.

Henley, J. R., and Adams, L. D.
1973   "Marihuana Use in Post-Collegiate Co-horts: Correlations of Use, Prevalence Patterns, and Factors Associated with Cessation." *Social Problems* 20: 514–520.

Hills, S. L.
1980   *Demystifying Social Deviance*. New York: McGraw-Hill.

Hilton, M. E., and Clark, W. B.
1987   "Changes in American Drinking Patterns and Problems, 1967–1984." *Journal of Studies on Alcohol* 48: 515–522.

Inciardi, J. A.
1981   "Marijuana Decriminalization Research: A Perspective and Commentary." *Criminology* 19: 145–159.
1990   "HIV, AIDS and Intravenous Drug Use: Some Considerations." *Journal of Drug Issues* 20: 181–194.

Inciardi, J. A., Pottieger, A. E., Forney, M. A., Chitwood, D. D., and McBride, D. C.
1991   "Prostitution, IV Drug Use, and Sex-for-Crack Exchanges among Serious Delinquents: Risks for HIV Infection." *Criminology* 29: 221–235.

Institute for Health Policy
1993   *Substance Abuse: The Nation's Number One Health Problem*. Princeton, NJ: Robert Wood Johnson Foundation.

Jellinek, E. M.
1952   "Phases of Alcohol Addiction." *Quarterly Journal of Studies on Alcohol* 13: 673–684.
1960   *The Disease Concept of Alcoholism*. New Haven, CT: Hillhouse Press.

Johnson, B. D.
1973   *Marihuana Users and Drug Subcultures*. New York: Wiley.

Johnson, B. D., Goldstein, P. J., Preble, E., Schmeidler, J., Lipton, D. S., Spunt, B., and Mither, T.
1985   *Taking Care of Business: The Economics of Crime by Heroin Abusers*. Lexington, MA: Lexington Books.

Johnson, B. D., Williams, T., Dei, K. A., and Sanabria, H.
1990   "Drug Abuse in the Inner City: Impact on Hard Drug Users and the Community." Pp. 9–67 in M. Tonrey, and J. Q. Wilson (eds.), *Drugs and Crime*. Chicago: University of Chicago Press.

Johnston, L. D., O'Malley, M., and Backman, J. G.
1987   *National Trends in Drug Use and Related Factors among American High School Students and Young Adults, 1975–1986*. Rockville, MD: National Institute on Drug Abuse.

Kandel, D. B.
1991   "The Social Demography of Drug Use." *Milbank Quarterly* 69: 365–414.

Kandel, D. B., Treiman, D., Faust, R., and Single, E.
1976   "Adolescent Involvement in Legal and Illegal Drug Use: A Multiple Classification Analysis." *Social Forces* 55: 438–458.

Kane, S.
1991   "HIV, Heroin and Heterosexual Relations." *Social Science and Medicine* 32: 1037–1050.

Kaplan, H. B., Martin, S. S., Johnson, R. J., and Robbins, C. A.
1986   "Escalation of Marijuana Use: Application of a General Theory of Deviant Behavior." *Journal of Health and Social Behavior* 27: 44–61.

Kaplan, J.
1983.   *The Hardest Drug: Heroin and Public Policy*. Chicago: University of Chicago Press.

Kornblum, W.
1991   "Drug Legalization and the Minority Poor." *Milbank Quarterly* 69: 415–435.

Kozel, N. J., and Adams, E. H.
1986   "Epidemiology of Drug Use: An Overview." *Science* 234: 970–974.

Kraar, L.
1988   "The Drug Trade." *Fortune*, June 20, pp. 27–38.

Krauss, M. B., and Lazear, E. P.
1991   *Searching for Alternatives: Drug-Control Policy in the United States*. Stanford, CA: Hoover Institution Press.

Kupfer, A.
1988   "What To Do About Drugs." *Fortune*, June 20, pp. 39–41.

Kwitny, J.
1987   *The Crimes of the Patriots: A True Tale of Dope, Dirty Money and the CIA*. New York: W. W. Norton.

Lender, M. E., and Martin, J. K.
1987   *Drinking in America: A History*. New York: Free Press.

Levine, H. G., and Reinarman, C.
1991   "From Prohibition to Regulation: Lessons from Alcohol Policy for Drug Policy." *Milbank Quarterly* 69: 461–494.

Linsky, A. S.
1971   "Theories of Behavior and the Image of the Alcoholic in Popular Magazines, 1900–1966" *Public Opinion Quarterly* 34: 573–581.

Linsky, A. S., Colby, J. P., and Straus, M. A.
1986   "Drinking Norms and Alcohol-Related Problems in the United States." *Journal of Studies on Alcohol* 47: 384–393.

1987   "Social Stress, Normative Constraints and Alcohol Problems in American States." *Social Science and Medicine* 24: 875-883.

Linsky, A. S., Straus, M. A., and Colby, J. P., Jr.
1985   "Stressful Events, Stressful Conditions, and Alcohol Problems in the United States: A Partial Test of the Bales Theory." *Journal of Studies on Alcohol* 46: 72–80.

Loehlin, J. C., Willerman, L., and Horn, J. M.
1988   "Human Behavior Genetics." *Annual Review of Psychology* 39: 101–133.

MacAndrew, C., and Edgerton, R. B.
1969   *Drunken Comportment: A Social Explanation.* Chicago: Aldine.

Marcos, A. C., Bohr, S. J., and Johnson, R. E.
1986   "Test of a Bonding/Association Theory of Adolescent Drug Use." *Social Forces* 65: 135–161.

McCaghy, C. H.
1968   "Drinking and Deviance Disavowal: The Case of Child Molesters." *Social Problems* 16: 43–49.

McCoy, A. W.
1972   *The Politics of Heroin in Southeast Asia.* New York: Harper and Row.

McGee, Z. T.
1992   "Social Class Differences in Parental and Peer Influence on Adolescent Drug Use." *Deviant Behavior* 13: 349–372.

McNicoll, A.
1983   *Drug Trafficking: A North-South Perspective.* Ottawa: North-South Institute.

Michalowski, R. J., and Kramer, R. C.
1987   "The Space Between the Laws: The Problem of Corporate Crime in a Transnational Context." *Social Problems* 34: 34–53.

Miller, J. D.
1983   *National Survey on Drug Abuse: Main Findings, 1982.* Rockville, MD: National Institute on Drug Abuse.

Mills, J.
1986   *The Undergraduate Empire: Where Crime and Governments Embrace.* Garden City, NY: Doubleday.

Mizruchi, E. H., and Perrucci, R.
1970   "Prescription, Proscription and Permissiveness: Aspects of Norms and Drinking Behavior." Pp. 234–253 in G. L. Maddox (ed.), *The Domesticated Drug.* New Haven, CT: College and University Press.

Mooney, L. A., Gramling, R., and Forsyth, C.
1992   "Legal Drinking Age and Alcohol Consumption." *Deviant Behavior* 13: 59–71.

Moore, M.
1988   "Drug Trafficking." *National Institute of Justice, Crime File.* Washington, DC: U.S. Department of Justice.

Morales, E.
1989   *Cocaine: White Gold Rush in Peru.* Tucson: University of Arizona Press.

Morgan, J. P., Riley, D., and Chesher, G. B.
1993   "Cannabis: Legal Reform, Medical Use and Harm Reduction." In N. Heather, A. Wodak, E. Nadelmann, and P. O'Hare, *Psychoactive Drugs and Harm Reduction: From Faith to Science.* London: Whurr.

Musto, D. F.
1987   "The History of Legislative Control over Opium, Cocaine, and Their Derivatives." Pp. 37–71 in R. Hamowy (ed.), *Dealing with Drugs: Consequences of Government Control.* Lexington, MA: D. C. Heath.

Nadelmann, E. A.
1988   "U. S. Drug Policy: A Bad Export." *Foreign Policy* 70: 83–108.
1989   "Drug Prohibition in the United States: Costs, Consequences and Alternatives." *Science* 245: 939–947.
1992   "Thinking Seriously about Alternatives to Drug Prohibition." *Daedalus* 121: 85–132.

Newcomb, M. D., Maddahian, E., and Bentler, P. M.
1986   "Risk Factors for Drug Use among Adolescents: Concurrent and Longitudinal Analyses." *American Journal of Public Health* 76: 525–531.

New York State Division of Substance Abuse
1981   "Drug Use among New York State Household Population." Unpublished paper.

Oppenheimer, G. M.
1991   "To Build a Bridge: The Use of Foreign Models by Domestic Critics of U. S. Drug Policy." *Milbank Quarterly* 69: 495–526.

Office of National Drug Control Policy
1991   "What America's Users Spend on Illegal Drugs." Technical report. Washington, DC: Department of Health and Human Services.

Orcutt, J. D.
1975   "Deviance as a Situated Phenomenon: Variations in the Social Interpretation of Marijuana and Alcohol Use." *Social Problems* 22: 346–355.
1976   "Ideological Variations in the Structure of Deviant Types: A Multivariate Comparison of Alcoholism and Heroin Addiction." *Social Forces* 55: 419–437.

Orcutt, J. D., and Turner, J. B.
1993   "Shocking Numbers and Graphic Accounts: Quantified Images of Drug Problems in the Print Media." *Social Problems* 40: 190–206.

Owen, D.
1934   *British Opium Policy in China and India*. New Haven, CT: Yale University Press.
Park, P.
1983   "Social-Class Factors in Alcoholism." Pp. 365–404 in B. Kissen and H. Begleiter (eds.), *The Pathogenesis of Alcoholism*. New York: Plenum.
Pastor, P. A., Jr.
1978   "Mobilization in Public Drunkenness Control: A Comparison of Legal and Medical Approaches." *Social Problems* 25: 273–384.
Pattison, E. M., Sobell, M. B., and Sobell, L. C.
1977   *Emerging Concepts of Alcohol Dependence*. New York: Springer.
Peele, S.
1985   *The Meaning of Addiction*. Lexington, MA: Lexington Books.
1986   "The Implications and Limitations of Genetic Models of Alcoholism and Other Addictions." *Journal of Studies on Alcohol* 47: 63–73.
1988   *Visions of Addiction: Major Contemporary Perspectives on Addiction and Alcoholism*. Lexington, MA: Lexington Books.
Peterson, J. L., and Bakeman, R.
1989   "AIDS and IV Drug Use among Ethnic Minorities." *Journal of Drug Issues* 19: 27–37.
Ratner, M. S.
1993   "Sex, Drugs, and Public Policy: Studying and Understanding the Sex-For-Crack Phenomenon." Pp. 1–36 in M. S. Ratner (ed.), *Crack Pip as Pimp: An Ethnographic Investigation of Sex-For-Crack Exchanges*. New York: Lexington.
Reinarman, C., and Levine, H. G.
1989   "Crack in Context: Politics and Media in the Making of a Drug Scare." Contemporary Drug Problems (Winter): 535–573.
Reiss, A. J., and Roth, J. A.
1993   *Understanding and Preventing Violence*. Washington, DC: National Academy Press.
Reuter, P.
1992   "Hawks Ascendant: The Punitive Trend of American Drug Policy." *Daedalus* 121: 15–52.
Ridlon, F. W.
1988   *The Fallen Angel: The Status Insularity of the Female Alcoholic*. Lewisburg, PA: Bucknell University Press.
Robinson, D.
1976   *From Drinking to Alcoholism: A Sociological Commentary*. New York: Wiley.
Rogers, J. M.
1971   "Drug Abuse by Prescription." *Psychology Today* 5:16 ff.

Rubin, V., and Comitas, L.
1975   *Ganja in Jamaica: A Medical Anthropological Study*. The Hague: Mouton.
Schmeisser, P.
1988   "Pushing Cigarettes Overseas." *New York Times Magazine*, July 10, p. 16 ff.
Schneider, J. W.
1978   "Deviant Drinking as Disease: Alcoholism as a Social Accomplishment." *Social Problems* 25: 361–372.
Schrag, P.
1978   *Mind Control*. New York: Pantheon.
Schuckit, M. A.
1987   "Biological Vulnerability to Alcoholism." *Journal of Consulting and Clinical Psychology* 55: 301–309.
Singer, M.
1986   "Toward a Political Economy of Alcoholism: The Missing Link in the Anthropology of Drinking." *Social Science Medicine* 23: 113–130.
Skolnick, J. H.
1992   "Rethinking the Drug Problem." *Daedalus* 121: 133–160.
Slevaggio, K.
1983   "WHO Bottles Up Alcohol Study." *Multinational Monitor* 4: 9.
Snyder, C.
1958   *Alcohol and the Jews*. New Haven, CT: Yale University Press.
Spradley, J. P.
1970   *You Owe Yourself a Drink: An Ethnography of Urban Nomads*. Boston: Little, Brown.
Stall, R., Watters, J. K., and Case, P.
1989   "Intravenous Drug Use and AIDS: Introduction." *Journal of Drug Issues*, Winter, pp. 1–7.
Stephens, R. C.
1991   *The Street Addict Role: A Theory of Heroin Addiction*. Albany: State University of New York Press.
Tarter, R. E., and Edwards, K. L.
1987   "Vulnerability to Alcohol and Drug Abuse: A Behavior-Genetic View." *Journal of Drug Issues* 17: 67–81.
Trebach, A. S.
1982   *The Heroin Solution*. New Haven, CT: Yale University Press.
1987   *The Great Drug War*. New York: Macmillan.
Trice, H. M., and Roman, P. M.
1970   "Delabeling, Relabeling, and Alcoholics Anonymous." *Social Problems* 17: 538–546.
U.S. Bureau of the Census
1993   *Statistical Abstract of the United States: 1993*. Table 209. Washington, DC: U.S. Department of Commerce.

U.S. Department of Health and Human Services
1987   *Alcohol and Health*. Rockville, MD: National Institute on Alcohol Abuse and Alcoholism.
1993   Preliminary Estimates from the 1992 National Household Survey on Drug Abuse, Advance Report Number 3. Rockville, MD: Author.

U.S. Department of Justice
1993   Uniform Crime Reports: Crime in the United States. Washington, DC: Federal Bureau of Investigation.

U.S. Senate Hearings
1977   *Occupational Alcoholism Prevention and Treatment Act of 1977*. Hearings of the Subcommittee on Alcoholism and Drug Abuse. Washington, DC: U.S. Government Printing Office.

Vaillant, G. E.
1983   *The National History of Alcoholism*. Cambridge, MA: Harvard University Press.

Van Dyke, C., and Byck, R.
1982   "Cocaine." *Scientific American* 246: 128–141.

Vlahov, D., Anthony, J. C., Munoz, A., Celentano, D. D., Solomon, L., and Polk, B. F.
1991   "The Alive Study: A Longitudinal Study of HIV-1 Infection in Intravenous Drug Users: Description of Methods." *Journal of Drug Issues* 21: 759–776.

Wallace, J. M., and Bachman, J. G.
1991   "Explaining Racial/Ethnic Differences in Adolescent Drug Use: The Impact of Background and Lifestyle." *Social Problems* 38: 333–357.

Watters, J. K.
1989   "Observations on the Importance of Social Context in HIV Transmission among Intravenous Drug Users." *Journal of Drug Issues* 19: 9–26.

Weinberg, T. S., and Volger, C.
1990   "Wives of Alcoholics: Stigma Management and Adjustments to Husband-Wife Interaction." *Deviant Behavior* 11: 331–343.

Weisheit, R.
1990   *Drugs, Crime, and the Criminal Justice System*. Cincinnati: Anderson.

Wen, U. C.
1961   "Opium in the Straits Settlements, 1867–1910." *Journal of Southeast Asian History* 2: 52–75.

Winick, C.
1991   "Social Behavior, Public Policy, and Nonharmful Drug Use." *Milbank Quarterly* 69: 437–459.

Wiseman, J. P.
1991   *The Other Half: Wives of Alcoholics and their Social-Psychological Situation*. New York: Aldine de Gruyter.

Wisotsky, S.
1986   *Breaking the Impasse in the War on Drugs*. New York: Greenwood Press.

Yamaguchi, K., and Kandel, D. B.
1985   "On the Resolution of Role Incompatibility: A Life Event History Analysis of Family Roles and Marijuana Use." *American Journal of Sociology* 90: 1284–1325.

Zimmer, L., and Jacobs, J.
1992   "The Business of Drug Testing: Technological Innovation and Social Control." *Contemporary Drug Problems* (Spring): 1–26.

Zimmer, L., and Morgan, J. P.
1995   "The Social Pharmacology of Smokeable Cocaine: It's Not All It's Cracked Up to Be." In C. Reinarman, and C. Levine (eds.), *Crack in Context*. Berkeley: University of California Press.

Zinberg, N. E.
1984   *Drug, Set, and Setting: The Basis for Controlled Intoxicant Use*. New Haven, CT: Yale University Press.

7 | Violence in the Family

For most people, the word *family* brings forth strong images of warmth, caring, security, and love. However, the facts about families reveal a striking paradox: In American society, the family is also one of the most violent institutions. The paradox is all the more curious because frequently evidence of both caring and violence coexists in the same home (Straus, 1977).

The violence found in families ranges from the use of physical punishment in the discipline of children to homicide. Discipline is generally thought to be "normal," even necessary under some conditions, while homicide is clearly regarded as deviant. The facts concerning homicide provide some of the strongest evidence that the family is a violent institution. In 1992 approximately 22,500 homicides were officially recorded in the United States, in 12% of which its murder victims were related to their assailants. Among all females killed, 29% were slain by husbands or boyfriends, but only 4% of males were killed by wives or girlfriends (U.S. Department of Justice, 1993).

Less extreme levels of violence are more common. Numerous studies have reached the same conclusion: "the average citizen is much more likely to be assaulted in his or her own home than on the streets of the most dangerous city in the United States" (Hotaling and Straus, 1990: 466). Researchers have found that one-half to three-quarters of all women have experienced some physical violence from their partners. For about 1 out of 5 women the abuse is not an isolated incident but occurs repeatedly; severe battering happens to about 1 out of 15 to 20 of them (Steinmetz, 1986). A large national survey in 1985 (Straus and Gelles, 1986) revealed that about 1.8 million women were severely assaulted by their partners. Children are spanked in 85% to 95% of families, but more severe physical force is used with surprising frequency. The 1985 study found that over 10% of American children, about 1.5 million, had experienced severe violence by their parents—kicking, biting, punching, hitting or trying to hit with an object, beating, or threatening with or using a gun or a knife. Approximately 1.7 million cases of child maltreatment are reported annually (Barth and Derezotés, 1990). Estimates for 1991 were that 2–4 million children were abused or neglected; nearly 2 million women were battered; and 1 million elderly persons were mistreated (Kroll, 1993). Siblings, parents, and older relatives, as well as spouses and children, may all be victims of family violence.

In considering why violence happens so frequently in families, attributes of the family as a social group and the social context in which the family functions may be contributing factors. They include the following:

- *Time at risk.* Because the proportion of time spent interacting with family members is high, there are many opportunities for disagreements or confrontations that escalate into violence.
- *Range of activities and interests.* There are many occasions, from child rearing to leisure, over which disputes may arise.
- *Intensity of involvement.* What happens in families is important to people. How family members should act and how things should be done can be sources of intense disagreement.
- *Impinging activities.* Conflicts are apt to arise because many actions in families result in one person losing while another gains. Which TV program to watch, which car to buy, where to go on vacation, and the like can become sources of dispute.
- *Right to influence.* Family membership usually implies the right to influence the values, attitudes, and behaviors of others. Parents expect to be able to control their children; many husbands have similar expectations regarding their wives. Older siblings often expect younger ones to conform to their wishes. When these expectations are not met, conflicts may be initiated or intensified.
- *Age and sex discrepancies.* The family is made up of very different individuals, especially during the child-rearing years. It often becomes the arena for conflict rooted in the cultural differences between young and old, boys and girls, men and women.
- *Ascribed roles.* Family relationships usually reflect and reproduce social inequalities. Often roles and responsibilities are assigned according to age and sex rather than interest or competence. In addition, there are widespread sexist beliefs about the "proper" role of family members in decision making and even the appropriateness of violence directed at others to enforce domination.
- *Family privacy.* The belief in American society that whatever happens in families is private and not of concern to outsiders insulates families from outside controls.
- *Involuntary membership.* Leaving one's family is difficult, even when the situation is violent. This is obviously true for young children but often the case also for spouses, especially women who may become trapped by social, emotional, economic, or legal contingencies.
- *High level of stress.* The changes in the structure of families as their members move through the life cycle can increase the susceptibility to conflict and violence. Matters affecting one member, such as illness, unemployment, or emotional problems, usually affect others.
- *Normative approval.* Cultural norms, both legal and informal, are sometimes quite accepting of family violence. Historically, in Western culture it has been legally acceptable for parents to use violence against their children and for husbands to use violence against their wives.

- *Socialization into and generalization of violence.* The family is the place where most people first see and experience violence—particularly in the form of physical punishment. Love can become associated with violence. Children can learn that those who love them "are also those who hit and have the right to hit…, that early experience with physical punishment lays the groundwork for the normative legitimacy of all types of violence but especially intrafamily violence" (Gelles and Straus, 1979: 554).

In this chapter we will expand on these themes as we consider several types of violence in families, the theories that have been proposed to explain them, and social policies directed at reducing domestic violence.

FAMILY VIOLENCE AS A SOCIAL PROBLEM

Historical and Cross-Cultural Perspectives

Historically, family violence—particularly that directed against children and women—has been common. In ancient Greece and Rome, children had no rights to life; infanticide was condoned or even required for premature, deformed, or weak infants (Radbill, 1987). Only very recently have laws provided much protection of children from violence at the hands of their parents at home. Likewise, women have historically been at the mercy of their husbands, with few legal protections. The prevailing notion in Western societies that "a man's home is his castle" and his wife and children are property he can treat as he pleases has also been challenged in recent years.

Before the 19th century there were only minor signs of reform. The first laws anywhere against "wife beating and 'unnatural severity' to children" (Pleck, 1987) were enacted between 1640 and 1680 by the Puritans in Massachusetts. In the early 1800s, the "house of refuge" movement directed some attention to children, but its goal was more child control than child protection (Pfohl, 1976). The plight of abused children first gained public attention in the United States in 1875, when the Society for the Prevention of Cruelty to Animals intervened in the case of a nine-year-old girl who had been viciously maltreated by foster parents. Public concern resulted in formation of the New York Society for the Prevention of Cruelty to Children, but interest in child abuse quickly declined and did not surface again until the early 1960s. The reemergence of child abuse as a social problem coincided with technological advances and more widespread use of X-rays as diagnostic tools in medicine. A group of pediatric radiologists described the evidence of child battering they found in their analyses of X-rays in a famous article, "The Battered Child Syndrome" (Kempe et al., 1962). By endowing the problem of child abuse with medical legitimacy, this article stimulated a major movement against it. Within four years, all 50 states had created reporting procedures for suspected abuse incidents and had made reporting mandatory for teachers, medical personnel, and social service workers.

Some concern for battered women paralleled the late-19th-century efforts on behalf of children, but it was fleeting and had little impact. The first major form of assistance for women, the shelter movement, appeared about a decade later than the 1960s child-abuse initiatives. In 1974, a book by an English woman, Erin Pizzey, *Scream Quietly or the Neighbors Will Hear*, vividly recounted the battering experiences of women. She founded the first English shelter for battered women in 1971 and was influential in the early development of shelters in the United States after her book was published here in 1977. Initiatives on behalf of battered women differed from those directed at child abuse because this issue did not have as long a history of prior concern, and wife battering did not have the medical legitimacy of a syndrome attached to it. Feminist groups have been largely responsible for increasing public awareness of wife battering and urging the use of public and private funds to provide assistance and alternatives to women who have been battered by men (Tierney, 1982; Breines and Gordon, 1983; G. Walker, 1990).

While violence directed at women and children is more common in Western industrialized societies, it is also found in less-developed societies throughout the world. A study of 60 small-scale, nonindustrialized societies found that wife beating was common or frequent in 4 out of 10 and physical punishment of children was common or frequent in about one-fourth of them. Overall, women are the victims of family violence in most societies (Levinson, 1981; Dobash and Dobash, 1981). Summing up cross-cultural evidence, Gelles and Cornell (1983) conclude that the likelihood of violence in families varies considerably from country to country.

> The accumulated evidence from both empirical studies and position papers is that child abuse and spouse abuse are probably most common in Western, industrialized, developed nations. Developing countries also seem to have problems of abuse and violence, but these are interpreted as being grounded in the social disorganization caused by modernization and the resultant changes in family, clan, tribal, and social situations. China is frequently described as a society with little or no problem with child or wife abuse, as are the Scandinavian countries. (161)

How We Know What We Know

Collecting accurate information on family violence poses difficulties because activities within families are generally regarded as private matters, and people are understandably reluctant to admit the occurrence of incidents that might be considered deviant or illegal. Most data reported on family violence probably *underestimate* its actual prevalence.

Sources fall into three main categories: clinical samples, official statistics, and random-sample surveys. Clinical samples consist of cases that come to the attention of medical personnel, such as the battered children identified by radiologists in the early 1960s. In addition these cases include, for example, battered women who come to shelters for refuge or counseling. Clinical samples have proven to be a rich source of information about the experience of family violence by victims, but they are not a good way to estimate prevalence or provide firsthand information about perpetrators. Even when clinical samples include both victims and perpetrators (as in Shupe, Stacey, and Hazlewood, 1987), the data gathered by this means are limited; we can only generalize findings to people who seek shelter or treatment, which excludes the majority of victims and perpetrators.

Official statistics, such as data from police records or child-abuse reports, tell us more about the response of government agencies to the problems than about actual incidence. For example, *reports* of child abuse have gone up dramatically since the late 1960s, when the laws requiring the recording of suspected cases by school and health workers were enacted. Still, the official data surely underestimate the actual amounts of violence. In addition, because law enforcement personnel and service providers may be biased in their inclination to record a case as violence or abuse, depending on the person's social class or race, people in the lower classes and racial and ethnic minorities tend to be overrepresented in official statistics.

Random-sample surveys provide the ability to go beyond cases that come to the attention of legal or health authorities. While surveys thus can provide more accurate estimates of prevalence, they are also likely to be underestimates, due to people's reluctance to admit certain actions. Data from this source is also not likely to be as detailed as that from clinical samples. In addition, the assessment of trends is made more difficult by recent changes in the structure of many American families. U.S. Bureau of the Census (1993) data indicate that:

- The proportion of married-couple family households declined from 61% in 1980 to 55% in 1992.
- The number of unmarried-couple households tripled between 1970 and 1980 and grew by 80 percent between 1980 and 1990, from 1.6 to 2.9 million. There were 3.3 million such households in 1992.
- The proportion of family households with children declined from 57% in 1970 to 47% in 1990 and in 1992.
- The proportion of children under 18 years of age living with two parents declined from 85% in 1970 to 73% in 1990 and to 71% in 1992.
- In 1992, 23% of all children under 18 lived with their mothers only—18% of white, 54% of black, and 28% of Hispanic children. Only 3% of all children lived with their fathers only.
- Census Bureau reports in August 1994 indicated that 27% of all children (18 million) were living with only one parent, twice as many as in 1970. For the first time, these children were as likely to be living with a parent who had never married as with one who had divorced. One-third of all family households were headed by a single parent.

Reiss and Roth (1993) caution that

> Trends in family violence must be interpreted against a decline in the fraction in households containing exclusively married couples and their natural children. Violence between growing numbers of same-sex and opposite-sex cohabiting partners is increasingly regarded as family violence regardless of legal marital status. Those who record statis-

tics may or may not classify violence between increasing numbers of divorced or separated ex-couples as family violence. (222)

Contemporary Family Violence: Extent, Costs, and Trends

Each year the U.S. Bureau of Justice Statistics conducts a National Crime Survey (NCS) designed to uncover one measure of the amount of crime in the United States by asking a large, random sample of members of representative households about their *victimization* from crime during the previous year. This survey is designed not to measure domestic violence specifically but to estimate true rates of crimes such as burglary, robbery, larceny and aggravated assault. Estimates of domestic violence drawn from it undoubtedly fall far short of actual numbers. Between 1973 and 1981 the NCS found a total of over 4.1 million victimizations by relatives, a yearly average of over 450,000 crimes, 88% of them assaults. Women were victims of family violence at a rate three times that of men; in violence involving spouses, 91% of the victimizations were women attacked by husbands or ex-husbands, while 5% were attacks by wives or ex-wives. Weapons were used in about 30% of all violent crimes by relatives (Klaus and Rand, 1984). In 1992, over 447,000 violent victimizations (excluding homicides) by relatives were reported, and weapons were used in over 30% of violent crimes involving nonstrangers (U.S. Department of Justice, 1994).

Several national random-sample surveys have provided the best estimates of incidence. Richard J. Gelles and Murray A. Straus (1987), using a representative sample of 6,002 American families, estimated an annual incidence rate of spousal violence (physical assault) at 161 per 1,000 couples. Most of these incidents were relatively minor, such as slapping or throwing an object. The rate for more serious incidents against wives (kicking, biting, punching, choking, beating, and use of weapons) was 34 per 1,000 couples. This translates into an estimated 1.8 million wives annually experiencing serious assaults. The same study found an annual rate of severely assaulted children (using the same incidents as criteria) of 110 per 1,000, or about 6.9 million children annually. When hitting with an object is omitted, because many people do not regard "paddling" as severe discipline, the estimated rate is 23 incidents per 1,000, or 1.5 million children seriously assaulted per year in this country.

One measure of the costs of this violence is the effect it has on the victims, as Gelles and Straus (1987) point out:

> [S]everely assaulted women averaged almost double the days in bed due to illness than did other women; a third fewer severely assaulted wives reported being in excellent health than other women, and three times as many severely assaulted wives reported being in poor health. Severely assaulted women had much higher rates of psychological distress than other women, including double the incidence of headaches, four times the rate of feeling depressed, and five-and-a-half times more suicide attempts.…
>
> [T]he child victims of severe violence had two to three times higher rates of trouble making friends, temper tantrums, failing grades in school, disciplinary problems in

school and at home, physically assaultive behavior at home and outside the home, vandalism and theft, and drinking and drug use.… [A]bused children were arrested four times more often than other children. (638–640)

Such differences between children who are abused and those who are not hold regardless of socioeconomic status, suggesting that it is abuse, rather than social class, that accounts for the effects.

Historically, it is impossible to establish family violence trends in any detail. Probably families are no more violent in the United States today than they ever were before, and possibly they are even less so. Two nationally representative surveys conducted by Straus and Gelles (1986) provide the best evidence we have to assess contemporary trends. Between 1975 and 1985, physical child abuse (measured by the number of children who were kicked, punched, bitten, beaten up, or attacked with a gun or a knife) decreased by 47%. Wife beating (measured by occurrence of the same acts, plus hitting with an object) decreased by 27%, while similar violence directed at husbands by wives decreased by 4.3%. Thus, although overall rates of family violence have remained high, the trend in this ten-year period was downward.

According to Straus and Gelles, these findings were not an artifact of methodological differences in the two surveys but were due to several changes in American society during the 1975–1985 period. First were the changes in family structure: age at first marriage and at birth of the first child increased, number of children per family decreased, and American families were slowly becoming more equalitarian. All of these factors reduced the likelihood of family violence. There also was an improved economic climate (especially for intact families—the population studied) during this period, probably resulting in lowered economic stress by 1985. Social policies aimed at reducing abuse may also have had some effect. The number of alternatives, particularly shelters for battered women, rose during the period, and treatment and prevention programs were expanded. There also is evidence that the public has become less accepting of family violence and that law enforcement agencies have responded by becoming more willing to take it seriously.

While the toll of family violence remains extremely high, there is reason to appreciate what has been achieved and grounds for optimism about continued improvements. Public awareness of the problem is higher than it has ever been, and political awareness is now strong. In 1983 President Reagan commissioned a Task Force on Family Violence, giving national recognition to the problem but little action. Legal changes paralleling those on behalf of children continue to be made to benefit women, and research on domestic violence has grown enormously in the past 25 years (Straus, 1992). As basic research accumulates and programs aimed at intervention and prevention are evaluated, we are also learning more about successful approaches to dealing with the problem (Shupe, Stacey, and Hazlewood, 1987).

These trends are likely to continue, with growing concern for other victims of domestic violence such as siblings, parents, and the elderly.

TYPES OF FAMILY VIOLENCE

Child Abuse and Neglect

Child abuse takes several forms. *Physical violence* ranges in severity from the serious assaults that called attention to the battered child syndrome in the early 1960s to milder forms of physical punishment. *Psychological abuse* can have harmful consequences for a child's development, but we will not consider it here. *Child neglect* takes the form of victimization of children through such circumstances as poverty, lack of child care, and inadequate provisions for education, what Breines and Gordon (1983) call "problems for which social and economic organization of our society is most to blame." From the viewpoint of family violence, however, *child sexual abuse* is particularly troubling.

In this section we will concentrate on physical and sexual abuse and note the important differences between them. We should note, however, that the largest share of child abuse and neglect cases substantiated annually by the National Center on Child Abuse and Neglect is categorized as neglect. One reason is the large numbers of children living in poverty in the United States. In 1991 there were 13.7 million children under the age of 18 in families living below the poverty level, 21% of all children, including 5.3 million children under 6 years old, 23% of children that age (U.S. Bureau of the Census, 1993: 469, 470). The poverty rate for children under 6 was 14% in white, non-Hispanic families, 49.5% in black, non-Hispanic families, and 40% in Hispanic families. Despite the numbers, child neglect has not captured the attention of researchers to the same extent as abuse. Not only is neglect far less sensational, but acknowledging its existence in an affluent society raises fundamental questions about the society's values and social and economic organization. Research funding to investigate such matters is hard to find.

Incidence. Official reports of child abuse and neglect have been rising sharply. Between 1976 and 1987, reports of suspected child abuse and neglect nationwide rose from an estimated 669,000 to 2,163,000—an average of more than 10% each year (Finkelhor, 1990). Among the three major maltreatment categories—physical abuse, sexual abuse, and neglect—reports of sexual abuse rose the fastest. The reasons for the increase in *official reports* were greater public awareness and, in some states, deteriorating economic conditions (U.S. Congress, House Select Committee, 1987). Data for 1991 from the National Center on Child Abuse and Neglect indicate that 1,767,673 child neglect and abuse cases, involving 2,695,010 children, were reported and investigated in the United States, and cases involving 811,709 children were substantiated. Out of 801,143 victims of substantiated maltreatment, 46% involved neglect, 25% physical abuse, 16% sexual abuse, 6% emotional maltreatment, and 8% other types of maltreatment (U.S. Bureau of the Census, 1993: 209).

While official reports have risen, we have noted evidence from national random-sample surveys of households that the actual incidence of cases has not. A combination of legislation that encourages more aggressive searches for cases and greater public willingness to bring abuse to the attention of authorities probably accounts for the discrepancy between official data and the incidence studies.

Factors Associated with Child Abuse. Research has revealed a number of factors associated with child abuse. In general, the youngest children are at greatest risk of being physically abused and sons are slightly more likely to be victims than daughters. Younger parents are more apt to be abusers, and, because mothers are the primary caregivers for children in most families, they are more likely to be child abusers than fathers (Gil, 1970; Gelles, 1978). Worldwide, certain categories of children are more vulnerable to maltreatment: children in poor health, females, unwanted children, and those born into difficult circumstances or under conditions of rapid socioeconomic change (Finkelhor and Korbin, 1988).

Numerous studies show that the strongest predictor of child abuse by a parent is similar abuse of the parent as a child: "The rate of abuse among individuals with a history of abuse (30%, plus or minus 5%) is approximately six times higher than the base rate for abuse in the general population (5%)" (Zigler and Kaufman, 1987). Although this is a strong predictor, it is by no means a certain one. Being abused as a child does increase the likelihood that one will be an abusive parent, but this outcome is far from inevitable (Gelles, 1987). The correlation that does exist seems to be related to attitudes toward violence—the experience of childhood violence is one of the most important determinants of approving attitudes toward violence as an adult (Owens and Straus, 1975).

Stress is another major contributing factor, particularly when combined with other conditions. Families experiencing high levels of stressful events, such as trouble at work, job loss, death of someone close, or serious sickness or injury, have higher rates of child abuse by both mothers and fathers. However, the rates of child abuse are even higher when the stress occurs in families where the parents engage in physical fights, have low status in education, income, or occupation, or are socially isolated and do not participate in clubs, unions, or other organizations. Abuse rates are also high when the marriage is unimportant or unrewarding to the parents. The stress of single parenthood, especially for poor mothers, is evident from research findings. Single parents are more likely than married-couple parents to use abusive forms of violence toward their children. This abusive violence is generally a function of poverty in mother-only homes but is unrelated to income in father-only homes (Gelles, 1989). The effects of stress are less of a factor in more equalitarian marriages and in families that are imbedded in supportive social networks (Straus and Kantor, 1987). It has also been found that subsequent acts of child abuse are significantly explained by a combination of stressful events and the seriousness of the initial assault (D. Browne, 1986).

Parental unemployment, an obvious stressor, requires special attention. Children with unemployed fathers are more likely to be abused, often by mothers, the primary caregivers and household managers. The risk of maternal abuse becomes even greater if the father is unemployed and the mother is working. In this instance, because mothers are apt to retain their responsibilities even while they are the primary breadwinners, their burdens can be overwhelming. Findings from a study by Gelles and Hargreaves (1981) provide evidence that unemployment among men "has serious noneconomic, negative consequences for their families. One of the major burdens of the father's unemployment falls on the shoulders of the working wife and then, through her violence, onto the children" (525).

One area of controversy is whether stepparents are more likely than genetic parents to be child abusers. Some evidence suggests that stepchildren are not disproportionately abused (Gelles, 1991), while other evidence suggests that stepchildren are at higher risk (Daly and Wilson, 1991). Less in doubt are the findings regarding race and ethnicity. Overall, the violence rate for Hispanic families is much greater than for non-Hispanic white families, and child abuse rates in Hispanic families persist regardless of economic circumstances (Straus and Smith, 1990c). Trends in the violence rates of black families are also disturbing: Hampton, Gelles, and Harrop (1991) compared 1975 and 1985 national survey rates and found that "While rates of severe violence were nearly the same in black and white homes in 1975, the rate of severe violence toward black children was double the rate toward white children in 1985" (16).

Alcohol abuse is associated with severe child maltreatment. Famularo et al. (1986) compared parents who had come to the attention of the courts when physical abuse, sexual abuse, or neglect required court-ordered removal of children from the home with parents in a control group. They found that parental alcoholism occurred in only 8% of the control families but in 38% of the maltreatment families. The authors conclude that "periods of active drinking increase the likelihood of direct child abuse. During such periods parents can show increased aggression toward their children and each other, family stress and arguments, decreased attention to children's basic needs, decreased job performance, lowered income, and poor health. Each of these problems not only has a negative impact on parental and family functioning but also makes it more difficult to reunite parents with children who have been removed" (484). Overall, according to Straus and Smith (1990), research suggests that

> [A] large part of the explanation of child abuse is in the very nature of American society and its family systems. This has profound implications for the prevention of child abuse. Although psychotherapy may be appropriate in some cases, a more fundamental approach lies in such things as a more equal sharing of burdens of child care, replacement of physical punishment with non-violent methods of child care and training, reducing the stresses and insecurity that continue to characterize our economic system for many families, and strengthening the ties of individual families to the extended family and the community. (260–261)

Child Sexual Abuse

The sexual abuse of children in families is different in several ways from physical abuse. Physical abuse is committed about equally by men and women—with somewhat higher rates for females, due to their greater routine contacts with children. In child sexual abuse the offenders are predominantly (85% to 95%) males, and about 95% of the victims are females. Sexual abuse can occur both inside and outside the family, but we will focus on that occurring in the family. Most sexual abuse, unlike physical maltreatment, does not involve physical trauma (although it is often coercive), and sexual abuse offenders enjoy what they are doing. More than physical abuse, sexual abuse is a middle-class phenomenon (Finkelhor, 1985).

Prevalence. Estimates of the amount of sexual abuse vary widely. It is likely that many incidence reports relying on adults' recall of childhood experiences underestimate the true incidence because people are reluctant to admit the incidents or have repressed them. One extensive review of studies of groups of adults looking back on their childhoods found that anywhere from 9% to 54% of the women and 3% to 9% of the men had been sexually abused (Finkelhor, 1984b: 20). In the first national survey of American adults concerning childhood sexual abuse, victimization was reported by 27% of women and 16% of men (Finkelhor et al., 1990).

Within the family, incest is a fairly common event in females' lives: 10% to 20% of females report at least one experience during childhood and adolescence, compared to 1% to 3% of males (Meiselman, 1990). The predominant form in the family is molestation of daughters by fathers or stepfathers. A study of historical case records dating back to 1880 confirms both the persistence of the father-daughter pattern and the long-term history of incest as a form of family violence (Gordon and O'Keefe, 1984). One of the largest studies of incest (Russell, 1986b) was based on a sample of 930 women residents of San Francisco in 1978. Incest was found to have affected 16% of the women before the age of 18, but only 2% of all experiences had been reported to the police. This is a form of deviance that remains effectively hidden from official agents of control.

Victims and Perpetrators. Children at high risk of sexual abuse, in addition to being female, tend to be young. Incestuous incidents usually start between the ages of 8 and 12, but cases occurring earlier are probably more apt to be underreported. In Russell's (1986b) San Francisco study, middle-class girls reported as much incest as those in the lower class; whites were victims in the same proportion as black and Latino girls; and Asians were least likely to be victims. Incest was seven times more frequent by stepfathers than by biological fathers. Uncles were slightly more frequent perpetrators than fathers. Incest was not always committed by adults; about a quarter of the cases were perpetrated by someone under 18. Brother-sister incest, contrary to popular myth, was not usually reciprocal and mutual. Only rarely (5%) do incest cases involve female perpetrators, who tend to be less abusive in terms of frequency and severity of sex acts, amount of force used, and age disparity between offender and victim.

Additional studies have found that the risk of child sexual abuse is increased (1) if the child has ever lived without the natural father; (2) if the mother is employed outside the home; (3) if the child has had a poor relationship with the incestuous parent; and (4) if the parents are in conflict (Finkelhor, 1986b; Finkelhor and Baron, 1986).

A number of studies have identified harmful short-term and long-term effects of childhood sexual abuse (Herman, Russell, and Trocki, 1986; Russell, 1986b). With its infusion of secrecy, guilt, and shame, incest corrupts children and deprives them of their childhood (May, 1991). Browne and Finkelhor (1986) describe other effects:

> Adult women victimized as children are more likely to manifest depression, self-destructive behavior, anxiety, feelings of isolation and stigma, poor self-esteem, a tendency toward revictimization, and substance abuse. Difficulty in trusting others and sexual maladjustment, such as sexual dysphoria, sexual dysfunction, impaired sexual self-esteem, and avoidance of or abstention from sexual activity has also been reported by empirical researchers, although agreement among studies is less consistent for the variables on sexual functioning....
>
> A number of good studies agree that longer-lasting experiences are more traumatic. Children who suffer more than one incident of abuse also seem to have more long-term effects. The preponderance of studies indicate that abuse by fathers or stepfathers has a more negative impact than abuse by other perpetrators. Presence of force seems clearly to result in more trauma for the victim. In addition, when the perpetrators are males rather then females, and adults rather than teenagers, the effects of sexual abuse appear to be more disturbing. (162–175)

Findings from other studies indicate that childhood sexual abuse increases the likelihood of disrupted marriages, leads to dissatisfaction in sexual relationships, and increases the likelihood of women's later victimization by nonincestuous rape or attempted rape (Finkelhor et al., 1989; Russell, 1986a).

A Model of Child Sexual Abuse. Given that the overwhelming majority of child sexual abusers are male, the problem is probably best understood as one of *masculine socialization*. David Finkelhor (1984a; 1986b) has identified several differences between the socialization of men and women that can account for why women are far less likely to be child sexual abusers.

- Women learn earlier and much more completely than men to distinguish between sexual and nonsexual affection. Men, far more than women, are apt to seek fulfillment of dependency and affectional needs in a sexual form. Through their socialization for motherhood, women learn to get this fulfillment through children in *non*sexualized relationships.
- Men, more than women, grow up feeling a stronger need for heterosexual success as a part of their gender identities. While sex with children could be expected to be only a weak confirmation of sexual adequacy, it may be so regarded as some under certain conditions.
- Men learn to focus their sexual interest on sexual acts isolated from the context of the relationship more than women do. Women learn to focus more on the romantic context and the overall relationship in connection with sex.
- Men are socialized to see as potential sexual partners those who are younger and smaller than themselves, while women learn to see those with the opposite characteristics as appropriate sexual partners. This makes it easier for a man than a woman to see a child as a sex object.

While these factors help to explain why men are more likely sexual abusers than women, they do not indicate why particular men become abusers while others do not. David Finkelhor (1986b) has further proposed a four-step model which serves as an organizing framework for possible explanations. Each of the four major elements in the model is intended to address a question about the abuser:

1. *Emotional congruence.* Why would a person be emotionally gratified by relating to a child sexually?
2. *Sexual arousal.* Why would a person be sexually aroused by a child?
3. *Blockage.* What might block or frustrate a person from obtaining sexual and emotional gratification from more acceptable sources?
4. *Disinhibition.* Why would a person not be deterred from sexual relations with a child by conventional social restraints and inhibitions?

Several possible answers to each of these questions are given in Table 7.1, which also describes the research evidence regarding them. Araji and Finkelhor (1986) summarize the research as follows:

> …(1) the best experimental research has been directed toward establishing that sexual abusers do show an unusual pattern of sexual arousal toward children, although no substantial theory yet exists about why this is so; (2) a number of studies have concurred that molesters are blocked in their social and heterosexual relationships; (3) alcohol is well established as a disinhibiting factor that plays a role in a great many sexual abuse offenses; (4) at least one study gives support to the "emotional congruence" idea that children, because of their lack of dominance, have some special meaning for pedophiles; and (5) there is evidence that many sexual abusers were themselves victims of abuse when they were children. (117–118)

Prevention. The existence of widespread child sexual abuse, particularly incest, has long been denied. Anthropologists and sociologists have traditionally classified incest as a *taboo*—an extraordinarily strong prohibition so thoroughly rooted in the natural or social order that its occurrence is extremely rare. Likewise, Freud chose to reject evidence that many of the problems of his female patients were rooted in seductive or incestuous relationships with their fathers. Instead, he concluded that references during clinical sessions to such experiences in their childhood were based on imaginary rather than real incidents (Masson, 1984). Both interpretations of child sexual abuse in the family—the anthropological idea of taboo and the Freudian insistence on imaginary fabrication—appear to be wrong in the face of emerging evidence. Clearly, incest occurs far too frequently to be taboo, and a large number of children, especially girls, do experience sexual abuse in their families.

The avenues to prevention must begin with recognition of the fact that child sexual abuse is overwhelmingly committed by males. This suggests that the key is to be found in male socialization: "As long as males are socialized with a predatory approach to obtaining sexual gratification, and as long as this is seen as so acceptable that to point it out is considered offensive, we will make little progress in our efforts

Table 7.1   Summary of Empirical Evidence for Explanations of Child
Molestation (Araji and Finkelhor, 1986)

Theory	Research Evidence
I. Emotional Congruence	
Children attractive because of lack of dominance	One positive study
Arrested development/immaturity	Some support from psychological testing, but inferences are weak
Low self-esteem	Some support from psychological testing, but inferences are weak
Mastery of trauma through repetition	Several studies show frequent histories of sexual abuse in offenders' backgrounds
Identification with aggression	Several studies show frequent histories of sexual abuse in offenders' backgrounds
Narcissism	Untested
Male socialization to dominance	Untested
II. Sexual Arousal	
Heightened arousal to children	Clear experimental evidence, except for incest offenders
Conditioning from early childhood experience	Several studies show frequent histories of sexual abuse in offenders' backgrounds
Modeling from earlier childhood experiences	Several studies show frequent histories of sexual abuse in offenders' backgrounds
Hormonal abnormalities	Mixed evidence
Misattribution of arousal	Untested
Socialization through child pornography or advertising	Untested
III. Blockage	
Difficulty relating to adult females	Generally positive evidence
Inadequate social skills	Suggested by two studies
Sexual anxiety	Some support from uncontrolled studies
Unresolved Oedipal dynamics	Family problems evident, but not necessarily the ones Oedipal theory would predict
Disturbances in adult sexual romantic relationships	Suggestive evidence from uncontrolled studies
Repressive norms about sexual behavior	Suggested by two studies
IV. Disinhibition	
Impulse disorder	True for some small group of offenders, but not for all
Senility	Negative
Mental retardation	Negative
Alcohol	Present in great many instances, exact role unclear
Failure of incest avoidance mechanism	Two studies show higher rates of abuse in stepfather families
Situational stress	Only anecdotal evidence
Cultural toleration	Untested
Patriarchal norms	Untested

Source: Araji and Finkelhor, 1986: 93–94.

to stop sexual assault, including incestuous abuse" (Russell, 1986b: 392). While some might conclude that the most effective way to prevent child sexual abuse is to keep men away from children—to avoid using boys as baby-sitters or placing men in nurturing roles—the opposite should be the case. Men will learn the distinction between nonsexual and sexual affection better by becoming *more* involved in bringing up children, and they will be less likely to be child abusers if they are socialized to be attracted to women who are their social equals, because they will be less likely to seek as sexual partners those who are smaller, less powerful, or younger than themselves (Finkelhor, 1985).

In addition to positive changes in male socialization, there need to be stronger barriers inhibiting the potential abuser. Vander Mey and Neff (1986) state that incest is not a true taboo, sufficiently abhorrent that the act is prohibited, and, because the perpetrators are rarely psychotic, it cannot be regarded as originating in bizarre personality problems. They propose instead an alternative orientation:

> Namely, it may be that many if not most fathers experience an occasional sexual desire in response to their daughters. They do not act on that impulse—because of certain barriers. Perhaps one of the most important barriers is a strong concern for the daughter's welfare. Partially because of harsh, unemotional, and unsupportive environments in their own childhoods, and partially because of subcultural factors, incest perpetrators have often failed to develop a capacity for such altruistic responses—even in relation to their own children. (168)

This suggests that child sexual abuse would be reduced if more people were aware of its deleterious effects and if potential perpetrators could be made more sensitive to the welfare of the victims. Programs aimed at teaching children to distinguish between acceptable and unacceptable displays of affection are certainly beneficial in this regard (Finkelhor, 1986a). They should help those most at risk as victims to be vigilant, as well as establish early in the minds of those most likely to be perpetrators norms of sexual conduct against the abuse of children. More generally, the cultural patterns of denial and refusal to confront child sexual abuse that have characterized the past need to be replaced by open recognition of it and confrontation with its causes.

Dating Violence

The Conflict Tactics Scale (CTS) developed by Murray Straus (1979) is a measure of interpersonal violence that has been applied to numerous family studies and has also been used to study violence in unmarried couples who are romantically involved. The prevalence in dating situations of any CTS behavior—including slapping, shoving, hitting, beating, or threatening with a gun or knife—ranges from about 12% of high school students to 36% of those in college (Lane and Gwartney-Gibbs, 1985). Similar to the patterns for married couples, in dating situations both women and men are perpetrators and victims, although women are more likely to experience severe violence and suffer injury (Makepeace, 1986).

monly jealousy, drinking behavior, and denial of sex (Makepeace, 1981). The longer the relationship, the greater the likelihood the partners will have experienced violence. Couples living together are much more apt than those who are romantically involved but living separately to resort to aggression in conflicts (Lane and Gwartney-Gibbs, 1985; Stets and Straus, 1989). Relationships characterized by dependency are more violence prone and violence in the family background of the aggressor is common. Alcohol is also a contributing factor.

Thus, dating violence is in many respects similar to marital violence, and it becomes more likely the more closely the dating relationship approximates marriage. Carlson (1987) says,

> Although a marriage license may in fact be a "hitting license," as has been asserted by Straus (1980), marriage is not a precondition for violence in loving relationships. However, the appearance of a serious, family- or marriage-like relationship does appear to be a precondition.… Thus, it appears that being in a quasi-marital relationship increases the likelihood of interpersonal aggression for many of the same reasons that being married does. (21)

In other words, some of the same characteristics of families—for example, time at risk, range of activities and interests, intensity of involvement, and the like—probably contribute also to violence in dating situations, particularly as the dating relationship comes closer to resemble marriage.

Marital Violence

Lenore Walker, a sociologist who called attention to violence directed against women by men in *The Battered Woman* (1979), provides one wife's account of such an incident:

> We sat down and started eating, the whole while Lew screaming at me that the food was lousy and that I was a lousy cook. I tried hard not to answer him back, even though I was getting angrier and angrier. I thought to myself, Why do I put up with all this stuff? Why do I have to stay? The kids are gone now. What's in it for me? Finally, I couldn't take any more. I turned to him and said, "If you don't shut up, I'm leaving."
>
> Lew lunged at me and grabbed me, holding me with his left hand, pushing the plate of stew in my face with his right hand. The scalding pain was more than I could bear. I screamed and screamed. He slapped me, kicked me, and pulled my hair until I just didn't know what was happening anymore. I started to run, and he grabbed me and ripped my dress as I was running. I didn't know what to do. I ran into our bedroom, instantly realizing I had made a mistake. I knew he'd follow me there and beat me more.
>
> I quickly made it to our bathroom and locked the door and prayed that he wouldn't break the lock again, as he had done in previous fights. I was lucky this time. The shouting and screaming stopped. The banging on the door went away. I just sat down on the floor, just thinking and staring into space. I didn't know what to do.
>
> A few minutes after hearing it quiet down, I got up and washed my face off. I put cold water where he had thrown the food, hoping that nothing was going to swell and that I wouldn't get any burn blisters. I cleaned myself off, and I put on a bathrobe. I slowly opened the door and came out to see what had happened. Lewis was lying there. It looked like he had passed out on our bed. I tiptoed very quietly into the dining room

and cleaned up the mess, tears streaming down my face, realizing that no matter what I did, Lewis wasn't going to change. The beatings weren't going to get better…. (102–103)

Prevalence. The report by Straus and Gelles (1986) on national surveys of marital violence indicated that while overall rates appeared to drop between 1975 and 1985, they remained extremely high. Even with a 27% reduction of reported serious violence against wives during the period, an estimated 1.6 million women suffered severe violence ("wife beating") in 1985. Today experts suggest that this figure may be low, and "a more accurate national estimate may be as high as *4 million women severely assaulted by male partners in an average 12-month period*" (A. Browne, 1993: 1078; italics in original). A survey of family homicides in large counties by the U.S. Department of Justice reported in July 1994 that women are much more likely than men to be killed by spouses, accounting for 60 percent of cases. About half the victims were drinking at the time of the assault, 13% were unemployed, and 54% were shot to death. Among defendants in cases of family homicide, 60% were male, 54% were drinking, 25% were unemployed, and 53% used a gun. Also reported in July 1994 was a finding by the American Psychological Association that as the number of women killed by intimates dropped over the preceding 15 years, there was a sharp increase in the number of nonmarried female partners killed by boyfriends (Gest, 1994).

The National Crime Survey has shown that women who are victimized by domestic violence but are not killed are at high risk of being victims again; approximately 32% were repeat victims between 1978 and 1982. Nearly half of all domestic violence incidents are not reported to the police. Victims fail to report them for a variety of reasons, most commonly because they consider the incident a private or personal matter or they fear reprisal for alerting the authorities (Langan and Innes, 1986).

Numerous studies document that overall the rates for less-extreme forms of violent behavior are about the same for husbands and wives (Gelles, 1974; Steinmetz, 1977; Straus, 1980; Straus and Gelles, 1986). However, husbands represent only a small proportion of victims who suffer serious injury (Steinmetz, 1986). While women may say they initiate or employ violence in families about as frequently as men do, women victims sustain far more physical injury (Stets and Straus, 1990). In the most severe instances of violence, women are more likely to be killed than men; in two-thirds of the cases when a spouse is murdered, the wife is the victim (A. Browne, 1987). When wives do use violence, it is far more likely to be in self-defense (Straus, 1980). Thus, while the use of violence in the home by women against both children and husbands is undeniable (Steinmetz, 1978a; Shupe, Stacy, and Hazlewood, 1987), in terms of severe violence, marriage is a "hitting license" primarily for men (Pleck et al., 1978; Berk et al., 1983; Klaus and Rand, 1984; Okum, 1986; Dobash et al., 1992). In couple relationships, according to A. Browne (1993),

…(a) men perpetrate *more* aggressive actions against their female partners than women do against their male partners; (b) men perpetrate more severe actions, at least by the name of the action (e.g., punch, kick, choke, beat up, threaten with or use a knife or gun) than do women; (c) men are more likely to perpetrate multiple aggressive actions during a single incident than are women; and (d) women are much more likely to be injured during attacks by male partners than men are during attacks by female partners. (1078)

In the remainder of our discussion of marital violence we will concentrate on men as perpetrators and women as victims in American society.

The Effects of Wife Battering. The physical pain, anger, humiliation, and sense of injustice felt by battered women should be apparent to anyone reading the passage from Walker at the beginning of this section. In a large study of hospital emergency room visits, 21% of all women using surgical services and one half of *all* injuries were a result of a partner's aggression (Stark et al., 1981). Women who are beaten generally experience substantially poorer health than other women and have sharply elevated levels of psychological distress, including headaches, nervousness, depression, and feelings of worthlessness and hopelessness, which increase with the severity of violence (Gelles and Straus, 1987).

Battered women also are at much greater risk of suicide. Pagelow (1981) found that almost half of the battered women she interviewed had contemplated suicide, and 23% had attempted it at least once. In a very large national survey in the United States, women who experienced severe violence reported thinking about taking their lives over 20 times more frequently than women who had experienced no violence, and battered women actually made attempts on their own lives 5 times more frequently (Gelles and Straus, 1987). Wife battering as a precipitant for female suicide is apparently common worldwide. Counts (1987) concludes from case studies and data from Oceanic, African, and South American societies, that suicide may be "a culturally constructed way in which a powerless woman may avenge herself on her tormentor" (201). The price of wife beating can be even higher than bruised bodies and sleepless nights.

Risk Factors. In general, marital violence declines with age and is not directly related to race when social class is taken into account (Cazenave and Straus, 1990; Suitor, Pillemer, and Straus, 1990). Although as a group wife batterers are heterogeneous and fail to conform to a unified profile of personality correlates (Hamberger and Hastings, 1991), perpetrators of wife abuse tend to have low self-esteem and volatile personalities. They are quick to interpret a remark as a threat or insult and easily lose self-control. One of the most striking commonalties, shared with child abusers, is the childhood experience of violence in the home (O'Leary and Curley, 1986). A history of family violence is present in the backgrounds of many wife beaters. Indeed, "childhood experiences of family violence have a greater impact than either chronic economic strain or actually stressful circumstances on whether individuals perpetrate spouse abuse" (Seltzer and Kalmuss, 1988: 473). Moreover, "the socialization experiences of wife batterers, whether involving neglect, outright abuse, or merely witnessing parental or sibling abuse, appears to be directly related to the severity of their later adult violence in the family" (Carter, Stacey, and Shupe, 1988: 259). A typical profile would resemble this one from Shupe, Stacey, and Hazelwood (1987):

> This man is not violent in any areas of his life outside his home. A typical scenario involves a man in his late twenties, married for several years or living with a woman. Arguments and conflicts usually are nonsubstantive (that is, over minor issues or over implied and unspoken issues). The arguments escalate in rapid fashion to physical violence. Besides these explosions of anger and violence, the man is described by his wife as a good husband and father. He is usually a dependable and stable employee.
>
> This man witnessed his father beat up his mother over a relatively long period of time and identified with his mother's abuse. Most such boys attempt to intervene in the violence at least once to protect their mothers. One man reported that "every time I tried to stop my dad, he would push me out of the way or hit me. When I was big enough, I finally stopped him by beating the shit out of him when he tried to hurt my mom." Another man told a counselor that "When my dad went out drinking, I used to lay in front of my mother's door. Sometimes he would kick me to make me get out of the way." (42–43)

Because employment is a major source of masculine identity in American society, it should not be surprising that difficulties in this realm contribute to the abuse of wives as well as children. Indeed, unemployment or part-time employment is strongly and consistently associated with wife abuse (Prescott and Letko, 1977; Rounsaville, 1978). Straus, Gelles, and Steinmetz (1980) found that unemployed men were twice as likely as men employed full time to use severe violence on their wives, and men employed part time had a rate of wife beating that was three times the rate for men employed full time. Despite this strong correlation, overall the large majority of wife batterers *are* employed (Schwartz, 1990), and work stressors are associated with abuse directed at wives (Barling and Rosenbaum, 1986).

Alcohol is present in one-third to one-half the cases of wife beating, although the nature of its role is not clear (Gelles, 1985). It is probably not a direct cause but instead exacerbates the already violence-prone situation (Berk et al., 1983). One study has determined that although excessive drinking is associated with high wife-abuse rates, the highest rates occur when blue-collar status, drinking, and approval of violence appear together (Kantor and Straus, 1987). Wives in marriages with low socioeconomic status are more likely to experience batterings. The wife's status in relation to her husband may also be a factor if his status is *lower* than hers (Smith, 1988). In general, wife abuse is least frequent in families where power and decision making are shared relatively equally (Straus, Gelles, and Steinmetz, 1980). As Coleman and Straus (1990) put it, "since equality in marriage is associated with low rates of intra-family conflict and violence, laws, administrative decisions, and services that empower women and encourage men to value an equal partner are likely to be important steps to reduce violence and strengthen the family" (301).

Why Women Stay. Despite the severity of batterings and repeated incidents, a substantial number of women remain in abusive relationships. For example, when 24 women who sought assistance from a safe house were interviewed four to six months later, half of them had returned to the same man from whom they had sought refuge (Giles-Sims, 1983). Many battered women continue to live with the men who beat them without ever seeking shelter. Physically abusive relationships are often emotionally complex and include good aspects along with bad; for example, warmth and intimacy may actually increase after an attack. Women generally seek to leave violent husbands only when the violence becomes particularly severe or frequent. Those who stay generally have few resources and limited education and occupational skills and are more likely to have experienced violence in childhood (Gelles, 1976; Cappell and Heiner, 1990). Wives who are highly dependent on their marriages are less effective in discouraging, avoiding, or ending abuse than women who have a closer balance of resources with their husbands in their marriages (Kalmuss and Straus, 1982). Many women are also reluctant to leave because they fear retaliation. Such fear may be rational, given that the most severe violence, that with weapons, occurs most often between estranged spouses. The National Crime Survey found that about one-fourth of wife assaults are perpetrated by ex-husbands, and about half of all conjugal murders occur among couples no longer cohabiting (Okum, 1986: 229).

In interviews with 100 battered women, Ferraro and Johnson (1983) identified six rationalizations commonly used by women to justify staying with men who abuse them:

1. *An appeal to the salvation ethic.* This is grounded in the woman's desire to be of service to others. She wants to "stick by her man" and try to "save" him from whatever is causing the violent behavior.

2. *Denial of the victimizer.* This is the belief that the battering is beyond the perpetrator's control and therefore not his responsibility.

3. *Denial of injury.* Some women simply refuse to acknowledge their victimization; they attempt to return to the routine of daily life as quickly as possible after the violent incident.

4. *Denial of victimization.* Sometimes women blame themselves, feeling that they could have done something different—been more passive or more conciliatory—to prevent the violence.

5. *Denial of options.* Women may feel that they have no alternative place to go, no way to support themselves or make it on their own. They may also feel they have no options at an emotional level, and no one but the batterer can provide intimacy and companionship.

6. *An appeal to higher loyalties.* Some women, out of allegiance to tradition or religion, insist that staying with a battering husband is their "duty."

Ferraro and Johnson found that women who eventually left battering relationships began to shed these rationalizations for staying when they redefined themselves as true victims. This was more likely to occur with an increase in the level of violence, an improvement in the woman's resources, when the violence became visible to outsiders, or when she reached the point of despair.

Hoff (1990), in an in-depth study of 12 battered women, found their accounts suggested they were not merely passive victims, but when they used violence in self-defense it usually only led to more brutal retaliatory beatings. As for staying, "their reasons are embedded in traditional views about marriage and the family and the interpretation of violence as a private rather than a public issue. Clearly, though, staying in violent marriages exacted an enormous toll on the women's self-esteem" (54–55).

Leaving or Stopping the Violence. There is no evidence to support the myth that battered women stay in abusive relationships because they are masochistic. Indeed, a substantial proportion of abused women do eventually break off relationships with their abusers. In one study of 300 battered women at a shelter, over 30% terminated cohabitation with the abuser, beginning with the shelter stay; over 40% did so within two years of the first shelter visit. Economic independence is apparently central to a woman's capacity to escape an abusive relationship; those with the greatest economic resources are most likely to leave (Okum, 1986). Straus and Kalmuss (1982) conclude that economic—not psychological—dependency is the most important factor keeping women in severely abusive marriages.

Some women are successful at stopping the abuse and salvaging the relationship. Bowker (1983) conducted interviews with 136 women who had been beaten at least once but had not been beaten in the 12 months prior to the interview. Three kinds of techniques were used by these women:

1. Engaging in personal strategies—talking, promising, threatening, passive defense, and aggressive defense.

2. Seeking informal sources of help—family members, in-laws, neighbors, friends, and shelters.

3. Relying on formal sources—police, social services, lawyers, and the like.

No single technique worked the best. What mattered most was "the woman's showing her determination that the violence *must stop now*" (131).

The importance of shelters as a resource, even for women who choose to stay with a man who has battered them, cannot be underestimated. According to Giles-Sims (1983), many of the women who went back to their husbands "held the option of a return to the shelter like a trump card, saying to the man, in effect, 'If you hit me, I am going to leave, and now I have a place to go'" (63). In her opinion, having this resource may be enough to change the pattern of violence. Still, the success of shelters depends upon the approach of those who run them. Loseke (1991) found that shelter workers, having constructed images of the "appropriate" clients for their service, may exclude some women whose accounts of abuse do not correspond to the stereotype. Furthermore, as Hoff (1990) points out,

Even if such services were sensitive to the sociocultural and political aspects of the problem, many battered women either do not know of them, or, since they accept the problem as personal, something *they* are responsible for alone, would not think to use them. For a woman, then, to leave a violent relationship and avoid killing either herself or her mate requires external social resources, a "definition of the situation" that no longer targets *her* as the source of the problem, and her ability to combine these external and internal resources in an action plan that preserves her own and others' lives. (78)

Other Victims: Siblings, Parents, and the Elderly

Sibling violence is the most common form of violence in the family. Brothers and sisters fight with one another, and frequently the altercations become physically abusive. A great deal of this violence is accepted as part of growing up, especially for boys, and even encouraged by the notion that it toughens them up both physically and psychologically. While most sibling violence is relatively minor—pushing, shoving, slapping, and throwing things—about 50% of American children each year attack a sibling so severely it would be classified as an assault if it occurred outside the home. In general, sibling violence declines as children get older; boys are more violent than girls; and the highest level of violence occurs when a boy has only brothers (Straus, Gelles, and Steinmetz, 1980: 80).

Although violence directed at parents by their children is far less common than parent-to-child violence in American society, it does occur frequently enough to be of concern. Several studies report the finding that around 10% of children and adolescents commit a violent act against their parents each year (Gelles and Cornell, 1985). Most children who attack their parents are adolescents or young adults. The most likely victim is the mother, although older males are more likely to hit their fathers. As with other kinds of family violence, the experience of violence as a child—either being abused or seeing parents abuse one another—is related to violence directed at parents by children. Agnew and Huguley (1989) conclude that "In general, adolescents who assault parents are more likely (a) to have friends who assault parents; (b) to approve of delinquency, including assault, under certain conditions; (c) to perceive the probability of official sanction for assault as low; (d) to be weakly attached to parents; and (e) to be white" (710).

Abuse of the elderly has recently drawn public attention because, as life expectancy increases and birth rates stabilize, the elderly are a growing proportion of the population. The amount of elder abuse has not been accurately determined, but estimates are increasing. In the 1980s they ranged from half a million to a million victims annually (Pierce and Trotta, 1986; Crystal, 1987); in the early 1990s the annual estimate was about 1.5 million (Boudreau, 1993). The victim is most likely to be 75 years old or older, female, and living with relatives or living alone and dependent on a caregiver. Abused elders also are more likely to be socially isolated (Pillemer, 1986). Women, who are nearly always the primary caregivers, are most often the abusers. Elder abusers are apt to be experiencing mental or emotional problems and involved in personal crises such as alcoholism, physical illness, or financial difficulties. The extent to which elder abuse fits into the cycle of violence common to other forms of family violence is open to question (Pierce and Trotta, 1986; Pillemer, 1986).

While child abuse and elder abuse are similar in the dependency of their victims, there are important differences. The elderly often become dependent after their adult children have reared their own families and may resent the burden of care and responsibility when they are forced to become caregivers again. While children become more independent as they grow up, the elderly usually become more dependent as they grow older, which makes the responsibilities especially stressful for the caregiver (Steinmetz, 1978b).

THEORIES OF FAMILY VIOLENCE

Abuse as Psychopathology: A Critique

Before the mid-1970s the assumption in the predominant theory of family violence was that the perpetrators must be psychopathic. Most family violence was hidden and believed to be relatively rare. It was hard to imagine that parents responsible for the battered child syndrome or husbands who severely battered their wives could be other than "sick." In general, the theory was that early childhood experiences—including abuse and emotional or psychological abandonment—led to psychopathic adult personalities that, in turn, led to abuse.

Another psychodynamic formulation growing out of frustration-aggression theory suggested that aggressive behavior represents a form of psychological release, and aggression expressed in one sphere reduces the need to express it in other spheres. In other words, venting emotion through aggression acts as a catharsis or safety valve.

As evidence accumulated about family violence, both the psychopathological and catharsis explanations were shown to be inadequate. The latter is not supported by the evidence because the types of family violence are related to one another, and, as Straus (1977) found, many studies not only fail to support the idea of catharsis, but almost always show that increased aggression in one sphere also increases it in others. Criticisms of the psychopathological model are grounded in evidence that multiple factors are associated with family violence. In his analysis of child abuse as psychopathology, Richard J. Gelles (1973) argued that social factors such as situational stress and the social position of parents are crucial to an understanding of the problem. He concluded that "it is now necessary to stop thinking of child abuse as having a single cause: the mental aberrations of the parents" (620). The alternative he proposes is the social psychological model shown in Figure 7.1, which includes many of the social variables we have discussed in this chapter.

The sharpest attack on the psychopathological model has come from feminists. From this point of view, violence in the family—particularly that directed against women and children—is not unusual, either now or historically. It is the means used by the more powerful to enforce their will on those who are less powerful. In

Figure 7.1   A Social Psychological Model of the Causes of Child Abuse (Gelles, 1973)

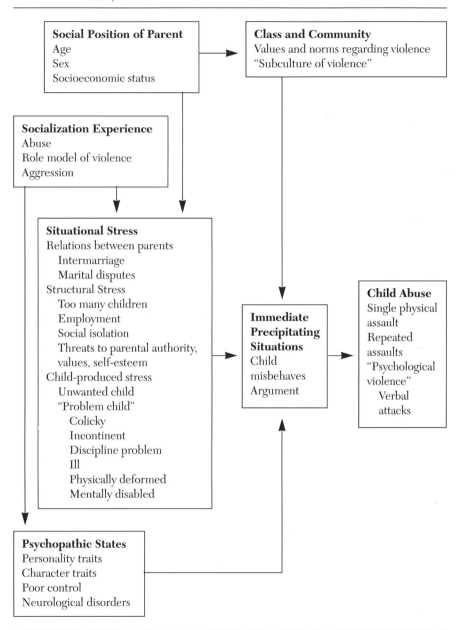

Source: Adapted from Gelles, 1973: 619.

this sense violence by males is not the isolated, idiosyncratic activity of a few but a widespread norm sanctioned by custom and law. To declare the perpetrators of violence "sick" is to deny their responsibility for their actions and ignore the ways in which men have historically enforced their dominance in the family by physical coercion.

Family Dynamics and Social Learning

Resource Theory. The characteristics of families that make them likely arenas for conflict and violence that were listed at the beginning of this chapter provide a foundation for an explanation of violence in the home that is based on family structure. In addition, Goode (1971) suggests that lower-class families may experience comparatively more family violence because they have insufficient resources to achieve their aims. When people's work lives allow them little control or provide little power, money, or prestige, they receive minimal respect outside their homes and are apt to experience greater frustrations in their family lives. They also have fewer social and economic resources to cushion those frustrations.

Exchange/Control Theory. Gelles (1983a) proposes that people will use violence in the family if the costs of being violent do not outweigh the rewards. The costs are minimized if violence is normatively accepted in the home ("Spare the rod and spoil the child") and if the "privacy" of the family reduces the chance of discovery and the threat of social control. Gelles describes the reasoning for his "exchange/social control theory" as follows:

> People abuse family members because they can. There are rewards to be gained from being abusive: the immediate reward of getting someone to stop doing something; of inflicting pain on someone as revenge; of controlling behavior; or of having power. All of these rewards are evident in other social settings. Why don't people beat up their neighbors when they return the lawn mower broken? Why don't people beat up their boss, when he makes them stay late on the night that they have show tickets that cannot be returned? Why don't people beat up their annoying co-workers? The motivation is there and is, perhaps, as strong as the motivation in families. They do not because the costs are too high. Beating up a boss could result in being kicked back, fired or having the police called. The police are known to respond faster when people are beating up a stranger than when they are beating up a family member. Beat up a stranger and the result could be assault charges or incarceration. Very few of those controls operate in families. A person does not lose his job for beating his wife or beating his children. The risk of official social controls is rarely run; judges are despondent when faced with a choice of leaving a family intact or criminally prosecuting the abuser. The tradition in families is for a more powerful person to beat on someone less powerful, someone who cannot return and inflict even physical costs. (1985b: 6–7)

Intergenerational Transmission of Violence. In addition to engaging in violence because they *can*, family members may do so because they have learned from experience that the family is an appropriate place for violence. No other finding in the research on family violence is more consistent than the appearance of family violence in the backgrounds of abusers. There is a cycle of family violence. However, although the evidence for intergenerational transmission is strong, we must be careful *not* to assume that *all* who have been abused as children will become adult abusers or that *all* adult abusers have been victims as children (Gelles, 1993b). The intergenerational transmission of family violence probably results because social learning that occurs early in life is a powerful influence on a person's norms, values, attitudes, expectations, and behaviors as an adult. When children learn from their parents that those who love are also those who hit, they are being prepared to act the same way as parents themselves.

The implications of social learning theory suggest controversial consequences for social policy. In an article titled "Discipline and Deviance," Straus (1991a) argues that even though over 90% of American parents use physical punishment to correct their children's misbehavior, and even if such punishment may produce conformity in the immediate situation, "in the longer run it tends to *increase* the probability of deviance, including delinquency in adolescence and violent crime inside and outside the family as an adult" (133). Therefore he calls for steps to encourage parents to avoid all use of physical punishment in child discipline. Critics have questioned Straus's conclusions (Kurz, 1991; Loseke, 1991; McCord, 1991), and the "spanking debate" goes on (Straus, 1991b).

Social Structure and Culture

Social Inequality.   Related to Goode's ideas on why families with limited economic resources are more likely to experience violence is evidence that stress can contribute to abusive actions by family members (Barling and Rosenbaum, 1986; D. Browne, 1986; Farrington, 1986; Straus and Kantor, 1987). The theories that relate family violence to inequalities assume that life as an underdog is more stressful and frustrating. For example, David Gil's (1986) thesis is that

> ...violence in human relations, including its domestic version, is rooted in socially evolved and institutionalized inequalities of status, rights and power among individuals, sexes, ages, classes, races and peoples. All social formations which involve such inequalities as a basis for domination and exploitation, from patriarchy and slavery to feudalism, capitalism, colonialism, imperialism, and authoritarianism, are therefore intrinsically violent societies. They violate the individual development of their members and they bring forth violent reactions from oppressed individuals and groups. (124–125)

Gil argues that in the United States deep inequalities are inherent in the management of resources, in the organization of work and production, in the distribution of goods and services, and in access to social, civil, and political rights. Indeed, our dominant ideology is oriented toward inequality, selfishness, competition and domination. As a result, he says, in American society there is widespread frustration of people's fundamental needs. A high level of family violence is only one product of these frustrations.

Patriarchy. Feminist theory places the causes of family violence in the same context as that offered by Gil, but with a sharper focus on the historical relationship between men and women. Gil is mainly concerned with the frustrations of inequality; feminist theorists focus on the attempts of males to maintain their power in the society. Feminists see violence by men directed at women as having a long tradition that reflects the institutions and beliefs supporting male dominance. The society thus is a male-dominant *patriarchy* supported by two interacting elements: structure and ideology (Dobash and Dobash, 1979).

The structure of patriarchy is reflected in the social institutions that have traditionally kept women subordinate. The specific techniques range from the segregation of women into low-paying occupations, unequal pay for comparable work, gender-exclusive social organizations, and laws that formerly permitted men to claim their wives as property. For example, the expression "rule of thumb" refers to 19th-century laws in the United States that allowed husbands to beat their wives without official interference as long as the stick they used was no bigger than a thumb. Likewise, the sayings "A woman's place is in the home" and "A man's home is his castle" capture the intent behind the historical structure of patriarchy.

The ideology of patriarchy is reflected in religious institutions, including Christianity (Martin, 1987). In their liturgy and dogma, religions traditionally place men in positions of authority over women in the church, often excluding them as ministers or priests. The highest authority, God, is typically characterized as male, and religious texts are interpreted to justify the dominance of men and the obligation of women to obey their husbands—under penalty of physical coercion, if necessary.

According to the feminist perspective, the explanation of family violence is not to be sought in deviant or pathological individuals or family structures. Rather, violence is seen as one among many "usual" and "normal" activities that are used by men to maintain their superordinate status. As Dobash and Dobash (1979) put it:

> The use of physical force against wives should be seen as an attempt on the part of the husband to bring about a desired state of affairs. It is primarily purposeful behavior and not the action of deviant or aberrant individuals or the prerogative of deviant or unusual families....Rather, men who assault their wives are actually living up to cultural prescriptions that are cherished in Western society—aggressiveness, male dominance, and female subordination—and they are using physical force as a means to enforce that dominance. (23–24)

Cultural Context. The case for cultural context as an explanation of family violence was enhanced by a study by Shupe, Stacey, and Hazlewood (1987) comparing about 230 batterers on active duty in the military with a sample of other male batterers. To the extent that the military represents an institutional segment of American society that encourages toughness, masculinity, the fighting spirit, and violence, we might expect the levels of domestic violence by military personnel to be higher than those of civilians. This hypothesis was strongly confirmed by the data.

The researchers say they were unprepared for the severity of violence in the military cases:

> In both groups (active military and civilian) there was a high incidence of verbal abuse (name-calling, swearing, and so on). Likewise, in both groups the majority of men slapped and punched women.... But almost twice as many soldiers as civilians actually used weapons on women. Four in ten military batterers used everything from guns and knives to baseball bats, lamps, and belts. A total of sixteen military men shot or pistol-whipped their wives, and twenty-two soldiers injured women with knives. (76)

Their analysis suggests further that there is a military effect on communities where the presence of a military establishment is strongly felt. The most important factor encouraging domestic violence was not military status per se but residence in a military-dominated community.

As a cultural context, the military base, with its heightened emphasis on masculinity and aggression, increases the violence of families within the surrounding community. To the extent that most religions also stress the importance of male dominance, we might also expect them to play a role in perpetuating violence among religious families. However, the relationship between religion and violence is not straightforward; religion has the potential to have positive or negative effects in relation to family violence. On the one hand, religious values may justify male dominance over wives and the violence to enforce it—as suggested by feminist theorists. On the other hand, clergy could be of positive assistance when family violence occurs by encouraging women to seek shelter and batterers to seek counseling. Nevertheless, on the basis of information given to counselors by violent partners, Shupe, Stacey, and Hazlewood (1987) concluded that "The overwhelming role played by religion in the lives of the violent couples we studied was a regressive, unwholesome one. Religion typically provided violent men with a rationale to dominate women and excused their occasional violence as necessary discipline" (97–98). Another recent study on problems associated with counseling battered women who attended fundamentalist churches is consistent with this finding (Whipple, 1987). While there were occasional instances of positive religious effects, the tentative conclusion supports the role of religion as an ideological support for male domination and violence.

The importance of cultural support for male violence as a factor in rape, which we noted in Chapter 2, applies to sexual assault and family violence more generally. The male perpetrator does not violate the predominate norms governing the masculine ideal—dominance, assertiveness, aggressive expression of sexuality, and acceptance of violence. Rather, he takes these ideals to a legally unacceptable extreme. The norms of a sexist, patriarchal society can be implicated in violence against women both inside and outside the home. However, although women and children are overwhelmingly the victims of the most severe domestic violence, they also commit such violence (Straus, Gelles, and Steinmetz, 1980; Shupe, 1987). This suggests that while patriarchy may be a powerful explanation for family violence, it does not suffice alone.

SOCIAL POLICY: INTERVENTION, REDUCTION, AND PREVENTION

Intervention

Victims. Since child abuse first came to public attention with the publication in 1962 of "The Battered Child Syndrome" by Kempe et al., there have been major changes in the law and social policy. Legislation requiring the reporting of suspected cases of child abuse to the authorities, with follow-up procedures for investigation, has been passed in every state. As public concern grew, there was a huge increase in the *reported* cases of child abuse and neglect, and simultaneously there was evidence that the actual *incidence* of these cases (at least physical abuse) was dropping. The legal changes appear to have been an effective initial step in social policy. Further reductions in child abuse depend on additional measures.

Since the early 1970s there also have been major changes in the availability of alternatives for women victims of domestic violence. The number of shelters for battered women has grown, in part as a result of the women's movement (Tierney, 1982). Indeed, the availability of shelters in a given state is closely tied to the level of feminist organization in that state; according to Kalmuss and Straus (1983), "the level of feminist organization is a more potent predictor of programs for battered women than is per capita income, political culture, individual feminist sentiment, or domestic violence legislation that allocates funds for services" (372). In this respect, women have taken the initiative in helping themselves.

Are the shelters helpful in preventing future violence? The answer is yes, with some qualifications. Loseke and Cahill (1984) found that shelter operators often ascribe motives and goals to victimized women that question their competence and capacity to manage their own affairs. In some instances, battered women may be denied shelter services because they do not fit the typical victim profile (Loseke, 1992). Another study (Berk, Newton, and Berk, 1986) concluded that while shelters have benefits, the extent may depend on the attributes of the victim: "When she is actively taking control of her life, a shelter stay can dramatically reduce the likelihood of new violence. Otherwise, shelters may have no impact or perhaps even trigger retaliation for disobedience" (488). This is consistent with the observation that women intent on stopping the violence against them can effectively use the availability of a shelter to back up a threat to leave the abusive relationship if it does not change (Giles-Simms, 1983).

Shelters might be even more effective if they were combined with more vigorous legal action resulting in a formal complaint and arrest of the assailant. Initial results from a police experiment in Minneapolis seemed to indicate that arrest was an effective deterrent against further violence by batterers (Sherman and Berk, 1984). The study tested three conditions—arrest, "advice" from the police, and an order to leave for eight hours. There was significantly less subsequent violence by arrested suspects than by those who were advised or ordered to leave. In the wake of considerable publicity, mandatory arrest policies became widespread throughout the country. Subsequent research has qualified the apparent breadth of the original study's results. Some have found that arrest does not deter violent husbands (Dunford, Huizinga, and Elliott, 1990), and others that it does so only under certain conditions—particularly if, by virtue of marriage or employment, the perpetrator has something to lose (Williams and Hawkins, 1989). Gelles (1993a) concluded that arrest alone did not appear to be the deterrent it was said to be in the Minneapolis study, but "when combined with other criminal justice sanctions, and in combination with particular attributes of the offender, arrest may be a deterrent" (583). At least, rigorous criminal intervention against wife batterers has not been found to place victims at risk of new violence (Ford, 1991).

Perpetrators. Counseling is the most common intervention for those who commit domestic violence. There have been very few evaluations of child-abuse treatment programs. One study found that group counseling by lay therapists is both less costly and more effective than one-on-one therapy with professionals (Gelles, 1985). A recent evaluation of three counseling programs for wife batterers in Texas found that it was possible to stop or reduce the violence in a majority of cases. Shupe, Stacey, and Hazelwood (1987: 119) concluded that successful programs have three dimensions:

1. Holding violent persons personally responsible for their actions and stressing that they have the power to stop being violent.
2. Trying to get objective, independent information on violent persons and whenever possible monitoring their behavior while they are in the program.
3. Creating a moral atmosphere in counseling sessions that conveys the idea that physical violence and emotional abuse are not appropriate or excusable, nor are they macho or normal.

While evidence that counseling programs can work is encouraging (Tolman and Bhosley, 1991), it is often difficult to get abusive individuals into them. The legal system is not well suited to discovering and prosecuting cases of family violence. Family members are often reluctant to testify against one another, and, in respect to child abuse, it is difficult to fit children's testimony to the legal requirements of the courtroom. Ensuring that those who can benefit from counseling get it remains a real problem.

Reduction and Prevention

Intervention efforts on behalf of family violence victims are necessary and worthwhile, as are programs aimed at changing the behavior of perpetrators. However, much of the violence in American homes is not committed by sick individuals or pathological family structures, but is congruent with long-standing beliefs, practices, and institutions. To focus only on intervention efforts to be implemented after the commission of family violence is inadequate. Such a strategy is like running an ambulance service at the bottom of the cliff while ignoring the problems with the road at the top that are *causing* the accidents (Gelles, 1973). To begin reducing family violence, we must recognize its connection to the violence in the society of which every family is a part.

Straus, Gelles, and Steinmetz (1980) suggest five steps that would move Americans toward a reduction of violence in the home. Some of these suggestions would require profound changes in social and economic institutions, but given the close ties between family violence and these institutions, there is little reason to hope that less far-reaching changes would be sufficient (Straus and Smith, 1990b).

Step 1. *Eliminate norms that legitimize and glorify violence in the family and society.* The majority of Americans believe that hitting children occasionally is necessary and beneficial. In too many cases, the same belief is held by husbands in respect to their wives. Most people learn early, in their most intimate environments, that violence is a legitimate way to express one's feelings or get one's way. The public must be made to understand that how people are brought up and interact in families has much to do with how they act in situations outside the home. People from exceptionally violent family backgrounds are far more apt to be the violent individuals whom we fear as street criminals and who fill our prisons (Straus, Gelles, and Steinmetz, 1980: 74).

The means for perpetrating lethal violence must be reduced in American society. In recent years the rates at which Americans, both the public and criminals, have been arming themselves with handguns and assault weapons have accelerated rapidly, despite legislative attempts to control them. When lethal weapons are readily available in the home, often what would have been a family fight turns into a murder. Hand guns kept in the home have been found to kill family members far more often than intruding strangers. In a Detroit study, Zimring (1988) found that more people were killed in one year by handgun accidents than were killed by home-invading burglars in four and one-half years. The best way to substantially reduce lethal family violence is by controlling the easiest way to commit it—with guns.

The symbols of legitimate violence range from the death penalty to the movies and music videos. Every time someone is killed by the state, the unspoken message is that the proper, legitimate, necessary response to violence is more of the same. Because there is no evidence that the death penalty is a deterrent to capital crime, we should carefully weigh its only apparent justification—retribution—against the symbolic costs of legitimizing the ultimate violent act—killing a person.

Likewise, we need to continue to raise public awareness of the harmful effects of media violence. In Chapter 2 we noted strong evidence that identifies the violent (as opposed to the sexual) component of pornography as the primary stimulus to male aggression against women. While the costs of outright censorship may be too great in an open, democratic society, people need to be aware of the consequences of the connection between media violence and violence in the streets and at home. Parents have to control children's exposure to media violence; public education programs, both in the schools and in the media, should be expanded. Studies have shown that such programs can be effective.

Step 2. *Reduce violence-provoking stresses in the society.* The connection between work-related stress and family violence has been substantiated in research. Gil (1986) calls for a reconceptualization of our view of work from activity in which the employer attempts to get the most out of employees at the least expense to work as an arena for the fulfillment of human needs. This requires better recognition of the connection between home and work. For example, employers must take account of working parents' needs by supporting or expanding federal family leave provisions, providing help with day care centers, and making allowances for the care of sick children or other family emergencies. By relieving stresses associated with conflicting work and family obligations, employers can increase the productivity of their employees, as well as alleviate sources of conflict and frustration that trigger family violence.

Likewise, businesses, unions, and governments should all work toward eliminating poverty, unemployment, and underemployment and providing jobs at decent wages for everyone who is willing and able to work. Every family should be able to secure for itself a minimal income, food, housing in a crime-free neighborhood, and health care. Many argue that to guarantee these necessities to every man, woman, and child is too costly. This is simply wrong. In global terms the United States is an extraordinarily wealthy country; the problem is not insufficient resources but a maldistribution of resources. The gap between richest and poorest sectors of the economy continues to widen, and a tiny proportion of very rich individuals and corporations controls a vastly disproportionate share of the country's wealth. (Confirmation of this assertion can be found in the discussion of the American class structure in Chapter 9.) One of the first acts of the Clinton administration was to begin to reformulate tax policies that have favored the rich and have produced an increasingly inequitable distribution of resources. Gil (1986) sketches the basics of such a plan:

> What is needed is a simple, fair, loophole-free progressive tax on income, irrespective of source, above the level of the "low standard of living" as measured by the Bureau of Labor Statistics. Income below that level ought to be defined as "basic" and should, therefore, be tax-free. There should also be taxes on income-producing capital once income from its use exceeds the basic income level, and there should be sales taxes on luxury goods but not on nonluxury goods. Income tax rates would have to be adjusted periodically upward or downward to assure a relatively balanced budget and avoid government borrowing and wasted debt services. (148)

To this should be added a close look at the laws governing the taxation of inheritances. Relatively meager estate taxes allow huge economic, social, and political advantages to be passed on from one generation of the upper class to the next, at the expense of those not born with silver spoons at their lips. Put simply, the provision of basic needs in this society is well within its means; only the will to do so is found wanting.

Step 3. *Integrate families into a network of kin and community.* Social isolation is strongly associated with the abuse of children and wives (Garbarino, 1977; Straus and Kantor, 1987; Walker, 1979; Pagelow, 1981). When a family is far from relatives and has few social bonds to outside individuals or groups, the members will find it harder to cope with stressful situations. Social supports of all types—financial and moral—are the most effective mediators of stressful life events. In addition, when families are socially isolated, their members are less constrained by the informal social controls made manifest in the concerns noticed and expressed by outsiders. A woman who regularly goes outside her home to see relatives or friends is less likely to be beaten by her husband because he knows that cuts and bruises are apt to raise questions.

The movement of people from one community to another throughout their lives has become commonplace for many Americans. It is becoming an oddity to live from birth to death, surrounded by one's lifelong relatives and friends, in the same community. Much of this mobility is related to the policies of large corporations that move managerial employees around the country and disrupt workers with sudden plant closings or relocations. Likewise, urban renewal projects often tear apart communities and neighborhoods, deteriorating though they may be, and relocate the residents with little concern for social relationships or for rudimentary housing. Social policies ought to discourage such practices, which destroy communities, build stress and resentment, and promote social isolation—all negative outcomes that contribute to higher rates of family violence.

Step 4. *Change the sexist character of the family and the society.* The expectation by many men, supported by the ideology of patriarchy, that they have an inherent right to dominate their families justifies much of the violence in the home. Many men beat their wives because they believe that beating is their right, and some women, regrettably, concur. Studies show that family violence is least likely when family decision making is democratic and shared between spouses (Straus, Gelles, and Steinmetz, 1980). In addition, the dependency of children and many women makes them vulnerable to violence. The inescapable vulnerability of children has been recognized in the laws requiring reports of child abuse, which are designed to ensure intervention on their behalf when necessary. The vulnerability of women needs to be addressed by ensuring their equal treatment as adults under the law, in the economy, and in the family. As a practical matter, this means ending discriminatory practices that disadvantage women and providing equitable pay for comparable work, equal access to all of the society's institutions of power, and the legal guarantee of equal rights under the Constitution. It also means much stronger mechanisms for enforcing child support to prevent children and their mothers from being held economic hostages in violent homes (A. Browne, 1993).

Changing the sexist character of the society also requires changes on the part of men. Boys as well as girls need to be taught nurturing attitudes and skills. As parents, both men and women ought to become equal partners in child rearing, sharing tasks and responsibilities. This would serve to teach their children more equal expectations for men and women, while it spreads the burden of caregiving. At the societal level, businesses, unions, and governments need to recognize the importance of child rearing for the society and make available to parents such arrangements as flexible work hours, child care and sick days, and paternity leave so working fathers and mothers can share the burdens of family life.

Step 5. *Break the cycle of family violence.* None of the preceding steps offers a "quick fix" for family violence. In Gil's words:

> Social transformations toward a nonviolent, egalitarian, democratic, and humanistic order are not a brief, cataclysmic event but an extended process. Prevention of domestic violence, which depends on such fundamental social transformations, is therefore also an extended process. It involves many steps, each of which needs to challenge consistently the destructive elements of the prevailing violent social order: its values and ideology; its legal definitions of the rights of people and especially of children and women; and its inegalitarian institutional arrangements such as poverty and the prevailing organization of work and production which...result inevitably in stunted human development, insecurity, frustration, and stress. (1986: 142)

The answers to the problem of family violence lie in the social organization of American society. Violence tends to "run in families" because when people learn as children that those who love them hit them, it becomes easier for them as adults to hit those they love. Violence also runs in families because those at the bottom are caught in a cycle of poverty, frustration, and stress that repeats itself from one generation to the next. The key to breaking the cycle of violence is breaking with the beliefs and institutional inequalities that feed it.

SUMMARY

Families are paradoxical: They are simultaneously the places where we seek love and warmth and among the most violent social groupings in our society. The reasons why the family is a violent setting have to do with the frequency and intensity of the relationships among family members. Family violence is also linked to the inequalities and patriarchal values in American society that create family stresses and justify aggression by males.

Contemporary concern for family violence in the United States began with the movement to prevent child abuse initiated by identification of the battered child syndrome in 1962, followed by the shelter movement to assist battered women in the early 1970s. Since then, public awareness and political action in respect to family violence have increased. Today every state has laws requiring reports to authorities of suspected child abuse, and the shelter movement for women made shelters generally available in the United States. A comparison of two national surveys done in 1975 and 1985 revealed that actual rates of physical child abuse and, to a lesser extent wife abuse, were declining.

Despite these positive developments, the rates of family violence remain frighteningly high. Statistics from national surveys show that each year millions of children and women are victims of severe assaults in their homes. The costs are measured in injury, illness, psychological distress, and suicide attempts for women and in poor school performance, disciplinary problems, delinquency, and drug use for children. One of the effects of family violence most consistently found is that it perpetuates itself. People who were abused as children are much more likely to become abusive parents.

Other factors associated with child abuse include stressful events affecting family members, social isolation, inequalitarian marriages, unemployment, and alcohol abuse. The sexual abuse of children differs from physical abuse in several ways. While physical abuse of children is committed as much by women as by men, most sexual abuse offenders are men. The incidence of child sexual abuse has been shown in recent studies to be much higher than previously thought. For instance, one large study found that incest had affected 16% of women before the age of 18. In general, sexual-abuse victims tend to be young girls who are victimized by stepfathers, uncles, fathers, or older male siblings. The evidence points to the conclusion that child sexual abuse should be seen primarily as a problem of masculine socialization.

Violence among intimates includes dating couples. As with assaults in marriage, the seriously harmed victims tend to be women. In general, the closer a dating relationship approximates a marriage—that is, the couple has a sexual relationship and is living together—the more likely the occurrence of violence. Men are not alone as perpetrators of violence in married couples, but women are victims of the most severe forms. The perpetrators of wife battering tend to have low self-esteem and volatile personalities, and they are likely to have been abused as children. Work stress, unemployment, alcohol abuse, blue-collar status, and inequalitarian marriages are also associated with wife beating.

Women often stay in battering relationships because they feel they must; economic dependency is a central factor in keeping women in severely abusive marriages. Many women rationalize or deny the violence inflicted upon them, in part because they believe that it is somehow their fault or a private matter. Shelters appear to give women more options to leave a batterer or, when they choose to stay, a means for leverage to change the violent behavior.

The earliest theories of family violence focused on the apparent psychopathology of the perpetrator. This model is inadequate because evidence shows that venting aggression is *not* a release or catharsis—violence does not reduce the likelihood of future violence. Moreover, multiple factors in the social situations characterizing families are associated with violence in the home. The social learning perspective is strongly supported by repeated findings that experiencing family violence as a child increases the chances of being a perpetrator as an adult.

Goode's resource theory argues that the people with fewest resources to achieve their aims will be quickest to resort to violence. Gelles proposes an exchange/social control theory which proposes that people will use violence when the costs of being violent do not outweigh the rewards. The reason why the cost/benefit ratio favors violence so often in families is that the privacy of what goes on decreases the likelihood of outsiders discovering the violence—and even if they do, the privacy norm reduces the chances that anything will be done about it.

The consistent finding that domestic violence is associated with stress suggests that social inequalities contribute to child abuse and wife battering. Economic inequalities account for the frustrations faced by lower-class parents trying to raise families with limited or inadequate resources. Feminist theory places domestic violence in the historical context of patriarchy—the institutions and beliefs behind the domination of men over women. From this viewpoint, male violence in the home is simply one among many techniques that have been used to keep women subordinate to men. The importance of the cultural context as an encouragement to family violence is supported by findings about the effects of military bases on the severity of domestic assaults against women and the role that religion often plays in justifying male aggression.

Social policies include intervention to assist victims, to treat perpetrators, and to prevent family violence. Legal changes appear to have helped children; the shelter movement has helped women. It has also been shown that arrest deters some batterers and that counseling programs can be effective. Ultimately, however, the reduction and prevention of family violence require fundamental changes in the culture and structure of American society.

REFERENCES

Agnew, R., and Huguley, S.
1989   "Adolescent Violence toward Parents." *Journal of Marriage and the Family* 51: 699–711.

Araji, S., and Finkelhor, D.
1986   "Abusers: A Review of the Research." Pp. 89–118 in Finkelhor (3rd.), *A Sourcebook on Child Sexual Abuse.* Beverly Hills, CA: Sage.

Barling, J., and Rosenbaum, A.
1986   "Work Stressors and Wife Abuse." *Journal of Applied Psychology* 71: 346–348.

Barth, R. P., and Derezotes, D. S.
1990   *Preventing Adolescent Abuse: Intervention Strategies and Techniques.* Lexington, MA: Lexington Books.

Berk, R. A., Berk, S. F., Loseke, D. R., and Rauma, D.
1983   "Mutual Combat and Other Family Myths." Pp. 197–212 in D. Finkelhor, R.J. Gelles, G.T. Hotaling, and M.A. Straus (eds.), *The Dark Side of Families,* Beverly Hills, CA: Sage.

Berk, R. A., Newton, P. J., and Berk, S. F.
1986   "What a Difference a Day Makes: An Empirical Study of the Impact of Shelters for Battered Women." *Journal of Marriage and the Family* 48:481–490.

Boudreau, F. A.
1993   "Elder Abuse." Pp. 142–158 in R. L. Hampton, G. R. Adams, E. H. Potter, III, and R. P. Weissberg (eds.), *Family Violence: Prevention and Treatment.* Newbury Park, CA: Sage.

Bowker, L. H.
1983   *Beating Wife-Beating.* Lexington, MA: Lexington Books.

Breines, W., and Gordon, L.
1983   "The New Scholarship on Family Violence." *Signs* 8: 490–531.

Browne, A.
1987   *When Battered Women Kill.* New York: Free Press.
1993   "Violence against Women by Male Partners: Prevalence, Outcomes, and Policy Implications." *American Psychologist* 48: 1077–1087.

Browne, A., and Finkelhor, D.
1986   "Initial and Long-Term Effects: A Review of the Research." Pp. 143–179 in D. Finkelhor (ed.), *A Sourcebook on Child Sexual Abuse.* Beverly Hills, CA: Sage.

Browne, D. H.
1986   "The Role of Stress in the Commission of Subsequent Acts of Child Abuse and Neglect." *Journal of Family Violence* 1: 289–297.

Cappell, C., and Heiner, R. B.
1990   "The Intergenerational Transmission of Family Aggression." *Journal of Family Violence* 5: 135–152.

Carlson, B. E.
1987   "Dating Violence: A Research Review and Comparison with Spouse Abuse." *Social Casework* 68: 16–23.

Carter, J., Stacey, W. A., and Shupe, A. W.
1988   "Male Violence against Women: Assessment of the Generational Transfer Hypothesis." *Deviant Behavior* 9: 259–273.

Cazenave, N. A., and Straus, M. A.
1990   "Race, Class, Network Embeddedness, and Family Violence: A Search for Potent Support Systems." Pp. 321–339 in M. A. Straus and R. J. Gelles (eds.), *Physical Violence in American Families.* New Brunswick, NJ: Transaction.

Coleman, D. H., and Straus, M. A.
1990   "Marital Power, Conflict, and Violence in a Nationally Representative Sample of American Couples." Pp. 287–304 in M. A. Straus and R. J. Gelles (eds.), *Physical Violence in American Families*. New Brunswick, NJ: Transaction.

Counts, D. A.
1987   "Female Suicide and Wife Abuse: A Cross-Cultural Perspective." *Suicide and Life-Threatening Behavior* 17: 194–204.

Crystal, S.
1987   "Elder Abuse: The Latest 'Crisis'." *Public Interest* 88: 56–66.

Daly, M., and Wilson, M.
1991   "A Reply to Gelles: Stepchildren Are Disproportionately Abused and Diverse Forms of Violence Can Share Causal Factors." *Human Nature* 2: 419–426.

Dobash, R. E., and Dobash, R.
1979   *Violence against Wives*. New York: Free Press.

Dobash, R. P., and Dobash, R. E.
1981   "Community Response to Violence against Wives: Charivari, Abstract Justice and Patriarchy." *Social Problems* 28: 563–581.

Dobash, R. P., Dobash, R. E., Wilson, M., and Daly, M.
1992   "The Myth of Sexual Symmetry in Marital Violence." *Social Problems* 39: 71–91.

Dunford, F. W., Huizinga, D., and Elliott, D.
1990   "The Role of Arrest in Domestic Assault: The Omaha Police Experiment." *Criminology* 28: 183–206.

Famularo, R., Stone, K., Barnum, R., and Wharton, R.
1986   "Alcoholism and Severe Child Maltreatment." *American Journal of Orthopsychiatry* 56: 481–485.

Farrington, K.
1986   "The Application of Stress Theory to the Study of Family Violence: Principles, Problems and Prospects." *Journal of Family Violence* 1: 131–147.

Ferraro, K. J., and Johnson, J.M.
1983   "How Women Experience Battering: The Process of Victimization." *Social Problems* 30: 325–339.

Finkelhor, D.
1984a   *Child Sexual Abuse: New Theory and Research*. New York: Free Press.
1984b   "How Widespread Is Child Sexual Abuse?" *Children Today* 13: 18–20.
1985   "Sexual Abuse and Physical Abuse: Some Critical Differences." Pp. 21–30 in E. H. Newberger and R. Bourne (eds.), *Unhappy Families: Clinical and Research*

Perspectives on Family Violence. Littleton, MA: PSG Publishing.
1986a   "Prevention Approaches to Child Abuse." Pp. 296–308 in M. Lystad (ed.), *Violence in the Home: Interdisciplinary Perspectives*. New York: Brunner/Mazel.
1986b   *A Sourcebook on Child Sexual Abuse*. Beverly Hills, CA: Sage.
1990   "Is Child Abuse Overreported?" *Public Welfare* 48: 22–29, 46.

Finkelhor, D., and Baron, L.
1986   "Risk Factors for Child Sexual Abuse." *Journal of Interpersonal Violence* 1: 43–71.

Finkelhor, D., Hotaling, G. T., Lewis, I. A., and Smith, C.
1989   "Sexual Abuse and Its Relationship to Later Sexual Satisfaction, Marital Status, Religion, and Attitudes." *Journal of Interpersonal Violence* 4: 379–399.
1990   "Sexual Abuse in a National Survey of Adult Men and Women: Prevalence, Characteristics, and Risk Factors." *Child Abuse and Neglect* 14: 19–28.

Finkelhor, D., and Korbin, J.
1988   "Child Abuse as an International Issue." *Child Abuse and Neglect* 12: 3–23.

Ford, D. A.
1991   "Preventing and Provoking Wife Battery through Criminal Sanctions: A Look at the Risks." Pp. 191–209 in D. Knudsen, and J. L. Miller (eds.), *Abused and Battered: Social and Legal Responses to Family Violence*. New York: Aline de Gruyter.

Garbarino, J.
1977   "The Human Ecology of Child Maltreatment." *Journal of Marriage and the Family* 39: 721–735.

Gelles, R. J.
1973   "Child Abuse as Psychopathology: A Sociological Critique and Reformulation." *American Journal of Orthopsychiatry* 43: 611–621.
1974   *The Violent Home: A Study of Physical Aggression between Husbands and Wives*, updated edition. Beverly Hills, CA: Sage.
1976   "Abused Wives: Why Do They Stay?" *Journal of Marriage and the Family* 38: 659–668.
1978   "Violence toward Children in the United States." *American Journal of Orthopsychiatry* 48: 580–592.
1983a   "An Exchange/Social Control Theory." Pp. 151–165 in D. Finkelhor, R. J. Gelles, G. T. Hotaling, and M. A. Straus (eds.), *The Dark Side of Families*. Beverly Hills, CA: Sage.
1983b   "Family Violence: What We Know and Can Do." Pp. 1–8 in E. H. Newberger and R. Bourne (eds.), *Unhappy Families: Clin-*

ical and Research Perspectives on Family Violence. Littleton, MA: PSG Publishing.

1985   "Family Violence." *Annual Review of Sociology* 11: 347–367.

1987   "What to Learn from Cross-Cultural and Historical Research on Child Abuse and Neglect: An Overview." Pp. 15–30 in R. J. Gelles and J. B. Lancaster (eds.), *Child Abuse and Neglect: Biosocial Dimensions.* New York: Aldine de Gruyter.

1989   "Child Abuse and Violence in Single-Parent Families: Parent Absence and Economic Deprivation." *American Journal of Orthopsychiatry* 59: 492–501.

1991   "Physical Violence, Child Abuse, and Child Homicide: A Continuum of Violence, or Distinct Behaviors?" *Human Nature* 2: 59–72.

1993a   Constraints against Family Violence." *American Behavioral Scientist* 36: 575–586.

1993b   "Family Violence." Pp. 1–24 in R. L. Hampton, G. R. Adams, E. H. Potter, III, and R. P. Weissberg (eds.), *Family Violence: Prevention and Treatment.* Newbury Park, CA: Sage.

Gelles, R. J., and Cornell, C. P.
1983   *International Perspectives on Family Violence.* Lexington, MA: Lexington Books.

1985   *Intimate Violence in Families.* Beverly Hills, CA: Sage

Gelles, R. J., and Hargreaves, E. F.
1981   "Maternal Employment and Violence toward Children." *Journal of Family Issues* 2: 509–530.

Gelles, R. J., and Straus, M. A.
1979   "Determinants of Violence in the Family: Toward a Theoretical Integration." Pp. 549–581 in W. R. Burr, R. Hill, F. E. Nye, and I. L. Reiss (eds.), *Contemporary Theories about the Family.* New York: Free Press.

1987   "The Cost of Family Violence." *Public Health Reports* 102: 638–641.

Gest, T.
1994   "Home Violence." *U.S. News and World Report,* July 18, 1994, p. 17.

Gil, D. G.
1970   *Violence against Children: Physical Child Abuse in the United States.* Cambridge, MA: Harvard University Press.

1986   "Sociocultural Aspects of Domestic Violence." Pp. 124–149 in M. Lystad (ed.), *Violence in the Home: Interdisciplinary Perspectives.* New York: Brunner/Mazel.

Giles-Sims, J.
1983   *Wife Battering: A Systems Theory Approach.* New York: Guilford Press.

Goode, W.
1971   "Force and Violence in the Family." *Journal of Marriage and the Family* 33: 624–636.

Gordon, L., and O'Keefe, P.
1984   "Incest as a Form of Family Violence: Evidence from Historical Case Records." *Journal of Marriage and the Family* 46: 27–34.

Hamberger, L. K., and Hastings, J. E.
1991   "Personality Correlates of Men Who Batter and Nonviolent Men: Some Continuities and Discontinuities." *Journal of Family Violence* 6: 131–147.

Hampton, Robert L., Gelles, R. J., and Harrop, J.
1991   "Is Violence in Black Families Increasing? A Comparison of 1975 and 1985 National Survey Rates." Pp. 3–18 in R. L. Hampton (ed.), *Black Family Violence: Current Research and Theory.* Lexington, MA: Lexington Books.

Herman, J., Russell, D., and Trocki, K.
1986   "Long-Term Effects of Incestuous Abuse in Childhood." *American Journal of Psychiatry* 143: 1293–1296.

Hoff, L. A.
1990   *Battered Women as Survivors.* New York: Routledge.

Hotaling, G. T., and Straus, M. A.
1990   "Intrafamily Violence and Crime and Violence Outside the Family." Pp. 431–470 in M. A. Straus and R. J. Gelles (eds.), *Physical Violence in American Families.* New Brunswick, NJ: Transaction.

Kalmuss, D. S., and Straus, M. A.
1982   "Wife's Marital Dependency and Wife Abuse." *Journal of Marriage and the Family* 44: 277–286.

1983   "Feminist, Political, and Economic Determinants of Wife Abuse Services." Pp. 363–376 in D. Finkelhor, R. J. Gelles, G. T. Hotaling, and M. A. Straus (eds.), *The Dark Side of Families.* Beverly Hills, CA: Sage.

Kantor, G. K., and Straus, M. A.
1987   "The 'Drunken Bum' Theory of Wife Beating." *Social Problems* 34: 213–225.

Kempe, C. H., Silverman, F. N., Steele, B. F., Droegemueller, W., and Silver, H. K.
1962   "The Battered Child Syndrome." *Journal of the American Medical Association* 181: 107–112.

Klaus, P. A., and Rand, M. R.
1984   "Family Violence." *Bureau of Justice Statistics, Special Report.* Washington, DC: U.S. Department of Justice.

Kroll, L.
1993   "AMA Family Violence Campaign." *Journal of the American Medical Association* 269: 1875.

Kurz, D.
1991   "Corporal Punishment and Adult Use of Violence: A Critique of 'Discipline and Deviance'." *Social Problems* 38: 155–161.
Lane, K. E., and Gwartney-Gibbs, P. A.
1985   "Violence in the Context of Dating and Sex." *Journal of Family Issues* 6: 45–59.
Langan, P. A., and Innes, C. A.
1986   "Preventing Domestic Violence against Women." *Bureau of Justice Statistics, Special Report.* Washington, DC: U.S. Department of Justice.
Levinson, D.
1981   "Physical Punishment of Children and Wifebeating in Cross-Cultural Perspective." *Child Abuse and Neglect* 5: 193–196.
Loseke, D. R.
1991   "Reply to Murray A. Straus: Readings on 'Discipline and Deviance'." *Social Problems* 38: 162–166.
1992   *The Battered Woman and Shelter: The Social Construction of Wife Abuse.* Albany, NY: State University of New York Press.
Loseke, D. R., and Cahill, S. E.
1984   "The Social Construction of Deviance: Experts on Battered Women." *Social Problems* 31: 296–310.
Makepeace, J. M.
1981   "Courtship Violence among College Students." *Family Relations* 30: 97–102.
1986   "Gender Differences in Courtship Violence Victimization." *Family Patterns* 35: 382–388.
Martin, D.
1987   "The Historical Roots of Domestic Violence." Pp. 3–20 in D. J. Sonkin (ed.), *Domestic Violence on Trial.* New York: Springer.
Masson, J. M.
1984   *The Assault on Truth: Freud's Suppression of the Seduction.* New York: Farrar, Straus and Giroux.
May, W. F.
1991   "The Molested." *Hastings Center Report* 21: 9–17.
McCord, J.
1991   "Questioning the Value of Punishment." *Social Problems* 38: 167–179.
Meiselman, K. C.
1990   *Resolving the Trauma of Incest: Reintegration Therapy with Survivors.* San Francisco: Jossey-Bass.
Okum, L.
1986   *Woman Abuse: Facts Replacing Myths.* Albany: State University of New York Press.
O'Leary, K. D., and Curley, A. D.
1986   "Assertion and Family Violence: Corre-

lates of Spouse Abuse." *Journal of Marital and Family Therapy* 12: 281–289.
Owens, D., and Straus, M. A.
1975   "Childhood Violence and Adult Approval of Violence." *Aggressive Behavior* 1: 193–211.
Pagelow, M. D.
1981   *Woman-Battering: Victims and Their Experiences.* Beverly Hills, CA: Sage.
Pfohl, Stephen
1976   "The 'Discovery' of Child Abuse." *Social Problems* 24: 310–323.
Pierce, R. L., and Trotta, R.
1986   "Abused Parents: A Hidden Family Problem." *Journal of Family Violence* 1: 99–110.
Pillemer, K. A.
1986   "Risk Factors in Elder Abuse: Results from a Case-Control Study." Pp. 239–263 in K. A. Pillemer and R. S. Wolfe (eds.), *Elder Abuse: Conflict in the Family.* Dover, MA: Auburn House.
Pizzey, Erin
1977   *Scream Quietly or the Neighbors Will Hear.* Short Hills, NJ: Ridley Enslow.
Pleck, E. J.
1987   *Domestic Tyranny: The Making of Social Policy Against Family Violence from Colonial Times to the Present.* New York: Oxford University Press.
Pleck, E. J., and Pleck, J., Grossman, M., and Bart, P.
1978   "The Battered Data Syndrome: A Comment on Steinmetz's Article." *Victimology* 2: 680–683.
Prescott, S., and Letko, C.
1977   "Battered Women: A Social Psychological Perspective." Pp. 72–96 in M. Roy (ed.), *Battered Women: A Psychosociological Study of Domestic Violence.* New York: Van Nostrand Reinhold.
Radbill, S. X.
1987   "Children in a World of Violence: A History of Child Abuse." Pp. 2–22 in R. E. Helfer and R. S. Kempe (eds.), *The Battered Child*, 4th edition. Chicago: University of Chicago Press.
Reiss, A. J., Jr., and Roth, J. A. (eds.)
1993   *Understanding and Preventing Violence.* Washington, DC: National Academy Press.
Rounsaville, B. J.
1978   "Theories of Marital Violence: Evidence from a Study of Battered Women." *Victimology* 3: 11–31.
Russell, D. E. H.
1986a   "The Incest Legacy: Why Today's Abused Children Become Tomorrow's Victims of Rape." *Sciences* 26: 28–32.

1986b   *The Secret Trauma: Incest in the Lives of Girls and Women.* New York: Basic Books.

Schwartz, M. D.
1990   "Work Status, Resource Equality, Injury and Wife Battery: The National Crime Survey Data." *Free-Inquiry in Creative Sociology* 18: 57–61.

Seltzer, J. A., and Kalmuss, D.
1988   "Socialization and Stress Explanations for Spouse Abuse." *Social Forces* 67: 473–491.

Sherman, L. and Berk, R. A.
1984   "The Specific Deterrent Effects of Arrest for Domestic Assault." *American Sociological Review* 49: 261–272.

Shupe, A. D., Stacey, W. A., and Hazlewood, L. R.
1987   *Violent Men, Violent Couples: The Dynamics of Domestic Violence.* Lexington, MA: Lexington Books.

Smith, C.
1988   "Status Discrepancies and Husband-to-Wife Violence." Paper presented at the Annual Meeting of the Eastern Sociological Society.

Stark, E., Flitcraft, A., Zuckerman, D., Grey, A., Robison, J., and Frazier, W.
1981   *Wife Abuse in the Medical Setting: An Introduction for Health Personnel.* Monograph No. 7. Washington, DC: Office of Domestic Violence.

Steinmetz, S.
1977   *The Cycle of Violence: Assertive, Aggressive, and Abusive Family Interaction.* New York: Praeger.

Steinmetz, S. K.
1978a   "The Battered Husband Syndrome." *Victimology* 2: 499–509.
1978b   "Battered Parents." *Society* 15: 54–55.
1986   "The Violent Family." Pp. 51–67 in M. Lystad (ed.), *Violence in the Home: Interdisciplinary Perspectives.* New York: Brunner/Mazel.

Stets, J. E., and Straus, M. A.
1989   "The Marriage License as a Hitting License: A Comparison of Assaults in Dating, Cohabiting, and Married Couples." *Journal of Family Violence* 4: 161–180.
1990   "Gender Differences in Reporting Marital Violence and Its Medical and Psychological Consequences." Pp. 151–165 in M. A. Straus and R. J. Gelles (eds.), *Physical Violence in American Families.* New Brunswick, NJ: Transaction.

Straus, M. A.
1977   "Societal Morphogenesis and Interfamily Violence in Cross-Cultural Perspective." *Annals of the New York Academy of Sciences* 285: 717–730.

1979   "Measuring Intrafamily Conflict and Violence: The Conflict Tactics (CT) Scales." *Journal of Marriage and the Family* 41: 75–88.
1980   "Victims and Aggressors in Marital Violence." *American Behavioral Scientist* 23: 681–704.
1991a   "Discipline and Deviance: Physical Punishment of Children and Violence and Other Crime in Adulthood." *Social Problems* 38: 133–154.
1991b   "New Theory and Old Canards about Family Violence Research." *Social Problems* 38: 180–197.
1992   "Sociological Research and Social Policy: The Case of Family Violence." *Sociological Forum* 7: 211–237.

Straus, M. A., and Gelles, R. J.
1986   "Societal Change and Change in Family Violence from 1975-1985 as Revealed by Two National Surveys." *Journal of Marriage and the Family* 48: 465–479.
1990   "How Violent Are American Families? Estimates from the National Family Violence Resurvey and Other Studies." Pp. 95–112 in M. A. Straus and R. J. Gelles (eds.), *Physical Violence in American Families.* New Brunswick, NJ: Transaction.

Straus, M. A., Gelles, R. J., and Steinmetz, S. K.
1980   *Behind Closed Doors: Violence in the American Family.* Garden City, NY: Anchor.

Straus, M. A., and Kalmuss, D. S.
1982   "Wife Marital Dependency and Wife Abuse." *Journal of Marriage and the Family* 44: 277–286.

Straus, M. A., and Kantor, G. K.
1987   "Stress and Child Abuse." Pp. 42–59 in R. E. Helfer and R. S. Kempe (eds.), *The Battered Child*, 4th edition. Chicago: University of Chicago Press.

Straus, M. A., and Smith, C.
1990a   "Family Patterns and Child Abuse." Pp. 245–261 in M. A. Straus and R. J. Gelles (eds.), *Physical Violence in American Families.* New Brunswick, NJ: Transaction.
1990b   "Family Patterns and Primary Prevention of Family Violence." Pp. 507–526 in M. A. Straus and R. J. Gelles (eds.), *Physical Violence in American Families.* New Brunswick, NJ: Transaction.
1990c   "Violence in Hispanic Families in the United States: Incidence Rates and Structural Interpretations." Pp. 34J–367 in M. A. Straus and R. J. Gelles (eds.), *Physical Violence in American Families.* New Brunswick, NJ: Transaction.

Suitor, J. J., Pillemer, K., and Straus, M. A.
1990   "Marital Violence in a Life Course Per-
         spective." Pp. 305–317 in M. A. Straus
         and R. J. Gelles (eds.), *Physical Violence
         in American Families*. New Brunswick,
         NJ: Transaction.
Tierney, K. J.
1982   "The Battered Wife Movement and the
         Creation of the Wife Beating Problem."
         Social Problems 29: 207–220.
Tolman, R. M., and Bhosley, G.
1991   "The Outcome of Participation in a Shel-
         ter-Sponsored Program for Men Who
         Batter." Pp. 113–122 in D. Knudsen, and
         J. A. L. Miller (eds.), *Abused and Bat-
         tered: Social and Legal Responses to Fam-
         ily Violence*. New York: Aldine de
         Gruyter.
U.S. Bureau of the Census
1993   *Statistical Abstract of the United States:
         1993*. Tables 62, 70, 75, 80, 340, 341, 736,
         737. Washington, DC: U.S. Department
         of Commerce.
U.S. Congress, House Select Committee on Children, Youth, and Families
1987   *Abused Children in America: Victims of
         Official Neglect*. Washington, DC: U.S.
         Government Printing Office.
U.S. Department of Justice
1993   *Uniform Crime Reports: Crime in the
         United States*. Washington, DC: Federal
         Bureau of Investigation.

1994   *Criminal Victimization in the United
         States, 1992*. Tables 37 and 72. Washing-
         ton, DC: Bureau of Justice Statistics.
Vander Mey, B. J., and Neff, R. L.
1986   *Incest as Child Abuse: Research and Ap-
         plications*. New York: Praeger.
Walker, G. A.
1990   *Family Violence and the Women's Move-
         ment: The Conceptual Politics of Strug-
         gle*. Toronto: University of Toronto Press.
Walker, L. E.
1979   *The Battered Woman*. New York: Harp-
         er & Row.
Whipple, V.
1987   "Counseling Battered Women from Fun-
         damentalist Churches." *Journal of Marital
         and Family Therapy* 13: 251–258.
Williams, K. R., and Hawkins, R.
1989   "Controlling Male Aggression in Intimate
         Relationships." *Law and Society Review*
         23: 591–612.
Zigler, E., and Kaufman, J.
1987   "Do Abused Children Become Abusive
         Parents?" *American Journal of Orthopsy-
         chiatry* 57: 186–192.
Zimring, F. E.
1988   "Gun Control." *National Institute of Jus-
         tice, Crime File*. Washington, DC: U.S.
         Department of Justice.

8 | Street Crime and Delinquency

Ask a sample of Americans what they mean by crime and most would refer to such disreputable activities as murder, robbery, theft, and the like. Customarily, the problem of crime is conceptualized as "crime in the streets," despite the fact that this activity results in far less economic and physical loss than do the corporate illegalities discussed in the next chapter. Nevertheless, street crime *is* a serious problem in American society, and in the public mind and political arguments, it is increasing.

Many of the activities commonly called *street crimes*, such as auto theft or robbery, occur in public. Others, such as larceny-theft, are frequently committed in private homes or businesses. Rather than the location where they are committed, two other characteristics distinguish street crimes: they are illegal acts that are widely regarded as seriously harmful, and minimal resources are required to commit them. To engage in a white-collar crime such as Wall Street insider trading, the offender must have a lofty position in the corporate world, to say nothing of sophisticated skills in persuasion, manipulation, and business practices. Snatching a purse or mugging an unwitting victim or robbing a storekeeper takes little more than boldness and, in the absence of a weapon, physical strength and speed. Illegal acts such as these thus are characterized as deviance committed by the relatively poor and powerless.

Official definitions place street crimes in the FBI's Uniform Crime Index of eight *serious crimes*, sometimes referred to as *Index crimes*. These include the *personal crimes* of homicide, forcible rape, robbery and aggravated assault, along with the *property crimes* of burglary, larceny-theft, motor vehicle theft, and arson (defined in Table 8.1). Arson was added to the list only recently, and data concerning it are frequently incomplete in official tabulations. Therefore, in this chapter we will concentrate on the other seven Index crimes.

SOURCES OF INFORMATION ON STREET CRIME

There are two primary sources of information on the amount of street crime in the United States. The first is data collected from police agencies nationwide and compiled by the Federal Bureau of Investigation annually in *Uniform Crime Reports (UCR)*. This information is of two types: (1) crimes *reported* but not necessarily solved, and (2) a record of arrests for crimes that the police have solved. The second major source of information is the *National Crime Survey (NCS)*, a random survey

Table 8.1   Definitions of Personal and Property Crimes on the FBI Uniform Crime Index

Personal Crimes	Property Crimes
Criminal Homicide—a. Murder and non-negligent manslaughter: the willful (non-negligent) killing of one human being by another. Deaths caused by negligence, attempts to kill, assaults to kill, suicides, accidental deaths, and justifiable homicides are excluded. Justifiable homicides are limited to: (1) the killing of a felon by a law enforcement officer in the line of duty; and (2) the killing of a felon by a private citizen. b. Manslaughter by negligence: the killing of another person through gross negligence. Traffic fatalities are excluded. While manslaughter by negligence is a Part I crime, it is not included in the Crime Index.	**Burglary, Breaking and Entering**—The unlawful entry of a structure to commit a felony or a theft. Attempted forcible entry is included.
Forcible Rape—The carnal knowledge of a female forcibly and against her will. Included are rapes by force and attempts or assaults to rape. Statutory offenses (no force used—victim under age of consent) are excluded.	**Larceny-theft (except motor vehicle theft)**— The unlawful taking, carrying, leading, or riding away of property from the possession or constructive possession of another. Examples are thefts of bicycles or automobile accessories, shoplifting, pocket-picking, or the stealing of any property or article which is not taken by force and violence or by fraud. Attempted larcenies are included. Embezzlement, "con" games, forgery, worthless checks, etc., are excluded.
Robbery—The taking or attempting to take anything of value from the care, custody, or control of a person or persons by force or threat of force or violence and/or by putting the victim in fear.	**Motor Vehicle Theft**—The theft or attempted theft of a motor vehicle. A motor vehicle is self-propelled and runs on the surface and not on rails. Specifically excluded from this category are motorboats, construction equipment, airplanes, and farming equipment.
Aggravated Assault—An unlawful attack by one person upon another for the purpose of inflicting severe or aggravated bodily injury. This type of assault usually is accompanied by the use of a weapon or by means likely to produce death or great bodily harm. Simple assaults are excluded.	**Arson**—Any willful or malicious burning or attempt to burn, with or without intent to defraud, a dwelling house, public building, motor vehicle or aircraft, personal property of another, etc.

Source: U.S. Department of Justice, *Uniform Crime Reports: Crime in the United States*, 1993: 381.

of households conducted by the U.S. Bureau of Justice Statistics each year. In 1992, for example 110,000 people age 12 and over in about 66,000 housing units took part in the telephone interviews, which asked whether they had been victimized in various types of crime. The *UCR* data tell something about street crimes reported to the police and the characteristics of individuals for whom contact with the criminal justice system is initiated at the point of arrest. Because many crimes are not reported to the police, however, the NCS data provide a better sense of the amount of street crime in the United States, whether or not it is counted in official police statistics.

According to NCS estimates based on the victimization surveys, there were about 33,649,000 total crime victimizations in 1992 (U.S. Department of Justice, 1994: 4). Over 6.5 million of them were violent crimes (rape, robbery, and assault); 12.2 million were personal theft; and 14.8 million were household crimes (burglary, household larceny, and motor vehicle theft). During the past 20 years the peak year of victimization was 1981, when nearly 41.5 million total victimizations were reported. Since then, total victimization levels have dropped by 18.8%; personal theft and household crimes have declined by 23% and 22%, respectively; and violent crimes have risen only slightly, by 0.6%. Thus, according to this measure, overall levels of street crime have been trending downward.

Table 8.2 presents information on crimes known to the police, using *UCR* data, and Table 8.3 shows NCS victim data, including the percentage of victims who said they had reported the crime to police. Note the following highlights in these tables:

- Rates of property crime (crimes of theft) far exceed those for violent crime.
- A substantial portion of crimes are not officially reported; less than 40% of all crimes on the NCS, taken together, are reported to the police.
- Crimes of violence are more apt to be reported to the police than are crimes of theft. The greatest exception is motor vehicle theft, the crime most likely to be officially reported.

FEAR OF STREET CRIME

Loss of property, injury, or death is an obvious cost of street crime to an individual victim. The social costs are more subtle. In certain American communities, particularly urban areas, residents and others have for some time reported an abiding fear of criminal victimization (Furstenberg, 1971; Skogan, 1981). Whether or not this fear is justified, it is accompanied by a suspicion of strangers, an increased intolerance for the unfamiliar, a constricted sense of community, and restricted freedom to use public streets and facilities. The fear of crime imposes a toll on our individual and collective well-being and quality of life.

In general, public beliefs about crime correspond remarkably to official statistics. In one study (Warr, 1980), survey respondents were, on average, able to estimate rather closely the official incidence of crimes reported to the police for 17 offenses, including the *UCR* Index crimes. This is despite portrayals of street crime on television and in the movies that exaggerate the extent of violent crime and the effectiveness of law enforcement agencies in solving cases (Lichter and Lichter, 1983). Apparently most people's perceptions of crime are more influenced by their own experience and reports in the news than by the inaccuracies conveyed by the media.

Table 8.2   FBI, Uniform Crime Index, Crimes Known to the Police, United States, 1992

Type of Crime	Number	Rate per 100,000 Population
Crime Index total	14,458,200	5,660.2
Violent crime	1,932,270	757.2
Murder and nonnegligent manslaughter	23,760	9.3
Forcible rape	109,060	42.8
Robbery	672,480	263.6
Aggravated assault	1,126,970	441.8
Property crime	12,505,900	4,902.7
Burglary	2,979,900	1,168.2
Larceny-theft	7,915,200	3,103.3
Motor vehicle theft	1,610,800	631.5

Source: U.S. Department of Justice, *Uniform Crime Reports: Crime in the United States*, 1993: 58.

Crime Waves: Fact or Myth?

Some 30 years ago, Daniel Bell wrote an article, "The Myth of Crime Waves" (1960), to show that the incidence of crime in the United States had not spiraled upward relentlessly since the country's founding. Instead, the amount of street crime has oscillated throughout our history. Most historians of crime agree that there was a surge in the amount of crime from the Revolution into the middle of the 19th century. For the next half to three-quarters of a century, street crime declined, for reasons that included lower per capita alcohol consumption, more effective urban services, such as street lighting and policing, and more disciplinary control imposed on workers by the factory system.

Contemporary records for tracking crime trends begin with establishment of the FBI Uniform Crime Index in 1933. After a drop during the first decade, the overall crime rate on this measure began to climb steeply, and, with only minor interruptions, it continued to do so into the 1980s. There is some evidence that it may be leveling off in the 1990s. However, this picture, based on crimes reported to the police, may be somewhat misleading. For example, while the NCS reported about a 25% *decrease* in both personal crimes and households touched by crime from 1973 through 1991, the *UCR* index of crimes reported to the police rose about 42%. Thus the most widely disseminated indicator of "crime rates" indicates a growing incidence of crime, while the NCS truer measure of incidence has declined. This discrepancy may be due to people's increased willingness to report crimes to the police, more accurate police reporting procedures, or increases in criminal justice expenditures and policing activity.

Table 8.3   Victimizations and Percent Reported to the Police, NCS Data, United States, 1992

Type of Crime	Number of Victimizations°	Percent Reported to the Police
All crimes	33,649,000	39%
Crimes of violence	6,621,000	50
Rape	141,000	53
Robbery	1,226,000	51
Aggravated assault	1,849,000	62
Crimes of theft	12,211,000	30
Personal larceny with contact	485,000	31
Personal larceny without contact	11,726,000	30
Burglary	4,757,000	54
Household larceny	8,101,000	26
Motor vehicle theft	1,959,000	75

Source: U.S. Department of Justice, *Criminal Victimization in the United States, 1992*, 1994: 5, 7.
°Estimated from the sample survey.

In spite of a fluctuating crime rate over the past 200 years, many Americans, fearful particularly of youthful street crime, look back with nostalgia to the "good old days," idealizing a crimefree past that never was while condemning the present. Public panics over "hooliganism" are not new; they have periodically infected British society, for example, at least since the 1500s (Pearson, 1983). In contemporary American society, the apparent heightened fear of street crime may have less to do with its *amount* (in fact, the incidence of many categories is actually dropping) than with its changing *quality*. For instance, high-powered, automatic weapons capable of firing rapid rounds of ammunition have facilitated multiple shootings in supposedly safe locations, from restaurants and workplaces to public transportation. While these highly publicized acts, which can reasonably be described as random and senseless massacres, are statistically rare, they certainly add to public fears that violent crime is widespread, out of control, and growing. Such fears may even be welcomed by politicians and government officials, who can use them to inflame public concern and, through "war on crime" and "law and order" campaigns, divert attention away from such major public policy issues as universal health care, corporate downsizing, falling standards of living, and the provision of social services. Moreover, playing to public fears of street crime can be in the interest of elites who wish to justify repressive measures against the "dangerous classes" and to focus attention on "crime in the streets" while diverting attention away from "crime in the corporate suites."

THE "FACTS" OF STREET CRIME

Like most social phenomena, crimes and crime rates are patterned. The patterns show up most distinctly as differences in the amounts of crime among countries, states, geographic areas, and social categories such as the sexes, age cohorts, racial groups, and social classes of perpetrators and victims. When these differences are large and persistent, they constitute the "brute facts" of street crime and criminality with which any theory devised to explain them must contend.

International Comparisons

Establishing in detail the relative crime rates of various countries is exceedingly difficult because little comparable data exist. Countries vary in how they define specific crimes, the efficiency of their reporting systems, and the accuracy of their tabulations. With homicide, such problems are minimal, and therefore comparisons are most meaningful. In various years from 1984 to 1990, the rates among countries ranged widely, as shown in Table 8.4. The homicide rate for the United States, 9.3 per 100,000 population in 1992, was among the highest in the world, from three to ten times higher than any other industrialized country. Rates for most categories of street crime in the United States are generally higher than those in other Western, developed countries, although the differences are not as extreme as those for homicide (Archer and Gartner, 1984).

Regional Differences in the United States

Until recently, the most distinctive feature of regional street crime variations in the United States has been the high rate of homicide in the South. To explain this pattern, Wolfgang and Ferracuti (1967) propose that in some areas, or among some groups, violence is an expected response to insult or injury. Such a norm, supported by the value of machismo (an exaggerated sense of masculinity or strength) and the ready availability of guns, sets the stage for greater amounts of lethal criminal violence.

Regardless of the historical pattern, however, a trend in recent years has been the growing similarity in crime rates, including homicide, across the regions of the United States. This probably reflects the relative weakening of regional cultures and the development of an American society as people who have been culturally homogenized by the national media and have become more mobile move from place to place. As our ways of life among the various regions of the country have grown more similar, so have our patterns of crime.

Far sharper than regional variations are differences in crime rates according to the size of the location in which crime takes place. As Table 8.5 shows, the *UCR* total Index rate for metropolitan statistical areas (large, densely populated urban areas together with adjacent communities with a high degree of social and economic integration) is over three times that for rural areas. For every individual crime there is a positive, monotonic or unvarying relationship between the size of place and the Index rate. A detailed analysis of data for 1960, 1970, and 1980

Table 8.4   Homicide Rates in Selected Countries and Years, 1984–1990, in Rate per 100,000 Population

Country	Rate	Year
El Salvador	40.4	1984
Mexico	19.9	1986
Puerto Rico	16.2	1990
Brazil	14.8	1986
United States	8.9	1988
Panama	6.9	1987
Argentina	5.4	1987
Dominican Republic	4.8	1985
Costa Rica	4.0	1988
Bulgaria	3.2	1990
Hungary	3.1	1990
Poland	2.9	1990
Australia	2.4	1988
Israel	2.4	1989
Belgium	2.1	1986
Canada	2.1	1989
Czechoslovakia	2.0	1990
France	1.1	1989
Germany (Federal Republic)	1.0	1990
Netherlands	1.0	1989
Japan	0.6	1990
England and Wales	0.5	1990

Source: United Nations, *1991 Demographic Yearbook*, 1992: 438–459.

showed that the cities that had extremely high crime rates tended to be the largest, most economically depressed, and most socially disintegrated (Land, McCall, and Cohen, 1991).

Offender Characteristics

Sex. In 1992 in the United States, males accounted for 99% of the arrests for rape, about 91% of those for robberies and burglaries, about 90% of those for murders and motor vehicle theft, 85% of those for aggravated assault, and 68% of those for larceny thefts. In virtually every category of serious street crime, in virtually every time and place enumerated, males have much higher rates than females. Throughout the world, overwhelmingly, street crimes are male activities.

Currently, the most interesting question about these facts is whether females are "catching up" to males in criminality. If women are becoming more like men in their opportunities outside the home, we might expect diminishing differences between men and women on numerous behavioral indicators, including rates of street

Table 8.5   FBI Uniform Crime Index Crimes Known to the Police, by Population Areas, United States, 1992

| | RATE PER 100,000 POPULATION | | |
Type of Crime	Metropolitan Statistical Areas	Other Cities	Rural Areas
Crime Index total	6,272.3	5,316.6	2,025.7
Violent crimes	871.2	486.2	220.2
Murder and nonnegligent manslaughter	10.4	5.4	5.2
Forcible rape	46.1	37.2	25.1
Robbery	323.2	70.1	16.3
Aggravated assault	491.5	373.5	173.6
Property crimes	5,401.1	4,830.3	1,805.5
Burglary	1,265.1	1,011.9	660.6
Larceny-theft	3,378.1	3,601.4	1,035.8
Motor vehicle theft	757.9	217.0	109.1

Source: U.S. Department of Justice, *Uniform Crime Reports: Crime in the United States*, 1993: 59.

crime. In the United Sates, up to about 1980, evidence indicated that the answer was yes with respect to petty property crimes, particularly among the young (Smith and Visher, 1980; Steffensmeier, 1978). However, the answer was no in regard to most *UCR* Index crimes. Women typically were nonviolent, petty offenders, and while they did make large gains on men in arrests for such minor crimes (Steffensmeier, 1978; Steffensmeier and Cobb, 1981), they were *not* catching up with males in the commission of violent, masculine, male-dominated, serious, or white-collar crimes, with the exception of larceny (Steffensmeier, 1980). One reason is that because traditional sex roles still largely persist in the world of work, women's criminal opportunities there are limited. On the streets there is an absence of viable female criminal subcultures (aside from those surrounding prostitution), and women often do not have access to the subcultures organized by males (Hagan, 1990). Although most studies have found little evidence for a convergence of male and female rates in patterns of street crime, a reanalysis of the UCR Index rate for 1965–1986 by Austin (1993) led to the conclusion that there is evidence to support some convergence. This issue remains controversial.

Age. The young are, by far, most frequently the perpetrators of street crime. As Gottfredson and Hirschi (1986) put it, "the propensity to commit criminal acts reaches a peak in the middle to late teens and then declines rapidly throughout life....Further, this distribution is characteristic of the age-crime relation regardless

Figure 8.1   Arrest Rates for Total Index Crimes, Males and Females, United States, 1992

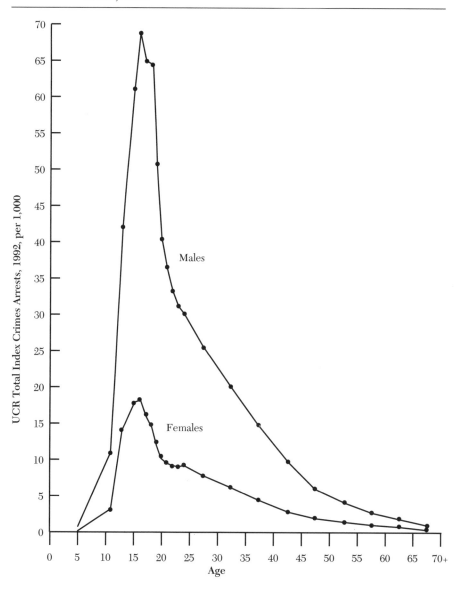

Sources: U.S. Department of Justice, *Uniform Crime Reports: United States,* 1993, Tables 39, 40; U.S. Bureau of the Census, *Current Population Reports,* P–25, No. 1092 (1992), Table 2.

Table 8.6   FBI *UCR* Arrests for Index Crimes, by Percent Male, Under Age 25, and White/Black, United States, 1992

	PERCENT ARRESTED			
	Male	Under 25	White	Black
Crime Index total	77.9%	55.9%	62.7%	35.2%
Violent crime	87.5	47.5	53.6	44.8
Murder and nonnegligent manslaughter	90.3	55.0	43.5	55.1
Forcible rape	98.7	43.8	55.5	42.8
Robbery	91.5	61.7	37.7	60.9
Aggravated assault	85.2	42.4	59.5	38.8
Property crime	74.5	58.9	65.8	31.8
Burglary	90.8	63.9	67.8	30.4
Larceny-theft	67.9	55.3	66.2	31.4
Motor vehicle theft	89.2	74.1	58.4	39.4

Source: U.S. Department of Justice, *Uniform Crime Reports: Crime in the United States*, 1993: 229–235.

of sex, race, country, time, or offense" (219). The pattern of arrests in the United States by age and sex is apparent from Figure 8.1. Table 8.6 shows that 56% of those arrested for *UCR* Index crimes in 1992 were under 25 years of age and that property crimes, especially, are likely to be youthful offenses. In every case, over half the arrests for each type of property crime are of people under 25.

Because age is such a robust variable in relation to crime, changes in the age distribution of the society's population can be expected to affect crime rates. Any increase in the youth population, as occurred in this country in the 1970s as a result of the post–World War II baby boom, increases the number of people in the high-crime age categories. Some of the increases in crime during the seventies were surely related to the increase in the population of youths coming of age to commit crimes. At the same time, of course, as the average age of the population increases, we could expect the crime rate to fall. A study of *UCR* and NCS rates between 1980 and 1984, a period when crime rates were declining, revealed that "about 40% of the reported drop in the nation's Crime Rate is due to shifts in the age structure alone" (Steffensmeier and Harer, 1987: 40). As the population continues to grow older and less crime-prone, crime rates could continue to decline.

Race. Overall, arrest rates for blacks in the United States are three to four times greater than those for whites. Although blacks constitute about 12% of the U.S. population, in 1992 they accounted for 35% of total Crime Index arrests—45% of violent crime arrests and 32% of property crime arrests (see Table 8.6). Incarceration rates of minority youth are also much higher than those of whites the same age (Krisberg et al., 1987). They also constitute nearly half of the country's federal and state prisoners. On any given day in the District of Columbia, our nation's capitol, in 1992, 42% of all black males ages 20–29 were either in jail, on probation or parole, awaiting trial, or being sought on arrest warrants (Kramer, 1993: 1726). There is evidence that some of these racial differences may be due to discrimination in the criminal justice system (Unnever, Frazier, and Hanretta, 1980; Fagan, Slaughter, and Hartstone, 1987; Johnson, 1993). At the same time, evidence from victimization studies indicates that blacks commit street crimes—particularly serious Index crimes—at a higher rate than whites (Huizinga and Elliott, 1987; Sheley, 1993). Blacks may be overrepresented as offenders in prison, then, both because they commit more street crimes and because they are more likely than whites to get arrested, convicted, and sentenced.

Unlike the age-crime relation that is invariant across times and places, higher black crime rates appear to be tied to social circumstances. No evidence exists that blacks in the United States are more predisposed genetically to street crime than whites, nor is there evidence that whites, despite their phenomenally high rates of white-collar crime relative to blacks, are more predisposed genetically to commit corporate or business crimes. Rather, the reasons for the differences can be explained by historically rooted variations in family structure, socialization patterns, and economic opportunity that have been shaped in a context of racial and ethnic discrimination and prejudice. In particular, high levels of disinvestment and relocation of heavy manufacturing have severely undermined the African-American communities in many cities. Sheley (1993) points out that

> These cities, more than others, have been marked by illegal activity for financial gain, especially drug trafficking. Changes in the larger culture, communicated primarily through the media, have encouraged young males to pursue visible material wealth, with aggression as an acceptable means of accumulating and maintaining that wealth. This leads to an increased risk of homicide among residents of cities where opportunities for illegal enterprises and the accompanying subcultural values flourish. (2287)

Social Class. The relationship between street crime and class is complex and somewhat controversial (Hindelang, Hirschi, and Weis, 1981; Tittle, 1983). The evidence for a strong relationship in a given study largely depends on the measures of class and crime used—for example, whether the measures of street crime are arrest statistics or self-report responses. Results of studies investigating the class-crime relationship also are influenced by whether the population studied is juvenile or adult.

Self-report studies that focus on minor offenses among juveniles have tended to show little differences among social classes (Braithwaite, 1981). Probably such surveys exaggerate the amount of middle-class delinquency because they concentrate on the kinds of minor activities that are widely regarded as a normal part of growing up and are readily admitted by survey respondents. Studies of official records tend to show higher rates of street crime in the lower class. This is especially true for adults (Thornberry and Farnworth, 1982). Furthermore, there is strong evidence that economic inequality increases rates of criminal violence for those on the lower end (Blau and Blau, 1982). This is especially the case for members of the urban underclass who suffer recurrent unemployment, intergenerational poverty, and welfare dependency (Brownfield, 1986; Messner and Tardiff, 1986). In research on delinquency among homeless youths, McCarthy and Hagan (1992) found "consistent evidence of the effects of adverse situational conditions: hunger causes theft of food, problems of hunger and shelter lead to serious theft, and problems of unemployment and shelter produce prostitution" (597).

Studies relating unemployment-rate fluctuations to rates of street crime have also found a positive relationship (Chiricos, 1987). However, these correlations are not consistently strong (Cantor and Land, 1985), probably because the people reflected in marginal changes in unemployment rates are not likely to commit serious crimes. Rather, street crime is and remains high among the more or less permanently unemployed in the underclass, regardless of the business cycle (Parker and Horwitz, 1986). Unemployment and crime tend to be mutually reinforcing over a person's life course (Thornberry and Christenson, 1984). An experimental study which examined the effects of financial and employment assistance on the likelihood of subsequent street crime found that "For ex-offenders at least, unemployment and poverty do cause crime on the microlevel. Modest amounts of financial aid can reduce recidivism among ex-felons. Experimentally induced unemployment can increase recidivism" (Berk, Lenhan, and Rossi, 1980).

Drugs, Recidivism, and Criminal Careers

Alcohol is present in a significant portion of the street crimes committed in the United States. In a survey of state prison inmates, nearly 30% said they had been drinking heavily just before they committed the offense for which they were convicted (U.S. Department of Justice, 1983). Evidence has also pointed to the role of alcohol in exacerbating violent confrontations that may end up in homicides (Wolfgang, 1958). Reiss and Roth (1993) found long-term, heavy alcohol use to be a predisposing factor for violent behavior, particularly for adults who had demonstrated chronic aggressive behavior and alcohol abuse in childhood and early adolescence. In Scandinavian countries a number of studies have shown reductions in crimes of violence when the availability of alcohol was curtailed by labor strikes that interrupted the supply (Room, 1983).

Whereas alcohol use is more strongly associated with crimes against persons, addiction to hard drugs is implicated more in property crimes. There is no evidence that nonaddictive drug use leads to crime or that addictive drug use has a direct causal relationship to crime either. The illegal market for psychoactive drugs accounts for far more violence than their pharmacological effects do (Reiss and Roth, 1993). To be sure, the use of addictive narcotics is associated with the commission of street crime. Offenders who are using drugs heavily commit crimes up to six times more frequently than nonusing offenders (Blumstein, Cohen, and Visher, 1986: 74–75). Serious heroin users commit crimes virtually daily, and the rate at which they do so is tied to the frequency of their heroin use. In one study, the number of crimes per year committed on average by each heroin user ranged from nearly 500 for irregular users to almost 1,500 per year for daily users (Johnson et al., 1985). Annual offense incidence rates of heroin addicts have been found to be remarkably consistent in various cities: Baltimore, 567 offenses per year; New York, 603; and Philadelphia, 631 (Ball, 1991).

The heroin addict's motive for committing street crimes is economic; money is needed to support an addiction made expensive by its illegality (see Chapter 6). Most of the ill-gotten gains from addicts' crimes go toward drugs, including alcohol (Johnson, Anderson, and Wish, 1988). The crimes that addicts commit, therefore, are mostly robbery and other property offenses. The best evidence that the addiction itself does not cause crime comes from England, where an extensive addict maintenance program supplies drugs to addicted individuals. Under these conditions, addicts are no more likely to be convicted of offenses than nonaddicts (Mott, 1980). Still, the precise connections between narcotics and criminal offenses are complex and not clearly understood (Speckart and Anglin, 1986; Faupel and Klockars, 1987).

The extraordinarily high offense rates by addicts suggests the possibility that relatively few street criminals are responsible for most of the street crimes. If this were true, and, further, if it were possible to identify among potential or current offenders who is likely to offend again, authorities might be moved to impose prison sentences on the basis of *predicted future* criminal activity. Under such a policy of *selective incapacitation*, longer sentences would be imposed on offenders who are predicted to be future recidivists (those who repeat or relapse into criminal activity). Some studies did report that a small proportion (from 1% to 6%) of offenders appear to account for a large proportion (from 50% to 75%) of offenses (Mednick and Christiansen, 1977; Wolfgang, 1972). This has led to studies designed to identify and study what are called *chronic offenders* or *career criminals* (Blumstein and Cohen, 1987). Studies also have shown that delinquency is a good predictor of adult criminality and that for some individuals there is remarkable stability of aggression, crime, and deviance over the life course. At the same time, high levels of desistance from delinquency after age 16 have been found, and situational factors such as employment and marital stability can have powerful effects in preventing adult crime that otherwise would have been likely in light of youthful criminality (Wolfgang, Thornberry, and Figlio, 1987; Sampson and Lamb, 1992). The existence of chronic offenders, the capacity to identify them accurately, to what extent they contribute to crime rates, and the ethical dilemmas of selective incapacitation as criminal justice policy all remain hotly disputed (Gottfredson and Hirschi, 1986; Messinger and Berk, 1987).

Victims of Street Crime

National Crime Survey (NCS) interviews over the years have shown certain population groups to be crime victims more than others. NCS data for 1992 indicated that blacks were more likely than whites to be victims of violent crime; people under age 25 had higher victimization rates than older people; and members of households in the lowest income category were more likely to be violent crime victims than those in households in the highest income bracket (U.S. Department of Justice, 1994: 3). A significant trend in the 1992 victimization report was a 23% increase in the number of juvenile (ages 12–17) crime victims between 1987 and 1992. Juveniles generally make up a tenth of the U.S. population, but they accounted for a fourth of all violent crime victims in 1992. They were five times more likely to be the victims of rape, robbery, and assault than adults age 35 and over.

Homicide. The odds of being a victim of homicide are higher for men than for women, for younger than for older people, and for blacks than for whites. In about 60% of homicides, the victim and offender are known to one another as family members, friends, or acquaintances. Over 90% of homicides are *intra*racial—cases of a person being killed by another of the same race. Given the proportion of black perpetrators, this means that blacks, especially black males, are at extremely high risk of dying by murder. For white males the chances of being a homicide victim over a lifetime are about 1 in 186; for black males the odds are 1 in 29 (Karmen, 1984: 10). According to Reiss and Roth (1993), compared to whites blacks were 41% and Hispanics 32% more likely to be victims of violent crime in 1990. They also found homicide rates highest for minorities; for blacks, the rate is five times that for whites, and for Native Americans, it is about double the rate of the entire population. Studies examining international data have demonstrated that economic deprivation, especially when shaped by racial discrimination, is associated with higher homicide rates (Messner, 1989; Gartner, 1990). Similarly, in the United States levels of legitimate violence, poverty, and economic inequality are significantly associated with differences in homicide rates among the states (Baron and Straus, 1988).

The most common motive for homicide, in about 40% of cases, is an argument—over property, a romantic triangle, or a similar matter. Fewer than 20% of homicides are committed in conjunction with felonies, and in these cases the elderly are disproportionately victims of theft-based homicide (Kennedy and Silverman, 1990). Guns, the most common murder weapon in the United States, are used in about 68% of homicides. The typical homicide results from an intense argument between two people who know each other, often intimately; when a weapon, particularly a lethal one such as a gun, is present, what might have been an aggravated assault turns into a murder. The higher the rate of firearm possession in a population, the greater risk of homicide victimization (McDowall, 1991). Although when a crime victim has a weapon it appears to inhibit attack by the perpetrator, and in case of attack it reduces the probability of injury, if injury does occur the presence of a firearm increases the probability of the victim's death (Kleck and McElrath, 1991). While homicide most frequently involves a victim and a killer who know each other, the number of homicides in which the victim and perpetrator are strangers has been increasing.

Although multiple or mass murders receive intense media attention, they are rare, and the odds of being a victim are small. Contrary to impressions after mass murderers or serial killers have been discovered, it is virtually impossible to identify them in advance. This type of violence is increasing in the United States, and it can claim both family members and strangers as victims (Levin and Fox, 1985).

Forcible Rape. Official crime statistics reflect only a portion of the rapes annually experienced by women in the United States, as we noted in Chapter 2; for instance, police data tend to exclude attacks by husbands or other intimates. In this chapter we will consider only how rape is defined and reflected in official records.

Forcible rape is a crime of violence whose victims are overwhelmingly women with annual incomes below the official poverty level (Schwendinger and Schwendinger, 1983). The perpetrators of the rapes against these women are from the same poor communities they are, and the majority of the "illegal" rapes included in official crime statistics are both intraclass and intraracial. Messerschmidt (1986) points out that in the same way economically marginalized men are more likely to be robbed by other marginalized men, marginalized women are more likely to be raped by marginalized men. The socioeconomic status of the offenders and the victims in this type of rape therefore is similar.

For young black males, poor economic opportunities heighten frustrations, and physical violence often remains the sole resource they can control. Young females who live in poverty-stricken areas become ready targets for this pent-up rage. These circumstances, combined with the stereotype of black women as being promiscuous and a black male street culture which promotes a "superstud" image, increase the probability of forcible rape in impoverished communities.

STREET GANGS

Public fear of street crime has been growing rapidly in the last decade of the 20th century. Crime and violence are the No. 1 concern in public opinion polls, and crime maintains its potency as a political issue even in the face of overall declining rates of criminal victimization. Two perceptions account for this more than others. First is the vulnerability felt by many Americans as a result of highly publicized, apparently random acts of violence committed by single perpetrators in "normal" settings like post offices, fast-food restaurants, or commuter trains. Second are the apparently group-oriented violent and otherwise criminal activities alleged to be associated with inner-city ethnic street gangs. Since the mid-1980s the volume of published work on gangs has expanded enormously, although a concern for gangs is not at all new.

Historical Perspective

Concentrations of youth-gang research have occurred at three fairly distinct times in this century. The earliest studies were part of the more general concern for the effects of social disorganization in rapidly growing urban areas by researchers at the University of Chicago (Thrasher, 1927; Shaw, 1930; Shaw and McKay, 1942). The second wave of studies commenced in the mid-1950s and ran through the mid-1960s (Cohen, 1955; Miller, 1958; Yablonsky, 1959; Cloward and Ohlin, 1960;

Short and Strodtbeck, 1965). In both periods the research interest in gangs was accompanied by public fascination and alarm. Significantly, the initial popularity of the musical *Westside Story* coincides with the second period of sociological writing on gangs.

Recent gang research dates from the mid-1980s to the present. In many respects the youth gangs of the 1920s bore similarities to those of today. Then, like now, the tendency was to associate gangs and gang violence with urban poverty; members saw their gangs as a source of security and identity in the face of harsh community living conditions, and gangs operated according to moral principles that diverged sharply from professed middle-class standards. The late 1980s and early 1990s, however, have brought new, more troublesome developments. As Skolnick (1992) notes, "Male bonding groups and delinquency exist in all communities. But gangs are a correlate of impoverishment, blocked economic opportunity, and social disintegration. As Thrasher's (1927) work shows, this pattern is long standing. The distinctive element now is an explosive combination of drugs, advanced weaponry, *de facto* racial segregation, and severely declining opportunity" (117). It appears that members are involved in gangs for longer periods of time, starting younger and extending into early adulthood, and that gangs have become increasingly entrenched in the economically depressed communities that nourish them (Short, 1990a).

Definition and Diversity

Defining a gang is not easy. In the widely cited attempt by Short (1990b), a gang is defined as "a group whose members meet together with some regularity, over time, on the basis of group-defined criteria of membership and group-determined organizational structure, usually with (but not always) some sense of territoriality" (239). This rather general definition omits reference to the gender or age of the gang's members or where it is likely to be found. Thus the definition might apply to groups as diverse as a middle-class women's club or members of college fraternities and sororities. A definition that casts the net this widely might be useful because, to the extent that gangs are associated with illegality and violence, some college fraternities, for example, might well be considered to engage in activities usually associated with gangs, including rape (Martin and Hummer, 1989). Middle-class teen gangs have disturbed the peace of suburbia with their violence (Davis, 1991), and hate-crime-oriented gangs such as "skinheads" have emerged as well. Hamm (1993) puts them in a different category from street gangs, saying that "much of the research and theory on traditional juvenile gangs has little relevance for understanding the American neo-Nazi skinheads. Because of their overt racism, political violence, and international links to a broader hate movement, the skinheads are properly defined as a *terrorist youth subculture*" (71; italics in original).

Our focus, however, will be primarily on the ethnic, inner-city, male-dominated street gangs that are most associated in the popular mind with crime. The evidence we have about female gangs and female auxiliaries to male gangs indicates that female gang participation is not nearly as frequent, committed, or violent as that of males, although female street gangs certainly exist in their own right (Campbell, 1984 and 1990; Harris, 1988; Swart, 1991). One recent study of Denver gangs found that 25% of gang members in that city were female (Esbenson and Huizinga, 1993). Even within this narrowed focus on male-dominated, urban, street gangs, their diversity is enormous. While the earliest researchers and those of the 1950s and 1960s studied mostly white, ethnic (Irish, Italian, Polish) gangs, the 1980s and 1990s research includes gangs whose members may be African American (Huff, 1989), Mexican American (Moore, 1979; 1991), Puerto Rican (Padilla, 1992), Chinese (Joe and Robinson, 1980; Chin, 1990), or Vietnamese (Vigil and Yun, 1990). Because the community contexts in which street gangs are found vary immensely today, generalizations that apply to all street gangs are nearly impossible.

Emerging Patterns

Since the urban riots of the mid-1960s, the economic conditions in the minority ghettos of American cities have deteriorated sharply (Wilson, 1987; Wacquant, 1989; Massey, 1990). Especially noteworthy is how this poverty has become concentrated in a handful of urban areas where minority neighborhoods are characterized by high youth unemployment (often approaching rates of 50%), illegal drug markets, other forms of street hustling, and violence. Street gangs thrive in such environments.

Martin Sanchez Jankowski (1991) studied 37 gangs in New York, Boston, and Los Angeles over a ten-year span. His theory of gangs is based on two key concepts: (1) the social character of gang members, and (2) the organizational principles that permit members to cohere in a gang. First, gang members tend to have developed a "deviant individualist character" that is rooted in their quest for survival in a mean environment. Gang members tend to be competitive, mistrustful, and self-reliant. Second, certain organizational characteristics are necessary for a group of such individualists to persist as an identifiable group. Therefore, gangs will exist only if they provide their members with prestige and valued services such as entertainment, protection, and financial assets. Doing so requires an efficient authority structure (usually hierarchical, top-down leadership) which provides the capacity to organize and discipline the often defiant, individualist membership. Establishing and maintaining authority can be a source of intragang violence. In addition, gangs bear a symbiotic relationship to their communities. Gangs can help to provide social organization in disordered communities, sometimes by offering such services as escorts to the elderly, protection for local businesses, and defense against outside intruders. Their communities, in turn, aid gangs by providing a safe haven, refusing to inform authorities, and providing information to gang members. In other words, gangs survive because they fulfill social functions, both for their members and for their communities.

Street-gang involvement in drug trafficking apparently varies greatly. Some gangs are highly entrepreneurial and well organized as drug-dealing businesses (Padilla, 1992; Williams, 1989). Their members have essentially learned an illegal trade that permits them to succeed materially, at some considerable risk, in an environment of limited legitimate opportunity. On the other hand, while many if not most gang members use and sell drugs, most gangs appear not to be primarily drug-trafficking organizations. The connection between crack-related violence and gangs may not be as great as commonly believed (Fagan, 1990; Klein, Maxson, and Cunningham, 1991; Esbensen and Huizinga, 1993), but violence is common and frequently lethal. Conflicts can arise from intragang authority struggles, intergang quarrels over turf (often but not always related to drug markets) and perceived threats to a gang's reputation or honor. What is especially disturbing in this regard is the increased firepower of heavy automatic weapons, which makes outbursts of violence more deadly. Nevertheless, much of gang life is fairly mundane (Spergel, 1992). Huff (1989) found in Cleveland and Columbus, Ohio, that "Gang members actually spend most of their time engaging in exaggerated versions of typical adolescent behavior (rebelling against authority by skipping school, refusing to do homework, and disobeying parents; wearing clothing and listening to music that sets them apart from most adults; and having a primary allegiance to their peer group instead of their parents or other adults" (530). For members of the Brooklyn gangs Sullivan (1989) studied, the rewards of criminal activities were both economic and psychological. Getting away with a criminal endeavor was symbolic of having beaten a system that they saw as stacked against them. Sullivan explains:

> They call success in crime "getting paid" and "getting over," terms that convey a sense of triumph which is not accounted for in the grim depiction of their acts as the economic strategies of the disadvantaged....What they "get over on" is the system, a series of odds rigged against people like themselves. Both phrases are spoken in a tone of defiant pride. They are phrases in the shared language of youths who are out of school, out of work, and seriously involved in crime. (245)

A number of observers have noted that the street gangs of the 1980s and 1990s have more older members. Hagedorn and Macon (1988) say that in Milwaukee "Gang members tend to stay involved with the gang as adults, and many have turned to the illegal drug economy for survival" (529). Likewise, Fagan (1990) notes that

> In the "new gangs," there are more older members (in their 20s) and more members with prison records or ties to prison inmates. Participation in these new gangs may be motivated by instrumental goals of profit rather than the cultural or territorial affinities that unified gangs in earlier decades. These events have coincided with basic social and economic transformations in inner cities that have weakened the formal and informal controls that in the past have mediated gang behaviors and adolescent violence. (185)

Thus the apparent fact that gangs have been becoming older, more utilitarian, and more violent is rooted directly in the deteriorating conditions of the underclass in America's urban ghettos, which are associated with the deindustrialization of the American economy. Well-paying, working-class jobs in factories have disappeared. As industrial plants close, communities are left with no viable economic base to support basic services, including schools, adequate policing, and refuse collection.

The entire neighborhood takes on an aura of decay and disorder. Huff (1989) depicts the situation in the Ohio cities he studied:

> An economically and socially marginal youth who has dropped out of or been expelled from school, and/or is without job skills, is in deep trouble in either Cleveland or Columbus. In Cleveland, he is competing for a rapidly shrinking pool of manufacturing jobs (more than 36,000 of these jobs were lost between 1970 and 1980 alone) and cannot qualify for other jobs....To make matters worse, the military, a traditionally available alternative career path for the poor, is increasingly inaccessible due to the higher quality of applicants generated by an economy with relatively few attractive entry-level positions for unskilled workers....[P]overty is increasingly victimizing families with children under 18 years of age. With little income to buy flashy clothes and other consumer goods advertised throughout our society, a poor minority youth may find the "illegitimate opportunities" available through gangs, crime, and drug sales more compelling than the legitimate options available to him. (527–528)

Moreover, as poverty and illegal markets increase, so do general community disorder and the effectiveness of legitimate community institutions to compete with the attractions of gangs and crime (Skogan, 1990). The term *social capital* refers to sources of legitimate role models for young people in a community. In communities where "old heads"—"respectable, and respected, middle- and working-class adults who made it a point to advise young people as to acceptable conduct" (Short, 1991)—have left, the milieu for youth street gang and criminal activity is further enriched. As Short notes,

> When social capital is weakened by demographic and economic shifts that concentrate poverty and destabilize community institutions, conventional socialization and control processes fail. When intergenerational relationships break down or are distorted by such developments, disorder and decline of neighborhoods inevitably follow, and the likelihood that gangs will emerge and flourish and compete with one another over territory, status, or drug markets, often with deadly consequences, is enhanced. (512)

Public Policy and Gangs

A survey of recent research on gangs reveals two points that relate to public policy strategy: (1) gang activities are highly variable in ways that are tied subtly to unique aspects of the gangs' particular communities, and (2) the roots of dangerous, illegal gang activities are to be found in the deteriorating economic conditions of America's inner cities. In respect to the first point, individual communities must be encouraged to develop techniques for greater social control such as community policing, increased police foot patrols, gang intervention units, improved school security, and the like—all of which should be developed with maximum local community consultation and support. It is important to distinguish between the hard-core gang leaders who are involved in the most serious criminal violence and the many youngsters whose participation is more peripheral. The former should be the primary targets of a criminal justice response; the latter should be the objects of inducements to make gang affiliation less attractive.

Community-level responses will never enjoy lasting success, however, until the underlying causes of economic deprivation are addressed. The changes from an industrial to a service-oriented economy that have destroyed legitimate life chances for the poor and undereducated is at the heart of the problem. Deindustrialization, due largely to technological advances, competition in the global economy, and the ease with which large corporations can shift unskilled production jobs to countries with much cheaper supplies of labor, has been responsible for the loss of numerous jobs at a living wage for American workers. It is essential that public policies cushion the blows of job loss, lack of employment prospects, and community disintegration which are most severe for young people and families at the bottom of the American income structure during its postindustrial transition. Huff (1989) concludes:

> Youth gangs are symptomatic of many of the same social and economic problems as adult crime, mental illness, drug abuse, alcoholism, the surge in homelessness, and multi-generation "welfare families" living in hopelessness and despair. While we are justly concerned with replacement of our physical infrastructure (roads, bridges, sewers) our *human* infrastructure may be crumbling as well. Our social, educational, and economic infrastructures are not meeting the needs of many children and adults. Increases in the numbers of women and children living in poverty (the "feminization" and "juvenilization" of poverty) are dramatic examples of this recent transformation.
>
> To compete with the seductive lure of drug profits and the grinding despair of poverty, we must reassess our priorities and reaffirm the importance of our neighborhoods by putting in place a number of programs that offer hope, education, job skills, and meaningful lives. It is worth the cost of rebuilding our human infrastructure since it is, after all, our children whose lives are being wasted and our cities in which the quality of life is being threatened. (536)

EXPLANATIONS OF STREET CRIME

Are people with certain physical or mental characteristics, more likely than others to commit street crimes? The evidence for street crime in the United States cited above certainly suggests so. For instance, men have higher murder rates than women. In this sense, we could say that a genetically determined characteristic (sex) is *related* to the tendency to commit street crime—but this is not necessarily to say that the tendency to commit street crime is genetically transmitted. Likewise, race is related to rates of street crime, but it does not follow that because skin color is a genetically determined characteristic criminality also is. The sharp differences in this country between the social environments in which whites and blacks and others are typically born, reared, and live are sufficient to explain racial differences in crime rates. Thus, in evaluating the evidence in respect to street crime it is essential to remember that any given relationship may have numerous possible causes. The task of explanation is to establish causes, and even in the case of the strongest relationships causes are not easily established.

Biogenetic Explanations

During certain periods of the history of criminology, the focus has been on biological or "constitutional" variables in the search for the causes of crime. The most famous such theory was by Cesare Lombroso (1836–1909), who maintained that the criminal is "an atavistic being who reproduces in his person the ferocious instincts of primitive humanity and the inferior animals" (cited in Taylor, Walton, and Young, 1973: 41). *Atavisms* were thought to be people who were throwbacks reflecting earlier stages of evolutionary development. A similar approach, also popular in the 19th century, emphasized particular shapes of heads and facial features that were thought to reflect the functioning of the brain. The theories of these early physiognomists and phrenologists have been discredited, but biological theories continue to be generated.

In the late 1940s William Sheldon proposed that somatotypes (types of body build) were linked to specific temperaments that, in turn, were related to criminality. *Mesomorphs* (strong, muscular, athletic people) were thought to have more criminogenic temperaments than *ectomorphs* (tall, thin people) or *endomorphs* (plump, round people). Research does indicate that delinquents have greater tendency to be mesomorphs. However, this apparently has to do with the fact that many delinquent acts call for strength and agility, so mesomorphs are slightly more likely to participate in delinquent activities. There is no evidence that body types are linked to "crime-prone" personalities, as suggested by Sheldon.

Studies in the 1960s suggested that sex chromosome abnormalities in some men might be a cause of crime. Normally males have two sex chromosomes, one X and one Y. In rare instances a male may have an extra Y chromosome, and some research has indicated that such men might have higher rates of criminality. The most thorough study (Witkin et al., 1976) found no evidence for violence among XYY men but significantly more criminal behavior. The XYY abnormality is related to crime; however, it is so rare a phenomenon that it does not account for a significant share of total crimes committed.

A more general biogenetic theory of criminality proposes that genetically caused abnormalities in the autonomic nervous systems of some people inhibit their ability to learn and apply the social norms of their society effectively (Mednick and Volavka, 1980). Overall, the research findings point to the evidence of a genetic component in the causation of some antisocial behavior (Pollock, Mednick, and Gabrielli, 1983; Mednick, Gabrielli, and Hutchings, 1984; and Rowe and Osgood, 1984). Even in cases where genetic factors may contribute to criminal behavior, however, they no doubt do so as part of a complex process involving the individual's environment (Ellis, 1982). As Reiss and Roth (1993) point out,

> Strong evidence from Scandinavian studies points to genetic influences on antisocial personality disorder in adults, a diagnostic category that includes persistent assaultive behavior. Evidence of a genetic influence specific to violent behavior is mixed, however....If genetic predispositions to violence are discovered, they are likely to involve many genes and substantial environmental interaction rather than any simple genetic marker.

By themselves, genetic influences cannot explain either short-run temporal fluctuations in violence rates or variation in rates among countries. Genetic processes may, however, account for individual or family-level deviations from aggregate patterns within a society. (11–12)

Intelligence and Street Crime. Numerous studies have shown that delinquents have lower IQs than nondelinquents. The interpretation of the relationship is, however, very controversial. First, there is a question about the measurement of intelligence. Critics argue that IQ tests measure social learning rather than "native ability"; moreover, the content of the learning the tests measure is culturally biased to enhance the scores of people who are white and middle class. Second, there is disagreement about how to explain the IQ–delinquency relationship. Even those who minimize the methodological limitations of IQ testing, such as Hirschi and Hindelang (1977), suggest that no evidence exists to show that intelligence has a direct impact on delinquency. Rather, a lower IQ affects school performance; poor school performance elicits negative attitudes toward school and teachers; and such attitudes lower the person's "stake in conformity," thus increasing the likelihood of delinquency.

An alternative interpretation proposes that low intelligence is not a cause of delinquency at all. It is possible that being in a lower-class family leads to both delinquency and trouble in school; trouble in school then inhibits learning and lowers IQ test performance. From their research, Menard and Morse (1984) argue that the IQ–delinquency association exists because schools do not provide positive roles and positive reinforcement for those who do not perform well academically, and the resulting alienation leads to delinquency. This approach places the burden of explanation on the school's response to the individual rather than on the individual alone.

Social Psychological Explanations

Socialization and Control. At the social psychological level of explanation there are two particularly influential theories. In one approach emphasizing socialization, the central idea is that people commit street crimes because they learn to commit them from others in their surroundings. The other approach has little to say about what motivates people to commit crime; instead, it places the burden of explanation on the social controls that inhibit people from engaging in illegal activities.

Edwin Sutherland's (1939) theory of differential association attempts to explain what motivates people to commit crime. It proposes that people are motivated by what they learn from those around them. Sutherland makes the point by stating that criminal behavior is *learned* from others in face-to-face interaction. Each person, he claims, is constantly exposed to definitions favorable to violating the law as well as definitions unfavorable to violating it. If the learning of values, attitudes, and techniques favorable to law violation exceeds the learning of those favorable to law abidance, the individual will commit crime. Depending on the frequency, duration, priority, and intensity of their exposure to criminal as compared to noncriminal definitions, people will or will not engage in crime. Because the exposure to differing definitions occurs in association with others, Sutherland called this the theory of *differential association*.

In respect to theft, for example, everyone is continually exposed to ideas that discourage stealing ("Taking what isn't yours is wrong") and others that encourage it ("In this world you've got to take what you can get, regardless"). Over time, a person who is more thoroughly exposed to values that encourage theft than those that discourage it is more likely to steal. The kinds of values individuals adopt depend upon what they learn from the words and behavior of parents, friends, and other influential people around them.

While differential association theory begins with the assumption that it is necessary to explain what motivates a person to be deviant, control theory makes no such assumption. The underlying assumption of control theory is that *conformity*, not crime, requires an explanation. Crime, after all, may be committed for fun, profit, out of impulse, or any number of other motives. The real question for control theory is: What prevents people from doing what they would do if left uninhibited? The answer, according to the theory's leading proponent, Travis Hirschi (1969), is that people will deviate when they have no stake in conformity—when their "bond to society is weak or broken" (16). Crime is unlikely when a person (1) is attached to others and eager to be seen by them in a positive light, (2) is committed to conventional avenues to success, (3) is involved in conventional activities, and (4) believes in the moral validity of social rules. The individual is bound to society, then, by attachment, commitment, involvement, and belief. A strong bond to the society controls natural tendencies to deviate.

These two explanations, differential association and control theories, differ in their assumptions about basic human nature and the mechanisms by which people become criminal. In differential association theory the assumption is that people are neither good nor bad, and it is necessary to account for what motivates them to go wrong. In control theory it is that, left unrestrained, people will do naturally whatever they can get away with. Therefore, the control theorist seeks to explain what restrains the criminal desires that we all possess but only some of us occasionally enact.

Both differential association and control theories have been tested most frequently in reference to delinquency, especially *status offenses* such as truancy which apply only to minors. In research on adolescent drinking and drug use designed to assess a social learning model, Akers et al. (1979) found differential association to be the most powerful variable they measured. Hirschi (1969) and others (Krohn and Massey, 1980; Wiatrowski, Griswold, and Roberts, 1981; Gove and Crutchfield, 1982) have reported support for control theory. And, despite Hirschi's (1979) protests that integration of the two theories is bound to fail because their underlying assumptions are incompatible, such combinations have been attempted. For instance, Elliott and his colleagues (1985) found that involvement with delinquent peers directly affects delinquency, and its effect is strongest when conventional controls are weakest. Likewise, Johnson (1979) concluded from a test of his integrated theory that the best model appeared to be a combination of the social learning perspective with a social bonding orientation.

At present, neither of these two theoretical contenders has managed to establish clear predominance. This is due in part to the fact that many research findings appear to be compatible with *both* theories. For example, Agnew and Petersen (1989) found that involvement in non-deviant leisure activities makes delinquency less likely. But this finding can be interpreted in two ways:

1. In nondeviant leisure activities, young people are *learning* nondeviant norms and values, consistent with differential association theory.

2. *Involvement* in conventional activities simply eliminates the opportunity for involvement with delinquent activities, consistent with control theory.

Labeling and the Situation. In labeling theory, the assumption is that the very process of attempting to admonish, chastise, punish, or control can contribute to delinquency and crime. This theory posits the social psychological process whereby people are labeled by members of the community, especially those in official positions (teachers, law enforcement professionals, doctors, and the like) and then react in conformity to the expectations applied to them. Frank Tannenbaum (1938), one of the early proponents of this perspective, puts it this way:

> The process of making the criminal, therefore, is a process of tagging, defining, identifying, segregating, describing, emphasizing, making conscious and self-conscious; it becomes a way of stimulating, suggesting, emphasizing, and evoking the very traits that are complained of....The child's isolation forces him into companionship with other children similarly defined, and the gang become his means of escape, his security. (19–20)

According to labeling theory, then, stigmatizing a person with a criminal label increases the likelihood of future crime. Because the stigma of labeling might also act as a deterrent to crime, it should not be surprising that research evidence has provided, at best, mixed evidence in support of the theory (Tittle, 1980; Braithwaite, 1989).

Labeling theory is distinguished by its focus on the immediate situation surrounding the crime—the process and effects of stigmatizing the alleged criminal *after* the criminal act has occurred. In other words, rather than turning to background factors (genetic influences, socialization, or even social class) to explain the crime, it concentrates on the "foreground"—the social processes immediately surrounding the criminal act that are alleged to contribute to further criminal acts. A related approach is suggested by Jack Katz in his book *The Seductions of Crime* (1988). In it he argues that many crimes, including murder, robbery, and petty theft, are not rationally motivated by materialistic considerations or ordinary conceptions of what would be "rational." Rather, many criminal activities can only be understood by looking at the "seductive qualities" experienced immediately in the midst of the criminal act: the release of righteous indignation in a murderous rage; the "sneaky thrills" for adolescents who shoplift or vandalize; the way in which the courage to commit a robbery contributes to the robber's thrilling self-image as a "hardman." In the tradition of intensive inspection of the situation from the viewpoint of the individual experiencing it (phenomenology), Katz suggests that one can hardly explain crime without a *subjective* understanding of what it feels like to actually *do* it.

Sociological Explanations

Theories at the sociological level attempt to explain street crime and delinquency in reference to the social environment. Some theories of this sort begin with the premise that, under "normal" conditions, mechanisms of control in a community will operate effectively to inhibit deviance; it is when the community suffers "social disorganization" that it will generate high rates of pathological behaviors, including excessive street crime. Another approach assumes that the way a particular society or community is organized for its normal, routine functioning will produce normal levels of deviance. For example, by failing to provide adequate employment opportunities for all, a society will be organized to leave some of its members out of the legitimate mainstream avenues to success. For these angry, alienated people closed off from realistic legitimate opportunities, a life of crime on the streets may seem the most attractive alternative. A society may also be "organized" to facilitate crime if, for example, employment patterns such as a large number of dual-income households, with both husbands and wives working, leave nobody home for extended time periods, thus increasing the number of potential crime targets.

Social Disorganization. Working in Chicago during the 1920s and 1930s, Clifford Shaw and Henry McKay (1942) noted that delinquency rates throughout the city varied widely. In general, the highest rates were in the center of the city, and they declined toward the periphery. This pattern conformed to the ecological model of cities in which urban core areas were identified as highly disorganized, as in the social and life-conditions hypothesis on the distribution of mental illness devised by Faris and Dunham (see Chapter 4). Social disorganization theorists proposed that the reason for the concentration of deviance in certain areas of the city was the breakdown of social relationships to the point where coordination, teamwork, morale, and social control are impaired. Areas where disorganization is likely to occur were said to have high mobility, few economic resources, and a high incidence of social ills such as disease and infant mortality. The disorganization was alleged to be a natural product of urban growth whereby the areas near the central business district were characterized by speculative real estate holding, slum housing, poverty, and transient populations. According to these theorists, these central areas of social disorganization, often the homes of the poorest and most recent immigrants, had high rates of street crime and delinquency due to the breakdown of their capacity for social control.

The crime rates in most cities today are consistent with the ecological pattern of crime rates noted by Shaw and McKay, but criminologists continue to disagree over whether the term *social disorganization* is a viable explanation for this pattern (Short, 1969; Miller, 1974). Perhaps the most vocal critic of social disorganization theory is C. Wright Mills (1942), who argues that the standards used to judge behavior in such communities are themselves biased, reflecting the views of the predominantly white, middle-class researchers who study them. However, recent evidence that social change can destabilize some communities and result in increased rates of delinquency is consistent with social disorganization theory (Bursik and Webb, 1982; Ebbe, 1989). As we noted in the section above on gangs, the transition to a postindustrial economy, with the attendant job loss and economic dislocation, has created community disruption of the sort that social disorganization theorists identify as the ideal breeding ground for gangs and violence.

Subcultural Theories. Among explanations that focus on community subcultures, the primary task has also been to explain delinquency in terms of the social environment. At least two theoretical perspectives offer conflicting alternatives. Albert K. Cohen (1955) argues that delinquent gangs are primarily a lower-class, male phenomenon. Lower-class boys have the same aspirations as middle-class boys; the problem is that their legitimate opportunities to succeed are often severely restricted. In school, their patterns of speech, dress, demeanor, and the like may close off avenues to success. As a result, Cohen (1983) says:

> When lower-class boys turn out to be failures in the society of young people, especially in the school, they draw together and elaborate alternative life-styles, codes, and criteria for judging themselves and others—in short, a subculture—in which they can do well. They create a game, so to speak, in which they can be winners, and this game is the delinquent subculture. (346)

Cohen argues that lower-class boys *create* a subculture of delinquency as a reaction to their environment. In contrast, Walter B. Miller (1958) holds that there is no need to create a delinquent subculture because lower-class culture itself embodies such "focal concerns" or characteristics as trouble, smartness, toughness, and excitement, and this accounts for the apparently higher rates of lower-class delinquency. More broadly, David Matza and Gresham Sykes (1961) claim that delinquency is, at least in part, simply an expression of "subterranean values" that are common throughout the American class structure, including the celebration of leisure, extravagant spending, the pursuit of excitement, and a cult of cowboy masculinity. At the same time, delinquents use rationalizations that are also common in the dominant culture (e.g., "It wasn't my fault," "It's just a little mischief that doesn't hurt anybody," "It's no worse than what the corrupt cops do") to excuse their behavior and neutralize its associated guilt (Sykes and Matza, 1957). This position on subterranean values and neutralization is consistent with the fact that delinquent activity is common among young males, from the top to the bottom of the class structure. Upper- or middle-class delinquency tends to be less violent and less visible than is typical in the lower classes, and it has less severe consequences for adult success (Hagan, 1991). As a result, the illegal street crime of more-affluent youths tends to be regarded by officials and the public as less threatening than the crime of poor youths (Chambliss, 1973).

The issue disputed among subcultural theorists is: In reference to whose values does the delinquent behave? Is he (for delinquents in this context are usually male) acting in reference to values constructed in reaction to those of the mainstream culture (Cohen)? Or is he merely expressing uniquely lower-class focal concerns (Miller)? A third alternative is that the delinquent is not expressing the values of a subculture or unique class culture at all, but his behavior reflects values, particularly those associated with masculinity, that are widely distributed throughout American society (Matza and Sykes, 1961).

Opportunity Structure. If a society does not provide all of its members with legitimate avenues to success, some of those who suffer from blocked opportunity—possibly due to discrimination, inadequate education, of lack of jobs to fit their skills—may turn to illegal activities to reach their economic goals. This is apt to occur especially in a society that defines success largely in terms of accumulating material goods and aggressively promotes the importance of these success goals, and America is just such a society, according to Robert K. Merton (1968). He argues that for many Americans there is a disjunction between the *cultural goals* of economic prosperity and the *institutionalized, legitimate means* available to achieve those goals. The result is a pressure or strain on those who experience blocked opportunity to forsake the legal norms and behave illegally in pursuit of the culturally approved goals. Thus the social structure—characterized by lofty standards for success but inadequate legal means for achievement to make them available to all—is said to create excessively high levels of *anomie*, or normlessness, which leads to high rates of crime.

The major prediction of Merton's anomie theory is that crime rates will be highest in the lower classes because people who are most apt to experience blocked opportunity. The evidence in support of the theory is mixed. Rates of street crime (the kind that most poor, powerless people are restricted to by their circumstances) do appear to be higher for those in the lower class. Still, crime more broadly defined is certainly not limited to the lower class; law-breaking among the society's elites is pervasive, as we will show in Chapter 9. Moreover, anomie theory does not fare well in tests that compare it to differential association and control theories as predictors of delinquency (Johnson, 1979; Elliott et al., 1985).

In an important extension of anomie theory, Richard Cloward and Lloyd Ohlin (1960) proposed that when legitimate opportunities are blocked, the *type* of behavior delinquents will engage in depends upon the kind of *illegitimate opportunities* open to them. They identified three kinds of delinquent subcultures: criminal, violent, and retreatist. The *criminal subculture* emerges in neighborhoods where adult patterns of criminal activity are well established and stable. In this situation, delinquents are well integrated into the local institutions and restrained from violence. The *violent subculture*, characterized by street fighting, flourishes in areas where youths have little communication with adult criminals—in other words, where opportunities for stable economic criminal activity are unavailable. The *retreatist subculture*, which focuses on drug-taking, arises among those who lack any other alternatives—legitimate, criminal, or violent. There is conflicting evidence that delinquents specialize in certain offenses, as suggested by Cloward and Ohlin; some researchers claim that delinquents rarely limit their activities to particular types of crimes (Gottfredson and Hirschi, 1990). However, recent research on gangs identifies three types—hedonistic, drug-oriented gangs; instrumental, theft-oriented gangs; and predatory, particularly violent gangs—which correspond remarkably well to Cloward and Ohlin's retreatist, criminal, and violent types (Huff, 1989: 528–529).

Social Organization. Rather than focusing on what *motivates* an offender to commit crime, some theorists have concentrated on how the ways people organize their routine daily activities either facilitate or inhibit the possibilities for criminal victimization. This approach focuses on how community structure contributes to crime by providing criminals with opportunities for their activities (Felson, 1983). It begins by recognizing that "Most criminal acts require convergence in space and time of *likely offenders, suitable targets*, and the *absence of capable guardians* against crime" (Cohen and Felson, 1979: 588). The "capable guardians" are not usually police or private security personnel but ordinary citizens going about their everyday activities, unaware that by their presence they are deterring crime. Therefore, circumstances that draw people away from home, decreasing the presence of guardians, will increase opportunities for crime.

The research evidence in support of this routine-activities approach is impressive (Jackson, 1984; Messner and Tardiff, 1985; Messner and Blau, 1987; Stahura and Sloan, 1988). In general, trends in social organization that characterize contemporary American life may contribute to increased opportunities for crime. Thus, Cohen and Felson (1979) say,

> It is ironic that the very factors which increase the opportunity to enjoy the benefits of life also may increase the opportunity for predatory violations. For example, automobiles provide freedom of movement to offenders as well as average citizens and offer vulnerable targets for theft. College enrollment, female labor force participation, urbanization, suburbanization, vacations and new electronic durables provide various opportunities to escape the confines of the household while they increase the risk of predatory victimization. Indeed, the opportunity for predatory crime appears to be enmeshed in the opportunity structure for legitimate activities to such an extent that it might be very difficult to root out substantial amounts of crime without modifying much of our way of life. Rather than assuming that predatory crime is simply an indicator of social breakdown, one might take it as a byproduct of freedom and prosperity as they manifest themselves in the routine activities of everyday life. (605)

Routine-activities theory focuses on the relationship between how we organize our daily lives and the risk of criminal victimization. It suggests that victimization is not entirely beyond our control; rather, we can alter the level of crime around us by changing the pattern of our routine activities. The changes we might make, however, are not without costs. For example, crime would be reduced if we had fewer valuables worth stealing, stayed home more to protect them, or invested heavily in alternative security arrangements.

Self-Control and Opportunity. Gottfredson and Hirschi (1990) combine some of the insights of the routine-activities approach with a concern for what is commonly characteristic of those who commit crimes. They begin by distinguishing between crime and criminality. *Crimes* are "acts of force or fraud undertaken in pursuit of self-interest" (15). While this includes most of what we commonly regard as street crime, they note that a number of other deviant activities (excessive alcohol and drug use, for example) are often highly associated with crime. What distinguishes all of these behaviors is that they produce "immediate, short-term pleasure or benefit to the actor," while entailing long-term costs to the perpetrator and/or others. In general, criminal acts provide immediate, easy gratification of desires; they are exciting, risky, or thrilling; they require little skill or planning; and they result in pain or discomfort for the victim.

Criminality refers to the propensities of individuals to commit criminal acts. Gottfredson and Hirschi argue that the common attribute in people who tend to commit crimes is *low self-control*. In their view, low self-control is not taught per se but arises in the *absence* of nurturance, discipline, or training. Its major cause thus appears to be ineffective child rearing, which begins with weak attachment of the parent to the child and inadequate parental supervision. The level of an individual's self-control is established early and remains relatively stable throughout life. Schools and other institutions of socialization are doomed to relative ineffectiveness in trying to compensate for an individual trait such as self-control which is established so young.

People with low self-control are apt to be attracted to all sorts of hedonistic activities often associated with deviance, including those commonly called crimes. This theory points to two plausible public policy interventions that could affect crime rates significantly. The first is to attend to crime-prone situations by minimizing the opportunities to be victimized by those with criminal propensities. This approach is consistent with routine-activities theory. The second is to reduce the number of individuals with low self-control produced by the society. For Gottfredson and Hirschi (1990),

> ...the origins of criminality, of low self-control, are to be found in the first six or eight years of life, during which time the child remains under the control and supervision of the family or a familial institution. Apart from the limited benefits that can be achieved by making specific criminal acts more difficult, policies directed toward enhancement of the ability of familial institutions to socialize children are the only realistic long-term state policies with potential for substantial crime reduction. (272–273)

Shame as Deterrence. A comparative examination of crime rates across the world reveals that some societies are far better than others at prevention. For example,

Table 8.4 above shows that some countries (England/Wales and Japan) have homicide rates under 1 per 100,000 population, while others (the United States) have rates ten times higher or considerably greater. The U.S. robbery rate of over 200 per 100,000 is over 150 times that in Japan, which is about 1.4 per 100,000 (Messner and Rosenfeld, 1994: 22). Criminologist John Braithwaite (1989) has proposed a theory to explain why which relates crime rates to social structure and would substitute the process of *reintegrative shaming* for labeling.

Braithwaite begins by asserting that labeling theorists are only partially correct, and they lead to a hopeless conclusion: If labeling is always harmful because it stigmatizes offenders, making their behavior worse than if there were no reaction to them at all, there is apparently little or nothing we can do about deterring crime. However, he argues, under certain conditions labeling is not permanently stigmatizing, and in countries where those conditions prevail, such as Japan, crime rates are notably low. Braithwaite calls this a theory of reintegrative shaming:

> The first step to productive theorizing about crime is to think about the contention that labeling offenders makes things worse. The contention is both right and wrong. The theory of reintegrative shaming is an attempt to specify when it is right and when wrong. The distinction is between shaming that leads to stigmatization—to outcasting, to confirmation of a deviant master status—versus shaming that is reintegrative, that shames while maintaining bonds of respect or love, that sharply terminates disapproval with forgiveness, instead of amplifying deviance by progressively casting the deviant out. Reintegrative shaming controls crime; stigmatization pushes offenders toward criminal subcultures. (12–13)

Thus societies that are highly successful at reintegrative shaming will have low crime rates, and those that are ineffective at it will have high crime rates. Compared to the United States, the conditions for reintegrative shaming in Japan are optimal. There people are enmeshed in powerful relationships of mutual interdependency at work and in their families. Occupational and residential mobility are relatively low. The society is communitarian, with an emphasis on the collective good as opposed to American individualism. Just as societies differ in their conditions of interdependency that are conducive to reintegrative shaming, within a society certain categories of individuals—males, youths (ages 15–25), the unmarried, the unemployed, and those who have low educational and occupational aspirations—will be the least interdependent, and the least susceptible to shaming, and they will have the highest crime rates.

U.S. offenders are stigmatized by harsh prison sentences, at higher rates than anywhere else in the world. A convict's time served is followed by little attention to reintegration into society after release. Japan relies far less on stigmatizing incarceration; there offenders are caught more efficiently but go to prison much less often. The mechanisms of social control depend more on the social approval of significant others; how one behaves is thought to reflect far more strongly on family, school, neighborhood, or employer than in the United States.

Reintegrative shaming may therefore be a more effective mode of crime control than purely deterrent punishment. However, the conditions for effective reintegrative shaming call for a society that is communitarian (as opposed to individualistic), that encourages relations of interdependency (as opposed to alienation), and that maximizes access to legitimate opportunities for all its citizens. In sum, reintegrative shaming is only possible in a society where people have strong bonds of mutual obligation and believe that the structure of opportunity is fundamentally just.

THE POLITICAL ECONOMY OF STREET CRIME

The political economy viewpoint is a sociological explanation which focuses on the relationships among political and economic processes in complex industrial societies. Theorists in this tradition link crime to the class structure of the society, arguing that the criminal law is made and enforced by elites to benefit their own interests (Quinney, 1970). The public is said to be conditioned by the government—mostly representatives of the dominant upper class—to regard street crime as a grave threat. Thus the "Crime Index" creates the impression that the "crime problem" is predominantly a lower-class phenomenon because it includes only street crimes; crimes committed by wealthy individuals or corporations are largely ignored or not treated as "real" crime. The mass media, also controlled by elites, tend to reinforce this picture, thus benefiting the upper classes by deflecting attention away from their own illegalities.

In such an approach, street crime is explained in reference to the class and power arrangements in a society. Often studies of this sort are historical or comparative and seek to show how the contemporary conditions that produce high levels of street crime grow out of evolving class relations. In such work the conclusion is that crime is endemic to capitalist economies. Others argue that crime is more a product of modernization—a process common to capitalist and noncapitalist societies alike.

Capitalism or Modernization?

The economics of precapitalist societies are local and agricultural. Virtually everywhere in the world prior to the 16th century, most people lived in rural communities, closely knit by traditions spanning hundreds of years. They made and used goods produced locally in small family units or shops, and young people's activities were thoroughly integrated into the daily work of adults. Between the 16th and 18th centuries, as the scientific, economic, and legal foundations for the industrial transformation of society were being laid, the first signs of severe disruption in the family and the community appeared. With the beginning of the Industrial Revolution in the middle of the 18th century, the capitalist mode of financing production, involving international markets and factory manufacture, uprooted many people and transformed them into urban laborers. The massive migrations of Italians, Irish, and Eastern Europeans to the United States during the 19th century were a part of this rapidly escalating process. The resulting dislocations and destruction of traditional social relationships, such as that between apprentice and master, are historical causes of youthful crime: "capitalism ripped apart the ancient regime and introduced criminality among youth in all stations of life" (Schwendinger and Schwendinger, 1985: 3). From this perspective, Palley and Robinson (1990) see the problems of the urban underclass, including chronic poverty, drug abuse, gangs, and crime, as "a phenomenon of uprooted peasant groups thrown into disorganized, socially chaotic urban development that lacks cohesion and basic shelter, health and social services."

Capitalism engenders chronically high levels of unemployment partly as a means for maintaining low wages (the "reserve army of unemployed") and partly as a result of technological progress which increases the efficiency of production and decreases the need for workers. Spitzer (1975) says modern capitalist societies progressively reduced the number of productive years in a worker's life and defined both the young and the old as "economically superfluous." The economically displaced and idle become "social junk" (the old, the chronically unemployed, and the poor), who are dependent on the welfare system, or they become "social dynamite" (the chronically unemployed, alienated, gang-oriented youth), who resort to street crime and are a burden on the criminal justice system.

Such accounts suggest that capitalist societies will have higher rates of crime than noncapitalist ones, but the evidence on this is far from clear. Some capitalist societies, such as Switzerland and Japan, have extremely low crime rates. A study comparing Switzerland and Sweden concluded that a centralized welfare state such as Sweden does not necessarily have lower crime rates (Clinard, 1978). More important, it appears, are (1) preservation of precapitalist units of production, (2) adherence to traditional community values, and (3) the integration of youths and adults in common activities. There does seem to be a widespread pattern of crime rate fluctuation as societies modernize, whether or not their economy is capitalistic.

In general, as societies develop from traditional, rural, preindustrial forms of organization to modern, urban, industrial forms they experience increases in crime— especially crimes against property. Shelley (1981) explains why:

> Property crime increased relative to violent crime because rural life characterized by relatively frequent crimes against the person declined in prominence while simultaneously urban life that promotes the rise in property crime became more pervasive. The general rise in the crime rate and its concentration in the urban environment are explained by other aspects of modernization. Increasing urbanization and prosperity contribute to the greater availability of goods, the increased feasibility of crime commission, and the increased likelihood of feelings of relative deprivation. The growth in female and juvenile participation in crime is explained by the changing roles of these two groups in modern society—by the increased participation of women in activities outside the home and by the decline of an established role for juveniles in society. These conditions of modern society have contributed to the transformation in quality and quantity of crime commission internationally in the last two hundred years. (144–145)

Inequality, Family, and Community

In American society, as elsewhere, most street crime is committed by young males. Moreover, serious patterned delinquency of the sort enumerated on the *UCR* seems to be more frequent in the lower class (Elliott and Ageton, 1980). To explain these facts, theorists have recently been proposing links between delinquency, patterns of socialization in families, and the ways families are affected by their position in the society's class structure. Colvin and Pauly (1983) propose that parents' class position affects the kind of control they experience in the workplace, which in turn affects their approach to child rearing. They describe the differences for working-class, middle-class, and upper-class families.

Lower-working-class parents generally are employed in jobs that provide little security and often are temporary or seasonal. As hourly employees who are easily replaced, they are subject to rigid, coercive controls backed up by an ever-present threat of job loss. People who work under such conditions often develop alienated or negative bonds to authority, which are translated in their family control structure as discipline that swings unpredictably between being lax and being highly punitive. Children reared under such conditions are apt to learn little self-control and to become alienated from authority. Higher up on the class structure, jobs traditionally have been more permanent and the approach to controlling workers less coercive and more utilitarian. As parents, middle-level workers tend to enforce a similar form of discipline at home. The children learn to calculate and predict the consequences of their behavior and have less alienated attitudes toward authority. At the top of the class structure, professionals, top managers, and owners of the means of production are usually in self-directing workplace situations. They are expected to exercise a great deal of discretion and self-control in their work and they tend to create a similar environment for child rearing. These children's attitudes toward authority are apt to be positive, and they are apt to learn effective self-control.

The Colvin and Pauly critique has received some direct research support (Messner and Krohn, 1990). Consistent with their ideas, also, are numerous studies that have found an association between physical, punitive approaches to child discipline and higher rates of delinquency, such as West and Farrington (1973). In general, coercive, physical, punitive child-rearing techniques are more likely to result in youths and adults who are aggressive toward others than are love-oriented, psychological approaches. Apparently, children disciplined by punishment-oriented techniques fail to develop strong internalized controls in the same way children reared by techniques that primarily employ the threat of withholding love do (Henry and Short, 1954). Moreover children reared in coercively controlled families are more likely to be placed in coercive, alienating control structures at school, where they form associations with similarly alienated peers. For these youths, the likelihood of serious delinquency is particularly great. Thus there is a hypothesized connection between the class structure of the society and the different ways parents' class positions affect their treatment at work, and this in turn affects their approaches to disciplining their children. Inconsistent, coercive discipline is more likely to result in serious delinquent behavior.

As we have noted, rates of street crime and delinquency are higher for people at the society's lower socioeconomic levels, and these are also far more frequently the victims of most types of street crime. The places where people live in America—

their neighborhoods and communities—are highly segmented into separate en-claves along class and racial lines. Those in the poorest communities almost always suffer the highest rates of street crime. What distinguishes these areas more than anything else is the lack of stable employment opportunities—especially jobs that provide a meaningful future for young people. It should not be surprising that in communities where teenage unemployment rates typically exceed 40% and dead-end jobs at minimum wage are the norm, the most rewarding activity many will find is in the illegalities of street life.

Elliot Currie (1985) concludes his survey of street crime in America with re-marks that cut to the heart of the matter:

> If we wanted to sketch a hypothetical portrait of an especially violent society, it would surely contain these elements: It would separate large numbers of people, especially the young, from the kind of work that could include them securely in community life. It would encourage policies of economic development and income distribution that sharply increased inequalities between sectors of the population. It would rapidly shift vast amounts of capital from place to place without regard for the impact on local commu-nities, causing massive movements of population away from family and neighborhood supports in search of livelihood. It would avoid providing new mechanisms of care and support for those uprooted, perhaps in the name of preserving incentives to work and paring government spending. It would promote a culture of intense interpersonal com-petition and spur its citizens to a level of material consumption many could not lawful-ly sustain. (278)

Such a model, Currie argues, comes remarkably close to American society in the late 20th century—a message that is both sad and hopeful. It is sad because it does not have to be so. We know this because other Western countries that have so-cial policies far more supportive of families and communities also have much lower rates of street crime. It is hopeful because it suggests that social policies *can* make a difference in preventing street crime and delinquency.

Societies vary enormously in amount and characteristic types of crimes, de-spite certain consistencies such as the predominant involvement in crime of youth-ful males and the increases in crime at certain stages of economic development. What determines the levels and types of street crime that will be found in a society depends on how the society is organized socially and economically—such factors as degree of cultural homogeneity, the patterns of routine daily activity, the extent to which shaming might be used as an effective mechanism of social control, and the nature and extent of structural inequalities. In large measure, societies will get the crime they are organized to produce.

STREET CRIME, DELINQUENCY, AND SOCIAL POLICY

The Politics of Street Crime and Delinquency

At various times, crime in the streets and law and order have been highly publicized issues on the political agenda. One reason is that street crime is a politically "safe"

Table 8.7   Political Ideologies Related to Causes and Solutions for Street Crime and Delinquency

	POLITICAL POSITION		
	Progressive Left	Liberal Center	Conservative Right
Location of the cause	The political economy	Social structure and culture	Individual constitution or character
Causal dynamics	Structural inequalities Injuries of class	Failed socialization Limited economic opportunity	Biogenetic constitution Flawed character Willful transgression
Policy implications	Redistribute wealth Eliminate gross social and economic inequities	Increase moral education Welfare-state subsidies Prisoner rehabilitation	Selective incapacitation Increase punishment
Consequences for the existing social order	Radical restructuring	Moderate reform	Maintenance of the status quo

issue. Fear often triumphs over reason. The general public is easily convinced that street crime is a serious problem (as it certainly is), and most middle-class voters (the ones most likely to exercise this right) are quite ready to believe that the problem is "caused" by the moral degeneracy of those at the bottom rungs of the social ladder. The law and order issue, therefore, does not raise questions about the inequities or injustices of the status quo. Instead it typically leads to calls for harsh, repressive measures including greater use of force and imprisonment.

People from differing political viewpoints find the problem of street crime and what to do about it good grounds for attacking one another over the relative effectiveness of their social policy strategies. For the most part in American society, the debate is confined to conservative and liberal political positions (see Table 8.7). Conservatives locate the causes of street crime in the individual's character or "constitutional factors such as gender, age, intelligence, and personality (Wilson and Herrnstein, 1985). Crime is considered bad behavior committed by bad people. Criminals may behave as they do because of a biogenetic abnormality, faulty upbringing, or simple meanness; regardless, there is not much to be done about it other than to apply severe sanctions.

Liberals are more likely to locate the causes of street crime in the social environment. Crime is considered bad behavior committed by people whose behavior has been shaped by bad social surroundings. Liberals argue that crime is linked to poverty, and they propose that social inequities ought to be reduced. Therefore, they put forward programs calling for aid to poor families, better education, job training, full employment policies, more attention to rehabilitation of prisoners, and the like. This approach adds up to a call for moderate reform.

Neither the conservative nor the liberal approach has been notably successful. For many years the United States imprisoned a higher proportion of its citizens than any industrialized country in the world except the Soviet Union and South Africa; now only Russia surpasses it atop this undistinguished list. The growth rate in imprisonments has been both huge and costly—it increased over 168% between 1980 and 1992 (Farmighetti, 1993: 965). Capital punishment resumed in 1977 after a ten-year moratorium, and 36 states had the death penalty in 1992. Nevertheless, American crime rates remain very high by international standards. Neither did the enormous growth in welfare programs and prisoner rehabilitation in the 1960s and 1970s have much effect on crime rates. Both conservatives and liberals might argue that their programs have not been given fair tests because they have not been permitted to go far enough—with either harsh sanctions or welfare reforms. Regardless, evidence is not encouraging for the overwhelming success of either.

A third alternative approach holds that the causes of street crime and the solutions to reducing it are embedded in the political economy. According to this progressive-left position, in order to reduce crime in America we must be prepared to provide every American family with opportunities to live in safe, secure, healthy homes and neighborhoods. Likewise, educational opportunities ought to be genuinely equal and not limited by residence or the ability to afford private alternatives or higher education. Unlike the liberal position, which calls for amelioration of inequities by welfare programs and handouts, the progressive-left position calls for a fundamental restructuring of resources through such mechanisms as minimum wage laws and income tax, inheritance tax, and corporate tax policies. Ideally, the poor would become richer while the rich become poorer. From the progressive-left position, crime is a by-product of gross class inequities, and the only way to decrease rates of crime substantially is to redistribute wealth more equally. That this approach receives little serious public discussion in the United States is not surprising, because its implications are most unsettling for those who benefit from the status quo.

Criminal Justice and Social Justice

Dealing with street crime is a vast enterprise in the United States. In 1990 over $31 billion was spent for police protection; nearly $25 billion for corrections (jails, prisons, probation, and parole); and about $10 billion for court activities (U.S. Department of Justice, 1992). To these public expenditures can be added billions of dollars spent annually on private security protection. Over the years vast resources have been poured into developing and implementing the techniques and technology of crime fighting, from neighborhood watch programs and prison reform to better bugging devices and more "humane" modes of capital punishment. In given situations, some of the techniques may decrease street crime slightly, some may increase it, and others may have no effect at all (Currie, 1985). On balance, alternative criminal justice techniques appear to yield only marginal differences in the levels of street crime. Neither international comparisons nor trends in the crime rate over time suggest that the justice system alone can make a major difference. It is unreasonable and unfair to place the primary responsibility for the levels of street crime and their reduction on the society's police, judges, and corrections personnel.

The many sociological explanations discussed in the preceding section lead to the conclusion that the causes of street crime are buried deeply in a society's social structure. Tinkering with policing techniques (types of patrols, communications, weapons), court procedures (bail policies, sentencing procedures), and punishment modes (prison reforms, selective incapacitation, ease of capital punishment, alternatives to incarceration such as fines and community service) will have minimal effects on overall patterns of crime. People may argue from various political positions for one approach or another, some of which may even be worth implementing on moral or humanitarian grounds. Past experience suggests, however, that we should not have great expectations for large changes in street crime as a result.

We repeat, societies will experience the kinds and amounts of crime that they are organized to produce. Some aspects of social organization, such as the availability of lethal weapons, are amenable to change through social policy—albeit at some cost (e.g., freedom to arm oneself as one pleases), and over a considerable period of time, possibly a generation or more. Other aspects of social organization may prove even more intractable. For example, class and racial stratification that debilitates and frustrates large portions of the population, or patterns of residence, work, and leisure that increase opportunities for criminal activity, are not easily altered. Surely it *is* possible to have lower rates of street crime in America; the experience of every other Western democracy suggests that this is so. However, policies to reduce street crime would also alter the privileges and freedoms of Americans—including the most wealthy and powerful people, those who benefit most from present social arrangements. Truly effective approaches to lowering street crime have costs as well as benefits. To think about social policies to lower street crime is to think about the kind of society we wish to live in, balancing the values of social justice, freedom, and exposure to personal risk.

SUMMARY

The problem of crime for most Americans is confined to crime in the streets. This image is reinforced by the official government measure of crime, the Uniform Crime Index. In *Uniform Crime Reports*, street crimes are typically divided into two categories: personal or violent crimes (homicide, forcible rape, robbery, and aggravated assault) and property crimes (burglary, larceny-theft, motor vehicle theft, and arson). A distinguishing mark of these street crimes is that they require minimal resources to commit, so they are the most readily available illegal activities for those among the poor who are attracted to them.

Our statistical knowledge of street crime in the United States is based on crimes reported to the police and arrest data (*UCR* reports) and the National Crime Survey of victimization. These data show that rates of property crime are much higher than rates of violent crime, and less than 40% of street crimes are reported to the police. Historically, rates of crime have gone up and down, as have levels of public concern. Politicians regularly play on the fear of crime for their own advantage.

The primary facts of street crime that theorists must confront in attempting to explain it include the following:

- U.S. crime rates are extraordinarily high compared to those of other industrialized countries, particularly for crimes of violence.
- U.S. crime rates for every category are highest in metropolitan areas and lowest in rural areas.
- Worldwide, serious street crime is overwhelmingly a youthful, a male activity.
- In the United States, blacks arrest rates for street crime are higher than those of whites; likewise, blacks' victimization rates are higher for most street crimes.
- Serious street crime, particularly violent crime, occurs more frequently in lower-class communities.

Urban street gangs have recently been the subject of three cycles of research attention in this century. In many respects, the accounts of the 1980s and 1990s bear striking similarity to those of the 1920s: Gangs are the product of inner-city poverty; they are a source of security and identity for their members in the face of a mean environment; and they operate according to moral principles that conflict with many professed middle-class standards. The "new gangs," however, are most often a product of a troubled inner-city environment. These gangs exist in racially segregated ghettos marked by extremely limited economic opportunities, where youths are plagued by an explosive combination of illegal drug markets, advanced weaponry, rage, and hopelessness. Members are involved in gangs for longer periods of time, and gangs have become more entrenched in their communities than in the past.

Theories of street crime range from biogenetic explanations of criminality at the individual level to social structural explanations that explain variations in crime rates between differing times, places, or social classes. Several theories provide contrasting explanations. For example, the theory of differential association states that people commit crimes when they have *learned* both the techniques and rationalizations for doing so, more than they have learned values that promote law abidance. In contrast, control theory is addressed to the question of why people do *not* commit crimes as opposed to why they do. Control theory proposes that people will commit crimes unless they are constrained by the various bonds imposed by the society.

Social structural theories also present conflicting alternatives. Social disorganization theorists locate the cause of crime in the breakdown of social norms when societies undergo periods of rapid social change. Thus the high crime rates of the central areas in American cities during the late 19th and early 20th centuries (and even today) are attributed to transient, unstable populations in communities with weak social ties. Subcultural theorists have searched for criminogenic values in the reaction formations of frustrated youths in delinquent subcultures; in lower-class focal concerns; and in the subterranean values of the dominant American culture. Anomie theory argues that blocked opportunities to achieve success legally leaves illegal means as the only alternative for many.

The routine-activities approach to explaining crime points to how the ways people's daily lives are organized either facilitate or inhibit the commission of crime. As our patterns of work and leisure create more goods to steal (autos, easily portable electronic gadgets) and greater opportunities to steal them (more people away from their homes for more time during work or play), street crime is made an easier, more attractive pursuit. Thus crime rates are affected by the presence of people motivated or inclined to commit illegal activity combined with the availability of opportunities for them to do so.

Gottfredson and Hirschi propose a theory that distinguishes between crime and criminality. Crimes are acts that satisfy the offender's desire for short-term pleasure or benefit. Criminality—the propensity to commit crime—is characterized by low self-control. People with low self-control will be attracted to a wide range of deviant activities, including crime. Because an individual's level of self-control is established early in life through the family, strengthening the family's capacity to socialize children carries with it the greatest hope for reducing crime rates significantly, according to this theory.

The theory of reintegrative shaming modifies the conclusions of labeling theory by suggesting that societal reaction to crime is not always counterproductive. On the contrary, in societies that successfully *shame* and then *reintegrate* rule-breakers, crime rates are much lower. In a communitarian, socially interdependent society like Japan, where crime rates are low, the conditions for successful reintegrative shaming are much better than in America, with its traditions of individualism and stigmatizing punishment accompanied by high crime rates.

Political economy theorists argue that street crime derives from the organization of class relations in a society. A person's class position is likely to determine parents' experiences with authority at work, their approaches to child rearing, and their capacity to provide support for their children—both material (food, clothing, health needs, recreational opportunities) and nonmaterial (supervision, language skills, educational advantages tied to residence, and academic encouragement). All of these can affect intellectual and personality development in ways that increase the probability of serious delinquency and street crime as an adult.

In addition, lawmaking and law enforcement are affected by class relations—usually to the advantage of the more affluent and powerful. Certainly some explanation of the excessive number of blacks who show up on official criminal justice statistics as perpetrators of street crime is the prejudice and discrimination they experience from arrest through sentencing. When they run afoul of the law, poor people have fewer legal resources to resist serious sanctions.

Social policy alternatives to deal with street crime and delinquency range from the conservative to the progressive left. Conservatives usually favor theories that place the causes of crime within the individual, as part of the person's biology, psychopathology, or undisciplined nature. To do so fixes the blame on the individual, justifies selective incapacitation and harsh punishments, and absolves the existing social structure from responsibility, thus protecting the status quo. Liberals blame the social environment for street crime and call for reform policies to ameliorate the offending conditions by improving nutrition, housing, health care, job training, and the like. Those on the progressive left agree with liberals about the importance of the social environment as a cause of crime, but they insist on the need to go beyond mere reform to a major redistribution of wealth and power for truly meaningful reductions of street crime.

REFERENCES

Agnew, R., and Petersen, D. M.
1989   "Leisure and Delinquency." *Social Problems* 36: 332–350.
Akers, R. L., Krohn, M. D., Lanza-Kaduce, L., and Radosevich, M.
1979   "Social Learning and Deviant Behavior: A Specific Test of a General Theory." *American Sociological Review* 44: 635–655.
Archer, D., and Gartner, R.
1984   *Violence and Crime in Cross-National Perspective.* New Haven, CT: Yale University Press.
Austin, R. L.
1993   "Recent Trends in Official Male and Female Crime Rates: The Convergence Controversy." *Journal of Criminal Justice* 21: 447–466.
Ball, J. C.
1991   "The Similarity of Crime Rates among Heroin Addicts in New York City, Philadelphia, and Baltimore." *Journal of Drug Issues* 21: 413–427.
Baron, L., and Straus, M. A.
1988   "Cultural and Economic Sources of Homicide in the United States." *Sociological Quarterly* 29: 371–390.
Bell, D.
1960   "The Myth of Crime Waves: The Actual Decline of Crime in the United States." Pp. 151–174 in *The End of Ideology.* New York: Free Press.
Berk, R. A., Lenhan, K. J., and Rossi, P. H.
1980   "Crime and Poverty: Some Experimental Evidence from Ex-Offenders." *American Sociological Review* 45: 766–786.
Blau, J. R., and Blau, P. M.
1982   "The Cost of Inequality: Metropolitan Structure and Violent Crime." *American Sociological Review* 47: 114–129.
Blumstein, A., and Cohen, J.
1987   "Characterizing Criminal Careers." *Science* 237: 985–991.
Blumstein, A., Cohen, J. R., and Visher, C. A. (eds.)
1986   *Criminal Careers and "Career Criminals."* National Research Council, Vol. 1. Washington, DC: National Academy Press.

Braithwaite, J.
1981   "The Myth of Social Class and Criminality Reconsidered." *American Sociological Review* 46: 36–57.
1989   *Crime, Shame, and Reintegration.* New York: Cambridge University Press.
Brownfield, D.
1986   "Social Class and Violent Behavior." *Criminology* 24: 421–438.
Bursik, R. J., Jr., and Webb, J.
1982   "Community Change and Patterns of Delinquency." *American Journal of Sociology* 88: 24–42.
Campbell, A.
1984   *The Girls in the Gang.* New York: Basil Blackwell.
1990   "Female Participation in Gangs." Pp. 163–182 in C. R. Huff (ed.), *Gangs in America.* Newbury Park, CA: Sage.
Cantor, D., and Land, K. C.
1985   "Unemployment and Crime Rates in the Post-World War II United States: A Theoretical and Empirical Analysis." *American Sociological Review* 50: 317–332.
Chambliss, W. J.
1973   "The Saints and the Roughnecks." *Society* 11: 24–31.
Chin, K.
1990   *Chinese Subculture and Criminality: Non-Traditional Crime Groups in America.* Westport, CT: Greenwood Press.
Chiricos, T. G.
1987   "Rates of Crime and Unemployment: An Analysis of Aggregate Research Evidence." *Social Problems* 34: 187–212.
Clinard, M. B.
1978   *Cities with Little Crime: The Case of Switzerland.* Cambridge, England: Cambridge University Press.
Cloward, R. A., and Ohlin, L. E.
1960   *Delinquency and Opportunity: A Theory of Delinquent Gangs.* New York: Free Press.
Cohen, A. K.
1955   *Delinquent Boys: The Culture of the Gang.* New York: Free Press.
1983   "Crime Causation: Sociological Theories." Pp. 342–353, in *Encyclopedia of Crime and Justice.* New York: Free Press.

Cohen, L. E., and Felson, M.
1979   "Social Change and Crime Rate Trends: A Routine Activities Approach." *American Sociological Review* 44: 588–608.
Colvin, M., and Pauly, J.
1983   "A Critique of Criminology: Toward an Integrated Structural-Marxist Theory of Delinquency Production." *American Journal of Sociology* 89: 513–551.
Currie, E.
1985   *Confronting Crime: An American Challenge*. New York: Pantheon.
Davis, P.
1991   "Violent Groups of Middle-Class Teens Disturb Peace of Suburbia." *Washington Post* (October 22): B1.
Ebbe, O. N.
1989   "Crime and Delinquency in Metropolitan Lagos: A Study of 'Crime and Delinquency Area' Theory." *Social Forces* 67: 751–765.
Elliott, D. S., and Ageton, S. S.
1980   "Reconciling Race and Class Differences in Self-Reported and Official Estimates of Delinquency." *American Sociological Review* 45: 95–110.
Elliott, D. S., with Huizinga, D., and Ageton, S. S.
1985   *Explaining Delinquency and Drug Use*. Beverly Hills, CA: Sage.
Ellis, L.
1982   "Genetics and Criminal Behavior: Evidence through the End of the 1970's." *Criminology* 2: 43–66.
Esbensen, F. A., and Huizinga, D.
1993   "Gangs, Drugs, and Delinquency in a Survey of Urban Youth." *Criminology* 31: 565–587.
Fagan, J.
1990   "Social Processes of Delinquency and Drug Use among Urban Gangs." Pp. 183–219 in C. R. Huff (ed.), *Gangs in America*. Newbury Park, CA: Sage.
Fagan, J., Slaughter, E., and Hartstone, E.
1987   "Blind Justice? The Impact of Race on the Juvenile Justice Process." *Crime and Delinquency* 33: 224–258.
Farmighetti, R. (ed.)
1993   *World Almanac and Book of Facts*, 1994. Mahwah, NJ: World Almanac.
Faupel, C. E., and Klockars, C. B.
1987   "Drugs-Crime Connection: Elaborations from the Life Histories of Hard-Core Heroin Addicts." *Social Problems* 34: 54–68.
Felson, M.
1983   "Ecology of Crime." Pp. 665–670 in *Encyclopedia of Crime and Justice*. New York: Free Press.

Furstenberg, F. F., Jr.
1971   "Public Reaction to Crime in the Streets." *American Scholar* 40: 601–610.
Gartner, R.
1990   "The Victims of Homicide: A Temporal and Cross-National Comparison." *American Sociological Review* 55: 92–106.
Gottfredson, M. R., and Hirschi, T.
1986   "The True Value of Lambda Would Appear to be Zero: An Essay on Career Criminals, Criminal Careers, Selective Incapacitation, Cohort Studies, and Related Topics." *Criminology* 24: 213–234.
1990   *A General Theory of Crime*. Stanford, CA: Stanford University Press.
Gove, W. R., and Crutchfield, R. D.
1982   "The Family and Juvenile Delinquency." *Sociological Quarterly* 23: 301–319.
Hagan, J.
1990   "The Structuration of Gender and Deviance: A Power-Control Theory of Vulnerability to Crime and the Search for Deviant Role Exits." *Revue Canadienne de Sociologie et d'Anthropologie* 27: 137–156.
1991   "Destiny and Drift: Subcultural Preferences, Status Attainments, and the Risks and Rewards of Youth." *American Sociological Review* 56: 567–582.
Hagedorn, J. M.
1991   "Gangs, Neighborhoods, and Public Policy." *Social Problems* 38: 529–542.
Hagedorn, J. M., and Macon, P.
1988   People and Folks: Gangs, Crime and the Underclass in a Rustbelt City. *Chicago*: Lake View Press.
Hamm, M. S.
1993   *American Skinheads: The Criminology and Control of Hate Crime*. Westport, CT: Praeger.
Harris, M. G.
1988   *Cholas: Latin Girls and Gangs*. New York: AMS Press.
Henry, A. F., and Short, J. F., Jr.
1954   *Suicide and Homicide: Some Economic, Sociological, and Psychological Aspects of Aggression*. New York: Free Press.
Hindelang, J., Hirschi, T., and Weis, J. G.
1981   *Measuring Delinquency*. Beverly Hills, CA: Sage.
Hirschi, T.
1969   *Causes of Delinquency*. Berkeley, CA: University of California Press.
1979   "Separate and Unequal Is Better." *Journal of Research in Crime and Delinquency* 16: 34–38.
Hirschi, T., and Hindelang, J.
1977   "Intelligence and Delinquency: A Revi-

sionist Review." *American Sociological Review* 42: 571–587.

Huff, R. C.
1989   "Youth Gangs and Public Policy." *Crime and Delinquency* 35: 524–537.

Huizinga, D., and Elliott, D. S.
1987   "Juvenile Offenders: Prevalence, Offender Incidence, and Arrest Rates by Race." *Crime and Delinquency* 3: 206–233.

Jackson, P. I.
1984   "Opportunity and Crime: A Function of City Size." *Sociology and Social Research* 68: 172–193.

Jankowski, M. S.
1991   *Islands in the Street: Gangs and American Urban Society.* Berkeley, CA: University of California Press.

Joe, D., and Robinson, N.
1980   "Chinatown's Immigrant Gangs." *Criminology* 18: 337–345.

Johnson, B., Anderson, K., and Wish, E. D.
1988   "A Day on the Life of 105 Drug Addicts and Abusers: Crimes Committed and How the Money Was Spent." *Sociology and Social Research* 72: 185–191.

Johnson, B. D., Goldstein, E. P., Schmeidler, J., Lipton, D. S., Spunt, B., and Miller, T.
1985   *Taking Care of Business: The Economics of Crime by Heroin Abusers.* Lexington, MA: Lexington Books.

Johnson, R. E.
1979   *Juvenile Delinquency and Its Origins: An Integrated Theoretical Approach.* Cambridge, England: Cambridge University Press.

Johnson, S. L.
1993   "Racial Imagery in Criminal Cases." *Tulane Law Review* 67: 1739–1805.

Karmen, A.
1984   *Crime Victims: An Introduction to Victimology.* Belmont, CA: Wadsworth.

Katz, J.
1988   *The Seductions of Crime: Moral and Sensual Attractions in Doing Evil.* New York: Basic Books.

Kennedy, L. W., and Silverman, R. A.
1990   "The Elderly Victim of Homicide: An Application of the Routine Activities Approach." *Sociological Quarterly* 31: 307–319.

Kleck, G., and McElrath, K.
1991   "The Effects of Weaponry on Human Violence." *Social Forces* 69: 669–692.

Klein, M. W., Maxson, C. L., and Cunningham, L. C.
1991   "Crack, Street Gangs and Violence." *Criminology* 29: 623–650.

Kramer, J. R.
1993   "Introduction: Symposium on Criminal Law, Criminal Justice and Race." *Tulane Law Review* 67: 1725–1738.

Krisberg, B., Schwartz, G. F., Eisikovits, Z., Guttman, E., and Joe, K.
1987   "The Incarceration of Minority Youth." *Crime and Delinquency* 33: 173–205.

Krohn, M. D., and Massey, J. L.
1980   "Social Control and Delinquent Behavior: An Examination of the Elements of the Social Bond." *Sociological Quarterly* 31: 307–319.

Land, K. C., McCall, P. L. and Cohen, L. F.
1991   "Characteristics of U.S. Cities with Extreme (High or Low) Crime Rates: Results of Discriminant Analysis of 1960, 1970 and 1980 Data." *Social Indicators Research* 24: 209–231.

Levin, J., and Fox, J. A.
1985   *Mass Murder: America's Growing Menace.* New York: Plenum.

Lichter, L. S., and Lichter, R. S.
1983   *Prime Time Crime: Criminals and Law Enforcement in T.V. Entertainment.* Washington, DC: Media Institute.

Martin, P. Y., and Hummer, R. A.
1989   "Fraternities and Rape on Campus." *Gender and Society* 3: 457–473.

Massey, D. S.
1990   "American Apartheid: Segregation and the Making of the Underclass." *American Journal of Sociology* 96: 329–357.

Matza, D., and Sykes, G. M.
1961   "Juvenile Delinquency and Subterranean Values." *American Sociological Review* 26: 712–719.

McCarthy, B., and Hagan, J.
1992   "Mean Streets: The Theoretical Significance of Situational Delinquency among Homeless Youths." *American Journal of Sociology* 98: 597–627.

McDowall, D.
1991   "Firearm Availability and Homicide Rates in Detroit, 1951–1986." *Social Forces* 69: 1085–1101.

Mednick, S., and Christiansen, K. O.
1977   *Biosocial Bases of Criminal Behavior.* New York: Gardner.

Mednick, S. A., Gabrielli, F., Jr., and Hutchings, B.
1984   "Genetic Influences in Criminal Convictions: Evidence from an Adoption Cohort." *Science* 224: 891–893.

Mednick, S. A., and Volavka, J.
1980   "Biology and Crime." Pp. 85–158 in N. Morris and M. Tonry (eds.), *Crime and Justice: An Annual Review of Research,* Vol. 2. Chicago: University of Chicago Press.

Menard, S., and Morse, B. J.
1984   "A Structural Critique of the IQ-Delinquency Hypothesis: Theory and Evidence." *American Journal of Sociology* 89: 1347–1378.

Merton, R. K.
1968   "Social Structure and Anomie." In *Social Theory and Social Structure*. New York: Free Press.
Messerschmidt, J.
1986   *Capitalism, Patriarchy and Crime*. Totawa, NJ: Roman and Littlefield.
Messinger, S. L., and Berk, R. A.
1987   "Review Essay: Dangerous People." *Criminology* 25: 767–781.
Messner, S. F.
1989   "Economic Discrimination and Societal Homicide Rates: Further Evidence on the Cost of Inequality." *American Sociological Review* 54: 597–611.
Messner, S. F., and Blau, J. R.
1987   "Routine Leisure Activities and Rates of Crime: A Macro-Level Analysis." *Social Forces* 65: 1035–1052.
Messner, S. F., and Krohn, M. D.
1990   "Class, Compliance Structures, and Delinquency: Assessing Integrated Structural-Marxist Theory." *American Journal of Sociology* 96: 300–328.
Messner, S. F., and Rosenfeld, R.
1994   *Crime and the American Dream*. Belmont, CA: Wadsworth.
Messner, S. F., and Tardiff, K.
1985   "The Social Ecology of Urban Homicide: An Application of the 'Routine Activities' Approach." *Criminology* 23: 241–267.
1986   "Economic Inequality and Levels of Homicide: An Analysis of Urban Neighborhoods." *Criminology* 24: 297–317.
Miller, W. B.
1958   "Lower Class Culture as a Generating Milieu of Gang Delinquency." *Journal of Social Issues* 14: 5–19.
1974   "American Youth Gangs: Past and Present." Pp. 210–239 in A. S. Blumberg (ed.), *Current Perspectives on Criminal Behavior*. New York: Knopf.
Mills, C. W.
1942   "The Professional Ideology of Social Pathologists." *American Journal of Sociology* 49: 165–180.
Moore, J. W.
1979   *Homeboys: Gangs, Drugs, and Prison in the Barrios of Los Angeles*. Philadelphia: Temple University Press.
1991   *Down to the Barrio: Homeboys and Homegirls in Change*. Philadelphia: Temple University Press.
Mott, J.
1980   "Opium Use and Crime in the United Kingdom." *Contemporary Drug Problems* 9: 437–451.

Padilla, F. M.
1992   *The Gang as an American Enterprise*. New Brunswick, NJ: Rutgers University Press.
Palley, H. A. and Robinson, D.
1990   "Black on Black Crime: Poverty, Marginality, and the Under-Class Debate from a Global Perspective." *Social Development Issues* 12: 52–61.
Parker, R. N., and Horwitz, A. V.
1986   "Unemployment, Crime, and Imprisonment: A Panel Approach." *Criminology* 24: 751–773.
Pearson, G.
1983   *Hooligan: A History of Respectable Fears*. London: Macmillan.
Pollock, V., Mednick, S. A., and Gabrielli, W. F., Jr.
1983   "Crime Causation: Biological Theories." Pp. 308–316 in S. H. Kadish (ed.), *Encyclopedia of Crime and Justice*. New York: Free Press.
Quinney, R.
1970   *The Social Reality of Crime*. Boston: Little, Brown.
Reiss, A. J., and Roth, J. A.
1993   *Understanding and Preventing Violence*. Washington, DC: National Academy Press.
Room, R.
1983   "Alcohol and Crime: Behavioral Aspects." Pp. 35–44 in *Encyclopedia of Crime and Justice*. New York: Free Press.
Rowe, D. C., and Osgood, D. W.
1984   "Heredity and Sociological Theories of Delinquency: A Reconsideration." *American Sociological Review* 49: 526–540.
Sampson, R. J., and Lamb, J. H.
1992   "Crime and Deviance in the Life Course." *Annual Review of Sociology* 18: 63–84.
Schwendinger, H., and Schwendinger, J.
1983   *Rape and Inequality*. Beverly Hills, CA: Sage.
1985   *Adolescent Subcultures and Delinquency*. New York: Praeger.
Shaw, C. R.
1930   *The Jack-Roller: A Delinquent Boy's Own Story*. Chicago: University of Chicago Press.
Shaw, C. R., and McKay, H. D.
1942   *Juvenile Delinquency and Urban Areas*. Chicago: University of Chicago Press.
Sheley, J. F.
1993   "Structural Influence on the Problem of Race, Crime, and Criminal Justice Discrimination." *Tulane Law Review* 67: 2273–2292.
Shelley, L. I.
1981   *Crime and Modernization: The Impact of Industrialization and Urbanization of*

Crime. Carbondale: Southern Illinois University Press.

Short, J. F., Jr.
1969   "Introduction to the Revised Edition." In R. Shaw and H. D. McKay, *Juvenile Delinquency and Urban Areas*, revised edition. Chicago: University of Chicago Press.
1990a   "Cities, Gangs, and Delinquency." *Sociological Forum* 5: 657–668.
1990b   "New Wine in Old Bottles? Change and Continuity in American Gangs." Pp. 223–239 in C. R. Huff (ed.), *Gangs in America*. Newbury Park, CA: Sage.
1991   "Poverty, Ethnicity, and Crime: Change and Continuity in U.S. Cities." *Journal of Research in Crime and Delinquency* 28: 501–518.

Short, J. F., Jr., and Strodtbeck, F.
1965   *Group Processes and Gang Delinquency*. Chicago: University of Chicago Press.

Skogan, W. G.
1981   "On Attitudes and Behaviors." Pp. 19–45 in D. A. Lewis (ed.), *Reactions to Crime*. Beverly Hills, CA: Sage.
1990   *Disorder and Decline: Crime and the Spiral of Decay in American Neighborhoods*. New York: Free Press.

Skolnick, J. H.
1992   "Gangs in the Post-Industrial Ghetto." *American Prospect* 8: 109–120.

Smith, D. A., and Visher, C. A.
1980   "Sex and Involvement in Deviance/Crime: A Quantative Review of the Empirical Literature." *American Sociological Review* 45: 691–701.

Speckart, G., and Anglin, D. M.
1986   "Narcotics and Crime: A Causal Modeling Approach." *Journal of Quantative Criminology*. 2: 3–28.

Spergel, I. A.
1992   "Youths Gangs: An Essay Review." *Social Service Review* 66: 121–140.

Spitzer, S.
1975   "Toward a Marxian Theory of Deviance." *Social Problems* 22: 635–651.

Stahura, J. M., and Sloan, J. J., III
1988   "Urban Stratification of Places, Routine Activities and Suburban Crime Rates." *Social Forces* 66: 1102–1118.

Steffensmeier, D. J.
1978   "Crime and the Contemporary Woman: An Analysis of Changing Levels of Female Property Crime, 1960–'75." *Social Forces* 57: 566–584.
1980   "Sex Differences in Patterns of Adult Crime, 1965–'77: A Review and Assessment." *Social Forces* 58: 1080–1108.

Steffensmeier, D. J., and Cobb, M. J.
1981   "Sex Differences in Urban Arrest Patterns, 1934–1979." *Social Problems* 29: 37–50.

Steffensmeier, D. J., and Harer, M. D.
1987   "Is the Crime Rate Really Falling? An 'Aging' U. S. Population and Its Impact on the Nation's Crime Rate, 1980–1984." *Journal of Research on Crime and Delinquency* 24: 23–48.

Sullivan, M. L.
1989   *Getting Paid: Youth Crime and Work in the Inner City*. Ithaca, NY: Cornell University Press.

Sutherland, Edwin H.
1939   *Criminology*. New York: J. B. Lippincott.

Swart, W. J.
1991   "Female Gang Delinquency: A Search for 'Acceptable Deviant Behavior'." *Mid-American Review of Sociology* 15: 43–52.

Sykes, G. M., and Matza, D.
1957   "Techniques of Neutralization: A Theory of Delinquency" *American Sociological Review* 22: 664–670.

Tannenbaum, F.
1938   *Crime and the Community*. New York: Columbia University Press.

Taylor, I., Walton, P., and Young, J.
1973   *The New Criminology: For a Social Theory of Deviance*. London: Routledge and Kegan Paul.

Thornberry, T. P., and Christenson, R. L.
1984   "Unemployment and Criminal Involvement: An Investigation of Reciprocal Causal Structures." *American Sociological Review* 49: 398–411.

Thornberry, T. P., and Farnworth, M.
1982   "Social Correlates of Criminal Involvement: Further Evidence on the Relationship between Social States and Criminal Behavior." *American Sociological Review*. 47: 505–518.

Thrasher, F. M.
1927   *The Gang: A Study of 1,313 Gangs in Chicago*. Chicago: University of Chicago Press.

Tittle, C. R.
1980   "Labeling and Crime: An Empirical Evaluation." Pp. 157–179 in W. R. Gove (ed.), *The Labeling of Deviance: Evaluating a Perspective*. Beverly Hills, CA: Sage.
1983   "Social Class and Criminal Behavior: A Critique of the Theoretical Foundation." *Social Forces* 62: 334–358.

United Nations
1992   *Demographic Yearbook, 1991*. Table 21. New York: Author.

Unnever, J. D., Frazier, C. E., and Hanretta, J. C.
1980   "Race Differences in Criminal Sentencing." *Sociological Quarterly* 21: 197–205.

U.S. Bureau of the Census
1992   *Current Population Reports*, Series P-25, No. 1,092. Washington, DC: U.S. Department of Commerce.

U.S. Department of Justice
1983   *Prisoners and Alcohol.* Bureau of Justice Statistics Bulletin, January.
1992   *Justice Expenditure and Employment, 1990.* Bureau of Justice Statistics Bulletin, September.
1993   *Uniform Crime Reports: Crime in the United States.* Washington, DC: Federal Bureau of Investigation.
1994   *Criminal Victimization in the United States, 1992.* Washington, DC: Bureau of Justice Statistics.

Vigil, J. D., and Yun, S. C.
1990   "Vietnamese Youth Gangs in Southern California." Pp. 146–162 in C. R. Huff (ed.), *Gangs in America.* Newbury Park, CA: Sage.

Wacquant, L. J. D.
1989   "The Ghetto, the State, and the New Capitalist Economy." *Dissent* 36: 508–520.

Warr, M.
1980   "The Accuracy of Public Beliefs about Crime." *Social Forces* 59: 456–470.

West, D. J., and Farrington, D. P.
1973   *Who Becomes Delinquent?* London: Heinemann.

Wiatrowski, M. D., Griswold, D. B., and Roberts, M. K.
1981   "Social Control Theory and Delinquency." *American Sociological Review* 46: 525–541.

Williams, T.
1989   *The Cocaine Kids: The Inside Story of a Teenage Drug Ring.* Boston: Addison-Wesley.

Wilson, J. Q., and Herrnstein, R. J.
1985   *Crime and Human Nature.* New York: Simson and Schuster.

Wilson, W. J.
1987   *The Truly Disadvantaged: The Inner City, the Underclass, and Public Policy.* Chicago: University of Chicago Press.

Witkin, H. A., Mednick, S. A., Schuslinger, F., Bakkestrom, E., Lundsteen, C., Owen, D. R., Phillip, J., Rubin, D. B., and Stocking, M.
1976   "Criminality in XYY and XXY Men." *Science* 193: 547–555.

Wolfgang, M. E.
1958   *Patterns in Criminal Homicide.* Philadelphia: University of Pennsylvania Press.

Wolfgang, M. E., and Ferracuti, F.
1967   *The Subculture of Violence: Towards an Integrated Theory in Criminology.* London: Tavistock.

Wolfgang, M., Figlio, R., and Sellin, T.
1972   *Delinquency in a Birth Cohort.* Chicago: University of Chicago Press.

Wolfgang, M. E., Thornberry, T. P., and Figlio, R. M.
1987   *From Boy to Man, From Delinquency to Crime.* Chicago: University of Chicago Press.

Yablonsky, L.
1959   "The Gang as a Near-Group." *Social Problems* 7: 108–117.

9 | Elite Deviance

This chapter deals with deviant behavior among those at the highest levels of the American social structure. Our initial task will be to identify who the elites are and to compare their wealth and power to those held by the rest of the people in the society. The elites whose deviance will concern us fall into two broad categories. First is the relatively small number of individuals who exercise great political power and are accorded exceptional prestige. Specifically, we will examine deviant behaviors that are closely linked to the occupations of these high-status individuals. Second is the relatively small number of large corporations whose decisions and operations control an ever-larger share of this nation's political economy. We normally conceive of any social behavior, deviant or normal, as the product of individual motives, initiative, choices, or responsibilities. In our society, however, corporations, as very large, complex, bureaucratic organizations in the private sector, have become actors whose behaviors affect people's well-being, for good or ill. A large portion of this chapter is devoted to corporate deviance and criminality.

For too long, say some critics (for example, Liazos, 1972, and Thio, 1973), students of deviance have concentrated on the poor, the powerless, or the pathological as the inspiration for their theories and the subjects of their studies. In the past 25 years, however, a growing body of research on deviance committed by elites has begun to shift this balance. With this change has come a clearer recognition that the study of deviance should never be limited by class boundaries or alleged individual psychopathology. As the evidence cited in this chapter amply demonstrates, deviance can become a way of life even for those at the top.

THE AMERICAN CLASS STRUCTURE

The American class structure is a social stratification system consisting of a number of social classes which are primarily indicative of economic standing in the society. Social class is determined by the economic opportunities available to individuals, the economic goods and resources they command, and the occupations or positions they hold (Longres, 1994).

Different sociologists and economists have designated various numbers and names of social classes. The General Social Surveys conducted by the National Opinion Research Center ask respondents to identify themselves as lower, working, middle, or upper class, and results have been consistent since the first survey in

1972. In 1993, less than 10% put themselves in either the lower class or the upper class; about 45% said they were in the working class and another 45% in the middle class (Leroux, 1993).

We will discuss the American class structure in terms of the model devised by Dennis Gilbert and Joseph Kahl (1993), which is more descriptive of the current economic structure. In this model there are six classes combined into four: capitalist, upper middle, middle and working, and working poor and underclass (see Table 9.1).

The Elites—Individuals and Corporations

Individuals. The tip of the American social hierarchy is occupied by roughly 1% of the population who control a disproportionate share of the country's wealth and exercise great economic and political power. The power of those in this class derives from the concentration of vast economic resources in relatively few hands. Smith (1987) found that one-half of 1% of American households owned 27% of the individual wealth and controlled 60% to 70% of the corporate wealth in the form of stocks and bonds; their ownership of over 40% of all corporate stock gave them virtual control over corporate America. As Gilbert and Kahl observe, it is this very small class of superrich capitalists whose investment decisions

> ...open or close employment opportunities for millions of others. They contribute money to political parties, and they often own newspapers or television companies, thereby gaining impact on the shaping of the consciousness of all classes in the nation. The capitalist class tends to perpetuate itself: It passes on assets and styles of life (including networks of contact with other influentials) to its children. This creation of lineage is of sufficient importance to them that they are active in creating and supporting preparatory schools and universities for their children and for carefully selected newcomers who can be socialized into their world view. (310)

Below the capitalist elite is the upper-middle class of university-trained managers, professionals, and bureaucratic administrators. Constituting about 14% of the population, this group is distinguished by a status grounded in educational credentials and relatively high income, rather than the inherited wealth and lineage of the capitalist class. The upper-middle class also is less culturally united by membership in elite social groups, enrollment in elite prep schools and colleges, listing in a social register, and the like, but its lifestyle incorporates the symbols that many Americans identify as the epitome of success. Taken together, the capitalist and upper-middle classes, the upper 15% of the American population in terms of wealth and income, can be considered to be comprised of the society's elite individuals. Characteristics of the classes making up the remaining 85% of the American social structure are summarized in Table 9.1.

While the individuals in this elite do change over time, due to death, economic misfortune, or other life events, the overall distribution of wealth in America has remained relatively stable over the past 40 or so years; that is, the proportions of people in the various classes have remained about the same. What did change in the

Table 9.1   Model of the American Class Structure: Classes by Typical Situations

Proportion of Households	Class	Education	Occupation of Family Head	Family Income, 1990
1%	Capitalist	Prestige university	Investors, heirs, executives	Over $750,000, mostly from assets
14%	Upper middle	College, often with postgraduate study	Upper managers and professionals; medium business owners	$70,000 or more
60% {	Middle	At least high school; often some college or apprenticeship	Lower managers; semiprofessionals; nonretail sales; craftspeople; foremen	About $40,000
	Working	High school	Operatives; low-paid craftspeople; clerical workers; retail sales workers	About $25,000
25% {	Working poor	Some high school	Service workers; laborers; low-paid operatives and clericals	Below $20,000
	Underclass	Some high school	Unemployed or part-time; many welfare recipients	Below $13,000

Source: Gilbert and Kahl, 1993: 311.

1980s was the *proportion of the nation's wealth* captured by the rich. Kevin Phillips (1990b) puts it this way:

> No parallel upsurge of riches had been seen since the late 19th century, the era of the Vanderbilts, Morgans and Rockefellers. It was the truly wealthy, more than anyone else, who flourished under Reagan. Calculations in a Brookings Institution study found that the share of national income going to the wealthiest 1 percent rose from 8.1 percent in 1981 to 14.7 in 1986. Between 1981 and 1989, the new worth of the Forbes 400 richest Americans nearly tripled. At the same time, the division between them and the rest of the country became a yawning gap. In 1980, corporate chief executive officers, for example, made roughly 40 times the income of factory workers. By 1989, C.E.O.s were making *93 times as much*. (26; italics in original)

This shift in wealth occurred at the same time those at the other end of the social scale—laid-off steel workers, foreclosed farmers, members of the urban underclass—were feeling intense economic pain. As Phillips notes, "A disproportionate number of female, black, Hispanic and young Americans lost ground in the 1980s….For example, the inflation-adjusted income for families with children headed by an adult under 30 collapsed by roughly one-fourth between 1973 and 1986" (Phillips, 1990b: 28). Families in the upper 1% of the U.S. income distribution, with an average income of over $400,000 in 1988, had improved their incomes by 50% since 1977. Those in the lowest 10% had an average income of $3,504 in 1988 and had *lost* 15% during the same period (Phillips, 1990a: 17). Thus, as the rich have been getting richer, the poor have been getting poorer. A report of the Commission on the Future of Worker-Management Relations issued jointly by the U.S. Labor and Commerce departments in June 1994 pinpoints a reason why: The gap between high-paid and low-paid workers had widened, and the number of low-paid workers "had grown greatly, with the result that a sizable proportion of U.S. workers are paid markedly less than comparable workers in other advanced countries." In contrast, high-paid workers were earning more than their counterparts in other nations (Associated Press, 1994). In 1992, according to the U.S. Census Bureau, 18% of year-round, full-time workers were earning less than $13,091 a year.

Corporations. In the same way a great deal of wealth and power are concentrated in the hands of a small proportion of individuals, a relatively few very large corporations control a large segment of the American economy. Clinard and Yeager (1980) put it: "The current size of U.S. corporations staggers the imagination" (31). Some representative recent indicators are:

- The five largest American corporations in 1993 were Federal International Mortgage, CitiCorp, Ford, General Motors, and BankAmerica, whose total combined assets exceeded $1 trillion.
- In 1993 the total annual sales of the *Fortune* 500 largest industrial corporations was $2.3 trillion ($2,340,164,300,000).
- In 1993, the annual revenues of General Motors, Exxon, and Ford each exceeded or approached $100 billion, greater than that of any government in the world except the United States.

- In 1993, five American corporations (General Motors, Wal-Mart, AT&T, Ford, and Pepsico) together employed over 2.25 million people (Martin, 1994; Teitelbaum, 1994).
- The 500 largest industrial corporations account for two-thirds of all industrial sales and three-quarters of all manufacturing assets in the United States.
- Of the more than 200,000 corporations in the United States, 2,000 (1%) account for one-half of all business.

Many key industries in the United States are dominated by a very small number of corporations; industries in which four corporations or fewer share over three-quarters of the market include aluminum, automobiles, synthetic fibers, flat glass, electric bulbs, telephone equipment, copper, cereal foods, gypsum, cigarettes, salt, rubber tires, soap, detergents, and steel ingots and shapes (Clinard and Yaeger, 1980). Moreover, the tendency toward concentration has been growing. The top 100 (or five-hundredths of 1% of industrial corporations) controlled 40% of all industrial assets in 1950 and 60% in 1986.

Contrary to the myth of laissez-faire capitalism that independent firms openly compete in open markets, the largest American companies are actually related to one another through shared memberships by individuals on their boards of directors. A study by Pennings (1980) of 797 of the largest American corporations revealed that only 62 of them had no interlocks (through interlocking directorships) with any of the other 735. Figure 9.1 shows how AT&T, in 1984, the year after divesting all of its 22 regional and local telephone companies in compliance with the court-ordered settlement of an antitrust suit, was connected to other large American corporations through interlocks between its board members and the boards of other large American corporations. Interlocks give firms an advantage because through their common bonds board members share valuable information about products, policies, and markets; there are positive correlations between the number of interlocks in a firm's board of directors and its earnings, return on sales, return on fixed assets, and sales on assets. Studies of interlocking directorships also point to the existence of a corporate elite, drawn from the top of America's largest companies and financial institutions, who are relatively unified and politically active on behalf of the business community (Mizruchi, 1982, 1989, 1990; Mizruchi and Koenig, 1991; Useem, 1984).

Elites and the Exercise of Power

The control of economic assets by elite individuals and corporations is important in the study of deviance to the extent that wealth can be effectively translated into political power—for with political power comes an enhanced ability to assure favorable enactment and enforcement of laws. Elites disproportionately influence the political process in three ways: (1) through direct control by individual participants, (2) through the indirect influence of organizations and institutions, and (3) through financial contributions (Jacobs, 1988).

Direct Control by Participants. The first way elites influence the political process is through their direct link to it at the national level as representatives and senators

Figure 9.1   Interlocking Directorships Held by AT&T Directors, 1984

Industrials	AT&T Directors	Banks and Insurance
DuPont	C. L. Brown	Chemical Bank of NY
General Foods	W. S. Cashel, Jr.	Manufacturers Hanover
Campbell Soup	C. B. Cleary	Citicorp
General Motors	W. M. Ellinghaus	Chase Manhattan
J.C. Penney	J. H. Evans	First Wisconsin
Zurn Industries	P. E. Haas	Northwestern Mutual
Jewel Companies	P. M. Hawley	Bankers Trust NY
Cummins Engine	J. H. Holland	Crocker National Bank
CBS, Inc.	E. G. Jefferson	Bank America
Southern Bell	B. K. Johnson	Continental Insurance
Dart & Kraft	J. M. Kreps	Pan American Banks
Kohler	J. E. Olson	First City Bancorp TX
Bristol-Myers	D. S. Perkins	
Continental	H. B. Schacht	
Deere & Co.	R. Warner, Jr.	
Corning Glass	T. H. Wyman	
Chrysler		

International Paper			
Pacific Tel. & Tel.			Freeport-McMo Ran
Union Pacific	Union Carbide	United Airlines	Inland Steel
Levi Strauss	Conoco	American Bell	Searle
Armco	Seagram	Bell Telephone Labs	Time, Inc.
Atlantic Richfield	Chaparrosa Ranch	Borg-Warner	Mobil
Walt Disney	Johnson Interests	NY Telephone	American Express
The Economist	Tenneco	Western Electric	Caterpillar Tractor
Culbro	Eastman Kodak	Firestone	Aurrera
Carter Hawley Hale	Federated Dept. Stores	Wheelabrator-Frye	R. J. Reynolds

Source: Dye, 1990: 178.
Note: Each line represents an interlocking directorship with AT&T; a double or triple line represents two or three interlocks.

in Congress or as Cabinet members. Since 1948, over three-quarters of the members of the House of Representatives have been lawyers, business owners, or professionals. The membership of neither the House nor the Senate represents the characteristics of the American population with respect to gender, race or ethnic origin, occupational categories, or social class. The 103rd Congress, which first convened in January 1993, was the most diverse to date. In the House, out of a total of 435 members, there were 48 women, as well as 39 blacks and 19 Hispanics. In the Senate, out of a total of 100, there were six women, and the only minority member was one black who was also a woman—Carol Moseley Braun of Illinois. Table 9.2 compares members of the House and Senate in the 103rd Congress with the American people as a whole on several characteristics associated with social status.

The representation of both blue-collar workers and white-collar employees in Congress has been slight. Gilbert and Kahl (1993) note that in the 102nd Congress (1991–1993), "Only two of the 535 members of the Congress have been union leaders—a background that is common for legislators in some Western democracies. Evidence going back to 1906 shows that this recruitment pattern has been consistent throughout the twentieth century" (215). The majority of senators had been professionals or business owners, and a significant minority could be described as upper class. At least half of the members of the Senate were millionaires; at least a third of House members had incomes in excess of $150,000. The members of Congress thus were recruited from the upper levels of the class structure, although typically "from a stratum a notch below that of the typical cabinet officer" (216).

While Congress, as the legislative branch of the federal government, makes the laws, the enforcement of laws falls to the judicial branch and the administrative policy and procedural decisions of the executive branch, which are influenced by the composition of the Cabinet. Here again, the domination of elites—especially the corporate elite—is remarkably evident. Freitag (1975) found that more than 76% of Cabinet members between 1897 and 1973 had interlocks with business as either corporate directors or officers (62%) or corporate lawyers (14%). The pattern was highly stable during the entire period and continues up to the present (Dye, 1990: 88–99).

To be sure, the strong tendency for Congress and Cabinet members to be recruited from the upper echelons of the society does not guarantee a uniform political viewpoint. However, people who share upper- or upper-middle-class origins are likely to be more sympathetic to views and interests common to those at the top of the class structure than to those toward the bottom. The historical pattern of legislation and enforcement *generally* favors the interests of the society's elites (Domhoff, 1970; 1983; 1990; Dye, 1990).

Indirect Influence of Organizations and Institutions. The second avenue through which elites affect the political process is more indirect. Upper-class members dominate numerous policy-forming organizations that heavily influence political candidates and often represent a major recruiting source for presidential appointees. Among such organizations are the Council on Foreign Relations, the Trilateral

Table 9.2   Characteristics of Members of the 103rd U.S. Congress, 1993, and General Population, 1992, in Percent

Characteristic	House	Senate	General Population
Females	11%	6%	51%
Blacks	9	1	12
Principal occupation			
Law	42	58	1
Business or banking	30	24	13
Politics or public service	20	10	—
Education	4	11	4
Agriculture	4	8	3
Journalism	6	9	—
Other professions	3	4	9
Other occupations	3	0	71
Religion			
Protestant	43	45	56
Roman Catholic	27	23	25
Jewish	8	10	2
Other	23	22	17

Sources: Ornstein, Mann, and Malbin, 1994; U.S. Bureau of the Census, 1993.

Commission, the Business Roundtable, the American Enterprise Institute, the Brookings Institution, the Center for Strategic and International Studies, the Ford, Rockefeller, and Carnegie foundations, and elite-sponsored research at major universities such as Harvard, Yale, Princeton, or Columbia. One researcher found that 42% of the directors of foundations, 25% of the directors of elite universities, and 40% of the directors of civic organizations could be classified as members of the upper class (cited in Kerbo and Fave, 1979: 17).

Thomas R. Dye's (1990) model in Figure 9.2 charts how elite organizations and institutions are linked to one another in ways that ultimately affect government policy and legislation. The model is based on the assumption that the initial resources for research, study, planning, and formulation of national policy are derived from corporate and personal wealth that is channeled into foundations, universities, and policy-planning groups in the form of endowments, grants, and contracts. Moreover, corporate presidents, directors, and top wealth-holders sit on the governing boards of these groups and organizations to oversee the spending of their funds. "In short, corporate and personal wealth provide both the financial and the overall direction of policy research, planning, and development" (250).

Figure 9.2   Elite Influences on National Policy Recommendations (Dye, 1990)

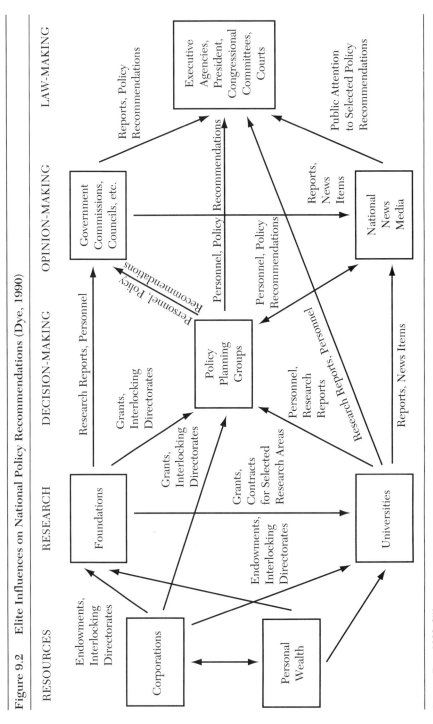

Source: Dye, 1990: 251.

In his extensive study, Dye (1990) found:

> Approximately 6,000 individuals in 7,000 positions exercise formal authority over institutions that control roughly half of the nation's resources in industry, finance, utilities, insurance, mass media, foundations, education, law, and civic and cultural affairs. This definition of the elite is fairly large numerically, yet these individuals constitute an extremely small percentage of the nation's total population—less than three-thousandths of 1 percent. (276)

This core elite continues to dominate the nation's top law firms, its corporations, its civic and cultural organizations, and its key posts in government, as it has for many years (see Salzman and Domhoff, 1979).

Financial Contributions. The third means by which elites influence the political process is through the money they inject into it. The cost of campaigns for national office runs into multimillions for the presidency and the Senate and only somewhat less for the House. Major sources of funds for this money-driven political campaigning are the political action committees (PACs) maintained by special interests. Studies have shown that through the use of PACs, America's largest businesses and corporations have been successful in implementing a political agenda in their particular interests (Jacobs, 1988; Clawson and Neustadtl, 1989; Mizruchi, 1989; 1990). Individual elites may dip into their personal fortunes to attain political office.

In sum, we can say that the American class structure is dominated by a relatively small elite of capitalists (1%) and upper-middle-class individuals (14%). Paralleling the concentration of wealth in the hands of these individuals is a comparable concentration of corporate wealth held by relatively few large corporations. The recent trend has been for these concentrations to increase. The evidence is very persuasive that America's elite individuals and corporations are able to translate their economic power into political decisions largely in their own interests, directly by political control of legislative and administrative positions; indirectly through organizations that influence public policy; and financially through PACs or personal wealth in the electoral process.

THE TRADITION OF WHITE-COLLAR CRIME

Edwin H. Sutherland challenged traditional criminology many years ago in his 1939 presidential address to the American Sociological Association. First he questioned the assumption, based on official statistics such as those in the Uniform Crime Index, that crime is concentrated in the lower classes. Sutherland charged that official measures of crime included only the sorts of offenses such as theft, burglary, and robbery that lower-class people are likely to commit, while excluding illegal activities common to the well-to-do such as tax evasion, embezzlement, and price fixing. Most students of deviance since have agreed with this critique.

Sutherland also argued that authorities on crime must extend their view beyond the strict violation of the criminal law in their identification of offenses and offenders. Criminologists should include administrative and civil law violations as well, because it is under these bodies of law that most crimes of the rich and powerful are committed. He even went so far as to suggest that because the wealthy and powerful create the law and have the law enforced largely in their own interests, criminologists should be the ultimate, unbiased arbiters of what constitutes crime for purposes of determining the subject of their research. In other words, criminologists should not confine their investigations to activities proscribed by the criminal law. Instead, they should invoke their own standard of those "wrongful and injurious practices" that should constitute crime, even if the behavior in question has not been officially labeled *criminal* by law.

In Sutherland's pioneering work *White Collar Crime* (1949), he reported on violations of the 70 largest corporations in the United States over a period from 1890 to 1945. He counted as crimes restraint of trade, misrepresentation in advertising, unfair labor practices, and financial fraud, among others, and found that these corporations had been involved in a total of 980 adverse legal decisions: "Every one of the 70 corporations has a decision against it, and the average number of decisions is 14....98% are recidivists; that is, they have two or more adverse decisions" (1956: 80). His conclusion was that "90% of the 70 largest corporations in the United States are habitual criminals." Only recently, with the publication of an uncut version of Sutherland's study that includes the names of these criminal corporations (Sutherland, 1983), have we learned exactly which ones they were. Originally, the names of Allied Chemical, American Tobacco, Armour, DuPont, General Electric, Swift, U.S. Steel, Westinghouse, and the like were excised because the publisher and Indiana University, where Sutherland was a faculty member, feared reprisals.

Although Sutherland has been rightly criticized for "overinterpreting" his data and inflating his rhetoric (Klockars, 1977), the thrust of his argument remains viable: Crime is not necessarily caused by (or even correlated with) poverty and its alleged attendant pathologies. Crime is not confined to the lower class. Moreover, crime is not necessarily due to psychological pathology. As Sutherland (1956) mockingly put it:

> Business leaders are capable, emotionally balanced, and in no sense pathological. We have no reason to think that General Motors has an inferiority complex or that the Aluminum Company of America has a frustration-aggression complex or that U.S. Steel has an Oedipus complex, or that the Armour Company has a death wish or that DuPonts desire to return to the womb. The assumption that an offender must have some such pathological distortion of the intellect or the emotions seems to me absurd, and if it is absurd regarding the crimes of businessmen, it is equally absurd regarding the crimes of persons in the lower economic class. (96)

The Problem of Definition

Sutherland defined white-collar crime as crime committed by a person of respectability and high social status in the course of his occupation. In practice,

Sutherland himself used the concept in reference to acts as varied as medical fee splitting by doctors, political corruption, embezzlement, tax fraud, antitrust violations, and labor law violations. More recently, the term has been applied to the production and sale of unsafe products and to environmental pollution, but these applications of Sutherland's original definition exceed its conceptual boundaries. For example, the original definition states that the crime is "committed by a *person.*" To be sure, this may be clearly the case in a physician's medical fee splitting or an individual's tax evasion. However, the legal actor in the case of antitrust or labor law violations is more likely to be a corporation, which suggests the need for care to avoid confusing deviant actions committed by individuals with those committed by corporations. Such a distinction forms the basis for the two major types of elite deviance we will consider is this chapter, elite occupational deviance (including official deviance) and elite corporate deviance.

Elite occupational deviance is an illegal or unethical act committed for personal gain by an individual of high social status and respectability in the course of that person's occupation or profession. The examples we will examine are certain practices in the professions among doctors, lawyers, and college professors, and political corruption among government officials. The central features that distinguish occupational deviance are the commission of the offense for direct personal gain and the relatively autonomous behavior of the offender.

Elite corporate deviance consists of actions that violate criminal, civil, or administrative law (acts of omission or commission) that are intended to benefit the corporation itself. Such actions result from decisions by officers in a corporation (executives or managers) in accordance with corporate goals (primarily profit), standard operating procedures, and cultural norms of the organization (adapted from Kramer, 1981: 7–8). Examples of corporate deviance include securities fraud, price-fixing, and violations of labor law, health and safety regulations, or pollution law. The key characteristics of corporate deviance are commission of the offense in the pursuit of corporate gain (profit, expanded market share, market stability), and the collective or organizational basis of the behavior. The decision to act illegally is made and implemented by numerous individuals through the bureaucratic procedures of the corporate organization. Many researchers in this field, following Sutherland's lead, use the term *corporate crime* to cover the actions encompassed by our definition of *elite corporate deviance.* In this chapter, the two terms will be taken to refer to the same general phenomena and will be used interchangeably.

ELITE OCCUPATIONAL DEVIANCE: PROFESSIONS

In an era when the term *professional* connotes proficiency in and dedication to one's work, there are few occupations—from streetwalker to paid athlete to brain surgeon—whose members do not claim to be professionals. As used by sociologists, however, the term is applied rather more narrowly to occupations of relatively high status invested with a great deal of trust on the part of clients that their affairs will be managed honestly and in the public interest. The work of doctors, lawyers, and professors nearly fits the ideal characteristics of a profession, including lengthy training to learn an abstract body of knowledge, autonomy and self-regulation on the job, the existence of a professional association, and specified standards or norms, usually set down in a code of ethics. In fact, both the professions and their clients rely heavily on the long educational process necessary for certification to practice as the principal means of social control. The professions seek to instill each practitioner with a strong ethical conscience, in the absence of which the license to practice becomes a license to steal, or worse.

Physicians

Doctors have been near the pinnacle of American society in income and prestige. The old-time dedication of a "Doc" in westerns and the wisdom of a television Marcus Welby are part of their image. Increasingly, however, physicians are being faced with public hostility, as manifested in malpractice suits, the disclosure of scandals such as Medicaid or Medicare fraud, and attempts to control doctors' charges and other health-care costs.

At least one of the offenses frequently committed by physicians is usually associated with street criminals—drug addiction. Physicians' rates of substance use, including sleeping pills, alcohol, and benzodiazepines, have been found in numerous studies to exceed those for the general population (Jex et al., 1992: 980); Hessler (1974) estimated that the rate of drug addiction was 100 times higher for physicians. Approximately 1% to 2% of doctors develop drug-abuse problems at some point in their careers, and 6% to 8% develop alcohol problems (Morrow, 1982: 92). The reasons are thought to be the stress of professional obligations, combined with easy access to drugs and a capacity to avoid detection. Other deviant activities such as performing unnecessary surgery, ordering excessive laboratory tests, fee-padding, or fee-splitting (referral of a patient to a specialist who then pays off the referring physician) appear to be motivated primarily by greed. The extent of such illegalities is frightening. Lewis and Lewis (1978) note estimates of administrators with long experience in this field that at least 1 in 20 physicians is a severe disciplinary problem, and between 15,000 and 20,000 private practitioners (as many as 1 in 9) are "repeatedly guilty of practices unworthy of the profession." These offenses are primarily unethical rather than illegal, such as providing substandard care, abandonment of patients, and overcharging, but some are narcotics violations, frauds, and other felonies.

One sociological answer to why so many high-status professionals engage in deviant behavior lies in an analysis of the degree of autonomy the profession provides. While professional autonomy lends an occupation prestige, it can also be a major contributor to deviance. As Lewis and Lewis (1978) put it about doctors:

> If you are like most laymen, you take comfort in the belief that doctors of medicine are kept in careful rein by stringent laws, rigorous government agencies, and exacting professional groups. Unfortunately, if you think this you are mistaken.
>
> Actually, the privately practicing physician is largely a free agent, scarcely subject to regulation. Once he secures a license he has virtually a lifetime franchise to practice at

his own discretion. There are few statutory standards he must meet, for the laws are generally silent as to what constitutes acceptable performance by physicians. Even where restrictions are clear, enforcement is spotty; the state boards charged with overseeing the profession are seldom active on matters of discipline. Within the profession itself the disciplining of colleagues has little support; physicians do not like to police their fellows, and this reluctance is reflected at every level of organized medicine. (248)

The opportunities for deviance built into the organization of the practice or specialty also appear to influence the likelihood of lawbreaking. For example, psychiatrists are disproportionately represented among those suspended from the Medicare or Medicaid programs for fraud or abuse. Psychiatrists charge their clients for time rather than service, which increases the opportunity for fraud as well as the likelihood of apprehension (Geis et al., 1985).

Physicians have been very difficult to police and control in respect to activities ranging from the persistent use of unnecessary or dangerous procedures to medical insurance fraud. Most are able to draw on their considerable influence and professional power to resist enforcement procedures and avoid damaging interpretations of acts when they violate the law (Bullough and Groeger, 1982; Pontell, Jesilow, and Geis, 1982).

Lawyers

Some lawyers engage in outright illegal activities such as criminal financial manipulation on behalf of clients, securing perjured testimony from witnesses, and threatening or intimidating witnesses. Between illegal and merely unethical acts are inflated fee setting and ambulance chasing, or watching for opportunities to offer accident victims legal services in suits for liability damages. The rise in the frequency and size of awards in medical malpractice suits lies behind increasing tensions between the medical and legal professions. Doctors charge that aggressive, greedy lawyers push clients to file malpractice actions. The lawyers counter that they are merely protecting their clients' interests in the face of an inadequately self-regulated medical profession.

The problem of fee-setting for legal services underscores how the autonomy, lack of regulation, and abstract quality of the services provided by lawyers coalesce into a virtual invitation to take unethical or illegal advantage of clients. Blumberg (1978), describing the practice of law as "a confidence game," says:

> In varying degrees, …, all law practice involves a manipulation of the client and a stage management of the lawyer-client relationship so that at least an *appearance* of help and service will be forthcoming. This is accomplished in a variety of ways, often exercised in combination with each other. At the outset, the lawyer-professional employs with suitable variation a measure of sales-puff which may range from an air of unbounding self-confidence, adequacy, and dominion over events to that of complete arrogance. This will be supplemented by the affectation of a studied, faultless mode of personal attire. In the larger firms, the furnishings and office trappings will serve as the backdrop to help in impression management and client intimidation. In all firms, solo or large-scale, an access to secret knowledge and to the seats of power and influence

are presumed to a varying degree as the basic vendible commodity of the practitioners. (267–277)

There are no statistics on the amount of illegal or unethical behavior among lawyers, although studies have found that the most frequent reason for disbarment is violation of the financial trust of a client (Reasons and Chappell, 1986). Certainly it would be unfair and incorrect to assume that every lawyer is a shyster or that every physician cares only for money. Indeed, it is probably a wonder, given the heavy reliance upon self-regulation, that deviance in these professions is not far more prevalent than it is. Dansereau (1974) summarizes the situation well:

> Given present goals and means, current practices are likely to continue. Persistence of the competition between the business and the professional ethic will probably find mere mortals frequently succumbing to the temptation to serve Mammon. As long as professional attention is poorly balanced between cure and prevention and oriented more toward the dollar than toward service, a favorable climate for professional deviance exists. The presence of interprofessional conflicts and competitions for client loyalty are other potential contributors to that climate. (89)

Professors

While feeling rather free to debunk those in other professions, college professors have been loath to expose their own deviant ways to the scrutiny of researchers or the public. Many people may regard professors as immune to temptation—after all, big money is not one of the inducements of academic life. However, money is not the only medium of exchange in our society that is liable to corruption. Especially in hierarchical situations in which women are subordinate to men, as is the situation of female students in relation to male faculty, sexual harassment is possible.

Equal Employment Opportunity Commission (EEOC) guidelines establishing what constitutes sexual harassment state:

> Unwelcome sexual advances, requests for sexual favors, and other verbal or physical conduct of a sexual nature constitute sexual harassment when (1) submission to such conduct is made either explicitly or implicitly a term or condition of an individual's employment or academic advancement, (2) submission to or rejection of such conduct by an individual is used as the basis for employment decisions or academic decisions affecting such individual, or (3) such conduct has the purpose or effect of reasonably interfering with an individual's work or academic performance or creating an intimidating, hostile, or offensive working or academic environment. (cited in Gutek, 1992: 337–338)

More concretely in an academic context, sexual harassment includes examples like the following from B. R. Sandler and associates (1981):

- A Yale undergraduate charged her political science professor with sexual harassment, alleging that he offered her an "A" in exchange for sexual favors. She refused, received a "C" in the course, and filed a lawsuit against the university.

- A senior communications major at a state university in California testified before the California state legislature in 1973 that she knew of "at least 15 professors who offered students 'A's for sex."
- A female cadet at West Point resigned from the military academy in 1977 after charging her male squad leader with improper sexual advances. The academy dismissed her charges when the squad leader denied any wrongdoing.

Survey data allow general estimates of the prevalence of sexual harassment on college and university campuses. In a random survey of 269 senior women at a major university 30% reported receiving unwanted sexual attention from at least one instructor during their four years of college (Benson and Thomson, 1981). In a smaller study, 8% of the women reported unwanted and offensive touching and 2.6% reported that a male instructor had suggested or demanded sexual relations in exchange for an academic reward (Wilson & Kraus, 1981). The overall picture emerging from numerous studies is that while sexual harassment by professors is not the norm in the university, it is nonetheless a serious problem for those who experience it (Reilly, Lott, and Gallogley, 1987).

Sexual harassment is complex, subtle, and can be emotionally traumatic. An example is this account from Sandler and associates (1981):

> A graduate student complained to her college counselor: "What was it that I did that led him to believe I was interested in him in anything but a professional sense? I am quite outgoing and talkative; could that be interpreted wrongly? I realized how utterly vulnerable I was in a situation like this. He is an immensely powerful person with many contacts and if I insult him, he can harm me and my career in a hundred different ways. Everything that happened would be interpreted in his favor, if it ever became public. It would be said that I got my signals wrong, that he was just truly interested in helping me in my career. I realized that should he try to hurt my professional advancement as a result of this kind of situation, there would be no person or formal mechanism to [whom I could] carry my grievances, no person I could complain to that would have any real power to help me. I was left feeling frustrated and defenseless...." (53)

Sandler also describes the emotional toll of sexual harassment. Symptoms reported by victims include insomnia, headaches, backaches, stomach ailments, lack of concentration, diminished ambition, listlessness, and depression. She says, "Sexual coercion makes the educational atmosphere intolerable, forcing the student, in many cases, to withdraw from a course of study or change her career plans. But the overwhelming feeling is helplessness—knowing that if one complains, nothing will likely be done or, worse yet, she will be labeled a 'troublemaker'" (54).

Certain qualities of higher education that impede an honest confrontation with the problem of sexual harassment have been identified (Dziech and Faaborg, 1982). The professional autonomy of faculty activity, sometimes couched in terms of academic freedom to teach and deal with students as professors see fit, can serve as a smoke screen for the sexual harasser. "Collegiality" can become a remarkable cohesive bond in the face of harassment charges. Other features of higher education that are conducive to harassment or protection of the harasser are: lack of uniform teaching methods; the absence of uniform goals in education; a diffusion of power and authority at college campuses; "tolerance" of "eccentric" faculty; and a tendency among educators to examine problems at great length before taking steps to resolve them.

Of course, sexual harassment is hardly confined to the university. Since the 1970s numerous studies have reported that between 20% and nearly 90% of women report having experienced sexual harassment at their jobs. After reviewing this evidence, Gutek (1992) concludes that "from one-third to one-half of all women have been sexually harassed at sometime in their working lives, although frequency rates in some types of work may be higher" (345). Young and unmarried women are especially vulnerable to workplace harassment, as are women in nontraditional jobs (e.g., truck driver, neurosurgeon, engineer, roofer) and in nontraditional industries such as mining and the military.

As Gordon (1981) puts it, "sexual harassment is not a matter of manners or style. It is a fundamental form of oppression, and one of the most widespread in our society" (14). By reinforcing woman's image as being "fair game" when outside the confines of the home, sexual harassment serves as a subtle but effective tool of domination. Academia should be one of the primary arenas in which the problem is openly recognized, confronted, and effectively fought. On many college campuses today there is an office or person students can go to with harassment complaints, usually without fear of identification or reprisals.

OFFICIAL DEVIANCE

With the growth of government in the 20th century, the opportunities for official corruption have expanded in kind. James Michael Curley, the colorful mayor of Boston in the early 20th century, is reputed to have looked into his shaving mirror each morning and said, "Well James Michael, what can I do for you today?" Apparently he managed to do very well, creating a political machine nearly as renowned as Boss Tweed's Tammany Hall of New York City almost 50 years earlier. However, even these legendary standards of political corruption among elected officials do not match today's possibilities because government is now comprised of so many more people, including elected, appointed, and career civil officials.

Official deviance is, to be sure, *occupational* deviance; but there are, as Geis and Meier (1977) note, several characteristics which justify treating it as a special category.

> Political white-collar crime differs from other forms of white-collar crime primarily in the occupational setting in which the offense takes place. A person who gains an elective or appointive office acquires with it considerable power to confer favors and to use public resources for personal gain. The officeholder also obtains control of persons and agencies which can be used to engage in illegal activities and to prevent their detection. Political white-collar crime, therefore, offers structural opportunities for violation that differ from those involved in other forms of white-collar crime.

There are, as well, additional variations which would appear to justify delineation of political white-collar crime as a separable entity. Among the more notable of these are that political office is regarded as a public trust, and the political incumbent has a specific duty to enforce the laws. Thus, one of the ugliest aspects of the Watergate affair was the contrast between the behavior of the participants and the public pronouncements of the leading members of the Nixon administration, with their demands for draconian measures against traditional offenders. (207)

Thus official deviance is unique because it is committed by those empowered to enforce the law, which makes it difficult to detect and prosecute. Moreover, since crime by those entrusted to uphold the law is morally repugnant, widespread disclosures of official deviance are apt to be met with considerable public outrage and, in the long term, to have a corrosive effect upon people's willingness to abide by the law throughout the society.

Among official elites there are two broad types of deviance oriented toward personal gain, through either money or power. The first is epitomized by the activities and events that led to Spiro Agnew's resignation as vice president in 1972. According to evidence collected by federal investigators, Agnew had accepted bribes from construction firms under contract in Maryland while he was Baltimore's county executive and continued to receive them while vice president. He was forced to resign as part of a plea bargaining arrangement in which he was allowed to plead *nolo contendere* ("I do not wish to contend") to tax evasion. Agnew, who was not independently wealthy, contended that he had continued to take bribe money because he needed supplementary income to keep up with the lifestyle of Washington's political elite.

In the second type of elite official deviance, exemplified by the Watergate scandal which led to the resignation of President Richard Nixon in 1974, the primary goal is to enhance or maintain power. Watergate began with a crude attempt at political espionage—a break-in and bugging of the Democratic Party national headquarters—and a subsequent failed attempt to cover up the president's knowledge of the scheme. Embedded in the complex machinations revealed by the Watergate investigations were the payoffs, bribes, and "hush money" characteristic of political corruption at all levels of government. The Iran-Contra scandal of the 1980s was a similar corruption of power in which a small group of presidential advisors sought to thwart the letter and the spirit of the law as enacted by Congress. In the case of the Reagan administration's Nicaraguan policy alone, at least 12 international laws and treaties and 11 domestic laws were violated (Pfost, 1987). Taken together, the Agnew, Watergate, and Iran-Contra episodes indicate that in some cases of official deviance the primary goal is ill-gotten money, while in other cases soiled money is a means employed to advance the end of retaining or enhancing political power.

In American cities, corruption is frequently associated with the supply of illegal services or commodities such as gambling, prostitution, or drugs. Because the demand is high and the business of providing these prohibited items is so profitable, politicians are frequent targets for bribes aimed at clearing the way for these illegal enterprises with minimal interference from the police. As Robert K. Merton (1957) puts it:

> The distinctive function of the political machine for their criminal, vice and racket clientele is to enable them to operate in satisfying the economic demands of a large market without due interference from the government. Just as big business may contribute funds to the political party war-chest to ensure a minimum of governmental interference, so with big rackets and big crime. In both instances, the political machine can, in varying degrees, provide "protection." In both instances, many features of the structural context are identical: (1) market demands for goods and services; (2) the operators' concern with maximizing gains from their enterprises; (3) the need for partial control of government which might otherwise interfere with these activities of businessmen; (4) the need for an efficient, powerful and centralized agency to provide an effective liaison of "business" with government. (80)

Theories of Official Deviance

Explanations of official deviance variously emphasize: (1) individual morality, (2) the social functions of corruption, (3) the expansion of government, or (4) corruption as integral to capitalism. The first, which attributes official deviance to lapses of individual morality, is a "bad person" theory. Thus, to explain the actions of Agnew, Nixon, or Oliver North in the Iran-Contra affair, we might search for the sources of character flaws that allowed them to fall to temptation. This is the most popular sort of theorizing among the general public; it is the least threatening to the status quo because it challenges only the integrity of the individuals involved and not that of the political-economic system; and it is the least satisfying sociologically.

The social functions approach is summarized in the preceding quote from Merton. Closely related is the argument that organized crime and the attendant corruption were inevitable because they provided one route by which immigrants, whose access to legitimate opportunities was often blocked, could achieve "social ascent and [a] place in American life" (Bell, 1953: 142). The result was a massive growth of illegitimate business which generated more than sufficient revenues to finance the corruption of political elites.

Jack Douglas argues that official deviance increases with the number of officials—that is, with the expansion of government. Government has expanded greatly with the emergence of the welfare state, and the inevitable result, according to Douglas (1977), is more official deviance and increasing public anger:

> There is a clear general principle in this. *The bigger the scale of government, and the more rules it seeks to enforce against its own agents, the more real official deviance there will be—inevitably.* So, it is not surprising to find that citizens see more acts of official usurpations of power. They are inevitably there, and they will continue to grow as government expands and its rules multiply. Since we have reason to believe the sense of moral outrage about official deviance is greater by some multiplier factor than that of private deviance, we can expect that the sense of moral outrage over increased government deviance, and the resulting sense of alienation and revolt, will accelerate. (407; italics in original)

Official deviance has also been explained as an endemic aspect of a capitalist system. Pearce (1976) suggests, for example, that elites may find it in their interests to tolerate or even encourage certain kinds of corruption and crime. For instance, organized crime can be a servant of the capitalist elite by performing such dirty work as labor racketeering, union busting, supplying drugs to defuse potentially revolutionary ghetto dwellers, and even as international assassins. The latter activity has been alleged in accounts of schemes to kill Fidel Castro. After an intensive case study of organized crime in an American city, William Chambliss (1977) concluded:

> I have argued, and I think that data demonstrate quite convincingly, that the people who run the organizations which supply the vices in American cities are members of the business, political, and law enforcement communities—not simply members of a criminal society. Furthermore, it is also clear from this study that corruption of political-legal organizations is a critical part of the life-blood of the crime cabal. The study of organized crime is thus a misnomer; the study should consider corruption, bureaucracy, and power. (328)

CORPORATE DEVIANCE

Characteristics of Corporations

Evans and Schneider (1981) provide a good idea of what a corporation is in the following quote:

> When you go out to choose between buying a Ford, Chrysler or Chevrolet, you probably do not think about the fact that if you had been buying a car at the beginning of the century you would have had 181 U.S. auto manufacturers competing to sell you their motorcars. When you decide between flying United or Eastern, it probably does not cross your mind that the Rockefeller family will be happy in either case since the Rockefellers' bank, Chase Manhattan, is a major stockholder in one and Laurance Rockefeller, in the other. Most of us know more about actors, actresses, football players and comic strip heroes than we do about corporate executives and stockholders. Yet, we are all aware that corporations play a central role in our lives. Two out of every five U.S. citizens work in them. They receive five out of every six dollars that we spend. And probably more than any other institution, what corporations do shapes our lives and our society.
>
> The market economy and bureaucratically administered organization together dominate our society. And the large corporation is both a model of a bureaucratically administered organization and the most important actor in the market economy. As such it is the core institution of modern society. Trying to understand the contemporary world without having a clear analysis of the modern corporation would be like trying to understand medieval society without examining the church. (216–217)

Three structural characteristics distinguish the modern corporation. First, a corporation is a large, bureaucratically administered organization. Second, the corporation is controlled from the top down through its managers. This is, however, a sticky point. Some analysts have argued that since the days of the great robber barons like Rockefeller and Carnegie, the control of corporations has passed effectively from stockholders to professional managers—the corporate executives. Others insist that control remains vested in the hands of superrich, capitalist owners who hold and manipulate critical masses of stocks through complicated financial institutions (Zeitlin, 1974; Johnson and Mintz, 1990; Fligstein and Brantley, 1992). Sorting out whether large stockholders or managers (who themselves are frequently large stockholders) exercise dominant control is important, but for our purposes we can say that corporate policy and operational decision making are in the hands of elite capitalists and managers.

The third characteristic is that the primary goals of the corporation are growth and profitability. While some corporate owners and executives have said that a corporation should widen its sights beyond the single-minded pursuit of profit to also fill obligations to the society, most would probably lean toward the position taken by the economist Milton Friedman—profit making must be uppermost. Noting the growing acceptance of the view that corporate officials have a "social responsibility" to do more than serve the interests of their stockholders, he observes that "Few trends could so thoroughly undermine the very foundation of our free society as the acceptance of a social responsibility other than to make as much money for their stockholders as possible" (1962: 134).

To understand large corporations in terms of deviance and criminality, we must also understand how they are organized and treated in law. Corporations officially come into existence when they are granted a state charter which specifies the purpose of the corporation and may place limits on its activities. The stockholders usually elect a board of directors who oversee corporate policies and management; day-to-day operations are controlled by the executive officers, who disperse their authority through the managerial chain of command. Legally, a corporation is treated as an intangible person. As one observer put it:

> Like natural (individual) persons, corporations are born (chartered), grow (enlarge assets, sales or profits), marry (merge), divorce (spin off), have children (organize subsidiaries), become healthy or ill (incur profits or losses), migrate (are licensed to conduct business in new jurisdictions), become parts of the hierarchical structures (become components in a holding company complex), and die (dissolve and surrender their charters). (Jacoby, 1973: 21)

Legally treating corporations as though they were individuals presents serious problems for controlling them. Stone (1975: 3) states that "the corporation *itself* (as lawyers are fond of reminding one another) is a *persona ficta*, a 'legal fiction' with 'no pants to kick or soul to damn.'" In this situation, trying to decide who or what to blame for misdeeds and figuring out how to punish them is difficult. Much of the discussion of corporate deviance that follows hinges on how the organizational complexity of the modern corporation and its curious status in law impinge on our capacity to understand and control it.

Why Study Corporate Crime?

During the 20th century, particularly the past 50 years, corporations have become the dominant actors in American society. The number of corporate actors has increased much faster than the number of individuals in the population. Corporate actors receive increasing attention in the media and match or exceed the involvement of individuals in court cases (Coleman, 1982). The fundamental nature of interactions in the society has changed accordingly—there are relations not only between individuals but between individuals and corporate actors (e.g., an employee and a company) and between corporate actors (e.g., a union and a company, one company and another, or a company and a government body). The study of corporate crime is one avenue to understanding the vast increase in interactions involving corporate actors in the United States.

Marshall B. Clinard and Peter C. Yeager's book *Corporate Crime* (1980) is the most comprehensive source on the subject. Drawing heavily upon another leading authority in the field, Gilbert Geis (1974), they offer a rationale for devoting attention to it:

> The study of corporate crime disputes traditional explanations of crime and offers insight into the distribution and exercise of power. More specifically, the argument that poverty or individual pathology "cause" crime, for example, fails completely to account for law-breaking by corporate executives, who are affluent and, presumably, well-adjusted persons....
>
> Corporate crime provides an indication of the degree of hypocrisy in society. It is hypocritical to regard theft and fraud among the lower classes with distaste and to punish such acts while countenancing upper-class deception and calling it "shrewd business practice." A review of corporate violations and how they are prosecuted and punished shows who controls what in law enforcement in American society and the extent to which this control is effective. Even in the broad area of legal proceedings, corporate crime generally is surrounded by an aura of politeness and respectability rarely if ever present in cases of ordinary crime. Corporations are seldom referred to as law-breakers and rarely as criminals in enforcement proceedings. Even if violations of the criminal law, as well as other laws are involved, enforcement attorneys and corporation counsels often refer to the corporation as "having a problem": one does not speak of the robber or the burglar as having a problem. (21)

Corporate Criminal Responsibility

Historically, the criminal liability of corporations grew out of common law; its development has been to some extent in England but mostly in the United States (Bernard, 1984; Coffee, 1983). While American corporations do face the possibility of criminal justice proceedings, most laws governing corporations are under civil codes. The distinction between civil and criminal liability for white-collar or corporate deviance is related more to precedent than to the seriousness of the offense. West and Carter (1983) point out the similarities in criminal and civil law: (1) the way liability is determined, (2) the moral judgments that are made of violations, (3) the purposes of the sanctions employed, (4) the objects of protection of the law, and (5) the behaviors that are regulated. That white-collar violations are most often treated as civil rather than criminal is due more to a procedural decision or an extralegal consideration than to the nature of the behavior. On this basis, most studies of corporate deviance have treated criminal, civil, or administrative law violations as crimes.

The Costs of Corporate Crime

John Conyers, chairman of the House of Representatives Subcommittee on Crime, reported in 1980 that, after extensive hearings, "it had become exceedingly clear that white-collar crime is the most serious and all-pervasive crime problem in America today" (288). The costs of corporate crime can be divided into three broad categories: (1) economic costs, (2) physical costs, and (3) social and moral costs (Kramer, 1981).

Economic Costs. As with ordinary street crimes, the costs of corporate crime are difficult to measure. Nevertheless, estimates consistently put the economic cost to the public at a very high level. Results of a joint congressional committee reported by Conyers (1980) conservatively estimated that "the short-term dollar cost to the American public of certain white-collar crimes—not including product safety, environmental, chemical, and antitrust violations such as price fixing, and not including fraud against government programs—is roughly $44 billion per year, eleven times the $4 billion estimate for annual losses attributable to crimes against property" (288). At about the same time, the Senate Judiciary Committee estimated that faulty goods, monopolistic practices, and other violations were costing consumers $174–$231 billion annually, and reported and unreported violations of federal regulations were costing taxpayers $10–$20 billion (Clinard and Yeager, 1980: 8). An attempt by Green and Berry (1985b) to assess the costs of corporate crime estimated the following: price-fixing and other restraints on the market, $32–$265.2 billion annually; discrimination against nonwhites and women, over $110 billion annually in lost jobs and inequitable salaries; commercial kickbacks and bribery, $3.5–$10 billion per year; cleaning up illegally dumped toxic wastes, possibly $100 billion. The largest "bill" for corporate crime was run up by failed savings and loan corporations in the 1980s; projected costs are in the hundreds of billions over several decades (see the subsection on collective embezzlement).

Kramer (1981) concludes that, taken together, these cost estimates lead inescapably to a single conclusion: "the economic costs associated with corporate crimes such as consumer fraud, antitrust and restraint of trade violations, commercial bribery, tax violations, and others, simply dwarf the financial costs of conventional property crimes like robbery, burglary and larceny" (9).

Physical Costs. The standard most Americans apply when gauging the seriousness of an illegal activity is physical harm (Schrager and Short, 1978). Recognizing this, some corporation executives have claimed that the accusations against them may be "sharp or shady business techniques," even "illegal," but hardly "criminal."

Such a claim is patently false. Much corporate crime can more appropriately be termed corporate violence. The toll is astonishing:

- Over 100,000 deaths per year are attributable to occupationally related diseases, the majority of which are caused by knowing and willful violation of occupational health and safety laws by corporations.
- Many of the industrial accidents that killed 10,000 workers and disabled 1.7 million others in 1991 would have been prevented but for dangerous working conditions in violation of federal law (U.S. Bureau of the Census, 1993: 433).
- Air, water, and soil pollution in violation of federal standards contributes to hundreds of thousands of deaths.
- The Consumer Product Safety Commission estimates that about 20 million serious injuries are annually associated with unsafe or defective consumer products such as food and drugs, autos, tires, appliances, and contraceptive devices; 110,000 result in permanent disability and 30,000 in death (Kramer, 1981).

To be sure, the public generally fears criminal activities like burglary, robbery, or homicide more than the disguised ripoffs of price-fixing or the creeping death of occupational diseases, industrial accidents, or pollution. Nevertheless, when compared to the average of 23,000 murders reported to the police annually and officially classified as criminal homicides, the physical, life-threatening costs of corporate violations amply earn the label *criminal violence.*

Social and Moral Costs. The economic losses and physical harms of corporate crime are severe, but some observers have found even greater damage to social relations. According to the President's Commission on Law Enforcement and Administration of Justice (1967), corporate crimes are "the most threatening of all—not just because they are so expensive, but because of their corrosive effect on the moral standards by which American business is conducted" (5). When the people at the top wantonly disobey the law, a dangerous example is set for those below—an example that threatens the legitimacy of existing economic and legal systems, as Conklin (1977) states:

> Business crime also sets an example of disobedience for the general population. Crimes by the upper class, especially if they do not lead to conviction and imprisonment, serve as rationalizations for the lower classes to justify their own criminal behavior. Bitterness at class and racial discrimination in the criminal justice system also makes traditional offenders resistant to rehabilitation. Unpunished violations by white-collar offenders create disrespect for the law and engender a desire for revenge against those who protect their own but punish society's outcasts. For example, consumer fraud and exploitation was one underlying cause of the frustrations which led to the riots in black ghettoes during the 1960s. (8)

To summarize, although many corporate crimes go undetected, those we know about verify the substantial costs. Corporate crime robs Americans financially, harms them physically, and corrupts the society morally. As a massive social problem, it deserves greater attention.

Types of Corporate Deviance

Of the several schemes for categorizing corporate deviance that have been devised (Edelhertz, 1970; Clinard and Yeager, 1980), the one best suited for our purposes applies the principle of who is victimized by the illegal activity. The most obvious recipients of potential harm are (1) customers, who may be victims of price-fixing, false advertising, or dangerous products; (2) employees, who may be subject to illegal, unsafe working conditions or whose economic power may be shrunk by unfair labor practices; and (3) the public at large, which suffers from pollution, public health and safety violations, and the corruption of government through such mechanisms as illegal political contributions (Schrager and Short, 1978: 413–415). A fourth group, owners or stockholders, can also be victims when an unscrupulous management commits securities fraud or mismanages corporate resources in a way that makes the stockholders' equity worthless (Ermann and Lundman, 1982: 24). Table 9.3 summarizes the gains to perpetrators and the losses to victims in several examples of illegal corporate actions in each of these four categories.

Customers as Victims.   Price-fixing is an agreement among the sellers of a particular product that they will charge a uniform price for it. The goals are to eliminate competition, stabilize the market, and increase profits for the companies involved. Even though price-fixing violates the Sherman Antitrust Act (1890), which was intended to ensure the maintenance of competitive markets in the economy, it has been frequently practiced. Sutherland's (1949) study of 70 large corporations in a 55-year period prior to 1945 found that legal decisions were made against 44 of them in 125 antitrust suits, and about 60% of the corporations were repeat offenders. The federal government processed around 300 cases in each decade throughout the 1940s, 1950s, and 1960s (Posner, 1970). Nevertheless, there has been no sign that either the amount of price-fixing or the legal actions against it are becoming less frequent (Clinard and Yeager, 1980: 141).

A famous price-fixing case was the electrical equipment conspiracy of 1960. Certainly one of the largest on record, it involved General Electric, Westinghouse, and 27 other firms which agreed to fix prices on heavy electrical equipment such as generators and turbines. In secret meetings, using coded messages and taking great care to destroy any incriminating evidence, the participants set prices in their industry in violation of the law (Geis, 1977). Despite elaborate precautions, evidence of the scheme slowly emerged from complaints by customers, employees who confessed to investigators, and numerous other sources.

The aspect that makes this case so noteworthy, aside from its magnitude, is the result. Short jail sentences were imposed on four executives, two division managers, and one sales manager; the more common penalties were fines, levied in amounts totaling about $2 million. The companies also had to settle claims against them by customers who were harmed by the price-fixing, but this did not diminish the prof-

Table 9.3   Gains to Perpetrators and Losses to Victims of Selected Types of Illegal Corporate Actions

Type of Illegal Corporate Action	Gain for the Perpetrator	Loss to the Victim
Against customers		
Antitrust violations	Reduction of competition; increased market share; increased economic power	Greater cost of consumer goods; reduced choice of products or manufacturers
False advertising	Increases market and consumption by creating an artificial demand for worthless or dangerous products	Waste of consumers' income on worthless or dangerous products
Production and sale of hazardous goods	Reduced costs of production; lowered expenses for engineering, testing, development, etc.	Increased danger to the consumer that may lead to injury or death
Against employees		
Occupational health and safety violations	Reduced costs of production; lowered expenses for safety equipment, medical tests, etc.	Increased danger to workers that may lead to danger or death
Labor law violations	Reduced labor costs through diminished collective bargaining power of the workers	Reduces workers' income
Against the public		
Pollution or public health and safety violations	Reduced costs of production; "solves" various "problems" like disposal of dangerous materials; lowers cost of pollution control	Increased danger to the public that may lead to sickness, injury, or death
Illegal political campaign contributions	Increased political power to influence the making and enforcement of laws in the violator's interest	Loss of legitimate capacity to influence the workings of government, particularly among people without substantial resources
Against corporate owners		
Securities fraud	Creation of financial capital by sale of fraudulent or falsely inflated stock	Owner of the security holds worthless stock similar to counterfeit money

itability of the conspiracy while it lasted, as indicated by the consequences for General Electric: 90% of some 1,800 claims had been settled by mid-1964 for a total of $160 million, but most of these payments were tax deductible (Geis, 1977: 120). Odd indeed is a system that encourages crime by subsidizing it through the tax laws.

Although price-fixing cases are regularly pursued by the authorities and some are successfully prosecuted, the ones that reach the courts represent only a small proportion of the total violations. A survey of major corporation presidents conducted by a Ralph Nader study group found that nearly 60% of the 100 who responded agreed that many industries or corporations fix prices (Nader and Green, 1972). In the 1990s alone, price-fixing incidents involving the following industries and products have been publicized: CDs, bread, drugs, electronics, air fares, chemicals, ink, cement, telephones, oil, gas, securities, infant formula, appliances, drug products, and machine tools. The cumulative costs to customers of undetected and unprosecuted violations constitute a major economic loss that can be attributed to corporate crime.

Employees as Victims. Among the examples of corporate crime outlined in the 1980 report of the U.S. House of Representatives Subcommittee on Crime was the knowing involvement role of several companies in the dangerous exposure of employees to asbestos. Asbestos is a heat resistant, strong, flexible, fibrous mineral that lends itself to a large number of commercial applications. The extent of risk from exposure of the general public to the material is unknown, but the risks to workers in the asbestos industry, where levels of contact with it are high, have been well documented. The report describes the conditions that can result as follows:

> Asbestosis, a nonmalignant scarring of the lungs, has been associated with 10% of the deaths among asbestos workers surveyed in epidemiological studies. The disease often makes breathing so difficult that victims are unable to climb stairs. Mesothelioma, a rare cancer of the linings of the chest or abdominal cavities, is associated exclusively with asbestos exposure and is usually fatal within a year after symptoms appear. Mesotheliomas have occurred in approximately 7% of worker exposures, and have even affected family members who reportedly contracted the disease by inhaling residue from a worker's clothing. The mineral also increases the risk of lung cancer, which accounts for the greatest number of asbestos-associated deaths. (U.S. House Subcommittee on Crime, 1980: 22)

Evidence that asbestos represents a health hazard began accumulating in the early 1900s, and by 1935, the main elements of the problem were known. Exposure to chyrsotile asbestos, about the only fiber then in use, could cause widespread, possibly fatal disease or malignancy. Nevertheless, until 1960 the problem did not attract major attention, and there were few regulations concerning it. Then several studies were published that provided clear evidence of the hazardous results from exposure to asbestos fibers.

Historically, the response of industry executives to evidence of danger to workers has been close to an outright cover-up. As the subcommittee report states: "During pretrial discovery proceedings in recent product liability suits against the asbestos industry, documents dating from 1933–1945 were obtained which included correspondence among senior executives, lawyers, physicians, consultants, and insurance representatives for Johns-Manville Corporation, Raybestos-Manhattan Incorporated and other asbestos companies."

When South Carolina Circuit Court Judge James Price reviewed the material, he found "a pattern of denial and disease and attempts at suppression of information" so persuasive that he ordered a new trial for the family of a deceased insulation worker whose claim had been dismissed. He noted that the correspondence reflected "a conscious effort by the industry in the 1930s to downplay, or arguably suppress the dissemination of information to employees and the public for fear of promotion of lawsuits." Compensation claims for disease had been filed by asbestos insulation workers against several companies that had quietly settled them, including 11 asbestosis cases settled out of court by Johns-Manville in 1933, "all predating the time (1964) when these companies claim they first recognized the hazard to insulators." Judge Price concluded that the settlements of these claims "constitute compelling proof of actual notice to certain manufacturers that asbestos-containing thermal insulation products indeed caused disease in the workers."

At the time of the 1980 report, an estimated 8 to 11 million workers were known to have been exposed since World War II, and the conclusion was that "the potential for asbestos-related occupational disease and cancer appears to be significant. Because of the latency period associated with this disease, it is reported that deaths from asbestosis and asbestos-related cancer in the year 2000, and later, will occur even if we ban the use of the substance today" (24). The asbestos industry has fought strenuously against proposals to tighten the minimal standards for exposure to the substance in the workplace. Similar accounts could be gathered for other industries, including mining (black lung), textiles (brown lung), and chemicals (numerous carcinogens). The cost in employees' health, quality of life, and life expectancy is dreadful.

The story of asbestos exposure is a long one of slow-motion death, but sometimes the employee victims of corporate crime die much more swiftly. Such was the case on September 3, 1991, when, at 8:30 in the morning, a fire broke out at the Imperial Foods chicken processing plant in Hamlet, North Carolina. Shortly after the flames ignited in a mechanized chicken fryer, thick, acrid smoke filled the building. About 200 employees, mostly women, tried to flee through the poorly marked exits, but the doors were *padlocked* and *bolted* from the outside—the result of a company policy allegedly intended to prevent the employees from stealing chicken parts. "'They were screaming "Let me out!"' Sam Breeden told The Associated Press.... 'They were beating on the door.'" (Smothers, 1991). Twenty-five died, mostly from smoke inhalation, and 55 were injured. The windowless building had no automatic sprinkler system, no properly marked fire exits, and there had not been a single fire drill in its 11-year existence. Due to lack of state regulatory resources, the plant had never been inspected for violations.

After an investigation, the company was fined $808,150 for 54 "willful" violations of state and federal safety regulations, 23 "serious" violations, and six "other-than-serious" violations. The local district attorney brought involuntary manslaughter charges against the company's owner, his son (director of operations), and the plant's manager. The owner eventually pleaded guilty to 25 counts of involuntary manslaughter and was sentenced to 19 years, 11 months in prison. He would be eligible for parole in about three years. Charges against the other two were dropped.

Due to its magnitude and the publicity it received, this murderous corporate crime was prosecuted successfully by the criminal justice system. In that respect, it is unlike tens of thousands of others which annually result in death or injury to workers.

The Public at Large as Victims. Sometimes the harm of corporate violations can be indirect and diffuse, as with campaign contribution violations in which companies seek to influence legislation or government regulation. Violation of pollution laws also may have a slow, cumulative effect on public health and mortality. However, there are cases in which corporate law violations have an immediate, devastating impact. The Buffalo Creek–Pittston Coal Company disaster, which "resulted from the company's knowing maintenance of an illegal dam" (Schrager and Short, 1978: 415), is such an example. The report of the House Subcommittee on Crime (1980) follows:

> ***Background.*** Buffalo Creek, West Virginia, is a mountain hollow, some 17 miles in length. Three small forks come together at the top of the hollow, to form the creek itself. In early 1972, approximately 5,000 people lived in this area, in what amounted to a continuous string of 16 villages.
>
> Middle Fork served for several years as the site of an enormous pile of mine waste, known as a "dam" to local residents and an "impoundment" to the Buffalo Mining Company. The impoundment was there because it solved two important disposal problems for the company:
>
> 1. Each time four tons of coal are removed from the ground, one ton of slag—a wide assortment of waste materials—is also removed, and must be disposed of.
> 2. Additionally, more than 500,000 gallons of water are required to prepare four tons of coal for shipment, and this, too, must be disposed of.
>
> The Buffalo Mining Company began to deposit its slag in Middle Fork as early as 1957, and by 1972 was dumping approximately 1,000 tons per day. Traditionally, the company had deposited its solid waste into Middle Fork, and its liquid effluent into nearby streams. However, by the 1960s, coal operators were under a great deal of pressure to retain this water until some of the impurities had settled out of it. The companies were also beginning to see the utility in having a regular supply of processing water on hand. Buffalo Mining Company responded to this by dumping new slag on top of old, in such a way as to form barriers behind which waste water could be stored and reused.
>
> Middle Fork was described as an immense black trough of slag, silt and water, a waste sink arranged in such a way as to create small reservoirs behind the first two impoundments, and a large lake behind the third.
>
> ***The Episode.*** According to subsequent accounts, during the night of February 25, 1972, Buffalo Mining Company officials continually monitored the Middle Fork waste site. They were reportedly uneasy because the lake water seemed to be rising danger-

ously close to the dam crest. The past few days had been wet ones, but such seasonal precipitation was not considered unusual. Toward dawn, company officials were concerned enough to have a spillway cut across the surface of the barrier in an effort to relieve pressure. The level continued to rise, but the company issued no public warnings. Testimony disclosed that the senior officials on the site met with two deputy sheriffs who arrived on the scene to aid in an evacuation in the event of trouble. The officials contended at the time that everything was under control, and the deputies left.

Just before 8:00 a.m., February 26, a heavy-equipment operator inspected the surface of the dam and found that not only was the water within inches of the crest—which he already knew—but that the structure had softened dramatically since the last inspection.

Within minutes the dam had collapsed. The 132 million gallons of waste water and solids roared through the breach. The wave reportedly set off a series of explosions, raising mushroom-shaped clouds in the air, and picking up "everything in its path." One million tons of solid waste were said to be caught in the flow.

Impact. A 20- to 30-foot tidal wave traveling up to 30 miles per hour devastated Buffalo Creek's 16 small communities. More than 125 people perished and hundreds of others were injured. Over 4,000 survived but their 1,000 homes as well as most of their possessions were destroyed.

A few hundred of the 4,000 survivors decided not to accept the settlement for real property damage offered by the coal company as reimbursement. Instead, they brought suit against the Pittston Corporation.

On Wednesday, June 26, 1974, two and one-half years after the incident, the 600 or so Buffalo Creek plaintiffs were awarded 13.5 million dollars by the Pittston Corporation in an out-of-court settlement. (1–3)

The Buffalo Creek flood was an incident involving an American company in the United States. Due to the complexities of today's economy, the harms of corporate violence and the question of how to cope with them also are global considerations. Transnational corporations are able to avoid the laws of home countries by operating in host countries with far less stringent regulations or enforcement (Michalowski and Kramer, 1987). In December 1984, a Union Carbide chemical plant in Bhopal, India, exploded, releasing deadly methyl isocyanate into the air. Three days later an eyewitness said:

There is something indescribable about the horror, the squalor, the sheer magnitude and force of death here. No one is counting numbers any longer. People are dying like flies. They are brought in, their chests heaving violently, their limbs trembling, their eyes blinking from photophobia. It will kill them in a few hours, more usually minutes. (Mokhiber, 1988: 87)

About 2,500 people died within the first week. Approximately 12,000 have since died, more slowly, from injuries; over half a million were injured. The secondary effects of birth defects also have become apparent. Years of international litigation among Union Carbide and the Indian and U.S. governments resulted in criminal charges being brought, then dropped, for negligent operation of the plant (inadequate equipment, improperly trained personnel, lack of safety precautions, etc.). There was a $470 million damage settlement, but most of the $3,500 payments ordered for each death were delayed for years (M. Moore, 1993).

Owners as Victims. Legally, a corporation is owned by its stockholders, many of whom are not superrich capitalists or huge institutional investors like banks or insurance companies but average individuals who buy shares with an investment of no more than a few hundred or a few thousand dollars. These investors entrust their money to the management of the company with the understanding that the company will be run to yield them a fair return on their investment. The Equity Funding securities fraud case, which began in 1960 but was not uncovered until 1973, is a dramatic instance in which stockholders became the victims of fraudulent management practices.

The Equity Funding Corporation of American (EFCA) was a combination insurance-investment company. The scandal involved inflating the value of Equity stock by creating fake insurance policies on the company's record books. As a result, there was a large number of phony customers: "When the fraud was discovered, there were 56,000 bogus policies as compared to 41,000 real ones. There were also accounting irregularities that claimed $200 million in nonexistent assets" (Ermann and Lundman, 1982: 43). The financial manipulation involved an estimated loss of $2 billion. According to Conklin (1977: 46), "The apparent motive behind this complex fraud was to create a good earnings record [which] would increase the value of the stock and thereby enrich the conspirators, who held large amounts of stock and who received more through the years as bonuses." The inflated reported earnings and assets enabled EFCA to acquire other companies in exchange for stock and to borrow money to make other acquisitions and underwrite company operations, which were losing heavily.

The scheme began to unravel only after Equity Funding fired a whistle-blowing employee (Seidler, Andrews, and Epstein, 1977). As a consequence of the fraud, the company's stockholders were left with little or nothing for their investment, and many of them could hardly afford the loss. William Blundell (1976) points out that the victims tended to be "the little people who bleed and suffer for months and years and perhaps the rest of their lives. In this sense the toll taken by Equity Funding was one of the most horrible of any modern crime." The Equity Funding conspirators who were convicted received relatively light fines and sentences.

Recent government investigations reveal that the pattern of fraud continues. The U.S. House Subcommittee on Oversight and Investigations (1990) concluded in an in-depth study of the four largest insurance company failures to date that fraud and illegal activity were significant factors in each of these insolvencies, which together would cost over $5 billion (Calavita and Pontell, 1991).

Collective Embezzlement: The U.S. Savings and Loan Crisis

Another type of crime has had the American taxpayer as the principal victim. The financial collapse of numerous savings and loan organizations in the 1980s involved billions of dollars in depositors' accounts, but because the accounts were insured by the Federal Savings and Loan Insurance Corporation, the taxpayers who under-write the financial stability of the government are paying the bill. The Congres-sional Budget Office estimated in September 1993 that handling losses in failed savings and loan institutions would cost $120 billion from 1990 through 1998, not in-cluding $60 billion spent before 1989 (Farmighetti, 1993: 107).

The savings and loan crisis constitutes the most costly crime wave in history. How and why these financial institutions had so many failures are complex ques-tions. Briefly, the answer is that the industry was undermined by the economy of the 1970s; at the same time long-term mortgages were paying interest in the sin-gle digits, there was double-digit inflation. The solution of the Reagan adminis-tration was to deregulate the industry, which allowed savings and loan banks to pay higher interest rates in order to attract deposits. Restrictions were also lifted on the risks they were permitted to take in making loans, and the FSLIC increased deposit insurance to $100,000 for each account held by a depositor. As a result, they were able to make many more (sometimes highly questionable) loans with no risk to themselves—the federal government was financially responsible. The stage was set for thrift institution owners and operators to commit widespread fraud of three types: (1) unlawful risk-taking, (2) "looting" their own institutions, and (3) covering up their crimes in collusion with government officials (Calavita and Pon-tell, 1990).

Federal investigators estimate that crime or misconduct played a role in about 80% of the more than 6,000 cases of savings and loan failures. The most costly cat-egory of crime was "looting," a form of collective embezzlement that Cavalita and Pontell (1990) refer to as "siphoning off funds from a savings and loan institution for personal gain, at the expense of the institution itself *and with the implicit or explicit sanction of its management*" (321; italics in original). This practice of "robbing one's own bank" represents crime by a corporation against the corporation itself. The individual crimes involved "innovative" financial transactions with names like "straw borrowers," " land flips," "linked financing," "daisy chains," "cash for trash," "dead cows for dead horses" and "cash for dirt." All occurred in an environment charged with a get-richer-quick mentality, government policies that encouraged minimal regulation and freedom from risk by bank officials, and complicity with govern-ment officials in covering up. Unlike typical corporate crimes undertaken to bene-fit the corporation, the savings and loan activities more closely approximated *orga-nized crime* in which "(1) the purpose of the corporation or company is primarily to provide a vehicle for the penetration of illegal activity for personal gain and (2) the crimes are premeditated, organized, continuous, and facilitated by the participation of public officials" (Calavita and Pontell, 1993: 529).

A number of expensive lessons can be learned from this crisis. First, govern-ment policies, by creating opportunities and minimizing risks to perpetrators, can actively *encourage* corporate, organized crime. Second, in a "criminogenic envi-ronment," regardless of social class, criminal perpetrators will emerge. Third, sav-ings and loan frauds may represent the leading edge of corporate crime's future. Calavita and Pontell (1993) conclude that:

As the primary locus of profit-making activity in the United States increasingly shifts from manufacturing enterprises to financial services, it is likely that the nature of much corporate illegal activity will shift as well. There is already some indication that "financial institution fraud" (FIF, as the Department of Justice now calls it) is beginning to outpace traditional corporate crimes in the manufacturing sector. It is in the nature of the financial services "production" process that financial institutions provide ideal vehicles for their own victimization. (542)

The Extent of Corporate Deviance

A study of legal actions against 582 of the largest U.S. corporations during 1975–1976 provides a baseline for estimating the volume of corporation violations. Marshall B. Clinard analyzed information from a variety of sources to study the legal actions initiated and completed against corporate violators. At the outset, he cautions that because many violations are not reported and others do not result in a formal charge, "official actions taken against corporations are probably only the tip of the iceberg of total violations, but they do constitute an index of illegal behavior by the large corporations" (Clinard and Yeager, 1980: 111). Therefore, the data reported represent minimal figures of government actions against major corporations. The undercount of detected violations may run as high as one-fourth to one-third.

With these qualifications, Clinard (1979) presents in its most positive light the fact that a majority of the corporations studied were the object of at least one enforcement action.

> *The world of the giant corporations does not necessarily require illegal behavior in order to compete successfully. The fact that (nearly) 40% of the corporations in this study did not have a legal action instituted against them during a two-year period by 24 federal agencies attests to this conclusion.* On the other hand, more than 60% had at least one enforcement action initiated against them in the period. An average of 4.8 actions were taken against the 300 parent *manufacturing* corporations that violated the law at least once. Moreover, a single instance of illegal corporate behavior, unlike "garden variety" crime, often involves millions of dollars and can affect the lives of thousands of citizens. This study found that almost one-half of the parent manufacturing corporations had one or more serious or moderate violations and these firms had an average of 3.1 such violations. (xix–xx; italics in original)

Among the firms Clinard studied, large corporations had a disproportionately greater number of violations. Those in the automobile, drug, and oil industries were the most frequent violators, accounting for almost one-half of all violations; 80% had one or more serious or moderately serious violations. As evidence that corporations are not usually subjected to the full force of the law, 80% of the fines imposed were $5,000 or less; less than 1% exceeded $1 million. Indeed, the most frequently imposed sanction of the 1,446 levied was a warning (44%), followed by monetary penalties (23%) and a variety of injunctions or consent orders. The type of violation also influenced the severity of the sanction. "Corporate actions that directly harm the economy were more likely to receive the greater penalties, while those affecting consumer product quality were responded to with the least severe sanctions" (Clinard, 1979: xx).

A certain number of violators are chronic repeat offenders. Clinard and Yeager (1980) put the problem this way:

> The rates of recidivism (relapse into prior criminal habits after punishment) vary from about 25 to as high as 60% for ordinary crime. It is interesting to compare these rates with those in the field of corporate sanctions. In Sutherland's (1949) study of 70 of the 200 largest nonfinancial corporations a high rate of recidivism was found. He studied sanctions imposed during the life of each corporation, an average of 45 years; he found that the average corporation had a decision rendered against it—that is, had an enforcement action taken against it—14 times and that 97.1% were recidivists in the sense of having two or more adverse decisions against them. (126–127)

The data from the Clinard (1979) study reveal a similar pattern of repeated offenses.

> Of the 477 manufacturing corporations, 210, or approximately one-half, had two or more legal actions completed against them during 1975 and 1976; 18.2% had five or more. For serious and moderately serious violations, 124 firms, or one-fourth, had two or more actions, and 7.8% five or more. If one could extrapolate the number of sanctions over the average equivalent time period used by Sutherland (1949), the result would far exceed his average of fourteen sanctions. (27)

Overall, these data reveal that:

- Corporate violations and repetitions are frequent.
- Offenders tend to be concentrated in certain large industries.
- The sanctions applied to violators are generally very light.

EXPLANATIONS OF CORPORATE DEVIANCE

The range of theories to explain corporate deviance is smaller than that for theories that explain other types of deviance. There are no biogenetic or hereditary theories of white-collar or corporate crime, and no explanations that begin with psychological factors such as an offender's parental relationships or faulty socialization. The categories of social psychological and sociological explanations used to organize the discussion in this section are: (1) social psychological theories, (2) the culture of the corporation, (3) the structure of the corporation, (4) the structure of the economy, and (5) societal reaction and social control theories.

Social Psychological Explanations

The earliest coherent explanation of corporate deviance is Sutherland's (1949) learning theory of white-collar crime, which is based on an application of the concept of differential association:

> The data which are at hand suggest that white-collar crime has its genesis in the same general process as other criminal behavior, namely, differential association. The hy-

pothesis of differential association is that criminal behavior is learned in association with those who define such behavior favorably and in isolation from those who define it unfavorably, and that a person in an appropriate situation engages in such criminal behavior if, and only if, the weight of the favorable definitions exceeds the weight of the unfavorable definitions. This hypothesis is certainly not a complete or universal explanation of white-collar crime or of other crime, but it perhaps fits the data of both types of crimes better than any other general hypothesis. (234)

Sutherland goes on to describe how a new corporate employee is introduced to the ways of corporate deviance and learns both the techniques for violating the law and the rationalizations for engaging in illegal practices:

As part of the process of learning practical business, a young man with idealism and thoughtfulness for others is inducted into white-collar crime. In many cases he is ordered by the manager to do things which he regards as unethical or illegal, while in other cases he learns from those who have the same rank as his own how they make a success. He learns specific techniques of violating the law, together with definitions of situations in which those techniques may be used. Also, he develops a general ideology. This ideology grows in part out of the specific practices and is in the nature of generalization from concrete experiences, but in part it is transmitted as a generalization by phrases such as "we are not in business for our health," "business is business," or "no business was ever built on the beatitudes." These generalizations, whether transmitted as such or abstracted from concrete experiences, assist the neophyte in business to accept the illegal practices and provide rationalizations for them. (240)

The importance of rationalization for high-status business executives who participate in corporate illegality cannot be overemphasized. Hills (1987) observes that "In view of the commitment of respectable corporate executives to the conventional social order, it is necessary for corporate officials who violate the law to neutralize the potential feelings of guilt and self-condemnation" (194). Excuses such as "Everybody does it," "The law only holds back free enterprise," or "It isn't really 'criminal'" are common. As Conklin (1977) states, rationalizations of this sort "may be even more important in explaining business crime than in explaining juvenile delinquency, because businessmen probably have a stronger need to deny criminal intent" (86–87).

A study of 80 incarcerated white-collar offenders, including antitrust violators, violators of financial trust, and those who had committed fraud or made false statements, found a strong tendency to deny criminality. The most consistent theme was denial of criminal intent—often linked to denying blame because of the complex laws that were violated. Offenders seemed convinced that what they had done was not really harmful and not really crime. As one antitrust violator put it, "It certainly wasn't a premeditated type of thing in our cases as far as I can see....To me it's different than _____ and I sitting down and we plan, well, we're going to rob this bank tomorrow and premeditatedly go in there....That wasn't the case at all....It was just a common everyday way of doing business and surviving" (Benson, 1985: 593).

A supplement to Sutherland's learning approach emphasizes the personal characteristics of those who climb to the top management of large companies. First we must understand that only a small proportion persistently strive for such top posts and that those who do are apt to be different from those who fail to make it to the top or do not try. Summarizing his analysis, Gross (1978) says:

> The men at the top of organizations will tend to be ambitious, shrewd and possessed of a nondemanding moral code. Their ambition will not be merely personal, for they will have discovered that their own goals are best pursued through assisting the organization to attain its goals. While this is less true, or even untrue at the bottom of the organization, those at the top share directly in the benefits of organizational goal achievement, such as seeing their stock values go up, deferred compensation, and fringe benefits.
>
> Further, being at or near the top, these persons are those most strongly identified with the goals of the organization...
>
> Finally, if the organization must engage in illegal activities to attain its goals, men with a nondemanding moral code will have the least compunctions about engaging in such behavior. Not only that, as men of power, pillars of the community, they are most likely to believe that they can get away with it without getting caught. Besides, they are shrewd. (71)

People who are ambitious, clever, and "morally flexible" are apt to find it easy to deny the criminality of their illegal activities, and even when they understand that they are committing a crime, they may find it easy to convince themselves that they can get away with it.

The Culture of the Corporation

While the evidence indicates that corporate deviance is widespread, it is by no means true that every large corporation is equally likely to commit crime. In the Clinard study, for example, 40% of the corporations had no legal actions brought against them during a two-year period. To explain why some corporations tend to deviate from the law more than others, some theorists have identified attitudes or motives that when overemphasized in the organization contribute to illegal behavior. Stone (1975: 237) cites (1) a desire for profits, expansion, and power; (2) a desire for security; (3) fear of failure; and (4) group loyalty and identification with corporate goals. Clinard and Yeager (1980) suggest that a significant factor is the moral tone established by the corporation's elite:

> Lawbreaking can become a normative pattern within a corporation, with or without pressure for profits or from the economic environment. In confidential interviews with a number of board chairmen and chief executive officers of very large corporations, a consensus emerged that the top management, particularly the chief executive officer, sets ethical tone. The president and chief executive officer of a large manufacturing corporation noted that "by example and holding a tight rein a chief executive...can set the level of ethical or unethical practices in this organization. This influence can spread throughout the organization." As another high executive pointed out, price fixing or kickbacks must be "congenial to the climate of the corporation." Still another board chairman said, "Some corporations, like those in politics, tolerate corruption." (60)

Possibly some industries are more inclined than others to engender a callous attitude toward obedience of the law. For instance, the pharmaceutical industry has a particularly poor record of violations, including international bribery, corruption, fraud in the safety-testing of drugs and criminal negligence in their manufacture (Braithwaite, 1984). Excessive violations may be related to the severity of competition, the risks attached to manufacture and use of the product, and the intensity of regulatory oversight. Concluding a study of illegal activity in the American liquor industry, Denzin (1977) quotes a high-ranking official in one distilling firm: "We break the laws every day. If you think I go to bed at night worrying about it, you're crazy. Everybody breaks the law. The liquor laws are insane anyway" (919).

Interviews with 64 retired middle managers from Fortune 500 companies revealed two factors they regarded as most important in establishing a climate conducive to corporate crime: (1) the role of top executives in establishing the ethical tone for a company's business, and (2) the pressures put on middle managers to attain corporate goals (Clinard, 1983). Indeed, a combination of the two in which there is excessive emphasis on the *goals* with insufficient insistence on the use of legitimate *means* produces the same social structure described by Merton (1957) in his theory of anomie as a precursor of deviance.

The Structure of the Corporation

Fundamentally, the structural characteristics of large, modern corporations are those of bureaucracies. The term *bureaucracy* refers to a mode of social organization based on (1) rationality in decision making, (2) impersonality in social relations, (3) the routinization of tasks, and (4) the centralization of authority.

Because of the nature of the organizational environment for those who work in corporate bureaucracies, they are prone to view problems from a narrow, technical perspective. As a result, Jackall (1980) says, "the rational/technical ethos of bureaucracy transforms even those issues with grave moral import into practical concerns" (355–356). For example, when the drug company Richardson-Merrill, manufacturer of the anticholesterol agent MER/29, discovered that the drug might cause side effects such as hair loss, reduced libido, cataracts, or partial blindness, the "company's executives considered the adverse reports as obstacles to be undercut, in this case with fabricated data, and concentrated on developing more aggressive marketing strategies to overcome the drug's tarnished image" (355–356). Corporate actors frequently tend to be morally blind because, as Hills (1987) puts it, "large corporate enterprises seem to generate a pragmatic *amorality*—an ethical numbness" (190).

Large, complex, bureaucratic organizations also tend to fragment work—to make members responsible only for a tiny portion of the final product. As a result, "bureaucracy separates men and women from the consequences of their actions; such depersonalization reinforces the avoidance of responsibility endemic to hierarchical, segmented structures" (Jackall, 1980: 356). In modern bureaucracies, the expectations of obedience to higher authority, coupled with a complex division of labor, provide the ideal setting to legitimize the excuse for almost any behavior (Kelman and Hamilton, 1989). With a clean conscience, most people in the organization can say, "I was only doing what I was told to do."

Referring to the large-scale organizations that dominate modern life, Gross (1978) states flatly that "all organizations are inherently criminogenic" (56). The seeds for criminality are sown into bureaucratic structures because "organizations find themselves under heavy pressure to meet their goals, with a structure which means that responsibility for tasks is delegated, enabling some units to pass off onto other units the risky consequences of questionable behavior, but in which trouble with the law is one of many environmental contingencies which must be handled" (61). Thus, modern bureaucratic organizations that provide a highly efficient, effective mechanism for the solution of complex technical problems do not provide a good setting for moral reflection or a sense of individual responsibility. An environment which facilitates crime is the result.

The Structure of the Economy

The underlying precepts of American capitalist business ideology include the primacy of profit as the goal of free enterprise. The bottom line—the final figure on an accounting statement that indicates a company's level of profitability or loss—is the ultimate criterion upon which most corporate executives are judged. This implies an anomic condition analogous to Merton's (1957) imbalance of cultural goals and institutionalized means, which creates structural pressures to deviate. As we noted in Chapter 8, Merton argues that an overemphasis on the success goals of American culture (ample money and comfortable surroundings), coupled with a lack of legitimate means to reach those goals (due perhaps to racial and ethnic discrimination in education or employment) will lead those whose opportunities are blocked to "innovate" by committing crimes to achieve success. The theory thus predicts that those most likely to be discriminated against—people at the bottom of the social hierarchy—will be most likely to commit crime, primarily in response to blocked opportunities. Obviously, the high-level corporate manager does not face the same sort of blocked-opportunity structure that a typical ghetto resident does. Instead, the pressure to deviate comes from the intense pressure to attain the corporate cultural goal—maximum profits. This powerful emphasis on goal attainment is frequently coupled with minimal concern for the legality or ethics of the means to succeed. Thus an excessive emphasis on goals as compared to means, which Merton used to explain lower-class deviance, may also be the structural foundation for deviance at the top (Passas, 1990). This is especially true when the economy's motivating dynamic is a "culture of competition" that simultaneously creates strong needs for material success and insecurities rooted in the fear of failure (Coleman, 1987).

In a capitalist economy, whether success is gained by legal or illegal means, it frequently is geared to eliminate competition. For example, the early U.S. domestic automobile industry, which had well over 150 manufacturers, is now dominated by three. Markets dominated by only a few suppliers are called *oligopolies*, and oligopolistic conditions are ripe for breeding certain kinds of corporate crime, especially price-fixing (Snider, 1991; Calavita and Pontell, 1993). When only a few firms

supply most of the goods in a particular industry, there are powerful pressures to stabilize the market and maximize profits by price-fixing.

The introduction of sophisticated technology into business and finance is another economic factor that has opened up new opportunities for crime. The use of
computers, electronic money transfers, and modern telecommunications to conduct banking and business have created entirely new ways to steal, as well as a jar-
gon to describe the techniques, including Trojan horse, salami, superzapping, logic
bombs, worms, viruses, data diddling, piggybacking, and scavenging (Forester and
Morrison, 1990). Research indicates that the rapid introduction of modern business technology, for all its obvious benefits, carries with it the potential for crimes
that are hard to detect, that amount to huge losses per incident, and that are radical
departures from the traditional images of criminals, crime, and crime control (Chang
and Chang, 1985). Modern society presents the predicament of a "criminal justice
cultural lag" in which the law and its enforcers are forever trying to catch up with the
criminal opportunities presented by new technologies and the inventiveness of those
who would put them to their own devious purposes (Collier and Spaul, 1992).

The growing preponderance of organizations as actors in American society can
itself contribute to the expansion of corporate crime. Obviously, the more of them
there are, the greater the chances of corporate illegality. Beyond this, however, is the
increasing number of interactions and relations in the society that are *between* corporate actors. Examples include electronic securities and financial transactions between corporations, contractual and regulatory arrangements involving other corporations or government agencies, and massive deliveries of goods, services, or
information from one corporate actor to another. Such transactions between large
organizations are often highly complex, specialized, and difficult to monitor—all
of which may facilitate unlawful behavior (Vaughan, 1982; Cunningham and Porter,
1992).

A Critique of Welfare-State Capitalism. A more general approach to economic
theorizing about the causes of corporate deviance is rooted in a critique of modern
capitalism. In broad outline, the analysis begins with the period of rapid industrial
growth and concentration of capital during the last half of the 19th century, when
capitalists like Carnegie and Rockefeller amassed huge personal fortunes and created vast industrial empires. Business was almost totally unregulated at this time, but
their success posed two dilemmas that paved the way for the growth of government. First, if the concentration of wealth were allowed to continue unabated, it
would destroy the competitive capitalist system; the most successful entrepreneurs
would eliminate their competition and consolidate control over industries. In part
to save the system from itself, regulatory laws like the Sherman Antitrust Act (1890)
were enacted. Second, the increasingly unequal distribution of wealth—the chasm
between the superrich and the rest of the people—became a source of mass dis-
content with potentially revolutionary consequences.

Thus, in fits and starts over the first three-quarters of the 20th century, government became an agency for redistributing wealth through such mechanisms as

progressive income taxation, social security, health benefits, unemployment compensation, and poverty programs. It has been argued that this redistribution mostly amounted to the transfer of wealth from the middle class to the lower class, leaving the upper-class elites relatively untouched. In any case, the federal government grew, both as the regulator of business and the redistributor of wealth, into what is now frequently called *welfare-state capitalism.*

Critics of welfare-state capitalism focus on how the relationship between large corporations and the state (the government), which is assigned the task of regulating corporate actions, actually encourages ineffective legal constraints and promotes corporate crime (Barnett, 1981). Ultimately, the reasons are grounded in the power of elites to influence government discussed at the outset of this chapter. As in the past, business elites continue to dominate the legislative and executive branches of government. To be sure, the state is under pressure from both corporate offenders and their victims (consumers, employees, and the public at large) to frame the law and have it enforced to their advantage. Snider (1990) observes that "Class power has shaped the laws that regulate corporate crime; it has a major impact on the behavior of state officials; and it is responsible for most of the difficulties they face in regulating effectively....[T]he entire agenda of regulation is the result of a struggle between the corporate sector opposing regulation and the much weaker forces opposing it" (384). In the end, says Barnett (1981), "the real economic impact and the control over information and financial resources which characterize large corporations grant to them an economic and political power that is great relative to that generally possessed by the victims of corporate crime" (4).

On balance, the law usually favors corporate interests, as do the funding and the priorities of regulatory and enforcement agencies. Due to this ineffective legal constraint, the relative risks and probable costs of corporate illegal activity are low compared to the likely gains, and the commission of corporate crime is a perfectly rational action. In brief, this critique maintains that overall the state is controlled by and operates in the interests of corporate capitalists, in opposition to the interests of consumers, workers, and the general social welfare.

Societal Reaction and Social Control Theories

Labeling, or societal reaction theory, proposes that attempts to control deviance often have the unintended consequences of increasing the likelihood of the undesired behavior rather than deterring it. For example, subjecting a young delinquent to the stigmatizing process of public trial is said to push him or her further into a criminal self-concept, while it closes off avenues to succeed in nondelinquent ways. Thus the efforts to control or deter the behavior actually end up encouraging or amplifying it. (For a detailed account of the dynamics of labeling theory, see the discussion in Chapter 4 of the nine propositions proposed by Thomas Scheff.) The policy implications of the theory are that officially labeling people as deviant should be avoided as much as possible to minimize its negative effects in stigmatizing them.

Experts on corporate deviance generally take a very different view of labeling as a deterrent against corporate illegality. They allege that a major reason for the failure to control corporate crime effectively is a lack of publicly imposed penalties. Braithwaite and Geis (1982) argue that such an observation has important implications:

> Although the labeling hypothesis makes it unwise to use publicity as a tool to punish juvenile delinquents, it is sound deterrence to broadcast widely the names of corporate offenders. Corporations and their officers are genuinely afraid of bad publicity arising from their illegitimate activities. They respond to it with moral indignation and denials, not with assertions that "if you think I'm bad I'll really show you how bad I can be," as juvenile delinquents sometimes do.

> Chambliss argues that white-collar criminals are among the most deterrable types of offenders because they satisfy two conditions: They do not have a commitment to crime as a way of life, and their offenses are instrumental rather than expressive. Corporate crimes are almost never crimes of passion; they are not spontaneous or emotional, but calculated risks taken by rational actors. As such, they should be more amenable to control by policies based on the utilitarian assumptions of the deterrence doctrine. (301–302)

Labeling theory may apply to many other types of deviance, but most analysts contend that it does not apply to white-collar or corporate criminality. Such a position leads inevitably to the conclusion that "corporate crime is a conceptually different phenomenon from traditional crime" primarily due to the high status and power of its perpetrators relative to its victims (Braithwaite and Geis, 1982: 294). Moreover, failure to vigorously enforce the laws against corporate violations can erode or neutralize moral indignation about these crimes, thereby legitimating them in a certain sense (McCormick, 1977). Both the failure to define many harmful corporate actions as criminal and the failure to enforce the laws that do exist have long been recognized. Sutherland (1949) maintains that various relationships account for the fact that the attitude of government toward businessmen is less critical than it is toward people with lower socioeconomic status:

> …(a) Persons in government are, by and large, culturally homogeneous with persons in business, both being in the upper strata of American society. (b) Many persons in government are members of families which have other members in business. (c) Many persons in business are intimate personal friends of persons in government. Almost every important person in government has many close personal friends in business, and almost every important person in business has many close personal friends in government. (d) Many persons in government were previously connected with business firms as executives, attorneys, directors, or in other capacities. In times of war, especially, many persons in government retain their business connections. (e) Many persons in government hope to secure employment in business firms when their government work is terminated. (f) Government work is often a step toward a career in private business. Relations established while in government, as well as inside information acquired at that time, carry over after the person joins a business firm. (f) Business is very powerful in American society and can damage or promote the governmental programs in which the governmental personnel are interested. (g) The program of the government is closely related to the political parties, and for their success in campaigns these political parties depend on contributions of large sums from important businessmen. (248–249)

Sutherland concludes that cultural homogeneity, close personal relationships, and power relationships protect businessmen from critical definitions by government. Because business is tightly organized and closely linked to government, corporate harms are less likely to be defined as criminal, or when so defined, are less apt to receive law enforcement attention. Consumers, employees, and the general public are neither as well organized nor as influential with government. Sutherland calls this situation *differential social organization* and says it must be redressed if harmful, illegal corporate actions are to be curbed.

While differential social organization persists, the public now is more likely to regard white-collar and corporate crime as serious offenses—in fact, as equal to, and even more serious than, many 'ordinary' crimes, such as burglary and robbery" (Clinard and Yeager, 1980: 5). As public perceptions of the seriousness of white-collar and corporate offenses have increased (Cullen, Link, and Polanzi, 1982; Cullen, Mathers, and Cullen, 1983; Cullen, Maakestad, and Cavender, 1987), the lack of strict laws and stringent enforcement can no longer be justified by claims that the public fails to view corporate crime as harmful and therefore views it as not worth legal attention (Meier and Short, 1985). Rather, the evidence indicates that the public regards corporate criminality as serious, generally supports existing laws aimed against it, and would like to see the laws more vigorously enforced (Conklin, 1977: 24).

SOCIAL POLICY ON THE CONTROL OF CORPORATE DEVIANCE

Approaches to controlling corporate crime can be organized into three broad categories: (1) legal, penal, and regulatory reform; (2) public action and government regulation; and (3) changes in corporate attitudes and structure.

Legal, Penal, and Regulatory Reform

The first step in initiating any criminal legal action is to uncover evidence that a crime has been committed. Usually, in the case of ordinary crimes such as theft or assault, the individual or organization that is harmed will report that a crime has occurred to the authorities. Corporate crimes, in comparison, frequently involve many victims, each of which is harmed so imperceptibly that none is motivated to report their victimization if they even know it has happened. Employees being harmed by illegally handled toxic substances at work or residents of a city exposed to health-endangering violations of pollution standards probably would not know of their victimization until it was too late unless there was monitoring of the situation. Thus ordinary street-crime control can rely heavily on *reactive enforcement*, activated when a victim makes a complaint, while corporate-crime control requires *proactive enforcement*, or monitoring and seeking-out violators.

The proactive nature of corporate-crime control suggests three strategies that might be used to pursue it. First, more could be done to protect *whistleblowers*—people in an organization who go to the authorities or to journalists to expose illegal or unethical corporate conduct. In some cases, whistle blowers have been subject to harsh discipline, harassment, job loss, or even physical harm. Although some protections already exist for informants, additional ones such as relieving them of the burden of legal fees if they win in court might encourage more to come forward (Ermann and Lundman, 1982: 165). Second, larger and more effective enforcement staffs are needed to pursue corporate crime because enforcement can deter. For example, increases in antitrust enforcement coupled with the credible threat of large damage awards to victims have been shown to be effective deterrents (Block, Nold, and Sidak, 1981). Third, some experts have advocated greater use of *covert facilitation*, "the practice of law enforcement officials who seek through the conscious use of deception to encourage criminal acts under circumstances where they can be observed by undercover operatives" (Braithwaite, Fisse, and Geis, 1987: 6). These advocates argue that use of such sting operations in proactive law enforcement is appropriate to offset the power of elite deviants to evade the law. Critics see dangers in any approach that uses the encouragement of crime to catch criminals (Marx, 1987; Skolnick, 1987).

The U.S. Justice Department spends less than 10% of its budget on white-collar crime. In 1984, for example, the Occupational Safety and Health Administration, with only 400 inspectors for 4 million workplaces, statistically could inspect a particular business only once every 80 years (Green and Berry, 1985a: 732). The massive publicity on recent Wall Street insider trading scandals to the contrary, Shapiro (1985) estimates that only 6 out of 100 parties investigated by the Securities and Exchange Commission ultimately are brought before a criminal court, and stock swindlers generally avoid criminal prosecution and are given civil or administrative treatment or diverted from legal action. Clinard and Yeager (1980) state flatly that "the regulatory agencies, both federal and state, lack resources to deal effectively with white-collar and corporate crime. Since corporate crime is organizational crime, its detection, investigation, and prosecution are time consuming" (316). Successful prosecution of corporate crime also requires an investment in highly specialized personnel such as accountants, engineers, and laboratory technicians. There is evidence, however, that if the probability of state detection can be increased by greater enforcement, corporate compliance with the law increases (Braithwaite and Makkai, 1991).

Even in cases reaching the courts and resulting in conviction, the penalties are generally very light, especially when compared to sanctions applied to typical street crimes (Snider, 1982). Eighty percent of the corporations fined between 1975 and 1976 received penalties under $5,000 (Clinard and Yeager, 1980: 125), and the $50,000 criminal fines handed out to the nine 1976 defendants of a major price-fixing case averaged well under the equivalent of $1 for an individual. Occasionally fines are considerable, as in the E. F. Hutton and Co. case in which the brokerage firm pleaded guilty to 2,000 felony counts of mail and wire fraud. Under the plea settlement the company agreed to pay a $2.75 million fine and to reimburse the banks it had defrauded. However, the fine agreement appears to have been a way to substitute punishment absorbed by the corporation as opposed to proceeding against two Hutton executives who were criminally responsible (Fisse and Braithwaite, 1993: 2–3). Thus fines, levied against the corporation and easily absorbed, sometimes serve as a shield protecting responsible corporate executives from facing criminal charges. Seymour (1973) underlines the disparities in the treatment of common criminals and white-collar criminals:

> To the family whose son has been sentenced to prison for four years for stealing a check from the mails, a suspended sentence for the man who has defrauded investors out of $150,000 represents rank injustice. To the inmates of Attica prison, newspaper accounts of a corporate executive who received a $41,000 fine for evading $60,000 in income taxes provide a reason for hatred. These disparities generate a practical threat to society in the form of unrest and bitterness. (821)

There is some evidence that when high-status white-collar offenders are convicted, they are more likely to be imprisoned than are low-status white-collar offenders (Wheeler, Weisburd, and Bode, 1982), but this finding has been challenged (Hagan and Parker, 1985; Hagan and Palloni, 1986; Benson and Walker, 1988; Benson, 1989). The fact remains that corporate and white-collar offenders are less apt to be arrested, convicted, and severely sentenced than are low-status offenders who commit street crimes. Moreover, when facing the courts, corporations have been shown to have an enormous advantage over individuals (Hagan, 1982; Kruttschnitt, 1985).

The Deterrent Effects of Prosecution.   Despite the obstacles to corporate criminal prosecutions, and with the understanding that the criminal law *alone* cannot stem corporate crime, the deterrent effects of the pursuit of corporate criminals through the criminal justice system apparently make it worthwhile (Cullen, Link, and Polanzi, 1987; Benson, Cullen, and Maakestad, 1990). Not only should at least minimal standards of justice be satisfied, but stiffer penalties for corporate wrongdoing can act as a deterrent. Braithwaite and Geis (1982) suggest that individual corporate criminals are likely to be deterred by severe penalties because "they have more of those valued possessions that can be lost through a criminal conviction, such as social status, respectability, money, a job, and a comfortable home and family life" (302). They apply the same argument to corporations:

> Corporations are future-oriented, concerned about their reputation, and quintessentially rational. Although most individuals do not possess the information necessary to calculate rationally the probability of detection and punishment, corporations have information-gathering systems designed precisely for this purpose....
>
>   Although the fine itself may be an ineffective deterrent when used against the corporate criminal, other sanctions associated with the prosecution—unfavorable publicity, the harrowing experience for the senior executive of days under cross-examination, the dislocation of top management from their normal duties so that they can defend the corporation against public attacks—can be important specific deterrents. (302–303)

Other effective sanctions might be to forbid repeat violators from acting in such roles as company directors, lawyers, accountants, and the like. At the most extreme level, "capital punishment for the corporation is one possibility: The charter of a corporation can be revoked, the corporation can be put in the hands of a receiver, or it can be nationalized" (Braithwaite and Geis, 1982: 307).

Public disclosure of corporate crime is itself an effective sanction. Clinard and Yeager (1980) found, from conversations with federal and state enforcement officials as well as with corporate executives, that "mass media publicity about law violations probably represents the most feared consequence of sanctions imposed on a corporation" (318). Likewise, Hopkins (1980) concludes that "for most companies, the real mechanism of deterrence was concern about loss of reputation, both that of the company and, more particularly, that of individual managers" (212). Fisse and Braithwaite (1983) studied 17 cases of large U.S. and Australian corporations that had experienced severe adverse publicity from allegations of gross misbehavior. In general, the financial effects (lost sales or revenues) were relatively slight, while the nonfinancial effects (changes in corporate behavior) were great; "in *every* case there was some worthwhile reform" (243). In other examples such as persuading American companies to cease international marketing of infant formula, it has been shown that publicity can change corporate behavior (Ermann and Clements, 1984; Gerber and Short, 1986).

The effectiveness of publicity may be enhanced by the public's interest in white-collar crime and the media's willingness to grant it news coverage. While newspapers failed to provide frequent, prominent attention to corporate criminal cases in 1961 and 1976, a content analysis of nightly network television newscasts between 1974 and 1984 revealed that 40% had at least one story about corporate crime (Evans and Lundman, 1983; Randall, 1987). The evidence suggests that stiff sanctions accompanied by widespread publicity can deter corporate deviance (Geis, 1984).

Public Action and Government Regulation

The consumer movement has grown slowly since the 1960s. Perhaps a watershed was Ralph Nader's carefully documented attack on General Motor's design and sale of the Corvair in *Unsafe at Any Speed* (1965). Private organizations such as the Consumer Union, which publishes *Consumer Reports*, have also had an influence in sharpening public awareness and increasing corporate responsibility. Government agencies such as the Consumer Product Safety Commission, the Federal Trade Commission, and the Food and Drug Administration regularly review complaints about products and order the suspension of sale or recall of items deemed unsafe. Snider (1991) argues that proregulatory pressure groups are central to the regulatory process, citing such examples as "environmental activities, 'green' politicians trying to eliminate chemicals from farmer's fields, unionists working to secure stronger health and safety laws in the workplace, and feminists trying to control the pharmaceutical industry." She concludes that "It is the pressure they exert, by maintaining a high level of struggle and dissensus, that provides the crucial leverage which forces the state to maintain enforcement activity in the area of corporate crime" (210–211).

Employees also exert pressure for healthful, safe working conditions, mainly through labor unions. The Occupational Health and Safety Administration is the federal agency created to oversee such standards in the workplace, and both consumer- and employee-oriented federal agencies have counterparts in many state and local governments. At the federal level, at least, there is reason to believe that regulatory agencies are not always dominated by those with direct relationships to big business. A study of links between corporations and seven major regulatory commissions (e.g., the Interstate Commerce Commission, Federal Trade Commission, and Security and Exchange Commission) revealed that commissioners frequently do *not* have past or future direct ties to the corporate community (Freitag, 1983). Particularly at the secondary levels of federal government, below the Cabinet, there is evidence that consumer, employee, and public interests have some chance of representation.

Several studies suggest a useful distinction between approaches to control that emphasize deterrence of corporate illegality and those intended to enforce compliance with regulations. Deterrence can be enhanced through the criminal justice system with a combination of stiff penalties and publicity as sanctions for criminal law violation. However, too much reliance upon deterrence of corporate crime through punitive measures is unwarranted, because the certainty and severity of punishment is low and, when punishment is inflicted, the costs to those not directly involved in the crime may be unacceptably high (C. Moore, 1987). For example, a punitive sanction that forces a company to curtail production sharply, close temporarily, or even go out of business could have devastating effects on employees and communities where plants are located. Compliance can be enhanced when governments, recognizing that prosecution of corporate crime is time-consuming, expensive, and effectively countered by skillful attorneys, give regulatory agencies bargaining clout to negotiate adherence to the law (Mann, 1985). Nonprosecutorial control strategies include "threats and use of adverse publicity, revocation of licenses, writing directly to consumers to warn them of company practice, and exerting pressure on reputable financial institutions and suppliers to withdraw support for the targeted company" (Braithwaite, 1985b: 10).

A combination of compliance-oriented, regulatory negotiating strategies with deterrence-oriented, criminal punishment could improve corporate crime control (Simpson and Koper, 1992). Reductions in corporate illegality are most likely when control tactics can be escalated in severity if there is failure to comply. Concluding a study of coal mine safety regulations, Braithwaite (1985a) advocates a hierarchy of regulatory response, from self-regulation to enforced self-regulation, command regulation with discretion to punish, and command regulation with nondiscretionary punishment. This pyramid of control measures, ranging from administrative to criminal, should be used to maximize compliance, deterrence, and the efficient use of scarce enforcement resources.

Fisse and Braithwaite (1993) have argued that moving toward greater accountability for corporate crime calls for a greater emphasis on the *individuals* within the corporation who are responsible for criminal acts. To do this in a cost-effective manner, however, requires greater reliance on the private justice system of the corporation to identify who is truly responsible. To achieve greater corporate responsibility through combining public law and corporate private justice, they say,

> ...the law should hold an axe over the head of the corporation that has committed the *actus reus* of a criminal offense. This may be almost literally an axe that ultimately can deliver the sanction of corporate capital punishment—liquidation, withdrawal of license or charter of the firm to operate. The private justice system of the firm is then put to work under the shadow of the axe. The axe would not fall if the private justice system of the corporation does what it is capable of doing—a self-investigation that fully identifies the responsible corporate policies, technologies, management systems, and decisionmakers and that comes up with a plan of remedial action, disciplinary action and compensation to victims that can satisfy the court. Should, however, the corporation cheat on its responsibility to make its private justice system work justly—by offering up a scapegoat, for example—then the axe would fall. (15–16)

The Effectiveness of Public Action. In evaluating the effectiveness of public action designed to achieve either deterrence or compliance, it must be recognized that not all government regulation necessarily benefits consumers, employees, or the public. Certain trade, pricing, or advertising regulations have actually increased consumer costs in the airline or trucking industries and professions such as mortuary or law. Some regulations may even encourage or facilitate crime. For example, regulations designed to control the removal, treatment, and disposal of hazardous wastes produced by corporations have turned out to be highly vulnerable to exploitation by organized crime. In response to lobbying by corporations, the regulatory structure allows them to limit their own liability and costs by contracting hazardous waste disposal to others—a service often supplied by organized criminals who then dispose of the wastes illegally (Szasz, 1986; Block and Bernard, 1988).

Nevertheless, isolated examples of bad regulations or poor judgment in enforcement should not be used to sustain a more general attack on efforts to control corporations. As Clinard and Yaeger (1980) note, "Although it is true that some rules may be overzealous, as also happens within a corporation itself, it is unreasonable to include in this category the vast majority of laws that regulate trusts, advertising, environment pollution, taxes, and other important areas of corporate behavior" (71). Government action in the public interest requires both sensible regulation and deregulation, with an eye not merely to the number but the intent and effect of the rules in question (Vaughan, 1983).

Ultimately, the effectiveness of public action depends upon improved information about corporate deviance. In order to achieve this, first, criminologists must be constantly aware of their responsibility as intellectual leaders to point out the existence and seriousness of corporate crime (Kramer, 1989). Second, there must be centralized collection of data on corporate violations as well as federal and state enforcement actions. At present, there is no standard system for the accumulation and publication of information on corporate crimes comparable to the FBI's *Uniform Crime Reports*, which is issued annually for street crimes. Conklin (1977) suggests that the development and regular issuance of such a "Business Crimes Report" would help to increase public awareness. Third, corporate crime is complex, and public understanding of it should be enhanced through informal channels such as investigative journalism and improved dissemination of information through the legal system. For example, publication of the details about corporate offenses could be used as a condition of court-ordered sentences imposed on corporate criminals (Fisse and Braithwaite, 1983). As Gerber (1990) observes, "Consumer activism, combined with negative publicity, may be the best hope for effective control of a variety of corporate behaviors" (108).

Changes in Corporate Attitudes and Structure

The most effective social control for individuals, it has been said, is achieved through their socialization to abide by the norms of the society. Similarly, underlying any strategy to control corporations is a viable set of ethical principles to guide the conduct of business. The strengthening of business ethics starts with the tone set by the board of directors and management of the corporation. The top management ought to write its own corporate code of conduct, distribute it to employees, and make it known that behavior in violation will not be tolerated. Beyond this, influential business organizations such as the U.S. Chamber of Commerce, the National Association of Manufacturers, and the Business Roundtable could direct attention to ethical standards. Business schools should continue to pay attention to ethics and social responsibility as part of the curriculum for the future corporate elite.

Changes in corporate organization have been identified as potentially fruitful ways of controlling corporate crime. Stockholders should be provided with more information on how the corporation is being run by management and should have more realistic opportunities to influence corporate decision making through the board of directors. As presently constituted and operated, most large corporations operate with little or no concern for the interests of small shareholders, even though collectively these people may own a majority of stock in the company. To correct this situation, Stone (1975) suggests:

- Large corporations should not be permitted to seat their managers on the board of directors.
- Steps should be taken to ensure that directors get critical information regarding company operations.
- The general public should have representation on the board of directors.

At the management level, McVisk (1978) argues that the liability of corporate executives for the behavior of their companies must be clarified. After all, in a giant organization employing thousands of people producing hundreds of products, how can the corporate executive legitimately be responsible for all possible criminal actions? The approach he proposes calls for a clear definition of the duties of all corporate personnel. The chief executive officer would be charged with the responsibility of introducing the necessary company systems to ensure compliance, and other officers and employees would share liability to the extent that their functions within these systems are not carried out. In this way, corporate executives would be made criminally liable for failure to institute adequate organizational safeguards against corporate crime. When a corporate executive *is* criminally liable, that person—as opposed to the corporation as a whole—ought to be the target of criminal justice procedures (Mills, 1986). Cressey (1989) argues that research and theory on corporate crime would benefit from the clear recognition that "only real persons have the psychological capacity to intend crimes," and it is essential to focus on the *managers* whose deliberate actions are responsible for such acts.

Even more sweeping reforms have been proposed. For example, Nader, Green, and Seligman (1976) call for federal as opposed to state chartering of corporations. At present, states compete for corporate chartering fees by trying to outdo one another in loosening restrictions on corporate behavior. The second smallest state, Delaware, has been the most successful (Davis, 1988); it hosts about half of the nation's 50 largest industrial firms. Of course, Delaware does not begin to have the resources necessary to cope with violations by these corporate giants. Clinard and Yaeger (1980) suggest a federal chartering system that could:

> ...require full disclosure of corporate operations, give stockholders the right to amend corporate bylaws and to recall any director, provide more opportunities for stockholders or stockholder groups to nominate some board members, provide a full-time staff to the board of directors to monitor independently corporate operations, establish safeguards to respect the privacy of all employees, and require a community impact statement when a corporation plant is to be relocated. Federal chartering would also make possible more effective regulation of corporations by various federal agencies, both in preventing illegal activities and in enforcement actions against violators. (212)

Control also might be more effective if such vast economic power were not allowed to concentrate in so few hands. A policy of deconcentration and divestiture could restrict the size of large corporations and their acquisitions, mergers, and general capacity to totally dominate a particular industry. In many countries, including the United States, federal ownership or nationalization of key monopolies or oligopolies, such as utilities and transportation systems, has been successful. But while public ownership is the most fundamental proposed reform, it is also the most controversial. The control of corporate deviance can be seen as an organizational problem as opposed to one of economic control. Ermann and Lundman (1982) argue that nationalization would not solve the problem of corporate deviance because:

> Nationalized corporations still would be organizations with essentially the same goals they currently have. Security, growth, and autonomy are important goals for *all* organizations. Corporate deviance is the product of organizational patterns that serve these goals. Deviance does not result from avarice by or for powerless shareholders. In fact, government and other nonprofit organizations also routinely are deviant. (175)

Whatever the social policy approach, whether through legal and penal reform, public action, changes in corporate organization, or altering the place of giant corporations in the economy, the options for controlling corporate deviance are varied and largely untried. Huge business organizations will continue to dominate the American economy and affect the society, and policies designed to encourage the best and restrain the worst that they have to offer should become a part of our public discourse.

SUMMARY

America's elites can be defined as the upper strata of individuals who form the superrich capitalist class and the upper-middle class, who together comprise about 15% of the population. There are also elite corporations whose staggering size and wealth permit them to dominate the American economy. These elite individuals and corporations are often able to transform their economic wealth into political power by a variety of direct and indirect means. As a result, a major factor in the evolving conceptions of crime and the administration of justice in the United States has been the ability of elites to have the law made and enforced in their interests.

The study of elite deviance is rooted in Sutherland's development of the concept of white-collar crime. The thrust of his argument is that crime is not merely a lower-class activity and need not be explained in terms of psychopathology. Extending Sutherland's pioneering work, others have identified deviant actions committed by high-status individuals and corporations. We defined elite occupational deviance as an illegal or unethical act committed for personal gain by an individual of high social status and respectability in the course of that person's occupation or profession. In contrast, corporate deviance consists of actions by corporations or individuals that violate criminal, civil, or administrative law and are intended to benefit the corporation. Such actions result from decisions by officers in a corporation (executives or managers) in accordance with corporate goals (primarily corporate profits), standard operating procedures, and cultural norms of the organization.

There are two major areas of elite occupational deviance: (1) illegal and unethical behavior among professionals, which includes problems like physicians' fee splitting, lawyers' fee-setting practices, and sexual harassment by academic professors, and (2) deviance by politicians and government officials. Four explanations of official deviance variously emphasize individual morality, the social functions of corruption, the expansion of government, and corruption as integral to the capitalist system.

Our review of corporate deviance began with a description of what a corporation is and how it operates. Although they are large, bureaucratic, hierarchically controlled organizations in pursuit of profits, corporations have a curious status in law as intangible persons. Both their organizational complexity and legal status are important for our understanding of corporate deviance.

The costs of corporate crime are immense. The economic toll certainly exceeds many times the annual losses from conventional property crimes like burglary, larceny, and robbery. The physical costs in damaged health and lost lives from violation of occupational health and safety and pollution laws are staggering. Possibly even more damaging are the social and moral costs from the disrespect for the law that wanton violation by the society's elites conveys to the rest of the population. All of these harms are apparent in four types of corporate deviance that have customers as victims, employees as victims, the public at large as victims, or owners as victims. The largest corporate crime wave in history occurred in the savings and loan debacle of the 1980s. This example of collective embezzlement represents a new, growing variety of organized corporate crime. A major study by Clinard provides a baseline for estimating the extent of corporate crime. He found that over a two-year period (1975 to 1976) among 582 of America's largest corporations 60% had at least one enforcement action initiated against them. Corporate offenders are concentrated in certain large industries; and penalties for violations generally are very light.

Explanations of corporate crime are either social psychological or sociological. Explicitly rejecting psychopathological explanations, Sutherland emphasized social psychological learning in his theory of differential association to account for corporate deviance. As part of their socialization in the corporation, people learn both the techniques for violating the law and how to rationalize having done so. The personal traits (ambition, shrewdness, and a nondemanding moral code) that often characterize people who rise to the top of large organizations also contribute to an atmosphere favoring corporate deviance. In fact, it appears that in some companies and industries, law violation has become a part of the corporate culture.

Sociological explanations focus on the structure of the corporation, the structure of the economy, and the failure of social controls. As large, bureaucratic organizations, corporations tend to fragment authority and responsibility for their actions. Deviance is more easily committed in this setting, which is not conducive to moral reflection or individual responsibility. Excessive emphasis on competition for maximum profits is central to one economic theory of corporate crime. A general critique of welfare-state capitalism emphasizes how corporate economic power is translated into political power. When the government proposes to control corporate crime through weak laws with inadequate enforcement provisions, the commission of corporate crime becomes a low-risk, rational action for the perpetrator. Put simply, efforts to control corporate crime have been feeble.

Numerous social policy reforms are aimed at controlling corporate deviance more effectively. These included legal, penal, and regulatory reform; public action and government regulation; and changes in corporate attitudes and structure. Political activism by consumer, environmental, and employee pressure groups, government regulation, and negative publicity on corporate wrong-doing may have the best hope of deterring corporate crime.

REFERENCES

Associated Press
1994   "Gap between High-Paid, Low-Paid Workers Widens," Rockford (IL) *Register Star*, June 3, 1994, p. 7A.

Barnett, H. C.
1981   "Corporate Capitalism, Corporate Crime." *Crime and Delinquency* 27: 4–23.

Bell, D.
1953   "Crime as an American Way of Life." *Antioch Review* 13: 131–153.

Benson, D. J., and Thomson, G. E.
1981   "Sexual Harassment on a University Campus: The Confluence of Authority Relations, Sexual Interest and Gender Stratification." Paper delivered at the Annual Meeting of the American Sociological Association, Toronto.

Benson, M. L.
1985   "Denying the Guilty Mind: Accounting for Involvement in a White-Collar Crime." *Criminology* 23: 583–607.

1989   "The Influence of Class Position on the Formal and Informal Sanctioning of White-Collar Offenders." *Sociological Quarterly* 30: 465–479.

Benson, M. L., Cullen, F. T., and Maakestad, W. J.
1990   "Local Prosecutors and Corporate Crime." *Crime and Delinquency* 36: 356–372.

Benson, M. L., and Walker, E.
1988   "Sentencing the White-Collar Offender." *American Sociological Review* 53: 294–302.

Bernard, T. J.
1984   "The Historical Development of Corporate Criminal Liability." *Criminology* 22: 3–17.

Block, A. A., and Bernard, T. J.
1988   "Crime in the Waste Oil Industry." *Deviant Behavior* 9: 113–129.

Block, M. K., Nold, F. C., and Sidak, J. G.
1981   "The Deterrent Effect of Antitrust Enforcement." *Journal of Political Economy* 89: 429–445.

Blumberg, A. S.
1978   "Practice of Law as a Confidence Game." Pp. 269–290 in J. M. Johnson and J. D. Douglas (eds.), *Crime at the Top*. New York: Lippincott.

Blundell, W. E.
1976   *Swindled*. Princeton, NJ: Dow Jones Books.

Braithwaite, J.
1984   *Corporate Crime in the Pharmaceutical Industry*. London: Routledge and Kegan Paul.

1985a   *To Punish or Persuade: Enforcement of Coal Mine Safety*. Albany: State University of New York Press.

1985b   "White Collar Crime." *Annual Review of Sociology* 11: 1–25.

Braithwaite, J., Fisse, B., and Geis, G.
1987   "Covert Facilitation and Crime: Restoring Balance to the Entrapment Debate." *Journal of Social Issues* 43: 5–41.

Braithwaite, J., and Geis, G.
1982   "On Theory and Action for Corporate Crime Control." *Crime and Delinquency* 28: 292–314.

Braithwaite, J., and Makkai, T.
1991   "Testing an Expected Utility Model of Corporate Deterrence." *Law and Society Review* 25: 7–40.

Bullough, V. L., and Groeger, S.
1982   "Irving W. Potter and Internal Podalic Version: The Problems of Disciplining a Skilled but Heretical Doctor." *Social Problems* 30: 109–116.

Calavita, K., and Pontell, H. N.
1990   "Heads I Win, Tails You Lose: Deregulation, Crime, and Crisis in the Savings and Load Industry." *Crime and Delinquency* 36: 309–341.

1991   "'Other People's Money' Revisited: Collective Embezzlement in the Savings and Load and Insurance Industries." *Social Problems* 38: 94–112.

1993   "Savings and Loan Fraud and Organized Crime: Toward a Conceptual Typology of Corporate Illegality." *Criminology* 31: 519–548.

Chambliss, W. J.
1977   "Vice, Corruption, Bureaucracy, and Power." Pp. 306–309 in J. D. Douglas and J. M. Johnson (eds.), *Official Deviance*. Philadelphia: Lippincott.

Chang, P. T., and Chang, R. H.
1985   "Social Issues and Computer-Based Management Information Systems." *Free Inquiry in Creative Sociology* 13: 75–79.

Clawson, D., and Neustadtl, A.
1989   "Interlocks, PACs, and Corporate Conservatism." *American Journal of Sociology* 94: 749–773.

Clinard, M. B.
1979   *Illegal Corporate Behavior*. Washington, DC: U.S. Government Printing Office.

1983   *Corporate Ethics and Crime: The Role of Middle Management*. Beverly Hills, CA: Sage.

Clinard, M. B., and Yeager, P. C.
1980   *Corporate Crime*. New York: Free Press.

Coffee, J. C.
1983   "Corporate Criminal Responsibility." Pp. 253–264 in *Encyclopedia of Crime and Justice*. New York: Free Press.

Coleman, J. W.
1987   "Toward an Integrated Theory of White-Collar Crime." *American Journal of Sociology* 93: 406–439.

Coleman, J. S.
1982   *The Asymmetric Society*. Syracuse, NY: Syracuse University Press.

Collier, P. A., and Spaul, B. J.
1992   "Problems in Policing Computer Crime." *Policing and Society* 2: 307–320.

Conklin, J. E.
1977   *"Illegal But Not Criminal": Business Crime in America.* Englewood Cliffs, NJ: Prentice-Hall.

Conyers, J., Jr.
1980   "Corporate and White-Collar Crime: A View by the Chairman of the House Subcommittee on Crime." *American Criminal Law Review* 17: 287–300.

Cressey, D. R.
1989   "The Poverty of Theory in Corporate Crime Research." Pp. 31–55 in W. S. Laufer and F. Adler (eds.), *Advances in Criminological Theory*, Vol. I. New Brunswick, NJ: Transaction Books.

Cullen, F. T., Link, B. G., and Polanzi, C. W.
1982   "The Seriousness of Crime Revisited: Have Attitudes toward White-Collar Crime Changed?" *Criminology* 20: 83–102.

Cullen, F. T., Maakestad, W. J., and Cavender, G.
1987   *Corporate Crime under Attack: The Ford Pinto Case and Beyond.* Cincinnati: Anderson.

Cullen, F. T., Mathers, R. A., and Cullen, J. B.
1983   "Public Support for Punishing White-Collar Crime: Blaming the Victim Revisited?" *Journal of Criminal Justice* 11: 481–493.

Cunningham, S., and Porter, A. L.
1992   "Communication Networks: A Dozen Ways They'll change Our Lives." *The Futurist*, January/February, Pp. 19–22.

Dansereau, H. K.
1974   "Unethical Behavior: Professional Deviance." Pp. 75–89 in C. D. Bryant (ed.), *Deviant Behavior: Occupational and Organized Bases.* Chicago: Rand McNally.

Davis, L. J.
1988   "Delaware Inc.: Fifty-Bucks—Credit Cards Accepted—Will Put You in Business." *New York Times Magazine*, June 6, Pp. 28+.

Denzin, N.K.
1977   "Notes on the Criminogenic Hypothesis: A Case Study of the American Liquor Industry." *American Sociological Review* 42: 905–920.

Domhoff, G. W.
1970   *The Higher Circles: The Governing Class in America.* New York: Vintage.
1983   *Who Rules America Now?: A View for the '80s.* Englewood Cliffs, NJ: Prentice-Hall.
1990   *The Power Elite and the State: How Policy Is Made in America.* New York: Aldine de Gruyter.

Douglas, J. D.
1977   "A Sociological Theory of Official Deviance and Public Concerns with Official Deviance." Pp. 395–410 in J. D. Douglas and J. M. Johnson (eds.), *Official Deviance.* Philadelphia: Lippincott.

Dye, T. R.
1990   *Who's Running America?*, 5th edition. Englewood Cliffs, NJ: Prentice-Hall.

Dziech, B., and Faaborg, L.
1982   *The Lecherous Professor.* Boston: Beacon Press.

Edelhertz, H.
1970   *The Nature, Impact and Prosecution of White-Collar Crime.* Washington, DC: U.S. Department of Justice, Law Enforcement Assistance Administration.

Ermann, M. D., and Clements, W. H., II.
1984   "The Interfaith Center on Corporate Responsibility and Its Campaign against Marketing Infant Formula in the Third World." *Social Problems* 32: 185–196.

Ermann, M. D., and Lundman, R. J.
1982   *Corporate Deviance.* New York: Holt, Rinehart and Winston.

Evans, P. B., and Schneider, S. A.
1981   "The Political Economy of the Corporation." Pp. 216–241 in S. G. McNall (ed.), *Political Economy: A Critique of American Society.* Glenview, IL: Scott, Foresman.

Evans, S., and Lundman, R. J.
1983   "Newspaper Coverage of Corporate Price-Fixing." *Criminology* 21: 529–541.

Farmighetti, R. (ed.)
1993   "The Savings and Loan Crisis." Pp. 107, 488 in *World Almanac and Book of Facts 1994.* Mahwah, NJ: World Almanac.

Fisse, B., and Braithwaite, J.
1983   *The Impact of Publicity on Corporate Offenders.* Albany, NY: SUNY Press.
1993   *Corporations, Crime and Accountability.* New York: Cambridge University Press.

Fligstein, N., and Brantley, P.
1992   "Bank Control, Owner Control, or Organizational Dynamics: Who Controls the Large Modern Corporation?" *American Journal of Sociology* 98: 208–307.

Forester, T., and Morrison, P.
1990   "Computer Crime: New Problem for the Information Society." *Prometheus* 8: 257–272.

Franklin, P., Moglen, H., Zatlin-Boring, P., and Angress, R.
1981   *Sexual and Gender Harassment in the Academy.* New York: Modern Language Association of America.

Freitag, P.
1975   "The Cabinet and Big Business: A Study of Interlocks." Social Problems 23: 137–152.
1983   "The Myth of Corporate Capture: Regulatory Commissions in the United States." Social Problems 30: 480–491.

Friedman, M.
1962   Capitalism and Freedom. Chicago: University of Chicago Press.

Geis, G.
1974   "Upper World Crime." In A. Blumberg (ed.), Current Perspectives on Criminal Behavior: Original Essays in Criminology. New York: Knopf.
1977   "The Heavy Electrical Equipment Antitrust Cases of 1961." Pp. 117–132 in G. Geiss and R. F. Meier (eds.), White-Collar Crime. New York: Free Press.
1984   "White-Collar and Corporate Crime." Pp. 137–166 in R. F. Meier, Major Forms of Crime. Beverly Hills, CA: Sage.

Geis, G., Jesilow, P., Pontell, H. N., and O'Brien, M. O.
1985   "Fraud and Abuse of Governmental Medical Benefit Programs by Psychiatrists." American Journal of Psychiatry 142: 231–234.

Geis, G., and Meier, R. F.
1977   White-Collar Crime. New York: Free Press.

Gerber, J.
1990   "Enforced Self Regulation in the Infant Formula Industry: A Radical Extension of an 'Impractical' Proposal." Social Justice 17: 98–112.

Gerber, J., and Short, J. F., Jr.
1986   "Publicity and the Control of Corporate Behavior: The Case of Infant Formula." Deviant Behavior 7: 195–216.

Gilbert, D., and Kahl, J. A.
1993   The American Class Structure, 4th edition. Belmont, CA: Wadsworth.

Gordon, L.
1981   "The Politics of Sexual Harassment." Radical America, Summer, pp. 7–14.

Green, M., and Berry, J. F.
1985a   "Capitalist Punishment: Some Proposals." The Nation 240: 731–734.
1985b   "White-Collar Crime Is Big Business." The Nation 240: 703–707.

Gross, E.
1978   "Organizational Crime: A Theoretical Perspective." Pp. 55–85 in N. K. Denzin (ed.), Studies in Symbolic Interaction, Vol. 1. Greenwich, CT: JAI Press.

Gutek, B. A.
1992   "Understanding Sexual Harassment at Work." Notre Dame Journal of Law, Ethics and Public Policy 6: 335–358.

Hagan, J.
1982   "The Corporate Advantage: A Study of the Involvement of Corporate and Individual Victims in a Criminal Justice System." Social Forces 60 (4) June: 993–1022.

Hagan, J., and Palloni, A.
1986   "'Club Fed' and the Sentencing of White-Collar Offenders before and after Watergate." Criminology 24: 603–621.

Hagan, J., and Parker, P.
1985   "White-Collar Crime and Punishment: The Class Structure and Legal Sanctioning of Securities Violations." American Sociological Review 50: 302–316.

Hessler, R. M.
1974   "Junkies in White: Drug Addiction among Physicians." Pp. 146–153 in C. D. Bryant (ed.), Deviant Behavior: Occupational and Organized Bases. Chicago: Rand McNally.

Hills, S. L.
1987   Corporate Violence: Injury and Death for Profit. Totowa, NJ: Rowman and Littlefield.

Hopkins, A.
1980   "Controlling Corporate Deviance." Criminology 18: 198–214.

Jackall, R.
1980   "Crime in the Suites." Contemporary Sociology 9: 354–371.

Jacobs, D.
1988   "Corporate Economic Power and the State: A Longitudinal Assessment of Two Explanations." American Sociological Review 93: 852–881.

Jacoby, N.
1973   Corporate Power and Social Responsibility. New York: Macmillan.

Jex, S. M., Hughes, P., Storr, C., Conrad, S., Baldwin, D. C., Jr., and Sheehan, D. V.
1992   "Relations among Stressors, Strains, and Substance Use Among Resident Physicians." International Journal of the Addictions 27: 979–994.

Johnson, E., and Mintz, B.
1990   "Organizational versus Class Components of Director Networks." Pp. 57–80 in R. Perrucci and H. R. Potter (eds.), Networks of Power: Organizational Actors at the National, Corporate, and Community Levels. New York: Aldine de Gruyter.

Kelman, H. C., and Hamilton, V. L.
1989   Crimes of Obedience: Toward a Social Psychology of Authority and Responsibility. New Haven, CT: Yale University Press.

Kerbo, H., and Fave, R. D.
1979   "The Empirical Side of the Power Elite Debate." *The Sociological Quarterly* 20: 5–22.

Klockars, C. B.
1977   "White-Collar Crime." Pp. 220–258 in E. Sagarin and F. Montanino (eds.), *Deviants: Voluntary Actors in a Hostile World*. New York: General Learning Press.

Kramer, R. C.
1981   "Toward the Study and Control of Corporate Crime: Some Preliminary Issues and Questions." Paper presented at the Annual Meeting of the Society for the Study of Social Problems, Toronto.
1989   "Criminologists and the Social Movement against Corporate Crime." *Social Justice* 16: 146–164.

Kruttschnitt, C.
1985   "Are Businesses Treated Differently?: A Comparison of the Individual Victim in the Criminal Courtroom." *Sociological Inquiry* 55: 225–238.

Leroux, C.
1993   "The American Middle Class is...." *Chicago Tribune*, March 7, sect. 4, p. 1.

Lewis, H. R., and Lewis, M. E.
1978   "A Crisis for Patients." Pp. 248–255 in J. M. Johnson and J. D. Douglas (eds.), *Crime at the Top*. New York: Lippincott.

Longres, J.
1994   *Human Behavior in the Social Environment*, 2nd edition. Itasca, IL: F. E. Peacock.

Liazos, A.
1972   "The Poverty of the Sociology of Deviance: Nuts, Sluts and 'Perverts'." *Social Problems* 20: 103–120.

Mann, K.
1985   *Defending White-Collar Crime: A Portrait of Attorneys at Work*. New Haven, CT: Yale University Press.

Martin, J.
1994   "The Service 500." *Fortune* May 30: 195ff

Marx, G. T.
1987   "Restoring Realism and Logic to the Covert Facilitation Debate." *Journal of Social Issues* 43: 43–55.

McCormick, A. E., Jr.
1977   "Rule Enforcement and Moral Indignation: Some Observations on the Effects of Criminal Antitrust Convictions upon Societal Reaction Processes." *Social Problems* 25: 30–39.

McVisk, W.
1978   "Toward a Rational Theory of Criminal Liability for the Corporate Executive."

Journal of Criminal Law and Criminology 69: 75–91.

Meier, R. F., and Short, J. F., Jr.
1985   "Crime as Hazard: Perceptions of Risk and Seriousness." *Criminology* 23: 389–399.

Merton, R. K.
1957   *Social Theory and Social Structure*. New York: Free Press.

Michalowski, R. J., and Kramer, R. C.
1987   "The Space between Laws: The Problem of Corporate Crime in a Transnational Context." *Social Problems* 34: 34–53.

Mills, E. B.
1986   "Perspectives on Corporate Crime and the Evasive Individual." *Criminal Justice Journal* 8: 327–361.

Mizruchi, M. S.
1982   *The American Corporate Network, 1904–1974*. Beverly Hills, CA: Sage.
1989   "Similarity of Political Behavior among Large American Corporations." *American Journal of Sociology* 95: 401–424.
1990   "Determinants of Political Opposition among Large American Corporations." *Social Forces* 68: 1065–1068.

Mizruchi, M. S., and Koenig, T.
1991   "Size, Concentration, and Corporate Networks: Determinants of Business Collective Action." *Social Science Quarterly* 72: 299–313.

Mokhiber, R.
1988   *Corporate Crime and Violence*. San Francisco: Sierra Club Books.

Moore, C. A.
1987   "Taming the Giant Corporation? Some Cautionary Remarks on the Deterrability of Corporate Crime." *Crime and Delinquency* 33: 379–402.

Moore, M.
1993   "Bhopal Gas Leak Victims Caught in Cycle of Despair." *Washington Post*, September 13, p. A1.

Morrow, C. K.
1982   "Sick Doctors: The Social Construction of Professional Deviance." *Social Problems* 30: 92–108.

Nader, R.
1965   *Unsafe at Any Speed: The Designed-In Dangers of the American Automobile*. New York: Grossman.

Nader, R., and Green, M. J.
1972   "Crime in the Suites: Coddling the Corporations" *New Republic* (April 29): 17–21.

Nader, R., Green, M., and Seligman, J.
1976   *Taming the Giant Corporation*. New York: Norton.

Ornstein, N. J., Mann, T. E., and Malbin, M. J.
1994   *Vital Statistics on Congress, 1993–1994.* Washington, DC: Congressional Quarterly Inc.

Passas, N.
1990   "Anomie and Corporate Deviance." *Contemporary Crises* 14: 157–178.

Pearce, F.
1976   *Crimes of the Powerful: Marxism, Crime and Deviance.* London: Pluto Press.

Pennings, J.
1980   *Interlocking Directorates.* Washington, DC: Jossey-Bass.

Pfost, D. R.
1987   "Reagan's Nicaraguan Policy: A Case Study of Political Deviance and Crime." *Crime and Social Justice* 27–28: 66–87.

Phillips, K.
1990a   *The Politics of Rich and Poor: Wealth and the American Electorate in the Reagan Aftermath.* New York: Random House.

1990b   "Reagan's America: A Capital Offense." *New York Times Magazine*, p. 26ff.

Pontell, H. N., Jesilow, P. D., and Geis, G.
1982   "Policing Physicians: Practitioner Fraud and Abuse in a Government Medical Program." *Social Problems* 30: 117–125.

Posner, R.
1970   "A Statistical Study of Antitrust Enforcement." *Journal of Law and Economics* 13: 365–419.

President's Commission on Law Enforcement and Administrative Justice
1967   *The Challenge of Crime in a Free Society.* Washington, DC: U.S. Government Printing Office.

Randall, D.
1987   "The Portrayal of Business Malfeasance in the Elite and General Public Media." *Social Science Quarterly* 68: 281–298.

Reasons, C. E., and Chappell, D.
1986   "Continental Capitalism and Crooked Lawyering." *Crime and Social Justice* 26: 38–59.

Reilly, M. E., Lott, B., and Gallogley, S. M.
1987   "Sexual Harassment of University Students." *Sex Roles* 15: 333–358.

Salzman, H., and Domhoff, W. G.
1979   "Corporations, the Civic Sector, and Government: Do They Interlock?" *Insurgent Sociologist* 9: 121–135.

Sandler, B. R., and associates
1981   "Sexual Harassment: A Hidden Problem." *Educational Record* 62: 52–57.

Schrager, L. S., and Short, J. F.
1978   "Toward a Sociology of Organizational Crime." *Social Problems* 25: 407–419.

Seidler, L. J., Andrews, F., and Epstein, M. J.
1977   *The Equity Funding Papers: The Anatomy of a Fraud.* New York: Wiley.

Seymour, W. N., Jr.
1973   "Social and Ethical Considerations in Assessing White-Collar Crime." *American Criminal Law Review*, 11: 833–834.

Shapiro, S. P.
1985   "The Road Not Taken: The Elusive Path to Criminal Prosecution for White-Collar Offenders." *Law and Society Review* 19: 179–217.

Simpson, S. S., and Koper, C. S.
1992   "Deterring Corporate Crime." *Criminology* 30: 347–375.

Skolnick, J. H.
1987   "The Risks of Covert Facilitation." *Journal of Social Issues* 43: 79–85.

Smith, J. D.
1987   "Wealth in America." *J.S.R. Newsletter* 14: 3–5.

Smothers, R.
1991   "25 Die, Many Reported Trapped, As Blaze Engulfs Carolina Plant." *The New York Times*, September 4, p. A1.

Snider, L.
1982   "Traditional and Corporate Theft: A Comparison of Sanctions." Pp. 235–238 in P. Wickman and T. Dailey (eds.), *White Collar and Economic Crime.* Lexington, MA: Lexington Press.

1990   "Cooperative Models and Corporate Crime: Panacea or Cop-Out?" *Crime and Delinquency* 36: 373–390.

1991   "The Regulatory Dance: Understanding Reform Processes in Corporate Crime." *International Journal of Sociology of Law* 19: 209–236.

Stone, C. D.
1975   *Where the Law Ends: The Social Control of Corporate Behavior.* New York: Harper & Row.

Sutherland, E. H.
1949   *White Collar Crime.* New York: Holt, Rinehart and Winston.

1956   "Crimes of Corporations." In A. Cohen, A. Lindesmith, and K. Schuessler (eds.), *The Sutherland Papers.* Bloomington, IN: Indiana University Press.

1983   *White Collar Crime: The Uncut Version.* New Haven, CT: Yale University Press.

Szasz, A.
1986   "Corporations, Organized Crime, and the Disposal of Hazardous Waste: An Examination of the Making of a Criminogenic Regulatory Structure." *Criminology* 24:1–27.

Teitelbaum, R. S.
1994   "The Fortune 500." *Fortune* April 18: 209ff
Thio, A.
1973   "Class Bias in the Sociology of Deviance." *American Sociologist* 8: 1–12.
Thurow, L. C.
1987   "A Surge of Inequality." *Scientific American* 26: 30–37.
U.S. Bureau of the Census
1993   *Statistical Abstract of the United States, 1992.* Table 441. Washington, DC: U.S. Department of Commerce.
U.S. House Subcommittee on Oversight and Investigations
1990   *Failed Promises: Insurance Company Insolvencies*, February. Washington, DC: Author.
Useem, M.
1984   *The Inner Circle: Large Corporations and the Rise of Business Political Activity in the U.S. and U.K.* New York: Oxford University Press.
Vaughan, D.
1982   "Transaction Systems and Unlawful Organizational Behavior." *Social Problems* 29: 373–379.

1983   *Controlling Unlawful Organizational Behavior: Social Structure and Corporate Misconduct.* Chicago: University of Chicago Press.
West, S. B., and Carter, T. J.
1983   "Bringing White-Collar Crime Back In: An Examination of Crimes and Torts." *Social Problems* 30: 545–554.
Wheeler, S., Weisburd, D., and Bode, N.
1982   "Sentencing the White-Collar Offender: Rhetoric and Reality." *American Sociological Review* 17: 641–659.
Wilson, K. R., and Kraus L. A.
1981   "Sexual Harassment in the University." Paper delivered at the Annual Meeting of the American Sociological Association, Toronto.
Zeitlin, M.
1974   "Corporate Ownership and Control: The Large Corporation and the Capitalist Class." *American Journal of Sociology* 79: 1073–1119.

10 | Deviance, Control, and Social Policy

This concluding chapter undertakes several tasks. First, we place the approaches to deviance and control in Western culture in a broad historical perspective. Second, we describe the process by which social policy concerning deviance has emerged in contemporary American society. Third, based on the theory and evidence set forth in the preceding chapters in this book, we make some recommendations for more effective alternatives to our present practice of social control. The parting remarks constitute a critical assessment of the persistent influence that those whose interest is in maintaining the status quo continue to have on the production, maintenance, and control of deviance in American society. The underlying theme is that deviance and control are inseparable from the broader social structures in which they are situated.

IMAGES OF DEVIANCE IN WESTERN HISTORY

Sin, Crime, and Sickness

Three approaches to explaining deviance have competed for ascendancy throughout Western history: deviance as sin, as crime, or as sickness. Sometimes two or all three have existed side by side, and in virtually every period there have been some adherents to each one. In a particular period, however, within very broad time frames , when one image of deviance has tended to dominate others, it should not be surprising that the dominant image is linked to that period's dominant groups and social institutions. For example, in medieval or feudal society, dominated by theological reasoning and ecclesiastical authority, theories of deviance emphasized sin, evil, and fall from grace. The clergy, whose authority was anchored in theological doctrine and tradition, were the primary social control practitioners. The social control practices, reflecting the apparent need to atone for sin or expunge evil, often involved penance or corporal punishment.

In contrast, the capitalistic welfare state, the model in current American society, is dominated by giant corporations, large, bureaucratic government, and *technocrats*—highly trained scientists, engineers, and other skilled professionals. In this technologically oriented society, the management of deviance is increasingly being placed in the hands of specialists. The ascendant image of deviance conceptualizes wrongdoing as evidence of sickness. Medical, psychiatric, and social scientists, along with various helping professionals (social workers, probation officers, counselors) increasingly preempt or share in social control decisions with the courts. Techniques of social control include drugs and surgery intended to "cure" the behavior in question.

Table 10.1 summarizes these broad historical trends in Western images of deviance and the practice of social control. Notice that in each historical period there tend to be characteristic images of deviance and approaches to social control.[1] Thinking in such a grand historical frame of reference is useful for uncovering large-scale patterns. However, there are specific exceptions to and reversals of the general tendency to move from images of deviance as sin, to crime, to sickness. Indeed, in American society within the past 100 years or so, there has been a cyclical pattern in deviance designations alternating between images of crime and sickness (Conrad and Schneider, 1993: 274). For example, from the 19th century to the present, opiate addiction has been alternately defined as no problem, a medical problem, a crime, and currently, a hybrid legal-medical phenomenon. Throughout the same period, alcoholism has carried a mixed connotation of immorality, illegality, and sickness; the medical model presently dominates. The prevailing definition of homosexual behavior has moved from sin to crime to sickness, and most recently, to demedicalization. After an intense struggle the American Psychiatric Association voted in 1973 to drop the classification of homosexuality as a mental illness, and various attempts have been made to recognize the civil rights of homosexuals, but at the same time efforts by some religious or conservative groups to brand homosexuality as sinful or to retain its definitions as illegal acts have been increasing.

The deeper implications of changing images of deviance must remain beyond the scope of this book. However, we can suggest at least one direction in which further thought on the subject may lead. From the viewpoint of images of deviance, the essential importance of a theory is not its truth or falseness, for virtually all theories become discredited, outmoded, or modified in time.[2] The impact of a theory explaining human behavior is its ability to make manifest underlying assumptions about the nature of humans and their interactions. As such, theories of deviance serve as guides for understanding how people treat one another and the kinds of societies they construct. Theories and images of deviance, modes of social control, everyday interaction, and the social structure of the society in which they exist are all of the same cloth.

The Medicalization of Deviance

American society in the 20th century has been a particularly receptive environment for medicalized conceptions of deviance. Peter Conrad and Joseph W. Schneider (1993), careful observers of the medicalization trend, summarize the reasons why:

> In a general sense, the American values of experimentation, newness, humanitarianism, pragmatism, and individualism have all contributed to a nurturing crucible for medicalization, for the medical perspective on deviance contains elements of all these values....

Table 10.1   Broad Historical Trends in Western Images of Deviance and Control

	Preindustrial, Feudal (pre-1500)	Mercantile & Early Industrial Capitalism (1500–1900)	Advanced Welfare-State Capitalism (1900–present)
Dominant groups and institutions	Church, clergy, monarchy, nobility	Landed gentry merchants and industrial capitalists	Industrial capitalists and technocrats
Image of deviance	Sin/evil	Crime/illegal	Sickness/madness/crime
Responsibility	Individual in relation to God and sovereign	Individual in relation to the law and the state	Individual denied responsibility
Social control	Clergy, monarchy, nobility	Judges, courts	Medical, psychiatric, and social scientists, helping professionals, courts
Legitimation of authority	Traditional, divine right, moral	Legal, rational, moral	Technical, rational, moral
Mode of response	Retributive—corporal, capital, penance	Restitutive—incarceration, capital, banishment	Rehabilitative—drugs or surgery; repressive—incarceration or capital
Image of the limits on human action	Supernaturalistic determinism—original sin	Free will—utilitarian, rational choice	Naturalistic determinism—biological, psychological, or social causes

...In recent years health itself has become a predominant value. American society, with its democratic system, is open to challenges of new definitions of deviance. Medical practice is independent and expansive. In a capitalist society, medicalization can create new markets and be highly profitable. In short, in American society medical conceptions of deviance have a cultural resonance both with dominant values and the organizational apparatus to promote and sustain them, creating a fertile environment for medicalization. (263, 265)

Deviance as Crime or Sickness. The most common alternative to medicalization in the 20th century has been to treat deviance as crime. Probably most significant of the underlying distinctions between deviance conceived as crime or as sickness is the attribution of responsibility in each case. Crime is assumed to be an act motivated by some gain—money, power, revenge, or pleasure. The criminal is presumed to be responsible for his or her own conduct, having made a moral choice to break rather than to abide by the law. In contrast, the sick person is seen as lacking responsibility for her or his condition. There is no moral decision to get sick or stay well; sickness merely involves a turn for the worse (Aubert and Messinger, 1958). Thus, when we treat someone as a criminal, we assume that the person's behavior involved a morally conscious choice for which that person can be held responsible. To say that behavior is a result of sickness implies that it occurred beyond the person's control, that the person is not responsible.

Beyond the attribution of responsibility, there are great differences in how crime and sickness are handled once they are suspected. Ideally, the determination of guilt or innocence in crime is made by citizen peers of the accused who make up a trial jury. In the case of sickness, decisions about whether one is ill or well are made by professional experts, primarily doctors.

The Blurring of the Distinction. The trend toward medicalization of deviance has not occurred as a sharp transformation in the definition of particular deviant activities, but rather through a subtle merging of the practices of law and medicine. We can see it in the increasing use of expert psychiatric testimony in "competency to stand trial" hearings and the successful use of the insanity defense in celebrated cases such as those of attempted presidential assassin John Hinckley, Jr., or Lorena Bobbitt's acquittal for cutting off her husband's penis.[3] Michael Foucault (1975) sees the emergence of a new form of law presided over by judges with an immense appetite for medicine which is manifested in their frequent appeals to psychiatric experts. The merging of law and medicine has had "a whole series of effects; the internal dislocation of the judicial power or at least of its functioning; an increasing difficulty in judging, as if one were ashamed to pass sentence; a furious desire on the part of judges to judge, assess, diagnose, recognize the normal and abnormal and claim the honor of curing and rehabilitation" (304).

In the day-to-day practice of decision making on questions of deviance and deviants, images of deviance as crime have become increasingly influenced by images of deviance as sickness. Moral judgments of right or wrong have coalesced with technical judgments of well or sick. The result is a subtle shift from a view of people personally responsible for their own behavior and who are judged guilty or innocent by citizen peers to a view of people who are irresponsible and whose behavior calls for evaluation by elite experts. The consequences extend well beyond the lives of deviants alone. With the blurring of the distinction between crime and sickness, the very capacity to view almost any misbehavior on a moral plane fades as moral-legal and medical-technical decision making meld. The moral frame required for a public understanding of popular protest breaks when virtually any sort of rule-breaking, including civil disobedience, is regarded as "sick" and therefore to be dismissed. Righteous indignation, even violent rage, can have their roots in serious injustice. However, if all we search for are hormonal imbalances, we will fail to see or understand the conditions that give some violent behavior its meaning. Medicalized deviant behavior loses all potential for political or social meaning, because sickness requires no motive.

Lawbreakers sometimes do have political motives. For instance, in the 1950s and the 1960s civil rights activists intentionally violated segregation laws that restricted where people could sit on public transportation or eat at restaurants; they wanted to demonstrate the injustice of the laws. In response, governments sometimes attempt to discredit people who have engaged in civil disobedience by implying their behavior was caused by mental illness or a character flaw. FBI activities against Daniel Ellsberg, who released the Pentagon Papers during the Vietnam War, and Dr. Martin Luther King, Jr., come to mind. Likewise, President Lyndon Johnson applied Eric Hoffer's (1952) thesis to anti–Vietnam War demonstrators, claiming that they merely represented the unfortunate attraction of society's "unstable and frustrated," who are normally dispersed and disorganized, to a single issue. In this way the demonstrators' behavior could be explained away as that of a "lunatic fringe," thereby denying its moral meaning. Indeed, during the 1960s, when the level of social unrest prompted a rush for explanations, the most common metaphor was that of a "sick" society. The terminology was medical rather than moral (for example, an "unjust" society). The United States is certainly not alone in the medicalization of civil disobedience. The former Soviet Union exercised social and political control by treating ideological dissidents as psychiatric cases and institutionalizing them. In respect to those on opposite sides of many contemporary political disputes involving fundamental values, from questions of abortion to capital punishment, it is not uncommon for partisans to label their opponents *sick* as opposed to charging them with being illogical, wrong-headed, immoral, or acting illegally. To dismiss one's adversary as sick is to foreclose on further philosophical discussion or political debate.

From a still wider perspective, a medicalized, therapeutic ethos directs the efforts of people searching to relieve their malaise not to the social arrangements into which they are bound but within themselves. They seek individualized "diagnoses" and "cures" as opposed to critically examining their society. And, whenever additional decisions leave the moral-legal domain for the medical-therapeutic one, people yield the power to control their own lives to medical, behavioral, and social "experts." Democracy is thereby diminished. The society is moved still closer to Aldous Huxley's *Brave New World* of genetic engineering, behavior modification, and total elite social control.

The Punitive Mode

As we noted in Chapter 1, the increased medicalization of deviance has by no means meant a corresponding reduction in punishment-oriented approaches to social control. The facts document quite the reverse—a massive increase in the funding and activity of the criminal justice system in the 1980s, and an emphasis on the control of street crime and violence in the 1990s. In 1970, there were approximately 196,000 prisoners in American state and federal correctional institutions; by 1994, that number had increased 410%, to over 1,000,000. Put another way, in 1970, 96 people per 100,000 in the U.S. population were imprisoned; by 1991 that rate was over 300 per 100,000—a 213% increase (U.S. Bureau of Justice Statistics, 1992d). More than 1 in every 300 U.S. citizens was in prison, and an additional 420,000, on average, were being held in local jails (U.S. Bureau of Justice Statistics, 1992b).

The high rate of imprisonment in the United States as compared to other industrialized countries is due both to higher crime rates and a greater reliance on imprisonment. According to the U.S. Bureau of Justice Statistics (1988), crimes of violence (homicide, rape, and robbery) are four to nine times more frequent in the United States than in Europe, and crimes of theft (burglary, theft, and auto theft) are also more frequent, but not to the same degree. A study comparing incarcerations in the United States with those in Canada, England, and West Germany (U.S. Bureau of Justice Statistics, 1987) revealed that for the same crimes, a much greater number of people were imprisoned each year in this country. For robbery, for example, the rates per 100,000 population were 26.8 in the United States, 15.5 in Canada, 4.3 in England, and 3.0 in West Germany. The analysis also indicated that the higher U.S. rates were due largely to higher arrest rates.

Continued increases in imprisonment have resulted in overcrowded prison populations in almost every type of facility in the United States, and this has put pressure on the criminal justice system to release offenders on probation or parole. In 1990 state and federal agencies reported over 2.6 million people on probation and over 500,000 on parole, which means that about 1.7% of all adults and 3% of all adult males in the United States were in one category or the other (U.S. Bureau of Justice Statistics, 1992a).

After a 10-year moratorium on capital punishment ended in 1976, executions increased from a single one the following year to 125 between 1985 and 1991 (Bureau of Justice Statistics, 1992a). As of April 1992, 2,600 prisoners were on death row, all but six of them in various state institutions. Perhaps as an indication of the increasing entanglement of medical and legal forms of social control, capital punishment is now carried out in a majority of states by lethal injection (Haines, 1989).

The characteristics of neither prisoners nor death row inmates correspond closely to the general population. In each case, males, blacks, and younger people are heavily overrepresented. Although blacks, for example, constitute about 12% of the population, they make up about 47% of prison inmates and over 40% of those on death row. Much, but not all, of this overrepresentation of blacks can be accounted for by the higher arrest rates (Blumstein, 1982; Dehais, 1987; Sheley, 1993). Over 60% of those entering state prisons in 1986 had less than 12 years of education.

Criminal justice and its associated punishment is costly. Overall, federal, state, and local governments in the United States spent $74 billion in fiscal year 1990 on civil and criminal justice (U.S. Bureau of Justice Statistics, 1992c). Corrections, in particular, have been requiring greater resources. For example, by 1990 corrections at all levels of government totaled nearly $25 billion—a figure that has nearly doubled since 1985. As more people are sent to prison on longer sentences, the need for prison space grows proportionately. Construction costs are now at about $100,000 per cell with operating costs of between $15,000 and $35,000 per prisoner each year (Jacobs, ND).

In general, despite the costs (or perhaps simply ignoring them), the American public supports stricter law enforcement, with more use of imprisonment and capital punishment. Politicians, often in the interests of powerful constituents, play up public fears of street crime and make demands for expanded criminal justice efforts. In recent years, the punitive mode of formal social control has expanded, to at least keep pace with the medical model.

THE CREATION OF DEVIANCE AND SOCIAL POLICY

The Social Construction of Deviance

Late in the 19th century the French sociologist Emile Durkheim made perhaps his most enduring observation about deviant behavior. It is not the intrinsic quality of a given act that makes it deviant but rather the definition of the act applied by the "collective conscience" of the society that confers on it a deviant character (Durkheim, 1938: 70). Howard S. Becker (1963) subsequently expanded on Durkheim's insight:

> ...*social groups create deviance by making the rules whose infraction constitutes deviance*, and by applying those rules to particular people and labeling them as outsiders. From this point of view, deviance is *not* a quality of the act the person commits, but rather a consequence of the application by others of rules and sanctions to an "offender." The deviant is one to whom that label has successfully been applied; deviant behavior is behavior that people so label. (9; italics in original)

Becker maintains further that "differences in the ability to make rules and apply them to other people are essentially power differentials (either legal or extra legal). Those groups whose special position gives them weapons and power are best able to enforce their rules" (18). Deviance designations therefore result from conflict and disagreement; they are part of the political process of society. Likewise, of course, social policies aimed at controlling what has been identified as deviant are the products of political struggles. Both deviance and the social policies adopted to control it arise from a complex set of interactions between interest groups: the society's elites, the government, media image makers, medical, behavioral, and social scientists, helping professionals, law enforcement personnel, the general public, and those who have been labeled deviant.

The Emergence of Social Policy

Neither images of deviance nor social policy is a static phenomenon. Rather than conceptualizing them as *things*, it is far better to see them as parts of a *process*—a process that is forever changing, forever in motion. Moreover, the process that creates images of deviance and social policies to control it is very complicated, not en-

Figure 10.1   The Process of Defining Deviance and Creating Social Policy

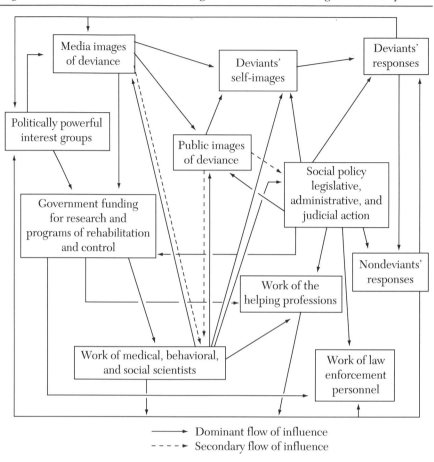

tirely understood, and difficult to convey in only a few sentences. Figure 10.1 is a simplified, general model of this process. Three things about it merit attention.

First, the model represents social action in motion. In the dynamic process of deviance definition and social policy formation concerning any particular behavior, almost all of the influences indicated by the arrows on the model are operating simultaneously. For illustration, we can take the example of how the model applies to the case of alcoholism. Beginning at the far left of the figure, politically powerful interest groups would include the liquor industry, organizations like Alcoholics Anonymous and the Women's Christian Temperance Union, university research groups and the professional associations of social workers, counselors, and law enforcement personnel. Taken together, these groups influence media images of alcoholism by the written material they produce (advertisements, papers, reports, brochures, and posters) and public statements on radio, television, and in the press. They also influence the types and amounts of government funding for research and the levels of support for programs to rehabilitate and control alcoholics.[4] The types and amounts of government funding directly affect the work of scientists doing research on alcoholism, professionals who implement programs for intervention and rehabilitation, and law enforcement personnel. Note that scientists, helping professionals, and law enforcement personnel simultaneously receive government support for their work and act as politically powerful interest groups that influence what types of government support will be offered and how much there will be. This kind of circular feedback of influence occurs at numerous other points throughout the model.[5]

Sometimes there is even more direct feedback. For instance, the work of medical, behavioral, and social scientists is reflected in media images of alcoholism. Newspaper, news magazines, and radio and television reporters rely on researchers' reports and public statements during interviews for various news stories. At the same time, however, media and public images of what constitute "hot topics" for research influence, to some extent, researchers' choices of particular problems to study. For example, increased media and public attention directed at women as problem drinkers is likely to stimulate greater study of that problem by social scientists, both directly in the scientists' selection of research problems and indirectly through the availability of funding.

Second, the social policy that emerges is embodied in the laws, administrative procedures, and judicial rulings made by public officials. For example, in the case of public drunkenness, social policy in most states has undergone a transformation from criminalization to decriminalization. Such a change usually involves eliminating some statutes concerning public drunkenness as a crime from the criminal law, the addition of regulations to the public health code, and administrative edicts declaring how people who are identified as public drunks are now to be treated. In addition to influencing the work of law enforcement agents and helping professionals such as social workers or detoxification specialists, the new social policy also will alter the self image of public drunks. Their condition will be redefined from a problem handled primarily by the criminal justice system to one managed by welfare and medical personnel.

Third, social policies produce responses from both nondeviants and those tagged with a deviant label. From the ranks of both may come politically powerful interest groups that either support or attempt to change whatever social policy is currently in force. In this sense, the deviants themselves must be seen both as objects and as participants in the process of social policy creation. To repeat, definitions of deviance and the social policies intended to control it emerge from a never-ending, dynamic set of interactions that influence one another in highly complex ways. Researchers have used sociohistorical analysis to unravel the details of specific cases of deviance, including drinking (Gusfield, 1963; Schneider, 1978), mental disorders (Szasz, 1961; Scull, 1989), prostitution (Hobson, 1987), marijuana use (Musto, 1973: Galliher and Walker, 1977), child abuse (Pfohl, 1976), and wife battering

(Tierney, 1982: Pleck, 1987; Dobash and Dobash, 1992). Continuing this tradition should remain an important item on the research agenda for students of deviance.

The Responsibility of the Human Sciences

Medical, behavioral, and social scientists should not underestimate the degree to which what they study and how they study it is influenced by government funding decisions and public and media images of what constitute worthy research targets. Nor should they minimize the impact of their work on (1) media images of deviance, (2) public images of deviance, (3) deviants' self-images, (4) the work of those in the helping professions, and (5) legal, administrative and judicial social policy. Theories widely accepted in the human sciences are part of the stuff of which deviance images are constructed and social policy decisions are implemented. The responsibility of the human sciences in this realm is significant.

Theories of deviance have an even more far-reaching, if diffuse, importance. For example, some argue that social scientists' explanations of deviance have too often been excessively deterministic (Matza, 1964; Taylor, Walton, and Young, 1973). In other words, the explanations seem to presume that the deviant is rather mindlessly driven down an inevitable path toward deviance by his or her genetic endowment, early childhood socialization, or pathology-producing social environment. The overriding image is a "billiard ball shot" conception of human behavior, whereby people appear to be propelled into their actions by prior causes over which they have little or no choice or control.

Such overly deterministic explanations are misleading in at least three ways. First, they ignore the role of human volition or free will as a determinant of social action. To be sure, social conditions do limit or alter people's behaviors. But humans, whether labeled deviant or not, have the capacity to think, anticipate, and reflect; they can and do make choices about how they will behave. Thus, excessively deterministic images of deviance can dehumanize our characterizations of those who are designated wayward; ultimately, they can dehumanize images of all others as well. Second, this conception of behavior removes the role of individual responsibility and accountability for actions. How can people be blamed, made ashamed, or found guilty if the underlying explanation for their actions is presumed to be beyond their personal control? Third, this model of human behavior erases or masks the moral and political meaning of deviant actions. When the elements of free choice and conscious decision are removed from explanations of deviance, the answer to the question "Why did he do it?" need not go beyond a narrow technical explanation of the person's physical or psychological condition. A more adequate framing of the question, "why did she *choose* to do it?" forces us to explore the conscious, human motivations—including the political and moral commitments—behind social action.

The main point is that theories of deviance inevitably embody fundamental assumptions about social action and human nature. Certainly far more attention is directed to the study of deviant than conforming behavior—especially the deviant behavior of the relatively powerless. After all, they are the ones who usually end up being defined as "the problems." However, in a certain sense, it is through our extensive observation of deviants and theorizing about them that the human sciences have produced what we think we know about human behavior. Not too much unlike the lowly white rat, powerless deviants have usually been docile research subjects. Thus the study of deviance and the underlying behavioral images that are part of deviance theories become part of general public discourse and explanations of human action. If we but listen carefully, we will hear them being applied to us all.

THE PRACTICE OF SOCIAL CONTROL

Since the 1960s, many social policy makers and their advisors in academe have called for the decriminalization of certain illegal activities, including prostitution, pornography, homosexual behavior, drunkenness, and drug use, as long as the behavior involves only consenting adults. The argument goes that because these activities amount to willing exchanges between a supplier of some good or service and a customer, no victim's complaint accompanies the "crime." With no complaint, the law is extremely difficult to enforce (Schur, 1965). Indeed, the attempt to enforce laws that, due to the nature of the activities they proscribe, are largely unenforceable may contribute to crime by enhancing disrespect for the law. As Morris and Hawkins (1970) put it:

> …in many cases the attempt to use the criminal law to prohibit the supply of goods and services which are constantly demanded by millions of Americans is one of the most powerful criminogenic forces in our society. By enabling criminals to make vast profits from such sources as gambling and narcotics; by maximizing opportunities for bribery and corruption; by attempting to enforce standards which do not command either the respect or compliance of citizens in general; by these and in a variety of other ways, we both encourage disrespect for the law and stimulate the expansion of both individual and organized crime to an extent unparalleled in any other country in the world. (27)

The leading humane alternative to criminalization of these activities is to treat them as medical problems, and we have already seen that the medicalization of deviance has its own dubious consequences. In addition, as Edwin Schur (1974) observes, the substitution of medical personnel for law enforcement officers amounts only to dressing up in different clothing a fundamentally punitive approach:

> There is now considerable recognition that, however progressive they may seem at first glance, these efforts to define problematic situations in medical terms are far from being universally successful. As the trend toward politicalization proceeds, the individuals involved become increasingly unwilling to accept medical definitions of their behavior; the gay liberation movement's repudiation of the concept that homosexuality is a disease or even "abnormal" is a striking case in point. Similarly, large scale service programs that leave the individual subject to substantial medical control (such as enforced "civil commitment" of addicts for treatment, or the granting of "therapeutic abortions" on approval by hospital medical boards) have been found to be inadequate modifications of what has remained a basically punitive policy. (43–44)

A Social Justice Alternative

Are there possibilities other than criminalization or medicalization of deviance? Yes. What we will call a *social justice approach* entails several steps we can take that are consistent with the conclusions of preceding chapters.

First, we can decriminalize for consenting adults most exchange activities, such as prostitution, homosexual behavior, and the sale of pornography and drugs, that generally yield no complaint by participants. The result may be short-term increases in some of these activities, no change, or even a decrease. Given the ineffectiveness of present policies, the hope is that in the long run decriminalization would at least diminish some of the present staggering economic, moral, and social costs of criminal law enforcement directed against these crimes.

Second, through public education we can discourage excesses and encourage responsible behavior. In regard to activities often considered deviant, this means, for example, encouraging individual responsibility for safe sex and moderation in the use of mind-altering substances. It also means informing the public about the negative effects of media violence (especially violence against women) and the facts about the sexual exploitation of children.

Third, for those who do create problems for themselves or others due to irresponsibility or excess, we can offer and provide genuine help in the form of clinics, alcohol and drug treatment programs, counseling centers, and the social services to support them. Many activities commonly designated as deviance *are* harmful. The thrust of social policy ought to be the most effective reduction of harm.

Fourth, we can acknowledge how deviance grows in complex ways out of the social organization of our society. High rates of serious domestic violence, street crime, and delinquency are related to the disintegration of families, neighborhoods, and communities—particularly among the poor. We must recognize how the disintegration is tied to fundamental social and economic inequalities in the distribution of wealth and power. Informal social controls embedded in the mutual respect, caring, and obligations of stable, prosperous communities are the most effective means for preventing the most harmful kinds of deviance. Establishing the foundation for more effective informal controls must have a high priority. Given the dominant position of huge corporations in the American political economy, social policy ought to take into account the influence they can have on the society. For instance, communities and families are adversely affected when factories are closed to send jobs to cheaper labor markets; they are harmed when continual transfer or displacement of workers creates social instability; and they cannot function effectively when the organization of work fails to account for responsible child rearing by single parents or in households where both parents are working.

Fifth, we must recognize how prejudice, racism, and sexism create conditions for discrimination, hatred, resentment and attitudes that justify violence. Through education and legal reforms we must transmit and validate values that encourage the acceptance of diversity, social justice, and freedom from domination.

In practical terms, a social justice model would, for example, ensure a respectable job and the realistic opportunity of an alternative livelihood for the street prostitute, as opposed to the revolving door (jail-to-street-to-jail) system of criminal justice in which she is now trapped. It would include legal reforms that guarantee women and minorities economic and political equity. The social justice alternative would protect against job discrimination and provide, at a minimum, freedom from legal stigma for consenting adults engaging in homosexual behavior. For the homeless alcoholic there would be (not unlike the present program of the Salvation Army) a place to sleep and a meal in a receptive environment, as opposed to court appearances and "three hots and a cot" in a drunk tank, serving a life sentence in 30-day increments "on the installment plan." For drug addicts, maintenance facilities would be readily available, along with medical and other social services. The social justice model would not allow the abandonment of the mentally ill to city streets in the name of deinstitutionalization, and it would devote greater resources to the victims of domestic violence, abuse, and neglect. Perhaps most important, it would provide the realistic prospect of a legitimate job as a viable alternative to the illegitimate ones that now flourish as the economic base for many who live amid the hopeless environment of America's urban ghettos.

This approach does *not* imply that harmful criminal offenses such as assault, theft, or robbery can be dealt with in any way that differs substantially from those presently used. Presumably, the social justice approach would eventually reduce the levels of these activities, but when crimes occur, punishment should be administered through the criminal justice system. Thus a drug addict on maintenance doses who can stay out of legal trouble should be left alone by the criminal law, but an addict who commits a serious crime like robbery should be subject to the full force of the criminal law for the act, regardless of addiction.

Such a program must raise questions about cost. Certainly some of the cost could be offset by reduction of the vast expenditures on criminal justice resources now directed at many marginal deviant activities. In 1991, prostitution and commercialized vice, other sex offenses (except rape), drunkenness, and drug abuse violations accounted for over 1.5 million arrests, or 15% of the total in the United States.[6] Each arrest represents valuable time spent by the police, to say nothing of legal fees, court costs, and prison expenses. And, given the low socioeconomic status of most of these offenders, fines hardly represent a cost-effective alternative. Processing through the criminal justice system is probably the *most* expensive means imaginable for dealing with these activities. In addition, there is the likely reduction in street crime if, for example, drug addicts did not have to engage in dangerous, often violent, activities to support a habit made more expensive because the supply is provided by the criminal underworld. The social justice approach would allow for the withdrawal of criminal justice attention from some activities that currently require large expenditures of time, money, and personnel. Over time, it anticipates a reduction in the resources devoted to criminal justice, because declining levels of street crime should follow from the more effective informal social controls that could be established by more stable families and communities.

Excesses and Limits of the Criminal Law. There are two main reasons why the social justice approach would decriminalize and treat as social welfare problems prostitution, drunkenness, and drug use. First, these activities and the people involved in them have proven to be undeterrable by a criminal justice system that is expensive, overburdened, and actually undermined by its attempts to enforce unenforceable laws. The corruption of officials seems endemic to the enforcement of laws against vice. Second, whatever harm there is in these activities (and undoubtedly there is some harm to the deviant and to others in the society), it can be minimized by treating them predominately as social welfare problems rather than criminal or medical issues. Thus, in respect to such deviant activities, present social policy represents an *overreach* of the criminal law that would be most beneficially retracted.

Along the same line of reasoning, social policy in respect to deviance by the relatively powerful can be characterized as a distinct underreach of the criminal law. Only recently have laws been enforced against the perpetrators of severe family violence, especially incest and the battering of women by men. Research evidence indicates that vigorous law enforcement in these cases does deter perpetrators, especially if they have something to lose in the enforcement. Likewise, elite individuals and corporations are both sensitive to negative publicity arising from brushes with the criminal justice system. They have a great deal to lose if convicted—economic resources, status, and prestige. Moreover, the deviant acts they commit are unlikely to be crimes of passion or desperate need. Rather, they are apt to involve very rational calculation of the relative gains and losses attached to lawbreaking. Thus strict law enforcement and severe sanctioning of elite deviance should be central to social policy. For one reason, the activities and people involved in elite deviance are very likely to be deterred by the application of criminal sanctions. Moreover, public respect for the criminal justice system would be enhanced by evidence that elite "crimes in the suites" were being handled with the severity applicable to "crimes in the streets." Another reason is that the considerable harm elite deviance does to clients, customers, employees, and the general public can be minimized through the deterrent effects of treating it as serious criminal behavior rather than with the benign neglect it often receives under present social policy.

While there is presently an underreach of the criminal justice system in respect to elite deviance and family violence, criminal sanctions cannot be relied on alone. As noted in Chapter 9, a prudent policy to reduce corporate crime would include reliance on a judicious combination of regulatory negotiation and criminal penalties. Likewise, the research cited in Chapter 7 assessing social policies on family violence suggests that taken together, arrest and counseling tend to decrease the frequency and severity of repeated violence by male perpetrators. But the fact that criminal sanctions are apparently effective controls for elite deviants and men who commit severe family violence suggests the possibility that the criminal law may be most potent as a deterrent when it is applied to those with positions of relative power who have the most to lose when criminal sanctions are threatened or carried out.[7]

The Limits of Social Policy.   Because many forms of deviance are embedded in the social and economic structures of a society, any social policies that fall short of altering those structures will have limited effects. In the preceding chapters we have identified the importance of socioeconomic relationships—especially the inequalities of wealth and power in the United States. We have also shown that power structures based on gender and race can foster attitudes and values of patriarchy and dominance that contribute to harmful deviance in the family and the community. Such broad structures, created and solidified over centuries, cannot be altered by a few new social policies, a few acts of the legislature. There are, of course, many Americans—most of the elites and many in the middle and working classes—who steadfastly oppose substantial changes. They feel they benefit from the present arrangements and fail to comprehend the related costs. The limits of social policy are marked by the barriers of this resistance.

The distribution of wealth and power is among the most basic sources of struggle and conflict in American society. This can be seen in the endless debates over the obligations of the welfare state and the pros and cons of free enterprise, tax policy, reproductive freedom, affirmative action, and health care. These debates over fundamental social structures and values will not be resolved quickly—if ever. What we have tried to do is show how deviance and control are tied to these structures, so it is not possible to "solve" problems of deviance without changing the structures themselves. The decision to change them is ultimately political. The conclusion we present in this book is that such changes are needed, first because they provide an avenue for effectively reducing and preventing the most harmful forms of deviance—elite deviance, family violence, street crime, and drug abuse. Second, such changes ought to be made because social justice demands them.

Deviance as Control

Deviants have long been recognized as harbingers of social change (Durkheim, 1938: 71). From Socrates in Athens to Bohemians in Greenwich Village or flower children in Haight-Ashbury, to many social and political observers and protest groups that today are actively questioning conventional ways of doing things in American society, nonconformists have played a role in the evolution of beliefs, lifestyles, and moral codes. For a balanced picture of deviance and control, we must take note of how the production, maintenance, and control of deviance have in effect contributed to the status quo.

First, the deviance-defining process has a symbolic value for those who succeed in discrediting others' customs or preferences by having them officially declared illegal, while their own remain legitimate. Status enhancement at the expense of others is the prize for the winners of deviance-defining "stigma contests" (Schur, 1980: 8). As we noted in Chapter 6, Gusfield (1963) interprets the mid-19th-century American temperance movement as a symbolic struggle of status politics between rural people, who were largely nativist, Protestant, and middle class, and city dwellers, who were on average immigrants, Catholic, and lower class. The passage of the Prohibition amendment provided, for a time, a way of declaring where the power in the society resided. When a group in power feels threatened and launches a stigma contest against the threatening party (which, of course, it wins), this is often the surest way to demonstrate relative status and dominance. More recently, some antipornography campaigns (Zurcher and Kirkpatrick, 1976) or the attacks on the gay rights movement (Bryant, 1977) can be viewed as efforts to keep or put the deviants, and those in sympathy with them, firmly in their place.[8]

Next, by successfully shaping popular images of deviance, public attention can be directed away from the transgressions of one social entity (usually the most powerful) at the expense of others (usually powerless). The process of deviance designation can be thought of as the identification and ordering of a particular set of social problems on the public agenda for social action. For example, if the majority can be convinced that *the genuine*, high-priority social problems in the country are street crime and allegedly related lower-class "pathological" activities such as street prostitution, gang membership, pornography, homosexual behavior, excessive drinking, and other drug-taking, they will be less receptive to searching for and finding deviance among those at the top of the social hierarchy. Beyond merely deflecting attention, labeled deviants become ready scapegoats who can be blamed by those in power and who provide targets for an aggressive populace when things are going badly. In a society with a faltering economy or failing foreign policy, the next best thing to war with another country to relieve the internal political pressure may be a "war on crime," a "war on drugs," an ideological witch-hunt like the McCarthyism of the 1950s, or a morality crusade against avowed "deviants" and misfits.

Deviance is profitable for those who study, prescribe, manufacture, and exercise social control techniques. It supports an "enormous enterprise" that includes, at all levels of government, police, judges, prison guards, probation officers, sociologists, psychologists, and doctors, in addition to private security firms, manufacturers of weapons, drugs, uniforms, vehicles, and so on (Palmer, 1973; 76). Deviance control is a sufficiently large enterprise with adequate political clout to ensure that its business will never decline substantially for want of offenders—real or imagined. In recent years the social control of deviance has been a growth industry for private security forces and private administration of correctional facilities contracted-out by governments, and the ratio of private to public policing and administration has increased accordingly. In both the public and private sectors, there has been an expanding cadre of social control entrepreneurs (Warren, 1981). If, as Erikson (1966) states, the amount of deviance found in a society is closely tied to "the size and complexity of its social control apparatus" (24), American society should not want for deviants in the foreseeable future.

Finally, popularly accepted images of deviance are central to the legitimization of patterns of domination in a society. To return to the theme with which we began this chapter, explanations and social policy in respect to deviance are generally consonant with the interests and ideas of the society's dominant groups. In medieval society the Church was the dominant institution; deviance was most com-

monly portrayed in terms of sin or evil; and social policy was predicated on reasoning that involved such concepts as original sin and demonic possession. Today,
in a world dominated by giant corporations, a massive government presence, and
high technology, one contemporary trend is for deviance to be portrayed as sickness. Social control consistent with this image of deviance becomes a less-public
enterprise. Rather than being open to public scrutiny, it is exercised by technical
experts who can hide behind a veil of professional-client confidentiality, a haze of
drugged psychotropic mind control, or the walls of large bureaucratic institutions.
At the same time, American society will continue to face the challenges of deindustrialization and the late-20th century transition to its place in the global economy. Elites in power frequently search desperately for others to blame and for issues that can deflect the attention of the great mass of people from their declining
standard of living and the eroding quality of their lives. Too often, part of the
grand strategy is to play upon fears and prejudices by calling for a repressive crack-
down on the activities (many of which are admittedly illegal) of the poor and powerless. Today, both the velvet-gloved manipulations of medicalized social control
and the iron-fisted display of punitive retribution have powerful adherents and
enjoy wide public acceptance. A contending alternative like the social justice model
sketched in this chapter may gain adherents. In any case, understanding the social
construction of deviance and the social policies intended to control it provides
one way to understand our present society and anticipate the one we can help to
make in the future.

THE POLITICS OF DEVIANCE AND CONTROL

Establishing what is deviant and how to control it are central to defining one's community and society. Often the most heated issues of the day boil down to matters of
designating what constitutes deviance and the measures that should be enacted to
deal with those who are officially so labeled. Should drug use be decriminalized?
Should prostitution be legalized? Should pornography be banned? Should openly
avowed homosexuals be allowed to serve in the military? Should greater public resources be put into building more prisons or into improving human services? Should
more public money be spent on enforcing laws to control corporate crime? Should
guns be subject to greater controls? Should the society's most severe sanction be
capital punishment?

Questions like these are inescapably political matters. Indeed, they are questions over which many politicians anguish in pursuit of positions that will benefit
them the most with voters. But where do voters get their opinions from? Opinion
leaders include the mass media (radio talk shows, television news, newspapers,
magazines, and books), educators, clergy, and politicians. As we showed in Chapter
9, the sources of information funneled to the public are funded and directed, for the
most part, by private and corporate wealth. Questions of deviance and its control are
often shaped in the interests of the society's most powerful, and the policy alternatives presented to the general public are often limited by those interests as well.

In a democracy the dominance of wealth and power is not absolute, however. When people have the right to vote, all of them—from the richest to the poorest—possess the power to influence public policy in the direction of their own interests and the collective benefit. In order to do so effectively, citizens must have the ability to critically assess what they see, hear, and read in the mass media. They must also get involved politically by exercising their right to vote and organizing in support of issues about which they feel strongly. Learning about the theory and research of deviance and control is, therefore, an important step toward becoming a democratic citizen. Actively taking part in the process of making public policy concerning deviance and its control is one means ordinary people have to realize their citizenship.

ENDNOTES

1. This point is related to Kai T. Erikson's (1966) observation that "Every human community has its own special set of boundaries (norms), its own unique identity, and so we may presume that every community also has its own characteristic styles of deviant behavior. Societies which place a high premium on ownership of property, for example, are likely to experience a greater volume of theft than those which do not, while societies which emphasize political orthodoxy are apt to discover and punish more sedition than their less touchy neighbors" (19–20).
2. This statement is no less true for the natural sciences such as physics, than it is for the behavioral and social sciences. See Kuhn (1970).
3. In trials involving psychiatric testimony, prestigious expert witnesses for both the prosecution and the defense frequently arrive at contradictory conclusions, despite vigorous claims of "scientific" precision and objectivity.
4. Of course, various nongovernmental organizations also support alcoholism research and rehabilitation programs. Their omission from the model is one example of how it is simplified. Generally in respect to most types of deviance, government-sponsored research and programs are the largest and most influential.
5. For a discussion of the theoretical rationale behind the type of feedback model proposed here, see Buckley's chapter, "Social Control: Deviance, Power, and Feedback Processes," in *Sociology and Modern Systems Theory* (1967).
6. This figure *excludes* arrests for driving under the influence of alcohol and other liquor law violations that together account for another 16% of the total annual arrests in the United States.
7. The more of a stake individuals have in their work, families, and communities—that is, the more they have to lose by misbehaving—the more sensitive their behavior becomes to the potential sanctions of the criminal justice system, provided those sanctions are fairly certain to bite. Thus, giving those at the bottom of the social scale a greater stake in the society can actually increase the deterrent effects of criminal sanctions.
8. In respect to pornography, there are crusaders from the political right who see the ready availability of sexually explicit materials as one sign of degenerate liberal politics and lifestyles. At the same time, antipornography campaigns are being initiated from the feminist left by women who object to the demeaning images of women these materials often portray.

REFERENCES

Aubert, V., and Messinger, S. L.
1958   "The Criminal and the Sick." *Inquiry* 1: 237–160.
Blumstein, A.
1982   "On the Racial Disproportionality of United States Prison Populations." *Jour-*

nal of Criminal Law and Criminology 73: 1259–1281.
Becker, H. S.
1963   *Outsiders*. New York: Free Press.
Bryant, A.
1977   *The Anita Bryant Story: The Survival of*

Our Nation's Families and the Threat of Militant Homosexuality. Old Tappan, NJ: Revell.

Buckley, W.
1967   *Sociology and Modern Systems Theory*. Englewood Cliffs, NJ: Prentice-Hall.

Conrad, P., and Schneider, J. W.
1993   *Deviance and Medicalization: From Badness to Sickness*. Philadelphia: Temple University Press.

Dehais, R. J.
1987   *Racial Discrimination in the Criminal Justice System: An Assessment of the Empirical Evidence*. Albany, NY: New York African American Institute.

Dobash, R. E., and Dobash, R. P.
1992   *Women, Violence and Social Change*. New York: Routledge.

Durkheim, E.
1938   *The Rules of Sociological Method*. Translated by S. A. Solovay and J. H. Mueller; edited by G. E. G. Catlin. New York: Free Press.

Erikson, K. T.
1966   *Wayward Puritans*. New York: Wiley.

Foucault, M.
1975   *Discipline and Punish*. Translated by A. Sheridan. Middlesex, England: Penguin.

Galliher, J. F., and Walker, A.
1977   "The Puzzle of the Social Origins of the Marijuana Tax Act of 1937." *Social Problems* 24: 367–376.

Gusfield, J.
1963   *Symbolic Crusade*. Urbana: University of Illinois Press.

Haines, H.
1989   "*Primum Non Nocere*: Chemical Execution and the Limits of Medical Social Control." *Social Problems* 36: 442–454.

Hobson, B. M.
1987   *Uneasy Virtue: The Politics of Prostitution and the American Reform Tradition*. New York: Basic Books.

Hoffer, E.
1952   *The True Believer*. New York: Harper & Row.

Jacobs, J. B.
ND   "Inside Prisons." The National Institute of Justice, *Crime File*. Washington, DC: U.S. Department of Justice.

Kuhn, T. S.
1970   *The Structure of Scientific Revolutions*, 2nd edition. Chicago: University of Chicago Press.

Matza, D.
1964   *Delinquency and Drift*. New York: Wiley.

Morris, N., and Hawkins, G.
1970   *The Honest Politician's Guide to Crime Control*. Chicago: University of Chicago Press.

Musto, D. F.
1973   *The American Disease: Origins of Narcotic Control*. New Haven, CT: Yale University Press.

Palmer, S.
1973   *The Prevention of Crime*. New York: Behavioral Publications.

Pfohl, S.
1976   "The 'Discovery' of Child Abuse." *Social Problems* 24: 310–323.

Pleck, E. H.
1987   *Domestic Tyranny: The Making of Social Policy against Family Violence from Colonial Times to the Present*. New York: Oxford University Press.

Schneider, J. W.
1978   "Deviant Drinking as Disease: Alcoholism as a Social Accomplishment." *Social Problems* 25: 361–372.

Schur, E. M.
1965   *Crimes without Victims: Deviant Behavior and Public Policy*. Englewood Cliffs, NJ: Prentice-Hall.
1974   "A Sociologist's View: The Case for Abolition." In E. M. Schur and H. A. Bedeau, *Victimless Crimes: Two Sides of a Controversy*. Englewood Cliffs, NJ: Prentice-Hall.
1980   *The Politics of Deviance*. Englewood Cliffs, NJ: Prentice-Hall.

Scull, A.
1989   *Social Order/Mental Disorder: Anglo-American Psychiatry in Historical Perspective*. Berkeley: University of California Press.

Sheley, J. F.
1993   "Structural Influences of the Problem of Race, Crime, and Criminal Justice." *Tulane University Law Review* 67: 2273–2292.

Szasz, T. S.
1961   *The Myth of Mental Illness*. New York: Harper & Row.

Taylor, I., Walton, P., and Young, J.
1973   *The New Criminology: For a Social Theory of Deviance*. New York: Harper & Row.

Tierney, K. J.
1982   "The Battered Wife Movement and the Creation of the Wife Beating Problem." *Social Problems* 29: 207–220.

U.S. Bureau of Justice Statistics
1987   *Imprisonment in Four Countries*. Washington, DC: U.S. Department of Justice.
1988   *International Crime Rates*. Washington, DC: U.S. Department of Justice.

1992a *Capital Punishment, 1991*. Washington, DC: U.S. Department of Justice.
1992b *Jail Inmates, 1991*. Washington, DC: U.S. Department of Justice.
1992c *Justice Expenditures and Employment, 1990*. Washington, DC: U.S. Department of Justice.
1992d *Prisoners in 1992*. Washington, DC: U.S. Department of Justice.
1992e *Probation and Parole, 1990*.Washington DC: U.S. Department of Justice.

Warren, C. A. B.
1981   "New Forms of Social Control: The Myth of Deinstitutionalization." *American Behavioral Scientist* 4: 724–740.

Zurcher, L. A., Jr., and Kirkpatrick, R. G.
1976   *Citizens for Decency: Antipornography Crusades as Status Defense*. Austin: University of Texas Press.

Author Index

Abernathy, J., 46
Acheson, E. D., 33
Achilles, N., 83
Adair, R. K., 114
Adams, E. H., 191, 192
Adams, L. D., 214
Ageton, S. S., 305
Agnew, R., 253, 296
Agrest, S., 143
Ajuluchukwu, D., 33
Akers, R. L., 8, 93, 128, 213, 214, 295
Allen, H. D., 161
Allman, C. J., 162
Alpern, D. M., 143
Altimore, M., 51
Amato, P., 123
Anderson, B., 16
Anderson, K., 285
Anderson, L., 138
Andrews, F., 348
Andrews, H., 131
Aneshensel, C. S., 125
Anglin, M. D., 222, 225
Araji, S., 244, 245
Archer, H., 278
Ardrey, R., 8, 10
Arif, A., 184
Armat, V. C., 138
Arnstein, R. L., 162
Arvanites, T. M., 142
Asberg, M., 165
Asher, R. M., 200
Atkinson, M., 38
Aubert, V., 378
Augoustinos, M., 131
Augustin, R. I., 61
Austin, R. L., 280
Aviram, U., 131

Bachman, J. G., 213
Bachrach, L. L., 134, 136, 137
Baden, M. M., 199
Bailey, J. M., 91
Bakeman, R., 199
Baker, S. J., 138
Bales, Robert, 203, 205, 207

Ball, J. C., 199, 285
Bandura, A., 8, 11
Banks, S. E., 33
Bankston, W. B., 161
Barkey, K., 166
Barling, J., 250, 257
Barnett, H. C., 357
Baron, J. H., 170
Baron, L., 51, 64, 242, 286
Barrett, S. A., 133
Bart, P. B., 65
Barth, R. P., 232
Bassuk, E. L., 138, 139
Bayer, R., 222
Beach, F. A., 73
Bean, G. J., 138
Becker, Howard S., 2, 4, 5, 6, 211, 212, 214, 381
Beiser, Morton, 139
Bell, A. P., 76, 77, 78, 79, 80, 93, 94
Bell, Daniel, 276, 336
Bell, V., 57
Benedict, R., 105
Bensen, M. L., 352
Benson, D. S., 333, 361
Bentler, P. M., 213
Berg, B., 206
Berger, R. M., 72
Berk, R. A., 248, 250, 260, 284, 285
Berk, S. F., 260
Bernard, T. J., 264, 339
Berry, J. F., 340, 360
Berry, R. E., 193
Bhosley, G., 261
Bieber, Irving, 92, 96
Bingham, J., 130
Black, A. J., 175
Black, D., 64
Blau, J. R., 284
Blau, P. M., 284, 300
Block, A. A., 364
Block, M. K., 360
Blumberg, A. S., 331
Blumstein, A., 284, 285, 380
Blundell, William, 348
Bode, N., 361
Boffey, P. M., 193

Subject Index

DEVIANCE AND CONTROL
Edited by Gloria Reardon
Production supervision by Kim Vander Steen
Designed by Jeanne Calabrese Design, Berwyn, Illinois
Composition by Point West, Inc., Carol Stream, Illinois
Paper, Finch Opaque
Printed and bound by McNaughton & Gunn, Saline, Michigan